The Rāmāyaṇa of Vālmīki

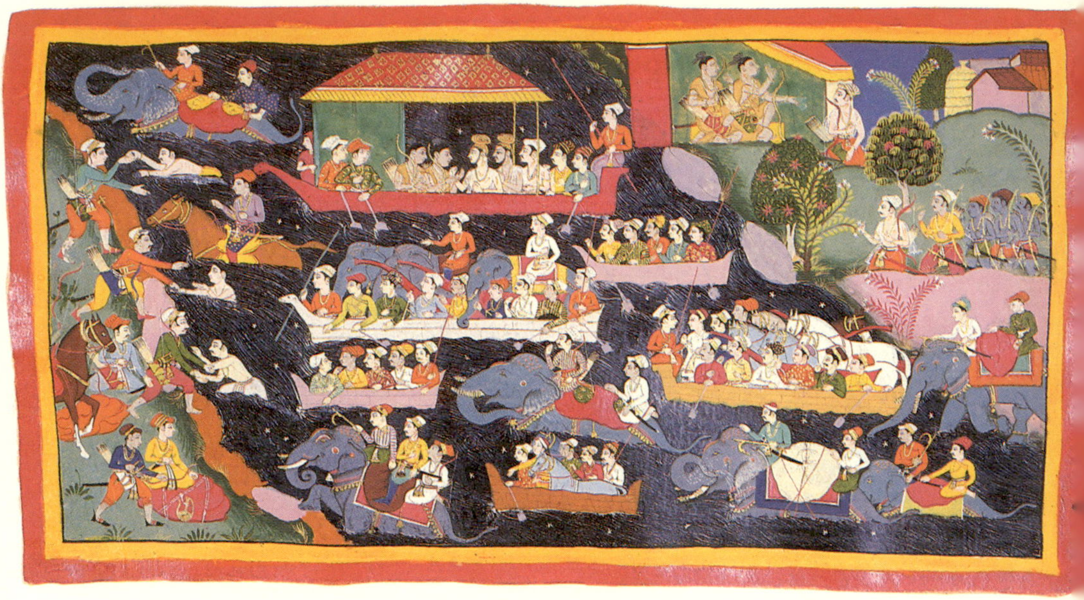

The Rāmāyaṇa of Vālmīki

AN EPIC OF ANCIENT INDIA

Volume II *Ayodhyākāṇḍa*

Introduction, Translation, and Annotation by

Sheldon I. Pollock * Edited by Robert P. Goldman

PRINCETON UNIVERSITY PRESS : PRINCETON, NEW JERSEY

For Estera Milman

Published by Princeton University Press, 41 William Street, Princeton, New Jersey 08540
In the United Kingdom: Princeton University Press, Guildford, Surrey

Library of Congress Cataloging in Publication Data will be found on the last printed page of this book

ISBN 0-691-06654-X

This book has been composed in Linotron Baskerville

Clothbound editions of Princeton University Press books are printed on acid-free paper, and binding materials are chosen for strength and durability. Paperbacks, while satisfactory for personal collections, are not usually suitable for library rebinding

Printed in the United States of America by Princeton University Press
Princeton, New Jersey

The translation of this volume was made possible through a grant from the translation program of the National Endowment for the Humanities, an independent federal agency, to which we would like to express our deep appreciation

Frontispiece: Bharata crossing the Ganges with his army. From the "Jagat Singh Ramayana," 17th c. British Library Add. 15296, Vol. I. By permission of the British Library

The Rāmāyaṇa of Vālmīki: An Epic of Ancient India

Robert P. Goldman, *General Editor*

Sally J. Sutherland, *Assistant Editor*

Leonard E. Nathan, *Editorial Consultant*

Translators: Robert P. Goldman, Rosalind Lefeber,
Sheldon I. Pollock, Sally J. Sutherland, Barend A. van Nooten

PRINCETON LIBRARY OF ASIAN TRANSLATIONS

idaṃ hi caritaṃ loke
pratiṣṭhāsyati śāśvatam

Theirs are exploits the world
will keep alive in memory forever.
—*Rām* 2.54.18

Contents

List of Abbreviations

Manuscripts, Commentaries, and Editions Used in Volume II, Following the Conventions Established in the Critical Edition of the Ayodhyākāṇḍa (see pp. iii-iv)

I. MANUSCRIPTS

Northern Manuscripts (N) forming the Northern Recension (NR) (15 MSS—including 7 Devanāgarī)

NW Northwestern Manuscripts
- i. Ś Śāradā
  - Ś1 undated

NE Northeastern Manuscripts
- i. Ñ Nepālī
  - Ñ1 A.D. 1020
  - Ñ2 A.D. 1675
- ii. V Maithilī
  - V1 undated
- iii. B Bengālī
  - B1 A.D. 1688
  - B2 A.D. 1789
  - B3 A.D. 1833
  - B4 undated
- iv. D Devanāgarī manuscripts allied with N
  - D1 A.D. 1456 W
  - D2 A.D. 1773 W
  - D3 A.D. 1717 W
  - D4 undated NE
  - D5 A.D. 1848 W
  - D6 undated NW
  - D7 A.D. 1639 NW

Southern Manuscripts (S) forming the Southern Recension (SR) (14 MSS—including 4 Devanāgarī)
- i. T Telegu
  - T1 undated
  - T2 undated
  - T3 undated
- ii. G Grantha
  - G1 A.D. 1818
  - G2 undated
  - G3 undated
- iii. M Malayālam
  - M1 A.D. 1512
  - M2 A.D. 1690
  - M3 undated
  - M4 undated
- iv. D Devanāgarī manuscripts allied with S
  - Dd the version of Devarāmabhaṭṭa A.D. 1840
  - Dg the version of Govindarāja A.D. 1775
  - Dm the version of Maheśvaratīrtha undated
  - Dt the version of Tilaka undated

II. COMMENTARIES (Note: Spelling follows the conventions established by the critical edition, see vol. 7, pp. 655-56.)

Cg	the commentary called *Bhūṣaṇa* (the name of the commentary on the *Ayodhyākāṇḍa* is the *Pītāmbarā*) of Govindarāja
Ck	the commentary called the *Amṛtakataka* of Kataka Mādhavā Yogīndra
Cm	the commentary called *Tattvadīpikā* of Maheśvaratīrtha
Cnā	the commentary of Sarvajña Nārāyaṇa (as cited by Lokanātha Cakravarti)
Cr	the commentary called *Śiromaṇi* of Bansidhara Śivasahāya*
Crā	the commentary of Rāmānuja*
Cs	the commentary of Satyatīrtha
Ct	the commentary called Tilaka of Nāgeśa Bhaṭṭa, composed in the name of Rāmavarmā
Ctr	the commentary called *Dharmākūtam* of Tryambaka Yajvan
Ctś	the commentary called Taniślokī of Ātreya Ahobala
Cv	the commentary called *Vivekatilaka* of Varadarāja Uḍāli (Uḍāri)

III. EDITIONS

CSS	Calcutta Sanskrit Series. *Vālmīki-Rāmāyaṇa*, Volume 2: *Ayodhyākāṇḍa*. Calcutta: Metropolitan Printing and Publishing House, 1933. Edited by Amareshwar Thakur.
GPP	Gujarati Printing Press (also called the vulgate). *Rāmāyan of Vālmīki*. 7 volumes. Bombay: Gujarati Printing Press, 1914-1920. With three commentaries called Tilaka, Shiromani, and Bhooshana.
VSP	Veṅkateśvara Steam Press. *Śrīmadvālmīkirāmāyaṇa*. 3 volumes. Bombay: Lakṣmiveṅkateśvara Mudraṇālaya, 1935. Edited by Gaṅgāviṣṇu Śrīkṛṣṇadāsa.

Journals

ABORI	*Annals of the Bhandarkar Oriental Research Institute*
BEFEO	*Bulletin de l'École Française d'Extrême Orient*
BSOAS	*Bulletin of the School of Oriental and African Studies*
IHQ	*Indian Historical Quarterly*
JA	*Journal Asiatique*
JAOS	*Journal of the American Oriental Society*
JAS	*Journal of Asian Studies*
JASB	*Journal of the Asiatic Society, Bengal*
JBBRAS	*Journal of the Bombay Branch of the Royal Asiatic Society*

* The critical edition uses Cr for the commentary of Rāmānuja, and gives no abbreviation for that of Bansidhara Śivasahāya.

JIP	*Journal of Indian Philosophy*
JOIB	*Journal of the Oriental Institute, Baroda*
JORM	*Journal of Oriental Research, Madras*
JRAS	*Journal of the Royal Asiatic Society*
PO	*Poona Orientalist*
ZDMG	*Zeitschrift der Deutschen Morgenländischen Gesellschaft*

Other Important Abbreviations

App.	Appendices to the critical edition of the *Rāmāyaṇa*
crit. app.	critical apparatus
crit. ed.	critical edition
PW	Petersburg Wörterbuch: Böhtlingk, Otto and Rudolph Roth. *Sanskrit-Wörterbuch.* St. Petersburg: Kaiserlichen Akademie der Wissenschaften, 1855-1875. Reprint in seven volumes, Osnabrück/Wiesbaden, 1966.
pw	Petersburg Wörterbuch (abridged): Böhtlingk, Otto. *Sanskrit-Wörterbuch im kürzerer Fassung.* St. Petersburg: Kaiserlichen Akademie der Wissenschaften, 1879-1889. Reprint in three volumes, Graz, 1959.
v.l.	varia lectio (a variant reading)

Sanskrit Texts Cited

AdhyāRā	Adhyātmarāmāyaṇa
AgniP	Agnipurāṇa
AitĀ	Aitareyāraṇyaka
AitBr	Aitareyabrāhmaṇa
AmaK	Amarakoṣa
ĀpaSm	Āpastambasmṛti
ĀpaŚS	Āpastambaśrautasūtra
ArthŚā	Arthaśāstra
ĀśvaGS	Āśvalāyanagṛhyasūtra
AV	Atharvavedasaṃhitā
BaudhDS	Baudhāyanadharmasūtra
BhagGī	Bhagavadgītā
BhāgP	Bhāgavatapurāṇa
BrahmāṇḍP	Brahmāṇḍapurāṇa
BrahmP	Brahmapurāṇa
BrahmSū	Brahmasūtra
BṛĀraU	Bṛhadāraṇyakopaniṣad
BṛDharmaP	Bṛhaddharmapurāṇa
Bṛhajjā	Bṛhajjātaka
BuddhaC	Buddhacarita
ChandaḥSū	Chandaḥsūtra

GautDS	Gautamadharmasūtra
GobhiSm	Gobhilasmṛti
HariVaṃ	Harivaṃśa
Hitopa	Hitopadeśa
KāśiVṛ	Kāśikāvṛtti
KāmSū	Kāmasūtra
KāṭhU	Kāṭhakopaniṣad
KātyŚS	Kātyāyanaśrautasūtra
KauṣīBr	Kauṣītakibrāhmaṇa
KauṣīBrU	Kauṣītakibrāhmaṇopaniṣad
Kāvyālaṅ	Kāvyālaṅkāra [of Rudraṭa]
KāvyPra	Kāvyaprakāśa
KumāSaṃ	Kumārasaṃbhava
KūrmaP	Kūrmapurāṇa
LāṭyāŚS	Lāṭyāyanīyaśrautasūtra
MahāBh	Vyākaraṇamahābhāṣya
MahāvīC	Mahāvīracarita
MaiU	Maitrāyaṇyupaniṣad
MaiS	Maitrāyaṇīsaṃhitā
ManuSm	Manusmṛti
MārkP	Mārkaṇḍeyapurāṇa
MatsyaP	Matsyapurāṇa
MBh	Mahābhārata
MīmāSū	Mīmāṃsāsūtra
Mṛcch	Mṛcchakaṭika
NāraSm	Nāradasmṛti
Nigh	Nighaṇṭu
Nir	Nirukta
NītiSā	Nītisāra
Pā	Pāṇini's Aṣṭādhyāyī
PadmaP	Padmapurāṇa
PañcBr	Pañcaviṃśabrāhmaṇa
PañcT	Pañcatantra
ParāSm	Parāśarasmṛti
PraśnaU	Praśnopaniṣad
RaghuVa	Raghuvaṃśa
Rām	Rāmāyaṇa
RāmāCam	Rāmāyaṇacampū
RāmāMañ	Rāmāyaṇamañjarī
ṚV	Ṛgvedasaṃhitā
SāhiDa	Sāhityadarpaṇa
Śāk	Abhijñānaśākuntala
ŚāṅkhāĀ	Śāṅkhāyanāraṇyaka

ŚāṅkhāBr	Śāṅkhāyanabrāhmaṇa
ŚāṅkhāGS	Śāṅkhāyanagṛhyasūtra
ŚāṅkhāŚS	Śāṅkhāyanaśrautasūtra
SarvaDaSaṃ	Sarvadarśanasaṃgraha
ŚatTrayī	Śatakatrayī = Bhartṛharisubhāṣitasaṃgraha
ŚatBr	Śatapathabrāhmaṇa
SatyāŚS	Satyāṣādhaśrautasūtra
Saund	Saundarananda
SkandP	Skandapurāṇa
SūktiRa	Sūktiratnahāra
TaiBr	Taittirīyabrāhmaṇa
TaiPrāti	Taittirīyaprātiśākhya
TaiS	Taittirīyasaṃhitā
TaiU	Taittirīyopaniṣad
UttaRāC	Uttararāmacarita
Vaija	Vaijayantī
VājaS	Vājasaneyisaṃhitā
VāmaP	Vāmanapurāṇa
VāsiDS	Vāsiṣṭhadharmaśāstra
VāyuP	Vāyupurāṇa
VetāPañ	Vetālapañcaviṃsati
ViṣṇuP	Viṣṇupurāṇa
ViśvaPra	Viśvaprakāśa
YājñaSm	Yājñavalkyasmṛti
YogSū	Yogasūtra
YogVā	Yogavāsiṣṭha

Preface

I WAS invited to participate in the Rāmāyaṇa Translation Project in the autumn of 1977. The *Ayodhyākāṇḍa* was substantially completed two years later in the summer of 1979, before I left for India to begin work on the third volume of Vālmīki's poem, the *Araṇyakāṇḍa*. During both the actual work on the text and what has seemed an interminable process of preparing the volume for publication, I have benefited from the kindness and advice of many friends and institutions.

Robert Goldman of the University of California, Berkeley, general editor of the Translation Project, read through the entire manuscript carefully and knowledgeably and offered numerous suggestions for improving the work. Perhaps even more than this, his enthusiasm for the enterprise has been infectious, and his good humor and calmness under pressure have been a support from the beginning. His friendship is one of the most valued outgrowths of my association with this project.

The University of Iowa has been extraordinarily generous to me during my work on the *Rāmāyaṇa*. Through the Faculty Scholars Program in particular it has provided me with extended periods of time for research and reflection, without which my labors would have been appreciably retarded.

In India I received substantial help from V. W. Paranjpe, Professor Emeritus of Deccan College, Poona, who made available to me the rich resources of the Poona Dictionary Project. Pt. Śrīnivāsa Śāstri answered my questions about Sanskrit with vast knowledge and great good will. Friends in America who kindly took time to comment on parts of the book include Paul Greenough and Ronald Inden. A. L. Basham read through the whole work, and with his wide learning and experience in India clarified a number of obscurities for me. That errors and excesses remain means only that I should have adopted more of my colleagues' suggestions than I have done.

Maureen Patterson, South Asia Librarian at the University of Chicago, helped to solve many frustrating bibliographical puzzles, and graciously made available to me several rare editions of Sanskrit texts. Margaret Case of Princeton University Press prepared the press copy with editorial skill and Indological acumen. Sally Sutherland of the Translation Project assisted in numerous ways in securing formal consistency between this and the previous volume of the series. Malinda Cox, with her impeccable literary taste and her generous hospitality, both improved the translation and made my frequent visits to Berkeley a great pleasure.

In Iowa City I have particularly to thank Chris Preuss of Weeg Computing Center. Without her technical expertise and willingness to help, the difficulties of computer translation between Iowa and Berkeley—at times more intractable than translating from Sanskrit into English—might never have been solved. I received a great deal of secretarial help from research assistants. Jey Flick entered well over six hundred pages of the commentary and has continued to oversee the progress of the volume through its final stages; her assistance has been more than one has the right to expect from one's student, and I am truly grateful to her. Martha Selby did a good deal of last-minute checking and assisted in the preparation of the glossary and index.

March 1984 *Sheldon Pollock*

Guide to Sanskrit Pronunciation

The pronunciation of Sanskrit is usually not very difficult for English speakers. A few guidelines will serve to clarify the basic pronunciation of the sounds. English examples are based on hypothetical "dictionary" pronunciation.

Vowels

a	like the u in "but"
ā	like the o in "mom"
i	like the i in "bit"
ī	like the ee in "beet"
u	like the first u in "suture"
ū	like the oo in "pool"
ṛ	something like the ri in "rig"
e	like the a in "gate"
ai	somewhat like the i in "high"; this sound becomes a diphthong to glide slightly into an "i" vowel
o	like the o in "rote"
au	somewhat like the ou of "loud" with a similar lip-rounding glide

Consonants

k	like the k in "skate"
kh	like the k in "Kate"
g	like the g in "gate"
ṅ	like the n in "sing"
c	like the ch in "eschew"
ch	like the ch in "chew"
j	like the j in "jew"
ñ	like the n in "cinch"
ṭ	like the first t in "start"
ṭh	like the first t in "tart"
ḍ	like the d in "dart"
ṇ	like the n in "tint"
t, th, d, dh, n	like the four preceding sounds, but with the tip of the tongue touching or extending slightly between the teeth
p	like the p in "spin"
ph	like the p in "pin"
b	like the b in "bin"

- m like the m in "mum"
- y like the y in "yellow"
- r like the r in "drama"
- l like the l in "lug"
- v produced generally with just the slightest contact between the upper teeth and the lower lip; slightly greater than that used for English w (as in "wile") but less than that used for English v (as in "vile")
- ś like the sh in "shove"
- ṣ produced with the tongue-tip further back than for ś, but giving a similar sound
- s like the s in "so"
- h like the h in "hope"
- ṃ a nasalization of a preceding vowel
- ḥ an aspiration of a preceding vowel pronounced, almost like an echo, as an "h" followed by the short form of the preceding vowel; for example: *devaḥ*, pronounced *deva(ha)*

INTRODUCTION

1. Prelude to the *Ayodhyākāṇḍa*

ALTHOUGH one can no longer claim with Jacobi's confidence that in its "original" form the *Rāmāyaṇa* began with the *Ayodhyākāṇḍa*,[1] nonetheless, the main narrative of the poem commences in this book. The name of Ayodhyā, the capital city of the ancient state of Kosala in east-central India, is an apposite choice for the title of the section. For in contrast to the other four central books of the epic, where the action takes place in the unpeopled wilderness (Book Three), the land of the monkeys (Book Four), and the island fortress of the *rākṣasas* (Books Five and Six), here the center of interest is the city, where social life reaches its greatest degree of complexity and intensity.

It was probably not much earlier than the seventh century B.C. that the major urban centers of aryan India came into existence,[2] and yet during the composition of the *Rāmāyaṇa* in pre-Mauryan times the city had already become the literary focal point of civilized life. Not surprisingly, given the conditions of their existence, the epic poets were primarily concerned with life as played out in the city. Their interest embraced both social life—especially the family with its inherent tensions, the responsibilities it imposes on the individual, and the often conflicting allegiances it exacts—and political life, the "state," and the powers of the state, which appeared in their most tangible manifestation in the city. For all the attention they pay it, the village might not have existed for the epic storytellers. Moreover, as we shall see in the *Araṇyakāṇḍa* (Book Three), they regarded the "desolate forest" as a zone of mystery, where supernatural forces came into play, yet where a certain Edenic quality had been preserved, as well.

The contrast—at times tension—between the city and the forest, which was increasingly to command the attention of the urban poet,[3] becomes palpable, perhaps for the first time in Indian his-

[1] Jacobi 1893, pp. 50ff., 64. See the General Introduction in Volume 1.

[2] A recent overview of the question can be found in Ruben 1978. Archaeology and philology are in accord; cf. Rau 1976, who notes (p. 51) that such words as *nagara* occur with the meaning "town" only in the very latest stratum of vedic literature.

[3] The theme becomes commonplace later on, as in the fifth-century poet Kālidāsa. See Ingalls 1976, especially pp. 22ff.

tory, here in the *Ayodhyākāṇḍa*. It is with an unmistakable sense of liberation that Rāma will find himself banished from Ayodhyā and its troubles, and declare:

> To set one's eyes on [Mount] Citrakūṭa and the Mandākinī [River], my lovely, is far better than living in the town.[4]

This attitude, partly a function of the innovative world view that we shall discover in the hero, seems also to be symptomatic of a new urban malaise.[5]

But this opposition remains secondary in the present book. For the most part, Vālmīki directs our attention to the city and its central concerns—those social and political features that are thrown into particularly high relief in an urban setting. As a consequence, the *Ayodhyākāṇḍa* is a remarkably human book; the story it tells is realistic and credible, and its subject-matter familiar and immediately understandable to an audience, village or urban, that would never march with an army of monkeys against a demon fortress.

Although these characteristics distinguish the *Ayodhyākāṇḍa* from the rest of the *Rāmāyaṇa*, the book by no means stands isolated from the main concerns of the poem as a whole. Quite the contrary. Because the scene later shifts beyond the human social order, the issues raised here may become attenuated, but they still remain the fundamental ones for Vālmīki.

These problems can be formulated through a large comparative generalization. If Homer, for example, addresses a transcendent problem, showing us what makes life finally impossible—in the words of one writer, "the universality of human doom"[6]—Vālmīki poses the more difficult question: What is it that makes life possible? This is more difficult because it is a social, not a cosmic question. The answer, as we might anticipate, is complex, raising additional questions that demand resolution: it is behavior in accordance with *dharma*, "righteousness," that alone makes life possible. But what

[4] 2.89.12; cf. 2.50.22 and 2.88.1ff., especially verses 3 and 19.

[5] The *Rāmāyaṇa*, and the *Ayodhyākāṇḍa* in particular, may well have contributed from the beginning—as it certainly did later—to the legend of the life of the Buddha, whose spiritual quest is at least partly conditioned by social problems of the sort noticed here (see Fairservis 1975, pp. 378-79). The city-forest antithesis does not, of course, exhaust the meaning of Rāma's exile, or fully explain it. Other themes are also present: a folkloric quest motif, for example, and perhaps that of a ritual enthronement (for the latter cf. Heesterman 1978).

[6] Griffin 1980, p. 69 (cf. p. 76).

exactly does "righteousness" mean? What are the kinds and limits of the obligations it imposes? Who is placed under these obligations, and to whom and how are they to be discharged?

Vālmīki, who represents the culmination of an epic tradition, was certainly not the first to explore this problem. On the basis of all the epic poetry we know, it seems safe to say that "the subtlest of things, *dharma*," had figured centrally in the genre from the start. That the interest in this issue was historically vital is demonstrated by the fact that an emperor of the third century B.C., toward the end of the creative epic period, had the question carved into rock: "*Dharma* is good. But what does *dharma* consist of?"[7] Vālmīki, however, subjected the matter to an especially sustained and profound analysis, and offered a set of answers that has deeply affected and durably fixed itself in the Indian imagination.

[7] Aśokan Pillar Edict II. For the subtlety of *dharma*, cf. *MBh* 2.34.3 and elsewhere in that epic. See also Cg on *Ayodhyākāṇḍa* 18.36: "The main concern of this *śāstra* (that is, the *Rāmāyaṇa*) is to validate *dharma*."

2. Synopsis of the *Ayodhyākāṇḍa*

THE STORY opens abruptly. Bharata, the king's second-eldest son, departs with his younger brother Śatrughna to the northwest land of Kekaya, to visit his maternal family. Rāma meanwhile carries out, on his father's behalf, the administrative duties of the kingdom, and his unique virtues begin to manifest themselves to the king, who consequently decides to consecrate him as prince regent. Daśaratha convenes an assembly of vassal kings and leading citizens, declares his resolution, and receives their ceremonial ratification (*sargas* 1-2). Rāma is informed of the decision, and then in a private meeting with his father learns that the ceremony is to take place the following day lest, as Daśaratha points out, Bharata have time to return and contest the succession. The people of Ayodhyā joyfully decorate the town, while the family priest Vasiṣṭha ritually prepares Rāma and Sītā for the ceremony (*sargas* 3-6).

Bharata's mother Kaikeyī, meanwhile, learns about the king's plans from her hunchback servant, Mantharā. At first delighted for Rāma, the queen is gradually convinced by the servant that the coronation poses a serious threat to Bharata. She resolves to secure her own son's succession and Rāma's banishment to the wilderness of Daṇḍaka for fourteen years (*sargas* 7-9). In her meeting with the king that follows, Kaikeyī attempts to realize her objectives by means of two boons Daśaratha had granted her long ago, the terms of which she now formulates in a devious way. Alternately threatening and pleading, the king in the end finds himself unable to change her mind (*sargas* 10-12).

Kaikeyī has Rāma summoned, and amid the joyful bustle of preparation for the consecration the prince makes his way to the king's palace (*sargas* 13-15). While Daśaratha lies prostrate and speechless with grief, Kaikeyī tells Rāma about the two boons and the demands she had made, and insists on his compliance. He agrees unhesitatingly, assuring her he will depart the same day (*sarga* 16). Rāma then leaves to inform his mother Kausalyā of the calamitous reversal of fortune, and both she and his youngest brother Lakṣmaṇa attempt to dissuade him from obeying Kaikeyī. Rāma stands firm in his resolve, and finally Kausalyā gives him her blessing for a safe journey (*sargas* 17-22). Returning then to his wife Sītā, he breaks the news to her and, though he is at first apparently reluctant, he is finally persuaded to take her along to the forest (*sargas* 23-27). He also grants Lakṣmaṇa permission to accompany him into exile (*sarga* 28). While preparing to leave, Rāma gives away all of his wealth to brahmans, mendicants, and his dependents, and then returns to his father to receive formal permission to depart (*sargas* 29-30).

The king at first remonstrates with Rāma, exhorting him to disobey—in fact, to depose him. When that course of action is rejected by Rāma, Daśaratha orders the whole army and treasury of Ayodhyā to accompany his son. But Rāma refuses it all and, dressing in the barkcloth garments of an ascetic, he takes leave of his parents and sets out, now amid the lamentation of the inhabitants of the city (*sargas* 31-36). The king desperately wants to follow Rāma, but his ministers prevail upon him to return. Back in the palace, Kausalyā laments and denounces her husband until she is calmed by the sage words of Sumitrā, Lakṣmaṇa's mother (*sargas* 37-39).

Many inhabitants of the city, however, resolutely continue to follow Rāma; on the next morning he deserts them, for their own good, and they return grief-stricken to Ayodhyā (*sargas* 39-42). Rāma makes his way south to the Ganges river, where he meets his old friend, the tribal chief Guha. After dismissing his charioteer Sumantra, he crosses the river and reaches the abode of Bharadvāja (*sargas* 42-47). This seer advises Rāma to establish his hermitage on Mount Citrakūṭa, and it is there that Rāma, his wife, and brother finally settle down (*sargas* 48-50).

On returning to Ayodhyā, Sumantra delivers Rāma's greetings to the king and queen, and attempts to console the sorrowing parents. Daśaratha and Kausalyā continue to grieve through the day and evening until late at night, when from out of the very depths of his misery, Daśaratha recovers the memory of something that had happened in his youth. He had accidentally killed a young ascetic, and the boy's father, a sage, had laid a curse on him that he, too, would end his days in grief for a son. A little after midnight on that, the sixth night of Rāma's exile, Daśaratha dies (*sargas* 51-58).

While the palace and city mourn the death of their king, the ministers, who are reluctant to perform the funeral with no prince at court, embalm the corpse. After consultation, they determine that the proper course of action is to fetch Bharata (who, after all, is now heir-apparent), in order to install him as king. Envoys are dispatched to the land of Kekaya (*sargas* 59-62). On the night of their arrival, Bharata has an ominous dream, and returning to the city of Ayodhyā, he learns to his horror of the crimes his mother has perpetrated in his absence (*sargas* 63-68). After protesting his own innocence to Kausalyā, Bharata performs the funeral rites for Daśaratha (*sargas* 69-72). The ministers afterward press the kingship upon him, but he adamantly refuses it, vowing instead to have Rāma brought back from the forest (*sargas* 73-76).

With a vast army Bharata goes out in pursuit of Rāma. Along the way he encounters Guha and Bharadvāja, and allays their suspicions concerning his intentions. At last he reaches Citrakūṭa (*sargas* 77-87). Rāma, strolling over the mountain, perceives the army of Bharata approaching. Lakṣmaṇa is convinced the expedition is a hostile one, but Rāma calms his fears and meets with Bharata (*sargas* 88-93). Assuming Bharata now to be king, Rāma interrogates him about his administration, only to learn of Daśaratha's death. After Rāma performs the funeral rites on his father's behalf, repeated attempts are made—by Bharata, the minister Jābāli, and the family priest Vasiṣṭha—to persuade Rāma to return and assume the kingship. But it is all to no avail: he is resolved to keep his father's promise and his own (*sargas* 94-103). He consents only to give his slippers to Bharata in token of his kingship, and after receiving them Bharata returns home and begins the period of his viceroyalty from the neighboring village of Nandigrāma (*sargas* 104-107).

Sometime later, the sages among whom Rāma is living decide to quit the hermitage on Mount Citrakūṭa because of repeated attacks of *rākṣasas*, and soon afterward Rāma departs as well. He heads further south, to the hermitage of Atri. The seer's wife Anasūyā bestows precious gifts on Sītā, and the princess tells her the story of her marriage to Rāma (*sargas* 108-110). The book ends with Rāma, Sītā, and Lakṣmaṇa leaving Atri's hermitage and entering at last the wilderness of Daṇḍaka.

3. The Central Issues

THE MEANING and significance of the *Ayodhyākāṇḍa* will come into focus more readily if we view the story against the background of other ancient Indian epic narratives and locate those narratives in their historical context.[1] Although the problems addressed by Vālmīki are typical of the epic genre, the manner in which he treats them is markedly innovative. History can suggest why these problems were addressed by resuscitating for us the crucial importance they once possessed. Just as, according to the first rule of interpretation, we determine the signification of a word in reference to the words surrounding it, so the literary text can be viewed as a semantic entity that acquires specific meaning in reference to the "texts" in which it is embedded: the literary genre, for example, and its historical situation. These are critical procedures the *Ayodhyākāṇḍa* presses upon us in an unusually insistent manner, though here it is not possible to do more than indicate their application in a brief and general way.

Indian epics—not only the other great epic, the *Mahābhārata*, but also the *Harivaṃśa* and a variety of lesser heroic tales—are admittedly interested in a wide range of issues. In the course of their transmission, in oral and afterwards in written form, and as a result of their appropriation by brahmanical orthodoxy, a congeries of topics—mythological, philosophical, religious, and so on—was incorporated into them. But at the root, in the very heart of many of these epic narratives, can be found a political problem similar to the one with which the *Ayodhyākāṇḍa* confronts us. This is true, for example, in the *Mahābhārata*. Here two claimants, Yudhiṣṭhira and Duryodhana, contend for the succession to the Kuru throne. They are related as *bhrātṛvya*, first cousins in the male line, called also *bhrātṛ*, which signifies in the first instance "brother," half- as well as full (Yudhiṣṭhira refers to Duryodhana's father as *pitṛ*, "father"). Their contention leads to the division of the kingdom and eventually to the exile of Yudhiṣṭhira. The dispute is finally resolved only by a cataclysmic struggle that spirals out to engulf the entire Indian world, besides resulting in the extermination of Duryo-

[1] What follows is an abbreviated version of a paper delivered at the Third Rāmāyaṇa Conference, Berkeley, summer 1978.

dhana and all his ninety-nine brothers. The *Harivaṃśa*, on the other hand, tells the story of Kṛṣṇa, the *bhrātṛ*[2] of the usurping prince Kaṃsa. He is likewise exiled, in a sense, but returns to slay the tyrant and reinstate the deposed ruler, the father of Kaṃsa himself. King Nala, in the *Nalopākhyāna*, finds his position usurped (by his *bhrātṛ*) and is driven into exile. In the stories of Yayāti, Śakuntalā, and Devavrata (Bhīṣma), to cite only a few more of the better-known examples, the struggle among "brothers" for succession to the hereditary throne forms the core problem of the narrative.

It seems, then, that an integral theme of Sanskrit epic literature is kingship itself and its attendant problems: the acquisition, maintenance, and execution of royal power, the legitimacy of succession, the predicament of transferring hereditary power within a royal dynasty. We are naturally led to wonder why this question should assume such importance for the Indian epic. We are not dealing here, as in other epic traditions, with just the heroic deeds of warrior kings, but with the nature and function of kingship as such; and these questions are not tangentially significant but central to the structure of the epic. One explanation may be that the problems of kingship addressed so insistently by the epic texts were new ones and, in their very nature, urgent.

This formative and referential relationship with historical reality that I propose holds true for certain other important aspects of the *Ayodhyākāṇḍa*, as well. The historical context is a complex one, and no less than the literary text an object of interpretation. But a couple of major developments and their consequences seem clear and especially relevant.

During the three or four hundred years following the middle vedic age (c. 800 B.C.),[3] a critical period of dynamic transition, fundamental and enduring changes came about in the Indian way of life. Besides the growth of cities like Ayodhyā and the rise of politically discrete polities like Kosala, the most important social development seems to have been a far more markedly defined hierarchical ordering of society.[4] The pyramidal social organization

[2] Cf. *HariVaṃ* 65.77, where Kṛṣṇa's father Vasudeva is called the husband of Kaṃsa's father's sister; cf. also verse 88.

[3] See most recently Mylius 1970.

[4] For example, according to Rau (1957, pp. 62ff.), "the classical Indian caste-order did not exist" at the time of the *Brāhmaṇas*; "the four orders of the Brāhmaṇa-

maintained by institutionalized inequality is now often met with; the assumptions about it are made clear enough in the *Rāmāyaṇa* itself:

> The kshatriyas accepted the brahmans as their superiors, and the *vaiśyas* were subservient to the kshatriyas. The *śūdras*, devoted to their proper duty, served the other three classes (*varṇa*s) (1.6.17).

However gross and ideal this schematization might be—whether, indeed, we are here presented with fact or, far more likely, hope or injunction—seems finally beside the point. It has now become the single paradigm of social relations, an inflexible hierarchy based on birth.

A second change, more pertinent to our immediate purpose, concerns the extraordinary expansion of the role of the king. Whether or not it is true that vedic India knew no "institution that we can usefully call kingship,"[5] the nature of monarchy in this period appears unlike anything existing earlier. As the *Rāmāyaṇa* represents it, the welfare of the "state"—the economic, social, political, and cultural welfare—was now felt to depend exclusively on the king.[6] Again, the model contained in this representation is of principal interest here, whether it was fully actualized or not—though it is a fact that the king's central position in the life of the community was steadily enhanced until, by the end of the epic period, his power would radiate out to encompass every sphere of social activity.

Political power, moreover, came to be concentrated in royal dynasties as exclusive proprietors. For the first time it became the conventional practice to transfer the kingship through heredity.[7]

---

period do not resemble the later castes in any one point." A vertical mobility is widely attested in the earlier period (p. 63). It is clear from his citations from the *Brāhmaṇas* that *varṇa* affiliation was not yet intimately connected with birth. As in the political sphere, it would seem to be only during the later *brāhmaṇa* period that the element of heredity unambiguously enters the picture, and the society makes "the transition from varna to caste" (Dumont 1980, p. 148).

[5] See Mabbett 1972, pp. 15, 19. On the various nonmonarchical structures existing before and into the epic period, see most recently J. B. Sharma 1968, pp. 15-80, 237-43.

[6] Cf. 2.46.18, 61.8ff., 94.37ff.

[7] A similar evolution has been suggested for "Celtic" kingship, where more or less strict primogeniture developed from the right to kingship of a much larger royal kin group. Cf. Binchy 1970, pp. 24-30.

This is a significant development because it implies a specific type of control of royal power; even more important, it is in itself problematic and regarded as such by the epics. Several consequences of hereditary monarchy are continually thrust upon our attention by their central position in the story of the *Ayodhyākāṇḍa*; none of them figures significantly in the pre-epic documents.

One such feature is the *yauvarājya*, "prince regency," whereby the still-reigning king appoints his successor (as Daśaratha intends to appoint Rāma). It is likely that this type of transfer of power would evolve as a response to the problem of legitimacy within a dynastic succession,[8] presumably because other, more communal mechanisms for legitimation, such as popular assemblies, are no longer effective (the assembly in *sarga* 2 of the *Ayodhyākāṇḍa* is clearly *pro forma*). Another feature is intertribal—or what is now really interstate—marriage. Its function is to secure a political alliance (such as the Kosala-Videha alliance here, or the Kuru-Pañcāla in the *Mahābhārata*), and that can be done effectively only when high office is transferred within a single dynasty. Closely related to this is the politically significant practice of *rājyaśulka*, "the brideprice consisting of the kingship (or kingdom)," which Daśaratha had offered to the king of Kekaya (99.3). Like the marital alliance, this brideprice, a pledge to the woman's male relations that her son shall succeed to the throne, would be practicable only when the kingship is proprietarily controlled.[9] Moreover, one must wonder whether there had actually been any clear conception of an

[8] Goody 1966, p. 8. He continues: "But the difficulties [of this type of premortem succession] are clear. For the sharp contrast that exists between king and ex-king . . . makes it well-nigh impossible for a man easily to cast off the authority he has held by right of birth. . . . This aura that attaches to the ex-king creates problems . . . which can often be resolved only by the banishment or killing of the king" (cf. Tod's remarks on the Rajputs of medieval India: "It is a rule [for an ex-king] never to enter the capital after abandoning the government; the king is virtually defunct; he cannot be a subject, and he is no longer king" [1920, vol. 3, p. 1,467]). The Ikṣvāku dynasty solved this problem by the institutionalized ritual exile of the king, his entering upon abdication into the *vānaprasthāśrama*, the stage of life of the forest hermit. It is not the least of the ironies of the *Rāmāyaṇa* that Rāma should fulfil in his youth this "vow" of the aged Ikṣvāku kings (see the pointed verses of Kālidāsa, *RaghuVa* 12.20 and Bhavabhūti, *UttaRāC* 1.22, and contrast the words of Lakṣmaṇa in *Ayodhyākāṇḍa* 20.20-21).

[9] Though we do find records of marital alliances between dynasties at a comparable geographical distance (for example, the alliance of the Śiśunāgas of Magadha with the northwestern Madras effected by Bimbisāra), the *rājyaśulka* of Daśaratha makes

exclusive royal dynasty in the vedic period. We almost never hear of heirs displaced either by rival claimants or because of incompetence,[10] so frequent an occurrence in the epics (as happens to Asamañja, 32.12-20). There seems to be no term for "royal dynasty," and the common epic word for it, *vaṃśa*, is not once employed in vedic texts in this signification (we hear only of undifferentiated, nonroyal lineages, *gotras*). Nor is any major role played by genealogy, which is the principal method of dynastic self-authentication and primogenitural validation.[11] Thus we have good reason to suppose that the special prominence dynasties and dynastic succession acquire in epic texts is at least partly the result of major changes in the structure of political power in late vedic times.

One final, and critical, intrinsic problem of kingship remains. The new restricted control of political power entailed a heightened competition attending its transfer. The process of transferring high office is inherently a perilous one, but the antinomies involved in hereditary monarchical succession posed the constant threat of the sharpest possible intensification of the process: the divisive and usually violent dynastic struggle.[12]

---

better political sense if we do not accept at face value the narrative of the *Ayodhyākāṇḍa*, which locates the kingdom of the Kaikeyas in their vedic homeland, the Punjab. It may be that, first, Rājagṛha-Girivraja (cf. *Ayodhyākāṇḍa* 8.22 and note, and 62.14) is to be taken as referring to the Magadhan capital (mentioned at 1.31.5); the itineraries of 2.62 and 65, then, might be regarded as a set piece, archaic or archaizing, at all events imperfectly transmitted to the monumental poet (cf. notes on 62.9 and 65.1). Second, the Kaikeyas may be identical with Haihayas (cf. Lüders 1940, p. 108 note 4; according to "Jain sources" cited by Kosambi 1952, pp. 188-89, the Haihayas seem to have had some relation to the ruling house of Magadha at the time of the Buddha: "Ajātaśatru's grandfather, the Licchavi [Haihaya] Ceḍago . . ."). In this light, the alliance of Daśaratha and Kaikeyī would have a strategic geopolitical function, paralleled by the historical Kosala-Magadha alliance secured during the reign of Prasenajit (see Kosambi 1952, pp. 185, 189). Note also that earlier in the "history" of the Ikṣvāku dynasty, Sagara fought and defeated the Haihayas (*MBh* 3.104.7; cf. *Rām* 2.102.14).

[10] Zimmer 1879, p. 165 on *ṚV* 7.104 is to be corrected according to Geldner's translation.

[11] As Vasiṣṭha shows in *sarga* 102. It is a matter of some labor to reconstruct the few vedic genealogies available. See Zimmer 1879, p. 162; Rau 1957, p. 86 and notes 2 and 3. (The examples usually cited, such as Spellman 1964, pp. 53, 57, derive from the end of the vedic period.)

[12] The "law of primogeniture," while an ideal repeatedly pointed to in the *Ayodhyākāṇḍa* (cf. 8.12-16, for example) as in other epic narratives, was liable to con-

If, as most evidence leads us to believe, the genesis of Sanskrit epic literature is to be located in the period that witnessed these historical changes, then our interpretation of the *Ayodhyākāṇḍa* may acquire some new points of leverage. Just as we have begun to comprehend how much fiction enters into the writing of history, so we are beginning to understand how much reality comes to be represented in fiction. The *Rāmāyaṇa* appears to derive much of its meaning from its intense engagement with the conditions of social and political existence. A work of fiction it no doubt is, but fiction that in both its genesis and its reference is historically constituted, that issues from and, in a complicated way, describes, interprets, and evaluates reality. From this perspective it is reasonable to see in the poem's preoccupation with kingship responses to unfamiliar and serious political questions. But, though this is a major concern of the poem, it is not its exclusive concern. Such problems (particularly the "laws" of political succession) are finally subordinated to and made a pretext for the epic's larger interests. On this higher level, attention is directed to broader patterns and expectations of behavior in the social hierarchy that are likewise constituted by historical conditions. Thus, although these patterns are elaborated on the basis of political problems, they are by no means restricted to that narrow focus of the narrative.

By its nature, epic seeks to embrace the totality of a society—as Hegel put it, both its "world-outlook" and its "concrete existence."[13] It is the most social, the most public of literary genres. We should

---

siderable variation in practice, as the same texts so often show. For if it were to be invariably employed, it would present a "challenging second" to the king by elevating the heir from the start to an "unambiguous second position" (Burling's terms). Indeterminacy, however, results in intensifying conflict among the possible heirs (see Goody 1966, pp. 2, 45; Burling 1974, pp. 58-83; Spellman 1964, p. 228 and note 3 [evidence from the *jātakas*]). Note that Rāma's succession is by no means a foregone conclusion; it comes as a surprise to Kausalyā, to Rāma's friends and enemies, and to Rāma himself. The important theme of the "disqualified eldest" was first clearly identified by van Buitenen (1973, especially pp. xvi-xix), and has more recently been analyzed from a psychoanalytic perspective by Goldman (1978).

[13] Hegel 1975, vol. 2, p. 1,044. He had the *Rāmāyaṇa* specifically in mind; he speaks of the "national bibles like the *Rāmāyaṇa*, the *Iliad* and the *Odyssey*" (p. 1,087). (The *Aesthetik* consists of lectures prepared during the 1820s. Presumably Hegel got what knowledge he had of the *Rāmāyaṇa* from A. W. von Schlegel and the fragmentary translations mentioned below, chapter 9 note 6. Contrary to the translator's identification of the "English translator" [p. 344], Charles Wilkins never published, to our knowledge, a translation of the *Rāmāyaṇa*.)

not lose sight of the broader concerns and larger audience of this poetry, even when, as in India, its selection of "concrete existence" has been conditioned by special factors. The most important of these factors in the case of the Sanskrit epic is that it was a literature composed by more or less professional poets for the politically dominant group, the kshatriyas.[14] Although the *Rāmāyaṇa* was also performed "on the streets and royal highways" of Ayodhyā (*Uttarakāṇḍa* 84.4), a popular function it has preserved to the present day, its primary and determinate audience, the one that authenticated and validated the work, was composed of kshatriyas; let us recall that Rāma, the hero of the poem, was also the original auditor (*Bālakāṇḍa* 4). It is natural that the issues addressed by the epic were those central to the lives of the kshatriyas who patronized it.

Thus, the genre itself and its primary social context restricted Vālmīki, like his predecessors and contemporaries, to a particular set of themes. But when we compare the *Rāmāyaṇa* with other examples of epic literature, it seems evident that Vālmīki found the previous treatments deficient not only aesthetically but ethically, as well.

As the *Mahābhārata* (and *Harivaṃśa*) makes clear, the early epic tradition had acknowledged, if sometimes reluctantly, only one means for the resolution of political and dynastic conflict: armed combat. For Vālmīki violence becomes, quite literally, the strategy of the inhuman. Although the position of the monkey prince Sugrīva resembles Rāma's own in many ways (4.4.19), he forcibly seizes the throne of the monkeys when, with Rāma's aid, he kills his elder brother, Vālin, who has "abandoned the path of kings" (4.18.12) through "sexual" excess (4.18.18ff.).[15] Here, in Kiṣkindhā, force is explicitly promoted as the only correct means of dealing with infringements of righteousness (4.18.21), and Rāma resolves to employ force as soon as he learns of the circumstances of Sugrīva's

[14] Oldenberg 1922, pp. 12-18, 96ff.

[15] Given the fact that royal proprietorship of the land is so often in the text expressed through sexual metaphors (the king is "husband" of the earth, 2.1.28, for instance, and his death leaves the earth a widow, 2.45.12, 97.11), one wonders whether the "sexual" perversity of Rāma's foils, Vālin, Rāvaṇa, and Daśaratha himself, is not in part to be read as proprietary rapacity, a correspondence the poet elsewhere implies (see 2.94.22 and note). Rāma's monogamy, contrasting sharply with the polygyny of the other kings, may continue and advance the correspondence. (On the possible symbolic resonances in the name "Sītā," cf. note on 110.30.)

exile (4.4.19). No attempt at peaceful reconciliation is made. In the sixth book, when the banished Vibhīṣaṇa, the younger brother of the demon king Rāvaṇa, takes refuge with Rāma, it is not—or not primarily—an act of disinterested altruism.[16] As Hanumān perceives (6.11.18)—and as Vibhīṣaṇa, in fact, later admits (6.40.18-19)—his defection is prompted in the first instance by his ambition to secure the kingship of the *rākṣasas* for himself. Rāma crowns him at once,[17] and repeats the ceremony after he kills Rāvaṇa (100.9ff.), another king who has erred, again through "sexual" immoderation. In Laṅkā, once more, the struggle for political power among brothers is settled by the sword.

These incidents establish instructive parallels with the events of the *Ayodhyākāṇḍa*. Bharata, too, has the chance to displace his elder brother in dynastic succession, while Rāma himself is dispossessed and driven from his country through a tyrant's unrighteous conduct (resulting from "sexual" excess). But the naked violence and unscrupulous political opportunism we encounter in Kiṣkindhā and Laṅkā are rigorously excluded from the city of Ayodhyā. For civilized society the poet inculcates, by positive precept and negative example, and with a sometimes numbing insistence, a powerful new code of conduct: hierarchically ordered, unqualified submission.

As we saw at the beginning of the poem, Vālmīki is shown to have developed a new form for his epic,[18] the *śloka* meter—itself an emotional response to violence and unrighteousness (1.2.13)—as the formal prerequisite for the communication of his new criticism of social life. In the context of the epic tradition, the ethics he advocates would have been thought an equally pronounced innovation.

Everyone in the *Ayodhyākāṇḍa* expects Bharata to mount a struggle for power: Daśaratha (*sarga* 4), Kausalyā (69), Guha (78), Bharadvāja (84-85), and, of course, Lakṣmaṇa (90). This was the established pattern of behavior. "There is no brotherly love among

[16] Note that in the *MBh*, Vibhīṣaṇa had gone into exile with Vaiśravaṇa when the latter was driven from the kingship of Laṅkā by his younger brother Rāvaṇa (3.259.36). Cg predictably tries to argue away Vibhīṣaṇa's political ambitions: the *rākṣasa* wants only to serve Rāma, as Lakṣmaṇa does (GPP 6.17.1, VSP vol. 3, p. 110).

[17] Perhaps to ensure his continued support. No further mention is made of Vaiśravaṇa, who, theoretically at least, is the rightful successor.

[18] But see the remarks below regarding the truth of this claim, chapter 6.

heroes," Rāvaṇa is told when urged to take up arms and drive his elder brother Vaiśravaṇa from the throne of Laṅkā (7.11.12). The *Mahābhārata* narrates in full the tragic consequences of this principle, which historical kings throughout the period—the young Aśoka, for example—tried to forestall by the summary execution of virtually all possible claimants, elder brothers among them. For Vālmīki such struggle must be averted at all costs. Bharata himself is the first to agree:

> It has always been the custom of our House that the kingship passes to the eldest son. . . . Rāma, our elder brother, shall be the lord of earth. (73.7-8)

> The kingship belongs to that wise prince. . . . How would a person like me dare seize it from him? How could a son born of Daśaratha usurp the kingship? The kingship, and I myself, belong to Rāma. . . . Righteous Kākutstha, the eldest son and the best . . . must obtain the kingship just as Daśaratha did. The other course is an evil one, followed only by ignoble men, and leading to hell.[19] Were I to take it I should become a blot on the House of the Ikṣvākus in the eyes of all the world. (76.10-13)

> There is an ancient practice of righteousness . . . established among us for all time. It is this: with the eldest brother living . . . a younger may not become king. (95.2)

And the way to obviate this deadly antagonism is by the doctrine of unqualified submission of the younger to the elder brother:

> The way of righteousness good people follow in the world is just this: submission to the will of one's elders [here, elder brothers]. (35.6)

Analogously, Rāma is urged to seize the throne of Kosala. Lakṣmaṇa (*sargas* 18 and 20; cf. Śatrughna's words in 72.3-4) and Daśaratha himself (31.23) exhort him to do so, with the kinds of arguments that might have been adduced in the many actual instances of usurpation occurring in this epoch and afterwards—as in the case of Ajātaśatru (himself both a parricide and a victim of

[19] "Followed only . . . ," a quarter verse appearing in the *Bhagavadgītā* (2.2c), where significantly it is used by Kṛṣṇa in reference to Arjuna's "fear" of engaging in the war against his kinsmen for the kingship.

parricide), or, in the ruling house of Kosala itself, Viḍūḍubha. For Vālmīki, the forceful seizure of power and the bloodshed that, as the *Harivaṃśa* shows, it inevitably brings in its train, must likewise be prohibited. And again the means is unqualified submission, now to one's father:

> And righteousness is this . . . : submission to one's mother and father. . . . My father keeps to the path of righteousness and truth, and I wish to act just as he instructs me. This is the eternal way of righteousness. (27.29-30)

The *Mahābhārata* is no doubt sensitive to the desperate dilemma of living made possible only through killing. But its interrogations are indecisive; it can conceive of no solution except the final one in heaven. Political violence is no less necessary for its impossibility. That the fratricidal doctrine is so often and positively enunciated and defended in the *Mahābhārata* suggests that for this and other epic stories, as for the historical kings of ancient India, the acquisition and retention of political power ultimately if tragically superceded all other concerns. We shall later have an opportunity to appreciate how starkly the *Rāmāyaṇa* differs in this regard from the *Mahābhārata* when we juxtapose Rāma's attitudes to those of Kṛṣṇa.[20] Here it is enough to remark that Vālmīki altogether inverts the priorities both literature and history had valorized, asking incredulously,

> How, after all, could a son kill his father, whatever the extremity, or a brother his brother, Saumitri, his very own breath of life? (91.6)

The question contains less rhetoric than admonition and instruction; and "just as you do not legislate against things nobody does," as one recent writer puts it, "so also no one needs to teach what everybody knows."[21]

Viewing the poem against such a literary and historical back-

[20] See chapter 10. At times the political restraint is so exaggerated that it seems nobody wants to be king (cf., for example, 16.33-34, 91.78). Kālidāsa appears very near the truth when he says that Rāma received his father's offer of the kingship in tears, and the order to go to the forest with deep delight (*RaghuVa* 12.7).

[21] The author continues: "ethical doctrines are in this sense to be understood as symptoms of a social situation which calls out for the supplement or the corrective of the doctrine in question" (Jameson 1976, p. 37).

ground, and keeping in mind its primary audience, we can appreciate more fully the significance and urgency of its contribution: the moral injunctions it seeks to place at the center of political life. The code of behavior Vālmīki prescribes in this context has a practical as well as an ethical dimension. If hereditary power could not be transferred smoothly, the consequences could be disastrous: the fragmentation of the state among rival claimants, or a dangerous interregnum entailing pressures for redistribution of power and liability to external attack.[22] The *Ayodhyākāṇḍa* seeks to solve this dilemma (one that may, in fact, be insoluble) by prescribing a pattern of behavior consonant with the demands of political order. Whatever the rival claims among the heirs themselves or of a single heir against the king, submission to the hierarchy—younger to elder prince, eldest prince to king—is essential, for only in this way is it possible to arrest the tendency in hereditary kingship toward ruinous fragmentation.

In addition to this practical vocation, the ethics represents a new and hopeful humanism in the realm of political behavior. Violence is brutality in the radical sense of the word, and belongs to the subhuman world of monkeys and demons; it is no longer to be regarded as a way of resolving social conflict. In this regard we may agree that the *Rāmāyaṇa* constitutes the first literary attempt in India to "moralize" the exercise of political power.[23]

Yet much of the *Ayodhyākāṇḍa* will remain unaccounted for if we restrict our analysis to this level of practical and ethical instruction designed for a kshatriya audience. Indeed, the larger audience of the epic might naturally be expected to extrapolate the narrative beyond the princely relationships and what is, after all, a remote struggle for dynastic control. The poem itself, however, urges us to penetrate the surface discourse to another set of references embedded in it. By both its explicit injunctions and the implications of its structure, the *Ayodhyākāṇḍa* invites and, in fact, has always been subject to wide social extension. "One must behave like Rāma" is the later proverbial formulation (one that was to receive encouragement from the kings of medieval India, who endowed pub-

[22] See Goody 1966, p. 10.

[23] Ruben 1975, p. 19. This humanism appears to have been a truly felt conviction of the poet, even beyond the strictly political sphere. Consider particularly his treatment of the forest-dwelling Niṣādas, whom the *MBh* regards as little more than animals. See the note on *Ayodhyākāṇḍa* 45.9.

lic recitations of the epic).[24] For Rāma represents a comprehensive model of behavior, enacting in particular two roles that encompass communal life in its totality.

After Rāma's banishment Kausalyā exclaims to Daśaratha:

> If only Rāma could have lived at home though it meant his begging in the city streets! You had the freedom to grant such a boon, which at the worst had made my son a slave. (38.4)

The verse directs our attention to an important aspect of Rāma's status: his absolute heteronomy. The status of junior members of the Indian household was, historically, not very dissimilar to that of slaves (as was also the case in ancient Rome), both with respect to the father and, again, hierarchically among themselves. The image of Rāma's bondage is enhanced by the fact that he is obliged to pay a debt that devolves upon him with the death of his father (104.6). More generally, like the slave, Rāma is "not his own master, he is subordinate to others and cannot go where he wishes," as an early Buddhist text defines the condition of slavery.[25]

On this level of signification, where Rāma's position is one of unqualified subservience to the will of his master, the relations that had come to characterize the social formation in general can be understood. As Lakṣmaṇa and Bharata submit to Rāma ("I am your

[24] On the endowments made by the Pallavas, Colas, and Paṇḍyas for *Rāmāyaṇa* recitation see Raghavan 1956, p. 504, who goes on to remark on the unbroken tradition of exposition, which at present "constitutes one of the leading forms of popular religious instruction all over South India. . . . The epic that holds the people enthralled is the *Rāmāyaṇa* . . . hardly a day passes without some expounder sitting in a temple, *maṭha* (centre of religious preaching), public hall, or house-front and expounding to hundreds and thousands the story of the *dharma* that Rāma upheld" (p. 505). For the proverbial formulation, see *SāhiDa* 1.2 *vṛtti*. The didactic function of poetry is repeatedly stressed in the later rhetorical tradition, which regards it as literature's primary function. See, for example, *Kāvyālaṅ* 5.3; *KāvyPra* 1.2 and *vṛtti*. Despite the view of one school that includes *itihāsa* within *kāvya* and ascribes this didactic function to it as well (Mahimabhaṭṭa, Bhoja; see Raghavan 1963, p. 694), we would argue that it is precisely *upadeśa*, "instruction," that distinguishes "poetry" from narratives of things "as they were" (*itihāsa*); it idealizes, exemplifies, and creates paradigms.

[25] See, for example, Bongert 1963, especially pp. 184-85. The definition cited is found in *Dīghanikāya* 2.72. The *MBh* repeatedly attests to the congruence in status of slave and son; for example: "There are three who control no wealth whatever: a wife, a slave, and a son" (1.77.22, 5.33.57, and elsewhere). Note too that the Pāṇḍava princes are temporarily reduced to slavery (through gambling, that is to say, debt; cf. Bongert 1963, pp. 151, 160, and note 2).

servant," says Lakṣmaṇa to Rāma, 20.35; "I am your slave," says Bharata, 97.12), and as Rāma himself submits and suffers ("the king [my] master is exercising his authority over . . . me," 21.17), so all the orders of society are to recognize and observe the strict boundaries of hierarchical existence. This is not something the poet is content merely to suggest. It is explicitly enunciated: "as I myself have shown you," Rāma tells the people of Ayodhyā, explaining the example he is setting, "you must obey your master's order" (40.9). Rāma's behavior is a paradigm to which all subordinates must conform. Where his status might seem to be different is in his apparent freedom to choose to obey. But this freedom is illusory, conjured by the poet only to dismiss it; it is precisely such freedom that Rāma himself denies: "It is not within my power to defy my father's bidding" (18.26); "I cannot disobey my father's injunction" (18.35). He acts, in fact, as if he had no choice, without deliberation, "without questioning my father's word" (16.37).[26] His obedience as unreflective action holds as much interest for the poet as its justification—indeed more, for the latter is consistently minimized.

On another socially symbolic level, where Rāma's filial relationship with the king is brought into prominence, the relations obtaining in the political organization at large are grasped. According to the paternalistic formulation of the text, the people are the *prajāḥ*, the "children," of the king. The institutionalization of dependency and loyalty would appear to be a major precondition for the centralization of power;[27] a basic problem, especially in the period of consolidation, is how to incorporate and manage the more traditional local allegiances. The mediating expression of a higher yet recognizable unity, the broadly integrating and richly allusive image of the state as family and the king as father would do this effectively—perhaps even more effectively than the ascription of divine status to the king (which, as we shall see in Book Three, likewise plays a significant role in the ideology of the poem). For the king comes to represent a superior kinship bond, drawing on and incorporating the symbolic power of those that had previously been dominant. The deeper resonances of "father" in the following verses would have been perceptible to any Indian audience "on the streets and highways of Ayodhyā":

[26] On the corroborative function of Rāma's fatalism, see chapter 5.

[27] Cf. also Thapar 1961, p. 147.

> There is no greater act of righteousness than this: obedience to one's father and doing as he bids. (16.48)

> It is this that is my duty on earth, and I cannot shirk it. Besides, no one who does his father's bidding ever comes to grief. (18.31)

> As long as Kākutstha lives, my father and lord of the world, he must be shown obedience, for that is the eternal way of righteousness. (21.10)

> Both you and I must do as father bids. He is king, husband, foremost guru, lord, and master of us all. (21.13)

> My father keeps to the path of righteousness and truth, and I wish to act just as he instructs me. That is the eternal way of righteousness. (27.30)

Thus the ideological dimension of the *Ayodhyākāṇḍa* comprises two principal components. Actual relations of subordination, on the one hand, and the identification of "state" and more localized political interests, on the other, can no longer be recognized as having a determinate and historical character; the one is now in every sense natural and inevitable; the other, an inextricable genetic bond. Social subordination and political domination now become "the eternal way of righteousness" and the ultimate horizon of possibility for human life. They thus acquire a heightened value, which in turn promotes their continuous reproduction.

It should come as no surprise to the reader of Spenser or Milton to find, as we do on our first level of signification, an extension of a private ethics into a public context,[28] a grounding of political success on moral success, and an embodiment of these concerns, with self-conscious didactic purpose, in epic poetry. In Vālmīki, however, no screen of allegory or allusion is interposed between the literary text and the political "subtext." The latter has a less ambiguous presence and is permitted a greater degree of transparency than most Western literature has prepared us to expect.[29] Similarly and more importantly, on the second level, the actual formulations of the larger social and political reality and its fictional

[28] See Hill 1977, pp. 345ff.

[29] It was left to the medieval commentators to rewrite the text according to an anagogical code. Much of the material for the *Ayodhyākāṇḍa* is made available in the annotations below (see for example on 47.22).

representation—the literary and "general" ideological discourses—are more simply and directly related than we are accustomed to finding.[30] They seem, in fact, to be fused into virtually total congruence, and they are enunciated with all the force and authority of a commandment of *śāstra*—precisely what the *Rāmāyaṇa* came later to be considered.

What external evidence substantiates the claim that the *Ayodhyākāṇḍa* incorporates such a "general ideological discourse"? Here we find ourselves in a more favorable position than that of students of many other oral epic traditions. The inscriptions of Aśoka (mid-third century B.C.) furnish an instructive historical analogue for the *Rāmāyaṇa*. The perspectives and attitudes, almost the very formulations that we find in the *Ayodhyākāṇḍa*, were also those of the king who consolidated and ruled the first great Indian empire:

> How might the people be made to advance in *dharma*? . . . This thought occurred to me: I shall have messages about *dharma* proclaimed.
>
> It is the supreme duty of the king to instruct people in *dharma*.
>
> [The people] must believe that the only true success is success through *dharma*.
>
> This world and the other are impossible to secure without a deep love of *dharma*, extreme vigilance, extreme obedience, extreme fear, and extreme effort. But thanks to my giving instruction, attention to and love of *dharma* grow day by day and will continue to grow.
>
> Whatever good deeds I have done the people have followed and will imitate. Thereby they have been made to progress and will be made to progress, in obedience to parents.
>
> One's parents must be obeyed, one's gurus must be obeyed.
>
> And this is *dharma*: . . . Obedience to one's mother and father.
>
> . . . that [the people] may learn that the king is to them like a father . . . that they are to the king like his children.

[30] Cf. Eagleton 1976, especially pp. 44-63 and 81.

All men are my children.[31]

Vālmīki's chronological relationship with the Mauryan king is problematical. But this should not conceal the essential and intriguing fact that so similar a discourse should come to be intimately shared. Whether it permits us to draw conclusions about the poem's "genetic" history, or restricts us to its "effective" history, in either case this fact invites us all the more readily to situate the ideological dimension of the *Ayodhyākāṇḍa* in the world of actual social experience.

[31] The nine citations are, respectively, from: Pillar Edict VII, Rock Edict IV, Rock Edict XIII, Pillar Edict I, Pillar Edict VIII, Minor Rock Edict II, Rock Edict XI, Separate Rock Edict II, Rock Edict I. For an informed analysis of Aśoka's *dharma* see Thapar 1961, pp. 147-75, also Tambiah 1976, especially pp. 56 and 59. There is no question but that many of its elements are old (cf. *TaiU* 1.11 and *Dīghanikāya* 3.188-89); what is important here is how these components, hitherto considered exclusively "sacred," are introduced into the political context (contrast Tambiah 1976, pp. 49-50).

4. A Problem of Narrative and Its Significance

When we speak of "Vālmīki," we are using the name as a convenient, shorthand way of referring to the composer of the monumental *Rāmāyaṇa,* which we have before us in the critically edited text. But we should bear in mind that this text is only the middle point of a poem in progress: we know that it continued to be amplified even after Vālmīki fixed the essential contours of the work; similarly, the monumental poem was itself not the beginning of the tradition, but a major synthesis of antecedent elements.[1] We would not expect such a synthesis to be seamless, but rather to show traces of elaboration or re-working.

The *Rāmāyaṇa* does contain such traces, which reveal themselves in the occasional discrepancies and inconsistencies of the narrative. We are surprised, for example, to find that the hero has such a superfluity of magical weapons—in fact, four different sets;[2] that now Sumitrā, now Kaikeyī, is the "middle mother" among the three (note on 18.22); that Sītā at one point is said to be wearing jewelry, then not wearing it, then again wearing it (34.17, 54.16, 82.13); that Rāma is shown to be crushed with grief at the news of his father's death (95.8ff.), and then described as one who is never "affected by sorrow, however insufferable" (99.45; see note to 99.15 and, more generally, note to 28.12-13). But, like the constitution of the embassy to Achilles or the death and later reappearance of the warrior Pylaimenes in the *Iliad,* such lapses are really trivial. There are, however, more instructive remnants of a premonumental version of the *Rāmāyaṇa* that do not appear to derive, like those, from poorly conflated traditions, imperfect transmission, the "inconsultability" of an oral text, or a faulty memory. Nor are they simple matters of formulaic amplification or thematic accretion. They may be seen, though with some caution, as revisions. They affect certain structural features of the *Ayodhyākāṇḍa,* and stand out as knots in the otherwise closely woven narrative of the book.

[1] See Volume 1, General Introduction.

[2] Given by Viśvāmitra (1.26), Varuṇa (2.28.12), Brahmā (2.39.11; see note there), and Agastya (3.11; this last will be used to slay Rāvaṇa, cf. *Yuddhakāṇḍa* 106).

By analyzing some of these remnants, we can try both to clarify a troublesome obscurity in the story and, in a more speculative way, to suggest how the narrative could have been adjusted by the monumental poet to serve his larger objectives.

Bharata's claim to the throne of Kosala, as the early chapters of our *Ayodhyākāṇḍa* present it, has an unsteady foundation. His mother Kaikeyī, we are told, once received two boons—the fulfilment of two wishes—from Daśaratha in gratitude for her somehow having saved him at a battle "when the gods and *asuras* were at war" (9.9-13). On the eve of Rāma's consecration as prince regent she claims her boons, demanding with one that her own son be made king, and with the other that Rāma be exiled (*sarga* 10).

There is no question that the theme of the two boons belongs to the monumental poem of "Vālmīki." The textual evidence for 9.9ff. is sufficient to guarantee its authenticity. Yet, on the face of it, the story Mantharā tells Kaikeyī has an unusually contrived appearance:

> When the gods and *asuras* were at war, your husband went with the royal seers to lend assistance to the king of the gods, and he took you along. . . . In the great battle that followed, King Daśaratha was struck unconscious, and you, my lady, conveyed him out of battle. But there, too, your husband was wounded by weapons, and once again you saved him, my lovely. And so in his gratitude he granted you two boons. (9.9-13)

The presence of a queen at a battle is extraordinary and virtually unparalleled in Sanskrit literature. The later manuscript tradition of the *Ayodhyākāṇḍa* evidently felt further explanation to be in order. It attempts to supply this by attributing some "magical knowledge" to Kaikeyī (see notes to 9.27 and 10.25), though that hardly suffices. Later adaptations of the *Rāmāyaṇa* are similarly troubled, but can do no more than replace the story with one still more improbable: Kaikeyī's service was to have held together the broken axle of Daśaratha's chariot.[3] All of this points to the adventitious, secondary character of the incident. It is like a makeshift part with no integral position in the structure of the story, which the tradition felt free or obliged to tinker with until it could be made to work.

[3] First in *BrahmP* 123.24ff. (cf. also *AdhyāRā* 2.2.63ff.). Here note also that Daśaratha rewards Kaikeyī with three boons, none of which she is ever said to use.

A close reading of *sargas* 9-10 reinforces this impression and strongly suggests that originally the two boons played no part in the scene. Kaikeyī has oddly forgotten about the boons, and even when reminded (9.14) she does not simply claim them as her due. Instead she is told, "recognize the power of your beauty" (9.19), and "when the great king Rāghava . . . offers you a boon, then you must ask him for this one, first making sure he swears to it" (9.22). In *sarga* 10, Daśaratha tries to mollify his angry wife: "I will do what will make you happy, I swear to you" (10.19), to which Kaikeyī directly replies, "Let the . . . gods . . . hear how you in due order swear an oath and grant me a boon. This mighty king . . . in full awareness grants me a boon—let the deities give ear to this for me" (10.21, 24). The queen thus "ensnared" the king, "who in his mad passion had granted her a boon" (10.25). With a quite casual indifference to the logic of the narrative, the text here continues, "I will now claim the two boons you once granted me" (10.26). Vālmīki clearly wanted to preserve the scene that originally, one would infer, must have shown Kaikeyī trick Daśaratha into offering, now for the first time, a single boon, to be used to exile Rāma.[4] For the poet can thus impugn her claim to the kingship for her son, transforming it into a deception when in truth it had been nothing of the sort.

Early in the *Ayodhyākāṇḍa* we are shown how Daśaratha fears the presence of Bharata and insists on holding the royal consecration while the prince is absent from the city (4.25-27). His motive is not merely to avoid the dispute which, given the problematic character of succession, a younger brother might be expected to raise. As Daśaratha knew, Bharata had a legitimate title to the throne, for near the end of the book we learn how the aged king, in order to gain the hand of the beautiful princess of Kekaya, had agreed to pay the highest brideprice. This was the *rājyaśulka*, a promise to the woman's male kin that her son shall succeed to the throne—a

[4] Since Rāma could not very well be killed outright, the purpose of this boon is to allow Bharata time to "sink deep roots" in the kingdom (9.25). In 6.114.5 only one boon is mentioned, used to banish Rāma (as also in 2.99.4, though here still, artificially, it is tied in with the Timidhvaja war). For the problems this poses the scribes and commentators, consult the critical apparatus. See also 3.45.7 and note. The *MBh* also knows only one boon (3.261.21ff.). The original scene would thus have been isomorphic, as was probably the design, with the Viśvāmitra incident in the *Bālakāṇḍa*: there, with similar rashness, Daśaratha offers the seer a boon, which likewise results in Rāma's departure to the forest (1.17.34-38; 18.3).

decision of major political significance. "Long ago, dear brother," Rāma explains to Bharata, "when our father was about to marry your mother, he made a brideprice pledge to your grandfather—the ultimate price, the kingship" (99.3). In the premonumental version, the armature of which is still visible here, it would have been on the basis of this pledge that Kaikeyī raised the legitimate demand that her son be crowned. This inference is corroborated by testimony from outside the *Rāmāyaṇa* tradition, namely, in the work of the first-century Buddhist poet, Aśvaghoṣa.[5]

Why, we must now ask, did Vālmīki revise the story, introducing the two boons and attempting to minimize, if not eliminate altogether, the *rājyaśulka*, at some cost in narrative coherence? Several answers suggest themselves.

First, the revision enables the poet to preserve the honesty and integrity of Daśaratha. The king is no longer endeavoring to repudiate his marriage pledge by a calculated and opportunistic political maneuver. On the contrary, he is now keeping his word to fulfill two promises given as a noble gesture of gratitude, however deceitfully and cruelly the terms of both of them were formulated by Kaikeyī. This would then be yet another in a series of attempts at idealizing the story that we find in the *Rāmāyaṇa* tradition. Just as, for instance, the later tradition will exculpate Kaikeyī by turning her slave Mantharā into an agent of the gods and making a divine virtue of her vicious ambition; just as it will maintain the chastity of Sītā by having Rāvaṇa abduct not the real princess but a magically enlivened simulacrum of her,[6] so already in the monumental version Daśaratha is to a large extent freed from guilt. He is transformed from an object of reproach into one worthy if not of admiration at least of commiseration. The necessity of this idealization

[5] In a verse describing the origins of the Śākyas, the tribe of the Buddha, Aśvaghoṣa writes as follows of their ancestors, the Ikṣvākus: "They did not try to seize the royal office that had come [to their half-brother] as the brideprice of their mother. No, instead they guarded their father's truth [that is, ensured that his word would be made good] and so retired to the wilderness" (*Saund* 1.21). Aśvaghoṣa knew the *Rāmāyaṇa*, the *Ayodhyākāṇḍa* in particular, with great intimacy and adapted it in his work repeatedly (see, for example, note on 2.51.4). Here we would submit that he is alluding to the incident of Daśaratha's brideprice agreement, in the awareness of a tradition in which it played a more conspicuous role.

[6] Mantharā as emissary of the gods already in the *MBh* 3.260.9-10; the simulacrum of Sītā first, it seems, in *KūrmaP* 2.33.112-41 (see note on *Araṇyakāṇḍa* 43.34), and cf. *AdhyāRā* 3.7. In the *Bālarāmāyaṇa*, a drama of the late ninth-century poet Rā-

from the political and ethical point of view is suggested in the *Ayodhyākāṇḍa* itself:

> Subjects will behave just like their king. The actions of a king must always be truthful and benevolent. The kingdom will thereby be true, the world firmly established on truth. (101.9-10)

And more pointedly by a verse in the *Mahābhārata*:

> A king must be an example to his people. If he lie let him be destroyed. In whatever the plight he finds himself, a king must never deceive. (1.77.18)

Second, a considerable intensification in the dramatic action has been achieved by the alteration. Like Shakespeare in adapting his sources for, say, *Macbeth* or *Othello*, Vālmīki may have chosen for aesthetic reasons to redirect the emphasis of his plot, diminishing such external factors as had hitherto been prominent (the marriage agreement) while magnifying the more personal motivation of the hero. How different the book would have been, to paraphrase the words of the Shakespearean critic, had the poet dwelt more on the reasons for Rāma's going into exile than on the reasons for his not going.[7]

Another explanation, similar to but more consequential than the last, is that, by amalgamating into a single act of Kaikeyī's perversity Rāma's dethronement and exile, the revision allows the poet to reinforce the principal didactic thrust of the book. For Rāma no longer abdicates the kingship and submits to his elders merely in recognition of the just claims of a contractual agreement (as in the version alluded to by Aśvaghoṣa, and like Bhīṣma in the *Mahābhārata*, whose father had made the identical pledge), nor does a *deus ex machina* demand compliance by asserting the validity of the agreement (as in the not dissimilar circumstances of the *Śakuntalā* story). He submits, instead, in the face of what is presented as a grave injustice—the unfounded, capricious, and selfish demand, indeed the deception (as Rāma sees, 21.8) of a junior wife. He submits in

---

jaśekhara, we are told that Śūrpaṇakhā took the form of Kaikeyī, and another *rākṣasa* that of Daśaratha, and they were the ones who banished Rāma to the forest (thus, as the poet explicitly says, Daśaratha is totally exculpated; cf. Raghavan 1963, pp. 882, 792).

[7] See Stoll 1961.

the face of repeated protestations of its injustice by all his loved ones, including his father and spiritual preceptor. The moral code exemplified in Bharata's self-abnegation before his elder brother, an innovation in political ethics already present, presumably, from the beginning of the Rāma legend, is effectively recapitulated by the hero's obedience to the word of his parents, regardless of the mendacity, unjustness, and avarice underlying it.

One wonders, then, why the later passage about the marriage pledge was retained, despite the serious inconsistency it presses upon our attention. Is it a simple question of the natural conservatism of oral poetry, or a function of its "inconsultability"? I think not. A closer scrutiny here discovers a basic and unresolvable problem in the argument of the poem. Later in the book Rāma must know of and reveal the agreement in order to justify his obdurate refusal to acquiesce in the pleas of his brother, his spiritual preceptor, and his people, and to fortify a position that appears increasingly untenable (for the argument is finally and forcefully made that what Daśaratha did was mad, "done in delusion"; it was "sinful, contrary to all that is right and good," he did it "just to please a woman," and thus Rāma is urged to save his father "from sin," 98.50-55, 66). Yet he cannot have known of the pledge if he is to have a tenable position at all: had he been aware of it in the early chapters of the book, he would then have been directly implicated in precisely the fraud he is so determined to avoid.[8] In much the same way, Rāma will later repeatedly justify his behavior by asserting that he must "obey his father's order." But nowhere in the book does Daśaratha issue any such order, nor even explicitly grant Kaikeyī's demands. At every crucial juncture where he might do so, he faints or remains speechless; at times we see the poet struggling to eliminate any suggestion of Daśaratha's involvement.[9]

[8] The commentators are baffled by the revelation in 99.3, and try to dismiss its relevance by claiming that Daśaratha's promise was not binding (see 99.3, 5, 6 and notes). If that were so on the story's own terms, Rāma would obviously not adduce the promise as an argument to support his position. For a more traditional interpretation of several of the problems raised here, see Ramaswami-Sastri 1944, pp. 78-82.

[9] For Rāma's obeying his father's express order, see 97.21; 98.38 and 69; 99.7; 101.16 and 24; 103.21. In 16.32 he in fact asks, "But there is still one thing troubling my mind and eating away at my heart, that the king does not tell me himself that Bharata is to be consecrated," but his question is never straightforwardly answered

We may have some reason to conclude that what Vālmīki found essential to underscore later in the story (the brideprice, the order) he found equally essential to bracket provisionally in the earlier portion. A direct royal order for banishment, which is a judicial punishment exacted only for the gravest offenses (cf. 66.37-38), would unavoidably have called into question the righteousness of the king and so the ultimate basis of his authority—a question now only rhetorically put, when not altogether suppressed. The same holds true, as we saw, if the brideprice had earlier been accorded the prominence it merits in the narrative. We are left to infer that these loose ends had to remain loose if the foundation of Rāma's obedience was to be secure. It is, once again, the necessity of obedience that the poem desires to emphasize, rather than the quality of the authority demanding it.

It may still be objected that this interpretation of the dramatic and didactic reasons behind the revision of the boon-motif shows an insensitivity to certain tensions and nuances within the poem. Doesn't Vālmīki himself actually demur before his hero's sacrifice? Indeed, the price of that sacrifice is deliberately shown to be high—maybe, by that very fact, too high for us to believe it to have been justified in the eyes of the poet. What are its consequences? Rāma's mother is left in a state of abject misery. His young wife and brother are to be exposed to the harshest trials. The city, whose protection should be Rāma's chief concern, is left without a king, as he would have anticipated, knowing that Bharata would never acquiesce in the fraud. The people are overpowered by their grief and desert Ayodhyā en masse to live out the period of his exile in the village of Nandigrāma. Last, and crucially, it is in part his very compliance that kills the man whose word he set out to make good. What results from Rāma's submission is despair, sorrow, and death. Can it be claimed that the poet means to endorse this, and not suggest by the crescendo of misery the need for reason to temper an obedience that might, in the end, destroy its own object?

These are considerable tensions, more easily exposed than resolved, which raise some delicate problems of the historical relativity

(16.41), nor is it ever posed again. The order is simply taken for granted. Furthermore, in 18.15 Kausalyā calls it Kaikeyī's order, and when not ignoring her argument (18.26-31), Rāma fails to explain clearly how Daśaratha is involved (18.35). See also chapter 9 note 9 below.

of cultural meaning. They may exist for us, but have we sufficient reason to believe they existed for the poet and his audience? The suffering brought about by the hero's sacrifice may be meant precisely to enhance its grandeur, not call it into question. Friction, severe friction, is necessary if heroic resolution is to keep its radiance and not fade into a common dullness. Rāma is aware of the suffering (47.19ff., for example, or 95.13), but he is never swayed from his purpose. He knows the price and is willing to pay it; the more he must pay the more precious the act becomes. And who is to gauge, for a work like an ancient Indian epic, the degree of suffering beyond which the value of a heroic act begins to depreciate? Finally, and most important, we must bear in mind that there was thought to exist no integral or causal relation between the sacrifice and the suffering. As the poem itself so often stresses, to have suffered was ineluctable.

5. The Philosophy

OBEDIENCE and the suppression of the individual will are not self-validating moral imperatives. On the contrary, the individual resists his abnegation, and empirical arguments to justify his sacrifice will necessarily fall short. The surest philosophical foundation would be provided by some transcendent authority that obviates the possibility of verification: a metaphysical category, a nontestable axiom. One function of the profound fatalism in the *Ayodhyākāṇḍa*, it would seem, is to supply this authority.

It has long been recognized that fate plays a central role in much epic poetry, but considerable variation in the role can be discerned among the different traditions.[1] Achilles may be doomed to choose between a short life of heroic glory and a long but obscure existence; nevertheless, the choice is his and he knows it. The characters of the *Rāmāyaṇa* believe themselves to be denied all freedom of choice; what happens to them may be the result of "their" own doing, but they do not understand how this is so and consequently can exercise no control. This essential difference implies another, equally weighty. Since the Greek hero in large measure makes and is aware of making his own fate, fate carries with it a substantial element of justice.[2] The fate of Rāma and the others is prepared for them, at some plane beyond their intervention or even comprehension. "Justice" never enters the picture in any demonstrable or even cognizable way. Further, since in the archaic Greek world fate has both a cosmic dimension and an aspect of justice, the gods can guarantee the whole process as guardians of a just and moral order. Significantly, the gods play no role whatever in the *Ayodhyākāṇḍa*. There is a mechanical quality to the course of human affairs, regulated only by some "dark, dumb force that turns the handle of this world." (The component of theodicy would, however, be affixed to the story at this point by the later *Rāmāyaṇa* tradition and elaborated in the medieval scholiastic allegories.)

In the *Ayodhyākāṇḍa* man is prohibited from making his destiny,

[1] An early meditation on the question is to be found in Hegel (1975, Vol. II, pp. 1,070ff.).

[2] Dietrich 1965, pp. 283, 333, etc. On the "justice" of fate, see, for example, p. 327.

and cannot truly comprehend the cause of his suffering. His predicament results from and is perpetuated by something entirely beyond his control. Fate—*daiva*, "what comes from the gods"; *kāla*, "time"; *adṛṣṭa*, "the unforeseeable"; *kṛtānta*, "doom" or "destiny"—is something one cannot understand and against which one cannot struggle:

> It is nothing but destiny, Saumitri, that we must see at work in my exile. . . . For why should Kaikeyī be so determined to harm me, were this intention of hers not fated and ordained by destiny? (19.13-14)

> What cannot be explained must surely be fate, which clearly no creature can resist; for how complete the reversal that has befallen her and me. What man has the power to contest his fate, Saumitri, when one cannot perceive it at all except from its effect? Happiness and sadness, fear and anger, gain and loss, birth and death—all things such as these must surely be the effect of fate. (19.18-20)

> No one acts of his own free will; man is not independent. This way and that he is pulled along by fate. (98.15)[3]

Rāma has no choice, as we saw; no one does. Choice is replaced by chance, and action is nothing more than reaction.

If the possibility of verification is obviated, the need for it cannot be denied. The doubts and hesitations in the face of so paralyzing an axiom are not suppressed; Lakṣmaṇa throughout much of the epic and the minister Jābāli in *sarga* 100 of the *Ayodhyākāṇḍa* are permitted to express them. They urge the antithetical position: reliance on *puruṣakāra*, "human effort," "free will":[4]

> For it is only the weak and cowardly who submit to fate; heroic men, strong of heart, do not humble themselves before fate. A man able to counter fate with manly effort does not give up for all that fate may frustrate his purposes. (20.11-12)

[3] Compare also *Bālakāṇḍa* 58.21-23 and *Araṇyakāṇḍa* 62.11.

[4] As the commentators are at pains to point out, this, significantly, is the *Lokāyata* or materialist posture. See, for example, Cg on 18.36, as well as 61.22 and 94.32-33.

But these characters are only foils, supplying a pretext for Rāma to advance his uncompromising position. His own convictions are never affected.[5]

Besides generally underpinning the action of the story, this fatalism takes on, in the recurrent appeal to *karma*, a more specific shape. Though the word *karma* seems not to be used in so technical a sense in the *Rāmāyaṇa*,[6] the belief is clearly present that there exists a latent and unfailing mechanism of retributive justice for transgressions committed in the past, usually in a former life.[7] No other explanation is ever available to the characters in the midst of their suffering. Without this, their suffering must remain inexplicable:

> It must be, I guess, that in the past I injured many living things or made many childless; that must be why such a thing has happened to me. (Daśaratha, 34.4)

> I guess, my mighty husband, yes, it must no doubt be that once upon a time, when calves were thirsting to drink, I ruthlessly hacked off the udders of the cows, their mothers. And so now . . . I who love my child so have been made childless by Kaikeyī. (Kausalyā, 38.16-17)

> It must be that in some past life women were separated from their sons by my mother's doing, Saumitri, and so this has happened to her. (Rāma, 47.19)

The cause of sorrow is hidden in a vast obscurity that effectively renders hopeless any attempt to remedy it—or to have prevented

[5] The controversy over fate and free will is not restricted to the *Rāmāyaṇa*, and it is often the antagonist (Duryodhana, for example, or Kaṃsa) who articulates the free-will position. There is one intriguing exception to this in the *Rāmāyaṇa*, near the end of the poem. In 6.103.4-5 Rāma does claim (despite such earlier statements as 6.39.28) that he, a human being, has overcome the adversity of fate through human effort. But by this point in the narrative we are too aware of the divine plan underlying the theft of Sītā and Rāvaṇa's death to fail to hear a certain irony in the words the poet places in Rāma's mouth.

[6] See note at 62.16 in the *Araṇyakāṇḍa*.

[7] "Normally the good or evil deed a person does bears its fruit in some other world or in some other life. Because [Daśaratha's] deed was so heinous it bore its fruit in this very world" (Cg on 57.8). On the logical problems involved in the coexistence of the doctrines of fate and *karma* see Hopkins 1906.

it. Only once is the connection ever perceived (by Daśaratha, *sargas* 57-58) between a specific deed and its grievous consequences, which might serve to clarify the mechanism, to explain or justify suffering. But as we shall see, Daśaratha's deed was accidental; the inscrutability of retribution is only intensified.

6. Aesthetic and Literary-Historical Considerations

ALTHOUGH the *Rāmāyaṇa*, in the form we have it, must represent the culmination of a long bardic tradition of heroic song, the poem is more easily considered as the first chapter in a new volume of Indian literary history than as the last of an old one. As the *Ayodhyākāṇḍa* well illustrates, little in antecedent literature can be brought to bear to situate the *Rāmāyaṇa* in a literary-historical continuum, and even less that prefigures its formal character.

The *Ayodhyākāṇḍa* does not in any consistent way presuppose the earlier sacred literary tradition. Though many stray allusions can be found (at one point a *yajurmantra* is quoted, at another a well-known *ṛkśloka*),[1] these are by and large oblique and sparse. One intriguing, if minor, exception is the poet's use of the *Taittirīya* corpus.[2] The *Taittirīya Saṃhitā* is virtually cited once (85.42), and it is probable that the *Brāhmaṇa* and later texts of the school are alluded to in at least four other places, which lends credence to the tradition associating Vālmīki with this branch of vedic learning.[3] With respect to the lawbooks, the situation is similar. Although parallels with many extant *dharmaśāstras* are not uncommon, no particular one appears to inform the *Ayodhyākāṇḍa*; the *Manusmṛti* tradition seems, however, to have particular affinities with it.[4]

I do not think it can be questioned that the monumental poet adopted certain motifs from folk literature as we find it represented in the Buddhist *jātakas*. The *Sāma Jātaka* (#540), for example, is closely related to *sargas* 57-58 and represents, as I shall argue, the prototype for that apparently rather late stratum of the text. Sim-

[1] We have been unable to trace the mantra (see 26.16 and note). For the *ṛkśloka* citation, see 68.14 and note.

[2] Contrast the note on *Bālakāṇḍa* 13.23, where it seems that the poet of the episode was most familiar with the Aśvamedha sacrifice known to the *VājaS*.

[3] See note on 29.13 for the possible allusions, and *Taittirīya Prātiśākhya* 5.36, 9.4, for Vālmīki's affiliation with this *śākhā*.

[4] For the eclectic use of the *dharma* tradition, see 69.14ff. and notes; for the *Manusmṛti*, see the notes on, for example, 2.22; 25.7; 69.22; 94.44 and 51; 99.12; 101.8 and 26; 103.9; 109.24.

ilarly, the tradition of *Rāmapaṇḍita*, "The Wise Rāma," which is preserved in the *gāthās* of the *Dasaratha Jātaka* (#461), seems to have been adapted in *Ayodhyākāṇḍa* 98.15ff., where it is tacked onto the narrative.[5] By contrast, several *jātakas* presuppose the Rāma legend in broad outline, and perhaps even the *Vālmīki Rāmāyaṇa* itself.[6] The *Jayadissa Jātaka* (#513) is a case in point. One *gāthā* found in it refers explicitly to the events—minor events after all—narrated in *sarga* 22 of the *Ayodhyākāṇḍa*:

> As Rāma's mother made her prayers for him when he was about to leave for Daṇḍaka wilderness, so I make my prayers for you . . .[7]

The vast body of early Indian legend and myth is only occasionally narrated or adumbrated, and then only in two contexts.[8] One is the rhetorical figure, where mythical allusions are quite common, but serve only to elevate the tenor of the figure by supplying a point of paradigmatic and nonspecific reference.[9] The second is the appeal to mytho-historical precedent, as when Kaikeyī cites the stories of King Śibi and others to show that Daśaratha must keep his promise, whatever the cost (*sarga* 12). Several of the stories contain archaic features, testifying to an origin antedating the rise of Vaiṣṇava syncretism.[10] There are also a few rather obscure tales that, as Vālmīki's passing references imply, must have been well known. But they remain obscure, for there are apparently no surviving versions elsewhere in Indian literature.[11]

The complicated issue of the relationship between the *Rāmāyaṇa* and the *Mahābhārata*, sketched in the General Introduction (in Volume 1), will not be simplified by a detailed analysis of the *Ayodhyākāṇḍa*. The evidence of the present book obliges us to regard

[5] See 98.15ff. and notes for the parallel verses and discussion.

[6] *Vessantara Jātaka*, #547, for example. See *Jātakas with Commentary*, vol. 6, p. 557.29-30. For a discussion of the date of the *gāthās* here see Cone and Gombrich 1977, p. xxix (possibly pre-Buddhist).

[7] *Jātakas with Commentary*, vol. 5, p. 29.1.

[8] For example, the stories of Alarka, Śibi, 12.4-5; Kaṇḍu, Rāma Jāmadagnya, 18.27ff.; Sāvitrī, 27.6; Surabhi, 68.15ff.; Anasūyā, 109.9-12.

[9] See note on 2.29.

[10] Indra (not Viṣṇu) and Bali, 12.8; the boar incarnation of Brahmā (not Viṣṇu), 102.3. See notes there.

[11] See, for example, 18.20 and 24 with notes.

the two epics as more or less co-extensive and to a high degree interactive traditions. We have already seen that the intractable problem of dynastic power lies at the heart of both. But there is a deeper structural affinity between them, and it emerges nowhere more dramatically than in their second books.

The *Ayodhyākāṇḍa* and the *Sabhāparvan*[12] follow an almost identical narrative pattern; their congruence is astonishing and quite involved. Both constitute the true commencement of their respective stories. All the action that follows depends directly on what happens here, just as everything that precedes serves no other function than to prepare this site. The problem of royal power is brought abruptly into sharp focus. Yudhiṣṭhira's claim to sovereignty, though ostensibly vaster than Rāma's, rests on a similar legitimacy of primogenitural succession,[13] and is asserted, as in the case of Rāma, by the decision to perform the royal consecration. This decision is likewise a provocation that evokes immediate and open opposition in the party of a rival claimant (a "brother"). It is the rival's maternal kin that promotes the opposition, and the means resorted to is comparable: the deception on the part of Bharata's mother finds its parallel in the trickery (at dicing) of Duryodhana's maternal uncle Śakuni. Like Kaikeyī, Śakuni aims at securing a long exile for his opponent so that in the interval Duryodhana can "sink deep roots" in the kingdom (*MBh* 2.66.22; cf. *Rām* 2.9.25). As in the *Ayodhyākāṇḍa*, the only voice of authority able to check the course of the tragic events, that of the aged king, is silenced by a weakness born of reckless affection (Dhṛtarāṣṭra's for his son Duryodhana parallels Daśaratha's for Kaikeyī; both kings, incidentally, justify themselves on the grounds of fatalism, *MBh* 2.45.57, 51.15, etc.; cf. *Rām* 2.34.4, 53.17). Like Rāma, Yudhiṣṭhira acts out of obedience to his "father's" order (*MBh* 2.52.15, 18); like Lakṣmaṇa, the prince's brothers exhort him to armed resistance (*MBh* 3.28-34), only to receive a response similar to Rāma's: Yudhiṣṭhira gave his word (at the time of the dicing, *MBh* 2.35.11, 14, 21); and so on.[14]

[12] Some of the relevant narrative spills over into the third book, the *Vanaparvan*.

[13] For dramatic reasons this legitimacy is deliberately complicated in Book One but clearly untangled in Book Five (see, for example, *adhyāya* 147, especially verses 29ff.).

[14] The public enactment of the drama unfolds in virtually identical ways. The justice

Although this isomorphism is remarkable and merits more detailed exploration, the disagreements are equally significant and instructive. A difference of vision, first, seems to be inscribed in the very names of the books, as it is in the texts throughout. There is a keen awareness of the broad social impact of political behavior, and consequently an exemplary figuration to it, in the "City of Ayodhyā," which is missing in the story of the idiosyncratic, at times erratic, conduct of the leaders who sit in closed session in the "Assembly Hall." Like Rāma, Yudhiṣṭhira is a victim of treachery and deceit, but he is in large measure also a victim of his own moral vacillation, lack of judgment, and ambition—characteristics that adhere to him throughout the poem, and that he himself recognizes.[15] He feverishly gambles for the crown that Rāma abandons with indifference; to put it another way, he confronts (and will be ruined by) the insoluble dilemma of the political problem transcended and so annulled by Rāma.

Bharata's temperamental distance from any participation in the political struggle finds an objective correlative in his removal from Ayodhyā to the land of the Kekayas. Duryodhana, by contrast, remains present all the while; his "humiliation" at the hands of the Pāṇḍavas (*MBh* 2.43) is the correlative of his clear recognition of, and sharp emotional response to their political challenge. Bharata's horror at learning of his mother's intrigues and his frantic attempt to conciliate and reinstate his brother stand in irreducible oppo-

---

of the hero's dispossession, for example, is called into question (*MBh* 2.60-64; cf. *Rām* 2.32), but the controversy ends in similar indecision. The prince in the end must strip and don the clothing of a beggar. His wife suffers the humiliation of public exposure (*MBh* 2.62.4ff.; cf. *Rām* 2.30.8ff.); in sorrow she takes leave of her mother-in-law and receives the latter's tearful parting advice (*MBh* 2.71.25ff.; cf. *Rām* 2.36.9ff.). The hero departs amid dire portents (*MBh* 2.71.25ff.; cf. *Rām* 2.36.9ff.). The people condemn the king for his weakness (*MBh* 2.61.50; cf. *Rām* 2.33.13) and denounce the victor, the prospect of whose coming rule terrifies them (*MBh* 3.1.12; cf. *Rām* 2.42.17ff., especially 21). They long to desert the city and follow the prince into banishment, but he urges them to return (*MBh* 3.1.16ff.; cf. *Rām* 2.40).

[15] These traits, of which Yudhiṣṭhira shows a clear understanding in 2.35.1ff., and which come into particularly distinct prominence in the fifth book, are difficult to dismiss on the basis of the role of dicing in the *rājasūya* ceremony as presented in the *Brāhmaṇas* (see van Buitenen 1975, pp. 3ff., especially pp. 27-30). The ritual explanation accounts only for the least interesting and least meaningful features of the narrative.

sition to Duryodhana's collusion at every step of the plot and his final exultation.

Finally, although the injustice surrounding the hero's exile is similar in the two books, in the *Mahābhārata* it is no pretext for brotherly submission. On the contrary, injustice is magnified into atrocity, which can only be cleansed in the blood of kinsmen. The symbolic focus of fratricidal conflict is the heroes' wife, Draupadī. The sexual outrages Duryodhana and the others commit against her in the *Sabhāparvan* call forth vengeful threats on the part of the Pāṇḍavas, and it is toward the fulfillment of these threats in the extermination of their "brothers" that all the remaining action of the poem inexorably moves. In the *Rāmāyaṇa*, Sītā functions as a comparable symbolic focal point, but its location is shifted. A sexual outrage is similarly perpetrated (Rāvaṇa's rape), but this will occur outside the assembly hall; it is, so to speak, strategically isolated in the forest, whereby its political charge is defused.[16]

The structural congruence of the two books thus seems to point to a more fundamental relationship between the epics than generic affiliation. Equally interesting, however, are their divergences. Their basic uniformity only illuminates the more distinctly the ways in which the *Ayodhyākāṇḍa* has sought to reformulate the terms of their common problem. This image of formative interaction remains if we examine the two poems on a more superficial level.

It is true that the *Ayodhyākāṇḍa*, like the rest of the poem, betrays no knowledge of the main narrative of the *Mahābhārata*, but it is reticent about much other early literature, as well. The *Rāmāyaṇa* has a single-minded purpose, with none of the encyclopedic interests of the *Mahābhārata* in its final form. Nor was it ever subjected to a literate, comprehensive redaction of the sort the *Mahābhārata* underwent. The *Rāmāyaṇa* has no interest in, and actually appears hostile to placing itself in history, as reference to the *Mahābhārata*—history for the Indian audience—would place it. It exploits only those features of the *Mahābhārata* narrative that can furnish a mythic paradigm: the story of Yayāti, for example (which the *Rāmāyaṇa* knows in detail and whose earliest known source is probably

[16] For a discussion, see the introduction to the *Rāmāyaṇa*, Volume III. If it is anything more than rhetoric, Rāma's willingness to surrender his wife Sītā to his brother Bharata (16.33-34, for example) would only reinforce the contrast between the two narratives.

the *Mahābhārata*).[17] Its silence about the *Mahābhārata* may come not from ignorance but from wilful disregard. As if it were attempting to supersede the second epic, the *Rāmāyaṇa* incorporates the great personages of the lunar dynasty into Rāma's solar lineage: Bharata, Nahuṣa, Yayāti, and perhaps even Janamejaya.[18]

By contrast, those specific themes that the *Ayodhyākāṇḍa* shares with the *Mahābhārata* by and large fit more appositely in Vālmīki's poem—if we are prepared to ascribe any cogency to the idea of narrative propriety. A good example is furnished by the *kaccitparvan, sarga* 94, where Rāma interrogates Bharata about his administration of the kingship. Many scholars, including the editor of this volume, Vaidya, have asserted the priority of the *Mahābhārata* version (2.5).[19] However, the scene plays a vital narrative function in the *Ayodhyākāṇḍa*. It serves in part to testify to Rāma's profound knowledge of righteousness and statecraft, and so to make his refusal to assume the kingship all the more poignant—and unarguable. No such integrating purpose can be discerned for *Mahābhārata* 2.5, where a divine sage puts the questions to a prince who, in fact, is not yet fully a sovereign. But, on the other hand, the very aptness of the *Ayodhyākāṇḍa*'s handling of the motif might lead one to conclude that it adapted and enlivened a stale, extraneous didactic catalogue with the careful attention to narrative functionality that is one of Vālmīki's talents.[20]

Problems like this, coupled with the numerous features of the folk tradition of storytelling in the *Rāmāyaṇa*, suggest that the question of priority with respect to preliterate epic or popular texts is in general misleading. The oral traditions of all the various genres and particular works must have been continuously interactive and

[17] *Ayodhyākāṇḍa* 5.9, 11.1, 71.10, etc.; *Araṇyakāṇḍa* 62.7; *MBh* 1.70ff. The vulgate of the *Uttarakāṇḍa* (GPP 7.58-59) relates the story, which seems to be a late addition, in a modified form.

[18] Cf. 2.102.13, 27; 1.69.30, 2.58.36 and note.

[19] Vaidya 1962, p. 702; cf. also more recently Kane 1966, pp. 51ff.

[20] See, for example, the note on 69.14ff. Besides the *kaccitparvan*, other sections the *Ayodhyākāṇḍa* holds in common with the *MBh* include the *arājaka* chapter (*sarga* 61) and the story of Surabhi (68.15ff.). See the notes there. Although a verse like *Rām* 2.61.22 seems to be a clear borrowing from the *MBh* (see note at 61.22), several introductory (and probably late) portions of the *MBh* appear to borrow from the *Ayodhyākāṇḍa*. Compare *MBh* 1.133.5ff., especially verse 12, with *Rām* 2.30.15ff.; *MBh* 1.138.15ff. with *Rām* 2.82.1ff. (the two motifs are irrelevant in the *MBh* contexts).

cross-fertilizing. Even more clearly than the *Rāmāyaṇa*, the *Mahābhārata* has roots that stretch back into the late vedic age. This fact, coupled with the structural similarity of the poems, forces us to think of the two epic traditions as coextensive processes that were underway throughout the second half of the first millennium B.C., until the monumental poet of the *Rāmāyaṇa* and the redactors of the *Mahābhārata* authoritatively synthesized their respective materials and thereby in effect terminated the creative oral process.

The impress of Vālmīki has been left particularly deeply on the formal aspects of the *Ayodhyākāṇḍa*. The reader who comes to it with an awareness of the literary character of late vedic myth and legend, the *jātakas*, or other early Pāli or Sanskrit Buddhist narratives, or of the central portions of the *Mahābhārata*, must be struck by the sophisticated artistry of the book, which nothing in the antecedent or contemporary literature had prepared him to expect.

We have already noted that the poet represents himself as developing a new formal vehicle for his work. Nothing of the sort really occurred, of course; the elements of the metric revert to vedic times (and were in great measure an Indo-European heritage). But Vālmīki's versification does unquestionably possess a polish and grace, a quiet elegance, that markedly differentiate it from anything known before.[21] We should also note the function of the "lyric" verses at the *sarga* ends. They are designed to mark closure, either by recapitulating the action (such as 76.27-30), or by providing a synoptic preview of what is to come (such as 21.25). There is no analogy for this device that I know of in early Indian literature.

If the balladlike refrain style to which Vālmīki is especially partial in the *Ayodhyākāṇḍa* has antecedents in the folk tradition,[22] nowhere else do we find it used with the same degree of skill. It is employed here with a fine sense of proportion and restraint, and is used only when there is compelling contextual motivation for the tone of pathos that it contributes. This kind of mature execution holds true for the poetic style of the book in general.

Unlike much early Sanskrit epic poetry, indeed, unlike oral epic

[21] There are very few technical problems: one apparently hypermetric *pāda*, in 95.31, and two verses that, no doubt because of the complexity and rarity of the meters, have suffered from an imperfect transmission (108.25, 26).

[22] For examples of the refrain, see 25.6ff., 61.8ff., 69.14ff., 77.3ff., 92.4ff., 103.4ff. For the relationship of this style to the folk tradition, which appears far more archaic, see the remarks of Oldenberg cited in the note to 25.5.

in general, with its natural impulse to subordinate the line to the paragraph, the paragraph to the book, and the book to the whole,[23] Vālmīki is particularly (though by no means exclusively) interested in sculpting the memorable individual line, often by the use of almost classical rhetorical devices. Consider the moving figure in the following verse, which concludes Sītā's supplication of Rāma to take her to the forest. Speaking of the pain of fourteen years of separation she says,

> I could not bear the grief of it even for a moment, much less ten years of sorrow, and three, and one. (27.20)

Or the very effective anaphora (in Sanskrit rhetorical terminology, an *ekāntarapādayamaka*) when Daśaratha is making ready to shoot the arrow that is to have such disastrous consequences for him:

> I drew out a shaft that glared like a poisonous snake, and I shot the keen-edged arrow, and it darted like a poisonous snake. (57.17)

Or the "poetic fancy" (*utprekṣā*) in Daśaratha's lament before his wife at the departure of Rāma:

> I cannot see you, Kausalyā! Oh please touch me with your hand. My sight has followed after Rāma and has not yet returned. (37.27)

In all these cases, which one could easily multiply, the listener or reader is asked to pause and relish, as he had not often been asked before.

Perhaps the most impressive formal feature, and the most sophisticated aesthetic advance, is to be found in the construction of the book. Besides its overall architectonic design and cohesion, it exhibits at times a complex narrative technique, quite unlike either the simple episodic or the emboxing procedures that are the norm in Sanskrit literature. This not only achieves a dramatic intensity of a very high order, but serves, on occasion, obliquely and for that reason the more effectively, to concretize certain aspects of the basic problematic of the story.

[23] Well described by Lewis 1942, pp. 1-2.

The *Ayodhyākāṇḍa* is probably the most skillfully structured of the seven sections of the poem; the links of the plot are securely and tightly concatenated. Our sight is never allowed to wander as the story progresses toward the final conflict and resolution (or provisional resolution, for the story does continue). And the progress has an implacable quality to it, marked by stirring and at times vehement and bitter encounters between the principal characters, by sudden and compelling reversals, and the stimulation and frustration of our expectations. This kind of artistry will be perceptible to even the casual reader, who will immediately appreciate how the narrative is propelled by the intensely dramatic series of confrontations: between Mantharā and Kaikeyī (*sargas* 7-9), Kaikeyī and Daśaratha (10-12), Rāma and Sītā (23-27), Bharata and Kausalyā (69), Rāma and Bharata (97-99, 103-104), to mention only the most prominent.

Beyond the mere linear development of the action, we can discern two other narrative modes that function as formal correlatives to the major problematic of the story. The first is distinguished by its spatial discontinuity, the second by its temporal synchrony.

The narrative time span for approximately the first two-thirds of the book is extremely brief. The action of *sargas* 1-40 (1-4 and 7-12 excepted) occurs in a single day; 1-63 all together occupy only ten days.[24] The feeling we get about Rāma's departure is a long ache rather than a single sharp pain. Moreover, if so much of the story occupies so limited a temporal framework, we would naturally expect a lingering, minute examination of what action there is from multiple perspectives—which, in fact, we do find. Whereas the narrative in the first mode proceeds directly forward, here we constantly find the scene shifting to register individual responses to the action. Diachronic narration starts in *sarga* 13, where for the first time the separate strands of the narrative are fully interwoven, but soon a spatial discontinuity sets in. With Rāma's departure from the city in *sarga* 35, the narrative focus begins to alternate frequently: to Ayodhyā (36-39), to Rāma (40-41), to Ayodhyā (42), back to Rāma (43-50), to Ayodhyā (51-87; on 51-58 in particular

[24] 2.64-104, with the seven days of Bharata's journey and the thirteen days of Daśaratha's funeral subtracted, take up some eight days. The narrative time-keeping pretty much ends with Bharata's departure from Mount Citrakūṭa and the commencement of Rāma's stay in the forest where, in a sense, normal time is suspended.

see below), to Rāma (88-91), to Bharata (92), when finally the action is again unified (93-104), only to disconnect once more into separate strands (105-107 concern Bharata, 108-11 Rāma).

Rāma's fate is not his alone; his family as well as the entire community are involved in it. From the hero's banishment result dilemmas of every sort—social, political, ethical. This kind of narrative presentation (which is not in any way a "natural" consequence of the story, as a comparison with the end of *Mahābhārata* 2 shows) permits us to witness each successive predicament as it is individually addressed. At the same time, it continually underscores the central importance of Rāma, and, by juxtaposing his response to those of the other characters, allows us to distinguish its uniqueness. Additionally, in a way less easily analyzed or demonstrated, the form of dyadic progression itself seems to incarnate the spirit of dilemma that so pervades the book.

A rather more subtle narrative procedure is discernible in the synchronous mode. Here the narrative does not move directly forward but retraces itself to examine the same narrative time frame from two different vantage points. A telling example is provided early in the book.[25] *Sargas* 7-9 backtrack to show us the previous day's conversation between Mantharā and Kaikeyī, which is taking place at the same moment as the one between Daśaratha and Rāma (*sarga* 4). The simultaneity of plot and counterplot produces the expectation of explosive fusion.

Less transparent but more elegant and expressive is the instance that occurs in *sargas* 50-58. In *sarga* 50 Rāma reaches the grove of asceticism and settles down, with a feeling almost of contentment, to his life in exile. It is the sixth evening of his banishment, as we can discover by following the poet's careful chronological indications.[26] At that very hour, back in Ayodhyā, Daśaratha lies plunged in sorrow and recovers at last the memory of the evil deed of his youth: he remembers that long ago he had slain a young ascetic and had been cursed by the boy's father. Now blind and feeble and

[25] The passage won the enthusiastic admiration of A. W. von Schlegel as early as 1838: "Not only is nothing confused in the ordering of events, but we can observe a marvellous artifice on the poet's part in ordering the narrative: presenting first everything that could awaken the most certain expectations of the happy event, he delays till the last possible moment the presentation of the fatal obstacle that will suddenly confound everything" (Schlegel 1838, p. 257).

[26] The six evenings of Rāma's exile: *sargas* 40, 45, 47, 48, 49, 50. See also 51.1, 4, and notes; 56.14, 57.3, where the poet becomes explicit.

as good as childless, Daśaratha is reduced to a condition identical to that of the seer he had bereaved, while Rāma, the son whom Kausalyā accuses her husband of having destroyed (55.20), has at the same moment been transformed into an ascetic of the sort Daśaratha had murdered.[27]

The synchronicity of the narrative here helps to make manifest a complex and richly suggestive set of latent correspondences. One further effect it has is to reinforce a dominant theme that we have already noticed: the role of fate, which blends together in an often violently interactive synthesis separate and perhaps otherwise benign destinies, and whose operations are as mysterious as they are inexorable.[28]

[27] Although Rāma mats his hair and adopts "the vow of forest hermits" in 46.55-58, he does not appear to enter fully on the renouncer's way of life until he reaches the grove of asceticism in *sarga* 50 (in 49.14, for example, he still eats meat, despite his claim in 17.15; see note to 48.15). For further parallels between the stories of Daśaratha/Rāma and the seer and his son, see 57.20, 27, 32 and notes, and note to 58.48. Jacobi underestimates the poet's narrative skill. He explains Daśaratha's death on the sixth day (rather than immediately after Rāma's departure, as *poetische Gerechtigkeit* demands) either as the result of the mistaken belief that narrative time must correspond to real time (that is, if Rāma's progress had been followed for six days, the scene in Ayodhyā that immediately ensues must be six days later), or for other, more implausible reasons (Jacobi 1893, pp. 47-50; addendum p. 255). See note on 57.3.

[28] Not so significant but nonetheless interesting as an indication of the poet's self-conscious artistry is the narrative parallelism of the *Ayodhyākāṇḍa*. The city and forest scenes where Rāma is begged to reconsider his decision unfold in similar ways: Kausalyā's demands for obedience, 18.16-21 = Vasiṣṭha's, 103.1-4; Lakṣmaṇa's counter-arguments, 18.1-15, 20.1-35 = Jābāli's, 100; Rāma's defense, 19.13-22 = 101; Kausalyā's threat to fast to death, 18.23 = Bharata's, 103.12-19; the sentiments of the people, 30.15-20 = 103.19-23. This was first pointed out, though with some not very persuasive conclusions, by Ruben (1956, pp. 48-49).

7. The Characters

If the style and narrative organization of the *Ayodhyākāṇḍa* often show great and easily accessible artistry, it may perhaps be more difficult for the modern reader to evaluate and gauge the quality of characterization. Since the characters are first fully introduced to us in this book, it is appropriate here to consider how they are depicted and to enquire whether there is any reason for us to temper our response, which initially may be unfavorable.

I think we can observe definite and important differences in the methods of characterization. Two distinct groups of characters seem to present themselves: those, on the one hand, who possess the natural uneven contours of imperfect human beings, depths where we can hear the cacophonous resonances of familiar emotions—hate no less than love, and ambition, remorse, fear, envy, rancor—and the many tones of moral uncertainty, of doubts, compunctions, scruples; and those, on the other, who seem to lack all this, who are more regular and flat, with almost emblematic features.

Daśaratha, Kaikeyī, and Kausalyā have a natural unevenness. They command full and complex emotional and moral registers, and a wide range of their modulations can be clearly heard throughout much of the book. Choices confront them with which they must grapple; they suffer and in their suffering engage in a painful and very human process of self-recognition. They thereby learn some fundamental truths about themselves and come to understand the consequences of reckless desire, or the hollowness of success achieved at the cost of one's integrity, or the futility of naive hope.

Yet we perceive all this only if we search for it; the culmination of these processes is rarely allowed into the foreground of the narrative. In the case of Daśaratha, the impact of recognition is deflected and appreciably diminished: it is turned into a useless if exonerating discovery of an act done long ago, over which he no longer has control—if, indeed, he ever had. With respect to Kaikeyī, although we see the groundwork prepared for her realization, we are never given the opportunity to witness it. After her principal narrative function is completed (*sarga* 33), she is given only several silent entrances (37.4, 60.1ff., 72.19ff., 86.16). What appears to be reconciliation (77.6) or contrition (86.16) is never developed or explained.

The treatment of Kausalyā is similar, and the many hints about her personal tragedy scattered throughout the book make the absence of some final resolution more conspicuous. Much of her story is only vaguely suggested, and we are left to reconstruct it inferentially. Her husband never loved her, and she set her hopes on finding in a son the joy and comfort denied her in her marriage (17.22, cf. 10.17 and note on 40). With the arrival of Kaikeyī she was "superseded" (see 28.7 and note), and from then on she sought retribution for her wrongs by her son's succession to the throne (4.38-39), living a life of religious austerity with the aim of securing her goals. But her realization is a bitter one:

> What a sorrowful thing that my vows, my gifts of alms, and acts of self-denial have all been to no avail, that the austerities I practiced for my child's sake have proved to be as barren as seed sown in a desert. (17.31)

But this limited discovery is all we are shown. The more important resolution of her relationship with Daśaratha is never provided. We get some sense of a final reconciliation through shared suffering (*sarga* 56; note on 57.7), but the poet does not take the trouble to substantiate it.

Vālmīki, rather clearly, is uninterested in these contingent characters. This whole rich ensemble of substantial and comprehensible human emotion is left incomplete, reduced to an epiphenomenon taking place on the periphery of Rāma's world. The poet's indifference is, of course, partly a result of the fact that Rāma and those who directly participate in his sacrifice—Lakṣmaṇa, Sītā, and Bharata—are the principal focus of his attention. But Vālmīki's unconcern has some other origin, which will become apparent if we examine his characterization of the second set.

The reader will probably be struck, despite the driving momentum of the action, by a feeling of stasis in these four characters. In contrast to those just discussed, they do not grow or change in the course of the narrative, or develop through inner struggle in the presence of moral choice.[1] They answer without hesitation the so-

[1] It has been argued that the poet disallows this by his bipartition of "whole" character types. Rāma's inner struggle is objectified in his alter ego Lakṣmaṇa, as less significantly Bharata's in Śatrughna (see Goldman 1980, pp. 164ff.).

cial and moral questions with which they are presented, for the most part secure in their particular patterns of behavior. Unlike Kaikeyī or Daśaratha, they define themselves in relation to others with an immutable and unnatural consistency. Their actions, consequently, have an emblematic regularity about them.

This, I believe, is exactly what the poet wishes us to perceive in them. He was not restricted in his characterization by some metaphysical concepts peculiar to India about time, causality, or reality, which predisposed him to see the transcendent and enduring in the local and transient. We have just viewed in the first set of characters the full range and clarity of his vision. Rāma and the others are evidently designed to be monovalent paradigms of conduct.

Vālmīki has not only an aesthetic intention but a didactic purpose, as well. And he has created these four great moral figures to achieve that purpose. The specific moral dimension of each is encapsulated in a formulaic, often alliterative, epithet, which augments the impression of stasis; no such tags are, or could have been, provided for Daśaratha, Kaikeyī, or Kausalyā. Rāma is the "champion of righteousness" (*rāmo dharmabhṛtāṃ varaḥ*); Bharata "a man of brotherly love" (*bharato bhrātṛvatsalaḥ*); Lakṣmaṇa "marked with goodness" (*lakṣmaṇaḥ śubhalakṣaṇaḥ*) in devotedly serving his eldest brother; Sītā is "like the daughter of the gods" (*sītā surasutopamā*), by reason of both her beauty and the virtue (that is, unwavering fidelity to her husband) that in Indian culture beauty is so often said to reflect.[2]

The two sets of characters thus serve very different literary func-

[2] The concomitance of beauty and virtue is stated most succinctly by Kālidāsa as a proverb: "Beauty cannot do wrong" (*pāpavṛttaye na rūpam, KumāSaṃ* 5.36; also *yatrākṛtis tatra guṇā vasanti*, "Virtue and beauty go hand in hand," *Śāk.* 4.0.7-8 [Pischel]). Cf. Kale's remark, "For beauty of person presupposes a degree of religious merit on the part of the person endowed with it; hence such a person cannot be expected to lead a sinful life" (Kale 1967 ad loc.), and the passages he adduces, especially *Mṛcch* 9.16, *na hy ākṛtiḥ susadṛśaṃ vijahāti vṛttam* ("Beauty and good conduct always go hand in hand," spoken by the judge).

The later purāṇic tradition clearly was aware of the four moral dimensions and the paradigmatic quality of the characters:

> [Kuśa and Lava sang the story of Rāma] wherein the ways of righteousness are set forth before one's very eyes [Rāma], and fidelity to one's husband [Sītā], great brotherly love [Bharata], and devotion to one's guru [Lakṣmaṇa]" (*PadmaP* 4.66.128).

tions. The four central ones embody permanent moral values in a society marked by generalized contingency.[3] The others (and this is the only sort known to the poets of the central portions of the *Mahābhārata*) typify precisely that uncertainty, hesitancy, and vacillation; it is for this reason that their personal fates are not pertinent. We may find it hard to respond to the former, since they will necessarily lack moral variety, although they retain a certain "freedom of sentiment" that often saves the work from lapsing into melodrama.[4] But we must remember that if they do not manifest a recognizable human complexity it is because they were never intended to do so; Rāma's "true feelings" will remain secret, and properly so, for they are quite irrelevant to the poem's purposes. These characters must be ideal because they are imaginary solutions to problems that do not admit of real solutions. The didactic exigencies of the work required perfect moral types, and perfection, by definition, does not alter.[5]

[3] This manner of characterization has parallels in other traditions (cf. Fränkel 1962, pp. 30, 37), and it has even been argued that it is fundamental to much western epic (not just to "altorientalische Despotismus," as claimed by Ruben 1936, pp. 34-35). One authority has remarked that "what epic can't do is to accommodate private, esoteric states of feeling or complex analyses of character. From Virgil to screen westerns the characters act out the *type* of a Roman, a barbarian" (Lawrence Kitchen cited by Merchant 1971, p. 83). But these kinds of generalizations are less helpful than specific explorations of the reasons enforcing the convention. We see in the *Rāmāyaṇa* that it is only partially observed, and in that part quite purposefully. Thus, with respect to the *Rāmāyaṇa*, it is not possible to agree that "there are no individuals in Sanskrit literature, there are only types" (Ingalls 1968, p. 17).

[4] This point is well brought out by D.H.H. Ingalls, whose remarks are worth quoting at length:

> "In the *Rāmāyaṇa*, which sets the pattern for much in Sanskrit literature, we witness the making of decisions, but there is never any doubt what the decisions will be. Rāma could not disobey his father without ceasing to be the Rāma he has been from the moment we first see him in childhood. Nor can one imagine a Sītā who would not join Rāma in his banishment. How different are Rāma and Sītā from the characters that set the patterns of European literature! An Antigone only comes to be Antigone by the tragic choice that we see her make. And yet, the predestination of action in the Indian poem does not produce a mechanical effect. The characters have a certain freedom of sentiment as opposed to a freedom of action. What they will do is not in doubt, but they may do it with compassion or stoicism, with laughter or eagerness or fear, sentiments which seem to arise from within as much as to be occasioned from without" (1968, p. 17).

[5] Rāma's madness in the *Araṇyakāṇḍa* (56-60) is a unique deviation, which will be discussed in the introduction to that volume.

With all that said, it will still be useful to consider more closely several of the main characters of the *Ayodhyākāṇḍa*: the female figures as a group, Daśaratha, and Rāma. In the first case, we must investigate an apparent disjuncture between precept and practice; in the second, we have to examine further the poet's idealizing treatment of a problematic character; and in the third our attention is commanded by a figure who represents a new attitude in the history of Indian thought.

8. The Women of the *Ayodhyākāṇḍa*

LIKE THE *Rāmāyaṇa* as a whole, the *Ayodhyākāṇḍa* is as interested in the domain of sexual relations as in socio-political life in general. The structure of relationships in the one sphere is fundamentally congruent with that of the other, not surprisingly, given their constitutive (if complex) interaction.[1] We have already seen that the poet is reluctant to let the message of the story emerge on its own, that he intervenes to explain what the fictional events are supposed to mean to the social formation at large. The same thing happens with respect to sexual relations, and to a much greater degree.

"A woman's first recourse is her husband," Kausalyā says to Daśaratha, "her second is her son, her third her kinsmen. She has no fourth in this world" (55.18). Here we have, possibly for the first time in Indian literature, a formulation of what was to become the normative view, strictly enforced in practice, on the status of women. The *locus classicus* is found in the *Lawbook of Manu*,[2] which recasts the idea and unambiguously appends the logical conclusion:

> In childhood a woman must bow to the will of her father, in adulthood, to the will of the man who marries her, and when her husband is dead, to the will of her sons. She must never have independence. (5.148)

Inasmuch as the *Ayodhyākāṇḍa* deals chiefly with marital relationships, it is the woman's position vis-à-vis her husband that is the principal subject of explicit didactic intervention, and the poet seems never to tire of repeating the categorical imperative:

> So long as she lives, a woman's one deity and master is her husband. (Rāma to Kausalyā, 21.17)

> You must not feel disdain for my son in his banishment. He is your deity, whether he be rich or poor. (Kausalyā to Sītā, 34.21)

[1] This interaction is apparent to some degree in the text itself, in the political doctrine of paternalism and in the sexual metaphors used to express a primary economic relationship, the king's possession of the land (see chapter 3 note 15 above). More particularly, one might consider such a verse as 2.61.9.

[2] The *Rām* commentators ad loc. make the same connection with *Manusmṛti*, only they point to the doublet, 9.3.

> I fully understand how to behave toward my husband. . . . A husband is a woman's deity. (Sītā to Kausalyā, 34.23 and 27)

> Ever venerate the feet of my lord [your husband], as if he were a god. (Rāma to Kausalyā, 52.14)

> To a woman of noble nature her husband is the supreme deity, however bad his character, however licentious or indigent he might be. (Anasūyā to Sītā, 109.24)

> A woman must show her husband obedience and earnestly strive to please and benefit him. Such is the way of righteousness discovered long ago, revealed in the *veda* and handed down in the world. (Rāma to Kausalyā, 21.21)

There is a close congruence between these precepts and the broader social interpretation offered by the *Ayodhyākāṇḍa*. Although the poet portrays some expression of resistance to this interpretation (Lakṣmaṇa, Jābāli), this seems to be little more than artifice, enabling the hero to argue out his position; no one enacts opposition. In the case of the female characters, however, we find some essential contradictions between the ideal and the actual, between the accepted norms and the specific behavior. For the women of the story do seem to be strong, self-willed, in fact independent.

Whatever the real purpose behind Rāma's initial reluctance to take her with him to the forest,[3] Sītā is by no means ready to submit to his command. She argues vigorously, at one point insulting her husband:

> What could my father Vaideha, the lord of Mithilā, have had in mind when he took you for son-in-law, Rāma, a woman with the body of a man? . . . like a procurer, Rāma, you are willing of your own accord to hand me over to others. (27.3, 8)

Her declared position is that "Even if my husband were wholly lacking in good behavior, . . . still I would always obey him wholeheartedly" (110.3). Yet here we see her caustically disputing and engaging with her husband as an equal.

Kausalyā similarly opposes her husband, with equal spirit and even greater frequency (38.1-7; 51.24-27; 55). If she can say that a woman has but three recourses in her life, she can also tell her

[3] See the notes on 23.23 and 27.26.

husband, "And you are no recourse for me." When Rāma informs her of his banishment, she insists that she shall desert her husband and go with her son. Rāma must remind her that

> For a woman to desert her husband is wickedness pure and simple. You must not do so despicable a thing, not even think it. (21.9)

In the same way, later in the story, during Kausalyā's harshest attack against her husband, Daśaratha himself must reacquaint her with the imperative:

> And as you know, my lady, a woman who has regard for righteousness should hold her husband, whether he is virtuous or not, to be a deity incarnate. (56.5)

The contradiction between precept and practice that surfaces in these episodes is concretely realized in the character of Kaikeyī.

There are substantial ambiguities in Kaikeyī's character. If, by formula, Sītā is beautiful and therefore good (as the servant Mantharā is ugly and therefore wicked), Kaikeyī occupies some ambivalent middle zone. "The golden Kaikeyī," Vālmīki calls her—fair as gold and just as malleable, as one commentator explains.[4] And indeed the impression is unavoidable, for the modern reader at least, that here is a good and trusting woman who is being slowly corrupted (*sargas* 7-9). But for nearly everyone in the story—Lakṣmaṇa (90.20-21), Kausalyā (60.3ff.), Bharata (*sarga* 67), and the people at large (42.18-21)—she is simply an evil woman, blinded by her ambition to the cruelty of her acts. Her inclination to do wrong was natural and was only activated by her servant:

> A greedy person is oblivious to risks; he will eat even fruit that makes one sick. And thus, at the instigation of the hunchback, Kaikeyī has destroyed the House of the Rāghavas. (60.6)

One branch of the *Rāmāyaṇa* tradition, in fact, adds an illustrative story to prove that her evil nature was inherited,[5] and Daśaratha discerns inimical scheming in her family as well as in the woman herself (53.15).

The poet cannot refrain from judging Kaikeyī. He calls her guile-

[4] See 9.44 and note.

[5] Properly rejected by the critical edition; see note on 32.1.

ful (10.3), unscrupulous (12.8), ignoble (16.54), artful (66.14), and so on. More effectively, he illustrates these traits through her behavior in the skillfully crafted scene of her reunion with Bharata (*sarga* 66), where the calculated nonchalance of her horrific disclosures evinces a brutality that has numbed her to all normal emotional response. As we have seen, Vālmīki also goes out of his way to eliminate the one factor that can extenuate her guilt, the legitimacy of her claim to the kingship. Only Rāma affirms the propriety of her behavior (103.29),[6] or excuses it on the grounds that she was compelled by fate (19.16-22). And only the seer Bharadvāja is vouchsafed the larger view:

> Bharata, you must not impute any fault to Kaikeyī. The banishment of Rāma will turn out to be a great blessing. (86.28)

Vālmīki, it appears, meant Kaikeyī to serve largely as a negative exemplar. The scene, for example, where the impudent queen forces her husband to grovel before her (*sarga* 10.40-*sarga* 11) is hard to forget, and not only because of its drama. The poet will not let us forget, for he later shows how a good wife is to behave in such circumstances (55.7-13). Kaikeyī, then, would be intended as an illustration of what happens when a woman seeks to act autonomously: she destroys the foundation of her life, her husband:

> Without strings a lute cannot be played, without wheels a chariot cannot move, without her husband a woman finds no happiness, though she have a hundred sons. (34.25)

And it is no doubt this aspect of her portrait that makes the greatest impact on the reader.

But if, like both Bharadvāja and the later *Rāmāyaṇa* tradition, we are disposed or even supposed to see her primarily as an instrument, a catalyst, a "dramatic mechanism," we may be approaching a vantage point where the contradictions between the poet's stubbornly reiterated homilies and the behavior of the other female characters can be transcended and so resolved. From such a perspective we see that these characters actually function on the whole either to enact the emotional content of the narrative, or as sound-

[6] His words in 47.14-18 may well be, as the commentators suggest, only pretense: he is trying to persuade Lakṣmaṇa to return to Ayodhyā in order to take care of Kausalyā.

ing-boards by means of which the proper role of women may be clearly articulated. They are merely instruments of the narrative, passively acted upon but not significant agents of the action. If superficially they deviate from the pattern, structurally, in their fully subservient functionality, they conform to it. In this sense, then, there is no conflict: in their "real" practice they are permitted no independence and exercise none.

9. Daśaratha

I HAVE ALREADY argued that in the course of the development of the Rāma story, alterations appear to have been made in order to secure a more idealized action and characterization. The effects of this revision are particularly noticeable in the case of the portrait of Daśaratha.

Initially Daśaratha is presented to us as the venerable, dignified, self-disciplined, and virtuous monarch. He tells us that as king he has "always kept to the path my ancestors followed" (2.4). We are invited to infer his integrity when he says, "I have grown weary bearing the burden of righteousness for the world. For it is heavy, one must have self-discipline to bear it" (2.7). Early in the story he advises Rāma, "exercise constant self-control, and avoid all the vices that spring from desire and anger" (3.26), giving us every reason to suppose that he practices what he preaches.

In the development of the story, however, the conflict between these professions and his behavior becomes irreconcilable. For other traits, elements of the structure of the narrative, slowly but with unmistakable clarity emerge: Daśaratha is weak, tyrannical, and reckless.

If these traits can be subsumed under any single character flaw, it is the king's unmastered sexual desire.[1] In the magnificent scene in *sarga* 10, under the pressure exerted by this desire, the king's whole personality begins to disintegrate. The unspeakable deeds of which it makes him capable now come out into the open. Pathetically attempting to ingratiate himself with his capricious young wife, the king asks her,

> Is there some guilty man who should be freed, or some innocent man I should execute? What poor man should I enrich, what rich man impoverish? (10.10)[2]

If the reader should overlook the enormity of this offer, the text itself, once again, is there to remind and instruct him. When Bha-

[1] On the possible multivalence of this theme, see chapter 3 note 15 above.

[2] The first line is one of the very few from the *Ayodhyākāṇḍa* that appears verbatim in the *Rāmopākhyāna* (*MBh* 3.261.22), an indication of its power if not of its antiquity.

rata is told that Rāma has been banished, he fears it might have been as the result of some heinous crime:

> Concerned for the greatness of his dynasty, he began questioning her further: "Rāma did not seize the wealth of any brahman, did he? He did not harm some innocent man, whether rich or poor?" (66.36-37)

Later on we learn from Rāma that what Daśaratha has proposed to Kaikeyī is the kind of conduct a king must avoid at all costs:

> No noble, honest man is ever charged with theft, I hope, without being interrogated by men learned in the sacred texts; and if innocent, is never imprisoned out of greed. And when a thief . . . has been seized and interrogated, I hope he is never set free . . . out of greed for money. . . . For the tears people shed when falsely accused come to slay the livestock and children of the king who rules for personal gain. (94.47-48, 50)

Daśaratha, in fact, should be viewed as one of several studies in calamitous passion, along with Vālin and Rāvaṇa himself,[3] and like them a figure designed as a foil to Rāma. He conspicuously lacks the emotional control of his son, the self-discipline, equanimity, and dignity. Rāma's strictly monogamous sexuality likewise stands in sharp contrast to the habits of his father. And whereas Daśaratha offers the kingship as brideprice for Kaikeyī (the *rājyaśulka*), Rāma wins Sītā by a "feat of heroic strength" (the *vīryaśulka*, *sarga* 110; *Bālakāṇḍa* 66ff.). Daśaratha's own character is distinctly projected when at one point he imagines Rāma's banishment as a kind of holiday outing: in the forest "there will be deer and elephants to kill, forest liquor to drink" (32.5). Rāma conceives of his sacrifice in considerably different terms:

> But it is righteousness . . . that I am set on following today. (27.28)

> I will . . . live a life of purity in the forest, restricting my food to holy things, roots, fruit, and flowers. . . . My five senses will have contentment enough, and I shall be maintaining the world on its course. (101.26-27)

As Daśaratha's transgression was committed, in Bharata's words, "out of anger [v.l., greed], delusion, and recklessness" (98.52), so

[3] For a full discussion cf. Ruben 1950, especially p. 352.

Rāma says to Jābāli that "not out of greed, delusion, or ignorance" would he himself ever act untruthfully (101.17). Although Rāma seems clearly to recognize the failings of his father, the latter is not once shown to possess any awareness of the need to uphold righteousness. At one point Rāma makes him the object of an important—perhaps the most important—gnomic utterance of the book:

> Whoever forsakes righteousness [*dharma*] and statecraft [*artha*] and follows the urgings of desire [*kāma*], will soon come to grief, just like King Daśaratha. (47.13)

The portrait, then, is constructed with careful, effective, and tragic irony—we suppose. But standing against the whole spirit and much of the letter of the story are many disavowals. The "truthful Rāma" himself assures us that the king is "noble and self-controlled" (46.20), "a truthful man, true to his word, ever striving for truth" (19.7). Is this wilful blindness, one wonders, a son's attempt to reassert his father's rectitude in the face of so much evidence to the contrary? Yet when the poet begins to describe the king as "the truthful and righteous lord of men, like the ocean in profundity and as free from taint as the sky" (31.6), our suspicions are aroused, and they focus on Vālmīki himself.

We might conclude that there is a fundamental ambiguity in Vālmīki's conception of Daśaratha. But it is even more probable that he was reluctant to reproduce unchanged the received characterization of the king.[4] It was too fundamental to discard, but it could be transfigured by some extenuating incident.

The earlier tale, as we saw, must have turned on the brideprice offer Daśaratha attempted to reverse and the one boon the reckless king was seduced into bestowing during his interview with Kaikeyī. This Vālmīki revised into the present story: two boons granted as a noble gesture of gratitude at a war of gods and demons, Kaikeyī's claim to the throne being now complete deception. A further transmutation, in the same spirit of exoneration, seems to have been effected elsewhere.

[4] Epic bards participated in a world of social relations like anyone else. Open criticism of legitimate kings is rare, and if weakness and tyranny are represented, an attempt is usually made to palliate this representation. An instructive example is *MBh* 15.15, especially verses 15ff., where this mechanism leads the poet to an encomium on Dhṛtarāṣṭra and Duryodhana that is irreconcilable with the description of their actions in the first fourteen books of the epic.

The text suggests that originally the tale recounted the tragedy of an old king overmastered by his passion for a beautiful young woman, who then had to face the disastrous consequences of the grave commitments he rashly made and later found impossible to keep. Daśaratha himself at one point is shown to perceive and admit his guilt. He fell into the trap set for him by Kaikeyī and her family, and abdicated the responsibility incumbent upon him as king to make rational political and moral judgments:

> Kaikeyī, a woman of evil family and evil designs, forced me, and I failed to seek the advice of elders skilled in counsel. I failed to take counsel with my friends, my ministers, and wise brahmans. It was on my own, in delusion, for a woman's sake that I did the rash thing I have done. (53.15-16)

But then there follows the defense that the poet will shortly expand into the only[5] fully developed subnarrative of the book:

> Or perhaps—yes, surely charioteer, this great calamity was something destined to be, that had somehow to happen, to bring ruin upon this House. (53.17)

Under the impact of Kausalyā's harsh criticism of him (*sarga* 55), Daśaratha plumbs "the very depths of his grief, and there a memory was revived of something evil he once did" (55.21). Later, as he continues to brood, the recollection of an evil deed of his youth again flashes momentarily across his mind (56.2). Finally, in the dark night of his soul, there emerges into full consciousness the remembrance of the event that made Rāma's exile inevitable, and doomed Daśaratha (57.3).

Sargas 57-58 constitute a brilliantly composed and moving section with considerable poetic power.[6] But at present its narrative function is of principal interest. Daśaratha here still recognizes the weakness and imprudence that led him to spurn Kausalyā and come under Kaikeyī's power (57.6-7), traits that he seems to recognize as part of his own character even in youth. As a young man he was proud of the reputation he had earned as an archer who could

[5] With the possible, if minor, exception of *sarga* 110.

[6] It caught the attention of early European scholars. Aside from the rudimentary attempts of Friedrich Schlegel in 1808 (cf. Oppenberg 1965, pp. 54ff.), it was the first extended passage of the *Rāmāyaṇa* to be correctly translated in Europe (Chézy 1814; the work of Carey and Marshman, 1806-1810, was carried on in India).

strike a target without looking, merely by hearing it move. And with this pride was coupled a natural intemperance (57.8-9,15). But perhaps we should believe that it is less Daśaratha's weakness that opens the door to doom than the compulsion of doom that causes the weakness to begin with.[7] Out hunting, Daśaratha shoots blindly in the night at a sound coming from the deserted riverbank. What he had thought to be an elephant was a young ascetic who had renounced all violence, and whose murder will entail the death of his two blind parents. The fact that the crime was wholly unintentional only secures for Daśaratha a temporary reprieve (58.20-21); it cannot avert the curse of the boy's father that ultimately the king, like the sage, "will end his days grieving for a son" (58.45-46).

Vālmīki appears to have reworked and inserted a narrative derived from the folk tradition (preserved for us in the form of the *Sāmajātaka*), one that could be adapted to harmonize with the pervasive fatalism of the *Ayodhyākāṇḍa*.[8] By means of this, the poet was able to effect yet another alteration in his idealization of Daśaratha, and to relieve him of any direct responsibility for what happened to his son.[9] "How unlike me it was . . . to do what I did to Rāghava!" the king protests one last time before he dies. It was not an act, we now are told, that was in any way characteristic of him, or for which he is to be held accountable, but the doing of some hidden power, as inexplicable and uncontrollable as the force that guided an arrow shot in the dark to the heart of an ascetic boy. The king is no longer

[7] "When a man is to be ruined by implacable doom," we are told later in the *Rāmāyaṇa*, "he loses all sense of right and wrong—and it is this that dooms him" (3.54.16; cf. 2.98.51 and *MBh* 2.72.8-11).

[8] See note on 57.10. The degree of inter-recensional divergence for these two chapters is unusually high. This may well indicate that the episode originates in the latest compositional stratum of the *Rāmāyaṇa*, and was imperfectly absorbed into the oral tradition. Oldenberg, on stylistic grounds, likewise puts the *Rām* version later than the Pāli *jātaka* ("One sees how the simple presentation of the other text is here [in the *Rām*] enriched, nuanced, lent accents," and so on, 1918, p. 459).

[9] This tendency is evident elsewhere in the *Ayodhyākāṇḍa*. Nowhere in our text does Daśaratha explicitly command Rāma to leave; in 31.25ff., he only gives the prince permission to depart, and even here some manuscripts, including the critical edition, seem reluctant to attribute the words directly to Daśaratha; see note ad loc. and on 12.16ff. A problem never conclusively solved by the text is the lie of which Daśaratha becomes guilty by *failing* to consecrate Rāma after having declared in open assembly that he would do so (*sarga* 2). The king himself, in a curious aside, recognizes his dilemma (11.2), and later in the epic Lakṣmaṇa pointedly reverts to it (6.70.27).

a victim of his own choices, as all the previous narrative would seem to have us believe; he is instead a victim of chance. And thereby, again, his probity is preserved intact.[10]

[10] Despite the purely accidental character of the deed, the later *Rāmāyaṇa* tradition apparently felt it necessary to minimize even this degree of Daśaratha's guilt. The ascetic boy seems originally to have been described as the son of a brahman, and was subsequently changed, in our *Rāmāyaṇa*, into the son of a *vaiśya* (and a *śūdrā*). See the notes on 57.37, 58.46 and 47.

10. Rāma

IN SOME respects it may be erroneous for us to think of the protagonist of the *Rāmāyaṇa* as a hero. Properly understood, heroes are those who do great things in the face of certain defeat, such as Achilles, Siegfried, Roland, Cuchulain.[1] They far transcend us and are not figures we are supposed to emulate. Rāma emphatically is; and the various types of behavior that he exemplifies—filial devotion, for example, or obedience—we have already observed.

Moreover, as has often been remarked, heroes generally set themselves apart from their community, and it is the latter that asserts the true values of the society, to which the hero as an outsider is unable to accommodate himself. In the *Ayodhyākāṇḍa*, just the reverse is true: the community itself is shown to be in the wrong. At every step of the way, Rāma must instruct each in his proper role: his mother (18.26-31, 21.9-22), his father (31.25, 32), his brothers Lakṣmaṇa (18.32-36, 20.36, 91.2-6) and Bharata (97.17-24, 98.37-39, 99.8-14), his ministers (101). The appeal to Rāma that is sounded throughout the book ends, finally, in the choruslike supplication made by his own spiritual teacher, Vasiṣṭha:

> I was your father's teacher and am yours, too, slayer of foes; in doing my bidding you will not stray from the path of the good. Here are the men of your assembly and the guildsmen gathered together; in practicing righteousness on their behalf, my son, you will not stray from the path of the good. Your mother is aged and righteous, and you must not disobey her; in doing as she bids you will not stray from the path of the good. If you do as Bharata bade when supplicating you, Rāghava, you will not go astray in your pursuit of truth and righteousness. (103.4-7)

But Rāma is uncompromising, secure in the conviction that the imperatives he is honoring must take precedence, since they are fundamental. This feature of his character is intimately related to another model role he plays in the poem, that of the ideal king.

Two primary considerations that underpin Rāma's behavior are

[1] Cf. Griffin 1980, pp. 81-102, especially pp. 92-93.

his concern for public opinion and for "righteousness" (*dharma*). The former has its parallels elsewhere in Indian epic poetry, but nowhere else is it so conditioned by a sense of "righteousness," and nowhere is "righteousness" itself invested with the special significance it possesses in the *Ayodhyākāṇḍa*.

A keen sense of honor and shame—an overriding emphasis on the opinion of other men—is characteristic of most protagonists in heroic epics. And this is no less the case with Rāma. Consider his statement to Lakṣmaṇa:

> In my rage, Lakṣmaṇa, all by myself I could overpower Ayodhyā or the world with my arrows. But truly force is useless. I fear the danger of unrighteousness [*adharma*], blameless Lakṣmaṇa, and I fear what other people might say. That is why I do not have myself consecrated at once. (47.25-26)

It is from this fear of what "other people" might say that Rāma wishes to free the king:

> Let my father . . . be freed from the fears he has of what other people might say. For if this rite were not called off, he too would suffer mental torment to hear his truthfulness impugned. (19.7-8)[2]

Lakṣmaṇa realizes that here Rāma is indirectly speaking of himself, and responds accordingly:

> Now is not the time for panic, the source of this sheer folly. Could a man like you talk this way were he not panicked, fearful of losing people's respect on account of some infraction of righteousness [*dharmadoṣa-*]? (20.5-6)

In the sixth and particularly the seventh books of the poem, this motivating factor in Rāma's character will be dramatically highlighted. For fear of public opinion (about the chastity of his queen), he will demand that Sītā undergo an ordeal, and for the same reason he will ultimately repudiate her, the wife for whom he suffered so deeply, just as here in the *Ayodhyākāṇḍa* he renounces his claim to the kingship.

[2] See note on 19.7 for a discussion of this interpretation of *paraloka-*, "what other people might say."

It is not so much concern for the "world to come" that conditions Rāma's behavior[3] as concern for this world and the opinion of the men who inhabit it. His desire for *yaśaḥ*, "glory," a good name that will outlive him, weighs heavily when he prepares to go into banishment:

> I cannot for the sake of mere kingship turn my back on glory [*yaśaḥ*], whose reward is great; nor, since life is so short, my lady, would I choose today this paltry land against all that is right [*adharmataḥ*]. (18.39)

That Rāma's abdication was meant to confer glory on him is reiterated in Sumitrā's address to Rāma's mother:

> What gain has your son failed to reap, who is waving the banner of his fame throughout the world by his self-restraint and devotion to truth? (39.7)

A thirst for glory is a quality everywhere associated with the heroic, and many analogies are to be found in Indian epic literature; a good example is Karṇa in the *Mahābhārata*. Normally it is prompted by fear of cowardice and ignominious behavior on the field of battle, and is quenched in suicidal struggle. In Rāma's case, however, the desire for fame is coupled with and qualified by his understanding of "righteousness." And for Rāma's valuation of righteousness the other epics provide no precise antecedents; it is virtually a new attitude.

Rāma is a kshatriya, and we are well informed by other epic texts about the conventional understanding of the *dharma*—the proper conduct, the duties, the "righteous" behavior—of a kshatriya. The *Mahābhārata* takes pains to set it out with special clarity:

> I shall explain to you the *dharma* of the kshatriya: He must give and not demand. . . . He must always be ready to slaughter the enemy, he must show bravery in battle. . . . The kshatriya who conquers in battle most effectively wins the [higher] worlds. Killing is the chief *dharma* of one who is a kshatriya. There is no higher duty for him than to destroy enemies. . . . [A kshatriya] who would satisfy the claims of his *dharma*, a king in particular, must fight. (*MBh* 12.60.13-18)

[3] Though this does play some role; see 101.8ab, 104.6, etc.

> The *dharma* of a kshatriya, as we have been told, includes great savagery. He lives by the sword and in due course dies by the sword in battle. . . . One's heart, a kshatriya's heart in particular, must be hard as adamant. . . . Indra was born the son of Brahmā, but he became a kshatriya by his actions: he slew his evil kinsmen, all ninety-nine of them, an act worthy of esteem and praise, and one that made him king of all gods. (*MBh* 12.22.5-12)[4]

Perhaps the most celebrated formulation occurs in the *Bhagavadgītā*, where Kṛṣṇa exhorts Arjuna before the cataclysmic battle:

> You must take regard for your proper code of conduct [*svadharma*] and not waver. There is no better thing for a kshatriya than to wage righteous war. . . . Fortunate the kshatriyas who are granted such a war as this. . . . Better to die in the adherence to one's own code of righteousness; to adopt another's is a greater peril. (2.31-32; 3.55)

The injustice of Rāma's banishment, the unrighteousness of everyone implicated in it, is repeatedly emphasized by the text. We have already seen how Rāma acts in response to the arguments in favor of resistance that Lakṣmaṇa and others offer (*sargas* 18, 20, 90, 100, etc.), arguments very like those made by Kṛṣṇa.[5] But how does Rāma answer the charge that he is acting contrarily in preferring the wilderness to the kshatriya order, "matted hair" to the government of men (98.56)? that he is neglecting "the code of righteousness appropriate" for him, the "code of kings" and the "traditional code of his House" (98.61, 104.10)? that, in essence, he is failing in his proper duty, his *dharma*? He answers by altogether reinterpreting what that proper duty is. He replies to Lakṣmaṇa:

> So give up this ignoble notion that is based on the code of the

[4] Note that for Rāma, Indra has achieved his position of preeminence not by slaughtering his kinsmen (vindicated by Vyāsa, 12.23.2), but rather by sacrificial rites (*Rāmāyaṇa* 2.101.29). (According to the *Mahāvāṃsa* [5.18-20], Aśoka likewise slew his ninety-nine brothers to secure the kingship.)

[5] Rāma's actions are consciously designed to ensure a moral order in society: "Were I to adopt this practice," he tells Jābāli, "the entire world would follow suit in acting as it pleases, for subjects will behave just like their kings" (101.8cd-9). This is exactly the position of Kṛṣṇa (*BhagGī* 3.21), but defends precisely the opposite course of action.

> kshatriyas [*kṣatradharma*]; be of like mind with me and base your actions on righteousness [*dharma*], not violence. (18.36)

Similarly, in his response to the *Realpolitik* of the minister Jābāli, Rāma asserts that he has a "personal code of righteousness" (*pratyagātma dharma*), one that he knows to be correct—a code that good men have always observed. He rejects out of hand

> the kshatriya's code [*kṣātraṃ dharmam*], where unrighteousness and righteousness go hand in hand [*adharmaṃ dharmasaṃhitam*], a code that only debased, vicious, covetous, and evil men observe. (101.20)

The glory at which Rāma aims, then, is not the martial fame his own guru Vasiṣṭha urges on him (102.31), but the fame of *dharma* in its new valuation (18.39) on behalf of which "force is useless." Rāma is unequivocal: it is not for the sake of political power (*artha*) that he suffers living in the world; he is only concerned with *dharma*, "like a seer" (16.46); he is like the sage "who has passed beyond all things of this world" (16.59), he has "given up attachment to everything" (33.2). And it is the seer alone whom Rāma considers to be deserving of esteem and emulation:

> Those men who are earnest in righteousness and keep company with the wise, who are supremely generous, nonviolent, and free from taint, those supreme and mighty sages are the ones truly worthy of reverence in this world. (101.31)

The path to the highest heaven for Rāma is not "conquest in battle," as in the *Mahābhārata*,[6] but "truth, righteousness, and strenuous effort, compassion for creatures and kindly words, reverence for brahmans, gods, and guests" (101.30).

We must not, however, leap from this to the conclusion that Rāma

[6] Yudhiṣṭhira in the *MBh*, especially in Book 2, before the royal consecration, and in Book 5, before the decision to fight is made, exhibits some of the traits we see in Rāma. But these are not consistent and constitutive aspects of his portrait. If anything they are simply *pūrvapakṣas*, raised only to allow Kṛṣṇa, Arjuna, and the others to refute them and reassert true kshatriya *dharma* (which Yudhiṣṭhira invariably, albeit reluctantly, accepts). This becomes particularly clear in Book 12, where Yudhiṣṭhira's desire to renounce is branded as *nāstikya* (atheism, heresy; cf. 12.25), while his brothers' arguments for his enjoying the fruits of victory, however bloody, are called *vedaniścaya* (in conformity with the teachings of the *vedas*; cf. 14.1); Vyāsa himself, the authorial voice, concurs (*sargas* 23, 25; cf. Bhīṣma's words in 12.55.14ff.).

represents a renouncer (though he is that in a special, restricted sense); he will come back to rule his kingdom. Here he is not so much rejecting the obligations of his social order as redefining them, transvaluating them. By subsuming his caste-specific *dharma* under a larger, superordinate *dharma*, he loosens the claims of the former by the same power that had given them their strength.

What is the significance of this reformulation? It has long been observed that there existed a fundamental dichotomy in the structure of power in ancient India. Although real power lay in the hands of the kshatriyas, its legitimation was in the hands of the brahmans. Hierarchy of status conferred supremacy on the brahman; the differentiation of actual power ("mere force") conferred supremacy on the kshatriya. There was a mutual dependence, the brahman depending for his material welfare (*artha*) on the kshatriya, the kshatriya for his spiritual welfare (*dharma*) on the brahman. The two domains remained separate:

> The supremacy of *dharma* is beyond question. . . . *Artha* is recognized only in second place, we may say in matters indifferent to *dharma*; *artha* remains finally contained within the all-embracing *dharma*, confined within *dharma*-prescribed limits. . . . Being negation of *dharma* in a society which continues to be ruled by *dharma*, the political sphere is severed from the realm of values.[7]

Or as another scholar has more pertinently formulated it:

> Kingship as an institution has no authority and legitimacy of its own. It is dependent on the uneasy relationship between king and brahmin. . . . [The brahmin's] monopoly of the source of authority and legitimation leaves the king with mere power and effectively bars kingship from developing its full potential as the central regulating force.[8]

[7] Dumont 1962, p. 66. See also Buss 1978 (Buddhist evidence). The legitimizing power exercised by the brahman derives ultimately from his magical control of the sacrifice, which he could manipulate for political purposes, as the *Brāhmaṇa* texts show (cf. Rau 1957, pp. 60-61).

[8] Heesterman 1978, p. 4. The *Rāmāyaṇa* evidence suggests conclusions different from those drawn by these authorities. Dumont argues that the bifurcation is a "necessary institution" (p. 54) that makes kingship "in some way . . . 'rational' " (p. 66). Heesterman appears to deny any competition for priority (p. 5); he finds the king seeking his authority in a supernatural domain outside the community.

The characterization of Rāma seems to be a response to this politically incapacitating bifurcation.

We find this dichotomy manifested in a number of brahmanical and epic narratives. It is certainly no coincidence that several of the more striking examples are in one way or another intimately associated with the *Rāmāyaṇa* tradition—in particular the biography of the Buddha, for which the *Rāmāyaṇa* may well have served as a prototype, and the legend of Viśvāmitra, absorbed into Vālmīki's work itself. But in these accounts the dilemma is resolved in quite different ways. On the one hand (in the case of the kshatriya prince Śākyamuni), the problem is repudiated and a new *dharma* altogether extrinsic to society is introduced, the *śramaṇadharma*: communal asceticism as a self-sufficient and fully integrated way of life receives new valorization. On the other hand (in the kshatriya king Viśvāmitra),[9] we meet an isolated, unrepeatable, in effect a fantasy transcendence of the actual: by means of asceticism a kshatriya king is literally transformed into a brahman. Rāma, by contrast, resolves the contradiction through a new definition of the *dharma* incumbent on him as a kshatriya. By the increment of a hieratic component, not derived from but only enriched by his temporary ascetic vocation,[10] his code is enlarged to become simply "righteousness." It is made to intersect with and so absorb brahmanical *dharma* and its legitimizing ethics, nonviolence, and spirituality.[11] In this way the kshatriya becomes self-legitimizing, and the "full potential" of kingship as an integrating power can at last be activated. The political and spiritual spheres may now converge in a single locus: the king.[12]

[9] See especially *Rām* 1.53.15, 55.4, 23. The problem reverberates throughout the Viśvāmitra-Vasiṣṭha legend and is unusually well articulated in the story of Satyavrata (Triśaṅku) as given in the *HariVaṃ* (9.88-10.20), where Vasiṣṭha seizes control of the Ikṣvāku kingdom. The brahman thus not only possessed the legitimizing authority, but could present himself as an actual rival for power. Such passages as *AitBr* 8.23 presuppose that a brahman could be king (cf. Rau 1957, p. 63).

[10] Rāma's asceticism during his exile (cf. note on 25.7 and references) may be an "overdetermination" of this spiritualizing tendency: the political exile of the Pāṇḍava princes, of Nala, Triśaṅku, and so on, includes no ascetic features.

[11] Thus the remarkable ambiguity of Rāma's status, which will be repeatedly underscored in Book Three. See 3.2.10-12; 16.11, and especially note on 2.48.8. This may help account for the many similes in which Rāma is likened not to the divine embodiment of kshatriya power, Indra, but to Brahmā. See 2.29.11, 93.27, 96.27 and especially note on 46.64, where we read in the Southern Recension, "Rāghava . . . prayed like a brahman and a kshatriya."

[12] This conjunction may figure as an element in the *dharma* of Aśoka, and go some

By the resolution of the dichotomy through the character of Rāma, the conditions are provided for the poem's conclusion, with its utopian vision of peace and abundance on earth, of an enduring empire based on righteousness. This hopeful image at once cancels and justifies all the misery and suffering that had gone before and prepared the way. It carries us beyond the more or less negative functionality of the text's broad social prescriptions and beyond its positive political and ethical mission, standing as the ultimate incentive to both. And it is made possible, it appears, only by the presence of a moral or spiritualized king, for whom violence is inhuman and is to be exercised only against the bestial (Vālin) or demonic (Rāvaṇa).

The *Mahābhārata* ends in anomie, ascetic suicide, and apocalypse. Individual life on earth can have no meaning for those who fail to understand the true "syntax" of social existence: it becomes instead a "living death."[13] The *Mahābhārata* heroes failed to understand this syntax precisely because it was incomprehensible as such, in that its constituent elements, the political and the spiritual, could never be construed. In sharp contrast, the righteousness of Rāma, not only as exemplar for the collective sense of duty but also as the integrating force of these two realms of human life, restores a universal Golden Age, the perfectly harmonious existence of man with nature and man with man (6.116.80ff.).[14]

way to explain his political success. (The connection between the usual subordination of the "political element" to the "religious" and "India's political instability" is drawn by Dumont 1964, p. 53, cited and translated by Derrett 1976, p. 597.) One is again struck by the similarity between the inscriptions and the *Ayodhyākāṇḍa*. For Aśoka, too, "the only true conquest is conquest through *dharma*": through "compassion, generosity, truthfulness, and honesty," through "reverence for brahmans and ascetics." Glory, too, is desirable only on account of his aim that "men may [be induced] by him to practice obedience to *dharma*, that they may conform to the duties of *dharma*." The "drum of battle" (for another analysis of the phrase see La Vallée Poussin 1922, p. 515) is similarly transformed into the "drum of *dharma*," and the "abiding welfare of all the world" (*sarvalokahita*, as in the *Ayodhyākāṇḍa*, 52.22) becomes the fundamental concern (the citations come respectively from Rock Edict XIII, Pillar Edict II, Rock Edict IV, Rock Edict X [after Hultzsch 1925, p. 18], Rock Edict IV [for the *bherī* used to give the call to arms see, for example, *Rām* 6.24.19-20], Rock Edict VI [see lines 9, 11]).

[13] *Mṛtā jīvāmahe vayam*, says Yudhiṣṭhira (*MBh* 15.46.8), and he elsewhere articulates the fundamental contradiction between *kṣatriya dharma* as conventionally understood and social life (12.38.3, 76.15, 98.1).

[14] Much of the parallel passage in 1.1.5ff. may well be an adaptation of the *Yud-*

Although the compensatory aspect of *Rāmarājya* is in part responsible for the undiminishing vitality of the poem and its enshrinement in Indian culture, as well as for the ready acknowledgement of its often proscriptive admonitions, it may be less significant in itself than for its latent foundations. If, in his course of action, Rāma explicitly affirms hierarchical subordination, the spiritual commitment that allows for his utopian rule seems implicitly to oppose it. If we are prepared to accept that the separation of domains was an actual model for social behavior, one broadly sanctioned in historical India; if we agree that

> status and power, and consequently spiritual authority and temporal authority, are absolutely distinguished. . . . The supremacy of the spiritual was never expressed politically . . . [and] only once this differentiation has been made [can] hierarchy manifest itself,[15]

then we are obliged to see the characterization of Rāma as a judgment on that model. Rāma expressly seeks to cancel the dichotomy by integrating the two "forces"—a resolution that inaugurates the Golden Age. Hierarchical life and the separation of "powers" that underpins it, which the poem elsewhere unambiguously attempts to validate, appears at the highest and critical level to be questioned, and a reformulation is offered in its place. And it is this that makes it possible for real political stability and social harmony finally to be secured.[16]

Whatever the validity of these speculations, much of the meaning and significance of the *Ayodhyākāṇḍa* does seem to lie in its vigorous, sustained, and searching interpretation of the conditions of social existence. A great culture's exploration of such central issues as the nature and function of political power and of a hierarchical social

---

dhakāṇḍa, presumably included again with the aim of idealizing Daśaratha; the narrative of the *Ayodhyākāṇḍa* certainly stands in opposition to it. At all events, the important contrast drawn here is not between Daśaratha and Rāma but between the *Rāmāyaṇa* and the *Mahābhārata*.

[15] Dumont 1980, p. 72.

[16] That at a deeper level the significance of this complicated work may lie in questioning rather than in affirming social hierarchy will no doubt seem surprising. For the theoretical foundations that support this conclusion, see the work of Jameson (1981).

order is preserved for us in this poem. The formulation, on the one hand, of hopeful solutions to what may be insoluble political problems, and on the other, of a code of conduct that appears to call that social order into doubt, supplies the particular answers of India's first poem to the question of what makes life possible.

11. The Text, Annotations, and Translation

THE GENERAL Introduction (Volume 1) discusses the nature of the critical edition upon which this translation is based, with regard to both its merits and its limitations. A careful and prolonged scrutiny of all the published manuscript evidence for the *Ayodhyākāṇḍa* has validated the general principles adopted for the critical edition. The manuscripts for the *Ayodhyākāṇḍa*, however, make it clear that in some places the original form of the poem cannot be confidently recovered. The annotations here often suggest alternative approaches (such as the note to 12.16), but only in a hypothetical way. For such passages, certainty is unattainable with the evidence available to us.

The critical edition is, furthermore, occasionally subject to question. Both the unavoidable subjectivity of text-editing, even upon the most scientific principles, and the natural limits to every editor's knowledge force us to recognize that any such edition can secure only a provisional status. Thus, when I found myself in serious disagreement with the editor, I emended and translated as I thought necessary. All departures from the constituted text are listed in an appendix to the translation and explained in the notes. No large segments of the text have been affected. I did not find it necessary to remove anything from the critical edition, though had I been editing the work I would probably have made some different decisions.[1] There was only one occasion when it proved necessary to add something that had been discarded—a short passage of two verses.[2] At this higher level of the work, my disagreements with the critical text were rarely serious. I usually concur with the editor about the secondary character of the additional material. But because the *Rāmāyaṇa* is not only a discrete poem but a tradition as well, every insertion that holds interest for the general reader or scholar has been translated or summarized in the notes.

At the level of the phrase, the word, the syllable, however, I have

[1] See, for example, notes to 75.1 and 92.1.

[2] See 31.25 note. A second addition (after 95.19) is the editor's (cf. Vaidya 1962, p. 706).

introduced some seventy changes in the text. Sometimes this was required when the editor preferred the hazardous procedure of ignoring the absolute unanimity of the manuscripts (e.g., 23.30) or the principles upon which the critical edition is based (e.g., 43.14); when a good variant was apparently mistaken by the editor as a corruption (e.g., 12.22, 63.4), or when the text as printed seemed to be nonsense (e.g., 106.9, 111.5). In all these cases I emend on the basis of manuscript testimony, evaluated on the grounds I discuss in the General Introduction. In a few instances I have conjectured readings, but only when I had good reason to believe in their inherent probability (e.g., 20.5, 30.10, 101.22; contrast the notes on 45.24 and 87.13).

The annotations have been prepared in accordance with the guidelines collectively decided upon for this translation: to serve as expeditiously as possible the needs of both the general reader and the scholar. They are intended in the main to explain the translation where necessary and to indicate how and why I arrived at such an interpretation. While I have sought to keep my attention focused on the *Ayodhyākāṇḍa* text itself and to refrain from enlarging on cultural matters beyond what was essential for the immediate comprehension of the translation, the work presents a multitude of textual and philological problems that required more detailed investigation.

I have kept before me all the medieval commentaries on the *Ayodhyākāṇḍa* that are available in print.[3] My admiration for the learning and perspicacity of the commentators is as great as my indebtedness to them. Many of the verses owe their English shape directly to the exegetical labors of these scholiasts, although, as will be obvious on virtually any page of the annotations, I have never followed them uncritically. But even when I disagree with them, I often record their remarks if some interesting observation is offered. Their responses are the closest approximation we have to those of an original audience. In addition, since in their eyes the *Rāmāyaṇa* is a *dharmaśāstra* or manual of proper conduct as well as a work of theological significance, I have translated or summarized many of their comments of a more general sort (ritual, legal, al-

[3] These are the ten listed in the General Introduction. I have additionally made occasional reference to the *Taniślokī* of Ātreya Ahobala, printed in extracts in the VSP edition. The modern Sanskrit notes of K. S. Varadacharya, published in his edition of Kataka's commentary (1964-1965), have also proved useful.

legorical), though these may have no direct bearing on our understanding of the text.

All translators acutely feel the obligation of not disappointing their author, well aware, at the same time, that there is always someone to charge them, as Blake put it, with being "hired to run down men of genius under the guise of translator." Vālmīki has substantial elements of genius, and I have striven to discharge the duty his genius imposes. But he is uneven, and the temptation to improve—supposing I had been able to do so—had to be resisted. The *Ayodhyākāṇḍa* is roughly two-thirds the size of the *Odyssey*, and there is bound to be a certain amount of chaff in it. It is in large part an oral composition; the repetitions of formula and epithet are as essential to it as any other literary or narrative feature, and for this and other reasons, these can no longer simply be thrown overboard at the whim of the translator. It is a heroic epic, too, and for that sort of literature a truly appropriate diction is no longer available. The only serviceable medium is, predictably, the "idiomatic, living language," but, besides its clear limitations in the present case, it seems sometimes a disappearing target. There is a certain indeterminateness, a certain evanescence about it, and in those moments when it disappears bombast usually finds a way in.

Finally, the problem of tradition. The contemporary translator of the Greek epic, to take the most celebrated parallel, has behind him some four hundred years of attempts at producing an English Homer, in which solutions have been reached that he can accept, blind alleys followed that he can now safely ignore. The Sanskritist works in a tradition both much more recent and less useful, and cannot safely assume that a single problem, whether philological or literary, has already been solved. He must start from the ground up—in fact from the very word *dharma*—and the only reasonable hope he may entertain is to have cleared some of this ground satisfactorily.

AYODHYĀKĀṆḌA

Sarga 1

1. Time passed and then one day King Daśaratha, the delight of the Raghus, spoke to Bharata, his son by Kaikeyī:

2. "My mighty son, your mother's brother Yudhājit, the son of the king of Kekaya, has come and is waiting to take you back home with him."

3. When he had heard what Daśaratha told him, Kaikeyī's son Bharata prepared to depart with Śatrughna.

4. Taking leave of his father, of tireless Rāma, and of his mothers, the hero, the best of men, went off with Śatrughna.

5. Delighted to have Bharata and Śatrughna with him, mighty Yudhājit returned to his native city, to the great satisfaction of his father.

6. There Bharata lived with his brother, enjoying the warm hospitality of his uncle Aśvapati, who showered him with all the affection one shows a son.

7. And yet, as the mighty brothers stayed on, their every desire satisfied, they often thought with longing of aged King Daśaratha.

8. The great king likewise often thought of his two absent sons, Bharata and Śatrughna, the equals of great Indra and Varuṇa.

9. For he cherished every one of the four bulls among men, as if they were four arms extending from his body.

10. But still, of all of them, it was mighty Rāma who brought his father the greatest joy. For he surpassed his brothers in virtue just as the self-existent Brahmā surpasses all other beings.

11. In Bharata's absence Rāma and powerful Lakṣmaṇa showed reverence to their godlike father.

12. Following his father's orders, righteous Rāma did all that was required to please and benefit the people of the city.

13. He scrupulously did all that his mothers required of him and attended to his gurus' requirements with strict punctuality.

14. Thus Daśaratha was pleased with Rāma's conduct and character, as were the brahmans, the merchants, and all who lived in the realm.

15. Rāma was always even-tempered and kind-spoken. Even if he were to be harshly addressed, he would not answer back.

16. He would be satisfied with a single act of kindness, whatever its motive, and would ignore a hundred injuries, so great was his self-control.

17. With good men—men advanced in years, virtue, and wisdom—he would converse at every opportunity, even during breaks in his weapons practice.

18. He was of noble descent on both sides of his family, he was upright and cheerful, truthful, and honest. Aged brahmans had seen to his training, men who were wise in the ways of righteousness and statecraft.

19. And thus he understood the true nature of righteousness, statecraft, and personal pleasure. He was retentive and insightful, knowledgeable and adept in the social proprieties.

20. He was learned in the sciences and skilled in the practice of them as well. He was an excellent judge of men and could tell when it was appropriate to show his favor or withhold it.

21. He knew the right means for collecting revenue and the accepted way of regulating expenditure. He had achieved preeminence in the sum total of the sciences, even the most complex.

22. Only after satisfying the claims of righteousness and statecraft would he give himself up to pleasure, and then never immoderately. He was a connoisseur of the fine arts and understood all aspects of political life.

23. He was proficient in training and riding horses and elephants, eminently knowledgeable in the science of weapons, and esteemed throughout the world as a master chariot fighter.

24. He could head a charge and give battle and lead an army skillfully. He was invincible in combat, even if the gods and *asuras* themselves were to unite in anger against him.

25. He was never spiteful, haughty, or envious, and he had mastered his anger. He would never look down on any creature nor bow to the will of time.

26. By his eminent virtues the prince won the esteem of people throughout all the three worlds, for he was patient as the earth, wise as Bṛhaspati, and mighty as Indra, Śacī's lord.

27. Rāma's virtues were prized by all the people, a source of joy to his father, and lent the prince himself such splendor as the sun derives from its shining beams.

28. His conduct and invincible valor made him so like one of the gods who guard the world that Earth herself desired to have him as her master.

29. Now, as King Daśaratha, slayer of enemies, observed the many incomparable virtues of his son, he fell to thinking.

30. In his heart he cherished this single joyous thought: "When shall I see my dear son consecrated?

31. "His one desire is that the world should prosper, he shows compassion to all creatures and is loved in the world even more than I, like a cloud laden with rain.

32. "He is as mighty as Yama or Śakra, wise as Bṛhaspati, steady as a mountain, and far richer in virtues than I.

33. "O that at my age I might go to heaven seeing my son holding sway over this entire land."

34. Recognizing that his son was endowed with these consummate virtues, the great king consulted with his advisers and chose him to be prince regent.

35. The lord of earth then convened the chief men of the land from the various cities and provinces in which they lived.

36. The nobles arrived and in the different places he assigned to them they solemnly took their seats, facing the king.

37. The lord of men paid his respects to the nobles and the men of the city and provinces, and as they sat deferentially around him he resembled Indra, the thousand-eyed lord, surrounded by the deathless gods.

The end of the first *sarga* of the *Ayodhyākāṇḍa* of the *Śrī Rāmāyaṇa*.

Sarga 2

1-2. King Daśaratha, lord of earth, called the whole assembly to order, and rumbling like a storm cloud, his loud voice deep and resonant as a bass drum, he made this incomparable speech to their delight and benefit.

3. "The whole world has long been under the protection of Ikṣvāku kings. It is my desire to ensure its well-being, for continued happiness is its due.

4. "I myself have always kept to the path my ancestors followed and watched over my subjects unremittingly, to the best of my ability.

5. "And, in my striving for the benefit of the entire world, my body has grown old in the shade of the white parasol.

6. "I have lived a life of many, countless, years, and now I crave repose for this aged body of mine.

7. "I have grown weary bearing the burden of righteousness for the world. For it is heavy, one must have self-discipline to bear it and the royal powers it encompasses.

8. "I seek respite by entrusting my subjects' welfare to the care of my son, with the approval of all you twice-born men assembled here.

9. "My eldest son was born resembling me in every virtue. He is a conqueror of enemy fortresses, as powerful as Indra, breaker of fortresses.

10. "It is my pleasure to invest Rāma, champion of righteousness and bull among men, with the office of prince regent, a union as propitious as the moon's with the constellation Puṣya.

11. "The majestic eldest brother of Lakṣmaṇa will be a fit and proper master for you—indeed, the three worlds all together would find a superior master in him.

12. "Once I have ensured the well-being of this land by entrusting it to this son of mine, I shall be free from care."

13. So the king spoke, and the nobles rejoiced at his words like peacocks at the rumble of a rain-laden cloud.

14. They fully recognized that the aim of their aged king, Daśaratha, was embraced in the wisdom of righteousness and statecraft, and when they had reflected upon it they replied:

15. "You are old, your majesty, and have lived many, countless, years. You should consecrate Rāma as prince regent of the land."

16. But when the king heard their reply he pretended not to know it was their heart's desire, and in order to test them he asked:

17. "How can it be that, while I am ruling the land in righteousness, you want to see my son become prince regent?"

18. In concert with the men of the city and provinces they answered great Daśaratha: "Your majesty, the virtues of your son are many and excellent.

19. "They are divine virtues, which make valiant Rāma the equal of Śakra and elevate him far above all other Ikṣvākus, lord of the peoples.

20. "All the world knows Rāma to be a decent man, for truth and righteousness are his first concern. And he is wise in the ways of righteousness, true to his word, a man of character, and never spiteful.

21. "He is forbearing, conciliatory, kind-spoken, grateful, and self-disciplined. He is gentle, firm of purpose, ever capable, and unspiteful.

22. "He speaks kindly to all people, and yet he always tells the truth. He shows reverence for aged and deeply learned brahmans.

23. "Because of this his fame among us is without equal and his glory and power have steadily grown. He is proficient in the use of all the weapons of the gods, *asuras*, and men.

24. "Whenever he goes forth with Saumitri to battle in defense of a village or city, he always returns triumphant.

25-26. "And coming back from battle on chariot or elephant, Rāma always stops to ask the men of the city after their welfare as if they were his kinsmen—about their sons, sacred fires, wives, servants, and students, without omission and in due order, just as a father might ask his sons, his own flesh and blood.

27. " 'Do your students obey you? Are they prompt in their tasks?' This is how Rāma, tiger among men, always questions us.

28. "When misfortune strikes anyone Rāma feels the sorrow keenly, and he takes the pleasure a father might in all the people's celebrations.

29. "He is a great archer, a man who tells the truth, who seeks the counsel of the aged and is master of his senses. How fortunate you are to be blessed with a son like your Rāghava, who, like Mārīca Kaśyapa, has every virtue a son should have.

30-32. "The people of the kingdom and in this the foremost of cities wish the celebrated Rāma strength, health, and long life—all the people of the city and the provinces, outsiders as well as intimates. And at dawn and at dusk women young and old alike devoutly worship all the gods for glorious Rāma's sake. By your grace, O god, let what they pray for come to pass.

33. "Grant, great king, that we may see Rāma become prince regent, your son who is dark as the blue lotus, and deadly to his every enemy.

34. "O god, your godlike son is committed to the good of all the world, and so for our good, granter of boons, please consecrate the exalted prince joyfully and without delay."

The end of the second *sarga* of the *Ayodhyākāṇḍa* of the *Śrī Rāmāyaṇa*.

Sarga 3

1. All around him they held out their hands cupped like lotuses, and the king acknowledged them, adding these kind and beneficial words:

2. "Ah, how overjoyed I am. You have magnified my grandeur beyond all measure that you should want my beloved eldest son to become prince regent."

3. When the king had paid the brahmans this honor in return he addressed Vasiṣṭha and Vāmadeva as the others stood listening.

4. "This is the majestic, auspicious month of Caitra, when the woods are in full bloom. Let all the preparations be made for Rāma's installation as prince regent."

5. "It shall be done," the two brahmans replied with joy and delight as they approached the lord of the world, "just as you command."

6. Then the splendid king said to Sumantra, "Please bring Rāma, my accomplished son, here at once."

7. Sumantra assented and by order of the king went in his chariot to fetch Rāma, best of chariot-fighters.

8-9. Meanwhile the kings who were seated there—the eastern,

northern, western, and southern kings, aryan and barbarian, and others who lived in the forest and mountain regions—all paid homage to King Daśaratha, as the gods do to Vāsava.

10. From the terrace of the palace where he stood in their midst like Vāsava among the Maruts, the royal seer watched his son approaching in his chariot.

11. Rāma was the very image of the king of *gandharvas*, and renowned throughout the world for his manliness as well. His arms were long, his strength immense, and he carried himself like a bull elephant in rut.

12. He was extremely handsome and his face had the lovely glow of moonlight. With his beauty and nobility he ravished both the sight and the hearts of men.

13. He was like the rain that refreshes people parched by summer's heat, and the lord of men could not get enough of gazing at him as he drew near.

14. Sumantra helped Rāghava down from his splendid chariot and followed at the rear, hands cupped in reverence, as Rāma made his way into his father's presence.

15. Accompanied by the charioteer, Rāghava, bull among men, went to see his father, ascending to the rooftop terrace lofty as Mount Kailāsa's peak.

16. With hands cupped in reverence Rāma came before his father. He prostrated himself and, announcing his name, did obeisance at his father's feet.

17. Gazing at his dear son bowed down beside him with hands cupped in reverence, the king drew him up by his clasped hands and embraced him.

18. The majestic king then directed Rāma to the throne made ready for him, a splendid one brilliantly set with gems and gold.

19. As Rāghava sat down, the throne seemed to glow more brightly still from the prince's own luster, like Mount Meru when the bright sun rises.

20. As the autumn sky, for all its bright planets and constellations, is illuminated still further by the moon, so was the assembly hall lit up by the radiance Rāma shed.

21. Daśaratha observed his dear son with keen satisfaction. It was as if he were looking in a mirror and seeing an enhanced reflection of himself.

22. The king, and most blessed of fathers, turned to his son with a smile and in words Kaśyapa might once have used with Indra, lord of gods, he said,

23. "Rāma, my dear son, you were born of my eldest wife—a worthy son of a worthy woman—and you are most virtuous.

24. "And since by your virtues you have won the loyalty of these my subjects, you shall become prince regent on the day of Puṣya's conjunction.

25. "You are by nature disciplined and virtuous, as much as one could desire. But still, in spite of these virtues, I shall give you some beneficial advice, my son, because of my affection for you.

26. "Impose even stricter discipline on yourself, exercise constant self-control, and avoid all the vices that spring from desire and anger.

27. "Actively concern yourself with both overt and covert activities, to retain the loyalty of all your subjects, from the ministers down.

28. "He who protects the earth while keeping the people content and loyal will give his allies cause to rejoice like the deathless gods when they obtained nectar. So hold yourself in check, my son, and behave in this fashion."

29. Upon hearing this speech Rāma's friends hurried off bearing the good news, and at once conveyed it to Kausalyā.

30. The excellent lady directed that gold and cows and an assortment of precious objects be given to those who brought the news.

31. Rāghava, meanwhile, after doing obeisance to the king, mounted the chariot and started back to his splendid dwelling amid the acclaim of the multitude.

32. When the townsmen heard the king's announcement, it was as if they had secured some longed-for object and, on taking leave of the lord of men, they went home and worshiped the gods in deep delight.

The end of the third *sarga* of the *Ayodhyākāṇḍa* of the *Śrī Rāmāyaṇa*.

Sarga 4

1. After the townsmen had gone the king held further consultation with his counsellors. When he learned what they had determined the lord declared with determination,

2. "Tomorrow is Puṣya, so tomorrow my son Rāma, his eyes as coppery as lotuses, shall be consecrated as prince regent."

3. Retiring then to his private chamber, King Daśaratha instructed the charioteer Sumantra to fetch Rāma again.

4. Upon receiving his orders the charioteer set out at once for Rāma's abode to fetch him.

5. The guards informed Rāma that Sumantra had returned, and as soon as he learned of his arrival he felt uneasy.

6. Rāma had him shown in at once. "Tell me the reason for your returning," he said, "and omit nothing."

7. The charioteer replied, "The king wishes to see you. Such is the message, but you of course must be the judge of your comings and goings."

8. Such were the charioteer's words, and, upon hearing them, Rāma hurried out and went to the palace to see the lord of men once more.

9. When word was brought that Rāma had arrived, King Daśaratha had him shown into his chamber, anxious to pass on the important news.

10. As majestic Rāghava entered the residence he caught sight of his father, and at a distance prostrated himself, cupping his hands in reverence.

11. He bowed low until the protector of the earth bade him rise and embraced him. Then, directing him to a splendid seat, the king once again addressed him:

12. "Rāma, I am old, my life has been long. I have enjoyed all the pleasures I desired. I have performed hundreds of sacrifices rich in food, with lavish priestly stipends.

13. "The child I wanted—and you are he—was born to me, a son who has no peer on earth today, the very best of men. I have given alms, offered sacrifices, and studied the scriptures.

14. "I have experienced every pleasure, everything I wanted—and thus, my mighty son, I have discharged all my debts, to the gods, the seers, my ancestors, the brahmans, and to myself.

15. "There is nothing further required of me except your consecration. Therefore you must do for me what I am about to tell you.

16. "All the subjects today expressed their wish to have you for their king, and so, my dear son, I will consecrate you as prince regent.

17. "But there is more, Rāma: I have had dreams lately, inauspicious, ominous dreams. Great meteors and lightning bolts out of a clear sky have been falling nearby with a terrible crash.

18. "The astrologers also inform me, Rāma, that my birth star is obstructed by hostile planets, Aṅgāraka, Rāhu, and the sun.

19. "When such portents as these appear it usually means a king is about to die or meet with some dreadful misfortune.

20. "You must therefore have yourself consecrated, Rāghava, before my resolve fails me. For the minds of men are changeable.

21. "Today the moon has reached Punarvasu, just to the east of Puṣya; tomorrow, the astrologers predict, its conjunction with Puṣya is certain.

22. "On this very Puṣya day you must have yourself consecrated—I feel a sense of great urgency. Tomorrow, slayer of enemies, I will consecrate you as prince regent.

23. "Therefore today you and your wife must take a vow to remain chaste this night, to fast and sleep upon a bed of *darbha* grass.

24. "Have your friends guard you warily today at every turn, for there are many impediments to affairs of this sort.

25. "I believe the best time for your consecration is precisely while Bharata is absent from the city.

26. "Granted your brother keeps to the ways of the good, defers to his elder brother, and is righteous, compassionate, and self-disciplined.

27. "Still, Rāghava, it is my firm belief that the mind of man is inconstant, even the mind of a good man constant in righteousness. Even such a man is best presented with an accomplished fact."

28. Once told his consecration was set for the next day, Rāma was given leave to go, and after doing obeisance to his father, he went home.

29. In keeping with the king's instructions regarding the consecration, he entered his house but then left immediately and went to his mother's apartment.

30. There in the shrine-room he saw her, clothed in linen, solemnly and silently praying for his royal fortune.

31. Sumitrā and Lakṣmaṇa had already come, and Sītā had been sent for as soon as they heard the news of Rāma's consecration.

32. At that moment Kausalyā stood with her eyes closed, while Sumitrā, Sītā, and Lakṣmaṇa were seated behind her.

33. From the moment she received word that her son was to be consecrated as prince regent on Puṣya day, she had been controlling her breathing and meditating on the Primal Being, Janārdana.

34. While she was engaged in these observances Rāma approached her and did obeisance. Then to her delight he said:

35. "Mother, my father has appointed me to the task of protecting the people. On father's instructions my consecration will take place tomorrow.

36. "And as Father, with his priests and preceptors, directs, Sītā and I both are to fast tonight.

37. "Please see that any auspicious rites appropriate for my consecration tomorrow are performed today on behalf of Vaidehī and me."

38. Hearing him say what she had so long desired, Kausalyā spoke to Rāma in words muffled with sobs of joy:

39. "Rāma, my child, long may you live. May all who block your way be vanquished. And when you are invested with sovereignty may you bring joy to my kinsmen and Sumitrā's.

40. "Truly it was under a lucky star I bore you, my dear son, since by your virtues you have won the favor of your father, Daśaratha.

41. "Truly the vows of self-denial I made to the lotus-eyed Primal Being were not in vain, since the royal fortune of the Ikṣvākus will pass to you, my son."

42. So his mother spoke, and Rāma then turned to his brother. He smiled as he looked at him sitting diffidently nearby, hands cupped in reverence, and he said:

43. "Come, Lakṣmaṇa, rule this land with me. Sovereignty falls to your share, too, for you are my second self.

44. "You too shall enjoy every pleasure you desire, Saumitri, and all the fruits of kingship, for the kingship, and life itself, I covet only for your sake."

45. So Rāma spoke to Lakṣmaṇa, and then doing obeisance to his mothers and bidding Sītā take leave of them, he returned home.

The end of the fourth *sarga* of the *Ayodhyākāṇḍa* of the *Śrī Rāmāyaṇa*.

Sarga 5

1. When he had given Rāma his instructions regarding the consecration on the coming day, the lord of men summoned his family priest Vasiṣṭha and said:

2. "Go, ascetic, and assist Kākutstha and his wife in undertaking a fast today, so that my son, a man strict in his vows, may gain majesty, glory, and kingship."

3. "So be it," said the holy Vasiṣṭha, greatest of vedic scholars, in reply to the king, and he went himself to Rāma's residence.

4. Arriving at Rāma's dwelling, which looked like a bank of silvery clouds, the great sage entered and drove through the three courtyards in his chariot.

5. At the arrival of this venerable seer, Rāma hurried from his house in great excitement, to show him veneration.

6. Hurrying to the side of the wise man's chariot and lending him support, he helped him to climb down.

7. The family priest, noting Rāma's deference, addressed him with compliments, and then to the delight of the prince, who was deserving of every kindness, he said:

8. "Your father is well-disposed toward you, Rāma; you shall become prince regent. Today you and Sītā must fast.

9. "For tomorrow morning the lord of men, your father Daśaratha, shall consecrate you as prince regent, with all the joy Nahuṣa felt in consecrating Yayāti."

10. So the sage spoke, and then, with the appropriate vedic verses, he assisted Vaidehī and Rāma, a man of strict vows, in undertaking their fast.

11. Afterwards, when he had been duly honored by Rāma, the king's guru took leave of Kākutstha and left his residence.

12. Rāma remained a while sitting there in the company of his affable friends. Then with their best wishes he took leave of them all and went inside.

13. Delight filled the throngs of men and women in Rāma's house so that for the moment it resembled a pond of blooming lotuses, where cheerful birds are flocking.

14. As Vasiṣṭha emerged from Rāma's kingly residence he saw the highway filled with people.

15. Curious onlookers, crowd upon crowd of them, were jamming every inch of the royal highways in Ayodhyā.

16. Like waves the crowds dashed together, and the royal highway sent up a roar of delight, like the sound the ocean makes.

17. The city was being decked with fresh wildflower garlands, banners run up high above the houses, the thoroughfares swept and sprinkled.

18. All the people who lived in Ayodhyā—women, children, and the aged alike—were eagerly waiting for sunrise and Rāma's consecration.

19. They were anxious to witness Ayodhyā's greatest festival, a source of joy to the people, and an occasion for their adornment.

20. The royal highway was so jammed that the family priest seemed to part a flood of people as he slowly made his way back to the palace.

21. He ascended to the rooftop terrace, like a mountain peak wreathed in white clouds, and rejoined the lord of men as Bṛhaspati might rejoin Śakra.

22. Seeing he had come, the king left his throne and questioned him, and Vasiṣṭha informed him that his mission had been carried out.

23. Given leave then by his guru, the king dismissed the multitudes of people and withdrew into his private chamber, like a lion into a mountain cave.

24. His palace, rivaling great Indra's palace, was crowded with womenfolk in rich attire, and as the king entered he shed over it as brilliant a light as the hare-marked moon sheds over the sky with its crowds of stars.

The end of the fifth *sarga* of the *Ayodhyākāṇḍa* of the *Śrī Rāmāyaṇa*.

Sarga 6

1. When the family priest had gone Rāma bathed and then, restraining his desire, he worshiped Nārāyaṇa in the company of his large-eyed wife.

2. With bowed head he held out the oblation vessel. Then, in accordance with the ritual precepts, he offered the clarified butter in a blazing fire to the great divinity.

3-4. He consumed the remains of the oblation and earnestly made his wish. Meditating on the god Nārāyaṇa, maintaining silence and restraining his desire, the prince lay down to sleep with Vaidehī on a thick-spread bed of *kuśa* grass in the majestic sanctuary of Viṣṇu.

5. With one watch of the night remaining, he awoke and saw to the decorating of the entire house.

6. This done and hearing the pleasant voices of the bards, genealogists, and panegyrists, he began to intone his prayers in deep concentration, performing the morning worship.

7. Dressed in spotless linen, his head bowed low, he glorified Viṣṇu, crusher of Madhu, and had the brahmans pronounce their blessings.

8. The deep sweet sound of their benedictions was echoed by the sound of pipes and pervaded all Ayodhyā.

9. All the people who lived in Ayodhyā were elated to hear that Rāghava and Vaidehī had undertaken their fast.

10. All the people of the town had heard about Rāma's consecration, and so when they saw night brighten into dawn they began to adorn the city.

11-13. On sanctuaries that looked like mountain peaks wreathed in white clouds, at crossroads and thoroughfares, on shrines and watchtowers, on the shops of merchants rich in their many kinds of wares, on the majestic, rich dwellings of householders, on all the assembly halls, and on prominent trees colorful banners and pennants were run up high.

14. There were troupes of actors and dancers, there were minstrels singing and their voices could be heard everywhere, so pleasing to the ear and heart.

15. In public squares and private houses people spoke with one another in praise of Rāma, now that his consecration was at hand.

16. Even children playing in groups at their front doors talked together in praise of Rāma.

17. The townsmen beautified the royal highway, too, for Rāma's consecration, placing offerings of flowers there and perfuming it with fragrant incense.

18. And anticipating that night would fall, they set up lantern-trees for illumination everywhere along the thoroughfares.

19-20. Thus the residents decorated their city. Afterwards, eagerly waiting for Rāma's consecration as prince regent, they grouped together in public squares and in assembly halls. And there in conversation with each other they sang the praises of the lord of the people:

21. "Ah, what a great man our king is, the delight of the House of the Ikṣvākus, to recognize that he is old and to be ready to consecrate Rāma as king.

22-23. "What a blessing to us all that for a long time to come Rāma will be the lord of earth and our protector. For Rāghava can tell good people from bad, he is wise and righteous and not arrogant. He loves his brothers and shows us the same affection he shows to them.

24. "Long live the righteous king, blameless Daśaratha, by whose grace we shall witness the consecration of Rāma!"

25. As the townsmen conversed in this fashion, the people of the provinces listened; for they too had come from every quarter when they got word of the event.

26. The people of the provinces had come to the city from every quarter to witness Rāma's consecration, and they filled his city to overflowing.

27. And as the waves of people rolled in, one could hear a sound like that of the sea when its swell is raised on a full-moon night.

28. The city, resembling Indra's residence, grew so noisy and congested everywhere with spectators arriving from the provinces that it looked like the ocean waters teeming with all the creatures of the deep.

The end of the sixth *sarga* of the *Ayodhyākāṇḍa* of the *Śrī Rāmāyaṇa*.

Sarga 7

1. Now, Kaikeyī's family servant, who had lived with her from the time of her birth, had happened to ascend to the rooftop terrace that shone like the moon.

2-3. From the terrace Mantharā could see all Ayodhyā—the king's way newly sprinkled, the lotuses and waterlilies strewn about, the costly ornamental pennants and banners, the sprinkling of sandalwood water, and the crowds of freshly bathed people.

4-5. Seeing a nursemaid standing nearby, Mantharā asked, "Why is Rāma's mother so delighted and giving away money to people, when she has always been so miserly? Tell me, why are the people displaying such boundless delight? Has something happened to delight the lord of earth? What is he planning to do?"

6. Bursting with delight and out of sheer gladness the nursemaid told the hunchback Mantharā about the greater majesty in store for Rāghava:

7. "Tomorrow on Puṣya day King Daśaratha is going to consecrate Rāma Rāghava as prince regent, the blameless prince who has mastered his anger."

8. When she heard what the nursemaid said, the hunchback was furious and descended straightway from the terrace that was like the peak of Mount Kailāsa.

9. Consumed with rage, the malevolent Mantharā approached Kaikeyī as she lay upon her couch, and she said:

10. "Get up, you foolish woman! How can you lie there when danger is threatening you? Don't you realize that a flood of misery is about to overwhelm you?

11. "Your beautiful face has lost its charm. You boast of the power of your beauty, but it has proved to be as fleeting as a river's current in the hot season."

12. So she spoke, and Kaikeyī was deeply distraught at the bitter words of the angry, malevolent hunchback.

13. "Mantharā," she replied, "is something wrong? I can tell by the distress in your face how sorely troubled you are."

14. Hearing Kaikeyī's gentle words the wrathful Mantharā spoke—and a very clever speaker she was.

15. The hunchback grew even more distraught, and with Kaikeyī's best interests at heart, spoke out, trying to sharpen her distress and turn her against Rāghava:

16. "Something is very seriously wrong, my lady, something that threatens to ruin you. For King Daśaratha is going to consecrate Rāma as prince regent.

17. "I felt myself sinking down into unfathomable danger, stricken with grief and sorrow, burning as if on fire. And so I have come here, with your best interests at heart.

18. "When you are sorrowful, Kaikeyī, I am too, and even more, and, when you prosper, so do I. There is not the slightest doubt of this.

19. "You were born into a family of kings, you are a queen of the lord of earth. My lady, how can you fail to know that the ways of kings are ruthless?

20. "Your husband talks of righteousness, but he is deceiving you; his words are gentle but he is cruel. You are too innocent to understand, and so he has utterly defrauded you like this.

21. "When expedient, your husband reassures you, but it is all worthless. Now that there is something of real worth he is ready to bestow it upon Kausalyā.

22. "Having got Bharata out of the way by sending him off to your family, the wicked man shall tomorrow establish Rāma in unchallenged kingship.

23. "He is an enemy pretending to be your husband. He is like a viper, child, whom you have taken to your bosom and lovingly mothered.

24.* "For what an enemy or a snake would do if one ignored them, King Daśaratha is now doing to you and your son.

25. "The man is evil, his assurances false, and, by establishing Rāma in the kingship, dear child who has always known comfort, he will bring ruin upon you and your family.

26. "Kaikeyī, the time has come to act, and you must act swiftly, for your own good. You must save your son, yourself, and me, my enchanting beauty."

27. After listening to Mantharā's speech, the lovely woman rose from the couch and presented the hunchback with a lovely piece of jewelry.

28. And, when she had given the hunchback the jewelry, Kaikeyī, most beautiful of women, said in delight to Mantharā,

29. "What you have reported to me is the most wonderful news. How else may I reward you, Mantharā, for reporting such good news to me?

30. "I draw no distinction between Rāma and Bharata, and so I am perfectly content that the king should consecrate Rāma as king.

31. "You could not possibly tell me better news than this, or speak more welcome words, my well-deserving woman. For what you have told me I will give you yet another boon, something you might like more—just choose it!"

The end of the seventh *sarga* of the *Ayodhyākāṇḍa* of the *Śrī Rāmāyaṇa*.

Sarga 8

1. But Mantharā was beside herself with rage and sorrow. She threw the jewelry away and said spitefully:

2. "You foolish woman, how can you be delighted at such a moment? Are you not aware that you stand in the midst of a sea of grief?

3. "It is Kausalyā who is fortunate; it is her son the eminent brahmans will consecrate as the powerful prince regent tomorrow, on Puṣya day.

4. "Once Kausalyā secures this great object of joy, she will cheerfully eliminate her enemies. And you will have to wait on her with hands cupped in reverence, like a serving woman.

5. "Delight is truly in store for Rāma's exalted women, and all that is in store for your daughters-in-law is misery, at Bharata's downfall."

6. Seeing how deeply distressed Mantharā was as she spoke, Queen Kaikeyī began to extol Rāma's virtues:

7. "Rāma knows what is right, his gurus have taught him self-restraint. He is grateful, truthful, and honest, and as the king's eldest son, he deserves to be prince regent.

8. "He will protect his brothers and his dependents like a father; and long may he live! How can you be upset, hunchback, at learning of Rāma's consecration?

9. "Surely Bharata as well, the bull among men, will obtain the kingship of his fathers and forefathers after Rāma's one hundred years.

10. "Why should you be upset, Mantharā, when we have prospered in the past, and prosper now, and shall have good fortune in the future? For he obeys me even more scrupulously than he does Kausalyā."

11. When she heard what Kaikeyī said, Mantharā was still more sorely troubled. She heaved a long and hot sigh and then replied:

12. "You are too simple-minded to see what is good for you and what is not. You are not aware that you are sinking in an ocean of sorrow fraught with disaster and grief.

13. "Rāghava will be king, Kaikeyī, and then the son of Rāghava, while Bharata will be debarred from the royal succession altogether.

14. "For not all the sons of a king stand in line for the kingship, my lovely. Were all of them to be so placed, grave misfortune would ensue.

15. "That is why kings place the powers of kingship in the hands of the eldest, faultless Kaikeyī, however worthy the others.

16. "Like a helpless boy that son of yours, the object of all your motherly love, will be totally excluded from the royal succession and from its pleasures as well.

17. "Here I am, come on your behalf, but you pay me no heed. Instead, you want to reward me in token of your rival's good luck!

18. "Surely once Rāma secures unchallenged kingship he will have Bharata sent off to some other country—if not to the other world!

19. "And you had to send Bharata, a mere boy, off to your brother's, though knowing full well that proximity breeds affection, even in insentient things.

20. "Now, Rāghava will protect Lakṣmaṇa, just as Saumitri will protect Rāma, for their brotherly love is as celebrated as that of the Aśvins.

21. "And so Rāma will do no harm to Lakṣmaṇa, but he will to Bharata without question.

22. "So let your son go straight from Rājagṛha to the forest. That is the course I favor, and it is very much in your own best interests.

23. "For in this way good fortune may still befall your side of the family—if, that is, Bharata secures, as by rights he should, the kingship of his forefathers.

24. "Your child has known only comfort, and, at the same time, he is Rāma's natural enemy. How could the one, with his fortunes lost, live under the sway of the other, whose fortunes are thriving?

25. "Like the leader of an elephant herd attacked by a lion in the forest, your son is about to be set upon by Rāma, and you must save him.

26. "Then, too, because of your beauty's power you used to spurn your co-wife, Rāma's mother, so proudly. How could she fail to repay that enmity?

27. "When Rāma secures control of the land, Bharata will be lost

for certain. You must therefore devise some way of making your son the king and banishing his enemy this very day."

The end of the eighth *sarga* of the *Ayodhyākāṇḍa* of the *Śrī Rāmāyaṇa*.

Sarga 9

1. So Mantharā spoke, and Kaikeyī, her face glowing with rage, heaved a long and burning sigh and said to her:

2. "Today, at once, I will have Rāma banished to the forest, and at once have Bharata consecrated as prince regent.

3. "But now, Mantharā, think: In what way can Bharata, and not Rāma, secure the kingship?"

4. So Queen Kaikeyī spoke, and the malevolent Mantharā answered her, to the ruin of Rāma's fortunes:

5. "Well then, I shall tell you, Kaikeyī—and pay close attention—how your son Bharata may secure sovereign kingship."

6. Hearing Mantharā's words, Kaikeyī half rose from her sumptuous couch and exclaimed:

7. "Tell me the way, Mantharā! How can Bharata, and not Rāma, secure the kingship?"

8. So the queen spoke, and the malevolent hunchback answered her, to the ruin of Rāma's fortunes:

9-11. "When the gods and *asuras* were at war, your husband went with the royal seers to lend assistance to the king of the gods, and he took you along. He set off toward the south, Kaikeyī, to the Daṇḍakas and the city called Vaijayanta. It was there that Timidhvaja ruled, the same who is called Śambara, a great *asura* of a hundred magic powers. He had given battle to Śakra, and the host of gods could not conquer him.

12-13. "In the great battle that followed, King Daśaratha was struck unconscious, and you, my lady, conveyed him out of battle. But there, too, your husband was wounded by weapons, and once again you saved him, my lovely. And so in his gratitude he granted you two boons.

14. "Then, my lady, you said to your husband, 'I shall choose my two boons when I want them,' and the great king consented. I myself was unaware of this, my lady, until you yourself told me, long ago.

15. "You must now demand these two boons of your husband: the consecration of Bharata and the banishment of Rāma for fourteen years.

16. "Now go into your private chamber, daughter of Aśvapati, as if in a fit of rage. Put on a dirty garment, lie down on the bare ground, and don't speak to him, don't even look at him.

17. "Your husband has always adored you, I haven't any doubt of it. For your sake the great king would even go through fire.

18. "The king could not bring himself to anger you, nor even bear to look at you when you are angry. He would give up his own life to please you.

19. "The lord of the land is powerless to refuse your demand. Dull-witted girl, recognize the power of your beauty.

20. "King Daśaratha will offer gems, pearls, gold, a whole array of precious gifts—but pay no mind to them.

21. "Just keep reminding Daśaratha of those two boons he granted at the battle of the gods and *asuras*. Illustrious lady, you must not let this opportunity pass you by.

22-23. "When the great king Rāghava helps you up himself and offers you a boon, then you must ask him for this one, first making sure he swears to it: 'Banish Rāma to the forest for nine years and five, and make Bharata king of the land, the bull among kings.'

24. "In this way Rāma will be banished and cease to be 'the pleasing prince,' and your Bharata, his rival eliminated, will be king.

25. "And by the time Rāma returns from the forest, your steadfast son and his supporters will have struck deep roots and won over the populace.

26. "I think it high time you overcame your timidity. You must forcibly prevent the king from carrying out Rāma's consecration."

27. And so Mantharā induced her to accept such evil by disguising it as good, and Kaikeyī, now cheered and delighted, replied:

28. "Hunchback, I never recognized your excellence, nor how ex-

cellent your advice. Of all the hunchbacks in the land there is none better at devising plans.

29. "You are the only one who has always sought my advantage and had my interests at heart. I might never have known, hunchback, what the king intended to do.

30. "There are hunchbacks who are misshapen, crooked and hideously ugly—but not you, you are lovely, you are bent no more than a lotus in the breeze.

31. "Your chest is arched, raised as high as your shoulders, and down below your waist, with its lovely navel, seems as if it had grown thin in envy of it.

32. "Your girdle-belt beautifies your hips and sets them jingling. Your legs are set strong under you, while your feet are long.

33. "With your wide buttocks, Mantharā, and your garment of white linen, you are as resplendent as a wild goose when you go before me.

34. "And this huge hump of yours, wide as the hub of a chariot wheel—your clever ideas must be stored in it, your political wisdom and magic powers.

35. "And there, hunchback, is where I will drape you with a garland made of gold, once Bharata is consecrated and Rāghava has gone to the forest.

36. "When I have accomplished my purpose, my lovely, when I am satisfied, I will anoint your hump with precious liquid gold.

37. "And for your face I will have them fashion an elaborate and beautiful forehead mark of gold and exquisite jewelry for you, hunchback.

38. "Dressed in a pair of lovely garments you shall go about like a goddess; with that face of yours that challenges the moon, peerless in visage; and you shall strut holding your head high before the people who hate me.

39. "You too shall have hunchbacks, adorned with every sort of ornament, to humbly serve you, hunchback, just as you always serve me."

40. Being flattered in this fashion, she replied to Kaikeyī, who still lay on her luxurious couch like a flame of fire on an altar:

41. "One does not build a dike, my precious, after the water is gone. Get up, apprise the king, and see to your own welfare!"

42. Thus incited, the large-eyed queen went with Mantharā to her private chamber, puffed up with the intoxicating power of her beauty.

43. There the lovely lady removed her pearl necklace, worth many hundred thousands, and her other costly and beautiful jewelry.

44. And then, under the spell of the hunchback Mantharā's words, the golden Kaikeyī got down upon the floor and said to her:

45. "Hunchback, go inform the king that I will surely die right here unless Bharata receives as his portion the land and Rāghava, as his, the forest."

46. And uttering these ruthless words, the lady put all her jewelry aside and lay down upon the ground bare of any spread, like a fallen *kiṃnara* woman.

47. Her face enveloped in the darkness of her swollen rage, her fine garlands and ornaments stripped off, the wife of the lord of men grew distraught and took on the appearance of a darkened sky, when all the stars have set.

The end of the ninth *sarga* of the *Ayodhyākāṇḍa* of the *Śrī Rāmāyaṇa*.

Sarga 10

1. Now, when the great king had given orders for Rāghava's consecration, he gladly entered the inner chamber to tell his beloved wife the good news.

2. But when the lord of the world saw her fallen on the ground and lying there in a posture so ill-befitting her, he was consumed with sorrow.

3. The guileless old man saw her on the floor, that guileful young wife of his, who meant more to him than life itself.

4. He began to caress her affectionately, as a great bull elephant in the wilderness might caress his cow wounded by the poisoned arrow of a hunter lurking in the forest.

5. And, as he caressed his lotus-eyed wife with his hands, sick with worry and desire, he said to her:

6-7. "I do not understand, my lady, why you should be angry. Has someone offended you, or shown you disrespect, that you should lie here in the dust, my precious, and cause me such sorrow? What reason have you to lie upon the floor as if possessed by a spirit, driving me to distraction, when you are so precious to me?

8. "I have skilled physicians, who have been gratified in every way. They will make you well again. Tell me what hurts you, my lovely.

9. "Is there someone to whom you would have favor shown, or has someone aroused your disfavor? The one shall find favor at once, the other incur my lasting disfavor.

10. "Is there some guilty man who should be freed, or some innocent man I should execute? What poor man should I enrich, what rich man impoverish?

11-12. "I and my people, we all bow to your will. I could not bring myself to thwart any wish of yours, not if it cost me my life. Tell me what your heart desires, for all the earth belongs to me, as far as the wheel of my power reaches."

13. So he spoke, and now encouraged she resolved to tell her hateful plan. She then commenced to cause her husband still greater pain.

14. "No one has mistreated me, my lord, or shown me disrespect. But there is one wish I have that I should like you to fulfill.

15. "You must first give me your promise that you are willing to do it. Then I shall reveal what it is I desire."

16. So his beloved Kaikeyī spoke, and the mighty king, hopelessly under the woman's power, said to her with some surprise:

17. "Do you not yet know, proud lady, that except for Rāma, tiger among men, there is not a single person I love as much as you?

18. "Take hold of my heart, rip it out, and examine it closely, my lovely Kaikeyī; then tell me if you do not find it true.

19. "Seeing that I have the power, you ought not to doubt me. I will do what will make you happy, I swear to you by all my acquired merit."

20. His words filled her with delight, and she made ready to reveal her dreadful wish, which was like a visitation of death:

21. "Let the three and thirty gods, with Indra at their head, hear how you in due order swear an oath and grant me a boon.

22-23. "Let the sun and moon, the sky, the planets, night and day, the quarters of space, heaven and earth, let all the *gandharvas* and *rākṣasas*, the spirits that stalk the night, the household gods in every house, and all the other spirits take heed of what you have said.

24. "This mighty king, who is true to his word and knows the ways of righteousness, in full awareness grants me a boon—let the deities give ear to this for me."

25. Thus the queen ensnared the great archer and called upon witnesses. She then addressed the king, who in his mad passion had granted her a boon.

26. "I will now claim the two boons you once granted me, my lord. Hear my words, your Majesty.

27. "Let my son Bharata be consecrated with the very rite of consecration you have prepared for Rāghava.

28. "Let Rāma withdraw to Daṇḍaka wilderness and for nine years and five live the life of an ascetic, wearing hides and barkcloth garments and matted hair.

29. "Let Bharata today become the uncontested prince regent, and let me see Rāghava depart this very day for the forest."

30. When the great king heard Kaikeyī's ruthless demands, he was shaken and unnerved, like a stag at the sight of a tigress.

31. The lord of men gasped as he sank down upon the bare floor. "Oh damn you!" he cried in uncontrollable fury before he fell into a stupor, his heart crushed by grief.

32. Gradually the king regained his senses and then, in bitter sorrow and anger, he spoke to Kaikeyī, with fire in his eyes:

33. "Malicious, wicked woman, bent on destroying this House! Evil woman, what evil did Rāma or I ever do to you?

34. "Rāghava has always treated you just like his own mother. What reason can you have for trying to wreck his fortunes, of all people?

35. "It was sheer suicide to bring you into my home. I did it unwittingly, thinking you a princess—and not a deadly poisonous viper.

36. "When praise for Rāma's virtues is on the lips of every living soul, what crime could I adduce as pretext for renouncing my favorite son?

37. "I would sooner renounce Kausalyā, or Sumitrā, or sovereignty, or life itself, than Rāma, who so cherishes his father.

38. "The greatest joy I know is seeing my first-born son. If I cannot see Rāma, I shall lose my mind.

39. "The world might endure without the sun, or crops without water, but without Rāma life could not endure within my body.

40. "Enough then, give up this scheme, you evil-scheming woman. I beg you! Must I get down and bow my head to your feet?"

41. His heart in the grip of a woman who knew no bounds, the guardian of the earth began helplessly to cry, and as the queen extended her feet he tried in vain to touch them, and collapsed like a man on the point of death.

The end of the tenth *sarga* of the *Ayodhyākāṇḍa* of the *Śrī Rāmāyaṇa*.

Sarga 11

1-2. The king lay there, in so unaccustomed a posture, so ill-befitting his dignity, like Yayāti himself, his merit exhausted, fallen from the world of the gods. But the woman was unafraid, for all the fear she awoke. She was misfortune incarnate and had yet to secure her fortunes. Once more she tried to force him to fulfill the boon.

3. "You are vaunted, great king, as a man true to his word and firm in his vows. How then can you be prepared to withhold my boon?"

4. So Kaikeyī spoke, and King Daśaratha, faltering for a moment, angrily replied:

5. "Vile woman, mortal enemy! Will you not be happy, will you not be satisfied until you see me dead, and Rāma, the bull among men, gone to the forest?

6. "To satisfy Kaikeyī Rāma must be banished to the forest, but if I keep my word in this, then I must be guilty of another lie. My infamy will be unequaled in the eyes of the people and my disgrace inevitable."

7. While he was lamenting like this, his mind in a whirl, the sun set and evening came on.

8. To the anguished king lost in lamentation, the night, adorned with the circlet of the moon, no longer seemed to last a mere three watches.

9. Heaving burning sighs, aged King Daśaratha sorrowfully lamented in his anguish, his eyes fixed upon the sky.

10. "I do not want you to bring the dawn—here, I cup my hands in supplication. But no, pass as quickly as you can, so that I no longer have to see this heartless, malicious Kaikeyī, the cause of this great calamity."

11. But with this, the king cupped his hands before Kaikeyī and once more, begging her mercy, he spoke:

12. "Please, I am an old man, my life is nearly over. I am desolate, I place myself in your hands. Dear lady, have mercy on me for, after all, I am king.

13. "Truly it was thoughtless of me, my fair-hipped lady, to have said those things just now. Have mercy on me, please, my child. I know you have a heart."

14. So the pure-hearted king lamented, frantically and piteously, his eyes reddened and dimmed by tears, but the malicious, black-hearted woman only listened and made no reply.

15. And as the king stared at the woman he loved but could not appease, whose demand was so perverse—for the exile of his own son—he once again was taken faint, overcome with grief, and dropped unconscious to the floor.

The end of the eleventh *sarga* of the *Ayodhyākāṇḍa* of the *Śrī Rāmāyaṇa*.

Sarga 12

1. The evil woman watched as Aikṣvāka lay writhing unconscious on the ground where he had fallen, tortured with grief for his son. Then she spoke:

2. "How can you collapse like this and lie upon the floor, as though you deemed it a sin to fulfill the promise you made me? You must stand by your obligation.

3. "For people who understand the meaning of righteousness hold truth to be its essence. Now, I am simply appealing to truth and exhorting you to do what is right.

4. "Śaibya, the lord of the world, once promised his very own body to a hawk, and he actually gave it to the bird, your majesty, thereby attaining the highest goal.

5. "The same was true of mighty Alarka. When a brahman versed in the *vedas* begged him for his eyes, he plucked them out, his own two eyes, and gave them unflinchingly.

6. "The ocean, lord of rivers, respects the truth, keeping his narrow limits, and in accordance with the truth does not transgress the shore he pledged to keep.

7. "If you do not make good this pledge to me, my noble husband, then right before your eyes I will abandon my life, as you have abandoned me."

8. So the shameless Kaikeyī pressed the king, and he could no more free himself from her snare than Bali could from Indra's.

9. His heart began to beat wildly, his face was drained of color, he was like an ox struggling between the yoke and wheels.

10. His eyes so clouded he could hardly see, barely steadying himself by an act of will, the lord of earth said to Kaikeyī:

11. "Once, in accordance with the sacred hymn, I took and held your hand in mine before the marriage fire. I now repudiate you, evil woman, as well as the son I fathered on you."

12. Blind with rage, the wicked Kaikeyī again addressed the king in the harshest words at her command.

13. "What are these venomous and cutting words you are speaking? Just have your son Rāma brought here without delay.

14. "Not until you have placed my son on the throne, sent Rāma to live in the forest, and rid me of all my rivals, will you have met your obligations."

15. Subjected to this constant pressure, like a noble horse prodded by a sharp goad, the king finally said:

16. "I am bound by the bond of righteousness. My mind is failing me! I want to see righteous Rāma, my beloved eldest son."

17. When Kaikeyī heard the king's words she immediately said to the charioteer on her own initiative, "Go! Bring Rāma."

18. Then the righteous and majestic king, utterly joyless on account of his son, looked up at the charioteer through eyes red with grief and tried to speak to him.

19. Hearing the pitiful sound and seeing the king's desolate expression, Sumantra cupped his hands in reverence and withdrew some steps from his presence.

20. When in his desolation the lord of earth proved incapable of speaking, Kaikeyī, who well knew her counsels, addressed Sumantra herself:

21. "Sumantra, I will see Rāma. Bring the handsome prince at once." Thinking this meant all was well, he rejoiced with all his heart.

22. For as she pressed him to hurry Sumantra reflected, "Clearly the righteous king has exhausted himself in preparing Rāma's consecration."

23. This is what the mighty charioteer thought, and he departed in great delight, eager to see Rāghava.

24. As he rushed out he noticed first the lords of earth at the door and then saw various wealthy townsmen assembling, taking their positions before the door.

The end of the twelfth *sarga* of the *Ayodhyākāṇḍa* of the *Śrī Rāmāyaṇa*.

Sarga 13

1. When night was past the brahmans, who were masters of the *vedas*, together with the king's family priests, assembled at the assembly hall.

2. The ministers, the leaders of the army, and the leading merchants joyfully convened for Rāghava's consecration.

3. When the bright sun had risen and Puṣya day had come, the chief brahmans made the preparations for Rāma's consecration.

4-7. They set out golden ewers, a richly ornamented throne, a chariot draped with a resplendent tiger skin; water brought from the holy confluence of the Ganges and Yamunā, and from all the other holy wells, pools and lakes, from rivers flowing east, west, north, and south, and from all the oceans; honey, curds, clarified butter, parched grain, *darbha* grass, flowers, and milk; golden and silver pots of grain decked with sap-rich twigs, and pots brimming with pure water and adorned with lotuses and waterlilies.

8. A splendid yaktail fan stood ready for Rāma. It was inlaid with jewels, white and softly radiant as moonbeams.

9. A white parasol, majestic and luminous as the full moon's disk, was set out in readiness for Rāma's consecration.

10. Standing ready were a white bull, a flawless white horse, and a majestic rutting elephant, fit for a king to ride.

11. There were eight maidens to ensure good fortune, all adorned with jewelry; all sorts of musical instruments, panegyrists, and others.

12-13. Bringing with them the different sorts of princely equipment required for a royal consecration of the Ikṣvākus, they all convened there by order of the king. But the lord of earth was nowhere to be seen. "Who will inform the king of our arrival?" they asked.

14. "The sun has risen and wise Rāma's consecration as prince regent is ready to begin, but we do not see the king."

15. As they were speaking, Sumantra, the honored attendant of the king, said to all those lords of earth who had come from all over the land:

16. "I can easily go and inquire, as my lords direct, why the king has not come out if he is now awake."

17. With this, the master of ancient tales went to the door of the inner chamber, and there he spoke his blessings and sang the praises of Rāghava's virtues.

18. "Holy night is past, gracious day has begun. Awaken, tiger among kings, and attend forthwith to your duties.

19. "The brahmans, the leaders of the army, and the merchants have come, your Majesty. They await your presence. Awaken, Rāghava."

20. As Sumantra, the charioteer and skilled counsellor, was singing his praises, the king became aware of him and said:

21. "I have not been sleeping. Bring Rāghava here at once." So King Daśaratha spoke, again ordering the charioteer.

22. Hearing the king's command and bowing his head to him, he left the king's chamber, thinking there to be some good news.

23. As the charioteer entered onto the royal highway bedecked with banners and pennants, he could hear the people talking about Rāma.

24. Sumantra then saw the lovely residence of Rāma, resplendent as Mount Kailāsa or the residence of Śakra.

25. It was closed fast with massive gates, and adorned with a hundred terraces. There were golden images atop its pinnacles and a gateway fashioned of gems and coral.

26. It looked like a bank of autumn clouds, radiant as a grotto on Mount Meru, and was adorned with enormous wreaths of choice garlands.

27. The charioteer proceeded on his horse-drawn chariot, observing the crowds that filled the great and opulent royal palace, and when he reached it, a shiver of delight passed through him.

28. It resembled a mountain peak or a motionless cloud, with a complex of buildings more splendid than aerial palaces, and the charioteer made his way through it unchecked, like a dolphin through the gem-stocked sea.

The end of the thirteenth *sarga* of the *Ayodhyākāṇḍa* of the *Śrī Rāmāyaṇa*.

Sarga 14

1-2. The master of ancient tales passed through the inner chamber door where crowds of people thronged and reached the courtyard. It was nearly empty except for the young men who stood guard, armed with bows and arrows and wearing polished earrings, wary, alert, and unswervingly loyal.

3. He saw the aged warders of the women stationed at the door.

They were dressed in saffron-colored robes and richly ornamented, and stood watchfully holding their staffs.

4. At the sight of him approaching they at once informed Rāma and his wife, eager to announce the news.

5. On receiving the message, Rāghava at once had them usher in the charioteer, his father's confidant, for he was anxious for the news.

6-7. The charioteer saw the slayer of enemies seated on a richly covered golden couch. He looked like Vaiśravaṇa, lord of riches, in all his jewelry and with the precious sandalwood cream he had applied, red as a boar's blood, pure and fragrant.

8. Sītā now was with him—like the star Citrā with the hare-marked moon—standing at his side with a yaktail fan in her hand.

9. He blazed like the sun with his natural radiance, and the charioteer greeted him, the granter of boons, with the deference in which he was practiced.

10. His hands cupped in reverence, Sumantra, the honored attendant of the king, asked the prince if he had passed the time agreeably, and slept and rested well. Then he said to him:

11. "O god, worthy son of Kausalyā, your father and Queen Kaikeyī wish to see you. Please go there without delay."

12. So he spoke, and the splendid lion among men was delighted. He dutifully assented and then said to Sītā:

13. "My lady, the king and queen must surely have met and taken some counsel on my behalf relating to the consecration.

14. "The lady is agreeable and desires to please. Having divined his intention she must be urging the king in my favor, my lovely-eyed wife.

15. "A council's mood will be reflected in the messenger it sends. Surely the king is going to consecrate me as prince regent this very day.

16. "So then, I will go off at once and see the lord of earth. Remain here comfortably seated with your companions, and rejoice."

17. Dark-eyed Sītā, esteemed by her lord, followed her husband as far as the door, uttering prayers for good fortune.

18. Catching sight of the crowds of eager people, he approached and greeted them. Then he mounted his splendid chariot that glowed like fire.

19. With the luster of its gleaming gold it nearly blinded the onlookers, while harnessed to it were blood horses almost the size of young elephants.

20. As thousand-eyed Indra boards his swift chariot with its team of bays, Rāghava boarded and sped away, ablaze with royal splendor.

21. Raising a clamor like a storm-cloud rumbling in the sky, he emerged majestically from his residence like the moon from a massive cloud.

22. Rāma's younger brother Lakṣmaṇa, with a parasol and flywhisk in his hands, boarded the chariot at the rear, standing guard for his brother.

23. As he was departing a wild cheering broke out from the flood of people all around.

24. Rāghava could hear the comments of the crowd gathered there and the different things the people of the city were saying about him in their deep delight:

25. "There goes Rāghava now, on his way to wide sovereignty by the grace of the king. All our wishes have come true, now that we shall have him as our ruler. What a great gain for our people, that at long last this whole kingdom will pass into his hands."

26. Like Vaiśravaṇa he proceeded on his way, while master musicians sounded his praises, and eulogists, bards, and genealogists extolled him as they rode ahead, their horses neighing and elephants trumpeting.

27. The lovely thoroughfare came into Rāma's view, with its teeming elephants, chariots, horses, with the great floods of people overflowing the squares, with its profusion of precious objects and stocks of many wares.

The end of the fourteenth *sarga* of the *Ayodhyākāṇḍa* of the *Śrī Rāmāyaṇa*.

Sarga 15

1. Aboard his chariot in the midst of his delighted supporters, majestic Rāma beheld the city crowded with people of every description.

2-3. Rāma proceeded down the center of the royal highway. The splendid thoroughfare was fragrant with aloe-wood and adorned with white, cloudlike houses—gleaming and spacious, flanked with all kinds of wares and foodstuffs of every variety.

4. As he made his way he honored every man, each according to his rank, and heard the many blessings spoken by his supporters:

5. "May you, after your consecration, embark upon and keep to the path traveled by your grandfathers and great-grandfathers."

6. "Once Rāma is king we shall live in even greater happiness than when his father catered to us or his grandfathers in times past."

7. "What need have we now of earthly pleasure, what need of heavenly bliss? Would only that we might see Rāma return installed in the kingship."

8. "There is nothing more welcome to us than this, that Rāma, a man of immeasurable power, be consecrated as our king."

9. Such and others like them were the heartfelt comments of his supporters, and, however laudatory, Rāma listened impassively as he proceeded along the thoroughfare.

10. And there was not a man among them able to tear his eyes or thoughts away from Rāghava, best of men, even when he had left them far behind.

11. Righteous Rāma showed compassion to the people of all four social orders, in a way befitting their ages, and so they were all devoted to him.

12. On reaching the palace that resembled great Indra's abode, the prince ablaze with royal splendor entered his father's residence.

13. Passing through all the courtyards and turning back all his people, the son of Daśaratha came to the private inner chamber.

14. When the prince had gone into his father's presence, all the people were delighted, and they awaited his return as the ocean, lord of rivers, awaits the rising of the moon.

The end of the fifteenth *sarga* of the *Ayodhyākāṇḍa* of the *Śrī Rāmāyaṇa.*

Sarga 16

1. Rāma saw his father, with a wretched look and his mouth all parched, slumped upon his lovely couch, Kaikeyī at his side.

2. First he made an obeisance with all deference at his father's feet and then did homage most scrupulously at the feet of Kaikeyī.

3. "Rāma!" cried the wretched king, his eyes brimming with tears, but he was unable to say anything more or to look at him.

4. As if his foot had grazed a snake, Rāma was seized with terror to see the expression on the king's face, one more terrifying than he had ever seen before.

5. For the great king lay heaving sighs, racked with grief and remorse, all his senses numb with anguish, his mind stunned and confused.

6. It was as if the imperturbable, wave-wreathed ocean had suddenly been shaken with perturbation, as if the sun had been eclipsed, or a seer had told a lie.

7. His father's grief was incomprehensible to him, and the more he pondered it, the more his agitation grew, like that of the ocean under a full moon.

8. With his father's welfare at heart, Rāma struggled to comprehend, "Why does the king not greet me, today of all days?

9. "On other occasions, when Father might be angry, the sight of me would calm him. Why then, when he looked at me just now, did he instead become so troubled?

10. "He seems desolate and grief-stricken, and his face has lost its glow." Doing obeisance to Kaikeyī, Rāma spoke these words:

11. "I have not unknowingly committed some offense, have I, to anger my father? Tell me, and make him forgive me.

12. "His face is drained of color, he is desolate and does not speak to me. It cannot be, can it, that some physical illness or mental distress afflicts him? But it is true, well-being is not something one can always keep.

13. "Some misfortune has not befallen the handsome prince Bharata, has it, or courageous Śatrughna, or one of my mothers?

14. "I should not wish to live an instant if his majesty, the great king, my father, were angered by my failure to satisfy him or do his bidding.

15. "How could a man not treat him as a deity incarnate, in whom he must recognize the very source of his existence in this world?

16. "Can it be that in anger you presumed to use harsh words with my father, and so threw his mind into such turmoil?

17. "Answer my questions truthfully, my lady: What has happened to cause this unprecedented change in the lord of men?

18. "At the bidding of the king, if enjoined by him, my guru, father, king, and benefactor, I would hurl myself into fire, drink deadly poison, or drown myself in the sea.

19. "Tell me then, my lady, what the king would have me do. I will do it, I promise. Rāma need not say so twice."

20. The ignoble Kaikeyī then addressed these ruthless words to Rāma, the upright and truthful prince:

21. "Long ago, Rāghava, in the war of the gods and *asuras*, your father bestowed two boons on me, for protecting him when he was wounded in a great battle.

22. "By means of these I have demanded of the king that Bharata be consecrated and that you, Rāghava, be sent at once to Daṇḍaka wilderness.

23. "If you wish to ensure that your father be true to his word, and you to your own, best of men, then listen to what I have to say.

24. "Abide by your father's guarantee, exactly as he promised it, and enter the forest for nine years and five.

25. "Forgo the consecration and withdraw to Daṇḍaka wilderness, live there seven years and seven, wearing matted hair and barkcloth garments.

26. "Let Bharata rule this land from the city of the Kosalans, with all the treasures it contains, all its horses, chariots, elephants."

27. When Rāma, slayer of enemies, heard Kaikeyī's hateful words, like death itself, he was not the least disconcerted, but only replied,

28. "So be it. I shall go away to live in the forest, wearing matted hair and barkcloth garments, to safeguard the promise of the king.

29. "But I want to know why the lord of earth, the invincible tamer of foes, does not greet me as he used to?

30. "You need not worry, my lady. I say it to your face: I shall go to the forest—rest assured—wearing barkcloth and matted hair.

31. "Enjoined by my father, my benefactor, guru, and king, a man who knows what is right to do, what would I hesitate to do in order to please him?

32. "But there is still one thing troubling my mind and eating away at my heart: that the king does not tell me himself that Bharata is to be consecrated.

33. "For my wealth, the kingship, Sītā, and my own dear life I would gladly give up to my brother Bharata on my own, without any urging.

34. "How much more readily if urged by my father himself, the lord of men, in order to fulfill your fond desire and safeguard his promise?

35. "So you must reassure him. Why should the lord of earth keep his eyes fixed upon the ground and fitfully shed these tears?

36. "This very day let messengers depart on swift horses by order of the king to fetch Bharata from his uncle's house.

37. "As for me, I shall leave here in all haste for Daṇḍaka wilderness, without questioning my father's word, to live there fourteen years."

38. Kaikeyī was delighted to hear these words of Rāma's, and trusting them implicitly, she pressed Rāghava to set out at once.

39. "So be it. Men shall go as messengers on swift horses to bring home Bharata from his uncle's house.

40. "But since you are now so eager, Rāma, I do not think it wise to linger. You should therefore proceed directly from here to the forest.

41. "That the king is ashamed and does not address you himself, that is nothing, best of men, you needn't worry about that.

42. "But so long as you have not hastened from the city and gone to the forest, Rāma, your father shall neither bathe nor eat."

43. "Oh curse you!" the king gasped, overwhelmed with grief, and upon the gilt couch he fell back in a faint.

44. Rāma raised up the king, pressed though he was by Kaikeyī—like a horse whipped with a crop—to make haste and depart for the forest.

45. Listening to the ignoble Kaikeyī's hateful words, so dreadful in their consequences, Rāma remained unperturbed and only said to her,

46. "My lady, it is not in the hopes of gain that I suffer living in this world. You should know that, like the seers, I have but one concern and that is righteousness.

47. "Whatever I can do to please this honored man I will do at any cost, even if it means giving up my life.

48. "For there is no greater act of righteousness than this: obedience to one's father and doing as he bids.

49. "Even unbidden by this honored man, at your bidding alone I shall live for fourteen years in the desolate forest.

50. "Indeed, Kaikeyī, you must ascribe no virtue to me at all if you had to appeal to the king, when you yourself are so venerable in my eyes.

51. "Let me only take leave of my mother, and settle matters with Sītā. Then I shall go, this very day, to the vast forest of the Daṇḍakas.

52. "You must see to it that Bharata obeys Father and guards the kingdom, for that is the eternal way of righteousness."

53. When his father heard Rāma's words, he was stricken with such deep sorrow that he could not hold back his sobs in his grief and broke out in loud weeping.

54. Splendid Rāma did homage at the feet of his unconscious father and at the feet of that ignoble woman, Kaikeyī; then he turned to leave.

55. Reverently Rāma circled his father and Kaikeyī, and, withdrawing from the inner chamber, he saw his group of friends.

56. Lakṣmaṇa, the delight of Sumitrā, fell in behind him, his eyes brimming with tears, in a towering rage.

57. Reverently circling the equipment for the consecration, but careful not to gaze at it, Rāma slowly went away.

58. The loss of the kingship diminished his great majesty as little as night diminishes the loveliness of the cool-rayed moon, beloved of the world.

59. Though he was on the point of leaving his native land and going to the forest, he was no more discomposed than one who has passed beyond all things of this world.

60. Holding back his sorrow within his mind, keeping his every sense in check, and fully self-possessed he made his way to his mother's residence to tell her the sad news.

61. As Rāma entered her residence, where joy still reigned supreme, as he reflected on the sudden wreck of all his fortunes, even then he showed no sign of discomposure, for fear it might endanger the lives of those he loved.

The end of the sixteenth *sarga* of the *Ayodhyākāṇḍa* of the *Śrī Rāmāyaṇa*.

Sarga 17

1. Sorely troubled, heaving sighs like an elephant, Rāma of his own accord went with his brother to his mother's inner chamber.

2. He observed the venerable elder seated there at the door of the house and many other people standing about.

3. Passing through the first courtyard, he saw the brahmans in the second, old men expert in the *vedas* and held in honor by the king.

4. Rāma bowed to the old men and passed into the third courtyard, where he saw women old and young vigilantly standing guard at the door.

5. In delight the women congratulated him and then rushed into the house to pass on the news to Rāma's mother.

6. Queen Kausalyā had spent the night in meditation, and now in the early morning was worshiping Viṣṇu to secure the welfare of her son.

7. Dressed in linen, intent upon her vow and with deep delight, she was then pouring an oblation into the fire in accordance with the vedic verses and pronouncing benedictions.

8. Entering her lovely private chamber, Rāma saw his mother as she was pouring the oblation into the fire.

9. When she saw that her son, his mother's one joy, had finally come, she approached him in delight, as a mare might her colt.

10. In her deep maternal affection for her son, the invincible Rāghava, Kausalyā addressed him with these kind and beneficial words:

11. "May you attain the life-span of the great and aged royal seers who keep to the ways of righteousness. May you attain their fame and the righteousness that benefits a ruling house.

12. "See, Rāghava, your father is as good as his word. This very day the righteous king will consecrate you as prince regent."

13. Extending a little the hands he held cupped in reverence, Rāghava bowed low out of natural courtesy and profound respect. Then he said to his mother,

14. "My lady, I see you do not know of the great danger at hand. It will bring sadness to you, Vaidehī, and Lakṣmaṇa.

15. "For fourteen years I must dwell in the desolate forest, living on honey, fruit, and roots, giving up meat like a sage.

16. "The great king is awarding Bharata the office of prince regent and banishing me to Daṇḍaka wilderness and a life of asceticism."

17-18. A sorrow such as she had never known swept over her, and Rāma saw his mother fall down in a faint, like a broken plantain tree. He came to her side and helped her up, and as she stood there in her desolation, like a mare forced to draw a heavy load, he brushed away the dust that covered her whole body.

19. Tortured by such unhappiness as she had never known before, she spoke to Rāghava, tiger among men, as he attended on her, with Lakṣmaṇa listening:

20. "Rāghava, my son, had you never been born to bring me such grief, had I been childless, I would have been spared any further sorrow.

21. "A barren woman's grief is only of the mind and only a single grief—the painful thought, 'I have no child'; she never comes to feel another, my son.

22. "But the joy and comfort I had not found to be within my

husband's power to give me, Rāma, I cherished hopes I perhaps might find in a son.

23. "How their words will break my heart, the many, painful words I shall hear from those junior co-wives, being their senior as I am. And what could bring a woman greater sorrow?

24. "Even with you present this is how I am spurned. What will it be like when you are gone, my child? Surely nothing is left me but to die.

25. "For anyone who used to serve me or respect my wishes will look anxiously toward Kaikeyī's son without so much as a word for me.

26. "The ten years and seven since you were born, Rāghava, I have passed yearning to put an end to my sorrow.

27. "It was so difficult to raise you in my wretched state, and it was all in vain, the meditation and the fasts, and all the pains I took.

28. "How hard this heart of mine must be that it does not crumble, as the bank of a great river crumbles in the rains when the fresh waters wash over it.

29. "It must be that I can never die, or that no room is left for me in the house of Yama, if even now Death will not carry me off, as brutally as a lion carries off a whimpering doe.

30. "My heart must be made of iron that it does not split and shatter upon the ground, and my body, too, under this crushing sorrow. How true it is that no one can die before his fated hour.

31. "What a sorrowful thing that my vows, my gifts of alms, and acts of self-denial have all been to no avail, that the austerities I practiced for my child's sake have proved to be as barren as seed sown in a desert.

32. "For if a person broken by heavy sorrow could die before his fated hour, of his own free will, then left without you as I am, like a cow without her calf, I would go this very instant to the congregation of the dead."

33. When she looked at Rāghava and contemplated the great calamity to come, her unhappiness was too much for her to bear, and she broke out in lamentation, as a cow will do at the sight of her calf being bound and dragged away.

The end of the seventeenth *sarga* of the *Ayodhyākāṇḍa* of the *Śrī Rāmāyaṇa*.

Sarga 18

1. Lakṣmaṇa grew desolate while Rāma's mother Kausalyā made this lamentation and then, in the heat of the moment, he addressed her:

2. "I do not approve of it either, my lady, that Rāghava should abdicate the majesty of kingship and go off to the forest, bowing to the demands of a woman.

3. "The king is perverse, old, and debauched by pleasures. What would he not say under pressure, mad with passion as he is?

4. "I know of no crime on Rāghava's part nor any fault that could justify his banishment from the kingdom to a life in the forest.

5. "I do not know of a single man in this world, not an adversary, nor even an outcast, who would assert such a fault, even behind our backs.

6. "Who that has any regard for what is right could renounce, without any provocation, a son so godlike, upright, and self-restrained, who cherishes even his enemies?

7. "What son, mindful of the conduct of kings, would take to heart the words of a king who has become a child again?

8. "Before anyone learns of this matter, let me help you seize control of the government.

9. "With me at your side, bow in hand to protect you, who could prevail against you, Rāghava, when you take your stand like Death itself?

10. "With my sharp arrows, bull among men, I will empty Ayodhyā of men if it stands in opposition.

11. "I will slaughter everyone who sides with Bharata or champions his cause. Leniency always ends in defeat.

12. "Now that the king has provoked our implacable enmity, yours and mine, chastiser of foes, what power can he summon to bestow sovereignty on Bharata?

13. "Truly, my lady, the loyalty I feel to my brother comes from the bottom of my heart. I swear it to you by my truth and my bow, by my gifts of alms and sacrifices.

14. "Should Rāma enter the forest, or a blazing fire, my lady, rest assured that I shall have entered first.

15. "I will drive your sorrow away with all the power of the rising sun that drives away the dark. Let the queen behold my power! Let Rāghava behold it!"

16. When she heard great Lakṣmaṇa's words, Kausalyā, weeping and sick with grief, said to Rāma,

17. "My son, you have heard your brother Lakṣmaṇa speak. Whatever is best to do next you must do, as you see fit.

18. "But you must not, heeding the unrighteous words spoken by my co-wife, go away and leave me stricken with grief.

19. "You know what is right and if you would do it, my most righteous son, obey me. Stay here and do your supreme duty.

20. "Kāśyapa obeyed his mother, my son, and lived a life of self-discipline at home. In this way he acquired ultimate ascetic power and reached the highest heaven.

21. "In no way am I less deserving than the king of the respect you owe a guru. I will not give you permission, you may not go away to the forest.

22. "Parted from you what use have I for a life of comfort? Better for me to be with you and eat the grass of the fields.

23. "If you go to the forest leaving me sick with grief, I will fast to death right here, for I could not bear to go on living.

24. "And you will then be guilty of a crime held in infamy in the world, like the ocean, lord of rivers, who through unrighteous conduct incurred the guilt of brahman-murder."

25. So his desolate mother Kausalyā lamented, and righteous Rāma replied to her in a manner consistent with righteousness:

26. "It is not within my power to defy my father's bidding. I bow my head in supplication; I wish to go to the forest.

27. "Even the wise seer Kaṇḍu, a man strict in his observances, slew a cow at the bidding of his father, for he knew that it was right.

28. "And in our own family long ago the sons of Sagara at their father's command dug up the earth and thereby met with wholesale slaughter.

29. "Rāma Jāmadagnya, at his father's bidding, took an ax and by his own hand butchered his mother Reṇukā in the forest.

30. "So you see, it is not I alone who acts as his father instructs. I am only following the path sanctioned and taken by those men of old.

31. "It is this that is my duty on earth, and I cannot shirk it. Besides, no one who does his father's bidding ever comes to grief."

32. So he spoke to his mother, and then he turned to Lakṣmaṇa and said, "I well know, Lakṣmaṇa, the profound affection you bear me. But you fail to understand the real meaning of truth and self-restraint.

33. "Righteousness is paramount in the world and on righteousness is truth founded. This command of Father's is based on righteousness and is absolute.

34. "Having once heard a father's command, a mother's, or a brahman's, one must not disregard it, my mighty brother, if one would hold to what is right.

35. "I cannot disobey my father's injunction, mighty brother, and it is at Father's bidding that Kaikeyī has coerced me.

36. "So give up this ignoble notion that is based on the code of the kshatriyas; be of like mind with me and base your actions on righteousness, not violence."

37. So Lakṣmaṇa's eldest brother spoke affectionately to his brother. Then, with head bowed and hands cupped in reverence, he once more addressed Kausalyā:

38. "Give me your permission, my lady, to go away to the forest. By my very life I adjure you, bestow your blessings on my journey. Once I have fulfilled the promise, I will return to the city from the forest.

39. "I cannot for the sake of mere kingship turn my back on glory, whose reward is great; nor, since life is so short, my lady, would I choose today this paltry land against all that is right."

40. The bull among men earnestly pleaded with his mother—he wanted only to go to the Daṇḍakas—and firmly taught his younger brother the proper view of things. Then, in his heart, he reverently circled the woman who gave him birth.

The end of the eighteenth *sarga* of the *Ayodhyākāṇḍa* of the *Śrī Rāmāyaṇa*.

Sarga 19

1-2. Saumitri was shocked and desolate; this was all far more than he could bear. He heaved a sigh like a mighty serpent, and his eyes bulged with wrath. But Rāma steadfastly maintained his composure and in full self-possession he turned to his beloved friend and brother and spoke:

3. "Saumitri, let this flurry in preparation of my consecration, let it all now be directed toward stopping it.

4. "You must take care that our mother, to whom my consecration was a source of such heartache, be anxious no more.

5. "Not for a moment, Saumitri, can I disregard the anxious sorrow that has sprung up in her heart.

6. "I do not recall ever doing the slightest thing, intentionally or unintentionally, to displease my mothers or father.

7. "Let my father—a truthful man, true to his word, ever striving for truth—let him be freed from the fears he has of what other people might say.

8. "For if this rite were not called off, he too would suffer mental torment, to hear his truthfulness impugned, and his torment would torment me.

9. "So call off the consecration ceremony, Lakṣmaṇa. As soon as you have done so, I wish to leave the city for the forest.

10. "By my immediate banishment the princess will achieve her goal, and be able to consecrate her son Bharata without any hindrance.

11. "For only when I have gone into the wilderness, dressed in barkcloth garments and hides, wearing a crown of matted hair, will Kaikeyī find peace of mind.

12. "Since my mind is made up and my heart is set on it, I should not cause more pain. I shall go into banishment without delay.

13. "It is nothing but destiny, Saumitri, that we must see at work in my exile and in the revocation of the kingship, which had been awarded to me.

14. "For why should Kaikeyī be so determined to harm me were this intention of hers not fated and ordained by destiny?

15. "You know yourself, dear brother, that never in the past have I drawn any distinction between our mothers, nor did she ever differentiate between her son and me.

16. "I cannot credit anything but fate for those words of hers, those hard and brutal words that meant the revocation of the consecration and my exile.

17. "How could she, a princess, so good-natured and virtuous, speak to my harm in the presence of her husband, like the commonest of women?

18. "What cannot be explained must surely be fate, which clearly no creature can resist; for how complete the reversal that has befallen her and me.

19. "What man has the power to contest his fate, Saumitri, when one cannot even perceive it except from its effect?

20. "Happiness and sadness, fear and anger, gain and loss, birth and death—all things such as these must surely be the effects of fate.

21. "I do not feel sad even though my consecration has been thwarted, and neither must you. Comply with my wishes and at once put a stop to the rite of consecration.

22. "It is not our younger mother, Lakṣmaṇa, who should be blamed for preventing my becoming king. People overmastered by fate say things they never wanted to—you know fate has such power."

The end of the nineteenth *sarga* of the *Ayodhyākāṇḍa* of the *Śrī Rāmāyaṇa*.

Sarga 20

1. While Rāma was speaking Lakṣmaṇa kept his head lowered the whole time and listened with his mind poised, it seemed, midway between joy and sorrow.

2. But then that bull among men knit a frown between his brows and heaved a sigh like a great snake seized with anger in its lair.

3. His frowning face was terrible to see—it looked like the face of a raging lion.

4. He shook his hand as an elephant shakes its trunk, from side to side, up and down, and let his head fall on his chest.

5. Looking askance at his brother, from the corner of his eye, he said, "Now is not the time for panic, the source of this sheer folly.

6. "Could a man like you talk this way were he not panicked, fearful of losing people's respect because of some infraction of righteousness?

7. "You are a bull among kshatriyas, as powerful as fate is powerless. How in the world can you blame fate, a contemptible, feeble thing?

8. "How is it you harbor no suspicion of those two evil people? Don't you know, my righteous brother, that there are cunning people who wear the guise of righteousness?

9. "A thing the whole world would find despicable is under way: someone other than you is to be consecrated. I despise that 'righteousness,' my king, which has so altered your thinking, and about which you are deluded.

10. "Even if you think it fate that framed this plot of theirs, still you must reject it. I cannot approve of this course at all.

11. "For it is only the weak and cowardly who submit to fate; heroic men, strong of heart, do not humble themselves before fate.

12. "A man able to counter fate with manly effort does not give up for all that fate may frustrate his purposes.

13. "No, today the people will see the power of fate and the power of man. Today the disparity between the two will be clearly revealed.

14. "Today they will see fate checked by my power, just as they saw your royal consecration checked by fate.

15. "By my power I will turn back fate that is running wild, like a careering elephant beyond control of the goad, in a frenzy of rut and might.

16. "Not all the gods who guard the world, Rāma, not the entire three worlds—much less our father—could prevent your consecration today.

17. "Those who conspired to banish you to the wilderness, your majesty, will themselves be exiled to the wilderness for fourteen years.

18. "I shall crush their hopes, Father's and that woman's, of making her son the king by overturning your consecration.

19. "The might of fate in aid of one fallen within my mighty grasp will be no match for my terrible power and the sorrow it will work.

20. "Later on, many years from now, my brother, when your sons in turn are protecting the subjects, you can go to live in the forest.

21. "For according to the ways of the royal seers of old, living in the forest is prescribed only after entrusting one's subjects to one's sons, to protect as though they were their very own sons.

22. "If perhaps you are unwilling to assume the kingship without the king's wholehearted support, righteous Rāma, for fear of a revolt against your kingship:

23. "I swear to you, my heroic brother, may I never come to share in the afterworld of heroes if I do not guard the kingship for you as the shore guards the ocean.

24. "Have yourself consecrated with the holy implements; busy yourself with that. I shall be able all on my own to repulse any kings by force.

25. "Not for beauty's sake are these two arms nor is this bow merely to adorn me; this sword is not for the sake of ornament nor are these arrows just for filling a quiver.

26. "All four things exist for subduing my enemies, and I am not very eager that anyone be thought my match.

27. "With my sword held ready, its blade sharp and lustrous as flashing lightning, I count no one my match, be he Indra himself, god of the thunderbolt.

28. "Soon the earth will be impassable, knee-deep in the trunks, flanks, and heads of elephants, horses, and men hacked off by the strokes of my sword.

29. "Like clouds with lightning playing about them, like mountains engulfed in flames, elephants will drop to the ground today under the blows of my sword.

30. "When I stand before them with my bow held ready, with my arm-guards and finger-guards strapped on, how could any of those men fancy himself a man?

31. "Shooting now one man with many, now many men with one, I will ply my arrows in the vitals of men, horses, and elephants.

32. "Today the power of my all-powerful weapons shall prevail to strip the king of his power and make it over to you, my lord.

33-34. "Today these arms of mine, well-suited for wearing sandalwood cream, sporting bracelets, lavishing wealth, and protecting friends as well, will do their job, Rāma, repulsing those who stand in the way of your consecration.

35. "Just tell me, which of your enemies should I separate this very day from his fame, his loved ones, and his life? Just instruct me what to do to bring the land under your control. I am your servant."

36. Wiping Lakṣmaṇa's tears away and comforting him all the while, the heir of the Rāghava dynasty said, "You must understand, dear brother, that I am resolved to obey my father's command, for such is the way of the good."

The end of the twentieth *sarga* of the *Ayodhyākāṇḍa* of the *Śrī Rāmāyaṇa*.

Sarga 21

1. When Kausalyā saw that he was resolved to follow his father's orders, she said to her most righteous son, through her choking sobs:

2. "How will he who has never known sorrow, who is righteous and speaks kindly to all creatures, how will the son I bore to Daśaratha live by gleaning grain?

3. "When his servants and slaves are eating delicacies, how can the master eat fruit and roots in the forest?

4. "Who would believe it, who would not be seized with terror, to hear that virtuous Rāghava, the king's beloved, is being exiled?

5. "If you leave me here, a raging fire of grief, unlike any other, will consume me as the many-colored flames of fire consume a thicket when winter is past.

6. "How would a cow not follow her calf if it wanders off? I must follow you, my son, wherever you may go."

7. When he heard what his mother said in her deep sorrow, Rāma, bull among men, addressed her with these words:

8. "Deceived by Kaikeyī, and with me withdrawn to the wilderness, the king will surely not survive if you too should desert him.

9. "For a woman to desert her husband is wickedness pure and simple. You must not do so despicable a thing, not even think it.

10. "As long as my father and lord of the world, Kākutstha, lives, he must be shown obedience, for that is the eternal way of righteousness."

11. From these words of Rāma's, Kausalyā recognized what was proper. "So be it," she replied, though without joy, to tireless Rāma.

12. At this, Rāma, champion of righteousness, once more addressed his mother in her deep sorrow:

13. "Both you and I must do as father bids. He is king, husband, foremost guru, lord, and master of us all.

14. "Once I have passed these nine years and five in the great wilderness, I shall stand again at your bidding, with the deepest joy."

15. Tormented by his words, her face flooded with tears, Kausalyā replied to her son, whom she so loved:

16. "Rāma, I cannot bear to stay among my co-wives. Take me, too, Kākutstha, to the wilderness like a wild deer if, out of regard for your father, your heart is set on going."

17. As she wept like this, Rāma wept, too, and said, "So long as she lives, a woman's one deity and master is her husband. And today the king our master is exercising his mastery over you and me.

18. "Bharata is righteous, too, and speaks kindly to all creatures. He will respect your wishes, for he has always been earnest in doing what is right.

19. "When I have departed you must take care to ensure that the king not trouble himself in the least with grief for his son.

20. "Even the most excellent of women, one who earnestly undertakes vows and fasts, will come to a bad end if she does not respect her husband's wishes.

21. "A woman must show her husband obedience and earnestly strive to please and benefit him. Such is the way of righteousness discovered long ago, revealed in the *veda* and handed down in the world.

22. "The brahmans likewise, who are true to their vows, you must reverence for my sake, my lady. In this way you will pass the time, awaiting my return.

23. "Your fondest wish will be fulfilled when I return, if the champion of righteousness should remain alive."

24. So Rāma spoke, and Kausalyā, tortured by grief for her son, her eyes dimmed by tears, replied, "Go, my mighty son, and be careful. My blessings with you always."

25. When the queen saw how determined Rāma was to live in the forest, she made her prayers for him from the bottom of her heart and prepared to bestow her blessings on his journey.

The end of the twenty-first *sarga* of the *Ayodhyākāṇḍa* of the *Śrī Rāmāyaṇa*.

Sarga 22

1. Rāma's mother restrained her anguish and took a sip of water. Now pure again and in better spirits, she began to make her prayers for him.

2. "May the *sādhyas* bless you and the All-Gods, the Maruts and the great seers. May Dhātṛ and Vidhātṛ bless you, Pūṣan, Bhaga, and Aryaman, too.

3. "May the years and seasons bless you always, the months and half-months, the nights and days and hours.

4. "May your learning, fortitude, and righteousness protect you everywhere, my son. May Skanda protect you, the blessed god, and Soma and Bṛhaspati.

5. "May the Seven Seers and Nārada guard you everywhere, my wise son, may all the constellations, and all the planets with their presiding deities, as you wander in a sage's garb through the great forest.

6. "May you not be troubled by monkeys or scorpions, by gnats or flies in the woods, by snakes or insects in the jungle thickets.

7. "May the huge elephants not harm you, my dear son, nor the lions, tigers, bears, boars, or ferocious horned buffalo.

8. "May the other ferocious breeds of creatures that feed on human flesh not injure you, my son, for these fervid prayers I now offer them.

9. "May your way be safe, may your courage prevail, may all good things be plentiful, Rāma. Go with my blessings, dear son.

10. "May my blessings protect you hour by hour from all the things on earth, in the sky or in heaven that might beset your path.

11. "May Brahmā, the sustainer of creatures and lord of all the worlds, may the seers and the rest of the gods guard you while you are living in the forest."

12. The glorious large-eyed woman worshiped the hosts of gods with garlands and incense and fitting hymns of praise.

13. "May you have the same good fortune as thousand-eyed Indra, to whom all gods bow, when he slew the demon Vṛtra.

14. "May you have the same good fortune Vinatā secured for Suparṇa, when he went in quest of the nectar."

15. Then, of an herb of proven worth, a lucky herb that could ward off thorns, she made an amulet and whispered vedic verses over it.

16. The glorious woman had him bow his head, she kissed him on the forehead and embraced him, saying, "Go in happiness, Rāma my son, and may you achieve success.

17. "How happy I shall be to see you, my child, back again in Ayodhyā, healthy, successful, and firmly established in the house of the king.

18. "I have worshiped the hosts of gods, Śiva and all the others, the great seers, the spirits, great *asuras*, and serpents. When you have gone to the forest, Rāghava, may they, and every quarter of space, ever promote your welfare."

19. And so, her eyes brimming with tears, she concluded her blessings for his journey, as custom required. Then she reverently circled Rāghava, took him in her arms, and pressed him to her bosom again and again.

20. After the queen had circled him glorious Rāghava again and again pressed his head to his mother's feet. Then he proceeded to Sītā's residence, ablaze with his own royal splendor.

The end of the twenty-second *sarga* of the *Ayodhyākāṇḍa* of the *Śrī Rāmāyaṇa*.

Sarga 23

1. So Kausalyā bade him farewell and Rāma did obeisance to her, ready to depart for the forest, keeping to the path of righteousness.

2. Along the royal highway crowded with men, the prince went illuminating it and melting the hearts of the people, it seemed, with all his virtues.

3. Poor Vaidehī had heard nothing of all this; she still believed he was being consecrated as prince regent.

4. She knew the rites for the gods and had performed them in deep delight. Thus she waited for the prince, knowing the kingly attributes to expect.

5. As Rāma entered his residence—still decorated and thronged with delighted people—he lowered his head a little, in shame.

6. Sītā started up and began to tremble as she looked at her husband consumed with grief, his senses numb with anxious care.

7. When she saw how his face was drained of color, how he sweated and chafed, she was consumed with sorrow. "What is the meaning of this, my lord?" she asked.

8. "Today was surely the day for which the learned brahmans had forecast the conjunction of Puṣya, the majestic constellation ruled by Bṛhaspati. Why are you so sad, Rāghava?

9. "The hundred-ribbed parasol with its hue of white-capped water is not throwing its shade upon your handsome face.

10. "Your face, with eyes like the hundred-petaled lotus, is not fanned by the pair of splendid flywhisks, the color of the moon or the wild goose.

11. "And I see no eloquent panegyrists, bull among men, singing your praises in delight, no bards or genealogists with their auspicious recitation.

12. "Nor have the brahmans, masters of the *vedas*, sprinkled your head and poured honey and curds upon it, as custom requires.

13. "No one wishes to follow in your train, not the officials, nor the heads of guilds in their finery, nor the people of the city and provinces.

14. "How is it the splendid Puṣya chariot does not precede you, with its team of four swift horses with trappings of gold?

15. "I see no sign of the royal elephant, revered for its auspicious marks and resembling a mountain black with clouds. It is not leading your procession, my mighty husband.

16. "Nor do I see your escort, my handsome and mighty husband, proceeding with the gold-wrought throne held before them.

17. "What can all this mean, when your consecration is already under way? Never before has your face had such color, and I see no sign of delight."

18. Such were her anxious words, and the delight of the Raghus replied to her: "Sītā, my honored father is banishing me to the forest.

19. "O Jānakī, you are the daughter of a great house, you know what is right and always practice it. Listen to the course of events that has brought this upon me.

20. "Once, long ago, when Kaikeyī had found favor with him, my father King Daśaratha, a man true to his promise, granted her two great boons.

21. "Today, when my consecration was already under way at the instigation of the king, she pressed him for them. Since he had made an agreement, he was compelled by righteousness.

22. "For fourteen years I must live in Daṇḍaka, while my father will appoint Bharata prince regent. I have come to see you before I leave for the desolate forest.

23. "You are never to boast of me in the presence of Bharata. Men in power cannot bear to hear others praised, and so you must never boast of my virtues in front of Bharata.

24. "You must not ever expect to receive any special treatment from him. Life with him will be possible only by constant acquiescence.

25. "I will safeguard my guru's promise and leave this very day for the forest. Be strong, my sensible wife.

26. "When I have gone to the forest where sages make their home, my precious, blameless wife, you must earnestly undertake vows and fasts.

27. "You must rise early and worship the gods according to custom and then pay homage to my father Daśaratha, lord of men.

28. "And my aged mother Kausalyā, who is tormented by misery, deserves your respect as well, for she has subordinated all to righteousness.

29. "The rest of my mothers, too, must always receive your homage. My mothers are all equal in my eyes for their love, affection, and care.

30. "And what is most important, you must look on Bharata and Śatrughna as your brother and your son, for they are dearer to me than life itself.

31. "You must never show opposition to Bharata, for he is now both king of the country and master of our House.

32. "Kings show their favor when they are pleased with good conduct and sedulously attended to—and if they are not, they grow angry.

33. "Lords of men will repudiate their sons, their own flesh and blood, if they serve them ill, and will adopt even strangers, should they prove capable.

34. "My beloved, I am going to the great forest, and you must stay here. You must do as I tell you, my lovely, and not give offense to anyone."

The end of the twenty-third *sarga* of the *Ayodhyākāṇḍa* of the *Śrī Rāmāyaṇa*.

Sarga 24

1. So Rāma spoke, and Vaidehī, who always spoke kindly to her husband and deserved kindness from him, grew angry just because she loved him, and said,

2. "My lord, a man's father, his mother, brother, son, or daughter-in-law all experience the effects of their own past deeds and suffer an individual fate.

3. "But a wife, and she alone, bull among men, must share her husband's fate. Therefore I, too, have been ordered to live in the forest.

4. "It is not her father or mother, not her son or friends or herself, but her husband, and he alone, who gives a woman permanent refuge in this world and after death.

5. "If you must leave this very day for the trackless forest, Rāghava, I will go in front of you, softening the thorns and sharp *kuśa* grass.

6. "Cast out your anger and resentment, like so much water left after drinking one's fill. Do not be reluctant to take me, my mighty husband. There is no evil in me.

7. "The shadow of a husband's feet in any circumstances surpasses the finest mansions, an aerial chariot, or even flying through the sky.

8. "My mother and father instructed me in all these different questions. I do not have to be told now the proper way to behave.

9. "I shall live as happily in the forest as if it were my father's house, caring for nothing in the three worlds but to be faithful to my husband.

10. "I will obey you always and practice self-discipline and chastity. What pleasures I shall share with you, my mighty husband, in the honey-scented forests!

11. "O Rāma, bestower of honor, you have the power to protect any other person in the forest. Why then not me?

12. "You need not doubt that I can survive on nothing but fruit and roots; I shall not cause you any trouble by living with you.

13. "I want to see the streams and mountains, the ponds and forests, and nowhere shall I be afraid with my wise husband to defend me.

14. "I want to see the lotus ponds in full bloom, blanketed with geese and ducks, happy in your company, my mighty husband.

15. "What pleasures I shall share with you, my large-eyed husband, what bliss for me to be with you like this, were it for a hundred thousand years!

16. "If I were to be offered a place to live in heaven itself, Rāghava, tiger among men, I would refuse it if you were not there.

17. "I will go to the trackless forest teeming with deer, monkeys, and elephants, and live there as if in my father's house, clinging to your feet alone, in strict self-discipline.

18. "I love no one else; my heart is so attached to you that were we to be parted I am resolved to die. Take me, oh please grant my request. I shall not be a burden to you."

19. Despite what Sītā said, the best of men, who so cherished righteousness, was still unwilling to take her, and in order to dissuade her, he began to describe how painful life in the forest is.

The end of the twenty-fourth *sarga* of the *Ayodhyākāṇḍa* of the *Śrī Rāmāyaṇa*.

Sarga 25

1. When Sītā finished speaking, the righteous prince, who knew what was right and cherished it, attempted to dissuade her.

2. "Sītā, you are the daughter of a great house and have always been earnest in doing what is right. You must stay here and do your duty, not what your heart desires.

3. "My frail Sītā, you must do as I say. There are so many hardships in the forest. Listen to me and I shall tell you.

4. "Sītā, give up this notion of living in the forest. The name 'forest' is given only to wild regions where hardships abound.

5. "It is, in fact, with your welfare at heart that I am saying this. The forest is never a place of pleasure—I know—but only of pain.

6. "There are lions that live in mountain caves; their roars are redoubled by mountain torrents and are a painful thing to hear—the forest is a place of pain.

7. "At night, worn with fatigue, one must sleep upon the ground on a bed of leaves, broken off of themselves—the forest is a place of utter pain.

8. "And one has to fast, Maithilī, to the limit of one's endurance, wear clothes of barkcloth and bear the burden of matted hair.

9. "The wind is so intense there and the darkness, too. One is always hungry and the dangers are so great—the forest is a place of utter pain.

10. "There are many creeping creatures, of every size and shape, my lovely, ranging aggressively over the ground—the forest is a place of utter pain.

11. "There are snakes, too, that live in the rivers, moving as sinuously as rivers, and they are always there obstructing one's way—the forest is a place of utter pain.

12. "Moths, scorpions, worms, gnats, and flies continually harass one, my frail Sītā—the forest is wholly a place of pain.

13. "There are thorn trees, *kuśa*, and *kāśa* grass, my lovely, and the forest is a tangle of their branches and blades—the forest is a place of utter pain.

14. "So no more of your going to the forest, you could not bear it. The more I think about it the more I see how many hardships the forest holds."

15. When great Rāma had thus made up his mind not to take her to the forest, Sītā did not reply to him at once, but then in bitter sorrow she spoke.

The end of the twenty-fifth *sarga* of the *Ayodhyākāṇḍa* of the *Śrī Rāmāyaṇa*.

Sarga 26

1. Sītā was overcome with sorrow when she heard what Rāma said. With tears trickling down her face, she answered him in a faint voice.

2. "Do you not know that what you call the hardships of life in the forest would all be luxuries if your love accompanied them?

3. "By the order of our elders I must go with you, Rāma. I would die here and now if parted from you.

4. "But if I were by your side, Rāghava, not even Śakra, lord of the gods, could harm me for all his might.

5. "A woman whose husband has left her cannot go on living, regardless of what advice you give me, Rāma.

6. "Besides, my wise husband, long ago in my father's house I heard the brahmans prophesy that some day I should have to live in the forest.

7. "The twice-born could read the marks on a person's body, my powerful husband, and from that moment at home, when I heard what they foretold, I have constantly yearned to live in the forest.

8. "The prediction that I should have to live in the forest must some day be fulfilled. And it is with you that I would go there, my love, not otherwise.

9. "I will go with you and carry out the prediction. The moment has arrived; let the prophecy of the twice-born come true.

10. "I know that in living in the forest there is indeed much pain, my mighty husband, but it is only those who are unprepared that suffer from it.

11. "When I was a girl in my father's house I happened to hear, in the presence of my mother, all about forest life from a holy mendicant woman.

12. "And, in fact, I have begged you many times before to let us go and live together in the forest, my lord, so much do I desire it.

13. "Please, Rāghava, I have been waiting for the chance to go. I want nothing more than to serve my hero as he lives in the forest.

14. "If from feelings of love I follow you, my pure-hearted husband, I shall have no sin to answer for, because my husband is my deity.

15-16. "My union with you is sacred and shall last even beyond death. There is a holy scripture, my high-minded husband, which glorious brahmans recite: 'When in this world, in accordance with their own customs and by means of the ritual waters, a woman's father gives her to a man, she remains his even in death.'

17. "What then is the reason you are set against taking me away from here, your own wife, a woman of good conduct and faithful to her husband?

18. "I am devoted and faithful to my husband. I have always shared your joy and sorrow, and now I am so desolate. You must take me, Kākutstha: your joy has always been mine to share, and your sorrow.

19. "If you refuse to take me to the forest despite the sorrow that I feel, I shall have no recourse but to end my life by poison, fire, or water."

20. Though she pleaded with him in this and every other way to be allowed to go, great-armed Rāma would not consent to taking her to the desolate forest.

21. And when he told her as much, Maithilī fell to brooding, and drenched the ground, it seemed, with the hot tears that fell from her eyes.

22. And as Vaidehī brooded, wondering how to change his mind, anger took hold of her. But Kākutstha did not lose his self-composure and tried his best to appease her.

The end of the twenty-sixth *sarga* of the *Ayodhyākāṇḍa* of the *Śrī Rāmāyaṇa*.

Sarga 27

1. Rāma tried to appease her, but Maithilī, daughter of Janaka, addressed her husband once more in the hopes of living in the forest.

2. Sītā was deeply distraught, and out of love and indignation she began to revile broad-chested Rāghava.

3. "What could my father Vaideha, the lord of Mithilā, have had in mind when he took you for a son-in-law, Rāma, a woman with the body of a man?

4. "How the people lie in their ignorance. Rāma's 'great power' is not at all like the power of the blazing sun that brings the day.

5. "On what grounds are you so reluctant, what are you afraid of that you are ready to desert me, who has no other refuge?

6. "Do you not know, my mighty husband, that I bow to your will, that I am as faithful to you as Sāvitrī was to Satyavant, Dyumatsena's son?

7. "Were I to go with you, blameless Rāghava, I would not even think of looking at any man but you, unlike some women who disgrace their family.

8. "But like a procurer, Rāma, you are willing of your own accord to hand me over to others—your wife, who came to you a virgin and who has been a good woman all the long while she has lived with you.

9. "You must not leave for the forest without taking me. Let it be austerities, or the wilderness, or heaven, but let it be with you.

10. "As I follow behind you I shall no more tire on the path than on our pleasure beds.

11. "The *kuśa* and *kāśa* grass, the reeds, the rushes, and thorn trees will feel just like cotton or a pelt to me on the road with you.

12. "The dust raised by heavy winds that will settle on me, my love, I shall look upon as the costliest sandalwood cream.

13. "As I roam through the deep forest there will be meadows for me to rest in, and to rest on couches spread with blankets could not give more pleasure.

14. "The leaves and roots and fruit you gather with your own hands and give me, however much or little there is, will taste like nectar to me.

15. "There will be fruits and flowers in their seasons to enjoy, and I shall not think with longing of my mother or father or home.

16. "And when you are there you will not know any grief or displeasure on my account. I shall not be a burden.

17. "To be with you is heaven, to be without you hell. Knowing how deep my love is, Rāma, you must take me when you go.

18. "But if you will not let me go to the forest when I am so set on it, I will take poison this very day, sooner than come under the sway of those who hate us.

19. "Afterwards I could not live anyway, my lord, for the sorrow of being deserted by you. Better to die that very instant.

20. "I could not bear the grief of it even for a moment, much less ten years of sorrow, and three, and one."

21. Consumed with grief, she lamented long and piteously. Crying out in anguish, she shrieked and embraced her husband with all her might.

22. His many words had wounded her, the way poison arrows wound a cow elephant. And the tears she had held in so long burst forth like a flame from a kindling stick.

23. Water clear as crystal, springing from her torment, came gushing from all around her eyes, like water from two lotuses.

24. She was nearly insensible with sorrow when Rāma took her in his arms and comforted her with these words:

25. "If its price were your sorrow, my lady, I would refuse heaven itself. No, I am not afraid of anything, any more than is the Self-existent Brahmā.

26. "But without knowing your true feelings, my lovely, I could not consent to your living in the wilderness, though I am perfectly capable of protecting you.

27. "Since you are determined to live with me in the forest, Maithilī, I could no sooner abandon you than a self-respecting man his reputation.

28. "But it is righteousness, my smooth-limbed wife, the righteousness good men in the past have practiced, that I am set on following today, as its radiance follows the sun.

29. "And righteousness is this, my fair-hipped wife: submission to one's mother and father. I could not bear to live were I to disobey their command.

30. "My father keeps to the path of righteousness and truth, and I wish to act just as he instructs me. That is the eternal way of

righteousness. Follow me, my timid one, be my companion in righteousness.

31. "Go now and bestow precious objects on the brahmans, give food to the mendicants and all who ask for it. Hurry, there is no time to waste."

32. Finding that her husband had acquiesced in her going, the lady was elated and set out at once to make the donations.

33. Glorious Sītā was delighted, her every wish fulfilled by what her husband said, and in high spirits the woman set off to give money and precious objects to all who upheld righteousness.

The end of the twenty-seventh *sarga* of the *Ayodhyākāṇḍa* of the *Śrī Rāmāyaṇa*.

Sarga 28

1. Mighty Rāma then turned to Lakṣmaṇa, who came and stood before him, hands cupped in reverence, begging that he might be allowed to go, in the very lead.

2. "Saumitri, were you to go with me now to the forest, who would support Kausalyā and glorious Sumitrā?

3. "The mighty lord of the land, who used to shower them with all they desired, as a raincloud showers the earth, is now caught up in the snare of desire.

4. "And once the daughter of King Aśvapati gains control of the kingdom, she will not show any good will to her co-wives in their sorrow."

5. So Rāma eloquently spoke, and Lakṣmaṇa in a gentle voice replied to him with equal eloquence:

6. "Your own power, my mighty brother, will no doubt ensure that Bharata scrupulously honors Kausalyā and Sumitrā.

7. "The noble Kausalyā could support a thousand men like me, for she has acquired a thousand villages as her living.

8. "I will take my bow and arrows and bear the spade and basket. I will go in front of you, leading the way.

9. "I will always be there to bring you roots and fruit and such other produce of the forest as is proper fare for ascetics.

10. "You shall take your pleasure with Vaidehī on the mountain slopes while I do everything for you, when you are awake and when you sleep."

11. His words pleased Rāma, and he replied, "Go, Saumitri, and take leave of all your friends.

12-14. "And those two divine, awesome-looking bows that great Varuṇa himself bestowed on Janaka at the grand sacrifice; the two suits of divine, impenetrable armor; the two quivers with inexhaustible arrows and the two swords bright as the sun and plated with gold—all was deposited in perfect order in our preceptor's residence. Collect the arms, Lakṣmaṇa, and come back at once."

15. So, resolved to live in the forest, he bade farewell to his friends and to the guru of the Ikṣvākus, and gathered up the all-powerful arms.

16. Saumitri, tiger of the Raghus, displayed to Rāma all the divine arms, in perfect order still and adorned with garlands.

17. When Lakṣmaṇa had come back, Rāma, joyfully and with full self-possession, said to him, "You have come, dear Lakṣmaṇa, at the very moment I desired.

18-19. "I want your help, slayer of enemies, in giving away whatever wealth I possess to the poor brahmans, to the best of the twice-born who live here in firm devotion to my gurus, and in particular to all my dependents.

20. "Fetch at once the foremost of the twice-born, noble Suyajña, Vasiṣṭha's son. I will leave for the forest after paying homage to him and all the other twice-born men of learning."

The end of the twenty-eighth *sarga* of the *Ayodhyākāṇḍa* of the *Śrī Rāmāyaṇa*.

Sarga 29

1. Acknowledging his brother's most just and welcome order, he left and immediately entered Suyajña's house.

2. The priest was in the fire-sanctuary, and after greeting him Lakṣmaṇa said, "My friend, come visit the dwelling of the man who is doing what no man has ever done."

3. After performing the twilight worship he left straightway with Saumitri and entered Rāma's lovely, majestic house.

4. On the arrival of Suyajña, the master of the *vedas* who shone like a fire ablaze with the offering, Rāghava and Sītā cupped their hands in reverence and approached him.

5-6. Kākutstha honored Suyajña with gifts—magnificent armbands fashioned of gold, sparkling earrings, gems strung on golden chains, bracelets and wristbands, and many other precious objects. And then, at Sītā's urging, Rāma said to him,

7. "Take this necklace and golden chain to your wife, my dear friend. Here is a jeweled belt, too, which Sītā wishes to give you.

8. "She also wishes to bestow on you this couch with exquisite coverlets, adorned with a variety of gems.

9. "I have an elephant named Śatruṃjaya, given to me by my maternal uncle and worth a thousand others. I make you a gift of him, bull among the twice-born."

10. So Rāma spoke, and Suyajña accepted all the gifts and conferred gracious blessings on Rāma, Lakṣmaṇa, and Sītā.

11. As Brahmā might address Indra, lord of the thirty gods, Rāma then addressed his kind, attentive brother Saumitri with these kind words:

12. "Summon the two eminent brahmans Āgastya and Kauśika and in homage shower precious objects on them, Saumitri, as crops are showered with rain.

13-14. "As for the learned preceptor of the Taittirīyas, the master of the *vedas* who devotedly serves Kausalyā with his blessings—present that twice-born with a palanquin and slave-girls, Saumitri, and silken garments to his heart's content.

15. "And give precious objects, garments, and money enough to content Citraratha, the noble adviser and charioteer, who has lived with us so long.

16. "Present a thousand draft animals, two hundred oxen, and a thousand cows, Saumitri, to provide for dairy needs."

17. Then Lakṣmaṇa himself, tiger among men, gave the riches as ordered to the lordly brahmans, just as Kubera, giver of riches, might have done.

18. Now, after Rāma had bestowed great wealth on each and every one of his dependents, he spoke to them as they stood before him choked with tears.

19. "Both Lakṣmaṇa's dwelling and the house belonging to me may be occupied until I return."

20. After speaking with all his sorrowful dependents, he turned to the keeper of the treasury and said, "Have the treasure brought." His dependents then fetched all his treasure.

21. And the tiger among men, with Lakṣmaṇa's help, had the treasure distributed to the needy brahmans, young and old alike.

22. There came a sallow brahman then, by the name of Trijaṭa Gārgya, all the way up to the fifth courtyard without anyone stopping him.

23. Reaching the prince, Trijaṭa said, "Glorious prince, I am penniless and have many children. I must live by constant gleaning in the forest. Have regard for me."

24. Rāma replied to him jokingly, "There are one thousand cows I have not yet allocated. You shall have as many as you can cover by hurling your staff."

25. In a frantic rush he girded up the rag around his loins and, brandishing his staff impetuously, hurled it with every ounce of his strength.

26. Rāma then said to Gārgya, seeking to placate him, "You must not be angry, truly. This was only a joke on my part."

27. Then the great sage Trijaṭa along with his wife accepted the herd of cows and pronounced blessings on the great prince conducive to fame, strength, joy, and happiness.

The end of the twenty-ninth *sarga* of the *Ayodhyākāṇḍa* of the *Śrī Rāmāyaṇa*.

Sarga 30

1. Now, after the two Rāghavas and Vaidehī had bestowed vast wealth upon the brahmans, they went to see their father.

2. How brilliant they looked when they took up their formidable weapons, which Sītā had ornamented and hung with flower garlands.

3. The wealthy townspeople went up to the roofs of their palaces and mansions and to the tops of many-storied buildings and watched despondently.

4. The streets were so thronged with people as to be impassable, and so they went up to the roofs of their palaces and in desolation gazed down at Rāghava.

5. When the people saw Rāma going on foot and without the royal parasol, their hearts were crushed with grief, and they said many different things:

6. "The prince, whom a vast army of four divisions used to follow as he went forth, is all alone now, with only Lakṣmaṇa and Sītā to follow behind."

7. "Though he has known the taste of kingly power and has always met the needs of the needy, in his veneration for righteousness he refuses to let his father break his word."

8. "People on the royal highway can now look at Sītā, a woman whom even creatures of the sky have never had a glimpse of before."

9. "Sītā is used to cosmetics and partial to red sandalwood cream, but the rain and the heat and the cold will soon ruin her complexion."

10. "Surely it is some spirit that has possessed Daśaratha and spoken today, for the king could never bring himself to exile his beloved son."

11. "How could a man force his own son into exile, even an unvirtuous son, let alone one who has vanquished the world simply by his good conduct?"

12. "Benevolence, compassion, learning, good character, restraint, and equanimity—these are the six virtues that adorn Rāghava, the best of men."

13. "And so the people are sorely hurt by any injury to him, like water creatures when the water dries up in the summertime."

14. "When the lord of the world is hurt so is all the world, as the fruit and flowers of a tree are hurt by an injury to its root."

15. "Let us at once take our wives and kinsmen, and like Lakṣmaṇa follow Rāghava as he goes forth, wherever he may go."

16. "Let us abandon our gardens, our fields and homes, and follow righteous Rāma, to share his sorrow and joy."

17-18. "Let us unearth our buried treasure, remove our stores of grain and our wealth, and take all our valuables. And when the household gods have abandoned them, and their courtyards are falling into disrepair and the dust settling thick upon them, let Kaikeyī take possession of the dwellings we have left."

19. "Let the wilderness where Rāghava goes become our city, and the city we abandon turn into a wilderness."

20. "Let all the animals leave their haunts, the snakes their lairs, the birds and beasts their mountain slopes, and take possession of what we have left."

21. Such were the kinds of remarks people were making one after the other, and Rāma heard them, but for all that he heard his mind remained unmoved.

22. And even when Rāma looked at the people in their anguish, not the least anguish touched him—he was smiling instead as he walked on, eager to see his father, eager to carry out his father's order to the letter.

23. Rāma, the great son of Aikṣvāka, on the point of leaving for the forest, caught sight of the anguished Sumantra, and only then did he come to a halt, in order to gain admittance to his father.

24. Because he so cherished righteousness, Rāghava had his mind firmly made up to enter the forest on his father's order. With a glance at Sumantra, he said, "Announce my arrival to the king."

The end of the thirtieth *sarga* of the *Ayodhyākāṇḍa* of the *Śrī Rāmāyaṇa*.

Sarga 31

1. When Rāma dispatched him, the charioteer, his senses numb with misery, entered at once. He saw the lord of men heaving sighs.

2. The wise charioteer gazed at him grieving over Rāma in deep mental turmoil. He then approached with hands cupped in reverence.

3. "Tiger among men, your son is here waiting at the door. He has given away all his wealth to brahmans and his dependents.

4. "Let Rāma, who always strives for truth, come and see you, please. He has taken leave of all his friends and now wishes to see you.

5. "He is about to depart for the great forest. Lord of the world, grant him audience, a man whom all kingly virtues encircle as beams encircle the sun."

6. The truthful and righteous lord of men, like the ocean in profundity and as free from taint as the sky, replied,

7. "Sumantra, bring all my wives to me. I wish to see Rāghava in the company of all my wives."

8. He went straight into the inner chamber and said to the women, "The king your husband summons you. Go to him at once."

9. So Sumantra spoke by order of the king, and all the women proceeded to their husband's chamber in compliance with his command.

10. Half seven hundred ladies with coppery eyes, who held firm to their vows, gathered around Kausalyā and slowly made their way.

11. When the king and lord of the land observed that his wives had come, he said to the charioteer, "Sumantra, now bring my son."

12. Then, with Rāma, Lakṣmaṇa, and Maithilī, the charioteer at once came forward into the presence of the lord of the world.

13. Seeing his son at a distance approaching with hands cupped in reverence, the tormented king in the midst of his womenfolk started up suddenly from his throne.

14. At the sight of Rāma the lord of the peoples ran impetuously forward but, broken by sorrow, he fell to the ground in a faint before he reached him.

15. Rāma flew to him at once and so did Lakṣmaṇa, the great chariot-fighter, as the lord of men lay insensible with sorrow and lost in grief.

16. And suddenly a shrill screaming broke out in the king's chamber, as countless women cried, "Alas, alas for Rāma!" the cry made all the louder by the noise of their jewelry.

17. Rāma and Lakṣmaṇa both took him in their arms and with Sītā's help they laid him on a couch, all three of them in tears.

18. After a moment the lord of the land, overwhelmed by a sea of grief, regained consciousness. Then Rāma cupped his hands in reverence and said to him:

19. "I ask leave of you, your majesty, for you are lord of us all. I am about to set out for Daṇḍaka wilderness. Look kindly on me.

20. "Give leave to Lakṣmaṇa. Sītā, too, shall follow me to the forest. Neither of them would be dissuaded despite the many sound arguments I offered.

21. "Have done with grieving, bestower of honor, and give leave to us all, to Lakṣmaṇa, Sītā, and me, as Prajāpati once gave his children leave."

22. Rāghava waited intently for the lord of the world to grant him permission to live in the forest. The king looked at him and said,

23. "Rāghava, I was deceived by Kaikeyī into granting a boon. Depose me now and become king of Ayodhyā yourself."

24. So the lord of men, his father, spoke, and Rāma, champion of righteousness, cupped his hands in reverence and in full command of his words replied to him:

25. "You shall be lord of earth, your Majesty, for countless years to come, and I will live in the wilderness. You must not on my account act untruthfully.

816*. "After I have passed the nine years and five of life in the forest, I shall once again clasp your feet, lord of men, when the promise is fulfilled."

The king wept in anguish at the snare of truth in which he was caught. But under silent pressure from Kaikeyī, he said at last to his beloved son:

26. "Go in safety, my dear son, and may no harm befall you. May your way be safe and free from all dangers, and lead you to good fortune, prosperity, and home once more.

27. "But by no means must you go now, this evening, my son. Spend the night in the company of your mother and me. Tomorrow morning, with all your desires satisfied, you may set out."

28. When Rāma heard the words of his anguished father, he was desolate, and so was his brother Lakṣmaṇa. He said:

29. "Who will confer on me tomorrow the benefits I should have tonight? I prefer, to any objects of desire, merely to depart.

30. "I abdicate all claim to this treasure-laden earth, its kingdom and people, its stores of grain and wealth. Let it be made over to Bharata.

31. "Put an end to your sorrow, do not let tears overwhelm you. The indomitable lord of rivers, the ocean, remains forever unperturbed.

32. "It is not kingship or comfort or even Maithilī that I desire, but that you be truthful, bull among men, not false.

33. "The city, the kingdom, and the entire land I abdicate. Let it all be given to Bharata. I will follow your command and leave for my long stay in the forest.

34. "Let Bharata hold absolute rule over the land I abdicate—this kindly land with its firm boundaries, its mountain ranges, towns, and woodlands. Let it be as you have said, my king.

35. "Never to the same degree have I set my heart on great objects of desire or my own pleasure, Your Majesty, as on your command, which men of learning always endorse. Put an end to your sorrow on my account, my blameless father.

36. "If it meant entangling you in falsehood, my blameless father, I would reject sovereign kingship, reject all objects of desire, all comforts, Maithilī, life itself. The truth of your vow must be preserved.

37. "There will be fruit and roots in the forest for me to eat, mountains, rivers, and lakes to see, and the moment I find myself among the many-colored trees I shall be happy. You should feel joy as well."

The end of the thirty-first *sarga* of the *Ayodhyākāṇḍa* of the *Śrī Rāmāyaṇa*.

Sarga 32

1. Tormented by his promise, Aikṣvāka heaved a deep and tearful sigh, and then in an urgent voice he said to Sumantra:

2. "Charioteer, I want an army, a force of four divisions, to be provisioned with every luxury and marshaled at once as escort for Rāghava.

3. "Let there be eminent courtesans to adorn the prince's retinue and prosperous merchants with choice wares to display.

4. "Handsomely pay all his dependents and all whose acts of strength have pleased him and assign them to his suite as well.

5. "Killing deer and elephants, drinking forest liquor, and viewing the different rivers he will not think with longing of the kingdom.

6. "The entire contents of my granary and treasury are to go with Rāma while he lives in the desolate forest.

7. "His life in the forest will be pleasant, what with holding sacrifices at holy places, conferring fitting priestly stipends, and consorting with seers.

8. "Great-armed Bharata shall protect Ayodhyā. Let majestic Rāma be sent off with every object of desire."

9. While Kākutstha was speaking, Kaikeyī was gripped by fear. Her mouth went dry and her voice was choked.

10. Pale and frightened, Kaikeyī spoke out: "My good man, Bharata is not to take charge of a kingdom stripped of its wealth, like a cup of wine drained to the dregs, an empty kingdom without a single thing to whet his appetite!"

11. So Kaikeyī viciously spoke, abandoning all shame, and King Daśaratha answered his large-eyed wife: "Will you yoke me to a burden, malicious woman, and beat me even as I bear it?"

12. Kaikeyī's fury was redoubled. "It was in your House," she said to the king, "that Sagara dispossessed his eldest son—Asamañja was his name. This one must leave in the same way."

13. "Curse you!" was all King Daśaratha could say in reply. And though the people were all ashamed for her, she paid them no mind.

14. Then an aged minister named Siddhārtha, an honest man esteemed by the king, addressed Kaikeyī:

15. "But Asamañja was wicked. He took pleasure in seizing children playing on the road and then hurling them into the waters of the Sarayū.

16. "When the townsmen saw what he was doing they were all enraged and told the king, 'Increaser of the realm, you must choose one: either Asamañja or us.'

17. "The king asked, 'What has happened to cause this fear of yours?' and the citizens responded to the king's inquiry:

18. " 'When our little children are out playing, this madman hurls them into the Sarayū and enjoys it to no end in his insanity.'

19. "When he heard what the people said, the lord of men renounced his malevolent son in his desire to please them.

20. "It was thus righteous King Sagara renounced him. But what evil has Rāma done that he should be dispossessed like that?"

21. After listening to Siddhārtha's speech, the king, in a failing voice and words fraught with grief, said to Kaikeyī:

22. "I will accompany Rāma today, renouncing altogether the kingdom, pleasure, and wealth. And with King Bharata may you long enjoy the kingdom to your heart's content."

The end of the thirty-second *sarga* of the *Ayodhyākāṇḍa* of the *Śrī Rāmāyaṇa*.

Sarga 33

1. After listening to the minister's speech, Rāma addressed Daśaratha with the deference in which he was practiced.

2. "I have given up pleasures, your majesty, and shall live in the wilderness on things of the wild. I have given up all attachments; what use then have I of an escort?

3. "Would a man who gives away a prize elephant cling to the cinch-belt? Why cherish the rope once the animal is gone?

4. "So it is for me, too, best of men and lord of the world. What use have I for a bannered army? I must refuse it all. Let them bring me only barkcloth garments.

5. "Bring me a small basket, too, and a spade before I go to the forest to make my dwelling for fourteen years."

6. Kaikeyī herself then brought the barkcloth garments. "Put them on!" she said to Rāghava, unembarrassed before the crowd of people.

7. The tiger among men took a pair of them from Kaikeyī, and laying his delicate clothes aside, he dressed himself in the clothes of a sage.

8. Lakṣmaṇa too, then and there, removed his lovely clothing and put on the garb of an ascetic, in the presence of his father.

9. Then Sītā, who was dressed in silks, glanced at the barkcloth garment meant for her to wear, and she was frightened, like a spotted doe at the sight of a trap.

10. Disconcerted and embarrassed, she took it up. Then she said to her husband, the very image of the king of *gandharvas*, "How do the sages who live in the forest put on barkcloth?"

11. She picked one up in her hand and held it to her neck and stood there, the daughter of Janaka, awkward and ashamed.

12. At once Rāma, champion of righteousness, came up to her and with his own hands fastened it over Sītā's silks.

13. Dressed in barkcloth she stood there as if defenseless, though her defender was at her side, while the people all cried out, "A curse upon you, Daśaratha!"

14. Aikṣvāka heaved a burning sigh as he said to his wife, "Kaikeyī, Sītā must not go in garments of bark and *kuśa* grass.

15. "Surely it suffices you, evil creature, that Rāma is being exiled. Must you heap these vile crimes on top of that?"

16. With this, the king hung his head and sat still, and Rāma addressed him once more before leaving for the forest:

17. "Righteous father, Kausalyā here, my glorious mother, is an aged woman of noble character, and she does not reproach you, my lord.

18. "She has never known adversity before, and bereft of me she will be plunged into a sea of grief. Show her higher regard, please, granter of boons.

19. "Equal of great Indra, this mother of mine dotes on her child. Please, take care that she not be tortured with grief when I am in the forest, that she does not lay down her life and go her way to the house of Yama, god of death."

The end of the thirty-third *sarga* of the *Ayodhyākāṇḍa* of the *Śrī Rāmāyaṇa*.

Sarga 34

1. Hearing Rāma's words and seeing him dressed in the clothes of a sage, the king, along with all his wives, was stricken senseless.

2. He was so broken by sorrow he could not look at Rāghava, so sick at heart he could not address him to his face.

3. The great-armed lord of the land fell unconscious for a moment and then in sorrow he began to lament, thinking only of Rāma:

4. "It must be, I guess, that in the past I injured many living things or made many childless; that must be why such a thing has happened to me.

5-6. "Before one's fated hour has come life cannot slip from the body, for Kaikeyī has tortured me and still I am not dead—I who see before me my own son, brilliant as fire, taking off his delicate garments and dressing in the clothes of an ascetic.

7. "The people, too, are tortured, and all because one woman, Kaikeyī, resorted to this deception in the pursuit of her own ends."

8. So he spoke, his eyes dimmed by tears. Then he cried out "Rāma!" only once, and could speak no further.

9. When after a moment he regained his senses, the lord of the land, his eyes filled with tears, said to Sumantra:

10. "Harness the finest horses to a draft-chariot and return; you must convey my illustrious son out of this country.

11. "Such, I guess, must be the reward the virtuous earn by their virtues, if this good and heroic prince is exiled to the forest by his mother and his father."

12. Acknowledging the king's command, Sumantra left at a quick pace. He harnessed the horses to the decorated chariot and then returned to the chamber.

13. Cupping his hands in reverence, the charioteer informed the prince that the chariot was standing ready, ornamented with gold and harnessed with excellent horses.

14. The king hurriedly summoned the officer in charge of the treasury. He was a meticulous and altogether honest man, with an accurate knowledge of times and places.

15. "Go at once," he told him, "and fetch precious garments and choice ornaments for Vaidehī, calculating against the number of years."

16. Thus addressed by the lord of men, he went at once to the treasure-room and brought everything and presented it to Sītā.

17. Noble Vaidehī, on the point of leaving for the forest, adorned her noble limbs with the sparkling jewelry.

18. And in her rich adornment, Vaidehī shed a deep luster over the chamber—it was like daybreak when the radiant sun comes up and sheds its splendor over the sky.

19. Her mother-in-law took Maithilī in her arms and kissed her on the forehead, and then said to the virtuous princess:

20. "If a woman who has been constantly gratified with things to please her does not hold her husband in respect when he has fallen low, she is regarded as a bad woman in the eyes of all the world.

21. "You must not feel disdain for my son in his banishment. He is your deity, whether he be rich or poor."

22. Sītā knew her words were in harmony with what was right and good and, with hands cupped in reverence, she faced her mother-in-law and replied:

23. "I will act exactly as my noble lady instructs me. I fully understand how to behave toward my husband; I have learned well.

24. "My lady ought not to liken me to bad people. I could no more leave the path of righteousness than radiance can leave the moon.

25. "Without strings a lute cannot be played, without wheels a chariot cannot move, and without her husband a woman finds no happiness, though she have a hundred sons.

26. "There is a limit to what a father can give, a limit to what a mother or son can give, but a husband gives without any limit. What wife would not revere him?

27. "I for my part understand this; I am a high-born woman who has learned right from wrong. My lady, how could I be disdainful? A husband is a woman's deity."

28. As Kausalyā listened to Sītā, the words touched the good woman's heart, and she suddenly burst out in tears of joy and sorrow.

29. Then Rāma, who understood best of all the meaning of righteousness, cupped his hands in reverence and approached his mother where she stood in the place of honor among the others. And he said to her:

30. "Do not be sorrowful, mother. Have regard for my father. My stay in the forest will soon be over.

31. "The nine years and five will pass for you like a night's sleep, and you will see me come home safe and sound, in the company of my loved ones."

32. These few sensible words were all he said to the woman who bore him. Then he turned his gaze and looked at his other three-hundred and fifty mothers.

33. They were just as deeply anguished, and with hands cupped in reverence, the son of Daśaratha addressed them with these righteous words:

34. "If in our living together I ever showed you any rudeness, however unwittingly, please forgive me for it. I bid you all farewell."

35. As Rāghava spoke these words, a scream broke out like the crying of curlews, from the wives of the lord of men.

36. The palace of Daśaratha, where once tambourines and bass drums rumbled like stormclouds, was now filled with lamentation and wailing, so bitter was the sorrow of this calamity.

The end of the thirty-fourth *sarga* of the *Ayodhyākāṇḍa* of the *Śrī Rāmāyaṇa*.

Sarga 35

1. In desolation Rāma, Sītā, and Lakṣmaṇa clasped the feet of the king. Then, cupping their hands, they reverently circled him.

2. After taking leave of him, Sītā and righteous Rāghava, distraught with grief, did obeisance to his mother.

3. Directly after his brother, Lakṣmaṇa did obeisance to Kausalyā and then clasped the feet of his own mother, Sumitrā.

4. As great-armed Lakṣmaṇa Saumitri paid reverence to his mother, she wept and kissed him on the forehead, and with his welfare at heart she said to him:

5. "You are determined to live in the forest out of deep loyalty to your loved ones. Do not be inattentive, my son, when your brother Rāma is on his way.

6. "He is your one refuge in times of both adversity and prosperity, my blameless son. The way of righteousness good people follow in the world is just this: submission to the will of one's elders.

7. "Remember, too, the conduct that has been the age-old custom of this House: liberality, consecration for sacrifice, and readiness to give up one's life in battle.

8. "Look upon Rāma as Daśaratha, look upon Janaka's daughter as me, look upon the woods as Ayodhyā. Go in happiness, my dear son."

9. Then Sumantra, hands cupped in reverence and with the deference in which he was practiced, addressed Kākutstha as Mātali might address Vāsava:

10. "Be pleased to mount the chariot, glorious prince. I will at once convey you wherever you tell me, Rāma.

11. "For you must now commence the fourteen years of life in the forest, which the queen has forced upon you."

12. When fair-hipped Sītā had finished ornamenting herself, with a cheerful heart she boarded the chariot that stood gleaming like the sun.

13-14. Sumantra placed inside the chariot-box the brothers' collection of weapons, their armor, and the leather basket, and when he saw they both had boarded with Sītā, he briskly urged on the superb horses, in speed like the rushing wind.

15. As Rāghava set out for his long stay in the great wilderness, a wave of stupor passed through the city, overwhelming the army and the people.

16. There was turmoil and confusion in the town, the elephants became wild and unruly, and the horses clangored noisily.

17. The town was in utter agony. The people—young and old alike—began to run straight toward Rāma, as men tormented by summer's heat run toward water.

18. Clinging to the sides and the back, they raised their tearful faces and in their bitter sorrow they all cried out:

19. "Charioteer, draw in the horses' reins, go slowly, slowly! Let us look upon Rāma's face, for soon it will be lost to our sight.

20. "Surely the heart of Rāma's mother must be made of iron if it does not break though her godlike child is going off to the forest.

21. "Vaidehī has accomplished her purpose—she follows her lord like a shadow, earnest in doing what is right, and can no more leave him than sunlight can leave Mount Meru.

22. "Ah, Lakṣmaṇa, you have achieved your goal; you will have the chance to serve your kind-spoken, godlike brother all the while.

23. "This is a great achievement for you, a great blessing, the way to heaven, that you are following after him." As they said these things their tears welled up and they could not hold them back.

24. Then in his desolation the king, accompanied by his desolate wives, emerged from the palace exclaiming, "Let me see my beloved son!"

25. Before him could be heard a mighty din of women crying, like the wailing of cow elephants when their great bull is captured.

26. And his father, majestic King Kākutstha, looked as feeble as the full, hare-marked moon dimmed at the hour of eclipse.

27. Then, behind Rāma, a tumultuous clamor broke out among the men as they saw the king collapsing under his heavy sorrow.

28. "Oh Rāma!" some of the people wailed, and others, "Oh mother of Rāma!" while all the women of the inner chamber lamented over the crying king.

29. Rāma glanced back and saw his mother trailing behind and the king, too, dazed and wretched. But he was caught up in the bonds of righteousness and dared not gaze at them openly.

30. They were on foot who should have ridden, who had known only comfort and did not deserve such suffering. And when he saw them he exhorted the charioteer, crying out, "Go faster!"

31. For the tiger among men could not bear the heart-rending sight of his father and mother; it was like a goad tormenting an elephant.

32. Kausalyā ran weeping after the chariot, crying "Rāma, Rāma! Oh Sītā, Lakṣmaṇa!" He glanced back often at his mother, who seemed almost to be dancing.

33. With the king crying, "Stop!" and Rāghava, "Go on! Keep going!" Sumantra's very soul seemed caught between two wheels.

34. "You can tell the king you did not hear, if he should rebuke you," Rāma said to him. "To prolong sorrow is the worst thing of all."

35. He did as Rāma told him, and taking leave of the people, the charioteer urged on the already racing horses.

36. After they had reverently circled Rāma, the king's people did turn back, but their hearts did not, nor the rush of their tears.

37. To the great king Daśaratha his ministers then said, "A person one hopes to see returning should not be followed out too far."

38. The king listened to what they said and, despondent and wretched, his body bathed in sweat, he halted with his wives and gazed out after his perfect son.

The end of the thirty-fifth *sarga* of the *Ayodhyākāṇḍa* of the *Śrī Rāmāyaṇa*.

Sarga 36

1. When, with hands cupped in reverence, the tiger among men was departing, a loud cry of anguish broke out from the women of the inner chamber.

2. "Where can our defender be going, he who was the recourse and refuge of this weak, defenseless, and miserable people?

3. "He never grows angry, whatever the insult, he avoids giving cause for anger, he calms the angry and shares every sorrow—where is he going?

4. "The mighty prince who treats us as he treats his own mother Kausalyā—where can the great man be going?

5. "Kaikeyī hounded the king until he drove him into the forest. Where can the guardian of this people, of the entire world, be going?

6. "The king must be mad to exile Rāma to a life in the forest, a righteous prince, devoted to truth and who is loved by every living soul on earth."

7. So all the queens, like cows who have lost their calves, wept in the torment of their sorrow, and shrilly wailed.

8. Already inflamed with grief for his son, the lord of the land grew more sorrowful, still hearing the dreadful cry of anguish from the women of the inner chamber.

9. No fire-offerings were offered, and the sun vanished. Elephants let their fodder drop, cows would not suckle their calves.

10. The constellation Triśaṅku, the planets Lohitāṅga, Bṛhaspati, and Budha, too, all took ominous positions over the moon.

11. The stars lost their radiance, the planets lost their glow, and the constellation Viśākhā shone, clouded by smoke, in the sky.

12. A wave of despair swept suddenly over all the people of the city, and no one gave any thought to nourishment or amusements.

13. The faces of the people on the royal highway were awash with tears. No one showed any sign of delight; all were lost in grief.

14. The cool breeze stopped blowing, the hare-marked moon no longer looked serene, the sun did not warm the world, the universe was in chaos.

15. Husbands became indifferent to their wives, children became indifferent, and brothers, too. All turned their back on everyone else and gave their thoughts to Rāma alone.

16. As for Rāma's friends, they were all bewildered; crushed by the weight of their grief, they could not rise from where they lay fallen.

17. Abandoned by the great prince, Ayodhyā, with all its hosts of soldiers and herds of horses and elephants, was tormented by a heavy weight of fear and began to quake dreadfully and resound, just as the earth would, mountains and all, if abandoned by Indra, breaker of fortresses.

The end of the thirty-sixth *sarga* of the *Ayodhyākāṇḍa* of the *Śrī Rāmāyaṇa*.

Sarga 37

1. Now, as Rāma was departing he raised a cloud of dust, and as long as it was visible the best of the Ikṣvākus would not turn his eyes away.

2. As long as the king could see his beloved, righteous son, he seemed to stand firm on the ground just to have him in sight.

3. But once the lord of the land could no longer see even Rāma's dust, in anguish and despair he fell to the ground.

4. His wife Kausalyā came up and stood by his right arm, and to his left side came Kaikeyī, whose only love was for Bharata.

5. The king, a man of prudence, righteousness, and courtesy, stared at Kaikeyī, his senses reeling, and said:

6. "Kaikeyī, do not touch me, evil woman, I do not want to see you. You are not my wife, you have no relationship to me.

7. "And your dependents have nothing to do with me, nor I with them. In pure selfishness you repudiated righteousness, and I repudiate you.

8. "Once I took your hand and led you round the marriage fire, but now I renounce it all, both in this world and the next.

9. "And if Bharata should be pleased at securing sovereign kingship, may any funeral offering he makes never reach me."

10. As the lord of men lay coated with dust, Queen Kausalyā helped him up and, racked with grief, began to lead him home.

11. As if he had intentionally slain a brahman, or held his hand in a fire, the righteous king burned with remorse to think of his son living a life of asceticism.

12. Again and again he turned back, he collapsed in the ruts of the chariot, and his figure, like the sun's at the hour of eclipse, lost all its splendor.

13. Tortured with sorrow, he began to lament as he thought with longing of his beloved son. He imagined his son to be returning to the city, and said:

14. "I see the tracks in the road made by the splendid horses carrying my great son, but I do not see him.

15. "No, he is probably now resting somewhere, at the foot of a tree, where he will sleep using a log or perhaps a boulder for his pillow.

16. "Wretched and caked with dirt he will heave a sigh as he rises from the ground, like the bull of an elephant herd from out of a mountain stream.

17. "Men who live in the forest will probably be watching as long-armed Rāma, the defender of the world, gets up and pushes on defenselessly.

18. "I hope you are satisfied, Kaikeyī. Now inhabit the kingdom a widow. For without the tiger among men I cannot bear to live."

19. So the king lamented, and surrounded by a flood of people, he reentered the best of cities, the way a mourner enters a cemetery.

20-21. The squares and courtyards were empty, the shops and temples closed, the thoroughfares nearly deserted, the people haggard, feeble, and racked with sorrow—such was the sight that met the king's eyes. But his thoughts were for Rāma alone and, lost in lamentation, he entered his dwelling, like the sun passing behind a cloud.

22. Without Rāma, Vaidehī, and Lakṣmaṇa his chamber seemed like a great, placid pool from which Suparṇa has snatched the serpents.

23. "Quickly take me to the dwelling of Kausalyā, Rāma's mother," the king demanded, and the watchmen took him.

24. He entered Kausalyā's chamber and lay upon the couch, and his mind began to reel.

25. Looking around, the great and mighty king reached out his arms and cried at the top of his voice, "Oh Rāghava, you have abandoned me!

26. "How lucky those good men who will be alive at the hour when Rāma comes back, who will see him and embrace him.

27. "I cannot see you, Kausalyā! Oh please touch me with your hand. My sight has followed after Rāma and has not yet returned."

28. Seeing the lord of men on the couch lost in thoughts of Rāma, the queen sat down close beside him, in the greatest anguish. She heaved a deep sigh and then began to lament bitterly.

The end of the thirty-seventh *sarga* of the *Ayodhyākāṇḍa* of the *Śrī Rāmāyaṇa*.

Sarga 38

1. Kausalyā gazed at the lord of the land as he lay on the couch prostrate with grief. Racked with grief for her son, she spoke:

2. "Now that Kaikeyī like a fork-tongued viper has spit her venom on Rāghava, the tiger among men, she will behave like a snake that has shed its skin.

3. "Now that she has had her way and exiled Rāma, the charming creature will apply herself to further terrorizing me, like a vicious serpent in the house.

4. "If only Rāma could have lived at home though it meant his begging in the city streets! You had the freedom to grant such a boon, which at the worst had made my son a slave.

5. "But you let Kaikeyī at her own sweet pleasure throw Rāma from his place and assign him as a portion for *rākṣasas*, the way a sacrificer at the half-month rites throws a portion away for them.

6. "My mighty son, the great-armed bowman with a step like a king of elephants, is probably now entering the forest with his wife and Lakṣmaṇa.

7. "They have never known the sorrows of the forest, but you yielded to Kaikeyī and abandoned them to a life in the forest. What can be their lot?

8. "Stripped of everything of value and exiled at the very hour of their triumph, how are these three wretched young people to live with nothing but fruit and roots to eat?

9. "If only it were now the hour that mercifully will end my grief, when I set eyes on Rāghava again with his wife and brother.

10. "When will Ayodhyā hear that the two mighty brothers have come back and once again be a glorious city, crowded with delighted people, garlanded with high-flying banners?

11. "When will the city see those tigers among men returned from the forest and exult in delight like the ocean on a full-moon night?

12. "When will the great-armed mighty prince enter the city of Ayodhyā with Sītā on the chariot ahead of him, like a cow before her bull?

13. "When will people by the thousands go out onto the royal highway to scatter parched grain upon my two foe-taming sons as they make their entrance?

14. "When will maidens proffer flowers and fruit to the brahmans and reverently circle the city in delight?

15. "When will he come back to me—my righteous son, young as a deathless god yet with an old man's wisdom and boyishness that warms my heart?

16. "I guess, my mighty husband, yes, it must no doubt be that once upon a time, when calves were thirsting to drink, I ruthlessly hacked off the udders of the cows, their mothers.

17. "And so now, tiger among men, I who love my child so have been made childless by Kaikeyī, as brutally as a lion might do to a cow with a young calf.

18. "For I have but one son—he is gifted with every virtue, a master of all learning—and without my son I cannot bear to live.

19. "I have not the least bit of strength to live in this world if I cannot see my beloved and mighty great-armed son.

20. "Here, see, a fire kindled by grief for my son has burst forth and is ravaging me, as the earth is ravaged in summertime by the rays of the blazing, holy sun that brings the day."

The end of the thirty-eighth *sarga* of the *Ayodhyākāṇḍa* of the *Śrī Rāmāyaṇa*.

Sarga 39

1. While Kausalyā, best of women, was lamenting in this fashion, Sumitrā, standing firm by what was right, addressed her with these righteous words:

2. "My noble lady, your son is the very best of men and truly virtuous. What need have you to lament like this and wretchedly weep?

3-4. "You should never grieve over Rāma, my lady, so excellent a son. He left surrendering the kingship, powerful as he is, to ensure that his great father might be true to his word. He took his stand by righteousness as the learned scrupulously practice it, and which has its rewards everlastingly, at death.

5. "Blameless Lakṣmaṇa will be a blessing to the great prince. He has always behaved with perfect propriety toward him, and he shows compassion to all creatures.

6. "Though Vaidehī is fully aware how painful life in the wilderness is, though she has known only comfort, she is following your righteous son.

7. "What gain has your mighty son failed to reap, who is waving the banner of his fame throughout the world by his self-restraint and devotion to truth?

8. "Clearly the sun will recognize Rāma's purity and incomparable grandeur, and will not dare to burn his body with its rays.

9. "A pleasant breeze will attend on Rāghava, blowing through the woodlands, gracious at all seasons, with temperate warmth or coolness.

10. "As the blameless prince sleeps at night, the moon like a father will clasp him in its embrace, caress him with cool beams and refresh him.

11. "Then too, the mighty prince was given divine weapons by Brahmā, when he saw him slay in battle the lord of *dānavas*, Timidhvaja's son.

12. "With the land, with Vaidehī and majesty, with all these three in his possession will Rāma, bull among men, soon be consecrated.

13. "Your eyes will soon drop joyful tears for the one you watched depart with tears of sorrow falling.

14. "Soon you will see your child and his loved ones greeting you, and you will shed tears of gladness like a string of clouds in the rains.

15. "Your son will soon return to Ayodhyā to grant you every boon, will soon bow down and clasp your feet with his firm and gentle hands."

16. After the mother of Rāma, the wife of the god of men, had listened to the words of Lakṣmaṇa's mother, the grief in her suddenly dissipated, like a cloud in the autumn when it holds but little water.

The end of the thirty-ninth *sarga* of the *Ayodhyākāṇḍa* of the *Śrī Rāmāyaṇa*.

Sarga 40

1. Now, as the great prince Rāma, who always strove for truth, was setting out to make his life in the forest, men loyal to him continued to follow.

2. Though the multitude of his loved ones and the king had been forced to turn back, these would not stop following Rāma's chariot.

3. For to the men who lived in Ayodhyā the glorious and virtuous prince was as well-loved as the full moon.

4. His subjects kept pleading with him but Kākutstha, to ensure his father's truthfulness, would only press on to the forest.

5. Rāma gazed at his people with affection, as if to drink them in with his eyes. And he spoke to them affectionately as though they were his children:

6. "Let the love and respect the residents of Ayodhyā feel for me be transferred in full to Bharata, as a kindness to me.

7. "Bharata, the delight of Kaikeyī, is of exemplary conduct, and he will do all that is required to ensure your welfare and happiness.

8. "Though only a boy, he has an old man's wisdom, though gentle he is endowed with all the virtues of a hero. He will be a fit master for you and will shield you from all danger.

9. "He possesses all the virtues a king requires, and he has been recognized as prince regent. Then too, as I myself have shown you, you must obey your master's order.

10. "And, finally, if you would do me a kindness, please take care that the great king does not suffer when I have gone to live in the forest."

11. But the more committed to righteousness Dāśarathi showed himself to be, the more the subjects desired to have him as their lord.

12. By their virtues Rāma and Saumitri seemed to bind and draw to them the desolate, tearful people of the city.

13. Now, certain brahmans who were elders on three counts—by their years, wisdom, and authority—began to cry out from afar, their heads shaking with age:

14. "Ho there, you purebred horses speeding away with Rāma. Stop, turn back! Be good to your master. You should be carrying your master back, not away from the city to the forest."

15. When Rāma perceived the anguished outcry raised by the aged brahmans, he alighted at once from the chariot.

16. Rāma then, with Sītā and Lakṣmaṇa, proceeded on foot, with measured tread, directing his attention wholly to the forest.

17. For the brahmans were on foot, and Rāma looked with pity on them. He so cherished propriety that he could not ride off and leave them.

18. Seeing that Rāma only continued on, the brahmans were disconcerted and in deep agony they said to him,

19. "The entire brahman order will follow you, best friend of brahmans, and these sacred fires will accompany you, borne on the shoulders of the twice-born.

20. "Just see the umbrellas given to us at the *vājapeya* rite, which are following along behind you like geese when the rains have ended.

21. "You never got your royal parasol, and, when the sun's rays are burning you, we will shade you with these, our own *vājapeya* umbrellas.

22. "We have always turned our minds to the study of the vedic

hymns, but now our minds are made up on your account, dear child, to turn to a life in the forest.

23. "Our greatest treasure, the *vedas*, lies stored in our hearts; our wives shall stay at home protected by their chastity.

24. "Our decision will not be reconsidered; we have made up our minds to go with you. But, as you have always shown regard for righteousness, will any regard now be paid to what is right?

25. "We have bowed our heads, white-haired as the wild goose and covered now with dust from falling prone upon the ground; we have pleaded with you to return, you who have always done what is proper.

26. "Many of the brahmans who have come here have already commenced sacrifices. Their consummation depends on your returning, dear child.

27. "All living things, moving and unmoving, are filled with devotion for you. Show your devotion to these devotees, who are pleading with you.

28. "The trees, unable to follow you because their roots prevent their movement, seem to be mourning as the gusting wind uplifts them.

29. "Even the birds have stopped flitting about and foraging for food. They sit in one place in the trees, pleading with you, who have always taken pity on all creatures."

30. And, as the brahmans sent up this mournful wail in order to turn Rāghava back, the Tamasā River came into view to aid, so it seemed, in stopping him.

The end of the fortieth *sarga* of the *Ayodhyākāṇḍa* of the *Śrī Rāmāyaṇa*.

Sarga 41

1. Now, when Rāghava had reached the lovely bank of the Tamasā, with a glance at Sītā he addressed Saumitri:

2. "Night has come to the forest now, the very first of our life in the forest. But please, Saumitri, do not be sad.

3. "Look, the woods are empty but all around they seem to weep: birds and beasts are hidden within them, each gone to its own lair.

4. "Surely the city of Ayodhyā, my father's capital, will grieve tonight, every man and woman, for us who have gone away.

5. "But I know that righteous Bharata will comfort my father and mother, speaking words in harmony with what is right, beneficial, and desirable.

6. "I have been reflecting all the while on Bharata's goodheartedness, and I no longer feel grief for my father, Lakṣmaṇa, or even for my mother.

7. "You have done your duty in accompanying me, tiger among men. But let me seek your help, too, in looking after Vaidehī.

8. "I myself, however, will have nothing but water tonight. This is what I prefer, though all kinds of forest fare are at hand."

9. So Rāghava spoke to Saumitri, and turning to Sumantra he said, "Do not neglect the horses, dear friend."

10. Sumantra tethered the horses as the sun was setting, gave them abundant fodder, and then waited in attendance.

11. When Rāma had worshiped the gracious twilight and saw night closing in, the charioteer with Saumitri's help made a bed for him.

12. Escorted by Saumitri, Rāma found the bed of leaves made ready near the bank of the Tamasā, and he and his wife then retired.

13. When Lakṣmaṇa saw that his brother had fallen asleep with his wife, he engaged the charioteer in conversation, talking about Rāma's many virtues.

14. Saumitri stayed awake all night long, and even as the sun rose he was still speaking of Rāma's virtues with the charioteer on the bank of the Tamasā.

15. There, at a little distance from the Tamasā where herds of cattle crowded the bank, Rāma spent the night with his people.

16. And, when on rising mighty Rāma observed them, he said to his good brother Lakṣmaṇa:

17. "Look at them now, Lakṣmaṇa, asleep under the trees. They care for us alone, Saumitri, caring nothing even for their own homes.

18. "So solemn is their commitment to turn us back that the townsmen would sooner throw their lives away than abandon their resolve.

19. "While they are still sleeping, we must board the chariot and quickly go, taking a path free from danger.

20. "No resident of the city of the Ikṣvākus should now, or ever again, have to sleep at the foot of a tree out of loyalty to me.

21. "A prince should spare his townsmen any troubles that are his affair alone. Surely he must not involve the residents of the city in his own trouble."

22. Lakṣmaṇa replied to Rāma as though it were Righteousness that stood embodied before his eyes: "I agree, my wise brother. Let us board at once."

23. In haste then the charioteer harnessed the splendid horses to the coach and, with hands cupped in reverence, directed Rāma to it.

24. But in order to confuse the townsmen Rāma instructed the charioteer, "Board the chariot, Sumantra, and head northward.

25. "Hurry onward for a while, then circle back on the chariot. You must take care to ensure that the townsmen do not know where I have gone."

26. The charioteer did just as Rāma told him, and on returning he directed Rāma to the coach.

27. Rāghava boarded with all his equipment and crossed the swift-flowing, eddying Tamasā.

28. Once across, the great-armed, majestic prince entered upon a broad pathway, a gracious one free from obstacles and the dangers of dangerous beasts.

29. When night brightened into dawn and the townsmen found themselves without Rāghava, their minds were stunned, and they were paralyzed by a crushing grief.

30. Drenched in tears of grief, they searched high and low, but to their bitter sorrow they caught not a glimpse of Rāma.

31. For a short while they followed the track, and when it gave out a wild despair swept over them.

32. When the track of the chariot gave out, the sensible among them turned back, thinking, "What can this mean? What are we to do? Fate has crushed us."

33. Then all of them, with weary hearts, returned the way they had come to the city of Ayodhyā, where all good people were still in a state of shock.

The end of the forty-first *sarga* of the *Ayodhyākāṇḍa* of the *Śrī Rāmāyaṇa*.

Sarga 42

1. So the residents of the city returned from following Rāma, but all their strength seemed to have gone, and they were left insensible.

2. They went each to his own dwelling and there, surrounded by their wives and children, they all broke out in weeping, and their faces were bathed in tears.

3. No one felt any delight or gladness, merchants would not display their wares, no goods were set out to catch the eye. Householders would have no meals prepared.

4. People felt no joy at finding something long thought lost, or obtaining vast wealth. Mothers felt no joy at delivering a first-born son.

5. In one house after another the women cried when their husbands came home, and in the anguish of their sorrow they berated them with words as piercing as elephant goads:

6. "What good are homes or wives or wealth, what good are sons or pleasures to those who have lost the sight of Rāghava?

7. "The one decent man in the world is Lakṣmaṇa, who with Sītā is following Rāma Kākutstha to serve him in the forest.

8. "Fortunate the streams, the lotus ponds, and lakes where Kākutstha will bathe, plunging into the pure water.

9. "The woodlands and the lovely groves will adorn Kākutstha, and so will the streams with their broad shores, and the steep-sloping mountains.

10. "Every hill or grove Rāma visits will treat him like a welcome guest and not fail to accord him hospitality.

11-12. "The mountains will be crowned with many-colored blossoms and bear clusters of bouquets when Rāma comes, and in sympathy they will display for him choice fruits and flowers even out of season. They will afford him views of waterfalls as well, one after the other, and the trees on the summits will gladden Rāghava.

13. "Where Rāma goes there is nothing to fear, and no one ever comes to grief. He is a great-armed hero and the son of Daśaratha.

14. "So let us follow Rāghava before he is too far away from us. How pleasant the shadow of the feet of such a great master as he; for he is the one defender of this people, he their one recourse and refuge.

15. "We shall attend on Sītā, and you on Rāghava." Such were the things the townsmen's wives told their husbands. And in the anguish of their sorrow they continued:

16. "Rāghava will see to it that you are safe and sound in the wilderness, and Sītā will do the same for us, the womenfolk.

17. "Who could find any joy in living here, where the people are filled with longing, a place so cheerless, so unpleasant and dispiriting?

18. "If, with our one defender gone and against all that is right, the kingship should come into Kaikeyī's hands, we would have no further use for living, much less for children or riches.

19. "Kaikeyī, that disgrace to her family, renounced her son and husband both for the sake of kingly power. Why then should she be expected to spare anyone else?

20. "We will never remain in the kingdom as servants to Kaikeyī, so long as she lives, or we do. Upon our sons we swear it.

21. "Who could live at ease under that unrighteous, wicked woman, so heartless that she forced into exile the son of the lord of kings?

22. "For with Rāma banished, the lord of the land will not long survive, and in the wake of Daśaratha's death will clearly follow total devastation.

23. "Utterly impoverished, luckless men! Better to mix poison and take it now. For either you follow Rāghava or you shall never be heard from again.

24. "Rāma, his wife, and Lakṣmaṇa have been treacherously banished, and all of us delivered up to Bharata like livestock to the butcher."

25. Such was the lamentation raised throughout the town by the townsmen's wives, and they wailed in agony, as if they feared for their very lives.

26. The women were as anguished on Rāma's account as if a son of theirs or a brother had been exiled. Desolate they lamented and madly wept, for he meant more to them, in fact, than their own sons.

The end of the forty-second *sarga* of the *Ayodhyākāṇḍa* of the *Śrī Rāmāyaṇa*.

Sarga 43

1. Now, in what remained of the same night Rāma, tiger among men, traveled a great distance, mindful of his father's command.

2. As he traveled gracious night departed. He then worshiped the gracious morning twilight and afterwards pushed on to the frontier of the realm.

3-4. Drawn by his splendid horses, he proceeded swiftly—though it seemed so slow to him—observing the villages with their wide-spaced boundaries and the forests all in flower, hearing the cries of the people who made their homes in the villages: "A curse upon King Daśaratha for succumbing to the power of passion!"

5-6. "Ah, Kaikeyī is a vicious and evil woman always doing evil, a heartless woman who has gone beyond all limits. Today she has done a heartless deed in exiling the prince to a life in the forest, so righteous a prince, so wise, compassionate, and steadfast."

7. Such were the words of the people who made their homes in the villages, and the mighty lord of Kosala heard them as he passed beyond the land of Kosala.

8. He then crossed the Vedaśrutī, a river running with gracious water, and continued on toward the region where Agastya lived.

9. He traveled a long while and then crossed the Gomatī, a chilly river flowing to the sea, its shores teeming with cows.

10. After fording the Gomatī on his swift horses Rāghava crossed the Syandikā river, where the cries of geese and peacocks resounded.

11. Rāma pointed out to Vaidehī the land King Manu long ago bestowed upon Ikṣvāku, a rich land encircled by vassal kingdoms.

12-13. And often the majestic bull among men would address his chariot driver in a voice like the call of the wild goose, saying, "When shall I come back, charioteer, and again go hunting in the flowering forest beside the Sarayū, reunited with my mother and father?

14. "I so long to hunt in the forest beside the Sarayū. That is a pleasure without equal in the world, one the hosts of royal seers have always prized."

15. Of these and other matters Aikṣvāka spoke with the charioteer in his sweet voice as he continued on his way.

The end of the forty-third *sarga* of the *Ayodhyākāṇḍa* of the *Śrī Rāmāyaṇa*.

Sarga 44

1. After passing through the broad and lovely land of Kosala, Lakṣmaṇa's great-armed eldest brother reached the outskirts of Śṛṅgaverapura.

2-3. There Rāghava saw the Ganges, the heavenly river that goes by three paths, its gracious water unclogged by weeds; a holy river frequented by seers, ringing with the cries of geese and cranes and the calls of sheldrakes, swarming with dolphins, crocodiles, and snakes.

4. As the great chariot-fighter gazed over its wave-capped eddies, he said to the charioteer Sumantra, "We shall spend the night here.

5. "There, not far from the river, is a towering almond tree with luxuriant flowers and shoots. Charioteer, we shall spend the night there."

6. "As you wish," replied Lakṣmaṇa and Sumantra, and the two then turned the horses toward the almond tree.

7. On reaching the lovely tree Rāma, the delight of the Ikṣvākus, alighted from the chariot with his wife and Lakṣmaṇa.

8. Sumantra alighted as well, and after unhitching the splendid horses he cupped his hands in reverence and stood in attendance on Rāma at the foot of the tree.

9. Now, the king of the region was named Guha, a friend of Rāma and precious to him as life. He was of the Niṣāda tribe, a powerful man and famed as their chief.

10. He had heard that Rāma, tiger among men, had come into his realm, and accompanied by his aged ministers and kinsmen, he approached him.

11. Seeing that Guha, overlord of the Niṣādas, was waiting at a distance, Rāma went out with Saumitri to meet him.

12. Guha embraced Rāghava in anguish, saying: "This land, no less than Ayodhyā, belongs to you. What may I do for you, Rāma?"

13. Then at once he had the welcome-offering brought along with an assortment of choice foods and drinks, and he said:

14. "I bid you welcome, great-armed prince. This entire land belongs to you. We are servants, you the master. Come, our kingdom is yours to rule.

15. "There is food at hand, solid, soft, and liquid, and sweet things to lick; comfortable beds as well, and fodder for your horses."

16-18. So Guha spoke, and Rāghava replied, "You honor and delight us in every way by your coming here on foot and your display of affection." He clasped him tight in his well-shaped arms and added, "How fortunate to see you, Guha, you and your kinsmen, in good health. All is well with you, I hope, with your kingdom, your treasury, and your allies.

19. "I must, however, refuse everything you have so kindly made ready, for I am not in a position to accept.

20. "You must know that I am now an ascetic, whose home is in the forest, whose sole aim is to follow the ways of righteousness, who must dress in *kuśa* grass, bark, and hides, and live on fruit and roots.

21. "It is only fodder for the horses I need, nothing more. My honored friend will do me great homage with that alone.

22. "For these horses are cherished by my father, King Daśaratha, and it will be hospitality enough for me if they are well cared for."

23. Guha then straightway ordered water and fodder for the horses. "Fetch it at once," he told his men.

24. Wearing an upper garment of barkcloth, Rāma then performed the twilight worship and took as his only refreshment the water Lakṣmaṇa brought himself.

25. Afterwards, as Rāma lay upon the ground, Lakṣmaṇa washed his feet and his wife's, and then withdrew, taking up a position beside the tree.

26. Saumitri was engaged in conversation by the charioteer and Guha, who also kept vigilant watch over Rāma, his bow at the ready.

27. And so the great prince, a man who had never before known pain, but only pleasure, the wise and glorious Dāśarathi lay there as the night dragged slowly by.

The end of the forty-fourth *sarga* of the *Ayodhyākāṇḍa* of the *Śrī Rāmāyaṇa*.

Sarga 45

1. As Lakṣmaṇa Rāghava stood there wide awake on his brother's behalf, Guha burned with a burning sorrow and said to him:

2. "Here is a comfortable bed, my friend, made ready on your behalf. Come, prince, rest in comfort upon it.

3. "My people are all used to hardship; you are used to comfort. We will stay awake tonight to watch over Kākutstha.

4. "There is no one on earth dearer to me than Rāma. I am telling the truth, and by my truth I swear it to you.

5. "Whatever hope I may have in this world for great glory, for the full acquisition of righteousness, or of simple wealth, I have by reason of his grace.

6. "And I for my part, bow in hand and in the company of my kinsmen, will protect my dear friend Rāma, come what may, as he lies asleep with Sītā.

7. "I have wandered the forest all my life and nothing happens here without my knowing of it. Moreover, we are prepared to withstand even a vast army of four divisions."

8. Lakṣmaṇa replied to him, "With you protecting us here, blameless Guha, with righteousness alone in view, we could have nothing to fear.

9. "But how, while Dāśarathi is lying on the ground with Sītā, could I find sleep—or any happiness in life?

10. "Look at him, Guha, reposing with Sītā on the grass, a man whom all the gods and *asuras* could not withstand in battle.

11. "This is the only one of Daśaratha's sons to resemble him in every trait—a son obtained by means of austerities, vedic recitations, and all kinds of heavy labors.

12. "With him in banishment the king will not long remain alive. The earth will surely soon be widowed.

13. "The women must have cried out their last great cries and ceased in exhaustion. The din, I expect, has ceased in the king's palace, my friend.

14. "I have little hope that Kausalyā, the king, or my mother will live out this night.

15. "Even if my mother should live through it to look after Śatrughna, Kausalyā's sorrow is such that she, who bore this one heroic son, will perish.

16. "Caught up in the king's calamity the city, which once brought gladness with its pleasant aspect, will perish with all its loyal people.

17. "And my father, who never got the wish that just eluded him, who never installed Rāma in the kingship, will perish, too.

18. "And when that moment comes, when father passes away and they purify the lord of the land with all the rites for the dead, they will have attained their object.

19-21. "Then they will stroll at their ease through my father's capital, through its lovely squares and well-ordered thoroughfares; with all its mansions and palaces, with the fairest courtesans to lend it beauty, with its teeming chariots, horses, elephants; resounding with the sound of pipes, stocked with every luxury, thronging with delighted and prosperous people, dotted with orchards and gardens, a place of crowded fairs and festivals.

22. "If only we might return to Ayodhyā when our stay in the forest is over to find him well and his promise fulfilled."

23. So the night passed with the great prince standing there mourning, racked with sorrow.

24. And when the good prince had spoken these forthright words, Guha wept in deep compassion, crushed by the calamity and tormented by heartache, like an elephant tormented by a raging fever.

The end of the forty-fifth *sarga* of the *Ayodhyākāṇḍa* of the *Śrī Rāmāyaṇa*.

Sarga 46

1. When night had brightened into dawn, broad-chested glorious Rāma spoke to good Lakṣmaṇa Saumitri:

2. "It is the hour of sunrise, blessed night has gone. Over there, dear brother, the jet-black bird, the cuckoo, is calling.

3. "You can hear the sound of peacocks crying in the forest. Let us cross the Jāhnavī, dear Lakṣmaṇa, the swift river that flows to the sea."

4. Heeding Rāma's words, Saumitri, the delight of his friends, bade farewell to Guha and the charioteer and stood before his brother.

5. Then, after strapping on their quivers and buckling on their swords, the two Rāghavas took up their bows and went with Sītā down to the Ganges.

6. Now the charioteer deferentially approached righteous Rāma and, cupping his hands in reverence, he asked, "What then am I to do?"

7. "Go back," Rāma answered. "You have done enough for me. We shall relinquish the coach and proceed to the great forest on foot."

8. Finding himself dismissed, the charioteer Sumantra was anguished and replied to Aikṣvāka, tiger among men:

9. "There is no person in the world who would ever have expected this, your having to live in the forest with your brother and wife, like some common man.

10. "I guess there is no reward for chastity or vedic study, for lenience, or uprightness, if such a calamity has befallen you.

11. "Living in the forest with Vaidehī and your brother, mighty Rāghava, you will achieve as high an end as if you had conquered the three worlds.

12. "But surely we are lost, Rāma, even you have misled us. For we shall come under the power of evil Kaikeyī, and only sorrow can be our lot."

13. So the charioteer Sumantra spoke to the prince who was precious to him as life. And as he looked at Rāma, so far from home, he was racked with sorrow, and for a long while he wept.

14. His tears stopping, the charioteer sipped water, and when he was thus purified, Rāma addressed him gently but insistently:

15. "I do not know of any friend the Ikṣvākus have to equal you. It is you who must take care that King Daśaratha not grieve for me.

16. "The lord of the world is aged, his heart has been crushed by grief and a heavy burden of desire weighs him down. That is why I tell you this:

17. "Whatever orders the great lord of the land may give in his desire to please Kaikeyī must be obeyed without demur.

18. "For it is to this end lords of men take up the rule of kingdoms, that their will never be opposed in anything they require.

19. "So you must take care, Sumantra, that the great king's displeasure is not provoked and that he does not languish under sorrow.

20. "The king has never known sorrow before; he is aged, noble, and self-controlled. First do obeisance to him and then address him in my name as follows:

21. " 'I do not grieve at all, nor does Lakṣmaṇa or Maithilī, that we have been expelled from Ayodhyā or that we must live in the forest.

22. " 'As soon as the fourteen years are over we will come home, and you shall look upon each of us again, Sītā, Lakṣmaṇa, and me.'

23-24. "After speaking to the king, Sumantra, ask my mother, ask Kaikeyī and all the other queens after their health, each one in turn. And tell Kausalyā for me that Sītā, Lakṣmaṇa, and I, her noble son, send her respectful greetings.

25. "Then you must tell the great king, 'Send for Bharata at once. As soon as Bharata returns he must be installed in office with the approval of the kings.

26. " 'Once you have taken Bharata in your arms and consecrated him as prince regent, sorrow for our suffering will no longer oppress you.'

27. "And tell this to Bharata: 'You must treat your mothers, all of them without distinction, the same way you treat the king.

28. " 'Just as you draw no distinction between Kaikeyī and Sumitrā, so draw none at all with regard to Queen Kausalyā, my mother.' "

29. Though stricken with grief at being sent back by Rāma, Sumantra heard everything he said and then affectionately replied to Kākutstha:

30. "If, emboldened by my affection, I do not speak as a subordinate should, attribute it to my deep devotion and forgive me what I say.

31. "How shall I return without you, dear Rāma, to a city that, at parting from you, went mad with such grief as one feels for a son?

32. "Think how the people were, merely seeing Rāma aboard my chariot. When the city sees my chariot with Rāma gone, it will fall to pieces.

33. "The city will be desolated when it sees the chariot empty. It would be as if, out of its whole army only a charioteer survived, while all its brave warriors were slain in battle.

34. "Just now, while you still stood before them, the people felt sick at heart just to contemplate you, in their mind's eye, living far away.

35. "The cry of anguish the townsmen raised at your banishment will be increased a hundredfold when they observe me all alone in the chariot.

36. "And what am I to tell the queen? 'I have taken your son to your brother's family, so do not agonize'?

37. "Would I not have to say something like this, untruthful as it is? For how can I tell the truth when it is so painful?

38. "The splendid horses, it is true, respond to my command, but they are used to pulling you and your kinsmen. How will they pull the chariot when you are not in it?

39. "If, despite my pleading, you insist on leaving me, I will board the chariot and set it on fire the moment you do.

40. "There will be creatures in the forest that will disturb your austerities, Rāghava, and I could chase them off with the chariot.

41. "Thanks to you I have known the joy of tending your chariot, and I hope and pray that thanks to you I may know the joy of life in the forest.

42. "Oh, be gracious, I wish to wait upon you in the wilderness. My one wish is to have the pleasure of hearing you say, 'Wait upon me.'

43. "As I live in the forest I will obey you with bowed head. I am ready to give up everything, Ayodhyā and the world of the gods itself.

44. "I cannot in any case enter Ayodhyā without you, any more than a man of evil conduct can gain entrance to the capital of great Indra.

45. "And the horses too, mighty Rāma, will attain their highest destiny if they can render you any service while you live in the forest.

46. "My fondest dream is that, when your stay in the forest has come to an end, I may convey you back to the city in this same chariot.

47. "In your company the fourteen years in the forest will pass like so many minutes, and without you they will seem like as many centuries.

48. "You have always cherished your servants, and I am a devoted servant only following the path his master's son has taken, only following the proper course. Please, do not leave me."

49. So the desolate Sumantra implored him, over and over, in every way he knew, and Rāma, who always felt compassion for his servants, replied to him:

50. "I know the profound devotion you bear me, and how you cherish your master. But you must hear the reason I have for sending you back to the city.

51. "When my younger mother Kaikeyī sees that you have returned to the city, she will be convinced I have truly gone to the forest.

52. "And if the queen is satisfied that I have gone to live in the forest, she will no longer harbor suspicions that the righteous king has spoken falsely.

53. "This is my first consideration—that my younger mother should gain the kingdom for her son, and that it may thrive under Bharata's protection.

54. "As a kindness to me and to the king, you must go back to the city with the chariot and faithfully deliver each and every message imparted to you."

55. So Rāma addressed the charioteer and comforted him at length. Then in a manful and purposeful tone he addressed Guha: "I will mat my hair and go. Please fetch me some sap of the banyan tree.

56. Guha at once brought the sap to the prince, and with it Rāma matted his own and Lakṣmaṇa's hair.

57. As they stood there dressed in barkcloth and bearing a crown of matted hair, the brothers Rāma and Lakṣmaṇa resembled a pair of seers.

58. Having entered with Lakṣmaṇa upon the way of forest hermits and adopted their vow, Rāma turned one last time to his friend Guha:

59. "Never neglect your army, Guha, your treasury, stronghold, or populace. Nothing is deemed so hard to preserve as the position of a king."

60. The delight of the Ikṣvākus then dismissed Guha and with determination went off swiftly with his wife and Lakṣmaṇa.

61. Now, at the riverbank the delight of the Ikṣvākus saw a boat. Preparing to cross the swift-flowing Ganges, he said to Lakṣmaṇa:

62. "Carefully board the boat that is standing ready, tiger among men. Then take hold of the spirited woman Sītā and help her to board."

63. Hearing his brother's command and in no way opposing it, the self-respecting prince first helped Maithilī aboard and then boarded himself.

64. Only then did Lakṣmaṇa's mighty eldest brother go on board, along with some of Guha's kinsmen, who went at the urging of the overlord of the Niṣādas.

65. After dismissing Sumantra, Guha, and his army, Rāma took his seat in the boat and urged on the boatmen.

66. They in turn urged on the boat, which, guided by the helmsman and propelled by the rush of their strong oars, moved swiftly out across the water.

67. When they reached the middle of the Bhāgīrathī, faultless Vaidehī cupped her hands in reverence and addressed the river:

68. "This is the son of the great king, wise Daśaratha. Protect him, O Ganges, and let him carry out his instructions.

69. "After living in the woodlands a full fourteen years, may he return once again with his brother and me.

70. "And then, O beautiful goddess Ganges, when I have come back safely, I will sacrifice to you in gladness for making all my wishes come true.

71. "O goddess, you are the river of three paths, you behold the world of Brahmā and show yourself in our world as wife of the ocean-king.

72-73. "I pay you homage, goddess, I sing your praises, lovely one. When the tiger among men has safely returned and secured the kingship, I will give the brahmans a hundred thousand cows, garments, and exquisite food in hopes of pleasing you."

74. Addressing the Ganges in this fashion, the faultless and courteous Sītā soon reached the southern bank.

75. Arriving at the bank, the bull among men, slayer of foes, left the boat and prepared to set out with his brother and Vaidehī.

76. The great-armed prince said to his brother, the delight of Sumitrā, "Go in front, Saumitri, let Sītā follow behind you.

77. "I shall go last, to protect you and Sītā. But all the same, today Vaidehī will come to know the pain of life in the forest."

78. Now, while Rāma was speeding to the further shore of the Ganges, Sumantra had watched continuously, but when the distance grew too great he turned his gaze away, and in shock and misery he wept.

79. On the further bank the brothers killed four large animals—a boar, an antelope, a gazelle, and a great black buck. They were famished and took meat hurriedly, and at sunset made for a tree beneath which they could spend the night.

The end of the forty-sixth *sarga* of the *Ayodhyākāṇḍa* of the *Śrī Rāmāyaṇa*.

Sarga 47

1. On reaching the tree, Rāma, the most pleasing of men, performed the evening twilight worship and then spoke to Lakṣmaṇa.

2. "This is the first night we shall spend outside our country without Sumantra, but please, do not be sad about it.

3. "From now on we must remain constantly vigilant at night, Lakṣmaṇa, for the safety of Sītā is in our hands.

4. "We shall have to spend this night as best we can, Saumitri. We shall have to settle down upon the ground itself strewn only with what we gather with our own hands."

5. Later, as Rāma lay on the earth—a prince accustomed to a sumptuous bed—he began to talk with Saumitri, and these were the heartfelt words he spoke:

6. "It must be the sleep of sorrow, Lakṣmaṇa, that the great king is sleeping tonight. Kaikeyī, however, must be content since her desires have been satisfied.

7. "But is it not possible that Queen Kaikeyī, when she sees Bharata back home again, may try to take the great king's life, to make her son the king?

8. "And being old and defenseless and parted from me what will he do? Such is his desire for Kaikeyī that he is completely in her power.

9. "Reflecting on this calamity and how the king so utterly changed his mind, I have come to the conclusion that the urgings of desire far outweigh both statecraft and righteousness.

10. "For what man, even a fool, would forsake his own son—a son who ever bowed to his will—on account of a woman, as father forsook me, Lakṣmaṇa?

11. "Kaikeyī's son Bharata and his wife must indeed be joyful. Like an absolute monarch he will have the happy land of Kosala all to himself.

12. "Indeed, with father well on in years and me withdrawn to the wilderness, he will be the single head of the entire kingdom.

13. "Whoever forsakes righteousness and statecraft and follows the urgings of desire will soon come to grief, just like King Daśaratha.

14. "I am convinced, dear brother, that Kaikeyī came among us just to bring about Daśaratha's end, my banishment, and Bharata's accession to kingship.

15. "Is it not possible that even now, in the flush of her good fortune, Kaikeyī may be persecuting Kausalyā and Sumitrā because of me?

16. "May Queen Sumitrā never live in sorrow on my account. You must go straight back to Ayodhyā tomorrow morning, Lakṣmaṇa.

17. "I shall go on alone with Sītā to the Daṇḍakas, and you will be there to defend the defenseless Kausalyā.

18. "For Kaikeyī can be spiteful, and in her hatred she may do something reckless. You must commit my mother to the care of Bharata, who knows what is right.

19. "It must be that in some past life women were separated from their sons by my mother's doing, Saumitri, and so this has happened to her.

20. "For Kausalyā nurtured me long and with great difficulty raised me. And now at the very moment of her reward she has been separated from me—a curse on me!

21. "May no one who parts her hair ever bear a son like me, Saumitri, who have given my mother grief without end.

22. "Lakṣmaṇa, I think even her myna bird is a greater source of joy than I. The bird at least is there to cry out, 'Parrot, bite the enemy's foot.'

23. "What good am I, tamer of foes, a son who does nothing to help her as she grieves in her misfortune? She might as well be childless.

24. "Bereft of me, my unfortunate mother Kausalyā has been plunged into a sea of grief and lies there racked by bitter sorrow.

25. "In my rage, Lakṣmaṇa, all by myself I could overpower Ayodhyā or the whole world with my arrows. But truly force is useless.

26. "I fear the danger of unrighteousness, blameless Lakṣmaṇa, and I fear what other people might say. That is why I do not have myself consecrated at once."

27. Such and many other pitiful words of lamentation did Rāma utter that night, in that desolate place. Then he fell silent, his face bathed in tears.

28. When Rāma had broken off his lamentation and lay like a damped-down fire or a sea becalmed, Lakṣmaṇa tried to comfort him.

29. "It is true, Rāma, best of warriors, that the city of Ayodhyā will be gloomy tonight now that you have departed, like the night when the moon is gone.

30. "But it is to no avail, Rāma, that you torment yourself like this. You are only disheartening Sītā, and me, too, bull among men.

31. "Neither Sītā nor I could live an instant without you, Rāghava. We would be like fish plucked out of the water.

32. "No, without you, slayer of enemies, I would not care to see Father now, not Śatrughna, Sumitrā, or heaven itself."

33. Rāghava, slayer of enemies, listened to Lakṣmaṇa's earnest words and at last, recognizing it as the way of righteousness, he considerately gave him permission to live in the forest for all the years to come.

The end of the forty-seventh *sarga* of the *Ayodhyākāṇḍa* of the *Śrī Rāmāyaṇa*.

Sarga 48

1. After passing the gracious night under the great tree, they set out from that place when the bright sun rose.

2-3. Plunging into the great forest, they headed toward the place where Bhāgīrathī, the river Ganges, joins the Yamunā. And here and there, as the glorious party made their way, different types of landscape came into view, and charming places such as they had never seen before.

4. Rāma took the safest path, observing the different sorts of trees, and as day was drawing to a close he spoke to Saumitri:

5. "Look at the smoke, blessed Agni's banner, rising above Prayāga. I think the sage Bharadvāja must live nearby, Saumitri.

6. "We must have reached the confluence of the Ganges and Yamunā, for you can hear the sound of water dashing against water.

7. "Here are logs hewn by foresters, Bharadvāja's dependents, and there you can see the different sorts of trees around his ashram."

8. The brothers went on at an easy pace bearing their bows, and as the sun was hanging low they came to the sage's abode at the confluence of the Ganges and Yamunā.

9. The deer and birds were frightened as Rāma entered the ashram. Proceeding along the path, he soon came upon Bharadvāja.

10. With Sītā following behind, the mighty brothers arrived at the ashram and stood some distance off, eagerly awaiting the appearance of the sage.

11. The illustrious sage soon completed the fire-offering, and the moment Rāma saw him, he cupped his hands in reverence and with Saumitri and Sītā did obeisance to him.

12. Lakṣmaṇa's eldest brother then identified himself to him: "Holy one, we are two sons of Daśaratha, Rāma and Lakṣmaṇa.

13. "And this is my wife Vaidehī, the lovely daughter of Janaka. The faultless woman is following me to the desolate groves of asceticism.

14. "When my father banished me, Saumitri, my beloved younger brother here, faithfully accompanied me to the forest.

15. "On my father's orders, holy one, we are to enter a grove of asceticism. There we will strictly follow the way of righteousness, living only on roots and fruit."

16. Upon hearing the words of the wise prince, the righteous sage presented him with a cow, the welcome-offering, and water.

17. Then, sitting with deer and birds and sages all around him, the sage welcomed his visitor Rāma and showed him hospitality.

18. Rāghava accepted his hospitality and took a seat, and then Bharadvāja addressed him with these righteous words:

19. "So at last I see you here, Kākutstha. I have heard about this, about your unwarranted exile.

20. "This is an isolated spot, here at the confluence of the two great rivers. It is a sacred and delightful place, and you can live here comfortably."

21. So Bharadvāja spoke, and Rāma Rāghava made a forthright reply, for the welfare of all was his chief concern:

22. "Holy one, not far from here live people of both town and province, and they will come to visit Vaidehī and me. For this reason I cannot consent to our living here.

23. "Please think of some good site for an ashram, holy one, in a secluded place, one that will delight Janaka's daughter Vaidehī, who deserves every comfort."

24. The great sage Bharadvāja, hearing Rāghava's forthright words, answered him in a way that carried conviction.

25. "Twenty miles from here, my son, is a mountain where you may live. It is a sacred place where great seers make their home, with a pleasant prospect at every turn.

26. "Langurs range about it, and monkeys and apes live there. Its name is Citrakūṭa, and it looks like Mount Gandhamādana.

27. "As long as a man beholds the peaks of Citrakūṭa, he meditates on blessed things and does not turn his mind to evil.

28. "Many seers have passed their hundred autumns there, and by means of their austerities have ascended to heaven with skull-white heads.

29. "It is an isolated place to live, one that I think will please you; or you may live here with me, Rāma, for the duration of your stay in the forest."

30. Thus Bharadvāja, wise in the ways of righteousness, received his dear guest Rāma, his wife, and brother, and fulfilled their every desire.

31. And when holy night came on, Rāma was still at Prayāga in the company of the great seer, holding animated conversation.

32. But when night had brightened into dawn, the tiger among men came before Bharadvāja, a sage of brilliant powers, and said:

33. "Last night, holy one, we made our dwelling here, in your ashram. Now, truthful sage, give us leave to depart."

34. Now that they had passed the night, Bharadvāja replied, "Go, then, to Citrakūṭa, a place rich in honey, roots, and fruit.

35. "You will see herds of elephants there, Rāghava, and herds of deer that range through the expanses of forest.

36. "Establish your ashram when you reach that gracious mountain—the call of lapwing and cuckoo echoes there, the deer in rut and the many elephants make it very pleasant."

The end of the forty-eighth *sarga* of the *Ayodhyākāṇḍa* of the *Śrī Rāmāyaṇa*.

Sarga 49

1. After spending the night there, the princes, tamers of foes, did obeisance to the great seer and went off toward the mountain.

2. As the great sage observed them setting out, he followed behind as a father would follow his children, and he began to speak:

3. "Now, when you reach the swift-flowing Kālindī, the daughter of the sun, make a raft there and cross the river.

4. "There you will come upon a great banyan tree with lush green leaves, called Śyāma. It has grown dense with its many trunks and is the haunt of perfected beings.

5. "Two miles beyond it, Rāma, you will see a dark thicket, a mixture of flame-trees, jujubes, and Yamunā bamboo.

6. "That is the way to Citrakūṭa. I have traveled it many times, for it is pleasant and easy, and quite safe from forest fires." After describing the way to them, the great seer turned back.

7. When the sage had gone, Rāma said to Lakṣmaṇa, "How fortunate we are, Saumitri, that the sage has shown us such compassion."

8. Conversing in this fashion, the brothers, tigers among men, proceeded in high spirits to the Kālindī River with Sītā before them.

9. They lashed together logs to fashion a good-sized raft, and Lakṣmaṇa cut some wood to make a comfortable seat for Sītā.

10. Next, Rāma Dāśarathi helped her board the raft, and as he did so she was half embarrassed, his beloved wife, a woman as marvelous as the goddess Śrī.

11. Then on the raft they crossed the Yamunā, daughter of the sun, a swift-flowing, wave-wreathed river with trees growing thick along her banks.

12. Once across they abandoned the raft, and setting out from the Yamunā forest they reached Śyāma, the cool, green-leafed banyan tree.

13. "O that I may see Kausalyā again, and glorious Sumitrā." Such was the wish Sītā made as she walked around the tree, hands cupped in reverence.

14. Proceeding two miles further, the brothers Rāma and Lakṣmaṇa killed many animals such as are pure to consume and ate them in a grove by the Yamunā.

15. They passed the time pleasantly in the lovely grove resounding with flocks of peacocks and teeming with elephants and monkeys. Then, no longer looking sad, they repaired to a spot where the riverbank was level and found a suitable place to pass the night.

The end of the forty-ninth *sarga* of the *Ayodhyākāṇḍa* of the *Śrī Rāmāyaṇa*.

Sarga 50

1. When night ended Lakṣmaṇa dozed off, but straightway the delight of the Raghus gently roused him.

2. "Saumitri, listen to the sweet sounds the forest creatures are making. Let us be off, slayer of enemies, it is time for us to depart."

3. Even though his brother had roused him the very moment he was dozing off, Lakṣmaṇa at once shook off his sleep and lassitude and the fatigue of constant travel.

4. They all rose and sipped the gracious water of the river and then set out on the path to Citrakūṭa described by the seer.

5. As Rāma set out in the early morning with Saumitri, he began to speak to lotus-eyed Sītā.

6. "Look, Vaidehī, the *kiṃśuka* trees are in full blossom now that winter is past. Garlanded with their red flowers they almost seem to be on fire.

7. "Look at the marking-nut trees in bloom, untended by man, how they are bent over with fruit and leaves. I know I shall be able to live.

8. "Look at the honeycombs, Lakṣmaṇa, amassed by honeybees on one tree after another. They hang down large as buckets.

9. "Here a moorhen is crying, and in answer to it a peacock calls through delightful stretches of forest richly carpeted with flowers.

10. "And look, there is Citrakūṭa, the mountain over there with the towering peak, teeming with herds of elephants and echoing with flocks of birds."

11. So the brothers and Sītā proceeded on foot and reached the delightful mountain, charming Citrakūṭa.

12. And on reaching the mountain, where birds of every description came flocking, he said, "This will be our dwelling for now. We shall enjoy ourselves here, dear brother.

13. "Fetch wood, dear Lakṣmaṇa, good, hard wood, and build a place to live, for my heart is set on living here."

14. Hearing his words Saumitri, tamer of foes, went and brought different kinds of trees and built a leaf hut.

15. Then Rāma addressed him again, his single-mindedly obedient brother: "Bring flesh of a black antelope, and we shall offer sacrifice to our hut."

16. Powerful Lakṣmaṇa Saumitri killed a black deer, one pure enough for sacrifice, and then cast it into a well-kindled fire.

17. When Lakṣmaṇa observed that it was cooked, well-broiled, the bleeding staunched, he said to Rāghava, tiger among men:

18. "The black deer has been roasted black, with all its limbs intact. You may now sacrifice to the gods, my godlike brother, for you are proficient."

19. Rāma bathed and then, intently and with expertise, he intoned the prayers most skillfully and made a plentiful offering for averting evil.

20. It was a charming leaf-thatched hut, well built in a suitable spot protected from the wind, and they all entered it together to take up their dwelling, as the hosts of gods enter their assembly hall Sudharmā.

21. It was a splendid forest, too, teeming with many kinds of birds and beasts, where trees grew dense with brilliant clusters of flowers, and the cries of wild animals echoed. And they enjoyed themselves in perfect happiness there—all the while holding their senses under control.

22. Now that he had arrived at pleasant Mount Citrakūṭa and the river Mālyavatī, with its gentle fords where beasts and birds would congregate, Rāma felt a gladness and delight that made him forget the sorrow of being an exile from his city.

The end of the fiftieth *sarga* of the *Ayodhyākāṇḍa* of the *Śrī Rāmāyaṇa*.

Sarga 51

1. Racked with bitter sorrow, Guha had stood talking a long while with Sumantra until Rāma landed on the southern shore, and then he returned home.

2. Given leave to depart, Sumantra harnessed the splendid horses, and in profound dejection he proceeded directly to the city of Ayodhyā.

3. Fragrant forests came into view, streams and ponds, then villages and cities, but he sped past it all.

4. Then, on the third day at dusk, the charioteer reached Ayodhyā, and it was a dismal sight that met his eyes.

5. The city was silent and seemed deserted, and as he looked at it in deep dejection, Sumantra was overcome by a rush of grief and anxiously asked himself:

6. "Can it be that the entire city, with its elephants and horses, its people, and their lord, has been consumed by the fire of grief, in sorrow for Rāma's suffering?" Lost in these anxious thoughts, the charioteer hurriedly entered.

7. But as the charioteer Sumantra was advancing, men began to

run toward him by the hundreds and thousands, asking, "Where is Rāma?"

8-9. He told them, "I took leave of Rāghava at the Ganges. The great and righteous prince dismissed me, and so I returned. The three of them have crossed the river." When the people heard this, their faces filled with tears, they sighed, "Alas!" and cried out, "Oh Rāma!"

10. And he heard what they said as they stood about in groups: "Now we are lost indeed, for we shall not see Rāghava here again."

11. "We will never again show ourselves at feasts or sacrifices, at weddings or great assemblies, since righteous Rāma will not be there."

12. "Like a father Rāma watched over the city, pondering what was advantageous for the people, what would please them and bring them happiness."

13. Along the row of inner shops he heard the mourning of the women where they sat by their windows, suffering with grief for Rāma.

14. In the middle of the royal highway, Sumantra covered his face and went straight to Daśaratha's palace.

15. Alighting swiftly from the chariot, he entered the king's compound and passed in turn through the seven courtyards, which were crowded with men of importance.

16. Here and there in the mansions he could hear the hushed comments of Daśaratha's wives, grief-stricken over Rāma:

17. "The charioteer went away with Rāma and now has come back without him. What can he possibly say to Kausalyā in her grief?"

18. "As hard as it is for Kausalyā to live, it must be, I guess, no easier to die, if she still lives despite her son's departure."

19. Hearing the talk of the king's wives—and it was all too true—he quickly entered the palace that seemed engulfed in flames of grief.

20. He made his way through the eighth courtyard, and there in the pale white chamber he saw the king desolate and anguished, tormented with grief for his son.

21. Sumantra advanced to where the lord of men was sitting. Doing

obeisance to him, he delivered Rāma's message just as it had been told to him.

22. The king listened in silence, and then, his mind reeling, he fell to the ground in a faint, overwhelmed by grief for Rāma.

23. Pain swept over the women of the inner chamber as the lord of the land grew faint. And as the king fell to the floor, they lifted up their arms and wailed.

24. With Sumitrā's help Kausalyā raised up her fallen lord, and then she said:

25. "Illustrious king, here is the messenger come from the prince who has done what no man ever did. He has returned from his sojourn in the forest. Why do you not address him?

26. "Or are you at last ashamed, Rāghava, of the calamitous thing you have done? Stand up, and set things right. Grief will render you no aid.

27. "Kaikeyī, for fear of whom you dare not ask the charioteer about Rāma, is not here, my lord; you may speak freely."

28. So Kausalyā spoke to the great king, and then, sick with grief, she suddenly fell to the floor, the rest of her words drowned in her tears.

29. When the women saw Kausalyā fall lamenting to the ground and looked at their lord, they all broke out in shrill weeping.

30. And as the din arising from the inner chamber reached them, men young and old alike and all the women broke out in weeping, so that once again every quarter of the city was thrown into confusion.

The end of the fifty-first *sarga* of the *Ayodhyākāṇḍa* of the *Śrī Rāmāyaṇa*.

Sarga 52

1. When the king had revived and recovered from his faint, he summoned the charioteer to learn what had happened to Rāma.

2-3. The charioteer approached in desolation, his body coated with dust, his face bathed in tears—an old man deeply suffering like an elephant newly captured, and like the elephant heaving sighs, pensive and beside himself with grief. The king addressed him in deep anguish:

4. "Where is my righteous son living? Must he resort to the foot of a tree? Rāghava has known every comfort, charioteer, what must he now eat? How can the son of the guardian of the earth lie down upon the earth like some helpless wretch?

5. "Foot-soldiers, chariots, and elephants used to follow Rāma wherever he went. How can he have gone off to live in the desolate forest?

6. "Wild animals range through it, black snakes infest it. How can the two young men and Vaidehī have gone to the forest?

7. "How could the princes and poor Sītā, so delicate a young woman, have alighted from the chariot, Sumantra, and proceeded on foot?

8. "You at least have found fulfillment, charioteer, in seeing my sons entering the forest as the two Aśvins might enter onto Mount Mandara.

9. "What were Rāma's words, Sumantra, what were Lakṣmaṇa's and Maithilī's when they reached the forest? Tell me, charioteer, where Rāma sat, where he slept, what he ate."

10. So the lord of men pressed the charioteer, and in a sob-choked and breaking voice Sumantra answered the king:

11. "Rāghava cupped his hands in reverence and bowed his head, great king, and in perfect keeping with righteousness he said to me:

12. " 'Charioteer, in my name you must fall at the feet of my great and celebrated father, and pay him the homage he deserves.

13. " 'In my name, charioteer, you must ask the women of the inner chamber after their health, all of them without exception, and do obeisance to them according to rank.

14. " 'And you must ask my mother Kausalyā after her welfare and do obeisance to her, saying, "My lady, ever venerate the feet of my lord as if he were a god."

15. " 'Ask Bharata after his welfare and tell him in my name, "You must observe proper conduct toward each and every one of our mothers."

16. " 'And tell him further, the great-armed prince, the delight of the Ikṣvāku House, "When you become prince regent you must defer to father, who remains the king." '

17. "So glorious Rāma spoke to me, great king, and as he did the tears rolled in a flood from his lotus-coppery eyes.

18. "But Lakṣmaṇa was furious, and heaving a sigh he said, 'For what crime has the prince been exiled?

19. " 'Whether it was the granting of a boon or some other selfish motive that led to Rāma's banishment, in any event an evil thing has been done. I can see no reason at all for Rāma to have been abandoned.

20. " 'The banishment of Rāghava was a rash act, a perverse act of folly, that must provoke protest.

21. " 'I for one can no longer regard the great king as my father. Rāghava shall now be brother, father, master, and every kinsman to me.

22. " 'How could anyone in the world feel loyalty to you after doing such a thing, after abandoning the prince whom all the world loves and who is devoted to the welfare of all the world?'

23. "Poor Jānakī stood heaving sighs, great king, motionless and oblivious as though a spirit possessed her.

24. "The glorious princess, who has never known adversity before, only wept in her sorrow and could not speak to me at all.

25. "She gazed up at her husband and her mouth went dry, and as she watched me leaving she suddenly burst into tears.

26. "That is just how it was—Rāma standing still, his hands cupped in reverence, his face bathed in tears, protected by Lakṣmaṇa's arms; and poor Sītā weeping as she gazed at the king's chariot, and at me."

The end of the fifty-second *sarga* of the *Ayodhyākāṇḍa* of the *Śrī Rāmāyaṇa*.

Sarga 53

1. "Now, as I was about to return, the horses would not take the road, and they shed hot tears as Rāma set out to the forest.

2. "I cupped my hands in reverence to both princes and boarded the chariot, ready to set out despite the sorrow I felt for them.

3. "But I waited the whole day there with Guha in hopes that Rāma might yet send word for me.

4. "Throughout your realm, great king, even the trees are tormented by Rāma's calamity; they have wilted, flower, bud, and branch.

5. "No creatures are moving about, no beasts stirring forth. The forest is overcome with grief for Rāma, and its murmur has been stilled.

6. "In the lotus ponds the lilies have closed their petals, lord of men, and the waters have grown turbid. The lotuses have withered, and the fish and birds have hidden themselves.

7. "Blossoms that grow in water, flowers that grow on land, and fruits have lost their familiar luster, and their fragrance is all but gone.

8. "No one welcomed me as I entered Ayodhyā. The men, not seeing Rāma, heaved sighs incessantly.

9. "From mansions, many-storied buildings, and palaces the women observed the chariot come, and they raised cries of woe, tormented at losing the sight of Rāma.

10. "More anguished than ever before, the ladies looked at one another dimly, through large and once-bright eyes that rushing tears had overwhelmed.

11. "I could detect no disparity in the anguish felt by friends, enemies, or neutrals.

12-13. "The people have lost all delight, the elephants and horses are desolate, the city wilts at the cries of anguish and reverberates with sighs, joyless and tormented by Rāma's banishment. It almost seems to me, your majesty, as if Ayodhyā, like Kausalyā herself, had been bereft of her only son."

14. When he heard the charioteer's report, the king replied in a most desolate, sob-choked voice:

15. "Kaikeyī, a woman of evil family and evil designs, forced me, and I failed to seek the advice of elders skilled in counsel.

16. "I failed to take counsel with my friends, my ministers, and wise brahmans. It was on my own, in delusion, for a woman's sake that I did the rash thing I have done.

17. "Or perhaps—yes, surely charioteer, this great calamity was something destined to be, that had somehow to happen, to bring ruin upon this House.

18. "If I have ever done you a kind deed, charioteer, you must bring Rāma back to me at once—and hurry, for my life depends upon it.

19. "If only my express command might even yet make Rāghava turn back! I shall not be able to live a moment without Rāma.

20. "But then, my great-armed son must have traveled far away by now. Then put me on the chariot and swiftly bring me within sight of Rāma.

21. "Where is Lakṣmaṇa's eldest brother, the great bowman with pearly teeth? Oh please, I must see him and Sītā if I am to live.

22. "If I cannot see Rāma, those coppery eyes of his, those great arms, the jeweled earrings that he wears, I shall go to the house of Yama.

23. "What greater sorrow can there be than this, that in the state to which I am reduced, Rāghava, the delight of the Ikṣvākus, is not here for me to see.

24. "Oh Rāma! Oh younger brother of Rāma! Oh poor Vaidehī! You did not know I would die helplessly in sorrow. Too wide, my lady, is this ocean of grief, too wide for me to cross alive.

25. "What misfortune to be denied the chance to see them, Rāghava and Lakṣmaṇa, here and now when I so need to see them." Thus the glorious king lamented until suddenly he fell back in a faint upon the couch.

26. Thus the king lamented over Rāma before his mind went dark, and his words were so doubly piteous that as the queen, Rāma's mother, listened, terror seized her once again.

The end of the fifty-third *sarga* of the *Ayodhyākāṇḍa* of the *Śrī Rāmāyaṇa*.

Sarga 54

1. Trembling constantly as though a spirit possessed her, Kausalyā spoke to the charioteer from the ground where she lay almost lifeless.

2. "Take me where Kākutstha is, and Sītā and Lakṣmaṇa. I cannot bear to live here without them for even an instant.

3. "Quickly turn the chariot around and take me as well to the Daṇḍakas. If I cannot go after them, I will go to the house of Yama."

4. The charioteer cupped his hands in reverence, and in a breaking voice choked by rushing sobs, he tried to comfort the queen.

5. "Put away your grief and confusion, and your consternation over this sorrowful event. Rāghava himself is living in the forest free from any sadness.

6. "Lakṣmaṇa, too, by humbly serving Rāma in the forest, by his self-restraint, and sense of duty, is winning the higher world.

7. "Sītā is making her dwelling in the forest, desolate place though it is, as if she were at home. She has entrusted her heart to Rāma and is full of confidence and unafraid.

8. "I did not perceive that Vaidehī felt any despair, not the slightest. She seemed to me almost accustomed to the hardships of exile.

9. "Sītā takes the same delight in the desolate forests that she used to have when going out to the city gardens.

10. "The delightful Sītā with her full-moon face is enjoying herself like a young girl, delighting in Rāma and not at all despondent, in the desolate forest though she may be.

11. "For her heart belongs to him, and her life depends on him. Ayodhyā itself, with Rāma gone, would be far more of a wilderness to her.

12. "On the road Vaidehī asks about the villages and cities she sees, the courses of rivers and the different kinds of trees.

13. "No journey or gusting wind, no distress or scorching heat can dim Vaidehī's moonbeam radiance.

14. "Sweet Vaidehī's face has not suffered any change; it still resembles the hundred-petaled lotus, still looks as radiant as the full moon.

15. "Her feet, radiant as lotus cups, remain as rosy as liquid lac even now, when she must do without it.

16. "Even now when she has cast off her jewelry out of love for him, beautiful Vaidehī moves as gracefully as if she were dancing with anklets sounding.

17. "In the forest when she spies an elephant, a lion or tiger, she slips within Rāma's arms and so does not take fright.

18. "You must not grieve for them or for yourself; you must not grieve for the lord of the people. For theirs are exploits the world will keep alive in memory forever.

19. "They have shaken off their grief and their hearts are joyful. They are keeping firmly to the path the great seers have taken; they find delight in the forest, have fruit of the forest to eat, and are making good their father's promise."

20. Yet for all the charioteer's attempts to restrain the queen with such well-reasoned words, she was still tormented with grief for her child and would not stop moaning, "Rāghava!" "My darling!" "My son!"

The end of the fifty-fourth *sarga* of the *Ayodhyākāṇḍa* of the *Śrī Rāmāyaṇa*.

Sarga 55

1. Kausalyā wept for Rāma, the most pleasing of men, gone to the forest in his adherence to righteousness. And she said in bitter anguish to her husband:

2. "Your fame is great, widespread throughout the three worlds—Rāghava is compassionate, they say, generous and kind-spoken.

3. "How then, best of kings, could your sons and Sītā have been made to suffer so? They were raised in comfort, how will they endure the sufferings of the forest?

4. "How in heaven's name will Maithilī, a woman in the bloom of youth, so delicate and used to comfort, endure the heat and the cold?

5. "Large-eyed Sītā has always had savory dishes to eat, exquisitely seasoned. How will she eat the food of the forest, plain rice growing wild?

6. "The faultless woman has always heard agreeable sounds, the sounds of singing and musical instruments. How will she stand it to hear the awful roaring of flesh-eating lions?

7. "My great-armed son, like the banner of great Indra! Where must he be sleeping, with no pillow but his iron-hard arm?

8. "When shall I see Rāma's perfect face again, lotus-hued, with hair so thick, his eyes like lotus petals, his breath scented like a lotus?

9. "Surely my heart is made of adamant; how otherwise, with him gone from my sight, would it not shatter into a thousand fragments?

10. "Even if Rāghava should return in the fifteenth year, he would spurn both the kingship and the treasury, since Bharata will have possessed them.

11. "When a younger brother has had possession of the kingship like this, lord of the peoples, why would the eldest and best brother not disdain it?

12. "A tiger will not eat the food another beast has fed upon. In the same way the tiger among men will scorn what another has tasted.

13. "One does not use again in a sacrifice the oblation, clarified butter, rice-cakes, *kuśa* grass, or posts of *khadira* wood, once they have rendered their service.

14. "This kingdom, in like manner, will have no value for Rāma. It will have been consumed, like a cup of wine drained to the lees, like a sacrifice when the *soma* has run out.

15. "Rāghava will not suffer an insult of this sort, any more than a powerful tiger suffers having its tail pulled.

16. "Such a man, a bull among men, with the power of a lion, the eyes of a bull! That his own father should destroy him, the way a fish destroys its offspring!

17. "If only you had kept to the age-old way of righteousness followed by the twice-born and set down in the sacred texts, before you exiled a son so earnest in righteousness.

18. "A woman's first recourse is her husband, Your Majesty, her second is her son, her third her kinsmen. She has no fourth in this world.

19. "But you are no recourse for me, and Rāma is off in the forest. I do not want to go to the forest; you have totally destroyed me.

20. "You have destroyed this kingship and this kingdom, and all the people of the city; you have destroyed your counselors and yourself, destroyed me and my son! Your son and your wife should be delighted now."

21. As he listened to the harrowing words she uttered, the king grew faint, overcome with sorrow. He plumbed the very depths of his grief, and there a memory was revived of something evil he once did.

The end of the fifty-fifth *sarga* of the *Ayodhyākāṇḍa* of the *Śrī Rāmāyaṇa*.

Sarga 56

1. Such were the harsh words that Rāma's mother in grief and anger forced the king to hear. And he was overcome with sorrow and fell to brooding.

2. And as he brooded there suddenly flashed upon his mind an evil deed he had once done, unintentionally, long ago, when he was shooting arrows by the sound of the target alone.

3. This grief and his grief for Rāma were driving him out of his mind. The mighty lord of earth, consumed now by a double grief, said to Kausalyā:

4. "I beg your forgiveness, Kausalyā! Here, I cup my hands in supplication. Always, even to strangers, you have been kindly and never cruel.

5. "And as you know, my lady, a woman who has regard for righteousness should hold her husband, whether he is virtuous or not, to be a deity incarnate.

6. "You have always kept to the ways of righteousness; you can tell good people from bad. Sorrowful though you are, you ought not to speak so unkindly to one more sorrowful still."

7. As Kausalyā listened to the pitiful words the king uttered in his desolation, tears began to fall from her eyes like fresh rainwater down a runnel.

8. And as she cried she cupped her hands like a lotus and raised them to her head before the king. Confused and alarmed, she spoke, the syllables racing one after the other:

9. "Forgive me, I bow my head, I fall before you to the ground and beg you. It hurts me so that you should beg me, my lord, and you ought not to hurt me.

10. "She is counted no real wife in this world or the next, my mighty lord, whose wise husband, deserving of her praise, must beg her forgiveness.

11. "I do know what is right, my righteous husband, I know you speak the truth. What I said was something uttered in the anguish of grief for my son.

12. "Grief destroys restraint, grief destroys all one has learned, grief destroys everything. No enemy is the equal of grief.

13. "An unexpected blow from an enemy's hand might be withstood, but to withstand unexpected grief, however slight, is all but impossible.

14. "Only five nights all told have now passed with Rāma living in the forest; but this grief that robs me of every delight makes it seem like five years.

15. "As I think about him the grief grows here, in my heart, just as the waters of the ocean grow great with rivers ever rushing in."

16. Such were Kausalyā's heartfelt words, and while she was speaking, the sun's rays began to fade, and evening came on.

17. And the king, both gladdened by what Queen Kausalyā said and overburdened with grief, yielded to sleep.

The end of the fifty-sixth *sarga* of the *Ayodhyākāṇḍa* of the *Śrī Rāmāyaṇa*.

Sarga 57

1. A short time later, his heart crushed by grief, King Daśaratha awoke, and began to brood once more.

2. Heartache over the exile of Rāma and Lakṣmaṇa once more swept over him, the equal of Vāsava, as the demon's darkness sweeps over the sun.

3. It was at midnight, on that sixth night since Rāma's banishment to the forest, when King Daśaratha fully remembered the evil deed he had once done. He then addressed Kausalyā, who lay anguished with grief for her son.

4. "Whatever a person does, be it good or evil, my dear and precious wife, he receives in like measure, the direct result of the deeds he has done himself.

5. "One deserves to be called a fool who sets about a deed without understanding the gravity of its consequences, what he stands to gain or lose.

6. "A person who cuts down a mango grove and instead waters flame trees—made greedy for their fruit by the sight of their flowers—would be sorry when that fruit appears.

7. "I cut down a mango grove and watered flame trees instead. When the fruit appeared I had to give up Rāma, and now, too late, I see my folly and grieve.

8. "When I was a young man, Kausalyā, I earned a reputation as a bowman. It was said, 'The prince can shoot by the sound of the target alone.' But I did an evil deed, my lady, and it has now come home to me, this sorrow that I have brought upon myself.

9. "But just as a child might eat something poisonous out of ignorance, so I, too, was unaware of the fruits my shooting by sound would bear.

10. "We were not yet married, my lady, and I was still prince regent. The rains had come, the season that quickens lust and desire.

11. "After having drawn up the moisture of the earth and scorched the world with its rays, the sun had entered the awful region the dead inhabit.

12. "All at once the heat vanished, dark rain clouds appeared, and all creatures began to rejoice—frogs, cuckoos, peacocks.

13. "Engulfed by the rain that had fallen and continued to fall incessantly, the mountain with its wild white cuckoos looked like one vast body of water.

14. "At this most pleasant of seasons I decided to take some exercise, and with bow and arrows and chariot I set out along the Sarayū River.

15. "I was an intemperate youth, eager to kill a buffalo at the waterhole in the nighttime, an elephant coming down to the river, or some other wild animal.

16. "Now, in the darkness I heard a noise, beyond the range of vision, of a pitcher being filled in the water, but just like the sound an elephant makes.

17. "I drew out a shaft that glared like a poisonous snake. I shot the keen-edged arrow, and it darted like a poisonous snake.

18. "And there, as day was breaking, the voice of a forest dweller rang out clearly, 'Ah! Ah!'—the voice of a young man crying there as he fell into the water: 'Why should someone shoot a weapon at a person like me, an ascetic?

19. " 'I came to the deserted river at night only to fetch water. Who has struck me with an arrow? What have I done to anyone?

20. " 'I am a seer who has renounced violence, who lives in the wilderness on things of the wild. Why should someone take up a weapon to kill a person like me?

21. " 'The one burden I carry is my matted hair, my garments are nothing but barkcloth and hides. What could anyone stand to gain by killing me? What wrong could I have done him?

22. " 'No, he cannot have had any purpose at all in what he did; pure malice must have prompted it. No one shall ever forgive him, like the man who violates his guru's bed.

23. " 'But it is not for the loss of my own life that I am grieving so. It is for two others I grieve that am slain, my mother and father.

24. " 'For they are an aged couple and have long been dependent on me. When I am dead what sort of existence are they to lead?

25. " 'My aged mother and father and I all slain by a single arrow! Who can have been so reckless, so malicious as to strike us down all at once?'

26. "When I heard that piteous voice, I who had always striven to do right, I shuddered and the bow and arrow dropped from my hands to the ground.

27. "Desolate to my innermost being, in the depths of misery I went to the place and saw on the bank of the Sarayū an ascetic struck down by my arrow.

28. "He fixed me with his eyes—I was beside myself with terror—and he spoke these harrowing words as though ready to burn me up with his ascetic power:

29. " 'What harm have I, living here in the forest, ever done to you, your Majesty, that you should attack me when all I wanted was to fetch some water for my elders?

30. " 'The very same arrow that has pierced me to the quick has also struck down two blind old people, my mother and my father.

31. " 'The two of them are frail and blind; they are thirsty and waiting for me. And now they will have to bear their parching thirst, as long as they can, on the strength of hope alone.

32. " 'I now see there is no reward for austerity or learning, since my father does not know that I lie fallen upon the ground.

33. " 'And even if he knew, what could he do? He is helpless and unable even to move about, as helpless as one tree to save another that is being felled.

34. " 'You yourself, Rāghava, must go at once to my father and tell him, lest in his wrath he consume you as a raging fire consumes a forest.

35. " 'There is the footpath, your Majesty, leading to my father's ashram. Go and beg his forgiveness, lest he curse you in his rage.

36. " 'Draw out the arrow from me, your Majesty, the keen-edged shaft is tearing me apart at the quick, as a rushing water current tears a soft riverbank apart.

37. " 'I am not a brahman, your Majesty, set your mind at ease. For I was born of a *vaiśya* father and a *śūdra* mother, lord of the country.'

38. "So he spoke, in pain, and as he lay doubled over, I pulled out the arrow from where it pierced him to the quick.

39. "I stared at him lying there by the Sarayū, his body drenched in water, as he painfully lamented, all the while gasping from his mortal wound; and as I stared, my dear wife, I grew utterly sick at heart."

The end of the fifty-seventh *sarga* of the *Ayodhyākāṇḍa* of the *Śrī Rāmāyaṇa*.

Sarga 58

1. "It was a great sin I had committed, however unintentionally. I hardly had my wits about me as all alone I put my mind to the question of how might it be righted.

2. "At last I took the pot filled with pure water and went along the path he had told me of, until I reached the ashram.

3. "There I saw his parents, a frail, blind old couple with no one to guide them, like a pair of birds whose wings have been clipped.

4. "They could not move about and were sitting there listless and helpless, talking about him, their one hope that I robbed them of.

5. "Hearing the sound of my footsteps the sage spoke: 'Why did you take so long, my son? Bring the water at once.

6. " 'Your mother here was worried, my child, and all because you were playing in the water. Come into the ashram at once.

7. " 'If perhaps your mother or I have offended you in some way, my son, you should not take it to heart. For you are an ascetic, my child.

8. " 'You are the recourse for us who have no other, the eyes for us whose sight is gone. Our very lives are in your hands. Won't you say something to us?'

9. "The longer I looked at the sage, the more frightened I became, and in a choked voice, stammering and slurring the syllables, I spoke to him.

10. "With effort I managed to collect my thoughts and recover the power of speech. Then I began to tell him the frightful story of his son's calamity.

11. " 'I am Daśaratha, a kshatriya, not the great one's son. A sorrowful thing, which all good men would condemn, has happened by my own doing.

12. " 'Holy one, I came to the bank of the Sarayū, bow in hand, eager to kill some animal, an elephant perhaps, coming down to the water hole.

13. " 'There I heard the sound of a pitcher being filled in the water and, thinking it an elephant, I shot an arrow at it.

14. " 'I went to the riverbank and there I saw an ascetic lying on the ground with an arrow piercing his heart and his life ebbing away.

15. " 'Holy one, I was aiming at a sound, meaning to kill an elephant. I released the iron shaft toward the water, and it struck your son.

16. " 'When the arrow was pulled out he went to heaven, then and there, grieving for both of you holy ones, lamenting your blindness.

17. " 'It was unintentional, holy one, it was an accident that I struck down your son. Whatever awaits me now may the sage forgive me!'

18. "The mighty sage gasped when he heard these harrowing words, and broken with grief he spoke to me as I stood before him, hands cupped in reverence.

19. " 'If you had not told me yourself of this impious deed, your Majesty, your head would have instantly burst into a myriad fragments.

20. " 'If a kshatriya intentionally commits a murder—and the murder of a forest hermit at that—it topples him from his place, be he Indra himself, the wielder of the thunderbolt.

21. " 'But since this act was unintentional, and for that reason alone, you shall live. Were it not so, the entire House of the Rāghavas, not just you, would cease at once to be.

22-23. " 'Take us, your Majesty, to the place,' he said to me. 'We want to see our son now, to have one last sight of him, his body spattered with blood and his hide garments in disarray, lying on the ground unconscious, under the sway of the King of Righteousness.'

24. "So all alone I led the sage and his wife to that place, and brought the deeply grieving parents near to where they could touch their son.

25. "The wretched couple drew close, they touched their son and collapsed upon his body. And his father cried out:

26. " 'My son, don't you love me any more? At least have regard for your mother then, righteous child. Why don't you embrace me, my son? Speak to me, my tender child.

27. " 'Whom shall I hear late at night—how it used to touch my heart—so sweetly reciting the sacred texts or other works?

28. " 'And after the twilight worship, the ritual bath, and offerings to the sacred fire, who will sit down beside me, my son, to allay the grief and fear that anguish me?

29. " 'Who will bring me tubers and fruit and roots, and feed me like a welcome guest—me an invalid, without leader or guide?

30. " 'And how, my son, shall I support your poor mother, blind and aged as she is, wretched and yearning for her son?

31. " 'Stay! Don't, oh don't go, my son, to the abode of Yama. You may go tomorrow, with your mother and me to lend you strength.

32. " 'For we too shall soon be going to the house of Yama, bereft of you and left helpless in the forest, wretched and anguished with grief.

33. " 'And then, when I see Vaivasvata, I will make this speech: "May the King of Righteousness forgive me, but this boy is needed to support his parents."

34. " 'You were free of evil, my son, and were struck down by a man of evil deeds. By the power of this truth may you go straight to the worlds they win who fight under arms.

35. " 'Proceed to the supreme state those heroes reach, my son, who do not turn their backs in battle but die facing the foe.

36. " 'Go, my dear son, to the state attained by Sagara, by Śaibya, Dilīpa, Janamejaya, Nahuṣa, and Dhundhumāra.

37-38. " 'Go, my dear son, to the state awarded to all holy men for their vedic study and austerities, to one who donates land, who keeps the sacred fires, who is faithful to his one wife; to those who make a gift of a thousand cows, who support their gurus, who lay their bodies down. For no child of this family ever goes to the state of the accursed.'

39. "So he mourned there, wretchedly and without pause, and then with his wife he set about making the funeral libation for his child.

40. "But just then the sage's son appeared in a heavenly form procured by his own good deeds, and for one brief moment he addressed these words of solace to his parents:

41. " 'I have attained a high station because I took care of you. And both of you shall soon come into my presence.'

42. "With this, the sage's disciplined son ascended straightway to heaven upon a heavenly chariot of wonderful construction.

43. "The ascetic and his wife hurriedly made the libation, and as I stood before him, my hands cupped in reverence, the mighty sage said to me:

44. " 'Slay me this very moment, your Majesty; dying holds no terror for me. For I had but one son and you have taken him from me with your arrow.

45. " 'Since it was unintentionally that you struck down my pure son, I will only lay a curse on you, though it is a grievous and very dreadful one:

46. " 'Just as I now sorrow over my son's calamity, so you, too, your majesty, shall end your days grieving for a son.'

47. "The words of the noble sage have thus come home to me, dear wife, for now I am to lose my life grieving for my son.

48. "If only Rāma could touch me or speak to me now just once. How unlike me it was, my lady, to do what I did to Rāghava.

49. "I cannot see you with my eyes, Kausalyā, my mind is failing. Here, the messengers of Vaivasvata are here, hastening me on!

50. "What greater sorrow than this, that in the final moments of my life I cannot rest my eyes on righteous, truthful Rāma.

51. "They are not men, they are gods who in the fifteenth year will see Rāma's face again, that lovely face with flashing earrings.

52. "His eyes like lotus petals, his perfect brows, his perfect teeth and lovely nose: how fortunate the men who will see Rāma's face, so like the lord of stars, the moon.

53. "Like the autumn moon or a full-blown lotus, and so fragrant: how fortunate the men who will see the face of my defender.

54. "When Rāma has ended his stay in the forest and returns to Ayodhyā, what happiness for those who will see him, like the planet Śukra moving forward on its course.

55. "The grief arising here in my very soul has left me helpless and insensible. In its wild rush it is sweeping me away, as a raging river sweeps away its bank.

56. "Oh great-armed Rāghava, the one relief of my agony!" With this last cry of grief King Daśaratha reached the end of his life.

57. And so it came about, just after midnight, when he had finished his mournful tale, that the lord of men, a man of noble vision, anguished by the exile of his beloved son and afflicted with the most profound sorrow, breathed his last.

The end of the fifty-eighth *sarga* of the *Ayodhyākāṇḍa* of the *Śrī Rāmāyaṇa*.

Sarga 59

1. Night passed, and next morning the panegyrists arrived to attend at the bed-chamber of the king.

2. The skillful servants approached as usual, women and eunuchs mostly, people of impeccable conduct.

3. At the proper time and according to custom the bath attendants came, bringing golden pitchers of water scented with yellow sandalwood.

4. And a group of women appeared, young maidens for the most part, bearing auspicious articles, refreshments and accoutrements.

5. The women then assembled who waited in attendance on the bed of the Kosalan lord, and they went to awaken their master.

6. They suddenly felt apprehensive as to whether the king was indeed alive; a shudder convulsed them and they began to tremble like blades of grass that stand against the current.

7. Then, as the trembling women looked more closely at the king, their apprehension of evil became a certainty.

8. The lovely women were desolate and sent up a shrill wail, like cow elephants in the wilderness when their bull is driven from his place.

9. At the sound of their crying Kausalyā and Sumitrā awoke at once and came to their senses.

10. Kausalyā and Sumitrā looked at the king and touched him. Then, crying out "O dear husband!" they collapsed upon the floor.

11. The daughter of the lord of Kosala lay writhing upon the ground, coated with dust, her brilliance dimmed like that of a star fallen from the sky.

12-13. A place of panic and bewilderment, with throngs of heart-broken people, tumult and crying everywhere, and kinsmen anguished with grief; all its bliss shattered in an instant, with a desolate and frenzied look—such was the palace of the god of men when he had reached the end of his allotted span.

14. Realizing that the glorious bull among kings had passed away, his wives gathered around him, weeping wildly and piteously in their sorrow, and stretching out their arms in helpless lamentation.

The end of the fifty-ninth *sarga* of the *Ayodhyākāṇḍa* of the *Śrī Rāmāyaṇa*.

Sarga 60

1-2. Kausalyā gazed at the dead king—he looked like a blazing fire suddenly extinguished, or the ocean emptied of water, or the sun gone dark—and her eyes filled with tears. Broken now with a double grief, she clasped the head of the king and cried out to Kaikeyī:

3. "You should be satisfied, Kaikeyī, for now you can enjoy the kingship unchallenged. Wasn't this the one object you had in mind when you forsook the king, you vicious, wicked woman?

4. "Rāma has gone away without me, and my husband has gone to heaven. I am like someone left behind by a caravan and utterly stranded. I cannot bear to live.

5. "What woman who has lost her husband, her own deity, would want to live—except Kaikeyī, who has lost the way of righteousness as well?

6. "A greedy person is oblivious to risks; he will eat even fruit that makes one sick. And thus, at the instigation of the hunchback, Kaikeyī has destroyed the House of the Rāghavas.

7. "When Janaka learns that the king, acting on an illicit order, has exiled Rāma and his wife, he will suffer just as I do.

8. "Lotus-eyed Rāma has gone away dead in life! And poor Sītā, too, daughter of the king of Videha, she who has never known hardship, will tremble all over at the hardships of the forest.

9. "At night Sītā will hear the ghastly cries of birds and beasts, and will shrink back into Rāma's arms in terror.

10. "Her father is aged and has but one child. He will fret over Vaidehī. He, too, will be overpowered by grief and no doubt lose his life."

11. As poor Kausalyā lamented in the anguish of sorrow, her maidservants helped her up and led her away.

12. The ministers then took the lord of the world and placed him in a vat of sesame oil, and thereupon they assumed all the royal duties, as they were empowered to do.

13. The counselors, being prudent men, were reluctant to administer the final rites with no prince at court. And so for the meanwhile they kept watch over the lord of earth.

14. When the women learned that the advisers had laid the lord of men in the vat of oil, they broke out in lamentation, crying "Oh he is dead!"

15. Their faces streaming tears, weeping in their burning grief, they raised their arms up piteously and piteously lamented.

16. Like a night without stars, like a woman bereft of her husband, the city of Ayodhyā without its great king was cast into gloom.

17. The people were drenched in tears, the housewives were crying

woefully, the public squares and private courtyards were empty, and the brilliance the city once had was gone.

18. As heaven has no light without the sun, as night has none when the crowds of stars have paled, the city went dark when it lost its great king, and sob-choked people crowded the streets and squares.

19. Men and women had begun to gather in groups, and they denounced the mother of Bharata. They were anguished and found no comfort in the city, now that the god of men was dead.

The end of the sixtieth *sarga* of the *Ayodhyākāṇḍa* of the *Śrī Rāmāyaṇa*.

Sarga 61

1. Night passed, and when the sun rose the deputies of the king, the brahmans, convened and went to the assembly hall.

2-3. Mārkaṇḍeya and Maudgalya, Vāmadeva and Kāśyapa, Kātyāyana and Gautama and glorious Jābāli—these brahmans and the ministers all gave voice to their different opinions. But in the end they turned to Vasiṣṭha himself, the foremost among them, the family priest of the king.

4. "The night passed sorrowfully for us; like a hundred years it seemed, with our king dead of grief for his son.

5. "The great king has gone to heaven, Rāma has withdrawn to the wilderness, and glorious Lakṣmaṇa has gone with him.

6. "Both Bharata and Śatrughna, slayers of enemies, are in the land of the Kekayas, in the lovely city of Rājagṛha, the home of Bharata's grandfather.

7. "Let some other Ikṣvāku prince be appointed king here and now, lest our kingdom be without a king and thereby meet with destruction.

8. "In a land without a king the rumbling lightning-wreathed clouds do not rain down their heavenly water upon the earth.

9. "In a land without a king handfuls of grain are not sown. In a land without a king no son submits to his father's will, no wife to her husband's.

10. "Where there is no king there can be no wealth; one cannot have a wife where there is no king. And there is yet further peril, for how can there be honesty where there is no king?

11. "In a land without a king patrons take no delight in building assembly halls, lovely gardens, or sanctuaries.

12. "In a land without a king the twice-born men who customarily sacrifice, the self-restrained brahmans rigorous in their vows, institute no sacred rites.

13. "In a land without a king no festivals or celebrations are held, where actors and dancers come in troupes and which bring a kingdom prosperity.

14. "In a land without a king litigants receive no satisfaction, while storytellers find no favor with audiences by their stories.

15. "In a land without a king lovers and their ladies do not ride out to the countryside on swift horses.

16. "In a land without a king the rich who live by farming and cattle raising do not sleep securely, with their doors wide open.

17. "In a land without a king merchants traveling long distances with loads of goods for sale do not go their way in safety.

18. "In a land without a king there wander no solitary, disciplined sages, those who lodge where nightfall finds them and contemplate the Self within themselves.

19. "In a land without a king security is not maintained: without a king the army cannot withstand the enemy in battle.

20. "Like rivers without water, like a forest without vegetation, like cows without cowherds is a kingdom without a king.

21. "In a land without a king no one can call anything his own. For men, like fish, incessantly seek to devour one another.

22. "Atheists, too, who unscrupulously break all bounds, conform to decency only when royal punishment is there to check them.

23. "Ah, it would be like darkness, nothing at all remaining clear, were there no king in the world to separate good from evil.

24. "Even while the great king was alive it was your word alone we would not overstep, as the ocean does not overstep its shore.

25. "Best of the twice-born, consider what awaits us: without a king the kingdom will become a wilderness. Name some prince of the Ikṣvāku line and consecrate him yourself as our king."

The end of the sixty-first *sarga* of the *Ayodhyākāṇḍa* of the *Śrī Rāmāyaṇa*.

Sarga 62

1. When he had heard their speech, Vasiṣṭha replied to the brahmans and the hosts of ministers and allies.

2. "Bharata is living comfortably with his brother Śatrughna in the city of Rājagṛha, among his uncle's family.

3. "So let swift messengers go at once on speeding horses and bring back the two mighty brothers. Why do we delay?"

4. "Yes, let them go," they all replied, and when Vasiṣṭha heard their response, he said:

5. "Come, Siddhārtha, Vijaya, Jayanta, Aśoka, Nandana. Listen, I shall tell you all what must be done.

6. "Take swift horses and swiftly proceed to the city of Rājagṛha. You must keep your grief in check and tell Bharata the following on my authority:

7. " 'The family priest asks after your health, as do all the counselors. Please hurry back, for there is urgent business to which you must attend.'

8. "But do not go and tell him of this disaster that has befallen the Rāghavas, do not tell him of Rāma's exile or the death of the king.

9. "Take silk garments and choice ornaments as gifts for the king and Bharata, and depart at once." Vasiṣṭha dismissed the messengers and they hurried off.

10. They crossed the Ganges at Hastinapura after reaching the country of Pañcāla, and headed west, cutting through the middle of the Kuru jungle.

11. They swiftly forded the Śaradaṇḍā, a heavenly river running with clear water, the home of birds of every description and thronged with people.

12. They reached the venerable tree on the western bank, the heavenly Granter of Wishes, and after approaching it they entered the city of Kuliṅgā.

13. From there they arrived at Abhikāla, passing on from Tejobhibhavana, and proceeding by way of central Bāhlika they made their way to Mount Sudāman. Soon the Foot of Viṣṇu came into view, and the Vipāśā and Śālmalī rivers.

14. The road was long and their mounts exhausted, but the messengers pressed on with all haste to Girivraja, best of cities.

15. To bring their master the news, to ensure the safety of their master's House and his succession in the dynasty, the messengers wasted no time but hurried on and reached the city late in the night.

The end of the sixty-second *sarga* of the *Ayodhyākāṇḍa* of the *Śrī Rāmāyaṇa*.

Sarga 63

1. Now, the very night the messengers were making their way into the city, Bharata had a terrible dream.

2. The son of the king of kings had this terrible dream just as night was ending, and it sorely troubled him.

3. Observing how troubled he was, his affable companions tried to ease his distress by engaging him in conversation in the assembly hall.

4. Some made music and sang, while others danced or staged dramatic pieces or told various kinds of jokes.

5. But great Bharata Rāghava took no delight in the conviviality of his affable friends.

6. One close friend questioned Bharata as he sat in the midst of his friends: "Why are you not enjoying yourself, my friend, in the company of your companions?"

7. Bharata replied to his companion, "Listen to the reason why great desolation has come over me.

8. "I saw my father in a dream. He was filthy, his hair dishevelled, and he fell from a mountain peak into a foul pool of cowdung.

9. "I saw him bobbing in the pool of dung, drinking sesame oil from his cupped hands, and he seemed to be laughing all the while.

10. "Then he was eating rice and oil, his whole body was anointed with oil, and again and again he would plunge headfirst into the oil.

11-12. "And in the same dream I saw the ocean gone dry and the moon fallen onto the earth. A blazing fire was suddenly extinguished, the earth was split open, and all the trees dried up; the mountains smoked and crumbled.

13. "Then, the king lay collapsed on a black iron throne; he was dressed all in black, and there were women mocking him, women part yellow, part black.

14. "And a righteous man, wearing red garlands and smeared with red cream, was hurrying off toward the south on a chariot yoked with asses.

15. "This was the terrifying dream I had last night. Surely I myself, or Rāma, or the king, or Lakṣmaṇa is going to die.

16. "For when in a dream a man sets out in a carriage yoked with asses, it is not long before a wreath of smoke appears above his funeral pyre. It is because of this I am so desolate and do not respond to your courtesies.

17. "My throat feels as if it were drying up; I can find no peace of mind. I feel a loathing for myself and do not know the reason why.

18. "Observing the course of this nightmare, with all those images that never before had entered my mind, and thinking about the king and that unthinkable look he had, I am filled with a great fear, and it will not leave my heart."

The end of the sixty-third *sarga* of the *Ayodhyākāṇḍa* of the *Śrī Rāmāyaṇa*.

Sarga 64

1. As Bharata was telling his dream, the messengers on their weary mounts entered the lovely city of Rājagṛha with its unbreachable defenses.

2. They met with the king and the king's son and were received with honor. Then clasping the feet of the king they spoke these words to Bharata:

3. "The family priest asks after your health, as do all the counselors. Please hurry back, for there is urgent business to which you must attend.

4. "Here is a gift for the king worth two hundred million, great prince, and one for your uncle worth a full hundred million."

5. Bharata accepted it all and in return honored the messengers with all that they might desire. He then asked, out of deep loyalty to his loved ones:

6. "My father, King Daśaratha, fares well, I hope? Rāma and great Lakṣmaṇa are in good health?

7. "And noble Kausalyā, too, wise Rāma's mother, who is earnest in righteousness, who knows the way of righteousness and ever looks to it?

8. "My middle mother Sumitrā, who knows the way of righteousness, the mother of Lakṣmaṇa and mighty Śatrughna, she is in good health, I hope?

9. "And Kaikeyī, too, my ever selfish, hot-tempered, and irascible mother, who fancies herself so wise?"

10. So great Bharata spoke, and the messengers most diffidently replied, "All fare well, tiger among men, whose welfare you desire."

11. At this, Bharata addressed the messengers: "I will ask leave of the great king, telling him the messengers are pressing me to hurry."

12. After speaking with the messengers and at their urging, prince Bharata addressed his grandfather:

13. "Your Majesty, I must return to my father at the urging of the messengers. But I shall come back again whenever you may wish me to do so."

14. So Bharata Rāghava spoke, and his grandfather the king kissed him on the forehead and addressed him with these heartfelt words:

15. "Go, my child, I give you leave. Kaikeyī has a worthy son in you. Give your mother my best wishes, slayer of enemies, and your father.

16. "My best wishes also to the family priest, my child, and to the other chief brahmans and those two great bowmen, your brothers Rāma and Lakṣmaṇa."

17. The king of Kekaya honored Bharata with the gift of prize elephants, many-colored blankets, and hides, and gave him riches.

18. Two thousand gold ornaments and sixteen hundred horses were the riches he bestowed to honor the son of Kaikeyī.

19. And straightway Aśvapati presented Bharata with his ministers as travel companions, estimable men, trustworthy and virtuous.

20. His uncle gave him riches too: handsome elephants bred on Mount Irāvata and Mount Indraśira, and swift asses that easily took the yoke.

21. He made him a present of dogs raised in the inner chamber, huge dogs with fangs like spears and the strength and courage of tigers.

22. Taking leave of his grandfather and his uncle Yudhājit, Bharata boarded his chariot with Śatrughna and set out.

23. And servants yoked the camels, oxen, horses, and asses to the circle-wheeled chariots, more than a hundred of them, and followed in Bharata's train.

24. So great Bharata set out with Śatrughna, under the protection of an army and accompanied by the ministers whom his grandfather trusted like himself. And he left Gṛha untroubled by enemies, as a perfected being might leave the world of Indra.

The end of the sixty-fourth *sarga* of the *Ayodhyākāṇḍa* of the *Śrī Rāmāyaṇa*.

Sarga 65

1. Heading east, mighty Bharata, the majestic delight of the Ikṣvākus, departed from Rājagṛha and crossed the wide and westward-flowing Śatadrū, a deep river capped with waves.

2-3. Crossing the river at Eladhāna, he reached Aparaparpaṭa, proceeding on to eastern Śalyakartana after crossing the Śilāvahā, the "river trailing stones." The prince, honest, majestic, and ever true to his word, had the river in view until he passed the high mountains leading to the Caitraratha forest.

4. Crossing the Kuliṅgā, a deep and swift river bounded by hills, he finally rested his army upon reaching the Yamunā.

5. He rested the weary horses and cooled their limbs. Then, having bathed and drunk, he took a store of water and set out once more.

6. In his handsome coach the handsome prince passed through the vast, uninhabited wilderness as the wind passes through the sky.

7. Traversing the southern end of Toraṇa, the son of Daśaratha reached Jambūprastha and proceeded to the pleasant village of Varūtha.

8. He spent the night there in the pleasant forest and then went on, heading eastward to the garden of Ujjihāna, thick with *priyaka* trees.

9. But when he reached the *priyaka* trees, Bharata took leave of the army, and harnessing swift horses, he sped onward.

10-11. He spent the night at Sarvatīrtha, and after crossing the Uttānakā and several other rivers on his mountain-bred horses, he arrived at Hastipṛṣṭhaka, where he forded the Kuṭikā. At Lauhitya the tiger among men crossed the Kapīvatī River, at Ekasāla the Sthāṇumatī, and the Gomatī at Vinata.

12. At Kaliṅganagara, Bharata reached the forest of *sāla* trees and drove on swiftly though his mounts were near exhaustion.

13. He passed straight through the forest at night and at sunrise set eyes on Ayodhyā, the city King Manu built.

14. The tiger among men had spent seven nights on the road, and at last he saw before him the city of Ayodhyā. From within the chariot he addressed his charioteer:

15-16. "There is Ayodhyā in the distance, that glorious white-clay city with its blessed gardens, throngs of virtuous sacrificers, brahmans who are masters of the *vedas*, and prosperous subjects, all under the protection of the best of royal seers—but how unhappy it looks to me, charioteer.

17. "In the past one used to hear a loud, tumultuous sound in Ayodhyā, of men and women all about, but I do not hear it now.

18. "At other times all the gardens revealed men leaving off the sports they had played since dusk and hurrying home.

19. "But now, abandoned by the lovers, the gardens seem to be weeping. It looks to me as if the town has become a wilderness, charioteer.

20. "Prominent men are no longer to be seen, as in the past, going in and out on carriages, elephants, and horses.

21. "And I see various portents, ominous ones, evil and appalling, and my heart sinks at the sight."

22. He entered by the Gate of Victory, his horses exhausted. The gatekeepers rose and with cries of "Long live the king!" accompanied him in.

23. In bewilderment Rāghava returned the gatekeepers' greeting, and then addressed Aśvapati's weary charioteer:

24. "We have heard how people looked in times past when they lost their king—and I see those looks here, charioteer, I see them all.

25. "The people I see in the town, men and women both, are unkempt, their eyes are filled with tears, and they have a desolate look, haggard, forlorn, and pensive."

26. So speaking to the charioteer, Bharata proceeded to the palace, heartsick at the ominous sights in Ayodhyā.

27. As he gazed at the city that once looked like Indra's city—at the empty crossroads, streets, and houses, at the bars on the door-leaves red with dust—he was filled to overflowing with sorrow.

28. There were so many things he saw that troubled his heart, things he had never before met with in the city, that great Bharata hung his head, sick at heart and joyless, as he made his way into his father's residence.

The end of the sixty-fifth *sarga* of the *Ayodhyākāṇḍa* of the *Śrī Rāmāyaṇa*.

Sarga 66

1. Not seeing his father there in his chamber, Bharata went to see his mother in hers.

2. When Kaikeyī saw that her long-absent son had arrived, she sprang up in delight, leaving her golden seat.

3. As soon as righteous Bharata entered his house he noticed that the royal splendor was absent, and so he clasped his mother's lovely feet.

4. She drew glorious Bharata to her breast, embraced him and kissed him on the forehead, and then she began to question him:

5. "How many days is it now since you left your grandfather's residence? You must have flown along in your chariot. Are you not weary from the journey?

6. "Is your grandfather well, and your uncle Yudhājit? Did you enjoy your visit, my son? You must tell me everything."

7. So Kaikeyī fondly questioned him, and lotus-eyed Bharata, the delight of the king, told his mother everything.

8. "Last night was the seventh since I left grandfather's residence. Mother's father is well, and so is my uncle Yudhājit.

9. "The king, the slayer of enemies, gave me riches and precious objects, but they were an encumbrance, and so I left them on the road and came on ahead.

10. "The messengers who carried the order of the king urged me to make haste. Now I have something to ask my mother, and she must answer.

11. "This comfortable gold-worked couch of yours is empty. And the people of Ikṣvāku seem to me to have lost all delight.

12. "The king is usually here in mother's chamber. I have not yet seen him and came here in hopes that I would.

13. "I should like to clasp my father's feet. Answer my question, mother. Could he perhaps be in the chamber of my eldest mother, Kausalyā?"

14. Infatuated by her lust for kingship, Kaikeyī replied to him—an artful mother to an artless son—announcing the grievous event

as if it were good news: "Your father has followed the course all living creatures must follow."

15. When he heard these words Bharata, an honest son of a righteous family, fell suddenly to the ground, shattered by the violence of his grief for his father.

16. Enveloped in grief, sorrowing over the death of his father, mighty Bharata lamented, his mind reeling in confusion.

17. "This couch of Father's used to look so lovely to me. It does not look that way today, with the wise man gone from it."

18. Seeing her godlike son fallen on the ground, anguished and grief-stricken, Kaikeyī tried to help him up and spoke these words:

19. "Come now, get up. Why are you lying there? Men like you do not grieve, glorious prince—good men esteemed in the assembly."

20. But he continued to weep for a long time and to roll about on the ground. Then, shrouded in his many sorrows he said to his mother:

21. "I had imagined the king was going to consecrate Rāma or perform a sacrifice, and so I made the journey in delight.

22. "How differently it has all turned out! My very mind is torn apart, that I shall never again see my father, who always strove so earnestly for my happiness and welfare.

23. "Oh mother, of what illness did the king pass away before I could return? How fortunate are Rāma and all the others who were present to perform the last rites for Father.

24. "But surely the great and illustrious king does not yet know I have come. Otherwise my dear brother would hurry here and bend down to kiss me on the forehead.

25. "Where is that hand so pleasant to the touch, the hand of my tireless dear brother, with which he would always brush away the dust from me?

26. "Have my arrival announced to him at once, to tireless Rāma. That wise man is now father, brother, and every kinsman to me, and I his slave.

27. "For in the eyes of a noble man who knows the way of righteousness one's eldest brother is as one's father. His are the feet I would clasp, for he is my only refuge now.

28. "But my lady, what did the truthful king, my father, say? I just want to hear what last message he might have had for me."

29. So he questioned her, and Kaikeyī replied straightforwardly: "The great king, as good a man as ever lived, went to the next world lamenting, 'Rāma!' and 'O Sītā, Lakṣmaṇa!'

30. "And when at last the law of time caught your father up, the way a snare catches a great elephant, the last words he uttered were these:

31. " 'Fortunate the men who will see Rāma when he comes back with Sītā, and see great-armed Lakṣmaṇa when he comes home.' "

32. Hearing this Bharata became still more distraught, for he anticipated yet another calamity. With an expression of deep distress he questioned his mother further:

33. "But where can the righteous prince have gone, the delight of Kausalyā, with our brother Lakṣmaṇa and Sītā?"

34. Questioned thus his mother again answered straightforwardly. She promptly began to relate the grievous event, supposing it would be taken as good news:

35. "My son, the prince went off in barkcloth garments to the great Daṇḍaka forest, with Vaidehī and Lakṣmaṇa following after him."

36. Bharata was alarmed when he heard this, for doubts had been raised about his brother's conduct. Concerned for the greatness of his dynasty, he began questioning her further:

37. "Rāma did not seize the wealth of any brahman, did he? He did not harm some innocent man, whether rich or poor?

38. "The prince did not covet another man's wife, did he? Why was he exiled to Daṇḍaka wilderness like one who has slain an unborn child?"

39. His capricious mother then began to tell exactly what she had done, and with the same feminine disposition that had made her do it.

40. "No, Rāma did not seize the wealth of any brahman. He harmed no innocent man, rich or poor, and Rāma would never so much as cast his eyes upon the wife of another man.

41. "It was I, my son. As soon as I learned of Rāma's consecration, I demanded that your father award you the kingship and exile Rāma.

42. "Your father followed the proper course of action and did exactly that, and so Rāma and Saumitri were sent away with Sītā.

43. "His beloved son gone from his sight, the glorious protector of the earth was crushed with such grief for his son that he died.

44. "So now you must assume the kingship, as you know to be right. It was on your behalf I did all this, all that I could do.

45. "Therefore, my son, in concert with the chief brahmans—those who know the ritual precepts, under the lead of Vasiṣṭha—you must at once perform according to precept the last rites for the courageous king, and then have yourself consecrated to power over the wide earth."

The end of the sixty-sixth *sarga* of the *Ayodhyākāṇḍa* of the *Śrī Rāmāyaṇa*.

Sarga 67

1. When Bharata learned that his father had passed away and his two brothers were in exile, he was consumed with sorrow and spoke these words:

2. "What possible use have I for kingship, stricken as I am and grieving, bereft of both my father and the brother who is like a father to me?

3. "You have heaped sorrow upon my sorrow, rubbed salt into a wound, by killing the king and making Rāma an ascetic.

4. "Like the night of doom have you come to annihilate this House. My father had no idea he was holding a firebrand in his embrace.

5. "It will be a miracle if Kausalyā and Sumitrā survive this torture of grief for their sons—and all because of you, my very own mother!

6. "My brother is righteous and knows the proper way to behave toward his elders, and surely his behavior toward you was perfect, just as toward his own mother.

7. "My eldest mother, Kausalyā, far-sighted though she is, treated you like a sister in her adherence to the way of righteousness.

8. "And you have sent her accomplished son away in barkcloth garments, to a life in the forest! Can you feel no grief, evil woman?

9. "He is an accomplished and glorious hero who never contemplated evil. What possible purpose could you have had in sight to banish him in clothes of bark?

10. "Was it all for the sake of kingship that you brought about this great misfortune? In your greed, I suppose, you never understood how I felt toward Rāma.

11. "With those tigers among men, Rāma and Lakṣmaṇa, gone from my sight, by virtue of what power would I be able to guard the kingdom?

12. "The great and righteous king himself had great might, yet he would constantly retreat behind his mighty son, like Mount Meru behind its forest.

13. "What strength have I to bear such a burden? I am like a calf before a load only a great ox can draw.

14. "Even were I to acquire the power through stratagems or force of intellect, I would never grant you your wish—not you, a woman so blindly ambitious for her son. I will bring my brother back from the forest, the beloved of his people."

15. So great Bharata spoke—and how hard his words struck, the very opposite of what she had hoped—and he roared out once more in the anguish of his grief, like a lion inside a mountain cave.

The end of the sixty-seventh *sarga* of the *Ayodhyākāṇḍa* of the *Śrī Rāmāyaṇa*.

Sarga 68

1. So Bharata reviled his mother, and in the grip of a wild rage he addressed her once more:

2. "It is you who should be expelled from the kingdom, Kaikeyī, you vicious, wicked woman! And abandoned in accordance with all that is right, may you weep your eyes out without me.

3. "What possible wrong could the king or perfectly righteous Rāma have done you, that because of you they should have found death and banishment both at once?

4. "You are guilty of murdering the unborn by your destruction of this House. May you go to hell, Kaikeyī, and never come to share the afterworld of your husband.

5. "That you could be capable of such evil and so horrible a deed—renouncing the beloved of all the world—makes me fearful on my own account as well.

6. "Because of you my father is gone and Rāma withdrawn to the wilderness, and you have brought infamy upon me in the eyes of every living soul.

7. "O enemy of mine in a mother's guise, malicious woman lusting for kingship! Never speak to me again, depraved murderess of your husband!

8. "Kausalyā and Sumitrā and the rest of my mothers are afflicted by great sorrow and it is all your fault, polluter of our House!

9. "You are no true daughter of Aśvapati, a wise and righteous king, but a demoness born to lay your father's House in ruins.

10. "Because of you righteous Rāma, constant in his devotion to truth, has been driven to the forest, and father has gone to heaven in his grief.

11. "This evil for which you have striven falls upon my head: I am left without my father and abandoned by my brothers, to become an object of hatred to all the world.

12. "You have parted Kausalyā from her son, a woman who has never departed from righteousness. What afterworld can you attain now, evil-scheming creature? You can only go to hell.

13. "Are you not aware, cruel woman, that Rāma—a man of restraint, the refuge of his kinsmen, the eldest son and his father's one equal—that Rāma arose from Kausalyā's very self?

14. "Limb from mother's limb is a son born, and from her heart. That is why she loves him so, because he is her very own, and not mere kin.

15. "Once upon a time, the story goes, righteous Surabhi, the cow held in esteem by the gods, caught sight of two of her sons. They were plowing the broad earth, in a state of stupor.

16. "Seeing her sons upon the earth exhausted at mid-day, she wept in grief for them, and her eyes were flooded with tears.

17. "Clear and fragrant her teardrops fell, and they touched a limb of the great king of gods as he was passing below her.

18. "Indra, wielder of the bolt, saw how the glorious cow was consumed with grief, and the king of the gods was disquieted. He cupped his hands in reverence and addressed her:

19. " 'No great danger threatens us from any quarter, does it? What is the cause of your grief? Tell me, all-beneficent cow.'

20. "So the wise king of the gods spoke, and Surabhi composed herself and eloquently replied:

21. " 'Perish the thought! No, nothing threatens you from any quarter, overlord of the deathless gods. I am only grieving for two of my sons, who languish in their sorry plight.

22. " 'I see how haggard and desolate the oxen are, how the rays of the sun are burning them, and how the plowman beats them, overlord of the gods.

23. " 'They were born of my body, and for me to see them sorrowful and oppressed by burdens is agony. There is nothing so dear as a son.'

24. "The wish-granting cow had countless sons and even so she grieved. How much more will Kausalyā grieve, who must live without Rāma?

25. "The good woman has but one son, and you have made her childless. For this you shall reap sorrow forever, both in this world and when you die.

26. "As for me, there is no question but that I must make full amends to my brother and father, and so restore our glory.

27. "I will have Kausalyā's splendid son brought back and go myself into the forest where sages make their home."

28. So he spoke, and with the look of an elephant in the wilderness driven with prods and goads, he fell upon the ground in a rage, hissing like a snake.

29. His eyes bloodshot, his clothes in disarray, all his jewelry cast aside, the enemy-slaying prince lay fallen on the ground like the banner of Indra, Śacī's lord, when the festival is over.

The end of the sixty-eighth *sarga* of the *Ayodhyākāṇḍa* of the *Śrī Rāmāyaṇa*.

Sarga 69

1. As great Bharata was crying out, the sound reached Kausalyā, and she said to Sumitrā:

2. "Far-sighted Bharata, the son of that savage woman Kaikeyī has returned. I want to see him."

3. With this, she set out to Bharata, her face drained of color and her garment filthy, trembling and almost insensible.

4. But at that same moment Rāma's younger brother was setting out to Kausalyā's residence, accompanied by Śatrughna.

5. And when Śatrughna and Bharata saw Kausalyā, they were overcome with sorrow. She dropped down, unconscious in the anguish of her sorrow, and they took her in their embrace.

6. Then, in deep sorrow, Kausalyā spoke to Bharata. "You lusted for the kingship and here you have it unchallenged—and how quickly Kaikeyī secured it for you by her savage deed.

7. "But what advantage did that cruel and scheming Kaikeyī hope to gain by driving out my son in clothes of bark to live in the forest?

8. "Why doesn't Kaikeyī at once drive me out as well to where my son is staying, my glorious Hiraṇyanābha?

9. "Then again, I should be happy to go to Rāghava on my own, with Sumitrā to attend me and the sacred fires carried at our head.

10. "But no, truly it is up to you to send me there yourself, where my son, the tiger among men, is practicing austerities.

11. "For this vast kingdom is now yours; she has delivered it to you, with all its abundance of wealth and grain, all its teeming elephants, horses, chariots."

12. As Kausalyā lamented like this, shrouded in her many sorrows, Bharata cupped his hands in reverence and addressed her:

13. "My lady, why do you upbraid me? I am guiltless and knew nothing of this. You know how deep and enduring is my love for Rāghava.

14. "May that man never come to think in harmony with the sacred texts who sanctioned my elder brother's going—Rāma, the very best of men, who always keeps his word.

15. "May he come to serve the most wicked of men, may he pass

urine facing the sun and kick a sleeping cow, he who sanctioned my brother's going.

16. "May the unrighteousness attaching to a master who forces an onerous task upon his servant without remuneration attach to him who sanctioned my brother's going.

17. "May the sin that beings incur in turning traitor to a king who has protected them like his own children be reckoned to his account who sanctioned my brother's going.

18. "May the unrighteousness attaching to a king who levies a sixth portion in tax without guarding his subjects attach to him who sanctioned my brother's going.

19. "May the sin men incur who promise priests their fee at a sacrifice and then cry off be reckoned to his account who sanctioned my brother's going.

20. "May he never honor the code of the brave in battle where elephants, horses, and chariots are crowding and weapons flying thick, he who sanctioned my brother's going.

21. "The subtle meaning of the sacred texts, which the wise impart with so much care, may the evil-hearted man forever lose who sanctioned my brother's going.

22. "May he eat milk-rice, sesame-rice, and goat's flesh to no purpose; may he show contempt for his gurus, the ruthless man who sanctioned my brother's going.

23. "May his children and wife and servants huddle about him at home while he alone eats delicacies, the man who sanctioned my brother's going.

24. "May he be guilty of the sin laid to one who murders a king, a woman, a child, or an elder, or who abandons his dependents.

25. "May the sin charged to one who sleeps through both the morning and evening worship be reckoned to his account who sanctioned my brother's going.

26. "May he be guilty of the sins of arson, violation of a guru's bed, and treachery to allies.

27. "May he never show obedience to the gods, his ancestors, his mother or father, he who sanctioned my brother's going.

28. "May he be excluded at once, this very moment, from the deeds practiced by the good, from the praises of the good, from the world of the good, he who sanctioned my brother's going."

29. In this way the prince tried to reassure Kausalyā, bereft of her husband and son, and then, in the anguish of his sorrow, he collapsed.

30. They were heavy curses Bharata had called down upon his head, and as he lay insensible and consumed with grief, Kausalyā addressed him:

31. "This sorrow of mine, my son, has grown only greater. That you should curse yourself with such curses chokes the very breath of life within me.

32. "Thank God, my child, that your own thoughts never swerved from righteousness any more than those of Lakṣmaṇa. If what you promise me is true, you shall attain the world the good attain."

33. So great Bharata lamented in the anguish of his sorrow, his mind in turmoil from all the confusion and besieged by grief.

34. On and on he wildly lamented; he fell in a stupor to the ground; heaving deep sighs all the while he passed the night lost in grief.

The end of the sixty-ninth *sarga* of the *Ayodhyākānda* of the *Śrī Rāmāyana*.

Sarga 70

1. As Kaikeyī's son Bharata still lay consumed with grief, Vasiṣṭha, most eloquent of seers, came and eloquently spoke to him:

2. "Glorious prince, I pray you, enough of this grief. It is time you performed the obsequies for the lord of men."

3. Bharata regained his composure on hearing Vasiṣṭha's words, and wise in the ways of righteousness he commenced the performance of all the funeral rites.

4-5. The protector of the earth was removed from the oily liquid and laid upon the earth. His face had a yellowish tinge, and he seemed to be asleep. The son then had Daśaratha laid upon a sumptuous bed encrusted with all kinds of gems, and he began to lament over him in deep sorrow.

6. "Why did you take this decision, your Majesty, when I was away, before I could return, after sending righteous Rāma into exile with mighty Lakṣmaṇa?

7. "Where are you going, great king, leaving your people in sorrow when the lion among men, tireless Rāma, has already left them?

8. "Who is there, your Majesty, to maintain the security of your city, now that you have gone to heaven, dear Father, and Rāma has withdrawn to the forest?

9. "The earth has been widowed, your Majesty; bereft of you it is cast into gloom. And the city looks to me like the night without a moon."

10. So Bharata lamented, sick at heart, until the great seer Vasiṣṭha addressed him once more:

11. "The funeral rites must be performed for the lord of the people. Let it all be done fully, great-armed prince, and without delay."

12. "So be it," Bharata replied, heeding Vasiṣṭha's command, and he urged all the sacrificial priests, the family priests, and preceptors to make haste.

13. The sacred fires of the lord of men had been placed outside the fire-sanctuary, and the priests and sacrificers fetched them in accordance with the ritual precepts.

14. Disconsolate and choked with sobs, his attendants raised the lifeless king onto a litter and bore him out.

15. Ahead of the king went people strewing the way with gold and silver and different kinds of garments.

16. Others brought sandalwood, aloe, balsam, pine, *padmaka* and *devadāru* wood and built a pyre.

17. After placing various other fragrant substances on the pyre, the priests laid the protector of the earth in the center.

18. The priests made offering to the fire and intoned prayers for him, while the chanters of the *Sāmaveda* sang the hymns in accordance with the sacred texts.

19. In palanquins and carriages, according to their rank, his wives had come out from the city in the company of the elders.

20. And as the flames engulfed the king and the priests walked leftward around him, the grieving women did likewise, with Kausalyā at their head.

21. At that hour could be heard a cry like the cry of curlews as the anguished women by the thousands raised their piteous wail.

22. Afterwards, amid uncontrolled weeping and constant lamentation, the women went to the bank of the Sarayū and alighted from their carriages.

23. After making the funeral libation, the king's wives, the counselors, the family priests, and Bharata tearfully re-entered the city, where they sat upon the ground to pass the ten-day period of mourning.

The end of the seventieth *sarga* of the *Ayodhyākāṇḍa* of the *Śrī Rāmāyaṇa*.

Sarga 71

1. When the ten-day period was over, the prince purified himself, and on the twelfth day he had the *śrāddha* rites performed.

2. To the brahmans he gave precious objects, money, and abundant food—goat's flesh and much white rice—and cows by the hundreds.

3. Male and female slaves, carriages, and grand houses did the prince bestow upon the brahmans as the funerary gifts of the king.

4-5. On the thirteenth day at the hour of dawn, great-armed Bharata went out to perform the ceremony of purification at the foot of his father's pyre. Again he was stunned by grief, and he began to lament. His throat choked with sobs, he cried out in his deep sorrow:

6. "Oh dear Father, my brother Rāghava, to whose care you committed me, is banished to the forest, and you have left me in an utter void!

7. "My king, my father, where have you gone? You have left mother Kausalyā helpless, with her son, her one refuge, banished to the forest."

8. And when he saw the ash-brown circle where the charred bones lay, the place where his father's body had met extinction, he gave way to despair and cried aloud.

9. He was desolated by the sight of it and fell weeping to the ground, the way a pole-banner in honor of Śakra might fall while being fixed in place.

10. His ministers all flew to the aid of the pious prince, just like the seers when Yayāti fell at his final hour.

11. Seeing Bharata overwhelmed with grief, Śatrughna likewise fell senseless to the earth, fondly remembering the protector of the earth.

12. He was nearly out of his mind, and like a madman he began to lament in his profound sorrow, recalling with every passing minute another of his father's virtues.

13. "Churned up in all its fury by Mantharā, with Kaikeyī as its raging beast and the offer of the boon its overwhelming flood, a sea of grief has swallowed us!

14. "Where have you gone, dear father, leaving Bharata to lament, a boy so delicate and young, whom you always treated so indulgently?

15. "Remember how you used to give us all so many delicacies to choose from, so many drinks, garments, and ornaments—who will do that for us now?

16. "If the earth does not dissolve at once, though bereft of you, great and righteous king, it never will, not even at the hour of universal dissolution.

17. "With father gone to heaven and Rāma withdrawn to the wilderness, what strength have I to live? I will enter a blazing fire.

18. "Bereft of my brother and father, I will not enter an empty Ayodhyā that Ikṣvāku once protected. No, I will enter a grove of asceticism."

19. Hearing the brothers' lamentation and reflecting on their calamity, the attendants were all afflicted with an anguish even sharper than before.

20. In despair and exhaustion, both Bharata and Śatrughna lay writhing on the ground like bulls with shattered horns.

21. But their father's family priest, the wise Vasiṣṭha, maintaining his usual composure, helped Bharata to his feet and said to him:

22. "There are three dualities to which every living thing without exception is subject. They cannot be avoided, and so you must not act this way."

23. Meanwhile Sumantra helped Śatrughna to his feet, consoling him and sagely explaining how all living things are born and so must die.

24. The glorious tigers among men stood up, but they both looked like banners of Indra ruined by the sun and rain.

25. The sons wiped away the tears from their reddened eyes and mourned in desolation until, at the ministers' urging, they turned to the other rites.

The end of the seventy-first *sarga* of the *Ayodhyākāṇḍa* of the *Śrī Rāmāyaṇa*.

Sarga 72

1. Now, as the grief-stricken Bharata was making the journey back, Lakṣmaṇa's younger brother Śatrughna addressed him with these words:

2. "Mighty Rāma, the refuge of all creatures in sorrow, and of himself most of all, has been banished to the forest by a woman!

3. "And what of Lakṣmaṇa, the powerful, mighty Lakṣmaṇa? Why did he not free Rāma, even if it meant deposing father?

4. "If he had fully weighed both sides of the issue, he would have deposed the king at the very first—a man who was under a woman's power and bent on an evil course."

5. As Lakṣmaṇa's younger brother Śatrughna was speaking, the hunchback appeared at the front gate, all adorned with jewelry.

6. She was anointed with essence of sandalwood and dressed in queenly garments, and with her many-colored belts and sashes she looked like a monkey tied up with rope.

7. Catching sight of the hunchback, the cause of all the trouble, a gatekeeper ruthlessly seized her, at the same time calling to Śatrughna:

8. "Here is the evil, malicious woman! It is her doing that Rāma is in the forest and your father has given up his mortal body. Do with her as you see fit."

9. When he heard this the devoted and sorrowing Śatrughna cried out to all the servants of the inner chamber:

10. "This is the woman who has brought such bitter sorrow upon my brothers and my father. Let her now taste the fruit of her malicious deed."

11. And with this, he violently seized the hunchback as she stood among her female companions, so that the house resounded with her cries.

12. Her companions stared with wild consternation at the raging Śatrughna and then fled in every direction.

13. And they all took counsel together: "In the course of his mad attack he will annihilate us all.

14. "Glorious Kausalyā is compassionate, generous, and righteous. We must take refuge with her. She will ensure our safety."

15. With eyes coppery red in his fury Śatrughna, slayer of enemies, dragged the howling hunchback over the ground.

16. And as Mantharā was being dragged this way and that, her many-colored pieces of jewelry were shattered in fragments all over the ground.

17. Scattered around the majestic palace the jewelry made it sparkle all the more, like the sky in autumn.

18. In his rage, the powerful bull among men, still holding her in his powerful grip, cried out bitterly, heaping scorn on Kaikeyī.

19. Śatrughna's bitter and sorrowful words plunged Kaikeyī even deeper into sorrow, and terrified by his threats she sought refuge with her son.

20. Bharata glanced at her and called out to the raging Śatrughna, "If any creature is not to be slain it is a woman. Forbear!

21. "I would kill this woman myself, this evil, wicked Kaikeyī, were it not that righteous Rāma would condemn me for matricide.

22. "If righteous Rāghava were to learn that even this hunchback were slain, he would surely never speak to you or me again."

23. Upon hearing Bharata's words, Lakṣmaṇa's younger brother Śatrughna checked his fury and released Mantharā.

24. Panting and anguished with sorrow, Mantharā fell at Kaikeyī's feet, lamenting wretchedly.

25. Bharata's mother looked at the hunchback and began gently to soothe her as she lay anguished and stunned from Śatrughna's abuse, staring like a trapped curlew.

The end of the seventy-second *sarga* of the *Ayodhyākāṇḍa* of the *Śrī Rāmāyaṇa.*

Sarga 73

1. On the fourteenth day, at the hour of dawn, the deputies of the king convened and addressed Bharata.

2. "Daśaratha, our most revered guru, has gone to heaven, having first banished Rāma, his eldest son, and mighty Lakṣmaṇa.

3. "O glorious prince, you must become our king this very day. Our kingdom is without a leader, and only by mere chance has it not yet come to harm.

4. "Your people and the guildsmen await you, prince Rāghava, with all the materials for the consecration in hand.

5. "Assume the kingship, Bharata, the great office of your fathers and forefathers. Have yourself consecrated, bull among men, and protect us."

6. The devoted Bharata reverently circled all the articles for the consecration and then made this reply to all the people:

7. "It has always been the custom of our House that the kingship passes to the eldest son. You men are aware of this and ought not to ask such a thing of me.

8. "Rāma, our elder brother, shall be the lord of earth. As for me, I will live in the wilderness for the nine years and five.

9. "Let a great army be marshaled, complete with all four divisions; for I myself will bring my eldest brother Rāma back from the forest.

10. "And all the consecration materials standing ready here I will carry in the vanguard as I go to the forest on Rāma's behalf.

11. "Then and there I will consecrate Rāma, tiger among men, and bring him back in the vanguard, like a sacred fire from the place of sacrifice.

12. "I will never grant this woman her wish, she who but faintly resembles a mother. I will live in the trackless forest, and Rāma shall be king.

13. "Let a road be made by artisans, let the rough sections be leveled out, let guards accompany them, and men to scout out the trackless regions on the way."

14. When the prince had ended this speech on behalf of Rāma, all the people answered him with an earnest prayer for majesty:

15. "May Śrī of the Lotus ever attend you for what you have spoken here, for your willingness to bestow the earth upon the eldest prince."

16. When the nobles heard the earnest words the prince uttered for all to hear, tears of joy for him welled up in their eyes and ran down their cheeks.

17. The ministers and members of the council had listened joyfully to his words. Their grief was allayed, and they said to him, "On your orders, best of men, the devoted people and companies of artisans shall be given instructions concerning the road."

The end of the seventy-third *sarga* of the *Ayodhyākāṇḍa* of the *Śrī Rāmāyaṇa*.

Sarga 74

1-3. Now surveyors and men trained in measurement, powerful excavators who were zealous in their work; engineers, laborers, craftsmen, and men skilled in machinery; carpenters, road-levelers, woodcutters, well-drillers, pavers, cane-weavers, and capable guides all set out from the city.

4. Proceeding joyfully to the appointed region, that vast flood of people resembled the great rushing tide of the sea under a full moon.

5. The skilled road-builders took their places each in his own contingent, and with all their different kinds of tools they set out bright and early.

6. Through vines and creepers and shrubs, through stumps and boulders and all kinds of trees, the workers cut and built a road.

7. In treeless areas some of them transplanted trees, while elsewhere some set to work chopping with axes, mattocks, and scythes.

8. Others, stronger men, cleared the strong-rooted stalks of beard grass and the more impenetrable areas.

9. Still others took dirt and filled dry wells and gaping holes, while some leveled out the tracts of land wherever it was too steep.

10. Men then bridged the areas that needed bridging, pounded those that needed pounding, and drained those in need of draining.

11. In no time at all they enlarged the volume and shape of many streams so that they looked like the sea, and they built various kinds of reservoirs embellished with benches.

12-13. The road for the army was paved and whitewashed, lined with blossoming trees, sounding with the calls of flocks of wild birds; it was adorned with banners, sprinkled with sandalwood water, ornamented with all sorts of flowers, and it shone with the brilliance of the Milky Way.

14-15. Now, certain sites in the loveliest tracts where fruit grew rich and sweet were selected as rest areas for the great Bharata. The superintendents, diligently following the orders they had received, gave orders to beautify these places with special ornamental work till they looked like perfect ornaments.

16. Under auspicious constellations and at auspicious hours the experts laid the foundations for great Bharata's rest areas.

17-19. The workers spread heaps of sand around the sites, built moats to encircle them, erected poles and crossbeams and bars. The sites were adorned with lovely lanes and garlanded with banners. Well-constructed thoroughfares ran through them all. And with their lofty, spire-topped mansions that seemed to wander lost in the sky, they resembled the city of Indra itself.

20-21. Where the royal road met the Jāhnavī—with its groves of different trees, its cool, clear water and shoals of large fish—it sparkled like the clear vault of heaven at night when the moon and crowds of stars embellish it. It was a lovely road every step of the way, built by master artisans.

The end of the seventy-fourth *sarga* of the *Ayodhyākāṇḍa* of the *Śrī Rāmāyaṇa*.

Sarga 75

1. Late in the night of Nāndīmukha, bards and genealogists, masters of all the fine points of speech, came to sing the praises of Bharata and wish him good fortune.

2. Struck by golden drumsticks, the drum of the nightwatch resounded, while conches by the hundreds and high- and low-pitched instruments were sounded.

3. The loud sound of pipes seemed to fill the heavens, though it only brought more lacerating grief to the grief-stricken Bharata.

4. On awakening, he put a halt to the clamor, exclaiming, "I am not the king!" Then turning to Śatrughna, he said,

5. "See, Śatrughna, what great wrong these people are doing because of Kaikeyī. And King Daśaratha is gone, leaving me all these troubles.

6. "This royal majesty, founded on righteousness, belonged to him, the great and righteous king. And now it is adrift like a ship on the water without a helmsman."

7. So Bharata wildly lamented, and as the women watched, they all broke out in piteous, shrill weeping.

8. He was still lost in lamentation as glorious Vasiṣṭha, the authority in all matters of kingship, made his way to the assembly hall of the lord of the Ikṣvākus.

9. It was a lovely hall fashioned of gold and richly studded with jewels and gems, and it looked like Sudharmā as the righteous family priest entered with his attendants.

10. The master of all the *vedas* sat down upon a golden bench covered with a costly spread and gave his instructions to the heralds.

11. "Go at once and diligently fetch the brahmans, kshatriyas, soldiers, ministers, and commanders of the troops. There is urgent business to which we must attend."

12. Soon there arose a tumultuous din as the people began arriving on chariots, horses, and elephants.

13. And as Bharata approached, the subjects called out their greetings to him just as they used to greet Daśaratha, the way the deathless gods greet Indra, lord of the hundred rites.

14. The hall was like a pool filled with gems and shells and pebbles, its waters still despite the teeming fish and serpents. And the son of Daśaratha lent it such beauty as it had in the past, when Daśaratha himself was there.

The end of the seventy-fifth *sarga* of the *Ayodhyākāṇḍa* of the *Śrī Rāmāyaṇa*.

Sarga 76

1. Crowded with hosts of nobles all favorably inclined toward Bharata, the assembly hall appeared to the wise Vasiṣṭha like a night when the moon is full.

2. As the nobles took their seats according to custom, the hall looked like a full-moon evening when the clouds have vanished.

3. Observing that all the king's subjects were represented in full, the family priest, knowing the ways of righteousness, commenced this gentle address to Bharata:

4. "My son, King Daśaratha went to heaven in the performance of righteousness, after making over to you this prosperous land abounding in wealth and grain.

5. "Rāma likewise held fast to truth, mindful of the righteous ways that good men follow. He could no more cast aside his father's command than the rising hare-marked moon its light.

6. "Your father and brother have bestowed on you unchallenged kingship. You must take possession of it and gladden the ministers. Have yourself consecrated at once.

7. "Let the sovereigns of the north and west and south, and the westernmost ones who live by the sea, deliver up untold riches to you."

8. Hearing these words, Bharata was overwhelmed with grief. Knowing what was right and anxious to abide by it, he turned his thoughts to Rāma.

9. With words unclear because of his sobbing and in a voice like the call of the gray goose, the young prince began to lament and to rebuke the family priest in the midst of the assembly:

10. "The kingship belongs to that wise prince who has practiced chastity, perfected his knowledge, and always striven for righteousness. How would a person like me dare seize it from him?

11. "How could a son born of Daśaratha usurp the kingship? The kingship, and I myself, belong to Rāma. Please see to it that your advice is in keeping with righteousness.

12. "Righteous Kākutstha, the eldest son and the best, the equal of Dilīpa and Nahuṣa, must obtain the kingship just as Daśaratha did.

13. "The other course is an evil one, followed only by ignoble men, and leading to hell. Were I to take it I should become a blot on the House of the Ikṣvākus in the eyes of all the world.

14. "I do not condone the evil deed my mother has done. Though I am here and he in the trackless forest, I cup my hands in reverence and bow to him.

15. "I will go after Rāma—he is my king, the best of men. Rāghava deserves not only this, but kingship over all three worlds!"

16. When they heard these righteous words, the men of the assembly, whose thoughts were ever with Rāma, all shed tears of joy.

17. "If I cannot bring my noble brother back from the forest, then in that very forest will I stay, just like my noble brother Lakṣmaṇa.

18. "I will use every means in my power to force him to return to the presence of you just, virtuous, and honorable noblemen."

19. With this, righteous Bharata, who so cherished his brother, turned to the skillful counselor Sumantra standing by his side and said:

20. "Make haste and go, Sumantra! On my authority muster the army at once and give the command for the expedition."

21. So great Bharata spoke, and Sumantra went off in delight and gave all the orders as he had been directed and had hoped to do.

22. The subjects and the marshals of the army were delighted to receive the command for an expedition to bring Rāghava back.

23. The soldiers' wives, too, when they learned of the expedition, were all delighted, and in each and every house they pressed their husbands to hurry.

24. The marshals rallied the entire army, the soldiers, the horses, the fast oxcarts, and the chariots swift as thought.

25. Bharata saw that the army was ready as he stood in the midst of his gurus. Turning to Sumantra, who was at his side, he said, "Hurry and bring my chariot."

26. He received Bharata's command in great delight and came forth with a chariot harnessed with splendid horses.

27. Bharata Rāghava was a courageous prince who held fast to truth and strove to act truthfully. His glorious guru was away in the great wilderness, and he was ready to go and beg his forgiveness. The words he spoke were fitting when he said:

28. "Make haste, Sumantra, and go to the leaders of the army to have the troops marshaled. Rāma is in the forest, and I mean to beg his forgiveness and bring him back for the welfare of the world."

29. So Bharata duly commanded the charioteer, and thereby answered Sumantra's every wish. He gave instructions to all the leading subjects, to the heads of the army, and to all their many loved ones.

30. And then the men of every household, the kshatriyas, *vaiśyas*, *śūdras*, and brahmans too, made haste and harnessed their camel-carts, their elephants, asses, and purebred horses.

The end of the seventy-sixth *sarga* of the *Ayodhyākāṇḍa* of the *Śrī Rāmāyaṇa*.

Sarga 77

1. Bharata made haste, and at that early hour he boarded his excellent chariot and set forth swiftly, eager to see Rāma.

2. Before him went all the counselors and family priests in horse-drawn chariots that resembled the chariot of the sun.

3. Nine thousand elephants marshaled according to precept fol-

lowed Bharata, the delight of the House of the Ikṣvākus, as he went.

4. Sixty thousand chariots and archers with every sort of weapon followed the glorious prince Bharata as he went.

5. One hundred thousand horses, each with a rider, followed the glorious prince Bharata Rāghava as he went.

6. Kaikeyī, Sumitrā, and glorious Kausalyā traveled in a resplendent carriage, delighted to be bringing Rāma back.

7. Throngs of nobles went along in hopes of seeing Rāma and Lakṣmaṇa. With delight in their hearts, they held animated conversation about him:

8. "When shall we see Rāma, raincloud-dark, great-armed Rāma, steady of courage and firm of vows, who allays the grief of the world?"

9. "For the mere sight of Rāghava will dispel our grief, as the rising sun dispels the darkness of all the world."

10. The men of the city carried on such heartfelt conversation as this and embraced each other as they made their way along.

11. Every estimable subject, the merchants and all the others, set off in delight to find Rāma.

12-15. Jewelers and master potters, weavers and weapon-smiths, workers in peacock feathers, sawyers, bauble-makers, gem-cutters, workers in ivory, plasterers, perfumers, renowned goldsmiths, blanket-cleaners, bath attendants, valets, physicians, incense-merchants and vintners, washermen and tailors, headmen of villages and hamlets, actors with their women, and fishermen—all were making the journey.

16. And thousands of brahmans all together, masters of the *vedas* esteemed for their conduct, followed Bharata in their oxcarts as he went.

17. Everyone was handsomely attired in clean clothing and anointed with pure coppery cream, and on a great array of vehicles they slowly followed Bharata.

18. Delighted and cheerful the attendant army followed Kaikeyī's son Bharata, and soon it came to a halt.

19. Observing the army stop, and seeing the gracious waters of the Ganges, Bharata addressed all his advisers with these well-spoken words:

20. "Have my army pitch camp anywhere it chooses. Straightway tomorrow, when we are rested, we shall cross the great river.

21. "As for myself, I wish to go down to the river and offer water to the departed king as part of his obsequies."

22. So he spoke, and all together the ministers replied with a word of assent. Then they ordered each group to pitch camp separately and wherever they pleased.

23. When the army, magnificent with its equipment all arrayed, was encamped along the great river Ganges, Bharata took up his dwelling and began to ponder how to bring great Rāma back.

The end of the seventy-seventh *sarga* of the *Ayodhyākāṇḍa* of the *Śrī Rāmāyaṇa*.

Sarga 78

1. Now, the king of the Niṣādas, seeing the bannered army encamped along the river Ganges, hurried off at once to speak with his kinsmen.

2. "A great army has appeared here, as vast as the sea. I cannot imagine what its purpose might be, however much thought I give it.

3. "There is a huge standard upon a chariot, marked with a *kovidāra* tree. Has someone come to take us fishermen captive, or to kill us?

4. "Or is it perhaps Bharata, Kaikeyī's son, marching out to slay Rāma Dāśarathi, whom his father has exiled from the kingdom?

5. "Rāma Dāśarathi is both my master and my friend. We must champion his cause. Arm yourselves and take up positions here on the bank of the Ganges.

6. "All the fishermen are to take up positions along the river Ganges. Guard the river with your troops, provisioning yourselves with meat, roots, and fruit.

7. "Let the younger fishermen," he exhorted them, "arm themselves and take up their positions, a hundred each on five hundred boats.

8. "But should it turn out that Bharata is not ill-disposed toward Rāma, this army of his may safely cross the Ganges today."

9. With this, Guha, overlord of the Niṣādas, took gifts and fish, meat, and wine, and went forth to meet Bharata.

10. The valiant charioteer observed him approaching, and with the deference in which he was practiced he informed Bharata.

11. "Here is the chief with a large escort of kinsmen. He is an old friend of your brother's and knows the Daṇḍaka wilderness well.

12. "Let Guha then come to see you, Kākutstha. The overlord of the Niṣādas will undoubtedly know where Rāma and Lakṣmaṇa are."

13. When Bharata heard Sumantra's just words, he replied, "Have Guha come to see me at once."

14. Guha was delighted to receive permission, and escorted by his kinsmen he humbly advanced before Bharata and spoke:

15. "This region is your pleasure-garden. You caught us here quite unawares. But we all bid you a welcome stay among our tribe of fishermen.

16. "Here are roots and fruit provided by the Niṣādas, meat both fresh and dried and a great variety of forest fare.

17. "I hope your army will spend the night here—we shall supply it well with food. Then tomorrow, after we have honored you with all you could desire, you and your soldiers may go your way."

The end of the seventy-eighth *sarga* of the *Ayodhyākāṇḍa* of the *Śrī Rāmāyaṇa*.

Sarga 79

1. When Guha, overlord of the Niṣādas, had spoken, high-minded Bharata made this reasoned and purposeful reply:

2. "Dear friend of my guru, you have, in fact, already fulfilled my greatest wish, in that you are willing all on your own to show hospitality to such an army as mine."

3. Such were the earnest words of mighty, majestic Bharata. And once again he addressed Guha, overlord of the Niṣādas.

4. "What way do I take, Guha, to go to Bharadvāja's ashram? This region is densely forested and the lowlands by the Ganges are hard to traverse."

5. When he heard the words of the wise prince, Guha the forest dweller cupped his hands in reverence and replied:

6. "The fishermen shall go with you, alert and armed with bows, and so will I, glorious prince.

7. "But you are not setting out with ill will toward tireless Rāma, are you? This great army of yours somehow arouses my suspicions."

8. Thus Guha addressed him, and Bharata, who was pure as the sky, replied in an even voice:

9. "May the hour that brings such disaster never come! Please, harbor no suspicions about me. For Rāghava is my eldest brother and like a father to me.

10. "I am setting forth to bring back Kākutstha, who is living in the forest. Do not imagine otherwise, Guha. I am telling you the truth."

11. His face beamed with joy when he heard what Bharata said, and joyfully he replied to Bharata:

12. "How blessed you are! I know of no one to equal you on the face of the earth. For although the kingship came to you effortlessly, you are prepared to give it up.

13. "You are prepared to bring back Rāma when he is in such a plight, and for this you shall win everlasting fame throughout the worlds."

14. As Guha and Bharata were conversing in this fashion, the sun's light began to fade, and night closed in.

15. After their army was encamped and Guha had provided for them generously, majestic Bharata and Śatrughna went to bed.

16. But grief brought on by anxious thoughts of Rāma troubled great Bharata—and how little such a man deserved it, one who had always kept his eyes fixed on the way of righteousness.

17. Rāghava was consumed with a searing inner blaze; it was like the flame hidden within a tree that a forest fire has scorched.

18. From the fire of grief he broke out in sweat, and the sweat poured down his every limb, like the icy water Himālaya pours down when the sun's rays heat it.

19-20. The son of Kaikeyī was crushed under a great mountain of sorrow, with its deep gorge of brooding, its minerals of heaving sighs, thickets of desolation, numberless creatures of delirium, plants and rushes of misery, and peaks of grief, care, and woe.

21. And so high-minded Bharata, wakeful and utterly distraught, came out with his people to meet with Guha, and again Guha offered him solace over his elder brother.

The end of the seventy-ninth *sarga* of the *Ayodhyākāṇḍa* of the *Śrī Rāmāyaṇa*.

Sarga 80

1. Guha the forest dweller then began to describe to the exalted Bharata the fidelity of great Lakṣmaṇa.

2. "When virtuous Lakṣmaṇa was keeping his vigil, mounting close guard over his brother, his splendid bow and arrows in his hands, I said to him:

3. " 'Here is a comfortable bed, my friend, made ready on your behalf. Lie down and rest in comfort upon it, delight of the Rāghavas.

4. " 'My people are all used to such pains; you are used to comfort. Righteous prince, we will stay awake and stand guard over him.

5. " 'There is no one on earth dearer to me than Rāma. Do not be anxious. Would I speak a lie to your face?

6. " 'Whatever hope I may have in this world for great glory, for the full acquisition of righteousness or of simple wealth, I have by reason of his grace.

7. " 'And I for my part, bow in hand and with all my own kinsmen, will protect my dear friend Rāma as he lies asleep with Sītā.

8. " 'I have wandered the forest all my life, and nothing happens here without my knowing of it. Moreover, we are prepared to withstand in battle even an army of four divisions.'

9. "When we had addressed him in this way, great Lakṣmaṇa entreated us all, with righteousness alone in view:

10. " 'How, while Dāśarathi is lying on the ground with Sītā, could I find sleep—or any happiness in life?

11. " 'Look at him, Guha, reposing with Sītā on the grass, a man whom all the gods and *asuras* could not withstand in battle.

12. " 'This is the only one of Daśaratha's sons to resemble him in every trait; a son obtained by means of great austerities and all kinds of heavy labors.

13. " 'With him in banishment the king will not long remain alive. The earth will surely soon be widowed.

14. " 'The women must have cried out their last great cries and ceased in exhaustion. The din has surely ceased by now in the king's palace.

15. " 'I have little hope that Kausalyā, the king, or my mother will live out this night.

16. " 'Even if my mother should live through it to look after Śatrughna, Kausalyā is so sorrowful that she, who bore this one heroic son, will perish.

17. " 'And my father, who never got the wish that just eluded him, who never installed Rāma in the kingship, will perish, too.

18. " 'And when that moment comes, when father passes away and they purify the lord of the land with all the rites for the dead, they will have attained their object.

19-21. " 'Then they will stroll at their ease through my father's capital, through its lovely squares and well-ordered thoroughfares; with its mansions and palaces, adorned with every precious object; with its teeming elephants, horses, chariots; sounding with the sound of pipes, stocked with every luxury, thronging with delighted and prosperous people, dotted with orchards and gardens, a place of crowded fairs and festivals.

22. " 'If only we might happily return when this period is over, to find him well and his promise fulfilled.'

23. "So the night passed with the great prince standing there mourning like this.

24. "At daybreak, when the sun grew bright, the two of them matted their hair and went down to the bank of the Bhāgīrathī, where I had them comfortably ferried across.

25. "Their hair matted, dressed in garments of bark, carrying splendid arrows, bows, and swords, the two princes, slayers of enemies,

powerful as bull elephants, glanced back often as they left with Sītā."

The end of the eightieth *sarga* of the *Ayodhyākāṇḍa* of the *Śrī Rāmāyaṇa*.

Sarga 81

1. As soon as he heard Guha's painful words, Bharata was plunged into agonizing thought.

2-3. That delicate young man, so courageous and handsome, with the shoulders of a lion, great arms and large lotus-shaped eyes, recovered for a moment, but then in profound distress he suddenly collapsed, like an elephant pierced near the heart by goads.

4. Seeing Bharata in this state, Śatrughna came close to him, and as he clasped him in his embrace he wept aloud, grief-stricken and nearly insensible.

5. All of Bharata's mothers flew to him then, women already haggard from fasting, desolate, and tortured by the calamity that had befallen their husband.

6. They cried as they gathered around him where he lay fallen on the ground. But Kausalyā was most distraught; she edged close to him and clasped him in her embrace.

7. As a loving cow might nuzzle her calf, the poor woman nuzzled Bharata. Weeping and sick with grief she asked:

8. "My son, you have no illness, have you, that gives your body pain? The life of this royal House now depends on you.

9. "To see you, my son, gives me strength to live, with Rāma and his brother gone. Now that King Daśaratha has departed you are our only defender.

10. "You have not heard any bad news, have you, about Lakṣmaṇa or my son—the only son I have—who has gone to the forest with his wife?"

11. After a moment glorious Bharata revived and, still weeping, he reassured Kausalyā. Then he said to Guha:

12. "Where did my brother, Sītā, and Lakṣmaṇa spend the night? What bed had they to sleep on, what did they eat? Tell me, Guha."

13. Thus questioned, Guha, overlord of the Niṣādas, told Bharata what sorts of refreshments he had provided for Rāma, his dear and kindly guest.

14. "I offered a variety of foods in great quantity for Rāma's meal, cooked food and fruit of different sorts.

15. "But the truthful Rāma refused it all. He heeded the code of kshatriyas and would not accept it.

16. " 'It is not for us to take, my friend. Ours is always to give' were the words with which great Rāma entreated us, your majesty.

17. "Glorious Rāghava only drank water, which Lakṣmaṇa drew for him, and both he and Sītā then fasted.

18. "Lakṣmaṇa had a little of the water that was left over, and all three, silently and intently, performed the evening worship.

19. "Afterwards Saumitri himself fetched some straw and quickly made a lovely bed for Rāghava.

20. "Then Rāma lay down with Sītā upon the pallet, and after washing their feet, Lakṣmaṇa withdrew.

21. "It was at the foot of the almond tree over there, upon that very grass that the two of them, Rāma and Sītā, slept that night.

22. "Lakṣmaṇa, however, the slayer of enemies, strapped on palm-guards and finger-guards, bound upon his back a pair of quivers filled with arrows, and holding his great bow strung and ready he stood nearby the whole night through.

23. "I then grasped my great bow and arrows, and with my never-tiring kinsmen similarly armed I came and took up my position by Lakṣmaṇa, to stand guard over the man who is the equal of great Indra."

The end of the eighty-first *sarga* of the *Ayodhyākāṇḍa* of the *Śrī Rāmāyaṇa*.

Sarga 82

1-2. After listening attentively to all of this, Bharata went with his counselors to the foot of the almond tree, and gazing at Rāma's bed he said to all his mothers, "Here on the ground is where the great man slept that night. Here are the imprints he made.

3. "Rāma is a son of Daśaratha, that wise and illustrious king, and scion of an illustrious House. He should not have had to sleep on the bare earth.

4. "The tiger among men used to sleep on a pile of choice spreads overspread with furs. How is it possible that he slept on the naked ground?

5-6. "Before, he always slept in the finest palaces, mansions, and summer houses with inlaid floors of gold and silver, amid a profusion of choice spreads, dazzling with bouquets of flowers, scented with sandalwood and aloe—rooms that looked like white clouds, where flocks of parrots whistled.

7. "He woke to the sound of singing and musical instruments, the tinkle of gorgeous ornaments, and the roll of splendid bass drums.

8. "And panegyrists came at their appointed hour, and a crowd of bards and genealogists, to greet the slayer of enemies with well-suited verses and songs of praise.

9. "No one in the world would ever have believed this; it does not seem at all real to me. Have I lost my wits? Or no, I am certain I must be dreaming.

10-11. "Surely no divine power is mightier than Fate, if Rāma Dāśarathi and his beautiful, beloved Sītā, the daughter of the king of Videha, the daughter-in-law of Daśaratha, had to sleep on the ground.

12. "This is my brother's bed; this is where he tossed and turned upon the hard surface, crushing all the straw with his limbs.

13. "I guess Sītā fell asleep on this bed that night dressed in all her jewelry, for here and there you can see bits of gold adhering.

14. "Clearly she must have caught her upper garment here that night, for silken threads can be seen adhering still.

15. "Perhaps to sleep beside her husband brings such pleasure that poor Maithilī, delicate child though she is, felt no pain.

16. "But Rāghava was born in a House of emperors; he brings comfort to all the world and is prized by all the world, and he gave up the highest prize, the kingship.

17. "Handsome, red-eyed, lotus-dark Rāghava was destined for pleasure and deserves no pain. How could he sleep on the ground?

18. "Vaidehī truly has attained her highest goal by following her husband to the forest. But we, who are bereft of the great man, are all thrown into jeopardy.

19. "The world has lost its helmsman, and how empty it seems to me, with Daśaratha gone to heaven and Rāma withdrawn to the wilderness.

20. "And yet, no one even thinks to advance against our treasure-laden land, for the might of his arms protects it still, even though he is living in the forest.

21-22. "Though the guardposts on the ramparts of the capital stand empty, though the horses and elephants have grown unruly, the city-gates stand wide open, and the army is demoralized; though the capital is unprotected, weakened, and vulnerable in its plight, our enemies dare not covet it, like food prepared with poison.

23. "From this day forward I will sleep on straw spread upon the ground, eat nothing but fruit and roots, and wear bark garments and matted hair.

24. "On his behalf I will live with pleasure in the forest for what time remains, taking his promise upon myself. No falsehood will attach to him.

25. "As I live there on my brother's behalf, Śatrughna shall live with me, while my noble brother protects Ayodhyā with Lakṣmaṇa.

26. "And in Ayodhyā the brahmans shall consecrate Kākutstha. If only the gods allow this wish of mine to come true!

27. "I will bow my head and beg Rāghava's grace myself in every possible way, but if he should not give in, then I will live with him as long as it takes; if I stay in the forest, he will not be able to ignore me."

The end of the eighty-second *sarga* of the *Ayodhyākāṇḍa* of the *Śrī Rāmāyaṇa*.

Sarga 83

1. It was in that very place, on the bank of the Ganges, that Bharata Rāghava passed the night. He rose at daybreak and addressed Śatrughna:

2. "Arise, Śatrughna, why do you lie asleep? Please fetch Guha at once, the overlord of the Niṣādas. He will ferry the army across."

3. "I am awake," Śatrughna replied when his brother accosted him. "I am not sleeping but only musing, just like you, on my noble brother."

4. While the lions among men were conversing in this fashion, Guha paid a timely visit to them. He cupped his hands in reverence and said to Bharata:

5. "I trust you spent a comfortable night on the riverbank, Kākutstha, and that all is well with you and your army."

6. Hearing Guha's affectionate inquiry, Bharata answered, subordinating all other considerations to Rāma:

7. "Yes, we passed the night comfortably, your Majesty. You have shown us honor. Now let your fishermen ferry us across the Ganges in their many boats."

8. Upon hearing Bharata's instructions, Guha hurried back to the settlement and addressed his kinsmen:

9. "Arise, wake up, my blessings on you ever. Haul down the boats, and let us ferry the army across."

10. So he spoke, and they arose in haste and, on instructions from their king, gathered five hundred boats from every direction.

11. Some of them were fine ones distinguished by swastikas and fitted out with large bells, lovely well-built sailboats that easily caught the wind.

12. Guha brought up such a boat, distinguished by a swastika and covered with a white carpet, a beautiful boat that gave out sounds of festive music.

13. Bharata boarded it with mighty Śatrughna, Kausalyā, Sumitrā, and the other wives of the king.

14. Before the women came the family priest and the brahman gurus, next the wives of the king, and then the wagons and supplies.

15. As the men loaded equipment, fired the camp, and began plunging into the ford, the noise rose up to the highest heaven.

16. The sailboats, manned by the fishermen, flew swiftly along, transporting the people on board.

17. Some boats were laden with women, others with horses, while still others transported the vehicles and teams and the great treasures.

18. On reaching the further bank, the fisherfolk helped the people disembark, and as they returned they sailed their boats in lovely formations.

19. The caparisoned elephants were urged on by their drivers, and making the crossing, they looked like flag-topped mountains.

20. Only some of the people were able to board the boats; others crossed on rafts, in tubs or barrels, while still others had only their arms to use.

21. The auspicious army, ferried over the Ganges by the fishermen, struck out at the hour of Mitra for the great forest at Prayāga.

22. Thus did great Bharata allow his army to encamp at its pleasure and to rest, and then he set out in the company of his priests to visit Bharadvāja, preeminent among seers.

The end of the eighty-third *sarga* of the *Ayodhyākāṇḍa* of the *Śrī Rāmāyaṇa*.

Sarga 84

1. When the bull among men spied the ashram of Bharadvāja only a few miles away, he brought the whole army to a halt and proceeded with his counselors.

2. Knowing the ways of righteousness as he did, he laid aside his weapons and equipment, and dressed in a pair of linen garments, he proceeded on foot, with the family priest Vasiṣṭha ahead of him.

3. When he caught sight of Bharadvāja, Rāghava halted his counselors and advanced behind the family priest.

4. The moment Bharadvāja saw Vasiṣṭha, the great ascetic sprang from his seat, calling to his students, "The welcome-offering!"

5. Bharata then did obeisance to him. Since he had come in the company of Vasiṣṭha, the mighty seer knew him to be a son of Daśaratha.

6-7. He gave the two of them the welcome-offering and water for their feet, and afterwards fruit. Wise in the ways of righteousness he asked them in due order after the welfare of their House, of

Ayodhyā, their army, treasury, allies, and counselors. But knowing that Daśaratha had passed away he did not mention the king.

8. Vasiṣṭha and Bharata asked him after the well-being of his body, his sacred fires, his trees, students, birds, and beasts.

9. Bharadvāja assured them all were well, but then, in his abiding affection for Rāghava, the great ascetic addressed Bharata:

10. "What is your business in coming here when you should be ruling the kingdom? Explain this to me fully, for my mind is unclear on it.

11. "The son Kausalyā bore, a slayer of enemies and the one source of her delight, has been banished for a long time to the forest with his wife and brother.

12. "I am told that his father, acting on the orders of a woman, ordered the glorious prince to become a forest hermit for fourteen years.

13. "I trust you have no intention of harming this innocent man and his younger brother, thinking thereby to enjoy unchallenged kingship."

14. So Bharadvāja spoke, and with tears in his eyes Bharata replied to him in a voice breaking with sorrow:

15. "I am lost if even the holy one thinks such a thing of me! Oh, do not suspect evil of me, do not rebuke me so.

16. "I never wanted what my mother demanded on my behalf; it gives me no satisfaction, and I will not accede to her demand.

17. "On the contrary, I am on my way to beg forgiveness of the tiger among men, to do obeisance at his feet, and to bring him back to Ayodhyā.

18. "That is the reason I have come—believe me, holy one. Please show me your grace and tell me the present whereabouts of Rāma, the lord of earth."

19. Graciously Bharadvāja replied to Bharata, "Such behavior toward your guru, such restraint and adherence to the ways of the good, become you, tiger among men, as a son of the Rāghava dynasty.

20. "I knew what was in your heart and only questioned you to hear it openly confirmed and to see your fame magnified to the highest degree.

21. "Your brother is living on the great mountain Citrakūṭa. Tomorrow you shall go to that place, but stay here tonight with your counselors. Grant me this desire, wise prince. You are mindful of the desires and needs of others."

22. Prince Bharata, a man of noble vision, was overjoyed and replied with a word of assent, for he had decided that he would indeed spend the night in the great ashram.

The end of the eighty-fourth *sarga* of the *Ayodhyākāṇḍa* of the *Śrī Rāmāyaṇa*.

Sarga 85

1. Once Bharata, son of Kaikeyī, had decided to spend the night there, the sage offered hospitality to him.

2. Bharata replied, "But surely you have already done as much. The water for our feet and the welcome-offering are the hospitality appropriate to the forest."

3. With a chuckle Bharadvāja said to Bharata, "I know you are agreeable and would be satisfied with anything.

4. "It is for this army of yours I wish to make provision. This would give me pleasure, and you yourself, bull among mortals, deserve no less.

5. "But why in fact did you station the army so far away before coming here? Why did you not approach with your army, bull among men?"

6. Bharata cupped his hands in reverence as he replied to the ascetic, "I did not approach with my army, holy one, for fear of the holy one.

7. "Spirited horses, men, and huge rutting elephants follow in my train, holy one, covering the wide earth.

8. "I was afraid they would ruin the land and water, the trees and leaf huts of the ashram, so I came alone."

9. "Bring the army here," the great seer commanded him, and Bharata accordingly had the army advance.

10. Bharadvāja entered the fire-sanctuary, sipped water, and wiped his mouth. He then invoked Viśvakarman in order to provide the hospitality.

11. "I invoke Viśvakarman and Tvaṣṭṛ, too. It is my intention to provide hospitality, and to this end let all these arrangements be made for me:

12. "Let the rivers flowing eastward and flowing westward, on earth and in the sky, now come together from wherever they may be.

13. "Let some of them flow with date-palm liquor, and some with long-aged wine, others with cool water tasting like the juice of sugarcane.

14-15. "I invoke the *gandharvas* of the gods, Viśvāvasu, Haha, Huhu, the *apsaras* goddesses as well, and the *gandharva* women wherever they may be: Ghṛtācī, Viśvācī, Miśrakeśī, Alambusā, the beautiful women who wait on Śakra, and those who wait on Brahmā—all these do I invoke to come with Tumburu and with all their trappings.

16. "Let Kubera's heavenly forest come from the land of the Kurus, the forest whose foliage is raiment and jewelry, and which constantly bears fruit in the form of heavenly women.

17-18. "Let the blessed moon come and provide me with the most exquisite food, solid and soft, and things to suck and lick, in great variety and quantity; many-colored garlands, too, dropping from the trees, wine and every other type of drink and meats of different sorts."

19. So the sage spoke in his deep concentration, incomparable power, and ascetic energy, his words accented in full accord with the rules of pronunciation.

20. As he continued rapt in meditation, facing east, hands cupped in reverence, one by one all those heavenly things began to appear.

21. A soft breeze began to blow, with a faint touch of the spice hills of Malaya and Dardura, a most pleasant, comforting, and gracious breeze that cooled one's sweat.

22. Heavenly clouds rolled in, showering blossoms, and in every direction could be heard the sounds of the bass drums of the gods.

23. Gentle winds began to blow, troupes of *apsarases* danced, the *gandharvas* of the gods sang, and their lutes gave forth notes.

24. The sound they sent up carried to heaven and over the earth to the ears of the people, a smooth and even sound with graceful rhythm.

25. The heavenly sound charmed the ears of the men, and when it faded, Bharata's army beheld the creations of Viśvakarman.

26. The ground had been leveled out all around to a distance of five leagues, and luxuriant lawns carpeted it, glistening like sapphire or cat's-eye beryl.

27. *Bilva* trees sprang up on it, woodapples, jackfruit trees, and citrons, myrobalans and mangoes, all adorned with fruit.

28. From the land of the northern Kurus came the forest with its heavenly delights, and the heavenly river with trees densely covering its banks.

29. Splendid four-room houses suddenly appeared, stables for the horses and elephants, clusters of castles and mansions, and lovely archways.

30-33. And there was a royal palace that looked like a silvery cloud. It had a grand archway and was beautified with white garlands and perfumed with heavenly fragrances. It was four-cornered and spacious, complete with couches, chairs, and carriages, provisioned with heavenly delights to suit every taste, with heavenly delicacies and garments. It was stocked with all manner of food, with utensils polished spotlessly, seats properly arranged for everyone, and a magnificent couch with a sumptuous spread. It was a majestic residence filled with treasures, and with the permission of the great seer, great-armed Bharata, son of Kaikeyī, entered it.

34. Behind him followed all the counselors and the family priest, and they rejoiced to see the arrangements provided in the residence.

35. There was a heavenly throne in it, a fan and a parasol, and with his ministers Bharata approached as if the king were there.

36. He paid homage to the throne, prostrating himself before Rāma, and taking up the yaktail fan he sat down upon a minister's seat.

37. Then all the others sat down in due order, the counselors and the family priest, next the chief of the army, and finally the palace supervisor.

38. At Bharadvāja's command, rivers running with rice pudding instantly sprang up before Bharata.

39. Along either bank of the rivers, lovely heavenly dwellings plastered with white clay were produced by the grace of the brahman.

40. And at the very same instant there came twenty thousand women sent by Brahmā, decked out with heavenly jewelry.

41. Twenty thousand more women came, sent by Kubera, all adorned with coral, gold, gems, and pearls.

42. A troupe of twenty thousand *apsarases* came from Nandana, who could madden with passion any man they took in their arms.

43. The kings of the *gandharvas*—Nārada, Tumburu, Gopa, Parvata, Sūryavarcasa—began to sing in the presence of Bharata.

44. And before him danced Alambusā, Miśrakeśī, Puṇḍarīkā, and Vāmanā, at Bharadvāja's command.

45. All the garlands to be found among the gods and in the Caitraratha forest appeared there at Prayāga at Bharadvāja's command.

46. *Bilva* trees became drummers and fig trees dancers, with beddanut trees beating the time, by the ascetic power of Bharadvāja.

47. Pines and palmyra trees, evergreens and beeches massed together in delight, becoming hunchbacks or dwarfs.

48. *Śiṃśapa* and myrobalan trees, rose-apples and all the vines of the woodlands assumed the form of women and took up their dwelling in Bharadvāja's ashram.

49. "There is wine to drink for all who wish to drink," they cried. "There is rice pudding for those who are hungry and succulent meat to eat, as much as you desire!"

50. The women then rubbed the men with oil and bathed them at the murmuring riverbanks, fifteen women for every single man.

51. The eyes of the lovely ladies sparkled bright as they approached and massaged the men, and after drying them off they gave each other things to drink.

52. The draft-animals of the great Ikṣvāku soldiers—the horses, elephants, asses, camels, and oxen, the sons of Surabhī—were fed with sugarcane and sweet barley by strong men who bade them eat.

53. For the horse-trainers ignored their horses and the elephant-handlers their elephants; the whole army was delirious with drink and pleasure.

54. Their every desire gratified, anointed with red sandalwood cream, the soldiers shouted out from where they lay with the troupes of *apsarasas*:

55. "We will never go back to Ayodhyā, nor on to Daṇḍaka! May Bharata fare well, and good luck to Rāma too!"

56. So the foot-soldiers shouted, and the riders and trainers of the elephants and horses, for after such a reception they recognized no master.

57. By the thousands the men of Bharata's retinue roared in delight and cried out, "This is heaven!"

58. And no sooner would they finish some ambrosial treat than they would glance at the other heavenly foods and turn their thoughts once more to eating.

59. The female servants and slave girls, the wives and women accompanying the army all found themselves dressed in fresh garments and they too wanted for nothing.

60. The elephants, asses, and camels, the cows and horses, and even the wild birds and beasts were well provisioned, and no one had to provide for any of them.

61. There was not a man to be seen whose garments were not sparkling white, not one who was hungry or dirty or whose hair was begrimed with dust.

62-63. To their amazement the men beheld thousands of metal pots crowned with flowers and banners, filled to the brim with white rice, goat meat, and boar meat, with mounds of choice condiments and fragrant, flavorful soups prepared from fruit-stock.

64. Along the edges of the forest were wells thick with rice pudding; there were wishing-cows, too, and trees dripping with honey.

65. There were pools filled with date-palm wine and ringed about with mounds of savory meats prepared in steaming cauldrons—venison, peacock, and chicken.

66-67. There were thousands of platters made of gold, and well-fired trays and jars and jugs filled with curds. There were ponds filled with buttermilk scented with fresh yellow woodapple, filled with white curds or rice pudding, and there were mounds of sugar.

68-72. At the landing places on the river the men beheld ointments and fragrant powders and bathing requisites, all stored in containers. There were stacks of tooth brushes, white and bristled, white sandalwood ointment packed in vials, and sparkling clean mirrors. There were piles of clothing and pairs of shoes and sandals by the thousands. There were collyrium boxes, combs, and brushes; parasols, bows, and shining armor; couches and chairs. There were full streams for watering the asses, camels, elephants, and horses, and streams just right for bathing, with lovely landings, lotuses, and waterlilies.

73. All about they saw mounds of soft barley-grass the color of sapphire or cat's-eye beryl for strewing before the animals.

74. The men were lost in wonder at the sight of the marvellous hospitality—like something in a dream—that the great seer provided for Bharata.

75. And while they were enjoying themselves like this in Bharadvāja's lovely ashram, just like the gods in Nandana, the night slipped away.

76. Then the rivers, the *gandharvas*, and all the lovely women took leave of Bharadvāja and returned just as they had come.

77. But the men were still drunk and wild with liquor, still anointed with the heavenly creams of aloe and sandalwood, and the heavenly garlands were still there, the various splendid garlands, though now in disarray and crushed by the men.

The end of the eighty-fifth *sarga* of the *Ayodhyākāṇḍa* of the *Śrī Rāmāyaṇa*.

Sarga 86

1. After passing the night with such hospitality shown to him, Bharata went with his escort and of his own accord approached Bharadvāja.

2. Bharadvāja had completed his fire-offerings when he observed that Bharata, tiger among men, had come with hands cupped in reverence. The seer addressed him:

3. "I trust you spent a pleasant night here in our domain. Were your people content with the hospitality? Tell me, blameless prince."

4. The supremely powerful seer strode from his ashram, and Bharata, hands cupped in reverence, prostrated himself and replied:

5. "I, my ministers, and all my army, and even the draft animals, have passed the night quite pleasantly, holy one. You have gratified most amply our every desire.

6. "We have been well fed and well housed, and our fatigue and pain have been allayed. Yes, all of us, the servants included, have passed the night most pleasantly.

7. "And though I must now bid you farewell, holy one, foremost of seers, please turn a friendly eye upon me as I set out to find my brother.

8. "Direct me to the ashram of my great and righteous brother. Tell me which road to take, righteous seer, and how far I must go."

9. Questioned in this fashion, Bharadvāja, the great and mighty ascetic, answered Bharata, who was yearning for the sight of his brother.

10. "Bharata, at a distance of two and a half leagues through the lonely forest is Mount Citrakūṭa, a place of lovely caverns and woodlands.

11. "Along its northern flank runs the Mandākinī River, thickly bordered with flowering trees and lovely flowering woodlands.

12. "Between the stream and Mount Citrakūṭa their leaf hut will be standing, my son. I am certain the two of them are living there.

13. "Illustrious lord of the army, if you lead your army of elephants, horses, and chariots by way of the southern road, keeping toward the southwest, you will soon see Rāghava."

14. When the wives of the king of kings heard they were about to depart, they left their fine carriages—and fine carriages they always deserved—and crowded around the brahman Bharadvāja.

15. Trembling, haggard, and desolate, Kausalyā along with Queen Sumitrā grasped the sage's feet with her hands.

16. Kaikeyī, her every desire thwarted, an object of contempt to all the world, was overcome with shame as she, too, grasped his feet.

17. Reverently she circled the great and holy sage and with a desolate heart stood apart, not far from Bharata.

18. Then Bharadvāja, a sage strict in his vows, made a request of Bharata: "I should like to make the acquaintance of your mothers individually, Rāghava."

19. So Bharadvāja spoke, and the righteous and eloquent Bharata cupped his hands in reverence and spoke these words:

20-21. "This woman whom you see, holy one, who is like a goddess though desolate now and haggard with grief and fasting, is Kausalyā, my father's chief queen. It is she who bore Rāma, the tiger among men who moves with the gait of a lion, as Aditi bore Dhātṛ.

22-23. "The woman holding her by the left arm, with as wretched a look as a *karṇikāra* branch stripped of its blossoms in the heart of the forest, is the queen whose sons are the godlike Lakṣmaṇa and Śatrughna, mighty and valorous princes.

24-25. "She on whose account the two tigers among men went away dead in life, on whose account King Daśaratha was bereft of his sons and so went to heaven—behold her, the power-hungry Kaikeyī, an ignoble woman in a noblewoman's guise, a vicious and malevolent person—my mother, and the one in whom I see this great calamity of mine to have its source."

26. The tiger among men stopped, his voice choked with sobs, his eyes bloodshot, fitfully heaving sighs like an angry snake.

27. When Bharata had finished speaking, the great and wise seer Bharadvāja replied with words of great import:

28. "Bharata, you must not impute any fault to Kaikeyī. The banishment of Rāma will turn out to be a great blessing."

29. Bharata did obeisance and received his benediction, and after reverently circling and taking leave of him, he commanded the army, "Harness up!"

30. The different groups of people then harnessed the many heavenly horse-chariots with fittings of gold, and they boarded, eager to be off.

31. The elephants, both bulls and cows, girt with gold, their pennants flying, set forth with a rumble, like clouds at the end of summer.

32. The different kinds of vehicles set forth, large ones and small ones and some of great value, while the foot-soldiers set out on foot.

33. Eager to see Rāma, the women, with Kausalyā at their head, set forth cheerfully in their distinguished vehicles.

34. A handsome palanquin was standing ready, resplendent as the morning sun, and majestic Bharata got in and set forth with his escort.

35. Teeming with elephants, horses, and chariots, the great army, like a massive lofty cloud, set forth turning southward, traversing stretches of forest alive with birds and beasts.

36. Its soldiers, elephants, and horses all excited, terrifying the flocks of birds and beasts as it plunged into the great forest, the army of Bharata made a splendid sight.

The end of the eighty-sixth *sarga* of the *Ayodhyākāṇḍa* of the *Śrī Rāmāyaṇa*.

Sarga 87

1. As the great bannered army was making its way, the wild bull elephants that lived in the forest were thrown into confusion and ran off with their herds.

2. So, too, were the monkeys and droves of dappled gazelle and black antelope that were everywhere to be seen in the stretches of the forest, on the mountains, and at the riverbanks.

3. The righteous son of Daśaratha happily proceeded in the company of his great and clamorous army of four divisions.

4. Great Bharata's army was like the ocean's flood, or the clouds that blanket heaven in the rains, the way it blanketed the earth.

5. For the earth was inundated with a flood of swift horses and elephants, and for a long time it disappeared altogether from sight.

6. Majestic Bharata had covered a great distance, and his mounts had grown weary when he addressed Vasiṣṭha, the best of counselors:

7. "We have clearly come to the region Bharadvāja spoke of: the scene that appears before us is just as I heard it described.

8. "Here are Mount Citrakūṭa and the Mandākinī River, and there, at a distance, the forest can be seen, blue-black as a stormcloud.

9. "Even now my elephants, mountain-like themselves, are trampling the lovely slopes of Mount Citrakūṭa.

10. "The trees upon the mountain slopes are shedding their blossoms, as blue-black water-laden clouds shed water when the heat of summer is over.

11. "Just look at the mountain, Śatrughna. It is a place where *kiṃnaras* roam, and now the horses are swarming over it like dolphins through the ocean.

12. "Startled herds of deer are darting off—they look like banks of clouds in the sky shredded by the autumn wind.

13. "The trees, with their cloud-dark branches and the fragrant flower-chaplets they wear upon their crowns, look like men of the south.

14. "The forest had been still and dreadful in appearance, but now, with all these throngs of people, it seems like Ayodhyā to me.

15. "The dust kicked up by hoofs hung obscuring the sky, but a breeze has come and quickly dispelled it, as if to do me a kindness.

16. "Look, Śatrughna, how the master charioteers drive the horse-drawn carriages and how they fly along so swiftly through the woodlands.

17. "And now those lovely peacocks—look, they are frightened and scurrying off to the mountain, the dwelling-place of birds.

18. "I find this a perfectly charming spot, clearly a place where ascetics would live—it is like the very pathway to heaven.

19. "The many charming dappled deer with their mates in the forest appear as if it were the blossoms that lent them their brilliant coloring.

20. "Come, let soldiers set out and search the woodland, to see if those tigers among men, Rāma and Lakṣmaṇa, are anywhere to be found."

21. Receiving Bharata's order, warriors with weapons in hand entered the forest and soon caught sight of smoke.

22. On observing the column of smoke, they returned and reported it to Bharata. "Where there is fire there must be men," they said. "Clearly the two Rāghavas are somewhere nearby.

23. "Then again, those tigers among men, the two enemy-slaying princes, may not be here, but others clearly are, ascetics like Rāma."

24. Hearing these just and reasonable words, Bharata, crusher of enemy armies, addressed all the soldiers:

25. "Remain here and be on the alert; no one is to go on ahead. I myself shall go with Sumantra and our guru."

26. So he spoke, and all of them remained where they were, while Bharata directed his gaze toward the column of smoke.

27. The army, too, from where Bharata had made them halt, gazed at the smoke that rose before them and felt delight, thinking it would not be long before they rejoined their beloved Rāma.

The end of the eighty-seventh *sarga* of the *Ayodhyākāṇḍa* of the *Śrī Rāmāyaṇa*.

Sarga 88

1-2. Now, during the long time that godlike Dāśarathi had been living on the mountain, he had grown to love the mountains and the forest. Once, eager to please Vaidehī and beguile his own mind, he showed his wife around wonderful Citrakūṭa, as Indra, breaker of fortresses, might show Śacī.

3. "Neither my expulsion from the kingdom, my dear, nor being apart from my loved ones pains my heart when I am viewing this lovely mountain.

4. "Look at the mountain, my dear, home to flocks of many different birds, how its peaks almost scrape the sky and veins of minerals adorn it.

5-6. "What a brilliant sight the lordly mountain is with its different regions adorned with minerals. Some sparkle silvery; some look blood-red or are tinted yellow or madder-crimson; some gleam like the rarest gems; some shine like topaz or crystal or the pale white screw pine flower, or gleam like stars or quicksilver.

7. "What a sight the mountain makes, swarming with birds and teeming with herds of beasts, panthers, hyenas, and monkeys, all of them tame.

8-10. "The trees that cover the mountain heighten its majesty, flowering, fruitful trees, shady and enchanting: mangoes, rose-apples, *asanas*, *lodhras*, *priyālas*, jackfruit trees and *dhavas*, *aṅkolas*, the gnarled *tiniśas*, *bilva* trees, ebonies, bamboo, white Kashmiri teaks, soapnut trees, quince and butter trees, evergreens, jujubes and myrobalan trees, *nīpas*, cane, *dhanvanas*, and pomegranates.

11. "Look, my dear, there on the lovely hillsides are some spirited *kiṃnaras*, impassioned with desire and pairing off to make love.

12. "And look there, where those swords and delicate garments are hanging from the branches: those are the enchanting pleasure-bowers of the *vidyādhara* women.

13. "What a sight the mountain makes with its waterfalls, one here, one there, and with its springs and running streams—it is like an elephant running with ichor.

14. "The breeze out of the grottoes bears the fragrance of different flowers and approaches with such pleasing redolence—what man would it not gladden?

15. "If I might live here all the years to come with you, my flawless wife, and with Lakṣmaṇa, I would never feel the searing pain of grief.

16. "For I delight in this lovely mountain, my beautiful wife, with its magnificent peaks where fruit and flowers are so abundant and many different birds come flocking.

17. "And my living in the forest has brought me a twofold reward: my father has discharged his debt to righteousness, and Bharata has been pleased as well.

18. "Vaidehī, you take delight, don't you, in being with me on Citrakūṭa, with so many different marvels before your eyes to experience, to contemplate and talk about?

19. "Living in the forest—as the royal seers of old, my ancestors, used to say—is the real drink of immortality for kings, and leads to well-being after death.

20. "How beautiful the rocks of the mountain are, massive rocks, hundreds of them all around, so many and so colorful—blue-black, yellow, white, and pink.

21. "At night the plants growing on the lordly mountain seem like tongues of fire, blazing by the thousands in the beauty of their own luster.

22. "Some parts of the mountain, my lovely, look like dwelling-places or gardens, while others are sheer rock.

23. "It is as if Citrakūṭa had arisen, splitting open the earth, but over there its peak seems gracious in every way.

24. "There you can see the sumptuous beds of lovers, spread with leaves of the wild ginger tree, the laurel, waxflower, and birch, and interspersed with lotus petals.

25. "Their lotus garlands can be seen, too, cast aside now by the lovers and crushed. And there, my beloved, look at all those different fruits.

26. "So rich in fruit and roots and water is Mount Citrakūṭa that it almost surpasses Vasvaukasārā, Nalinī, or the land of the northern Kurus.

27. "Passing this time with you, my beloved Sītā, and with Lakṣmaṇa, will be a pleasure to me, and one that fosters the righteousness of my House, for I shall be keeping to the path of the good with the utmost self-restraint."

The end of the eighty-eighth *sarga* of the *Ayodhyākāṇḍa* of the *Śrī Rāmāyaṇa*.

Sarga 89

1. Then the lord of Kosala, making his way down the mountain, showed Maithilī where the clear waters of the lovely Mandākinī River ran.

2. Lotus-eyed Rāma spoke to the daughter of the king of Videha, his broad-hipped wife with a face as fair as the moon.

3-4. "Just look at the lovely Mandākinī River with its sparkling sandbanks, the geese and cranes that make their home there, the flowers embellishing it, the fruiting and blossoming trees of every sort that grow thick upon its banks. Wherever one looks it shimmers like Nalinī, the lake of Kubera, king of kings.

5. "Herds of animals have drunk here, and though the landing places are turbid now, they are lovely still and give me much pleasure.

6. "Over there seers wearing hides, matted hair, and upper garments of barkcloth are immersing themselves in the Mandākinī River, my beloved, for it is the appointed hour.

7. "Those others are sages who take rigorous vows and worship the sun, my large-eyed wife, with their arms held high in self-mortification.

8. "As the wind buffets the treetops, and they strew their leaves and flowers all about the river, the mountain seems almost ready to dance.

9. "Look at the Mandākinī River there, where its water flows crystal-clear, and there, where its sandy beaches stretch out, and over there, where perfected beings crowd about it.

10. "Look at the flowers the wind has shaken off and massed into drifts, or those others bobbing in the middle of the water.

11. "Those sweet-voiced birds are sheldrakes, my precious, the ones alighting on the drifts of flowers and uttering their pleasant cries.

12. "To set one's eyes on Citrakūṭa and the Mandākinī, my lovely, is far better than living in the town—in your eyes, too, I think.

13. "Come plunge with me into the river. Its waters, as always, are agitated only by perfected beings, men cleansed of all impurities and endowed with ascetic power, self-restraint, and tranquillity.

14. "Plunge into the Mandākinī, my lovely Sītā, as if it were an old friend of yours, submerging the lotuses and waterlilies.

15. "Just think of the wild animals as the townsmen all the while, my beloved, of the mountain as Ayodhyā, and this river as the Sarayū.

16. "You both bring me such joy, both righteous Lakṣmaṇa, who attends to my orders, and you, Vaidehī, who are so agreeable.

17. "Being here with you, bathing at the time of the three oblations, and eating sweet fruit and roots, I no longer yearn either for Ayodhyā or the kingship.

18. "The man does not exist who would not find repose and happiness beholding this river, the herds of elephants that stir it up, the lions, monkeys, and elephants that come to drink its water, and the blossoming trees in full bloom that lend it such adornment."

19. So Rāma, heir of the Raghu dynasty, spoke with his beloved about the river, fondly and at length, as he went strolling over lovely Citrakūṭa, a very balm to the eye.

The end of the eighty-ninth *sarga* of the *Ayodhyākāṇḍa* of the *Śrī Rāmāyaṇa*.

Sarga 90

1. Now, as Rāma was sitting there, he perceived the noise and the dust—they reached to heaven—of Bharata's approaching army.

2. The wild bull elephants, meanwhile, were frightened by the deafening noise, and in panic they and their herds ran scattering in every direction.

3. Rāghava heard the noise made by the army and noticed all the elephants running away.

4. And watching them run off, and listening to the din, Rāma addressed Lakṣmaṇa Saumitri, a man of blazing power:

5. "Ho there, Lakṣmaṇa, worthy son of Sumitrā, go and take a look. A tumultuous clamor has broken out, awesome and deep as thunder.

6. "Perhaps a king or royal officer is out hunting in the forest, or it could be something else, an animal maybe. Please find out, Saumitri, find out as quickly as you can exactly what this all might be."

7. Lakṣmaṇa hurriedly climbed a flowering *sāla* tree, and peering about in every direction, he turned to the east.

8. Craning his neck and peering out, he saw a vast army, a mass of chariots, horses, and elephants, and footsoldiers among them on the alert.

9. He informed Rāma of the army teeming with horses and elephants, decked out with chariot-standards, and then added:

10. "Put out the fire, brother, and let Sītā get to a cave. String your bow and take up your arrows and armor!"

11. Rāma, tiger among men, replied to Lakṣmaṇa, "Very well, but consider first, Saumitri: to whom do you think this army might belong?"

12. Like a raging fire ready to burn the army to ashes, Lakṣmaṇa replied to Rāma:

13. "Clearly now that he has got the consecration he wants to have the kingship wholly in his power and is coming to kill the two of us—who else but Bharata, the son of Kaikeyī!

14. "There, in fact, the lofty majestic tree is coming into view: the standard of the spreading *kovidāra* shining brilliantly atop his chariot.

15. "There are men mounted on speeding horses drawing close at will, and how excited those riders appear mounted on the elephants.

16-17. "Let us take our bows and fall back to the mountain, my mighty brother, or make our stand right here, armed for battle with our weapons at the ready. If only the *kovidāra* standard would come within our range in battle! If only I could catch sight of Bharata, the cause of the great calamity that has befallen you, Rāghava, Sītā, and me.

18. "Your enemy has arrived, mighty Rāghava, he who brought about your expulsion from the ancient kingship. It is Bharata, and I will kill him.

19. "I see no wrong, Rāghava, in slaying Bharata. No unrighteousness comes from ridding oneself of a man who was first to give offense. When he has been struck down you shall rule the whole treasure-laden earth.

20. "If only that power-hungry woman Kaikeyī could see her son killed by me today in combat—like a tree felled by an elephant—and feel the anguish of bitter sorrow.

21. "But no, I will slay Kaikeyī, too, and her supporters and kinsmen. Let the earth be cleansed today of this foul scum!

22. "Today, O giver of honor, I will cast out upon the enemy army my pent-up wrath and our dishonor, like fire upon dry grass.

23. "Today I will rend the enemies' bodies with my sharp arrows, and spatter the woodlands of Citrakūṭa with their blood.

24. "And when my arrows have rent the hearts of their elephants and horses, let wild beasts drag them off, and the men, too, when I have cut them down.

25. "I have always discharged my debt to my bow and arrows in great battles, and I have no doubt I shall again in destroying Bharata and all his army."

The end of the ninetieth *sarga* of the *Ayodhyākāṇḍa* of the *Śrī Rāmāyaṇa*.

Sarga 91

1. In an effort to calm Lakṣmaṇa Saumitri, who was so violently agitated and almost beside himself with rage, Rāma spoke these words:

2. "What need is there of a bow or sword and shield when it is the great archer, wise Bharata himself, who is coming?

3. "It is only to be expected that Bharata should wish to see us. He would not do us any harm, nor even contemplate it.

4. "When has Bharata ever opposed you, or made you any such threat that you should now have these suspicions of him?

5. "You must not speak disparagingly or abusively of Bharata. It is I who would be abused were any abuse directed against him.

6. "How, after all, could a son kill his father, whatever the extremity, or a brother his brother, Saumitri, his very own breath of life?

7. "If it is for the sake of the kingship that you are saying these things, I shall tell Bharata when I see him, 'Hand over the kingship to him.'

8. "For were I plainly to tell him, Lakṣmaṇa, 'Offer him the kingship,' Bharata's only response would be, 'Of course.' "

9. So spoke his righteous brother, whose welfare was his one concern, and Lakṣmaṇa seemed almost to shrink into himself for shame.

10. Rāghava noticed Lakṣmaṇa's chagrin and once again addressed him: "I think the great-armed prince has come here only to visit us.

11. "Or perhaps he wants to take Vaidehī home. He may have had second thoughts about her staying in the forest, a woman used to every comfort.

12. "There you can see the team of splendid horses, my mighty brother, those thoroughbred, magnificent swift horses, in speed like the rushing wind.

13. "And there is Śatrumjaya, our wise father's aged and massive elephant, lumbering at the head of the army."

14. Climbing down from the top of the *sāla* tree, Lakṣmaṇa, champion in battle, came and stood at Rāma's side, hands cupped in reverence.

15. On orders from Bharata that there be no disturbance, the army had pitched camp all around the mountain.

16. For a league and a half along the slope of the mountain the Ikṣvāku army encamped with its throngs of elephants, horses, and chariots.

17. The army made a brilliant sight when Bharata had marshaled it there on Citrakūṭa the day he came, shedding his pride and honoring the claims of righteousness, to conciliate the delight of the Raghus with all the diplomacy at his command.

The end of the ninety-first *sarga* of the *Ayodhyākāṇḍa* of the *Śrī Rāmāyaṇa*.

Sarga 92

1. After encamping the army, lordly Bharata, the best of men who walk the earth, set out walking to find Kākutstha, who was a guru to him.

2. As soon as the army was duly encamped as he had instructed, Bharata addressed his brother Śatrughna:

3. "Dear brother, you must at once explore the whole extent of the forest, with troops of our men and these hunters to accompany you.

4. "I shall find no peace until I see Rāma, powerful Lakṣmaṇa, and illustrious Vaidehī.

5. "I shall find no peace until I see the lovely moonlike face of my brother and his lotus-petal eyes.

6. "I shall find no peace until I bow my head to my brother's feet, which bear all the signs of sovereignty.

7. "I shall find no peace until he assumes, as he deserves, his position in the kingship of our fathers and forefathers, with the consecration water moist upon his head.

8. "Illustrious Vaidehī, the daughter of Janaka, has fulfilled herself by following her husband, master of the ocean-girdled earth.

9. "How fortunate is Citrakūṭa, that mountain equal to Himālaya, king of mountains, where Rāma is living like Kubera in Nandana.

10. "This trackless forest, the haunt of wild beasts, has fulfilled itself as well, to have become the dwelling-place of Rāma, the best of all who bear arms."

11. With this, mighty Bharata, bull among men, set out on foot into the great forest.

12. The eloquent prince made his way through the thickets growing on the mountain slopes, their treetops all in bloom.

13. Upon reaching the flowering *sāla* tree atop Mount Citrakūṭa, he spied the towering banner of the fire burning in Rāma's ashram.

14. Majestic Bharata and his kinsmen rejoiced to see it, knowing that Rāma must be there; the prince felt as if at last he had made the further shore of an ocean.

15. Perceiving upon Mount Citrakūṭa Rāma's ashram and the holy men there, great Bharata hurried off with Guha after again encamping the army.

The end of the ninety-second *sarga* of the *Ayodhyākāṇḍa* of the *Śrī Rāmāyaṇa*.

Sarga 93

1. Now, once the army was encamped, Bharata set out impatient to see his brother, showing the way for Śatrughna.

2. He had instructed the seer Vasiṣṭha to bring his mothers directly, while he himself hurried on ahead, out of deep love for his guru.

3. Sumantra likewise followed close behind Śatrughna, for he was no less ardent than Bharata to see Rāma again.

4. Majestic Bharata advanced and soon could see his brother's leaf hut and thatched cottage situated within an ascetic's retreat.

5. In front of the lodge Bharata saw the logs that had been cut and the flowers that had been gathered.

6. And in the forest he saw the dry dung of buffalo and other animals collected in great mounds for use against the cold.

7. As brilliant, great-armed Bharata proceeded he excitedly spoke to Śatrughna and the ministers all around him:

8. "I think we must have reached the spot Bharadvāja spoke of; the Mandākinī River cannot be far from here, I think.

9. "This must be the trail, for above strips of bark have been fastened. Lakṣmaṇa must have marked it for traveling at night.

10. "And that one must only be a path beaten on the mountain slope by the large-tusked elephants charging and trumpeting at one another.

11. "There you can see the thick smoke from black-trailed fire; it is customary for ascetics to maintain a fire continuously in the forest.

12. "It is here I shall have the delight of seeing my noble brother Rāghava, who is living like a great seer to do his guru honor."

13. Bharata Rāghava continued on and soon reached the place where Citrakūṭa abuts the Mandākinī. He addressed the people with him:

14. "The tiger among men must sit on the ground and practice the 'heroic' posture in yoga—the lord of all people in this unpeopled place. A curse on me that I was born and that I live!

15. "Because of me a calamity has befallen brilliant Rāghava, the master of the world. He has had to renounce all pleasures and make his dwelling in the forest.

16. "And the world condemns me for this. But now I will go and beg their forgiveness; I will throw myself down again and again at the feet of Rāma and Sītā."

17-22. As the son of Daśaratha was lamenting in this fashion, he saw a large, enchanting, and holy leaf hut in the forest, densely thatched with *sāla*, palmyra, and *aśvakarṇa* leaves. It was a spacious hut with soft *kuśa* grass spread about, like an altar at a sacred rite. Bows adorned it, gleaming like rainbows, heavy, sturdy, and backed with gold, of a sort that could rout any foe. Arrows flashing like sunbeams adorned it, too, like the serpents adorning Bhogavatī, awesome arrows packed in quivers, with heads blazing. A pair of swords in golden scabbards shed a luster over the hut, and two shields lent their adornment, brilliantly embossed with gold. Brilliant forearm-guards and finger-guards studded with gold were hanging there, too. It was a place as impregnable to enemy hordes as a lion's cave to deer.

23. Bharata saw a holy altar there in Rāma's residence, broad and sloping to the northeast, with a blazing fire upon it.

24. Glancing about, Bharata suddenly saw his guru Rāma seated in the thatched cottage, wearing a crown of matted hair.

25-27. He saw Rāma seated there, dressed in a black antelope hide and barkcloth garment. He was the image of fire in every respect, with the shoulders of a lion, great arms, and lotus-petal eyes—the righteous master of all the ocean-girdled earth. He looked like the eternal Brahmā as he sat together with Sītā and Lakṣmaṇa upon the floor strewn with *darbha* grass.

28. When majestic Bharata saw him, both sorrow and confusion overwhelmed him at once, and righteous Bharata, the son of Kaikeyī, went running to him.

29. The mere sight of Rāma anguished him, and he broke out in sob-choked lamentation. He could hardly endure it, and yet he steadied himself to speak:

30. "The man to whom his subjects in the assembly should rightly be paying homage, here he sits, my elder brother, receiving the homage of beasts of the wild.

31. "The man who in the past was accustomed to clothes worth many thousands, here he is, the great man, wearing deerskins in the performance of righteousness.

32. "How can Rāghava bear this burden of matted hair, when he used to wear many-colored flowers of every variety?

33. "The man who should rightly be gaining abundant merit through sacrifices performed according to precept now seeks it by mortifying his body.

34. "It had always been precious sandalwood cream that coated my noble brother's limbs. How is it possible they are now coated with dirt?

35. "It is my fault this misery has befallen Rāma, who had known nothing but happiness. A curse on my life, vile creature that I am, an object of scorn to all the world!"

36. So Bharata lamented in desolation and, his lotus face breaking out in sweat, he reached in vain for Rāma's feet and collapsed in tears.

37. Consumed with sorrow, the powerful prince Bharata exclaimed in desolation, "My brother," but could say nothing further.

38. He glanced at glorious Rāma, and through a sob-choked throat he cried out only "My brother!" unable to utter anything more.

39. Śatrughna was weeping, too, as he prostrated himself at Rāma's feet. And as Rāma embraced the two of them, he shed tears as well.

40. The two princes then met with Sumantra and Guha there in the wilderness—it was as if the day-bringing sun and the night-bringing moon were to meet with the planets Śukra and Bṛhaspati in the sky.

41. The inhabitants of the forest watched as the princes, men like bull elephants, were reunited there in the great wilderness, and they lost all delight as well, and every one of them burst into tears.

The end of the ninety-third *sarga* of the *Ayodhyākāṇḍa* of the *Śrī Rāmāyaṇa*.

Sarga 94

1. Rāma drew Bharata to his breast, embraced him, and kissed him on the forehead. Then he questioned him closely:

2. "What has become of your father, dear brother, that you have come to the wilderness? While he yet lives you should not be going off to the forest.

3. "It is a long time, indeed, since I have seen Bharata, who has come from so far into this wilderness. Why have you come to the forest, dear brother, looking so somber?

4. "King Daśaratha is in good health, I trust, still true to his given word, still performing royal consecrations and horse-sacrifices, and deciding points of law.

5. "I trust proper homage is still being shown the wise and brilliant brahman, dear brother, the preceptor of the Ikṣvākus, who is constant in righteousness.

6. "Dear brother, Kausalyā is happy, I hope, and Sumitrā, the mother of such good children. I trust noble Queen Kaikeyī rejoices, too.

7. "You honor your family priest, I trust, a highborn man, learned and disciplined, who gives instruction ungrudgingly.

8. "I hope you have appointed a man to tend your sacred fires who is sagacious and upright and knows the ritual precepts. I trust he always informs you in a timely fashion both before and after the oblations have been offered.

9. "I trust you continue to hold the preceptor Sudhanvan in esteem, dear brother. He is expert in the most formidable arrows and missiles, and a master of the science of statecraft.

10. "You have made brave men your counselors, I trust, dear brother, men you look upon as your very self—men who are learned, self-controlled, and highborn, and able to read a man's thoughts in his face.

11. "Counsel is the basis of a king's success, Rāghava—when it is well kept by counselors and ministers skilled in the science.

12. "You are not ruled by sleep, I trust, but are always awake early, while spending the late-night hours reflecting on what makes for prudent statecraft.

13. "I trust you take counsel neither all by yourself nor with a multitude. And once determined, your counsel does not, I hope, fly about the kingdom.

14. "I hope that the enterprises you decide on involve little expense and bring great profit, and that you undertake them quickly, without procrastinating.

15. "I trust kings learn of your every venture only when fully accomplished, or nearly so, and not beforehand.

16. "Your counsels, dear brother, or your ministers', even when not

betrayed, cannot be discovered, I hope, through reasoning or supposition.

17. "You prefer, I trust, a single wise man to a thousand fools. At times of political crisis a wise man can confer great benefits.

18. "A king may turn to thousands of fools, to tens of thousands, but they will not render him the least assistance.

19. "Yet even a single minister who is clever, brave, capable, and knowledgeable can secure great royal fortune for a king or his officer.

20. "I trust you have appointed servants to the tasks appropriate to them, the foremost servants to the most important tasks, the middling to the middling ones, and the lowly to the low.

21. "I trust you appoint your principal ministers to the principal tasks, men who hold hereditary positions, who are honest, and have passed the test of loyalty.

22. "People have no reason to despise you, I hope, as sacrificial priests despise an outcaste, or women a lover who takes them brutally.

23. "Remember, too, that a shrewd man with cunning schemes, a servant prone to corruption, or a man who is bold and hungry for power will slay you if you do not strike first.

24. "I trust you have appointed as your general a bold and brave man, one who is steady, sagacious, honest, highborn, loyal, and capable.

25. "You show honor and esteem to your foremost soldiers, I trust, the courageous, powerful men who are skilled in battle and have already evinced their heroism.

26. "I trust you pay, when payment is due, the appropriate wages and rations to your army, and do not defer them.

27. "If the time for their wages and rations is missed, servants grow angry with their masters and are easily corrupted—and this, as it is set down in the texts, can lead to very great misfortune.

28. "I hope everyone has remained loyal to you, especially the men of good family, and would willingly give up his life in your cause.

29. "I trust you always choose a man of the provinces as your envoy,

Bharata, a wise, diplomatic, perceptive, and discerning man, who repeats exactly what he is told.

30. "I trust you have come to learn the minds of the eighteen chief officials in each foreign state, and the fifteen of your own, by means of undetectable spies, three for every official.

31. "I hope, crusher of your foes, you do not wrongly view as harmless any hostile men who, once deported, have made their way back.

32. "You do not, I hope, associate with brahmans who are materialists, dear brother. Their only skill is in bringing misfortune; they are fools who think themselves wise.

33. "Although preeminent texts on righteous conduct are ready to hand, those ignorant fellows derive their ideas from logic alone and so propound utter nonsense.

34-36. "I trust you are keeping Ayodhyā content and prosperous, dear brother, the city where from ancient times our heroic ancestors have lived. I trust the city with its sturdy gates is still true to its name, 'The Impregnable,' still thronging with elephants, horses, and chariots, still crowded with nobles by the thousands—brahmans, kshatriyas, and *vaiśyas*—every one of them remaining, as always, prompt in his own tasks, self-controlled, and energetic. I trust the city is still crowded with mansions of various construction and thronged with learned people.

37-39. "I trust that the countryside is still prospering, Rāghava, and that life there continues comfortable, with shrines abounding by the hundreds, with sanctuaries, wells, and pools lending their adornment. I trust that the people are well settled, and the men and women happy; that fairs and festivals lend their adornment, and that the boundary lines are well spaced. The land is still rich in cattle and free from disasters, I trust, still nourished beyond the whim of the rain god, still lovely and safe from wild beasts.

40. "I hope you cherish all men who make their living by farming and cattle raising; for a well-founded economy, dear brother, promotes the world's happiness.

41. "I trust, then, that you support them with protective and defensive measures. A king must, in accordance with the ways of righteousness, guard all who live in his realm.

42. "I hope you gladden your women and guard them well, but do not place too much trust in them and tell them secrets.

43. "You are protecting the elephant forests, I trust, and attending to the needs of the elephants. I trust you often rise early, prince, and display yourself in full array to the people on the thoroughfares.

44. "I trust all the forts are well-stocked with money, grain, weapons, and water, with machines of war and craftsmen and archers.

45. "Your revenues far exceed your expenditures, I hope, and your treasure never passes into unworthy hands, Rāghava.

46. "I trust your expenditures go for the gods and ancestors, brahmans and guests, the soldiers and hosts of allies.

47. "No noble, honest man is ever charged with theft, I hope, without being interrogated by men learned in the sacred texts; and if innocent, is never imprisoned out of greed.

48. "And when a thief, either caught in the act or discovered with the stolen property, has been seized and interrogated, I hope he is never set free, bull among men, out of greed for money.

49. "I trust your wise ministers, Rāghava, render judgment impartially when a rich man and a poor man are engaged in a suit.

50. "For the tears people shed when falsely accused come to slay the livestock and children of the king who rules for personal gain.

51. "I trust you make use of the three means, Rāghava—affection, kind words, and gifts—in showing regard for children, the aged, and the foremost learned brahmans.

52. "You pay homage to your gurus, I trust, to the aged, to ascetics, guests, and gods, to shrines and all accomplished brahmans.

53. "You never deny the claims of righteousness in the name of statecraft, I trust, or again, the claims of statecraft in the name of righteousness, or either of them—from lust for pleasure—in the name of personal desire.

54. "Foremost of champions, I trust you make due allocation of time—and you are aware of the proper time for each, Bharata—and attend to all three, to matters of righteousness, of the state, and of personal desire.

55. "I hope the brahmans who comprehend the meaning of all the

sacred texts, and the people of the city and provinces, too, wish you happiness, my wise brother.

56-58. "I trust you avoid the fourteen errors of kings: atheism; falsehood; irascibility; inattention; procrastination; shunning the wise; indolence; sensual indulgence; solitary determination of political affairs; taking counsel with those ignorant of such affairs; failure to execute your decisions, to keep your counsel secret, or to employ auspicious rites; and indiscriminate courtesy.

59. "I trust you never eat savory foods all by yourself, Rāghava, and that you give aid to allies when they request it."

The end of the ninety-fourth *sarga* of the *Ayodhyākāṇḍa* of the *Śrī Rāmāyaṇa*.

Sarga 95

1. After listening to Rāma's words, Bharata replied, "What good is it for me to know the right conduct of kings, when I am wholly lost to righteousness?

2. "There is an ancient practice of righteousness, bull among men, one established among us for all time. It is this: with the eldest brother living, your Majesty, a younger may not become king.

3. "So come back with me, Rāghava, to the prosperous city of Ayodhyā, and have yourself consecrated for the good of our House.

4. "Some say a king is but a mortal; I esteem him a god. His conduct in matters of righteousness and statecraft, it is rightly said, is beyond that of mere mortals.

5. "While I was still in the land of the Kekayas, my brother, and you had withdrawn to the wilderness, the king, a man esteemed by the good, a performer of sacrifices, went to heaven.

6. "Arise, tiger among men, make the funeral libation to Father. Śatrughna here and I have already done so.

7. "It is said, Rāghava, that what a well-loved person gives to those in the world of the ancestors abides forever—and Father loved you well."

8-9. When he heard Bharata's piteous words that told him of his father's death—the dreadful words Bharata spoke, which struck him like a bolt of lightning—Rāma Rāghava, slayer of enemies, lost consciousness. Throwing out his arms he fell to the ground like a flowering tree in the forest cut down by an ax.

10-11. Fallen upon the earth, Rāma, the lord of earth, resembled a bull elephant asleep, grown weary from striking a riverbank. His three brothers and Vaidehī wept as they sprinkled water upon him, the great bowman, utterly broken by grief.

12. Soon Kākutstha revived, and with tears trickling from his eyes he began a long and sorrowful lament:

13. "What good was I, a wretched son, to my great father? He died of grief for me, and I could not even perform the final rites for him.

14. "Oh Bharata, my blameless brother, you have achieved your greatest goal, you and Śatrughna, since you could honor the king with all the rites for the dead.

15. "Ayodhyā is bereft of the lord of men; it no longer has its chief, no longer has direction. Even were my stay in the forest over, I could not bear to go back.

16. "When my stay in the forest is at an end, slayer of enemies, who will there be in Ayodhyā ever again to give me guidance, now that father has gone to the other world?

17. "In the past when Father noticed good conduct on my part, he would say such gratifying things to me, so pleasant to hear. From whom am I to hear them now?"

18. When he finished speaking to Bharata, Rāghava approached his wife, her face like the full moon, and consumed with grief he said to her:

19. "Sītā, your father-in-law is dead, and you, Lakṣmaṇa, have lost your father. Bharata has brought the sorrowful news that the lord of earth has gone to heaven."

2178*. As Kākutstha spoke, still more copious tears welled up in the eyes of the glorious young men. All three brothers did what they could to solace him, and they told him, "Let the funeral libation be offered to Father, the master of the world."

2179*. When Sītā heard that her father-in-law the king had gone to heaven, tears so flooded her eyes that she no longer could see her husband.

20. As the daughter of Janaka wept, Rāma comforted her. Lost in sorrow he then said sorrowfully to Lakṣmaṇa,

21. "Bring me a cake of almond meal and fetch an upper garment of barkcloth. I will go to make the funeral libation for our great father.

22. "Let Sītā proceed in front, and you next, while I go at the rear, for such is the procession of mourning."

23-24. Their constant attendant, the celebrated Sumantra, a high-minded and gentle man, self-restrained, tranquil, and staunchly devoted to Rāma, joined the princes in solacing Rāghava. Then, lending support, he escorted him down to the gracious Mandākinī River.

25-26. In pain the glorious princes made their way to the charming bathing place on the lovely Mandākinī River, where the woodlands were always in flower, and the current ran swiftly. And on reaching the landing, gracious and sparkling clear, they sprinkled water for the king with the words, "Father, let this be for you."

27. The protector of the earth held out a handful of water, and facing the direction of Yama he said, weeping:

28. "O tiger among kings, may this pure water I now give you be at your disposal in the world of the ancestors and abide forever."

29. Mighty Rāghava then ascended from the bathing place on the Mandākinī and in the company of his brothers made the offering of food to his father.

30. Upon a spread of *darbha* grass Rāma deposited the cake of almond meal mixed with fruit of the jujube tree. And weeping in the anguish of his deep sorrow, he said:

31. "Be pleased to eat this, great king, such food as we ourselves now eat, for a man's gods must feed on the same food as he."

32. The tiger among men ascended from the riverbank and by the same way he had come climbed up the lovely slope of the mountain.

33. On reaching the door of his leaf hut the lord of the world clasped both Bharata and Lakṣmaṇa in his arms.

34. All the brothers and Vaidehī began to weep, and the mountain echoed with the sound, as of lions roaring.

35. Bharata's soldiers were alarmed when they heard the tumultuous sound. "Bharata must surely have met with Rāma," they said. "The loud sound must be their grieving over their dead father."

36. With one mind they all left their camps and raced off in the direction of the noise, following where it led them.

37. Some went on horses or elephants, others—the delicate ones—on ornate chariots, while the rest of the men went on foot.

38. All the people rushed to the ashram, yearning to see Rāma, for, though his absence had been brief, it had seemed so very long.

39. Yearning to see the reunion of the brothers, they hurried off on every sort of vehicle, in a flurry of hoofs and wheels.

40. Struck by the hoofs and wheels of the many vehicles, the earth gave off a tumultuous sound, like the heavens when stormclouds gather.

41. The sound frightened the bull elephants and the cows in their train, and they ran off to another part of the forest, perfuming the way with their scent.

42. Boars, deer, lions, buffaloes, apes, monkeys, tigers, cow-eared antelopes, and wild oxen were terrified, as well as the dappled antelopes.

43. Sheldrakes, moorhens, geese, ducks, plovers, cuckoos, and curlews took to the horizons in a blind rush.

44. The sky appeared to be as covered with birds frightened at the sound as did the earth with men.

45. Righteous Rāma then caught sight of the tearful, sorrowing men, and like a father or a mother he embraced them.

46. The prince embraced some men, while others did obeisance to him; his presence restored to all of them, each according to his station, their one true kinsman or one true friend.

47. The great men wept, and the noise made earth and heaven echo incessantly, through the mountain caves and in all directions, with a sound like the roll of bass drums.

The end of the ninety-fifth *sarga* of the *Ayodhyākāṇḍa* of the *Śrī Rāmāyaṇa*.

Sarga 96

1. Placing the wives of Daśaratha before him, Vasiṣṭha set out for that spot, longing to see Rāma.

2. Proceeding slowly toward the Mandākinī, the wives of the king soon spied the bathing place Rāma and Lakṣmaṇa frequented.

3. Kausalyā's throat was choked with sobs, and her mouth went dry as she spoke in her desolation to Sumitrā and the other wives of the king:

4. "This must be where they come to bathe—poor children. It has recently been disturbed by them, whom nothing had ever disturbed before. Once it was deserted, off here in the forest—but they have been driven from their country!

5. "It must be from here, Sumitrā, that your son Saumitri, constantly and without flagging, has to fetch water himself on my son's behalf."

6. On the ground the large-eyed woman saw the cake of almond meal for the father deposited upon the *darbha* grass, whose blades pointed toward the south.

7. And when Queen Kausalyā observed what had been deposited on the ground by Rāma in anguish for his father, she said to all of Daśaratha's women:

8. "Look at this. It was offered by Rāghava according to precept to his father, the great Rāghava, the leader of the Ikṣvākus.

9. "But how unseemly a food I find it for the great and godlike king, who enjoyed so many delicacies.

10. "He had the whole four-cornered earth for his enjoyment; he was great Indra's equal on earth. How is it possible that the lord of the land has now but a cake of almond meal for food?

11. "No greater sorrow than this has the world to show me, that the once-prosperous Rāma should have only such meal to offer his father.

12. "And I have before my very eyes the cake Rāma offered his father—how is it, then, my heart does not burst for sorrow into a thousand pieces?"

13. Such were her anguished words, and her co-wives tried to comfort her. They continued on, then, and soon caught sight of

Rāma in the ashram, resembling a deathless god fallen from heaven.

14. As his mothers gazed at Rāma, who was denied now every luxury, they were anguished and racked with grief and broke out in shrill weeping.

15. Rāma, tiger among men, a man always true to his promise, rose and clasped the lovely feet of all his mothers.

16. And the large-eyed women brushed the dust from his back with their lovely hands, with their soft fingers and palms so pleasant to the touch.

17. Saumitri, too, was overcome with sorrow as he gazed at all his mothers. He did obeisance to them after Rāma, slowly and clingingly.

18. And all the women treated good Lakṣmaṇa, a son born of Daśaratha, exactly as they treated Rāma.

19. Sītā, too, sorrowfully grasped the feet of her mothers-in-law and stood before them, her eyes brimming with tears.

20. Just as a mother would embrace her own daughter, Kausalyā embraced Sītā as she stood anguished with sorrow, desolate and haggard from her stay in the forest. And she said to her:

21. "How is it possible that the daughter of the king of Videha, the daughter-in-law of Daśaratha, the wife of Rāma, should have to live a life of pain in the desolate forest?

22-23. "Your face is like a lotus scorched by sunshine, like a withered lily, or gold caked with dirt, or the moon obscured by clouds, and as I look at it, grief consumes me as fire consumes its bed—a wild grief, here, in my heart, Vaidehī, kindled by this calamity."

24. As his mother was speaking in her anguish, Bharata's elder brother made his way to Vasiṣṭha and clasped his feet.

25. Rāghava grasped the feet of the fiery and brilliant family priest just as Indra, overlord of the deathless gods, might grasp Bṛhaspati's, and together they took their seats.

26. Lastly, righteous Bharata sat down near his elder brother, and with him sat the counselors, the leading men of the city, the soldiers, and the people most wise in the ways of righteousness.

27. As mighty Bharata sat next to him and gazed at him dressed as an ascetic, yet radiant with majesty, he humbly cupped his hands in reverence, like great Indra before Prajāpati.

28. "Just what will Bharata say to Rāghava now, after bowing to him and showing him honor?" the nobles wondered and waited with truly great curiosity.

29. Surrounded by their friends the brothers sat—truthful Rāghava, high-minded Lakṣmaṇa, and righteous Bharata—like the three fires at a sacred rite with the officiants gathered all around.

The end of the ninety-sixth *sarga* of the *Ayodhyākāṇḍa* of the *Śrī Rāmāyaṇa*.

Sarga 97

1. Now, when Rāma had comforted his brother Bharata, who so cherished his guru, he and his brother Lakṣmaṇa began to question him:

2. "I should like to hear from your own lips what all this means, why you have come to this region in barkcloth, hides, and matted hair.

3. "For what reason did you leave the kingdom and enter this region wearing black hides and matted hair? Please, tell me everything."

4. So great Kākutstha spoke, and the son of Kaikeyī cupped his hands in reverence once more, and holding them out stiffly, replied:

5. "It was grave wrongdoing for our great-armed father to repudiate my noble brother. And grief for his son so tortured him that he went to heaven.

6. "Under the constraint of a woman—my mother, Kaikeyī—he committed this great evil, slayer of foes, which robbed him of his glory.

7. "But my mother never achieved her goal, the kingship. And now she is a widow racked with grief, who must fall into the most abominable hell.

8. "Please show your grace to me, your slave. Have yourself consecrated, like Indra the munificent, into the kingship this very day.

9. "All these subjects and your widowed mothers have betaken themselves to you. Please, show them your grace.

10. "It is proper both by reason of succession and by virtue of the man himself. O giver of honor, assume the kingship as is right, and grant your loved ones their desire.

11. "Let the earth be a widow no more, but once again complete, with you as her husband, just as the autumn night is made complete by the bright, hare-marked moon.

12-13. "I and all the advisers here are begging you with heads bowed low. Tiger among men, please, show your grace to me, your brother, your pupil and slave, and do not transgress against this whole order of advisers, this ancient, hereditary, and venerable order."

14. With these tearful words Bharata, the great-armed son of Kaikeyī, pressed his head once more to Rāma's feet.

15. And as his brother Bharata stood heaving sighs like an elephant in rut, Rāma embraced him and replied:

16. "You are highborn, valorous, and mighty, and keep your vows. How would it be it possible for one such as you ever to do evil for the sake of kingship?

17. "I find no fault with you, crusher of foes, not the slightest. But then too, you ought not, like a child, reproach your mother.

18. "Champion of righteousness, your mother commands as much reverence as our father, who was wise in the ways of righteousness and held in honor by the world.

19. "Our father and mother, righteous people both, bade me 'Go to the forest.' How can I do otherwise, Rāghava?

20. "It is for you to assume the kingship in Ayodhyā, held in honor by the world. I must live in the Daṇḍaka wilderness, wearing clothes of barkcloth.

21. "Such was the apportionment the great king made in the presence of all the world. And after giving his orders, the mighty Daśaratha went to heaven.

22. "The righteous king, the guru of the world, must be your guide. You must accept what Father bestowed, whatever your portion.

23. "For my part, dear brother, I will accept the portion bestowed by our great father and withdraw for fourteen years to the Daṇḍaka wilderness.

24. "It is what my great father—who was held in honor by the men of the world, the peer of Indra, overlord of the wise gods—bade me do that I regard as my ultimate good, not sovereign lordship over all the worlds."

The end of the ninety-seventh *sarga* of the *Ayodhyākāṇḍa* of the *Śrī Rāmāyaṇa*.

Sarga 98

1. The lions among men continued to grieve in the company of their hosts of friends, and the night passed, painfully.

2. When night had brightened into dawn, his brothers performed the morning offering and prayers by the Mandākinī in the company of their friends, and then returned to Rāma.

3. They sat together in silence, no one saying a word, until, from where he sat among their friends, Bharata addressed Rāma:

4. "My mother has been satisfied; the kingship has been bestowed on me. And I bestow it on you, and you alone. Enjoy unchallenged kingship.

5. "Like a dike washed away by a great flood when the rains come, the kingdom will utterly disintegrate unless you prevent it, and no one else can.

6. "An ass cannot match the pace of a horse, birds cannot match Tārkṣya's pace, nor have I the power to match yours, lord of the land.

7. "Life is ever easy when it is others who must depend on you, but how hard life is, Rāma, when you must depend on others.

8-9. "It is like when a man plants a tree and nurtures it till it becomes a great tree with spreading branches, impossible for a short man to climb. When the tree comes into flower but shows no fruit—the whole purpose for which it was grown—the man fails to take any pleasure in it.

10. "This is a simile, my great-armed brother—and you will easily

grasp its meaning—for your not ruling over us, a mighty master over his servants.

11. "Let the guildsmen, O great king, and all the leading subjects behold you installed in the kingship, tamer of foes, blazing like the sun.

12. "Let rutting elephants trumpet in your entourage, Kākutstha; let the women of the inner chamber rejoice with all their hearts."

13. The various classes of townspeople approved as just the words they heard Bharata speak in supplication of Rāma.

14. Accomplished Rāma gazed at glorious Bharata lamenting in his sorrow, and in full self-possession tried to comfort him:

15. "No one acts of his own free will; man is not independent. This way and that he is pulled along by fate.

16. "All accumulation ends in depletion, all rising ends in falling, in separation all union ends, and all life ends in death.

17. "Just as ripe fruit need fear one thing—to fall—so every man that is born need fear but death.

18. "Just as a stout-pillared house decays and collapses, so men collapse, succumbing to old age and death.

19. "The passing days and nights quickly deplete the life of all living things in the world, as water is dried up by the rays of the summer sun.

20. "You should be grieving for yourself, not for anyone else. Your life is steadily dwindling, whether you stand still or move.

21. "Death walks at your side, death sits next to you. Travel as far away as you like, death will come back with you.

22. "Wrinkles beset the body, the hair turns white; a man decays with old age, and what can he do to escape it?

23. "People are glad when the sun rises, or glad when it goes down, but they are wholly unaware that their life is slipping away.

24. "All things that breathe are delighted to see the face of each new season come, though with the turning of the seasons their life-breath is slipping away.

25-26. "As two pieces of wood might meet upon the open sea and, having met, drift apart after a few brief moments, so too do your wives and children, your relatives and riches meet with you and hasten away. To lose them is a certainty.

27. "No creature that draws breath in the world can escape this course of things. There is no cure to be found for it, grieve for the dead all you will.

28-29. "Like a man standing by the roadside and calling out to a passing caravan, 'I too am coming, right behind you'—so did our ancestors take this sure road, our fathers and our forefathers. Why should you grieve when you cannot avoid it, when you are following that very road yourself?

30. "Since life trickles away like the waters of a stream, never to return, happiness should be one's aim—and people have found happiness, or so it is recorded.

31. "By means of every holy rite, with fitting priestly stipends, our righteous father, the lord of earth, cleansed away his sins and went to heaven.

32. "Our father conscientiously supported his dependents, protected his subjects, levied taxes in accordance with righteousness, and by virtue of these acts he has gone to the highest heaven.

33. "Having offered up the various sacrifices and enjoyed abundant pleasures, the lord of earth attained a ripe old age and went to heaven.

34. "Our father abandoned a decrepit mortal body and found the heavenly treasure that awaits one in the world of Brahmā.

35. "This man no one should mourn, no one as wise as you, as learned and intelligent.

36. "The strong of heart will shun these different griefs, these words of lamentation, this weeping, and hold fast to wisdom in all circumstances.

37. "Compose yourself and do not grieve, most eloquent of men. Go back and take up your residence in the town, as Father of his own accord directed you to do.

38. "And the order this same man of holy deeds has given me I shall carry out, and exactly where our noble father directed.

39. "It would be wrong, tamer of foes, for me to cast aside his order. And you too must always respect it, for he was our kinsman, indeed, our father."

40. Such were Rāma's most sensible words, and when he finished speaking, righteous Bharata made this righteous and wonderful reply:

41. "Where in this wide world is your like to be found, tamer of foes, a man whom sorrow does not pain, and joy does not delight?

42-43. "You are esteemed by the elders, you have questioned them about your doubts and gained these insights about the living and the dead, and how alike they are in their existing and not existing both. What is there that could distress you? Such a man does not despair when calamity befalls him.

44. "Your courage is like that of a deathless god; you are a great man true to your word. You are all-knowing and all-seeing and a man of wisdom, Rāghava.

45. "In possession of such virtues and sage in matters of birth and death, you would not be affected by sorrow, however insufferable.

46. "When I was absent, my mother, that wretched woman, did an evil thing on my account, which I never sought. Please forgive me!

47. "I am bound by the bond of righteousness, and only because of that do I not inflict the harshest punishment now on my mother and kill her, as she deserves, for the evil she has done.

48. "How could I, a son born of Daśaratha—that man of honorable family and honorable deeds—knowing the meaning of righteousness, do a deed so abominable, so unrighteous?

49. "I would not reproach our father before the assembly; he was a god to us, a performer of sacred rites, our guru, elder, king, and father, now departed.

50. "But still, my righteous brother, what man knowing the meaning of righteousness would do so sinful a deed, contrary to all that is right and good, just to please a woman?

51. "There is an ancient saying: 'Creatures go mad when their end is near.' In acting as he did, the king has illustrated this saying for all the world.

52. "Mindful of what is correct, you must redress the transgression Father committed out of anger, delusion, and recklessness.

53. "Only the offspring who corrects his father's transgressions does the world consider a son—and the very opposite if he does otherwise.

54. "Be such a son, do not endorse the evil deed Father did, censured by every man of wisdom in the world.

55. "Save Kaikeyī, Father, and me, save your friends and our kinsmen, all the people of the city and provinces, this whole world.

56. "How incongruous they are, this wilderness and the kshatriya order, this matted hair and the government of men. You must not do so perverse a deed.

57. "Or, if it is your wish to follow the way of righteousness that demands physical exhaustion, then endure the exhaustion of righteously governing the four social orders.

58. "Those who understand righteousness—and you yourself understand it—say that of the four stages of life the foremost is that of householder. How can you renounce it?

59. "I am a child measured against you, both in learning and rank of birth. How should I govern the land when you are on hand to do it?

60. "I am a child, inferior in both virtue and intelligence, and junior in rank as well. Without you I could not carry on.

61. "In keeping with the code of righteousness appropriate for you, my righteous brother, govern the kingdom of our fathers, this whole, sovereign, unchallenged kingdom, in the company of your kinsmen.

62. "Let all the subjects in a body, and the priests under Vasiṣṭha's lead who are expert in vedic recitation, consecrate you here and now to the accompaniment of the vedic hymns.

63. "Once we have consecrated you, return and protect Ayodhyā, utterly triumphant over all peoples, like Vāsava with his Maruts.

64. "Discharge the three debts: completely eliminate your enemies, fulfill your friends' every desire, and give me guidance, as you alone can.

65. "My brother, let your friends now find delight in your consecration, let your enemies now take fright and flee in the ten directions.

66. "Bull among men, rid us now of this infamy, me and my mother, and guard our revered father from sin.

67. "I implore you with my head bowed low. Take pity on me, on all your kinsmen, as the Great Lord takes pity on creatures.

68. "But if you only turn your back and go off into the forest, I will go with you as well."

69. But for all that Bharata wearied himself begging Rāma's grace with head bowed low, the courageous lord of earth was resolved not to return, but to hold firmly to what his father had bidden him.

70. The people observed Rāghava's wonderful determination, and they felt joy and sorrow both at once: they were sorrowful he would not return to Ayodhyā and yet rejoiced to observe how determined he was to keep his promise.

71. The priests, the merchants, and the commanders of the troops—his mothers, too, stunned though they were and choked with sobs—commended what Bharata said, and they bowed low before Rāma and began to implore him all together.

The end of the ninety-eighth *sarga* of the *Ayodhyākāṇḍa* of the *Śrī Rāmāyaṇa*.

Sarga 99

1. When Bharata had finished speaking, Lakṣmaṇa's majestic eldest brother, the most honored among his kinsmen, replied to him once more:

2. "How fitting are the words you have spoken, like a true son of Kaikeyī and Daśaratha, the best of kings.

3. "Long ago, dear brother, when our father was about to marry your mother, he made a brideprice pledge to your grandfather—the ultimate price, the kingship.

4. "Later, at the battle of the gods and *asuras*, the lordly king of the land, pleased and delighted with your mother, granted her a boon.

5-6. "Your glorious fair-skinned mother then bound the best of men to his oath and demanded these two boons of him: the kingship for you, tiger among men, and my banishment. And under this constraint the king granted her the boon.

7. "And that is why, bull among men, father constrained me to do this, to live in the forest fourteen years, in accordance with the granting of the boon.

8. "And I for my part have come here, to the lonely forest, with Lakṣmaṇa and Sītā, and I will brook no opposition to my safeguarding Father's truthfulness.

9. "In just the same way you must likewise ensure, by your immediate consecration, that the truth of the lord of kings, our father, be preserved.

10. "Free the lordly king from his debt, for my sake, righteous Bharata. Save your father and give your mother cause to rejoice.

11. "They recite a verse sung long ago, dear brother, by glorious Gaya when he was offering sacrifice to his ancestors in the land of Gayā:

12. " 'Because a son rescues his father from the hell named Put, he is called *putra*; or because he protects his ancestors.

13. " 'One should strive to have many virtuous and learned sons, for among such a host perhaps one might be found who will make the journey to Gayā.'

14. "All royal seers have concurred in this, delight of the king. Save your father, then, from hell, my lordly brother, best of men.

15. "Bharata, my mighty brother, go back to Ayodhyā with Śatrughna and all the twice-born men, and win the loyalty of your subjects.

16. "I will enter Daṇḍaka wilderness without delay, your Majesty, and only these two shall join me, Vaidehī and Lakṣmaṇa.

17. "It is you, Bharata, who must become the king of men. As for me, I shall become sovereign king of the beasts of the wild. Go now in delight, to the best of cities, and in delight I too shall go off to the Daṇḍakas.

18. "Let the royal parasol cast its cool shade over your head, blocking out the rays of the sun, bringer of day. I shall have shade as well to retreat to for comfort, the deeper shade of these woodland trees.

19. "Quick-witted Śatrughna will be your companion and trustworthy Saumitri my chief ally. Let all four of us, his principal sons, preserve the truth of the lord of men. Do not despair."

The end of the ninety-ninth *sarga* of the *Ayodhyākāṇḍa* of the *Śrī Rāmāyaṇa*.

Sarga 100

1. As righteous Rāma was consoling Bharata, a prominent brahman named Jābāli addressed him in words at variance with righteousness:

2. "Come now, Rāghava, you must not entertain such nonsensical ideas like the commonest of men, and you a noble-minded man in distress.

3. "What man is kin to anyone, what profit has anyone in anyone else? A person is born alone, and all alone he must die.

4. "And thus, Rāma, the man who feels attachment thinking, 'This is my mother, this my father', should be regarded as a madman, for in truth no one belongs to anyone.

5-6. "A man traveling from village to village will spend the night somewhere and next day leave the place where he stopped and continue on—in the same way, Kākutstha, his father and mother, his home and wealth are mere stopping places for a man. The wise feel no attachment to them.

7. "You must not, best of men, abdicate the kingship of your fathers and embark upon this unwise course, painful, rocky, and full of thorns.

8. "Consecrate yourself in prosperous Ayodhyā; the city is waiting for you, wearing her single braid of hair.

9. "Indulge in priceless royal pleasures and enjoy yourself in Ayodhyā, prince, like Śakra in his heaven.

10. "Daśaratha was nobody to you, and you were nobody to him. The king was one person, you another. So do as I am urging.

11. "The king has gone where he had to go; such is the course all mortals follow. You are merely deluding yourself.

12. "The men I grieve for, and I grieve for no one else, are all who place 'righteousness' above what brings them profit. They find only sorrow in this world, and at death their lot is annihilation just the same.

13. "People here busy themselves because 'It is the Eighth Day, the rite for the ancestors.' But just look at the waste of food—what really is a dead man going to eat?

14. "And if something one person eats here could fill the belly of

someone else, one could simply offer *śrāddha* for a traveler, and he would need no provisions for the road.

15. "It was only as a charm to secure themselves donations that cunning men composed those books that tell us, 'Sacrifice, give alms, sanctify yourself, practice asceticism, renounce.'

16. "Accept the idea once and for all, high-minded prince, that there exists no world to come. Address yourself to what can be perceived and turn your back on what cannot.

17. "Give precedence to these ideas of the wise, with which the whole world concurs. Be appeased by Bharata and accept the kingship."

The end of the one hundredth *sarga* of the *Ayodhyākāṇḍa* of the *Śrī Rāmāyaṇa*.

Sarga 101

1. Upon hearing Jābāli's words, Rāma, the most truthful of men, replied with sound argument, his own convictions quite unshaken:

2. "What you have said in the hopes of pleasing me is wrong with only a semblance of right; it is harm that simulates help.

3. "A person wins no esteem among the wise when his conduct belies his tenets, and he acts in evil ways, recognizing no bounds.

4. "It is conduct alone that proclaims whether a man is highborn or base, honest or dishonest, brave or merely a braggart.

5-6. "It would be ignobility with a semblance of nobility, dishonesty with an outward show of honesty, dishonor masquerading as honor, indecency disguised as decency, were I to reject the good and accept such unrighteousness. For it merely wears the cloak of righteousness; it would throw the world into confusion, and is utterly in conflict with duty and precept.

7. "What sensible man anywhere in the world, aware of what is right and wrong, would hold me in high esteem—a man of evil acts, a corruptor of the world?

8. "To whose actions should I be conforming, and how then should I reach heaven, were I to adopt this practice and break my promise?

9. "Besides, the entire world would follow suit in acting as it pleases, for subjects will behave just like their king.

10. "The actions of a king must always be truthful and benevolent. The kingdom will thereby be true, the world firmly established on truth.

11. "It is truth and truth alone that both gods and seers hold in esteem, for the man who tells the truth in this world will attain the highest abode.

12. "As from a serpent do people recoil from a man who speaks falsely. Truth, it is said, is the ultimate form of righteousness in this world, and the very root of heaven.

13. "Truth is the lord of this world, the goddess of the lotus resides in truth, all things are rooted in truth, there is no higher goal than truth.

14. "The giving of alms, sacrifices, the offering of oblations, the practice of asceticism, and the *vedas* themselves are based on truth, and so it is truth that must be one's highest aim.

15. "One man protects the world, one protects his House, one is exalted in heaven, and one sinks down to hell.

16. "As for me, why should I not truthfully follow my father's command? I have always been true to my word, and I have pledged upon my truth.

17. "Not out of greed or delusion or ignorance would I blindly breach the dam of truth. I will remain true to my promise to my guru.

18. "Neither the gods nor the ancestors, we have heard, accept offerings from a man whose covenant is false, from an inconstant and irresolute man.

19. "This personal code of righteousness I know myself to be the true one. Wise men have always borne the burden it imposes, and I gladly accept it.

20. "I reject the kshatriya's code, where unrighteousness and righteousness go hand in hand, a code that only debased, vicious, covetous, and evil men observe.

21. "And sinful action is of three sorts: One can have evil thoughts, or do an evil deed, or tell a lie.

22. "Land, fame, glory, and wealth seek out the man who holds to truth and ever attend on him. Let a man then devote himself to truth alone.

23. "What you consider the best course is in fact ignoble; the statements you make urging me to 'do what is good for me' are mere sophistry.

24. "I have promised my guru to live in the forest. How then can I do as Bharata bids, and defy the bidding of my guru?

25. "I made a promise in the presence of my guru—it brought delight to the heart of Queen Kaikeyī—and that promise shall not be broken.

26-27. "I will thus live a life of purity in the forest, restricting my food to holy things, roots, fruit, and flowers, and satisfying the gods and ancestors. My five senses will have contentment enough, and I shall be maintaining the world on its course. Moreover, I myself shall remain a sincere believer, fully aware of what is right and what is wrong.

28. "On entering this realm of action one must do good deeds. And such deeds have their rewards: Fire, Wind, and the Moon have reaped them.

29. "After Indra brought a hundred rites to completion he became king of the gods in the highest heaven. After performing awesome feats of asceticism the great seers reached heaven.

30. "Truthfulness, righteousness, and strenuous effort, compassion for creatures and kindly words, reverence for brahmans, gods, and guests is the path, say the wise, to the highest heaven.

31. "Those men who are earnest in righteousness and keep company with the wise, who are supremely generous, nonviolent, and free from taint, those supreme and mighty sages are the ones truly worthy of reverence in this world."

The end of the one hundred first *sarga* of the *Ayodhyākāṇḍa* of the *Śrī Rāmāyaṇa*.

Sarga 102

1. Vasiṣṭha, perceiving that Rāma was angry, addressed him: "Jābāli likewise understands the true course of this world. He only said these things in his desire to dissuade you.

2. "I want you now, master of the world, to learn from me the origin of this world. Everything was once just water, and within this water the earth was fashioned. The Self-existent Brahmā then came into existence with the gods.

3. "He then became a boar, raised up the treasure-laden earth, and created the whole moving world with the help of his accomplished sons.

4. "Brahmā the everlasting, the eternal and imperishable, arose from space. He begot Marīci, and Marīci a son named Kaśyapa.

5. "Kaśyapa begot Vivasvan, the Sun. Manu is recorded as the son of Vivasvan—he was the first lord of creatures—and the son of Manu was Ikṣvāku.

6. "It was on him that Manu originally bestowed this prosperous land, and thus know that Ikṣvāku was the first king of Ayodhyā.

7. "The son of Ikṣvāku, we have heard, was majestic Kukṣi, and Kukṣi was the father of the heroic Vikukṣi.

8. "The son of Vikukṣi was the mighty, powerful Bāṇa, and Bāṇa's son, the great-armed, glorious Anaraṇya.

9. "When Anaraṇya, the best of men, was king, there was no drought, no famine, and not a single thief in the land.

10. "Anaraṇya had a great-armed son, King Pṛthu. Pṛthu was the father of the great king Triśaṅku, that heroic man who by virtue of his truthfulness went to heaven with his body.

11. "Triśaṅku had a glorious son, Dhundhumāra, and Dhundhumāra begot glorious Yuvanāśva.

12. "Yuvanāśva was the father of majestic Māndhātṛ, and Māndhātṛ the father of mighty Susandhi.

13. "Susandhi had two sons, Dhruvasandhi and Prasenajit. Dhruvasandhi had a son named Bharata, a glorious crusher of foes.

14. "To great-armed Bharata was born a son named Asita, against whom neighboring kings rose up in enmity: the Haihayas, the Tālajaṅghas, the Śūras, and Śaśabindus.

15. "The king marshaled his troops in battle against them all, but he was driven into exile and became a contented sage upon a lovely mountain. He had two wives, both of whom were pregnant, we have heard.

16. "A man of the Bhṛgu clan named Cyavana had retired to the Himālayas, and Kālindī once approached the seer and did obeisance to him.

17. "She was eager to obtain a boon for the birth of a son, and the sage greeted her. The queen then went home and soon gave birth to a son.

18. "Her co-wife had given her poison in order to slay the unborn child, but he was born nonetheless along with that very poison, and so they called him Sagara.

19. "This was the King Sagara who in the course of a sacrifice had the ocean dug, which even now frightens creatures when it swells under the full moon.

20. "Asmañja, we have heard, was the son of Sagara, but in the very prime of life he was expelled by his father for the evil deeds he had done.

21. "Heroic Aṃśumant was the son of Asamañja, Dilīpa was the son of Aṃśumant, and Bhagīratha of Dilīpa.

22. "Bhagīratha was the father of Kakutstha, from whom you have come to be known as the Kākutsthas. Kakutstha's son was Raghu, whence you are called the Rāghavas.

23. "Raghu's mighty son was the awesome eater of men known throughout the world as Kalmāṣapāda Saudāsa.

24. "The son of Kalmāṣapāda was called Śaṅkhaṇa, and whoever came up against his might perished utterly with his army.

25. "The son of Śaṅkhaṇa was heroic, majestic Sudarśana, Sudarśana's son Agnivarṇa, Agnivarṇa's son Śīghraga.

26. "Śīghraga's son was Maru, Maru's son was Praśuśruka, Praśuśruka's son the splendid Ambarīṣa.

27. "Ambarīṣa's son was valorous Nahuṣa, Nahuṣa's son the supremely righteous Nābhāga.

28. "Aja and Suvrata were the two sons of Nābhāga, and Aja's son was righteous King Daśaratha.

29. "And you, known far and wide as Rāma, are his eldest son and heir. Assume, then, the kingship that is your own and show regard for the world, your Majesty.

30. "For among all the Ikṣvākus the first-born has always become the king. When the first-born is living, it is not a younger son but only the eldest who is consecrated for kingship.

31. "This is the age-old custom of your own house, the House of the Rāghavas, and you must not abandon it now. You must govern the earth with its abundant treasures and abundant vassal kingdoms, and like your father win great fame."

The end of the one hundred second *sarga* of the *Ayodhyākāṇḍa* of the *Śrī Rāmāyaṇa*.

Sarga 103

1. When Vasiṣṭha, the family priest of the king, had finished this speech, he once more addressed Rāma in harmony with righteousness:

2. "A man born into this world has three gurus, Rāghava Kākutstha: his teacher, his father, and his mother.

3. "The father begets the man, bull among men, but the teacher imparts wisdom to him, and for this reason he is called guru.

4. "I was your father's teacher and am yours, too, slayer of foes; in doing my bidding you will not stray from the path of the good.

5. "Here are the men of your assembly and the guildsmen gathered together; in practicing righteousness on their behalf, my son, you will not stray from the path of the good.

6. "Your mother is aged and righteous, and you must not disobey her; in doing as she bids you will not stray from the path of the good.

7. "If you do as Bharata bade when supplicating you, Rāghava, you will not go astray in your pursuit of truth and righteousness."

8. Addressed in this gentle fashion by his guru, Rāghava, bull among men, for his part replied to Vasiṣṭha who sat beside him:

9-10. "The constant benefits parents confer upon their child are not easily repaid—all that a mother and father do, giving him things to the limit of their resources, bathing and clothing him, always speaking kindly to him and nurturing him, too.

11. "King Daśaratha was my father, he begot me, and the promise I made to him shall not be rendered false."

12. So Rāma spoke, and noble Bharata, in great distress, addressed the charioteer who was waiting in attendance:

13. "Charioteer, spread some *kuśa* grass on the ground for me at once; I will fast against my brother, until he shows me his grace.

14. "Eating nothing, seeing nothing, like a penniless brahman, I will lie before the hut until he consents to return."

15. He watched in distress as Sumantra remained with his eyes fixed on Rāma, and then he procured a layer of *kuśa* grass himself and spread it on the earth.

16. Mighty Rāma, the best of royal seers, said to him, "What have I done, dear Bharata, that you should fast against me?

17. "A brahman may have the right to coerce men by lying on his side, but there is no precept permitting those whose heads are anointed to fast against anyone.

18. "So stand up, Rāghava, tiger among men, and abandon this heartless vow. You must leave at once for Ayodhyā, the best of cities."

19. But Bharata remained seated and, looking all around at the people of the city and provinces, he cried, "Why do you not remonstrate with my brother?"

20. And the people of the city and provinces then said to the great prince, "We recognize that what Rāghava is telling Kākutstha is correct.

21. "But then too, this illustrious man is holding firm to what his father bade him do. That is why we are truly incapable of dissuading him."

22. Hearing their words, Rāma said, "Listen to the words of our friends, who see with the eye of righteousness.

23. "You have heard from both sides now. Consider it well, Rāghava. Stand up, my great-armed brother, touch me and sip water."

24. Bharata then stood up, took a sip of water, and said, "Hear me, men of the assembly, you counselors and guildsmen, too.

25. "I did not ask my father for the kingship; I gave my mother no instructions. But I do recognize that my noble brother Rāghava is supremely wise in the ways of righteousness.

26. "Thus, if someone must live here, if father's bidding must be done, I myself will live out the fourteen years in the forest."

27. Righteous Rāma marveled at his brother's forthright declaration, and glancing at the people of the city and provinces he said,

28. "What my father in his lifetime bought or sold or pledged neither Bharata nor I can in any way annul.

29. "I cannot allow a substitute to live in the forest; that would be repugnant to me. What Kaikeyī asked was proper; what my father did was rightly done.

30. "I know Bharata is forbearing and shows his gurus honor. All will be perfectly safe in his care, for he is a great prince and true to his word.

31. "When I return from the forest I shall rejoin my righteous brother and become supreme lord of the earth.

32. "Kaikeyī made her demand of the king, and I have done her bidding and saved my father, the lord of earth, from falsehood."

The end of the one hundred third *sarga* of the *Ayodhyākāṇḍa* of the *Śrī Rāmāyaṇa*.

Sarga 104

1. The great seers who had assembled to watch marveled, thrilled by the meeting of the two incomparably mighty brothers.

2. The hosts of seers, perfected beings, and supreme seers remained invisible as they sang the praises of the two brothers, the great Kākutsthas.

3. "Fortunate the man who has such sons as these, sons who know and follow the way of righteousness. How envious we are after hearing their conversation."

4. Then all at once the hosts of seers, eager for the destruction of ten-necked Rāvaṇa, spoke to Bharata, tiger among kings.

5. "You are a wise and highborn prince, a man of great rectitude and glory. If you have any regard for your father, you must agree to what Rāma says.

6. "It is our wish that Rāma forever keep his father free from debt. It is because Daśaratha was free from his debt to Kaikeyī that he has gone to heaven."

7. Saying no more, the *gandharvas*, great seers, and royal seers all departed for their separate abodes.

8. Splendid Rāma was gladdened by these splendid words, and his face beamed with delight as he paid homage to the seers.

9. But Bharata went limp in every limb. He cupped his hands in reverence and, in a breaking voice, once more addressed Rāghava:

10. "Please, show regard for the code of kings and the traditional code of our House. Oh Kākutstha, grant what we beg of you, your mother and I.

11. "I cannot, all by myself, protect this vast kingdom. Nor can I win the loyalty of the people of the city and provinces; their loyalty is already fixed.

12. "It is for you alone our kinsmen and soldiers, our allies and friends are yearning, as farmers yearn for rain.

13. "Oh my wise brother, accept the kingship and restore its stability. You are the only one, Kākutstha, who commands the power to govern the world."

14. So Bharata spoke, and throwing himself at Rāma's feet he continued to beseech his brother with earnest expressions of love.

15. Rāma gathered his brother Bharata, dark and lotus-eyed, into his embrace, and in a voice like the call of the wild goose he said:

16. "You have the wisdom in your possession, innately and from your training, dear brother; you too are perfectly capable of protecting the land.

17. "Take counsel with your ministers, your friends, and wise counselors, and you shall see all matters accomplished, however great they may be.

18. "The moon's splendor might forsake it, Himālaya might lose its snow, the ocean might overstep its shore, but not I my promise to my father.

19. "Whether it was love or greed that made your mother act as she did on your behalf, dear brother, should be none of your concern. You must treat her as what she is—your mother."

20. So the son of Kausalyā spoke, his brilliance like the sun's, his face like the waxing moon. And Bharata then said to him:

21. "Please place these gold-trimmed slippers upon your feet, my brother. They will serve to guarantee the security of all the world."

22. The mighty tiger among men put on the slippers. Then taking them off he presented them to great Bharata.

23. The mighty and righteous Bharata accepted the ornamented slippers, and after reverently circling Rāghava he placed them atop a splendid elephant.

24. Rāma paid homage to his people in due order: to his gurus and counselors, to the subjects and both his younger brothers. Then the heir of the Rāghava dynasty dismissed them, standing firmly as Mount Himālaya by his own code of righteousness.

25. In their sorrow, his mothers could not bid him farewell, their throats were so choked with sobs, but Rāma did obeisance to them all and then entered his hut, in tears.

The end of the one hundred fourth *sarga* of the *Ayodhyākāṇḍa* of the *Śrī Rāmāyaṇa*.

Sarga 105

1. Bharata took the slippers and placed them upon his head. Then in delight he boarded the chariot with Śatrughna.

2. All the counselors revered for their counsel—Vasiṣṭha, Vāmadeva, and strictly observant Jābāli—proceeded before them.

3. They passed the lovely Mandākinī River, heading east and keeping great Mount Citrakūṭa on their right.

4. In the company of his army, Bharata made his way along the mountainside, observing the thousands of lovely different minerals it held.

5. Not far from Citrakūṭa Bharata caught sight of the ashram where the sage Bharadvāja made his residence.

6. Thoughtful Bharata, the delight of his House, approached the ashram, and alighting from the chariot he prostrated himself at Bharadvāja's feet.

7. In delight Bharadvāja asked, "Have you done what had to be done, Bharata my son? Have you met with Rāma?"

8. So the wise Bharadvāja spoke, and Bharata, who cherished the ways of righteousness, replied:

9. "Both his guru and I entreated the steadfast Rāghava, but he was deeply displeased and made this reply to Vasiṣṭha:

10. " 'I will scrupulously keep my promise to my father, the fourteen years I promised to my father.'

11. "So Rāghava eloquently spoke, and the wise Vasiṣṭha replied to him with equal eloquence, and spoke these weighty words:

12. " 'Be pleased, wise prince, to give us these gold-trimmed slippers. In your stead they will ensure the welfare and security of Ayodhyā.'

13. "So Vasiṣṭha spoke, and Rāghava stood facing eastward and bestowed on me these gold-worked slippers, in order to rule the kingdom.

14. "Great Rāma gave me leave, and now I am returning. I am going back to Ayodhyā, taking the splendid slippers with me."

15. The sage Bharadvāja listened to the earnest words of great Bharata, and then even more earnestly he replied:

16. "It is not surprising, tiger among men, most upright and dutiful of men, that nobility should come to reside in you, like rainwater in the lowlands.

17. "Your great-armed father Daśaratha is not dead, not when he has such a son as you, a righteous son who cherishes the ways of righteousness."

18. When the great seer finished speaking, Bharata cupped his hands in reverence, and in preparation for bidding him farewell he clasped his feet.

19. Again and again majestic Bharata reverently circled Bharadvāja, and then, with his counselors, he set out for Ayodhyā.

20. Spread far and wide with all its coaches, wagons, horses, and elephants, the army made its way back in Bharata's train.

21. They all crossed the heavenly, wave-wreathed Yamunā River, and saw once more the gracious waters of the Ganges.

22. Crossing the river brimming with lovely water, he and his kinsmen and army entered lovely Śṛṅgaverapura.

23. Beyond Śṛṅgaverapura, Bharata once more beheld Ayodhyā, and he was consumed with sorrow as he said to his charioteer:

24. "Look, charioteer, Ayodhyā is darkened and in ruins. Its beauty is gone, its bliss is gone, it is desolate and silent."

The end of the one hundred fifth *sarga* of the *Ayodhyākāṇḍa* of the *Śrī Rāmāyaṇa*.

Sarga 106

1. The coach gave out a smooth deep sound as the glorious and lordly Bharata approached and directly entered Ayodhyā.

2. There were cats roaming everywhere, and owls circling; the people and elephants were in hiding, and the city lay shrouded in gloom. It lay dark as night itself with no light at all.

3. It looked like the constellation Rohiṇī, the majestically radiant and beloved wife of the Moon, the enemy of Rāhu, when that seizing eclipse encroaches and harries her left all alone;

4. Like a wasted mountain river, its water scant, hot, and turbid, the birds dazed by summer's heat, the minnows, fish, and crocodiles lying hidden deep below;

5. Like a flame that has leapt from the sacrificial fire, smokeless and golden when the oblation was poured, then abruptly snuffed out;

6. Like an army routed in a great battle, its armaments in ruins, its horses and elephants slaughtered, its chariots and standards shattered, its heroes slain;

7. Like a great wave raised foaming and roaring on the open sea and then, when the wind dies down, dispersed into silence;

8. Like an altar after the worthy sacrificers have left with all their sacrificial implements, the hour of the *soma* pressing has come and gone, and the din has ceased;

9. Like a herd of cows in the middle of a pasture when their bull has left them, and they no longer graze the new grass but are anguished and wistful;

10. Like a new pearl necklace when its precious gems have come unstrung, the most perfect, smooth, radiant, glistening gems;

11. Like a star suddenly tottering from its place when its merit is exhausted, and falling from heaven down to earth, its expansive luster dimmed;

12. Like a woodland vine at the end of spring, decked with flowers and swarming with drunken bees, then scorched by a racing forest fire and withered.

13. All the merchants were in a daze, the bazaars and shops closed up tight, and the city looked like the night sky covered with clouds, the hare-marked moon and constellations obscured;

14. Like a rowdy tavern littered with smashed goblets, the costly drinks drained, and the patrons lying in the open, dead drunk;

15. Like a ruined well, sunken and broken, its water used up, its pavement cracked, its buckets cracked and scattered all around;

16. Like a bowstring, once long and taut and fitted out with loops, fallen from the bow to the ground when cut by a champion's arrows;

17. Like a filly stripped of all her trappings and wildly whipped on by a battle-drunk rider, a weak filly, one that should still be running free;

18. Like the radiance of the sun gone behind a bank of clouds when the driving rains come, and the blue-black clouds obscure it.

19. The charioteer drove the excellent chariot onward, and seated inside, Bharata, Daśaratha's majestic son, addressed him:

20. "Why, I wonder, are the deep, pervasive sounds of singing and musical instruments not coming from Ayodhyā now, as they always used to?

21. "The heady fragrance of wine, the pervading fragrance of garlands, and the fragrance of aloewood incense are no longer carried on the breeze.

22. "The clangor of fine carriages, the rich sound of horses, the trumpeting of rutting elephants, and the deafening sound of chariots are no longer to be heard in the city, now that Rāma is in exile.

23. "No people are to be seen thronging together on Ayodhyā's thoroughfares, neither the youngsters in their finery nor the adults with their stately step."

24. With these and many similar comments he entered his father's residence, bereft now of the lord of men like a cave without its lion.

The end of the one hundred sixth *sarga* of the *Ayodhyākāṇḍa* of the *Śrī Rāmāyaṇa*.

Sarga 107

1. After resettling his mothers in Ayodhyā, the grief-stricken Bharata, firm in his vows, addressed his gurus:

2. "I have come to ask leave of you all; I am going to Nandigrāma. There I shall suffer through all this sorrow of being without Rāghava.

3. "With the king gone to heaven and my guru in the forest, I shall await Rāma until he assumes the kingship, for he is the glorious king."

4. When they heard great Bharata's heartfelt declaration, Vasiṣṭha the family priest and all the counselors replied,

5. "These are seemly and praiseworthy words you have spoken out of love for your brother, Bharata, and they befit you.

6. "Keeping to the noble way, always zealous on your kinsmen's behalf, and steadfast in your brotherly love—whose approval could you fail to win?"

7. On hearing the kind words of the counselors, all that he could hope for, he bade the charioteer, "Harness my chariot."

8. The face of the majestic prince beamed with delight as he did obeisance to all his mothers and boarded the chariot with Śatrughna.

9. Once aboard, Bharata and Śatrughna sped off in great joy, together with their counselors and family priest.

10. Before them went all their gurus, the brahmans led by Vasiṣṭha, heading east toward Nandigrāma.

11. And altogether unbidden, the army, a crush of elephants, horses, and chariots, set off as Bharata left, and so did all the inhabitants of the town.

12. Righteous Bharata, who cherished his brother, hurried in his chariot to Nandigrāma, still bearing the slippers upon his head.

13. Soon Bharata entered Nandigrāma, and hurriedly alighting from the chariot he told his gurus:

14. "My brother himself gave me the kingship as a trust—it is these gold-trimmed slippers that will guarantee its welfare and security—and I shall guard this trust until Rāghava's return.

15. "O that I might soon see the feet of Rāma Rāghava placed within these slippers, tying them on once again with my own hands.

16. "When I am reunited with Rāghava, I shall lay my burden down, making over the kingship to my guru and resuming toward him the conduct due a guru.

17. "When I have restored this trust to Rāghava, these splendid slippers, this kingship, and Ayodhyā, I shall be cleansed of sin.

18. "When Kākutstha is consecrated, when the people are delighted and glad once more, the joy and glory I shall gain will be worth four times the kingship."

19. So glorious Bharata lamented in his desolation, and in Nandigrāma with his counselors he commenced his rule in sorrow.

20-21. Heroic Bharata wore barkcloth and matted hair—the lord wore the garb of a sage—and lived in Nandigrāma with his army, longing for Rāma's return, cherishing his brother, doing his brother's bidding, and intent on carrying out the promise.

22. Bharata consecrated the slippers and lived in Nandigrāma, and before he would give any order he first apprised the slippers.

The end of the one hundred seventh *sarga* of the *Ayodhyākāṇḍa* of the *Śrī Rāmāyaṇa*.

Sarga 108

1. As Rāma lived on in the grove of asceticism after Bharata's departure, he began to observe with a growing dismay an uneasiness among the ascetics.

2. It was the ascetics who had earlier taken refuge with Rāma and were pleased with the ashram there on Citrakūṭa, whom he now observed to be so uneasy.

3. They regarded Rāma suspiciously, their brows knit in a frown, and they whispered softly to each other and held conversation among themselves.

4. And observing their uneasiness, Rāma began to suspect that he himself might be at fault. Cupping his hands in reverence, he addressed the seer who was chief of their community.

5. "Holy one, have you found my conduct changed from before? Is that why this change has come over the ascetics?

6. "Have the seers found my younger brother Lakṣmaṇa doing something unbefitting him, out of negligence?

7. "Has Sītā failed to maintain properly the conduct becoming a woman, neglecting, in overscrupulous obedience to me, her obedience to you?"

8. The seer, a man advanced both in years and in asceticism, was trembling slightly as he replied to the compassionate Rāma:

9. "How could Vaidehī ever err, my son, especially against ascetics, when she is so good-natured and always earnest for what is good?

10. "It is in fact on your account that the ascetics are in this state—because of the *rākṣasas*. That is why they are disquieted and hold conversation among themselves.

11-12. "One of Rāvaṇa's younger brothers—Khara is his name—is nearby. He is the one who uprooted all the ascetics dwelling in Janasthāna. He is an eater of men, audacious and impudent, vicious, haughty, and evil, and he cannot abide you, my son.

13. "From the moment you came to live in this ashram, my son, the *rākṣasas* have been molesting the ascetics.

14. "They show themselves in every form of deformation, loathsome, savage, and terrifying forms, a horror to behold.

15. "Enemies of all that is noble, they defile some ascetics with unspeakable impurities and strike terror into others by suddenly appearing before them.

16. "Stealthily they prowl the ashram sites, one after another, and take a mad delight in harassing the ascetics.

17. "They scatter the ladles and the other sacrificial implements; they douse the fires with water and break the vessels when the oblations are under way.

18. "The ashrams are infested with these wicked creatures. The seers are eager to abandon them and have been urging me to go to some other region.

19. "So before these foul creatures offer physical violence to the ascetics, we will leave this ashram, Rāma.

20. "Not far from here is a wonderful forest with many roots and fruit. It was our old ashram, and I will return there with my host.

21. "Before Khara does some harm to you, too, my son, you should come away from here with us, if you are of a mind to do so.

22. "For you to live here with your wife is perilous, Rāghava, ever alert and powerful though you may be. It will soon bring you sorrow."

23. So the ascetic spoke, and his uneasiness was such that nothing Prince Rāma offered in reply could hold him back.

24. The chief of the community blessed Rāghava, comforted him and asked his leave, and abandoning the ashram with his community he went away.

25. Rāma escorted the host of seers, following them out to some distance, and did obeisance to the seer, their chief. They were well pleased and, as they gave him leave, they repeated their advice. Then he returned to his own holy abode to take up his residence.

26. Lordly Rāghava did not for an instant leave the ashram now that the seers had quit it, the ascetics who had always attended Rāghava with the many virtues acquired from their sage conduct.

The end of the one hundred eighth *sarga* of the *Ayodhyākāṇḍa* of the *Śrī Rāmāyaṇa*.

Sarga 109

1. When the ascetics had departed, Rāghava fell to thinking, and he found that for many reasons his dwelling place no longer pleased him.

2-4. "It was here I saw Bharata, my mothers, and the townsmen," he reflected, "and my memory lingers on them still in their constant grief. Then too, the camps great Bharata pitched and the dung of his elephants and horses have left things in a terrible state. We shall therefore go somewhere else." And so Rāghava set forth with Vaidehī and Lakṣmaṇa.

5. Making his way to the ashram of Atri, glorious Rāma prostrated himself before the holy seer, and Atri received him like a son.

6. He himself provided Rāma with hospitality, lavish and honorable, and he cheered Saumitri and illustrious Sītā.

7. His aged and honored wife arrived, and the seer, wise in the ways of righteousness and earnest for the welfare of all creatures, invited her and cheered her, too.

8. This was Anasūyā, an illustrious ascetic who followed the way of righteousness, and the best of seers bade her receive Vaidehī.

9-10. And he told Rāma about his ascetic wife who followed the way of righteousness: "Once when the world was utterly ravaged by drought for ten years, it was Anasūyā who created roots and fruit and caused the Jāhnavī to flow, for the ascetic power she has acquired is awesome, and mortifications adorn her.

11. "She has practiced intense asceticism for ten thousand years, my son, and by her vows all obstacles have been removed.

12. "It was she who, to advance the cause of the gods, straightway reduced ten nights to one. Here she is, blameless prince; look on her as a mother.

13. "Now have Vaidehī approach her; she is a glorious woman worthy of every creature's adoration, an aged and ever amiable woman."

14. When the seer had finished speaking, Rāghava replied with a word of assent and then addressed Sītā, who was wise in the ways of righteousness:

15. "Princess, you have heard what the sage has said. Approach the ascetic woman at once, for your own good.

16. "Her name is Anasūyā, and her deeds have won her renown throughout the world. Approach the ascetic at once—she is most approachable."

17. Sītā, princess of Mithilā, who always had Rāghava's welfare at heart, listened to his words and then sought out Atri's wife, a woman wise in the ways of righteousness.

18-19. Anasūyā was very old, her skin was wrinkled and loose, her hair white with age, and her body trembled constantly, like a plantain tree in the wind. Sītā carefully did obeisance to the illustrious and faithful woman and announced her name to her.

20. After doing obeisance to the faultless ascetic, Vaidehī cupped her hands in reverence and delightedly asked after her health.

21. She, too, felt delight when she saw how illustrious Sītā was following the way of righteousness, and she cheered her, exclaiming, "How fortunate you have such high regard for righteousness!

22. "How fortunate you should abandon your kinfolk, your pride and wealth, proud Sītā, to follow Rāma when he was banished to the forest.

23. "A woman who holds her husband dear—whether he is in the city or the forest, whether he is good or evil—gains worlds that bring great blessings.

24. "To a woman of noble nature her husband is the supreme deity, however bad his character, however licentious or indigent he might be.

25. "I can see no kinsman to surpass him, Vaidehī, far as I might look. Like ascetic power, which once acquired is never lost, a husband is ready and able, come what may.

26. "But bad women have no such understanding of virtue and vice. Their hearts are the slaves of desire, and they lord it over their husbands.

27. "Indeed, women like that, Maithilī, who yield to what they should not do, are held up to infamy and fall away from righteousness.

28. "But women like you, virtuous women who can tell good from bad in this world, come to reside in heaven just the same as men who have gained great merit."

The end of the one hundred ninth *sarga* of the *Ayodhyākāṇḍa* of the *Śrī Rāmāyaṇa*.

Sarga 110

1. So Anasūyā spoke, and Vaidehī ungrudgingly paid her homage and softly replied:

2. "The instruction my noble lady has given me comes as no surprise. I myself am well aware that a husband is a woman's guru.

3. "Even if my husband were utterly lacking in good behavior, my noble lady, still I would always obey him wholeheartedly.

4. "How much more readily would I obey a man praised for his virtues, a compassionate, self-disciplined, and righteous man, who is constant in his love, who defers to his mother and holds his father dear?

5. "Great Rāma behaves toward all the women of the king exactly as he does toward Kausalyā.

6. "And any woman the king glanced at but once mighty Rāma would treat just like a mother, without the least resentment. For he cherishes the king and knows the meaning of righteousness.

7. "The instructions my mother-in-law imparted to me as I was coming to this desolate and frightening forest have remained firmly implanted in my heart.

8. "And I have retained as well the lessons my mother taught me long ago, when I gave my hand before the marriage fire.

9. "But your words, follower of righteousness, have reminded me afresh of all this: no other ascetic act is required of a woman than obedience to her husband.

10. "Sāvitrī is exalted in heaven because she showed obedience to her husband. Arundhatī, too, went up to the heavens by virtue of her obedience to her husband.

11. "And Rohiṇī, the very best of women and a goddess up in the heavens, is never seen an instant separated from the moon.

12. "Excellent women such as these, firm in their vows to their husbands, are exalted in the world of the gods by reason of their meritorious deeds."

13. Anasūyā was delighted to hear Sītā's words. She kissed her on the forehead, and to Sītā's delight she said:

14. "I possess great ascetic power, acquired through various austerities. I will now make use of it, chaste Sītā, for your enjoyment.

15. "Your words are fitting and proper, Maithilī, and they have pleased me. What is the most suitable thing I might do for you? Only tell me." "You have already done it," Sītā replied to the woman of ascetic power.

16. These words pleased the righteous woman all the more. "Come now, Sītā, I wish to repay the delight you have given me.

17. "Here is a choice heavenly garland, raiment and jewelry, and a cream, Vaidehī, a precious salve.

18. "This that I give you, Sītā, will beautify your body, it will suit you perfectly, never spoil, and be yours forever.

19. "With this heavenly cream applied to your body, daughter of Janaka, you will adorn your husband to the same degree that Śrī adorns the eternal Viṣṇu."

20. Maithilī accepted the raiment, cream, jewelry, and garlands, a gift of love without compare.

21. After accepting the gift, glorious Sītā cupped her hands in reverence and waited in steadfast attendance upon the ascetic.

22. Now, as Sītā was waiting on her, the pious Anasūyā put a question to her about a certain tale she was fond of.

23. "It was at a self-choice rite, they say, that glorious Rāghava obtained you, Sītā. This at least is the tale that has reached my ears.

24. "I should like to hear that tale in full, Maithilī, exactly as it happened, in its entirety. Would you tell it to me, please?"

25. So the righteous woman spoke, and replying, "You shall hear it then," Sītā told the tale:

26. "There is a righteous and mighty king of Mithilā; his name is Janaka. He honors the code of kshatriyas and rules his land with prudence.

27. "It was once when, plow in hand, he was tilling the circle of fields that I broke through the earth—so the story goes—and arose to become the daughter of the king.

28. "King Janaka was busy sowing grain by the fistful when he caught sight of me, my body all caked with dirt, and he was amazed.

29. "He was childless then, you see, and with his own two hands he took me affectionately on his lap. 'She shall be my daughter,' he said, and he showered me with affection.

30. "From out of the sky, they say, there came a voice—a human voice but unlike any ever heard: 'It is so, lord of men. By rights the child is yours.'

31. "My father, the righteous lord of Mithilā, was delighted. The lord of men had obtained vast wealth, he felt, in obtaining me.

32. "The virtuous king entrusted me to the care of his favorite queen, the eldest, and she raised me affectionately, with a mother's love.

33. "Now, when my father observed that I had reached the right age for marriage, he began to worry, and he grew desolate, like a man impoverished by the loss of his wealth.

34. "The father of an unmarried girl, though he be the equal of Indra on earth, finds himself humiliated by people, by his equals, and even his inferiors.

35. "When the king perceived how close he was coming to humiliation, he was launched upon a sea of worry, and like a man without a raft he could not make the shore.

36. "Seeing I was not born of a woman's womb, the protector of the land for all his thinking could not discover a fit and proper husband for me.

37. "But after giving it much thought he had an idea. 'I will hold the self-choice rite for my daughter,' the wise king decided.

38. "He had at that time a superb bow and pair of quivers with inexhaustible arrows. Great Varuṇa had graciously bestowed them on him at a great sacrifice.

39. "Because of its weight humans could not budge the bow, no matter how hard they tried; lords of men were unable to bend it even in their dreams.

40. "So after he had extended invitations to the kings and put the bow on display, my truthful father made this declaration before the convocation of the lords of men:

41. " 'The man who can raise this bow and string it shall have my daughter for his wife. Let no one doubt it!'

42. "The kings looked at the superior bow, like a mountain in weight, and they said farewell and departed, unable even to lift it.

43. "A long time passed until one day this splendid Rāghava arrived with Viśvāmitra to observe a sacrifice.

44. "My father paid special homage to valiant Rāma and his brother Lakṣmaṇa, and to righteous Viśvāmitra.

45. " 'Here are two Rāghavas,' the sage told my father, 'Rāma and Lakṣmaṇa, sons of Daśaratha. They are eager to see the bow.' Upon hearing this, my father had the bow brought out.

46. "In the twinkling of an eye mighty Rāma bent it, and all at once the mighty prince strung and drew it.

47. "And so impetuously did he draw the bow that it broke in two right in the middle, and the sound it made as it fell was dreadful, like a thunderclap.

48. "Thereupon my father, true to his agreement, raised up a splendid water vessel, ready to bestow me on Rāma.

49. "But ready though my father was to bestow me, Rāghava would not accept me right away, for he did not yet know the will of his father, the lordly king of Ayodhyā.

50. "So my father invited my father-in-law, aged King Daśaratha, and afterwards bestowed me on the celebrated Rāma.

51. "And my younger sister, the good and lovely Ūrmilā, my father of his own accord bestowed as wife on Lakṣmaṇa.

52. "And that is how I was bestowed on Rāma, there at the self-choice ceremony, and as is right I love my husband, the mightiest of men."

The end of the one hundred tenth *sarga* of the *Ayodhyākāṇḍa* of the *Śrī Rāmāyaṇa.*

Sarga 111

1. When righteous Anasūyā had heard this extraordinary tale, she embraced Maithilī with both arms and kissed her on the forehead.

2. "How wonderfully and sweetly you spoke, each word, each syl-

lable was clear, and now I have heard the whole story of how the self-choice rite took place.

3. "I am truly charmed by your tale, my sweet-voiced child. But now the majestic sun is setting, bringing on the gracious night.

4. "You can hear the twitter of the birds that by day range far and wide in search of food; now at twilight they are going to their roosts to sleep.

5. "And here, carrying their water pots, are the sages returning in a group, wet from their ablutions, their barkcloth garments soaked with water.

6. "The seers have made their fire-offerings according to precept—do you see the smoke, pearly as a dove's neck, carried by the wind?

7. "Though their leaves are really sparse, the trees all about, even in the distance, seem to have grown dense; the horizons are all lost to view.

8. "The creatures that wander by night are now beginning to move, and the deer of the ascetics' grove are settling down on the paths that lead to the altars.

9. "Night is coming, Sītā, adorned with stars. You can see the moon in his mantle of light rising in the sky.

10. "You may go now and attend on Rāma, I give you leave. Your sweet story-telling has brought me deep contentment.

11. "But first, would you adorn yourself, Maithilī, in my presence? Allow me to have the pleasure of seeing you, my child, beautified by these heavenly ornaments."

12. So Sītā adorned herself, and looking like the daughter of the gods, she bowed her head to her and went off to Rāma.

13. The eloquent Rāghava took great delight in seeing Sītā adorned with the ascetic's gift of love.

14. And Sītā, princess of Mithilā, explained everything to Rāma, how the ascetic had given her a gift of love—raiment, jewelry, and garlands.

15. Rāma was delighted, and so was Lakṣmaṇa, the great chariot-warrior, to see the honor conferred on Maithilī, an honor such as few mortals ever receive.

16. And so, with the warm reception accorded him by the perfected ascetics, the moon-faced delight of the Raghus happily passed the holy night.

17. And when night was over, and the forest ascetics had bathed and made their fire-offerings, the tigers among men asked leave of them.

18. The forest ascetics, who followed the way of righteousness, informed them that travel through the forest was impeded by *rākṣasas*.

19. "But there is one path through the forest," they said, "which the great seers use when they go to gather fruit. By this path, Rāghava, one can pass safely through the otherwise impassable forest."

20. Then the brahman ascetics cupped their hands in reverence and blessed the journey of the slayer of foes, and with his wife and Lakṣmaṇa, Rāghava plunged into the forest, like the sun into a bank of stormclouds.

The end of the one hundred eleventh *sarga* of the *Ayodhyākāṇḍa* of the *Śrī Rāmāyaṇa*.

The end of the *Ayodhyākāṇḍa*.

NOTES

Sarga 1

Ck, said to be missing for *sargas* 1-3 in the manuscripts used in preparing the crit. ed. (Vaidya 1962, p. 3), appears in the printed edition of the commentary (Mysore, 1964) and is utilized here.

1. "the delight of the Raghus" *raghunandanaḥ*: Raghu is the name of an eponymous ancestor of Daśaratha's clan, whence the normal patronymic Rāghava, cf. 102.22. The zero-grade form is also thus used, though much less frequently (see, for example, 6.96.20).

2. Yudhājit: See 1.72.1ff. After this verse several N and S manuscripts add: "Therefore you should go from here with him, to see your maternal grandfather, my son" (4*). Cg and Cr, from whose texts this verse is absent, remark that the king only indirectly tells his son to leave because he could not bear his absence (but cf. 4.25ff. below).

3. In an N interpolation after this verse, Kaikeyī learns and approves of her son's departure (7*; cf. 8.19 below). Some manuscripts append a long passage containing Daśaratha's parting advice to his son and his urging him to take Śatrughna along (App. I, No. 1; No. 2.1-32).

4. "tireless" *akliṣṭakāriṇam*: Literally, "acting without difficulty," an epithet used almost exclusively of Rāma (and Kṛṣṇa). (Cg, Ck, and Ct offer the traditional interpretation, "whose character it is to act in such a way that no one is hurt.")

Note how perfunctorily the poet dismisses Bharata and Śatrughna. The N recension, however, in various interpolations after verse 4, describes Bharata's departure, voyage, arrival, and stay among the Kekayas (App. I, No. 2.33ff.; No. 3); his course of education there (which includes learning how to write, No. 2.67, 117 = No. 4.4, 117); and his dispatch of a messenger to Daśaratha informing him that he is ready to return home (No. 2.64ff. = No. 4 [erroneously recorded after verse 14]).

5. "his father" *pitā tasya*: That is, Yudhājit's father. The city of the Kekayas was Rājagṛha (also called Girivraja), located in the Punjab (cf. note on 8.22 and *sarga* 62, where the journey to Rājagṛha is described).

6. "his uncle Aśvapati" *mātulenāśvapatinā*: Cg takes Aśvapati (literally, "lord of horses") to be another name of Yudhājit, while at the same time (like Cr) giving it a functional value: "He honored Bharata by giving him purebred horses and so on." Kaikeyī is called "the daughter of Aśvapati" below (9.16, 28.4), and in 64.19, 22 the king of the Kekayas is clearly named Aśvapati and distinguished from Yudhājit. That Vālmīki nods here is unlikely; asyndeton is possible: "by his uncle (and) by (his grandfather) Aśvapati" (see 66.6 and note); Cv (on 64.19) may be correct, however, in supposing Aśvapati to be a cognomen of the men of this family.

7. "they often thought with longing of . . . Daśaratha" *smaratāṃ . . . daśaratham*: This suggests to Cm (Ct) the brothers' fear that, considering the age of the king, they might have insufficient time to fulfill the proper *dharma* of sons, which is obedience. Cg finds the implication to be that they wondered whether the king would consecrate Rāma as prince regent, since he himself was now too old to bear the burden of kingship.

8. The simile, according to Cg, refers to the unwavering friendship of Indra and Varuṇa.

9. "as if they were four arms" *catvāra iva bāhavaḥ*: For Ct the verse metaphorically

represents the king as the four-armed Viṣṇu (this idea is made explicit in some N manuscripts, which read, "they were like the arms of Viṣṇu").

10. "just as the self-existent Brahmā" *svayaṃbhūr iva*: The simile owes its existence in part to alliteration (*svayaṃbhūr . . . bhūtānāṃ babhūva*). Cm extends it: Rāma, being more virtuous, pleased his father more, as Brahmā similarly pleases his father Viṣṇu.

After this verse the S recension inserts: "For he was eternal Viṣṇu born in the world of men when begged by the gods, who were seeking the destruction of haughty Rāvaṇa" (10*.1-2). Note that Rāvaṇa will not be mentioned in Book Two except at 104.4 (see note there) and 108.11.

14. "merchants" *naigamāḥ*: So Cg, Ck, Ct; Cm, "townsmen"; Cr construes with *brāhmaṇāḥ*, that is, "who followed the *vedas*." In the *Rām nigama-* always and *naigama-* usually (except at 2.53.16 and possibly 98.71) appear to refer to the merchant class.

15-28. This long catalogue of Rāma's virtues is not merely epic convention; it seeks to demonstrate that Rāma meets all the qualifications for kingship demanded by the *Arthaśāstra* (so Ctr vol. 1, pp. 5ff.).

18. "of noble descent" *kalyānābhijanaḥ*: Also possible: "both sides of his family were blessed in him" (so Cg, "with whom, by whom his mother's and father's family were distinguished"; for the idea see *MBh* 2.70.5).

19. "knowledgeable and adept in the social proprieties" *laukike samayācāre kṛtakalpo viśāradaḥ*: Ck and Ct, finding a chiasmus, join *kṛtakalpaḥ* with *laukike* ("had acquired skill in worldly affairs"), and *viśāradaḥ* with *samayācāre* ("clever, able in *dharma*"). We follow the more natural interpretation of Cm and Cg.

20. "skilled in the practice of them" *kṛtajñaḥ*: That this is the meaning of the compound seems clearly to be indicated by its juxtaposition to *śāstrajñaḥ*, "learned in the sciences," that is, in theoretical knowledge (cf. 16.31 and note, 23.4 and note, where the signification is similar; also possibly in *MBh* 7.36.4 and 50.31). The distinction between "theory" (*śāstra*) and practice (usually *prayoga*), which becomes so important in classical Indian culture, is drawn here for perhaps the first time.

"an excellent judge of men" *puruṣāntarakovidaḥ*: Less likely, "could tell the inner feelings of men (at first glance)," Ct and Cr.

"to show his favor or withhold it" *pragrahanigrahayoḥ*: The crit. ed.'s reading in *pāda* c, *pragrahānugrahayoḥ*, makes little sense; the gloss of Cm and Cg, "to win and keep friends," fits poorly with *yathānyāyam* ("when it was appropriate"). The formula in the epics consists either of the pair *pragraha-* and *nigraha-* (cf. 6.20.5; *MBh* 4.4.33 and Raghu Vira 1936 ad loc., as also 16* here), or *nigraha-* and *anugraha-* (cf. 4.17.28; Ct, Cr here are forced to gloss *pragraha-* as *nigraha-*). The segment *-ānu-* is sufficiently disputed in the manuscripts that preserve the verse to favor our conjecture, *pragrahanigrahayoḥ*.

21. "He knew the right means" *upāyajñaḥ*: "As a bee draws honey from flowers, that is, without oppressing the people," Cm and Cg; "as the sun draws water with its rays, that is, effortlessly," Cr.

"the accepted way" *saṃdṛṣṭa-*: Cm, Cg, Ct, and Cr cite: "Kings should pay their expenditures with [that is, should restrict their expenditures to] one quarter, or two or three, of their revenue [but never more]" (cf. *MBh* 2.5.60); Ck states simply, "The *dharma* is that expenditure should not exceed income." See 94.45 below.

"even the most complex" *vyāmiśrakeṣu ca*: Cm, Cg, Ck, Ct, and Cr explain, "(*śāstras*) composed in mixed language, that is, Sanskrit with the Prakrits," but no such *śāstras* exist (except in a certain special sense for the later *alaṃkāraśāstra* or science of rhetoric), and furthermore the word is nowhere attested with this meaning (*vyāmiśra-* in *MahāBh* on 3.1.26 end is not instructive, nor can we here follow Lüder's "bei Parteiungen" [1940, p. 421, n2]).

22. "all aspects of political life" *arthavibhāga-*: Cm, Cg, Ct, and Cr explain more specifically, "the various uses of wealth," and cite: "A man fares well both in this world and the next if he spends his money in these five ways: on *dharma*, glory, *artha*, himself, and his relatives"; Ck, for contextual reasons, interprets *artha* as the doctrines of the *Bharatīyanāṭyaśāstra*, the textbook on dramaturgy.

25. "bow to the will of time" *kālavaśānugaḥ*: This is a very literal translation, for we are not certain of the precise meaning of the compound. Presumably something like "fall victim to procrastination," or "wait upon events" is meant (cf. 94.14, 56 below). Less likely, "give in to fate" (literally, "to time"), as in *MBh* 13.1.44, which would be quite inappropriately used of Rāma, who throughout the poem will assert how irresistible is the power of fate. The commentators offer interesting if irrelevant theological interpretations emphasizing the Blessed One's transcendence of time.

26. "the three worlds" *triṣu lokeṣu*: Usually understood as earth, sky, and heaven, populated by mortal, semidivine, and divine beings.

"patient as the earth" *vasudhāyāḥ kṣamāguṇaiḥ*: *-guṇaiḥ* has probably been attracted into the plural by the presence of *guṇaiḥ* in *pāda* a.

28. "the gods who guard the world" *lokapāla-*: The gods who were thought of as guardians of the directions: Indra (east), Yama (south), Varuṇa (west), and Kubera (north). In the later epic period, world-protectors of the intermediate directions were included: Agni, Nairṛta, Vāyu, and Īśa.

30. "consecrated" *abhiṣiktam*: Literally, "sprinkled" with water at the ceremony for inducting the prince regent into office.

33. "that . . . I might go to heaven" *yathā svargam avāpnuyām*: This is best analyzed as an absolute use of *yathā* with the optative to express a wish (*yathā* with imperative used absolutely perhaps in 15.7; cf. *yadi* with imperative as absolute in 53.19). The commentators do not persuasively account for *yathā* (Cg, Ck, and Cr, for example, read in compound: *yathāsvargam*, "whatever heaven I deserve").

34. "prince regent" *yuvarājam*: Literally, "young king." The prince so appointed (and note here that it is not a foregone conclusion that Rāma would be appointed; cf. also 4.5ff., 4.38) would assume most of the duties and prerogatives of kingship, but not all of them. His powers were limited so long as the king remained alive or did not retire to the forest to live the life of a hermit (cf. 47.7ff., especially verses 11-12; 52.16).

All but the NE manuscripts add hereafter that Daśaratha had also been frightened by the appearance of ominous portents and, additionally, had suddenly come to realize how old he himself was (27*; cf. 4.17ff.).

NE manuscripts omit verses 34ff. up to 2.14. This omission of the preliminary meeting with the ministers led Ruben to speculate on the development of royal autonomy through the epic period: absolute in the period of the "original" poem (whether in fact or in theory only) and gradually delimited in the period reflected in what he thought the later stratum (S and NW) of the text (Ruben 1936, p. 68); obviously this is speculation only.

35. Many N manuscripts add after this: "Then the subjects gathered, the chief brahmans and kshatriyas" (29*), whereas the SR inserts 30*, which contains the interesting verse: "However, because of his haste he did not invite the king of Kekaya

or Janaka, thinking that they would hear the good news afterwards." The motive behind Daśaratha's haste and his reluctance to inform the Kekaya king will become clear in *sarga* 4.

36. "nobles" *nṛpāḥ*: The term seems to be used like *rāja-* in the *Brāhmaṇas* (cf. Rau 1957, pp. 47ff.). Possibly "(vassal) princes" of the monarch Daśaratha, though their position and authority are never clearly defined.

37. "the men of the city and provinces" *purālayair jānapadaiś ca*: This appears to refer—though no previous mention of them is included in the crit. ed.—to the leading citizens of Ayodhyā (so Ct and Cr; brahmans would of course be included among them) and of the outlying provinces, who, as we shall see, were present in addition to the nobles or vassal princes (cf. 2.18, 27 and note).

"the thousand-eyed lord" *sahasracakṣur bhagavān*: Ct suggests that the epithet applied to Indra is significant here: Daśaratha too has a "thousand eyes"—his spies—by which he knows what all his vassals and subjects are thinking.

Sarga 2

5. "The white parasol" *pāṇḍurasyātapasya*: A symbol of royalty.

6. "I have lived a life of many, countless, years" *prāpya varṣasahasrāṇi bahūny āyūṃṣi jīvataḥ: Sahasra*: need not always (in fact, occasionally must not) be taken literally in the *Rām*; cf. note on 31.16 and Cg on 2.1.11 vulgate, who cites: " 'Hundred,' 'thousand,' 'billion' are all used to connote simply 'countless.' " *Bahūni*, moreover, construes not with *āyūṃṣi* but with *pāda* a; cf. the NW lection *bahūny āyuś ca*, and the parallel phrase in verse 15 below. Finally, *āyūṃṣi* (the internal object to *jīvataḥ*), means "years of life" (not "lifetimes"); cf. the NW *āyuś ca pālitam*. Grammar and the human character and scale of the *Ayodhyākāṇḍa* force us to reject the interpretation of the commentators, who understand both *sahasrāṇi* and *āyūṃṣi* literally, specifying that Daśaratha has lived "60,000 years, many lifetimes" of one hundred years each. They have in mind, of course, the (textually later) statement of 1.19.10. There is no indication in *Rām* Books 2-6 that the narrative takes place during the Tretā Yuga, which might be thought to justify the king's longevity.

7. Inasmuch as Daśaratha is explaining why the kingship has wearied him, the first line of the verse should give substance to his explanation. I therefore understand as follows: A king is responsible for the maintenance of *dharma*; with this charge come royal prerogatives (*rājaprabhāva-*) for the enforcement of *dharma*; and the constant self-vigilance necessary for justly exercising these prerogatives (cf. 3.26) has consumed his strength.

8. "twice-born" *dvija-*: Men of the first three *varṇas* (brahmans, kshatriyas, and *vaiśyas*, though often the word is used to refer only to brahmans). They are said to be "born again" when they are inducted into Aryan society at the initiation ceremony, which takes place sometime between the eighth and twelfth year.

10. "a union as propitious as the moon's with the constellation Puṣya" *candram iva puṣyeṇa yuktam*: A particularly auspicious time, on which important ceremonies are by preference held (Draupadī's marriage, for example, *MBh* 1.190.5), or on which major events take place (for example, the Buddha's renunciation, enlightenment, and *parinirvāṇa* [cf. Przyluski 1926, p. 88], or indeed, according to the Southern tradition, Rāma's birth [see note on 1.17.5]). Rāma will return from exile

to Ayodhyā on Puṣya day (6.114.45). The simile is all the more apposite in that Rāma's consecration itself will be scheduled for that day (3.24). The constellation Puṣya consists of three stars of Cancer (Kirfel 1920, p. 36).

12. The SR inserts four lines after this verse, in which Daśaratha asks for the assembly's approval or, that failing, for further suggestions (35*).

13. "the rumble (of a . . . cloud)" (*mahāmegham*) *nardantam*: Cm, Cg, Ck, Ct, and Cr all read *nardanta* ("[peacocks] crying" [not recorded thus in the crit. app.]), but the crit. ed. reading fits better with verse 2, and Vālmīki uses the root *nard* frequently of clouds (e.g., 6.41.25). The monsoon marks the beginning of the mating season for peacocks; they are said to welcome the thundering clouds with cries of greeting.

14. The assembly's first response (verse 15) is pro forma, based on their recognition of the legitimacy of the succession. It is only when Daśaratha, not wanting merely to be humored on this account, presses them that they give a heartfelt answer (verses 18ff.). Ruben offers various other possible explanations for Daśaratha's behavior here (1950, pp. 297ff.).

After *pādas* ab, the SR inserts: "The brahmans and the chiefs of the army, together with the people of the city and provinces, after they had assembled and consulted, reached unanimity" (37*).

15. "have lived many, countless, years" *anekavarṣasāhasraḥ*: See the note on verse 6 above.

"(prince regent) of the land" (*yuvarājānam* . . .) *pārthivam*: For this literal sense of *pārthiva-* cf. 22.10 below.

18. "the virtues of your son are many and excellent" *bahavo . . . kalyāṇā guṇāḥ putrasya santi te*: Cg cites Yāmunācārya: "[The Blessed One is] endowed with a host of virtues—innate, boundless, countless, excellent" (this line is found in the *Gadyatraya*, which is dubiously ascribed to Rāmānuja).

21. "unspiteful" *anasūyakaḥ*: Having just been used in verse 20 ("never spiteful"), the adjective here is taken by Cv, Cm, Ct, and Cr as a *bahuvrīhi* compound, "he was the object of no one's spite," in their hopes of explaining the iteration.

"grateful" *kṛtajñaḥ*: Or, "skillful" (cf. note to 1.20).

22. The two *ca*'s here function as restrictive particles: Rāma would speak only kind words, and only true words; he would never give voice to a compliment that was untrue or to a truth that might be painful (so Cg). Compare the famous prescription of Manu cited in the note on 46.36-37 below.

27. Up until now the main participants in the assembly appear to have been the nobles (cf. 1.35ff., 2.13); the situation described here and in verse 26, however, would apply to brahmans (their presence is suggested in 1.37 and 2.8, 18, but faintly enough to call forth interpolations, cf. notes on verse 14 above, and on 1.35). Ck (Ct) attempts to rectify matters by addressing 27b to the kings ("are they [your servants] prompt"; cf. also 3.3 and note, and compare the make-up of the later assembly, 75.11). As Ruben remarks, our manuscripts no longer enable us to determine with certainty the constitution of the assembly (1936, p. 68 n228). Here, as elsewhere, Vālmīki shows himself to be unfamiliar with the actual workings of the monarchical state.

28. "When misfortune strikes anyone Rāma feels the sorrow keenly" *vyasaneṣu manuṣyāṇāṃ bhṛśaṃ bhavati duḥkhitaḥ*: The line has considerable importance in the history of South Indian Vaishnavism for the theological question about the nature of the pity (*dayā*) of God. The position of the Teṅgalai sect is that God's pity is His

sharing of man's sufferings: since everything the *Rām* says is true, this passage is speaking of real suffering on the part of Rāma. The Vaḍagalai doctrine is that God's pity consists in the desire to assuage the suffering of others: when in His avatars God appears to suffer, this is not real but only mimetic (*abhinaya*), for otherwise it would fundamentally contradict God's blissful essence (cf. Siauve 1978, pp. 62-63 with notes). We shall have frequent occasion to remark on the latter tenet and its impact on the *Rām* commentators both in the *Ayodhyākāṇḍa* and, even more, in the *Araṇyakāṇḍa*.

"celebrations" *utsaveṣu*: These are normally held to be the seasonal festivals (cf. Gonda 1947, pp. 149ff.); Cg more relevantly calls them "celebrations on the birth of a child."

29. After *pādas* ab, S manuscripts insert nine lines, including: "He has handsome brows, long coppery eyes, is like Viṣṇu in very person" (55*.3).

30-32. The articulation of these verses agrees with Cm, Cg, Ck, and Ct (against the crit. ed.'s implication).

32. "all the gods" *sarvān devān*: Cg remarks that the women worship the gods indiscriminately, making no distinctions among them according to whether they are superior or inferior gods, vedic or nonvedic, because they are infatuated by their love for Rāma. And that they do worship, he continues, is another consequence of their infatuation: they erroneously believe that the gods are able to protect Rāma, whereas, in fact, it is he who protects them.

"O god" *deva*: The vocative here and in verse 34 is addressed to Daśaratha.

33. "Grant . . . that we may see" *paśyāmaḥ*: Indicative for imperative (as in 4.4.21).

34. "O god" *deva*: This agrees with Cg (first explanation) and Ck in taking *deva* as vocative. Cm, Ct, and Cr take it in combination, " 'like the god of gods,' that is, Viṣṇu" (an appellation more often used of Śiva [see 1.35.9, 65.13] or of Brahmā in Sanskrit literature), but this locution is not found in *Rām* 2-6.

"granter of boons" *varada*: Usually a nonspecific commendatory epithet of a generous king, here taking on some color from the context. (The *Mbh* connects it with *putrapradāna*, "giving [fathering] a son," 14.93.26.)

Sarga 3

2. "grandeur" *prabhāvaḥ*: One might translate, "how matchless my *power* (must be)," and see some implication that the appointment of a prince regent rested on a king's ability to impose his will by virtue of his political power and influence. But Daśaratha would hardly be expected to voice so provocative a sentiment in open assembly. Furthermore, the tone of the assembly so far (and see the beginning of the next verse) suggests that the deliberative procedures described here are not consultative but more or less ceremonial. (When Daśaratha later comes to allow the accession of Bharata, no consultation with the assembly is required.)

3. "had paid the brahmans this honor in return" *iti pratyarcya tān . . . brāhmaṇān*: This agrees with Cg, syntactically the most natural interpretation of the verse. Ck (so Cm?) understands *nṛpān* with *tān*, whereas Ct and Cr read *paurajānapadān* and awkwardly construe *brāhmaṇān* with the main verb. The problem arises, again, from ambiguity as to who the king's principal interlocutors are (cf. note on 2.27).

4. "month of Caitra": Mid-March to mid-April.

After this verse most manuscripts include thirty-three lines (App. I, No. 6) in which Vasiṣṭha orders the various preparations for Rāma's consecration (63* shows the two brahmans writing out a list of things to be done).

5. "It shall be done" *kṛtam*: Past participle with immediate future sense (see 16.47 below), as often in the *Rām* (2.9.45, 23.22, 33.26, 34.17, 49.2, etc.). The usage is similar to, but not quite the same as *ādikarmaṇi kta* (*Pā* 3.4.71, which indicates the actual commencement of the action); it is closer to the finite perfect in Greek and Latin, which can denote a "certainty or likelihood that an action will take place" (Goodwin 1893, p. 15). Was it a misinterpretation of this usage that caused the insertion noted at verse 4?

"with joy and delight" *prītau harṣayuktau*: Cm, Cg, Ck, and Ct, here, as elsewhere, explain away the pleonasm by identifying the first as mental pleasure, the second as its physical manifestation.

"just as you command" *yathoktavacanam*: Cm, Cg, Ck, Ct, and Cr all explain the phrase as part of the brahmans' statement, even though direct discourse in the *Rām* is rarely articulated, like this, over the hemistich boundary.

9. "aryan and barbarian" *mlecchāś cāryāś ca*: " 'Aryans,' those who dwell in Madhyadeśa (north-central India)"—Ct; Cr reasonably, but awkwardly, construes "aryan" with the kings of the directions and "barbarians" with the kings of the forests and mountains. Cg and Ck read instead *mlecchācāryāḥ*, "teachers (that is, kings and at the same time spiritual guides) of the barbarians" (not recorded in the crit. ed.). This reading finds support in the *MBh* (12.4.8); see Belvalkar's note ad loc. Raghavan, too, favored this reading and gives various additional arguments in support of it (Raghavan 1968, p. 597). Some N manuscripts substitute *yavanāḥ*, "Greeks," and in 9b "the Śakas (Scythians) who live in the mountains."

10. "royal seer" *rājarṣim*: Daśaratha. The title "royal seer" is applied, it seems, to virtually any aged king.

11. "a bull elephant in rut" *mattamātaṅga-*: The commentators are not sure whether the bull elephant in rut carries himself in a proud and sportive manner or very slowly (Cm and Cg).

12. "he ravished both the sight and hearts of men" *puṃsāṃ dṛṣṭicittāpahāriṇam*: Cg comments as follows: if he can ravish the hearts of men, who are by nature insensitive, how much more easily can he steal away the hearts of women (so Cm); or "men" may be a general term for "self, soul" and thus connote "all creatures"; or, finally, men may, when seeing Rāma, conceive the desire to become women and so to experience Rāma completely, an idea which finds expression in the following verse: "The women who saw lotus-eyed Pāñcālī washing her full hips wished for a moment that they were men" (untraced).

15. "charioteer" *sūtena*: He combines the offices of charioteer and poet, in particular the singer of epic and puranic tales (see note on 6.6).

20. "By virtue of the simile we understand that the assembly hall was already to some extent irradiated by the presence of Daśaratha, Vasiṣṭha, and the others," Cm and Cg.

23. "worthy" *sadṛśa-*: The adjective is grammatically absolute (as in 107.5, 110.34, 36, etc.; Cr glosses, "similar to me," so Ck). Rāma and Kausalyā are "worthy" in the sense that they share a rank and status commensurate with the king's.

"most virtuous" *guṇaśreṣṭhaḥ*: *-jyeṣṭhaḥ*, "eldest (in virtue)" (as in *MBh* 2.68.4), is perhaps to be preferred to the *-śreṣṭhaḥ* of the crit. ed., for it is widely attested, establishes a characteristic symmetry with *pāda* a, and (if only obliquely) underscores a primary theme of the book, primogeniture. One manuscript, G1, offers what may be the authentic reading, "virtuous and the eldest."

27. "overt and covert activities" *parokṣayā . . . vṛttyā pratyakṣayā*: Covert activity would include espionage; overt activity, the king's personal handling of duties, and his close observation of events (Cg, Ct, and Cr). Cm paraphrases the two as personal and delegated supervision of royal business.

"subjects" *prakṛtīḥ*: The word can mean "the people" in general (for example, 40.4, or 6.116.33) or, more specifically, as perhaps here, the six constituent elements of the state besides the king himself: minister(s), realm, fortified city, treasury, army, and allies (cf. *ArthŚā* 6.1.1ff.; cf. 84.7 and note). Cg and Ck gloss the passage, "the ministers, general, urban police, the people of the city and provinces, and all the subjects."

29. "bearing the good news" *priyakāriṇaḥ*: Note the NR reading *priyanivedinaḥ*, which may be interpreted as a gloss, and the sense *priya-* must have in verse 30 and frequently elsewhere (4.9, 7.29, 10.1, 14.5, 62.15, etc.). PW curiously can adduce no citation but Indian lexica.

32. "worshiped the gods" *devān samānarcuḥ*: The purpose of the worship would be to ward off any hostile influences that might impede Rāma's consecration (Cm, Cg, Ck, Ct), not to offer thanksgiving.

Sarga 4

1. "When he learned what they had determined" *niścayajñaḥ*: The king learns from the brahmans that Puṣya is to come into conjunction with the moon on the very next day. *Niścayajñaḥ* is unlikely to be an ornamental epithet, despite the anaphoric use of *niścayam*; it is too rare for that, and the only other occurrence in the *Rām*, 6.25.15, tends to support this interpretation.

2. "his eyes as coppery as lotuses" *rājīvatāmrākṣaḥ*: A sign of beauty and youth (see Roşu 1969, pp. 37ff.).

7. "comings and goings" *gamanāyetarāya vā*: Literally, "going or the other," that is, coming (so Cm, Cg; with equal probability Ck, Ct, "going or not going": "a servant cannot order his master to go," Ck [but see 14.11]).

10. "at a distance prostrated himself" *dūrāt praṇipatya*: Rāma bows at a distance (contrast 3.16) for fear of what his father might have to tell him (Ck, Ct).

14. "I have discharged all my debts" *anṛṇo 'smi*: Every man is born with "debts" that he must pay before death. Normally three are recognized (to the seers, gods, and fathers, to be paid by vedic study, sacrifices, and male offspring, respectively); a fourth (to brahmans, to be paid by alms) and a fifth (to oneself, paid by pleasure or simply self-preservation) are later, and the commentators here feel obliged to defend them. In 98.64 only the three debts are mentioned.

17. "lightning bolts out of a clear sky" *-nirghātāḥ*: Thus explained by Cg (see *Bṛhajjā* cited on 3.22.15; for the Latins this was by contrast a good omen; see Vergil, *Aeneid*, 8.523ff.). A D insertion (92*) adds hurricanes and earthquakes.

18. Aṅgāraka: Mars.

20. "resolve" *cetaḥ*: So we translate (in agreement with Cm, Cg, Ck, Ct), especially in view of *pāda* d (see also verse 27), which cannot imply going mad (still less dying).

The omens warn Daśaratha of some terrible calamity in the offing, and in order to avert it, he fears he might ultimately be induced to abandon his plans for Rāma's consecration. The impression is given, however, that a more specific reason behind the king's fear of irresoluteness is being suppressed, namely, the possibility of Kaikeyī's demanding that he make good what he promised her (so too Cg, Ck, Ct; see note on verse 25 below). It may, in fact, be his very deception of her (and the unrighteousness it signifies) to which he tacitly attributes the appearance of the ominous portents.

21. Punarvasu: This constellation corresponds to two stars of Gemini (Kirfel 1920, p. 36).

"predict" *vakṣyante*: Ck notes simply that the tense and voice are archaic. The verb may be attracted into the future by *pāda* c, or is perhaps an example of the weakening of the future tense (so Cr; see 27.4 and note, and Renou 1968, p. 462).

25. Cm, Cg comment that Daśaratha is thinking of the promise he made when marrying Kaikeyī, that her son would succeed to the throne (see 99.3 and note; less attractive is Cm's second interpretation, that the king merely doubts Bharata's self-control as he does his own in verse 20). How much Rāma knows of the marriage promise at this point is open to question. Cr maintains that this passage implies Rāma does know, but this of course would mean that Rāma is assisting his father in breaking his word, whereas the whole *Rām* is predicated on his efforts "to preserve his father's truthfulness." However, we are never shown where Rāma does learn of it (see the Introduction, Chapter 4).

27. "is best presented with an accomplished fact" *kṛtaśobhi:* Literally, "is enhanced by (adorned by, appears to its best with) the act accomplished" (for the idea see *MBh* 5.38.16, *kariṣyan na prabhāṣeta kṛtāny eva ca darśayet,* "Before the deed is done one should not divulge it; one should reveal accomplished facts"). This interpretation agrees substantially with Cm's second suggestion: "The idea is this: If Rāma's consecration is performed immediately, then Bharata too would be pleased, or at least resigned, for there would be nothing he could do about it; if not, if it were still within his grasp, then Bharata might conceive a desire for the kingship himself." Ck (Ct) is just possible: "even such a man's mind 'is adorned with,' that is, is affected by, things 'brought about'—passion, hatred, etc.—through whatever cause. No person has all his emotions wholly under his control; if he did, he would not be here in the sea of transmigration, with waves of pain and joy cresting about him."

29. "In keeping with the king's instructions regarding the consecration" *rājñoddiṣṭe 'bhiṣecane*: A *viṣayasaptamī* (as in the previous verse), rather than *sati* (Cr), or *nimitta* (Cg, Ck, Ct). Rāma returns home as the king's directions for the consecration require, but leaves again on not finding Sītā.

31. "Sītā had been sent for" *sītā . . . ānāyitā*: Having no independent status, Sītā could not come of her own accord, like Sumitrā and Lakṣmaṇa; Kausalyā would have her brought by her servants (Cg) (see verse 45).

33. "the Primal Being" *puruṣam*: The cosmic man first described in *ṚV* 10.90; here, like Janārdana, a name of Viṣṇu, to whom this is one of the relatively few references in the *Ayodhyākāṇḍa* (see note on 22.18).

37. "auspicious rites" *maṅgalāni*: "She is to have costly perfumes made ready, and garlands, garments, jewelry, and so on, and to have ritual baths and similar acts performed," Ck, Ct.

39. "my kinsmen and Sumitrā's" *jñātīn me . . . sumitrāyāś ca*: Notice that no mention

is made of Kaikeyī. Only through vague intimations of this sort are we to learn of the profound enmity between the two women (see, for example, 8.26).

42. "He smiled" *smayann iva*: Probably we have here metrical shortening for *eva* (so Ck); less likely, "half-smiling" (Cg, Ct), the Gioconda smile often attributed to Kṛṣṇa.

43. "rule this land with me" *imāṃ mayā sārdhaṃ praśādhi tvaṃ vasuṃdharām*: Later Rāma will, in fact, offer to make Lakṣmaṇa heir-apparent, but the latter will refuse (6.116.77-78).

44. "the fruits of kingship" *rājyaphalāni*: Ck, Ct rightly gloss "*dharma* and *artha*." The rewards of sovereignty consist not only of one-sixth of the wealth of the kingdom (precious objects, clothes, ornaments—Cm, Cg), and of the fame produced by such wealth (Cr), but also of one-sixth of the spiritual merit of the people of the kingdom (as is emphasized in 3.5.13; see *ManuSm* 8.304).

Sarga 5

2. Kākutstha: Rāma. Like "Rāghava," this is a patronymic applied to all the members of the lineage (see also 102.22).

4. "courtyards" *kakṣyāḥ*: We should probably think of these "courtyards" or "enclosures" as concentric or emboxed (as in the description of Vasantasenā's palace in *Mṛcch* 4; see below 13.28 and note, and note on 15.12). To be allowed to proceed through the courtyards on a chariot appears to be a mark of high respect.

9. Yayāti: Son of Nahuṣa, he was "universal emperor" and father of five sons (Yadu, Puru, etc.), from whom were descended the five great clans of the *Mahābhārata* epic. (See *MBh* 1.70.29ff. and below, 11.1 and note. Observe that in 102.27 below, Nahuṣa is included in the solar dynasty, whereas in 1.69.29-30 both he and Yayāti are so reckoned; see also note on 58.36.)

10. After this verse a few eastern and D manuscripts add that Rāma "made his guru the gift of a thousand cows and ten" (98*).

15. "royal highways" *rājamārgāḥ*: A main thoroughfare leading directly from one of the city gates to the royal palace (Schlingloff 1969, p. 8 n5).

17. "thoroughfares . . . sprinkled" *sikta- . . . -rathyā*: The streets would be sprinkled with scented water, probably to lay the dust.

"fresh" *tadahar-*: This item is to be joined in compound with *vana-*, "flowers of that day," that is, fresh (see *ViṣṇuP* 5.6.12, *tadaharjāta-*), against the commentators, who construe it as an independent adverb ("on that day").

19. "an occasion for their adornment" *prajālaṃkārabhūtam*: The phrase is obscure. Cg comments, "[an occasion] rich in ornaments for, or of, the people," that is, richly distributed to them, or richly worn by them.

20. A verb governing *-mārgam* is wanting (unless it is *vyūhan*, with *janaugham* as a *bahuvrīhi* compound).

21. "a mountain peak wreathed in white clouds" *sitābhraśikhara-*: *madhyamapadalopi* (or elliptical) compound as in *agryaveṣapramadā-* in verse 24 below (see 23.15; so partially Cr on 6.11 [second interpretation]), not *upamānapūrvapada* ("peaks like white clouds," Ct, Cr).

24. "womenfolk in rich attire" *agryaveṣapramadājana-*: Represented in the simile by the stars; see 3.20.

Sarga 6

1. "worshiped" *upāgamat*: See 3.6.21 for this sense of the verb, which appears to be unattested elsewhere (thus too the commentators: " 'went to,' that is, in his thoughts," Ck, so Cr; Cm, Ct, "paid worship" [Ctś, " 'went to' the sanctuary of Nārāyaṇa"]). Many N manuscripts read, "went in with his wife, like Nārāyaṇa with Lakṣmī."

Ck notes, "In accordance with the shastric statement that 'no king exists without Viṣṇu,' Viṣṇu [Nārāyaṇa] must be worshiped for the sake of kingship." On the intimate relationship between the god Viṣṇu and kingship see Gonda 1969, pp. 58-59, and especially pp. 164-67.

3. "earnestly made his wish" *āśāsyātmanaḥ priyam*: Ctr (vol. 1, p. 83) cites *ĀpaŚS*: "After pouring the oblation one should meditate on what one desires" (1.5.1283 in the edition of Narasiṃhācār).

4. "restraining his desire" *niyatamānasaḥ*: As in verse 1 above, the underlying thought of the phrase is no doubt correctly explicated by the NE gloss, "suppressing [his desire for] sexual congress" with his wife (this too is likely to be the real function of the instrumental phrases in both verses). See 4.23 above.

"sanctuary" *āyatane*: It is uncertain whether we can infer from such passages as this (see verse 11) that any significant temple cult was in existence at the time this stratum of the *Rām* was composed; we have virtually no concrete information about the construction of such places of worship. (Ck and Ct note that the "sanctuary" would be located in Rāma's palace.)

5. "With one watch of the night remaining" *ekayāmāvaśiṣṭāyāṃ rātryām*: Night consists of three watches, each about three hours long.

6. "bards" *sūta-*: Royal charioteers and advisers, as well as reciters of the epics and *purāṇas*.

"genealogists" *māgadha-*: Apparently hailing originally from Magadha (modern Bihar), they recite the royal lineage.

"panegyrists" *bandin-*: Also called *vaitālika*; they perform praise-poems for the king, especially at the royal levee. The different functions of the three positions are not always distinguished in the *Rām* or later literature. The *sūta* Sumantra is called both "master of ancient tales" (*purāṇavit*) in 13.17, and *bandin* in 14.9; whereas the *bandins* go to awaken the king in 59.1, in 75.1 it is the *sūtas* and *māgadhas* who do so.

"he began to intone his prayers" *jajāpa*: Rāma's prayers would include the *Gāyatrīmantra* (Cg), the early-morning hymn directed to the sun (*ṚV* 3.62.10).

10. "they began to adorn the city" *cakre śobhayituṃ purīm*: We read, as in principle the crit. ed. should have, with the SR (the accepted NR reading is weak: "They once again made grand decoration"). The inconsistency, in light of 5.17, is of a sort not uncommon in the epic.

11. "shrines" *caityeṣu*: These need not be Buddhist shrines in particular (though that is how Cg and Ck gloss), nor "brick-piles for the vedic sacrifices" (Belvalkar on *MBh* 12.29.18). Cf. *MBh* 12.69.39-40, where clearly it is a tree shrine that is meant (see note on 62.12).

15. "In public squares and private houses" *catvareṣu gṛheṣu ca*: The fact that the people praise Rāma in private no less than in public shows there is nothing contrived about their love for him (Cg).

"in praise (of Rāma)" *(rām)ābhiṣṭava-*: Both here and in verse 16c below we read thus for the crit. ed.'s *(rām)ābhiṣeka-*, "(spoke . . . about Rāma's) consecration," which is, uncharacteristically for Vālmīki, redundant here in view of *pāda* c. The lection adopted has the important, virtually conclusive, concurrent testimony of Cm, Cg, most S and NE manuscripts (NW has a substitute verse); note also verse 20 below, which seems to be an analytical expression for the compound here (and see 6.97.28, *rāghavastavasaṃyuktā* [*vāk*]).

"now that his consecration was at hand" *rāmābhiṣeke saṃprāpte*: Perhaps the suggestion is that, with Rāma on the point of being crowned, the people no longer feel it necessary to conceal their preference for him as against any other Ikṣvāku claimant.

18. "anticipating that night would fall" *niśāgamanaśaṅkayā*: Before Rāma takes his postinaugural tour of the city.

"lantern-trees" *dīpavṛkṣān*: "Sorts of lamp-posts consisting of many branches, like a tree," Ck, so Cg, Ct (Cr, "trees characterized by branches fit for placing lamps there"; see Belvalkar on *MBh* 12.195.9).

22. "for a long time to come" *cirāya*: The common sense of the dative of this word (see 31.33, 3.16.21, etc.; so Cr here). Just possible also, "at long last" (see 47.33), with an implicit criticism of Daśaratha's reign.

"can tell good people from bad" *dṛṣṭalokaparāvaraḥ*: The phrase appears to be used in a moral sense in the *Rām*; see 56.6 (in reference to Kausalyā), and note the similar one in 34.27. Ck, Ct are close: "who understands exactly what is and is not praiseworthy in his people" (Cm, Cg struggle: "who has seen superior and inferior things in the world"). Most N manuscripts give, "who has seen [= come to distinguish] higher from lower principles," but it is unlikely that the phrase is ever used with a philosophical significance in the *Rām*, as it is in the *MBh* (see *MBh* 12.219.14, and 13.80.7 and the commentator cited ad loc. by Dandekar; but see *Rām* 3.10.15, 5.50.8).

28. "Indra's residence" *indrakṣaya-*: "That is, Amarāvati," Cm, Ct, Cr. *Kṣaya-* can also mean a structure (that is, a palace), and Cg defends this meaning here, claiming that the comparison of Ayodhyā not to Indra's city but to his palace, which is the very core of the city, serves to suggest even more Ayodhyā's marvelous beauty.

Sarga 7

1. Cg (so Cm) points out that, although the events of the previous *sarga* take place on the evening before (6.1-8) and the early morning of the day of the consecration (6.9-28), the events of *sarga* 7 are described as happening on the day before (since "only one thing can be told at a time"). For a discussion of this narrative technique, see Chapter 6 of the Introduction to this volume.

"from the time of her birth" *yato jātā*: This interpretation differs from that of the commentators, who understand "born somewhere or other," that is, of obscure origin (Cm, Cg). Their intention is either to debase further the wicked Mantharā, or to underscore the fact that, as "an agent of the gods," her provenance cannot be any more explicitly revealed (thus "the old teachers" cited by Cg). Ct mentions here the *Padmapurāṇa*'s revisionist account of Mantharā as an *apsaras* come to earth to effect the object of the gods (which is the story also in the *MBh*; see 3.260.9-10, Chapter 4 and note 6 of the Introduction to this volume). Ck ridicules the whole interpretation, which he ascribes to Yadvābhaṭṭa ("the master of equivocation," probably Cg; compare their comments on 5.49.27), but his own is just as unacceptable (" 'since she was a family servant' she descended 'in a fury' [verse 8], on hearing of Rāma's consecration").

3. "freshly bathed" *śirahsnāta-*: The townsfolk would take ritual baths for the auspicious occasion (Cm).

4. "a nursemaid" *dhātrīm*: The one Rāma had as a child, according to the commentators.

"has always been so miserly" *arthaparā*: Thus in agreement with Cm and Cg; Ck, Ct, Cr try variously to palliate the insult. Cg suggests further that Mantharā calls her "Rāma's mother" because she cannot bear to speak her name.

9. Before this verse, N manuscripts insert the following passage, in order to provide some kind of motive for Mantharā's ill-will: "She remembered a former injury, and was resolved on evil towards Rāma [read *niścitapāpā*?]. For once, when she had done something wrong, Rāma struck her with his foot and she fell to the ground" (124*; see 122*).

"malevolent" *pāpadarśinī*: Literally, "envisaging evil." Ct understands it in a causative sense, "pointing out the evil" (that is, the threat to Bharata); Cr, "instructing in evil."

11. "Your beautiful face has lost its charm" *aniṣṭe subhagākāre*: Understood as a *sati saptamī* (thus, with some minor differences, Ck); Cg analyzes as vocative: "You who are only superficially happy [see below], but really unloved [by the king]"; whereas Ct suggests a *viṣayasaptamī*, referring to the king: "(Why do you boast of your beauty's power) over him who, while outwardly 'providing marital felicity,' is really 'unkind' [to you]?" The phrase is echoed in the *MBh* version, 3.261.17-18.

"beautiful" *subhaga-*, "power of . . . beauty" *saubhāgya-*: The words connote additionally "marital felicity." See Ingalls 1962, p. 95: "When applied to men and women . . . *subhaga* maintains at least a portion of its ancient, etymological meaning, 'lucky, especially in love'. . . . When applied to a person one may explicate *subhaga* as 'possessing that sort of beauty which wins and holds the love of one's partner.' "

19. "queen" *mahiṣī*: Not "chief queen"; see 36.7 below.

"how can you fail to know" *katham . . . na budhyase*: For Ct, Mantharā is implying: when your rival comes to the throne, he will destroy you and your son.

26. "my enchanting beauty" *vismayadarśane*: This agrees with Cg, Cr (second explanation of both). As Cg notes, the epithet is meant to hint at the means Kaikeyī should employ to effect her goal: she must subjugate the king to her will by exploiting her special power over him (*pace* Ck, who rejects this interpretation as narratively inconsistent; see 9.19, 42 below).

27. "rose from the couch" *śayanāt*: Through eliminating the SR interpolation 129*, the crit. ed. leaves *śayanāt* (absent in the NR) without syntactical connection.

"presented . . . a lovely piece of jewelry" *ekam ābharaṇam . . . pradadau śubham*: Like Kausalyā in 3.30 (see also 6.101.16ff., 113.40ff., *MBh* 14.89.14, for other examples), Kaikeyī is here rewarding a bearer of good news (Ck), not trying to assuage Mantharā's anger (Cr).

29. "reporting" *ākhyātuḥ*: *ākhyātṛ* as a feminine (a reading based apparently on only one manuscript [G2] and two commentators [Cg, Cr]), is of course irregular (expect *ākhyātrī* [*Pā* 4.1.5]).

Ct notices the tautological quality of the verse and defends it on the grounds that the speaker is beside herself with joy.

31. "possibly tell . . . or speak" *suvacam*: The verbal is repeated to render more

intelligible the phrase *vaco varam* ("more welcome words"), which stands in apposition to *paraṃ . . . priyam* ("better news").

Sarga 8

1. "spitefully" *abhyasūya*: We read *abhyasūya* for the causative *abhyasūyya* (reported only by Ct; see the NR's *sāsūyam*), and we construe *enām* with *uvāca*. All S manuscripts hereafter insert:

> I find it ridiculous of you, my lady, while at the same time I am sorrowed, that you are delighted when you should be grieving in the face of this great disaster. I grieve for your stupidity, for what intelligent woman would be happy when prosperity comes to a deadly enemy, the son of a co-wife? (5) Rāma must fear Bharata, who has an equal claim on the kingship [*rājyasādhāraṇāt*], and realizing this I am dismayed, for where there is cause for fear there is danger. Now, Lakṣmaṇa the great bowman is wholly loyal to Rāma [and so no cause of fear to him], and Śatrughna is to Bharata as Lakṣmaṇa to Kākutstha [and so not a separate cause of fear]. Moreover, it is Bharata who is close[st] in order [of birth (see 1.17.6ff.), and thus of succession to the kingship], my lovely. (10) Succession to the kingship is far removed from the other two, who are younger. Rāma is prudent, he knows the things a kshatriya must do and he acts when he must. I tremble when I think about your son, from the danger Rāma poses. (134*)

rājyasādhāraṇāt in line 5 of this interpolation appears to be a key idea, but the precise meaning of the compound is not clear. The commentators are not very instructive: "because the kingship is a thing to be commonly enjoyed," Ck, Ct; "[Bharata being] equally fit for reigning," Cr; "[Bharata being one] of whom, to whom, the kingship is common," Cm, Cg; see note to 9.13.

3. The first line of this verse is repeated verbatim in *MBh* 3.261.18.

4. "cheerfully" *pratītām*: Against the commentators ("well-known," Cm, Ct; " 'trusted,' that is, by the king," Cr; "renowned," Cg [citing *AmaK*]); compare the use of the word in 9.27, 37.9, 42.17, 65.15, 6.110.23, etc.

5. "Rāma's exalted women" *rāmasya paramāḥ striyaḥ*: The plural has exercised some commentators, since Rāma's monogamy is repeatedly stressed in the text. The simple explanation, given and defended at length by Cg, is that all the women who attend Rāma are meant to be included (Ck, " 'Rāma's women,' namely, those who are on his side"; Cm [Ct] "the plurals [here and in the next clause] denote the friends of Sītā and those of Bharata's wife, respectively"). But in 5.16.15 (see 18.16), as in *MBh* 15.41.18, the locution seems to mean "wives," and to have almost a technical sense. Moreover, the plural "daughters-in-law" in the very next line would seem to suggest (despite Cg) that the princes, like their father, all had more than one wife (5.26.14, cited by Cg, supports this notion, to some extent, and see also Book Six, App. I, No. 10, line 91; for Bharata, see also 75.7 and 94.42). The NR reads the singular in both places (139*; we see no reason to believe that the NR has retained "a genuine older tradition," with Shah 1980, p. 98; M4 is a contaminated and virtually worthless manuscript).

"at Bharata's downfall" *bharatakṣaye*: Thus interpreted also by Cg, Ck, Ct. Possible too, but much less probable, is Cm's "in Bharata's house" (though this is how D1-3, 5 have interpreted, too: *bharatālaye*).

6. "deeply distressed" *param aprītām*: The two items have to be divided thus (so Cm, Cg, Ct), *param* being adverbial (see the NR variant *bhṛśam*; the phrase reappears at 105.9 and possibly 6.99.35, see Cg ad loc.).

9-16. Jacobi was troubled by this exchange between Kaikeyī and Mantharā, finding it unnecessary unless one assumed that the original audience lived under another form of government than that depicted in the text. He thus considered it a later interpolation, dating from the period in ancient Indian history when (as he believed) oligarchy had replaced monarchy (Jacobi 1893, pp. 106-107). There is not much to this argument. First, no social or political practice was too familiar to escape the encyclopedic didacticism of the epic; the law of primogeniture in particular is something the epics never tire of examining and illustrating, however late the text might be. Moreover, if the reasoning does have any validity, it is more probable that the political transformation in question was that from tribal oligarchy or elective chieftainship to hereditary monarchy (see the Introduction to this volume, Chapter 3), or from a system in which the eldest male member of the dynasty succeeded to the throne (as may have been the case with the Śakas of Ujjain, for example), to a primogenitural succession. Either would make Mantharā's instruction necessary.

9. The verse is most curious, for it makes the odd assumption that after Rāma's lifetime (of which one hundred years would be the proverbial epic span), Bharata, though born at the same time as Rāma (1.17.6ff.), would still be alive to succeed. The commentators are of no help. The reasonable inference is that in some earlier, still partly surviving, version of the story Bharata was represented as being considerably younger than Rāma (see below verse 19; also 40.8). Mantharā refutes Kaikeyī's supposition in verse 13 below, and will herself be refuted by the events: Rāma will make Bharata heir-apparent upon his return (6.116.79).

10. "when we have prospered in the past" *abhyudaye prāpte*: Against the commentators, we translate *prāpte* as connoting specifically past good fortune. The present good fortune the commentators take to be Rāma's consecration, the future, Bharata's (Ck's *kalyāṇa iti rāmābhiṣekalakṣaṇa* . . . appears to be a simple error).

S manuscripts include before *pādas* ef a half-verse giving an easier transition: "I feel the same esteem for Rāma as for Bharata, even more so" (141*).

After verse 10, most S manuscripts insert: "Then too, if Rāma has the kingship, Bharata likewise has it, for Rāghava looks upon his brothers as no different from himself" (142*).

13. "and then the son of Rāghava" *rāghavasya ca yaḥ sutaḥ*: Cg, Cr read *rāghavasyānu yaḥ*, "and after Rāghava his son" (not recorded in the crit. ed.). The verse is very close in sentiment to the words of Duryodhana in *MBh* 1.129.15-16.

14. "misfortune" *anayaḥ*: For this sense of the word see Dandekar on *MBh* 9.40.19 and see *Rām* 3.62.7,12; possible too, "it would be grave imprudence" (Cm glosses it, "disintegration of the kingdom"; Ck, Ct, "that is, mutual strife [and the oppression of the subjects, Ct] through 'impolitic' jealousy"; Cg, Cr more literally, "it would be 'contrary to political wisdom' to do so").

After this verse one manuscript (M4) inserts: "Whoever gets the kingship extirpates his other brothers who have ambition for the kingship, and rules the kingdom alone" (146*).

15. "however worthy the others" *guṇavatsv itareṣv api*: "That is, 'however worthy' the younger sons, and however unworthy the elder," Ct, Cr.

N manuscripts add hereafter: "And the eldest one in his turn makes over the whole kingship to his eldest son, indubitably, and never to his brothers" (147*).

16. After this verse most D manuscripts add: "You have heard about the many conflicts of the gods and *asuras*, how they cast brotherly love to the winds, each striving for his own advantage. Brothers, sons of the same father, will struggle over their family property, seeking to gain the upper hand, the one over the other—and nowhere have I ever seen brothers show each other brotherly love" (148*).

18. "unchallenged" *akaṇṭakam*: Cr takes this as a sort of proleptic adverb with *nāyayitā* ("will have . . . sent off," that is, so that no challenge can be made). It is true that the kingship cannot rightly be called "unchallenged" until Bharata is removed, but such syntax as he proposes is too hard, and the motive for it hypercritical.

19. "proximity breeds affection" *saṃnikarṣāc ca sauhārdaṃ jāyate*: Cm interprets the line to mean that, had Bharata remained in Ayodhyā, Rāma would have grown fond of him, and all enmity between the two would have been obviated (so Cr on verse 21). Quite differently Ct (Ck): the king's partiality for Rāma—which is the reason behind his consecration—is a result of the absence of Bharata, which Kaikeyī herself brought about [only according to the interpolation noted on 1.3]. If Bharata had been there, the kingdom would have been divided, and he would have received an equal share (so in part Cg).

"even in insentient things" *sthāvareṣv api*: Much of the SR adds a verse attempting to explain: "The story is told of foresters who intended to cut down a particular tree. The tree was saved from its fearful fate by thorny shrubs in close proximity" (151*.3-4). Ck reads *avareṣu* (not recorded in the crit. ed.), "(proximity breeds affection [in fathers]) for their sons."

22. Rājagṛha: A proper noun, the name of the city of the Kekayas (see 61.6, 62.2, 64.1, etc.). "The Kekayas lived near the Jhelam and had their capital at Rājagṛha or Girivraja (modern Girjak or Jalalpur on the Jhelam)" (Sircar 1967, p. 74). Distinguish this city from the ancient capital of Magadha of the same name (1.31.5, but see Chapter 3, note 9 of the Introduction).

23. Ct suggests another construction: "For in this way [if Bharata flees to the forest], good fortune may still befall our family (insofar as fear of Bharata, even if he is in exile, will prevent anyone from injuring us); or if Bharata might secure . . . [*yadi ced* = *yadi vā*, which in fact is read by N manuscripts], then good fortune might befall." The translation offered agrees with his second interpretation and that of Cg, Cr.

Sarga 9

5. After this verse most S manuscripts add, rather lamely: "Do you not remember, Kaikeyī, or do you remember but hide it, that you want to hear me tell you what will work to your advantage? But if, beautiful girl, you wish to hear me tell you, then listen, I shall, and once you have heard, you must ponder it well" (155*).

9. "took you along" *tvām upādāya*: That a king should have his wife accompany him into battle is virtually unparalleled in Sanskrit literature (though Kṛṣṇa did take his wife Satyabhāmā to the battle against the demon Naraka, *HariVaṃ* 91.39, *ViṣṇuP* 5.29). Kaikeyī is said, in an N interpolation (see note to verse 27), to possess some *vidyā* or magic power, which might account for her presence, though see note to verse 13. (Kālidāsa does not mention her presence when he refers to Daśaratha's exploit on Indra's behalf, *RaghuVa* 9.19. He knows two boons, however: 12.5-6.)

11. Śambara: Indra's enemy from the time of the *ṚV* (see Macdonell and Keith 1912, vol. 2, p. 355 for references). The name Timidhvaja seems to occur only here (and below, 39.11) in Sanskrit literature.

12. After *pāda* a, S manuscripts insert: "At night, while the men slept hurt and wounded, demons came all of a sudden and began to slay them, and a terrible fight ensued" (158*).

12-13. "conveyed" *apavāhya*: Kaikeyī executed the office of charioteer, according to Cm, Cg, Ck, Ct. Since she in effect guards her husband twice, as the commentators point out, he grants her two boons (so too in Bhoja's version, *RāmāCam* after 2.10, and see 2.19). As it stands, the text is clearly contrived. Only one boon would appear to have been granted, and that not in the absurd way recounted here but in the confrontation presented in the following *sarga* (see verse 22 and note below; 10.21 and note, and Chapter 4 of the Introduction).

14. "I . . . was unaware" *anabhijñā . . . aham*: Ck reads, *anabhijñāsi tad devi tvayaiva kathitā purā*, "Do you not recollect that, my lady? It was you who told me long ago" (not recorded in the crit. ed.; see M2).

Hereafter S manuscripts add: "I have borne this story in my mind out of love for you. You must forcibly prevent [the king] from instituting Rāma's consecration" (162*).

15. S manuscripts insert after this: "For during the fourteen years that Rāma is banished to the forest, your son will find affection in the hearts of the people and will become firmly established" (163*).

16. "private chamber" *krodhāgāram*: Literally, "room or house for anger" ("where women stay after love-quarrels and suchlike," Cg; an interesting analogy is presented by "boudoir" in its etymological sense, from French *bouder*, to sulk).

18. "to look at you" *tvāṃ . . . pratyudīkṣitum*: Many N manuscripts read instead, "to ignore you."

22. "offers you a boon" *te varaṃ dadyāt*: Evidently this stratum of the story knows nothing of any previous boon(s). Nor can the phrase be stretched to mean, "allows you to formulate the boons previously given you." The whole point of Mantharā's instructions in verses 9-15 is to remind Kaikeyī that she already has the means to coerce the king; it is nonsense to say that the king, having once granted her two wishes, should be forced to allow her the opportunity to specify them. Similarly in verses 16-19: the idea there is that Kaikeyī should exploit her power over the king, to seduce him into granting her a wish. And thus in 10.25 and later in 31.23, Daśaratha will maintain (justly, in view of the "earlier stratum") that he was "tricked" by Kaikeyī into offering a boon (which again makes little sense with regard to an open-ended wish granted long ago). Most of the NR attempts to improve matters by rearranging the verses (especially the problematic verse 21, which obviously disrupts the argument of verses 16ff.), but without appreciable gain.

24. "Rāma will . . . cease to be 'the pleasing prince' " *rāmo 'rāmo bhaviṣyati*: An etymological figure based on Rāma's name, which is traditionally etymologized as "he who pleases [his subjects]," *prajā ramayatīti rāmaḥ* (see 47.1; the etymology is explicitly given only in *MBh* 3.261.6, though see *Bālakāṇḍa* 17.16). In exile Rāma will not have the chance to win the affection of his subjects, and they will gradually forget him (so Varadacharya 1964-1965, vol. 1, p. 85n; similarly Cg, Ck, Ct).

25. "won over" *saṃgṛhīta-*: Cg (Ck, Ct) glosses, "will (through his good government) have won the loyalty of the people of the city and provinces, that is, because of his steadfastness"; Cr, "will have gained control of the army."

"steadfast" *ātmavān*: The NR reads more pointedly, "(will be) in control of the treasury" (*kośavān*).

26. After this verse, NW manuscripts insert the following vigorous passage: "False-hearted Kaikeyī accepted Mantharā's advice, unrighteous, pernicious advice that appeared beneficial, and so she was turned against [Rāma]. For that is the nature of women, to accept at once, without a second thought, what a person of their camp says, however foolish he may be. Like a wide-eyed doe charmed by a hunter's decoy call, she was brought into evil by the hunchback's words. Good can take the form of evil, and evil that of good, and bring a person to grief, with his full approval" (169*).

27. After *pādas* ab of this verse some N manuscripts insert all, some part of a passage of about fifty lines (App. I, No. 7) which, first, attempts to offer some reason why Kaikeyī should accept such malicious advice: as a child she is supposed to have angered a brahman, who cursed her one day to find herself an object of scorn among people (lines 1-6 [also reported by Ct, and see his remarks in note to 33.6]); second, repeats the account of the battle during which Daśaratha gave her the two boons and explains how she protected him: she possessed a magic power that made her unassailable to *rākṣasas*, a power she obtained from an aged brahman in a rather roundabout way (14-37); and third, shows Kaikeyī to be convinced of the danger in which Bharata will find himself if Rāma is crowned, "since power corrupts" (40-45).

28. "Of all the hunchbacks . . . there is none better at devising plans" *pṛthivyām asi kubjānām uttamā buddhiniścaye*: Cg finds here the implication that *kubjas* ("hunchbacks") were generally sagacious servants. Ck, Ct suggest that such servants were particularly desirable to queens, since they did not pose the threat of rivalry that a comely servant might.

31. "grown thin" *śātam*: We read thus (see the common compound *śātodarī*), with many S manuscripts (note agreement of V and B) and Cm, Cg, Ck, for the crit. ed.'s *śāntam*. As Cg explains, the verse contains the figure *utprekṣā* ("poetic fancy"): the waist, which is so thin, might be said to have grown thus for shame or envy after seeing the eminence of the chest.

33. After this verse S manuscripts and Ś1 insert: "The thousand magic powers that were in Śambara, overlord of *asuras*, have all been placed in you, and many more, by the thousands" (175*).

36. "liquid" *suniṣṭaptena*: This follows Cr in rendering the striking image, though it remains uncertain whether "liquid gold" in the strict sense of the term (German *Glanzgold*) is meant (or was even known in ancient India). Perhaps simply "refined" ("gold infused with sandalwood paste; or, a bodice made of gold," Cm, Cg; "a garland . . . made of gold" [connecting with verse 35], Ck, Ct).

38. "you shall strut" *gamiṣyasi gatiṃ mukhyām*: This follows Cg's suggestion that *gatim* is cognate accusative and refers to a particular style of movement; Ck, Ct, Cr understand, "you will reach the highest rank, preeminence."

"holding your head high" *garvayantī*: The causative appears to be *svārthe* or, rather, to be employed only to permit the verb a quasi-transitive aspect.

41. "apprise the king" *rājānam anudarśaya*: Uncertain. Cm, Cg, Ck, " 'show the king' to the chamber, or, await the king"; Ct, " 'have the king see,' that is, you in your chamber"; Cr, "go into the sight of the king" (contrast the use of the word in 28.8 and 93.1). The NR offers, "infatuate the king."

44. "golden" *hemopamā*: Varadacharya cleverly remarks that not only is Kaikeyī's body as beautiful as gold, but her mind, if just as pure, is also as malleable (1964-1965, vol. 1, p. 91n).

45. "the land" *kṣitim*: Accepting here the reading of the crit. ed., despite the weighty concord of Ś1, Ñ1, M1, G1, etc., for *śriyam* ("royal fortune," that is, the kingship), in order to preserve a significant contrast between the inhabited royal domain and the wild jungle.

It is very likely that hereafter the original contained a verse in which Kaikeyī vows not to drink or eat until Rāma has departed to the forest. Both recensions include the idea (181*, 183*.21-22), though in forms not easily reducible to a single source; moreover, later in the poem two references are made to Kaikeyī's threat (3.45.8, 5.31.16).

46. "fallen" *patitā*: "From heaven to earth, as a result of the diminution of merit," Cm, Ct.

Sarga 10

1. "Rāghava's consecration" *rāghavasyābhiṣecanam*: After this phrase Ś1 and all S manuscripts insert: "and having taken leave of the assembly [thus picking up the action from 5.23], he entered his dwelling, believing that Rāma's consecration had only just become known [and that therefore Kaikeyī would not yet have been informed of it]" (186*).

"gladly" *vaśī*: Literally, "of his own accord." The king believes that Kaikeyī will be as pleased as he is to learn of Rāma's consecration (is this a fatuous belief? see notes to 4.39, 8.10, 10.3). *Vaśin* in this sense is quite rare, attested in the *Rām* only two other times (see 17.1 and 98.37 and notes), and elsewhere only *TaiS* 3.4.2.2. The commentators fail to appreciate it. Ck, Ct, " 'self-controlled,' in all things except what concerns his wife"; Cg, " 'everything is under his own control,' that is, he is independent and would tell Kaikeyī himself."

After verse 1, the SR adds a passage in which Daśaratha, on entering his chamber, fails to find Kaikeyī there. He is troubled, for she has never before missed the appointed hour for their rendezvous, and he is desirous of making love with her (lines 13-15). A chambermaid then explains the situation to him (187*).

3. "guileless" *apāpaḥ*: "It is because the king is 'guileless' and infatuated with her that he fails to realize how painful to Kaikeyī the consecration of her co-wife's son would be," Cg.

4. "his cow wounded by the poisoned arrow of a hunter" *kareṇum . . . digdhena viddhāṃ mṛgayunā*: Though it has the ring of a commonplace, the simile may well be intended to refer to Mantharā and her poisonous counsel (see 27.22 below).

6. "why you should be angry" *krodham ātmani saṃśritam: Ātmani*: Cr, "that is, 'in your mind' "; Cm, Ck, Ct take this as referring to the king (anger "against me"; for this type of oblique reflexivity of *ātma-* see 64.24 and note), but this does not fit with his next question.

7. *pādas* ab are best taken with the previous verse, as Ck does (Cm, Cg, Ct, Cr explain as a self-contained sentence, but this is too hard syntactically).

"when you are so precious to me" *mayi kalyāṇacetasi*: Literally, "when I am one [or, when I am here, or, alive and one] of whom the mind is favorably disposed [toward you]." Ck, Ct analyze, "when I have done you no wrong."

8. "gratified in every way" *abhituṣṭāś ca sarvaśaḥ*: That is, by means of gifts, high regard being shown them, and so on (Cm, Cg, Ct; the variant reading in some N manuscripts, "well provided with payments," is simpler and more explicit).

10. "Is there some guilty man" *vadhyaḥ kaḥ*: Daśaratha's flagrant disregard for *dharma* (see 66.37 and 94.47-48) because of his passion for Kaikeyī is a theme Vālmīki's idealized treatment of the story has not eliminated altogether (see Introduction, Chapter 9). The verse is closely (in part, verbatim) reproduced in *MBh* 3.261.22-23.

12. "not if it cost me my life" *ātmano jīvitenāpi*: The *pāda* construes with verse 11 (thus too all commentators).

"the wheel of my power" *cakram*: So Cm, Ck; see 6.116.11 and *MBh* 2.68.3: "the wheel of the great king Dhārtarāṣṭra has been set in motion" (see also 1.69.45). The universal monarch is often referred to as "he who turns the wheel," *cakravartin* (the word, which is thought to be post-Buddhist, occurs only once in *Rām* 2-6, at 5.29.2). Less likely Cg, Ct, Cr: "the wheel of the sun's chariot," the disc of the sun.

In S and NW manuscripts the statement in *pādas* cd regarding the king's dominion follows somewhat more logically on his protestation (verse 19) that Kaikeyī should not doubt his ability to fulfil her desire. Placing verse 19 before 12 cd also allows the powerful verse 18 to stand at the end of the king's speech, as it was probably meant to.

After verse 12 the crit. ed. excludes a few verses (194*, in NW and S manuscripts) that provide a list of the peoples in the king's dominions: the eastern Sindhusauviras [Cg, Ct, Cr read "the Drāviḍas, the Sindhusauviras"], the Saurāṣṭras, the Dakṣiṇāpathas, the people of Vaṅga, Aṅga, Magadha, the Matsyas, the people of Kāśi and Kosala; Daśaratha at the same time asks Kaikeyī to *choose* (that is, offers as a boon; line 4) any precious thing she might want (see NE manuscripts, 195*).

14. "mistreated" *viprakṛtā*: Cg glosses, "(I am) not ill."

16. "with some surprise" *īṣadutsmitaḥ*: Cg offers three possible reasons for the king's surprise: that she insists on an oath even though he always does as she asks (= Cm, Ct); because he could easily do anything she might want done (= Ck); or that she was not ill, as he had feared.

17. "there is not a single person I love as much as you" *tvattaḥ priyataro mama manujo . . . na vidyate*: Crā, Cm, Cg, Ct, Cr suggest another way to understand the clause: there is none among women I love more than you, none among men I love more than Rāma (i.e., he does not love Rāma more than her). Their intention, apparently, is to emphasize that Daśaratha is blameless and Kaikeyī's malice wholly unprovoked.

An insertion in S and NW manuscripts, taking up the mention of Rāma in verse 17, has Daśaratha vow to do what Kaikeyī wishes by swearing an oath three times on the head of Rāma (without seeing whom he "could not live an instant," and whom he "would choose even at the cost of himself or his other sons" [200*]).

18. The cue for the literal interpretation of this verse is the NR variant 201*; the commentators are hopelessly confused here.

19. "Seeing that I have the power" *balam ātmani paśyantī*: "Seeing in [me my]self the power," Cm, Ck. Since *ātma-* is, strictly speaking, reflexive to the verbal subject (but see notes to 64.24 and 10.6), some commentators suggest the interpretation "seeing in [your]self the power," i.e., the power exerted by your beauty or by my love for you—Cm, Cg, Ct. (See *MBh* 3.261.24, which supports this latter explanation;

the problem is complicated by the uncertain position of the verse, see note to verse 12 above.)

"I swear . . . by all my acquired merit" *sukṛtenāpi . . . śape*: "That is, 'May my good *karma* not produce its beneficial effects [in my future births] if I do not do what you wish,' " Ct; see note to 18.13.

20. "like a visitation of death" *abhyāgatam ivāntakam*: The simile is poignantly apposite, since the ultimate consequence of her request will be that Daśaratha dies (*sarga* 58).

21. "in due order" *krameṇa*: Cm, Cg, Ck, Ct take the adverb with *śapase* alone, "you swear in turn," that is, by Rāma and by your good works. The passage where the king swears by Rāma is (rightly, see 3.45.7) excluded from the crit. ed. (note to verse 17 above). Here and in verse 24 it again seems clear that in some antecedent version of the story Daśaratha grants Kaikeyī a boon *during this* interview, as even here some "interpolations" would have it (see note to verse 12 above). See note to 9.13.

22. "heaven" *jagat*: So glossed by Cm, Cg (citing *AmaK*), Ck, Ct.

25. "called upon witnesses" *abhiśasya*: The lection is uncertain. Cg reads thus and we follow his explanation (" 'called to witness,' namely, all the gods"; Ck, Ct less persuasively explain, " 'having praised' him by calling him 'true to his word,' etc. in order to confirm him in his duty"). A good variant reading reported in some N manuscripts is *abhiśāpya*, "having caused him to swear" (see *sampratiśrāvya* in 99.5 and for the causative of the root *śap*, 3.23.12, 4.9.14).

After verse 25 the crit. ed. excludes a twelve-line passage (204*, found in most D and S manuscripts), which again and somewhat differently attempts to explain the two boons Kaikeyī is about to mention: "Remember, Your Majesty, what happened long ago, during the battle of the gods and *asuras*: There your enemy caused you to fall lifeless. [Remember] that then, my lord, you were protected by me; that when your body was smeared with blood in that battle of the gods and *asuras* [we omit here the meaningless *tatra covāca tacchaktaḥ*], the *rākṣasas* attacked you, and I foiled them with my secret knowledge, though their might and valor were great. And I kept watch and cared for you, and then you gave me two boons."

35. "thinking you a princess" *nṛpasutā*: We must understand *iti* after *nṛpasutā* (so Cm, Cg; see the NR gloss *rājaputrīti*).

38. "I shall lose my mind" *naṣṭā bhavati cetanā*: The present *bhavati* here signifies an action about to occur (*Pā* 3.3.131; NR accordingly reads optative); less likely is a general statement: when[ever] I cannot see Rāma I lose my mind, lose consciousness.

40. After this verse most S and NW manuscripts include a long and at times tiresome section (App. I, No. 9), in which Daśaratha, incredulous, hurt, and angry, pleads with Kaikeyī, admitting at one point how often he has withheld any show of affection toward Kausalyā because of her (118-121) and in the end refuses to grant her wishes no matter what she threatens to do.

41. Kaikeyī's extending her feet for her husband to touch in supplication is an act of extreme disrespect (Cg), or may suggest that she looks on him, king and husband though he be, as her slave or debtor (Ck, Ct). She would naturally be expected to retract her feet and to raise her husband off the ground (Cm, Cs understand, ingenuously, that suspecting her husband might try to bow down to her Kaikeyī "shifts her feet" elsewhere).

A NW interpolation has the night pass with the king lost in grief (219*); the SR transfers this insertion to the end of *sarga* 11.

Sarga 11

1. Yayāti: See note to 5.9 above. He reached heaven by means of his self-control, but because of his pride was thrown out by Indra (*MBh* 1.81). The story is alluded to in 3.62.7.

"his merit exhausted" *puṇyānte*: The good *karma* acquired in his previous life (the reward of which was his stay in heaven) had been used up. The depletion of his merit would suffice to eject him from heaven; presumably it made him prone to such vices as pride, which is elsewhere related as the cause of his fall.

2. "for all the fear she awoke" *bhayadarśinī*: The commentators explain variously: "showing the danger posed to Bharata by Rāma" (Cm, Ct); "exposing Daśaratha to danger [= Ck], or, reading *(a)bhaya-*, not seeing (reckoning) the danger to Daśaratha" (Cg [Cm]; perhaps correct: *bhayadarśinī* in 3.20.10 means, "seeing danger").

"had yet to secure her fortunes" *(a)siddhārthā*: Agreeing here with Crā, Cm, Cg, Ct (against the crit. ed.) on the *praśleṣa* of *a(siddha-)*.

3. "you are vaunted" *katthyase*: The passive (for the crit. ed.'s *katthase*) seems clearly indicated by the NR's *kīrtyase*.

6. A difficult verse, much complicated by the fact that the crit. ed. constitutes a text (*pādas* a-f) exhibited by no single manuscript. The third-person reference to Kaikeyī (understood to be in *oratio obliqua* in the SR by and large, through interpolation 221*; so too, it seems, in the NR, through 222*) must be taken as a sudden soliloquizing on the part of Daśaratha. However, *pādas* cd remain obscure, for the antecedents of the pronouns are uncertain. We follow Cm, Cg, Cr, who consider Daśaratha's lie to be his failing to consecrate Rāma after he had promised to do so (they cite 4.22; better is 3.24, and see note on 55.2-3). Such too is the opinion of Ruben (1950, p. 292 and note; 1956, p. 36 and note). The *Rām* never reverts to the issue (though see note on 55.2-3).

8. "to last a mere three watches" *triyāmā*: See note to 6.5. The compound must, because of *śarvarī*, be taken in a literal rather than metonymic sense (see the NR substitute: "though of three watches, the night . . . seemed like a hundred years," 224*; Cg understands *atriyāmā*, " 'the night was no longer only three watches,' that is, it was very long").

9. "his eyes fixed upon the sky" *gaganāsaktalocanaḥ*: Daśaratha proceeds in the next verse to address the night, for which the present phrase must suffice as reference. Both the NR (225*.5) and the SR (226*) make the apostrophe explicit.

10. "so that I no longer have to see" *nāham icchāmi . . . draṣṭum*: Daśaratha would be relieved of the sight of Kaikeyī at dawn either because the presence of the citizens (that is, men) would force her to withdraw (Cm, Ck, Ct, Cr), or because he would die the moment Rāma departed (Ct).

11ff. For the king's posture here and Kaikeyī's indifference, contrast the scene between Daśaratha and Kausalyā (56.4ff., especially verses 9-10).

11. "Daśaratha's alternating condemnation and supplication of Kaikeyī implies that he cannot bring himself to abandon either his son or *dharma*," Cg.

12. "Please, I am an old man" *sādhu vṛddhasya*: The reading with best manuscript

authority is *sādhu vṛddhasya*. The crit. ed.'s *sādhuvṛttasya* ("I have been of good conduct"), makes little textual or contextual sense. *Sādhu,* "please," emphatic initial position as in 3.51.12, 53.18, etc. "I am an old man," as in 4.12.

"I place myself in your hands" *tvadgatasya*: Close to Cg's interpretation, "having you as my last resort." Cm, Ck, Ct understand, " 'come into your power,' because of his being under the power of truth [that is, his promise]."

"after all, I am king" *rājño viśeṣataḥ*: N manuscripts have tried to alter the reading of the rather bathetic line, but it is in character (see for example 56.5 and note).

13. "it was thoughtless" *śūnyena*: Literally, "I was empty," "devoid of the discrimination of what one should and should not say, because of grief," Ct; Cm, Ck seem to take it, " 'I speak to you now empty,' namely, devoid of all self-respect," whereas Cm (first explanation), Cg, Ct (second) read *śūnye na* and explain, "this, namely, Rāma's consecration, was not announced 'in an empty place,' where no people were, but in the presence of all the people."

14. "made no reply" *na cakāra vākyam*: Less likely, "would not do what he said." The commentators are silent.

15. "for the exile" *vivāsaṃ prati*: Dependent on *pratikūlabhāṣiṇīm* (so, more or less, Cr).

Sarga 12

2. "as though you deemed it a sin" *pāpaṃ kṛteva*: Cm, Cg, Ck understand, " 'committing this evil,' namely, that of not keeping the promise" (and they take *iva* as *eva*). This translation agrees with Cr, in view of the explanation offered in verse 3.

"You must stand" *sthātuṃ tvam arhasi*: The poet probably intends the sarcastic *double entendre*.

4. Śaibya: King Śaibya (or Śibi), rather than go back on his promise of protecting a dove that took refuge with him from a pursuing hawk, offered up his own body by way of compensation (the story is a popular one; for one early version see *MBh* 3, App. I, No. 21). The appeal to mytho-historical precedent is noteworthy. It is a favorite device of Vālmīki's (for example, 18.20, 27-29, and *sarga* 102), but has a more than literary function: in questions of what constitutes proper behavior in a matter where no shastric injunctions exist, "the ways of good men in the past" is one of the authoritative standards.

5. Alarka: Referred to elsewhere in Sanskrit literature only in the *MBh*, but in a way unconnected with the events mentioned here (see 3.26.12, "Alarka, they say . . . was a good and truthful man, king of the Kāśikauruṣas, who gave up his kingdom and wealth"; in 14.30.1ff. he is said to have been a *rājarṣi* who learned the supreme bliss of yoga). The story told of him here appears in the *Jātakas* (#499), where, however, the principal actor is King Śivi. The learned commentator Rāmacandra on *RāmāCam* 2.18 is unable to cite a source for this story of Alarka.

6. "he pledged to keep" *satyānurodhāt*: For the *samaye* of the crit. ed. (Cm, Ct, Cr, " 'even at the time,' that is, of its swelling under the full moon"; Cg, "at some given time"), we read *samayam,* which is strongly indicated by the agreement of M1, G2 and NE manuscripts, by the parallelism with *pādas* ab, and by the next verse; our interpretation agrees with Ck.

8. "than Bali could from Indra's" *balir indrakṛtaṃ yathā*: All commentators un-

derstand the simile as referring to the trap of the promise made by the demon king Bali to Viṣṇu in his dwarf incarnation, and they take Indra here as standing for Upendra, "(Viṣṇu) sent by Indra" (a comparatively late cognomen of Viṣṇu; so understood also in the NR, see 235*; for the story see 1.28.11 and 6.105.24). However, in an earlier version of the Bali story, one unconnected with the dwarf incarnation of Viṣṇu, it is Indra who tricks Bali and binds him; see, for example, *MBh* 9.30.8 and Tripathi 1968, pp. 49ff. (contrast however *Rām* 3.59.22).

11. "in accordance with the sacred hymn, I took" *mantrakṛtaḥ*: This agrees with Ck, "a hand, the bearing of which is made [required] by the *mantra*, 'I take your hand [for happiness]' " [*ṚV* 10.85.36] (Cm, Cg, Ct, Cr understand, "purified by the *mantra*").

"I now repudiate you . . . as well as the son I fathered on you" *taṃ tyajāmi svajaṃ caiva tava putraṃ saha tvayā*: When, at the end of the *Yuddhakāṇḍa*, Rāma meets his dead father, his only request of him will be to lift this "terrible curse" (6.107.25).

After verse 11, most N manuscripts insert a passage (239*) that brings the night to a close and shows Daśaratha awakened in the morning by the praises of Sumantra, which he says cause him anguish. This insertion is followed by verse 19. SR 240* similarly shows the night to have passed.

13. "without delay" *akliṣṭam*: So Cg (see the NR gloss, *visrabdham*). Kaikeyī urges that Rāma be brought so that the decree of banishment can be made at once.

16. In the NR, this verse is addressed by Daśaratha to the charioteer; in the SR the king here is never said to order Rāma to be brought (the NW version says explicitly that Sumantra took Kaikeyī's words as the order of the king, 260*.1-2; thus the commentators of the SR explain 255*, but see note to verse 21; also 13.21 and note).

After this verse the SR inserts a passage of sixty-eight lines (App. I, No. 10: It is dawn and Vasiṣṭha enters the city with the equipment for the consecration. He sees Sumantra and tells him to inform the king that he has arrived and that it is time to commence the ceremony. Sumantra enters and recites the morning panegyric, which grieves the king). After comparing this passage with the one noted above, NR 239* (see note to verse 11), we believe the crit. ed. has imperfectly established the text for verses 17-21. The data are admittedly complex for this scene; Ruben felt a reconstitution of the archetype to be "excluded" (1950, p. 293 n4). But it seems possible, on the basis of the textual evidence, to come closer than the crit. ed. to what the poet must originally have intended. Here, then, follows an alternative reconstruction (the translation of the verses from the crit. ed. must be somewhat adjusted to fit with the new context):

> #10.44-45 [see 239*.4-5]. The charioteer Sumantra, it being the appointed hour, then entered the king's apartment and cupping his hands in reverence, he began to sing the praises of the lord of the world.
>
> #10.46-47 [see 239*.7-8]. "May you be joyful and with a joyful heart delight us with your presence, as the rising sun delights the mighty ocean."
>
> #10.67-68 [see 239*.11-12 + 251*]. The lord of the earth, as he listened to the charioteer's cordial and well-meaning words, was overcome once again with grief.
>
> (N.B. verse 17 of the crit. ed. is simply the NR variant of verse 21, and should be omitted.)

18. Then the righteous and majestic king, utterly joyless on account of his son, looked up at the charioteer through eyes red with grief, and said,

252* [=239*.14]. "You cut me to the very quick with these words of yours."

19. Hearing the pitiful words and seeing the king's desolate expression, Sumantra cupped his hands in reverence and withdrew some steps from his presence.

20. When in his desolation the lord of earth proved incapable of giving the command himself, Kaikeyī, who well knew her counsels, addressed Sumantra herself:

253*. "Sumantra, the king is exhausted from being awake the whole night in his eager delight over Rāma, and now he is sleepy. Go quickly, then, charioteer, to the glorious prince. Bring Rāma, please. You need have no qualms in doing so."

21 cd-255*. Thinking that this meant all was well he rejoiced with all his heart. Joyfully he departed, hurrying in consequence of the royal command.

This is what the manuscripts seem most persuasively to attest, but narrative inconsistencies still remain (see 13.20ff. and notes). In fact, the textual confusion in the whole scene seems to reflect an anxiety on the part of the custodians of the *Rām* tradition about Daśaratha's having any direct involvement in the process of Rāma's banishment.

18. "tried to speak" *uvāca*: By the deletion of the various "interpolations" the verb has been left without any direct speech to complement it, a construction without parallel in the *Rām*. Accepting the crit. ed., we have only one solution, to take this as a conative perfect (and to understand the king as attempting to confirm Kaikeyī's order?). For the occasional conative aspect of the perfect in the epic see 1.63.7, 3.24.7, 43.36, 59.28, 5.47.21, and *MBh* 3.102.6.

20. "who well knew her counsels" *mantrajñā*: The epithet is principally ornamental, allowing for alliteration (*sumantraṃ mantrajñā*, a sort of *pādamadhyayamaka*; see 13.20, *sumantraṃ mantrakovidam*, etc.).

21. Several D manuscripts add that Sumantra hesitated to go without receiving a direct order from the king (254*), and attribute verse 21 to Daśaratha.

22. "has exhausted himself in preparing Rāma's consecration" *rāmābhiṣekārtham āyasyati*: We read *rāmābhiṣekārtham* with all commentators, and with most of them *āyasyati* (mistaken by the editor of the crit. ed. as a corruption; see *āyasta-* in 17.1 and 27.21, and note also the "gloss" in 253*.2, [*prajāgara-*]*pariśrāntaḥ*). The crit. ed. would give, "Clearly Rāma will come here for the purpose of his consecration," a reading equally weak with regard to context and manuscript authority.

Sarga 13

2. "the leading merchants" *mukhyā ye nigamasya*: For *nigamasya* we agree with Ct, Cr (so Cm on verse 19 below; see note to 1.14 above, and 106.13. Cg understands, "the leading men of the city").

3. Some S manuscripts add, "When the sun had entered the sign of Cancer, when it was Rāma's birthday" (259*; see note to 1.17.5).

4-7. Ct supplies various verbs with the different objects; Cg construes all with *bhānti* in 7c, and we more or less follow him.

10. "flawless" *susthitaḥ*: The adjective (literally, "well-built") is rare with animate objects. The NR's *upakalpitaḥ* seems to speak in favor of the widespread SR variant *saṃsthitaḥ* ("was present").

11. Hereafter many S (265*) and NW (270*) manuscripts add a verse describing the presence of courtesans (see note on 32.3).

15. "from all over the land" *sārvabhaumān*: The word appears to be unique in this sense.

S manuscripts insert after this verse: "At the king's command I am setting off quickly to Rāma. But you are honored of the king, and of Rāma in particular" (275*).

16. "easily" *sukham*: We take this adverbially (as Cg, "without delay"); Ck, Ct interpret as direct object, "I shall inform him that you all ask after his 'comfort' ["whether he has slept 'well,' " Ct], (and shall ask why . . .)."

"if he is now awake" *saṃprati buddhasya*: We understand *saṃprati* independently, as an adverb, with Ck. The participle *buddhasya* is less likely concessive (Cm, Ck, Ct) than conditional: Sumantra proceeds as if the king is not yet awake (even though he has just left him in the previous *sarga*), and we must assume the charioteer believed him to have fallen asleep, since he has not yet come forth. After this verse S and NW manuscripts insert: "May the moon and sun, O Kākutstha, may Śiva and Vaiśravaṇa, Varuṇa and Agni and Indra ordain victory for you" (279*), thus attempting to furnish the blessings mentioned.

20. Many S manuscripts try to introduce order in the rather disorderly narrative by adding: "I had told you to bring Rāma, charioteer. For what reason do you disobey my order?" (288*; see 255*).

21. "So . . . Daśaratha spoke, again ordering" *iti . . . daśarathaḥ . . . anvaśāt punaḥ*: This implies that Daśaratha once already explicitly commanded Sumantra to bring Rāma, though the verses indicating that are identified as interpolations (see previous note and note to 12.16). It may be that we are to infer that by not openly countermanding Kaikeyī's order Daśaratha can be thought to have approved it, and here avers his full consciousness of it (as Cm, Cg, Ck suggest).

22. Sumantra's redundant inference is eliminated in the NR.

25. "terraces" *vitardi-*: See Schlingloff 1969, p. 26 and note 2.

"golden images atop its pinnacles" *kāñcanapratimaikāgram*: The compound is unclear. The commentators are not unanimous: "dense with golden images, or, in which the chief pinnacles (were surmounted) by golden images," Cg; "complete with chief golden images," Ck; "in which the predominant façade was provided with golden images," Cm, Ct, Cr.

"coral" *vidruma-*: It has been argued that coral (also *pravāla-*) was available to India only from the Mediterranean, and thus there is no reference to it in Sanskrit texts until the early Christian era, when trade with Rome became significant (a fact that, if true, might help date our passage; see Trautmann 1971, p. 178, citing Lévi 1936). This may be the case with respect to red coral, but we do not know whether the Sanskrit words refer exclusively to that variety, or also to others, such as the black coral once exported from the Persian gulf, or that which, according to the poem itself (see 3.33.24), is found along the south Indian coast.

27. "royal palace" *rājakulam*: There is no necessity to abandon (in agreement with Ck, Ct, Cr) the common meaning of the compound (see 15.12), and to understand

it in the very rare sense of "royal highway." Admittedly, to construe *pādas* b and c thus together is unusual. This difficulty appears to have called forth the passage rejected by the crit. ed., 303*; while otherwise vacuous, it in fact supplies the substantive required by 27c (*gṛham*, with which 27c would have construed were it not for other excisions made by the crit. ed. in verse 27). These lines should have been included since all manuscripts report them (B4 and D3 are missing for this portion of the *sarga*).

28. "with a complex of buildings more splendid than celestial palaces" *mahāvimānottamaveśmasaṃghavat*: Agrees with Cm.

Sarga 14

1. "the courtyard" *kakṣyām*: The NR describes it as the "seventh courtyard" (contrast 5.4, and see note there).

2. "the young men who stood guard" *yuvabhir . . . adhiṣṭhitām*: In accordance with Daśaratha's advice in 4.24 above.

5. "anxious for the news" *priyakāmyayā*: See note to 3.29. The commentators explain unsatisfactorily, as Ct, " 'desiring to do a kindness,' to wit, to his father"; Cg reads, " 'desiring to do a kindness to Rāghava,' that is, Daśaratha."

6. Vaiśravaṇa: Kubera, "lord of wealth," ruler of *yakṣas* and *gandharvas*, "world-protector" of the northern quarter, and, incidentally, half-brother of Rāvaṇa, who drove him from his hereditary kingship (see 3.46.4ff.). See also verse 26 below, and for this type of allusion, note to 2.29.

8. "Sītā now was with him" *upetaṃ sītayā bhūyaḥ*: In contrast to Sumantra's previous visit, 4.5ff. Our construction is close to Cg's ("once again with her at his side," though he goes on to add, "after she had anointed him or [he seems to say] after she had embraced him, overcome by his beauty"). Ct, Cr impossibly connect *bhūyaḥ* with *dadarśa* in verse 6 (Ct, "again and again"; Cr, "completely" [intensely]). Cm, Cg report another interpretation, which understands *virājamānam* ([gleaming] *the more* with Sītā at his side). The NR (312*) has "like Madhusūdana (Viṣṇu) attended by Śrī with her lotus in her hand."

9. In *pādas* cd there is a remarkable alliteration: "*vavande varadaṃ bandī vinayajño vinītavat*" (note that /b/ and /v/ are considered homophonic for all figures of sound).

10. "passed the time agreeably" *vihāra-*: Sumantra's question is unexpected, since Rāma was to have fasted, abstained from sexual intercourse, and entered into a state of consecration. Cm and Cg are perplexed; Ct, with some N support, reads differently and seems to understand, "having seen the handsome man upon the couch [that served] for pleasure and sleeping."

11. "worthy son of Kausalyā" *kausalyāsuprajāḥ*: In conformity with the general practice of the crit. ed., *kausalyāsuprajāḥ* should probably be printed as two separate words (see 1.22.2, 3.3.17, 5.62.30), though the commentators are not unanimous on whether or not this is in fact a compound, and what its specific sense is. Either "Kausalyā has good offspring in you" (noncompound, *suprajāḥ* as *bahuvrīhi* compound, so Cm, Cg; for the termination see note to 64.15), or, "good offspring of Kausalyā" (compound, *suprajāḥ* as *karmadhāraya*, so Cg, Ck). *Pā* 5.4.122, which prescribes the *samāsānta asic* for *bahuvrīhi* compounds, would support the first inter-

pretation (though Ck on 3.3.17 maintains that the suffix can exceptionally be used in *tatpuruṣas*); the use of the phrase in 64.15 (see note there) and 90.5 below likewise favors it.

13. "on my behalf" *madantare*: So Cm, Cg, Ck (citing *AmaK*), Ct, Cr; see note to 84.16. (Less likely, "in my absence.")

14. "my lovely-eyed wife" *madirekṣaṇe*: Read as the vocative with most S manuscripts (rather than the nominative of the crit. ed., a rather curious way for Rāma to speak of his "mother"; the adjective he applies to Kaikeyī in 99.5-6 has narrative relevance).

15. "A council's mood" *yādṛśī pariṣat*: We understand *pādas* ab in part as a general observation. The "council" at issue is Daśaratha's colloquy with Kaikeyī (so Cm).

17. "uttering" *abhidadhyuṣī*: The commentators (except Cr) derive this perfect participle not, as here, from the root *dhā* but from the root *dhyā*, "meditating."

19. "almost the size of young elephants" *kareṇuśiśukalpaiḥ*: According to Ck, however, the simile is meant to suggest that the horses are excited, strong, and so on.

20. "thousand-eyed Indra": What is meant to be compared to the thousand eyes on the body of Indra, Ct suggests, is the mass of different gems set in the ornaments on Rāma's body.

23. After verse 23, S manuscripts and Ś1 insert an eighteen-line passage (327*), in which, as Rāma passes through the streets, the women at the windows watch enraptured and sing his praises (see the similar scenes, perhaps modeled on this one, in *BuddhaC* 3 and *RaghuVa* 7).

24. "in their deep delight" *prahṛṣṭarūpasya*: *-rūpa-* is an intensifier, as often in the *Rām* (30.22, 84.22, 3.43.36, 56.19; 5.7.69). See *Pā* 5.3.66.

Sarga 15

4. "he honored every man, each according to his rank" *yathārhaṃ . . . saṃpūjya sarvān eva narān*: "That is, with glances, motions of his eyebrows, words, folded hands, bows, etc., according as these were appropriate," Cg, Ck, Ct. The poet elsewhere shows himself to be highly sensitive to the proprieties of social rank; see especially 95.46 and note.

5. "grandfathers and great-grandfathers" *pitāmahaiḥ . . . tathaiva prapitāmahaiḥ*: The plurals, according to Cr, are honorific.

7. "heavenly bliss" *paramārthaiḥ*: Literally, "ultimate benefits," "heaven, etc." (Cm, Ck).

"Would only that we might see" *yathā paśyāma*: Perhaps to be taken absolutely (Cg correctly interprets the imperative in the sense of requesting, *Pā* 3.3.162; several manuscripts read the optative).

10. After this verse the SR adds: "Whoever might fail to see Rāma, or be seen by Rāma, would live an object of the world's reproach, and of his own" (346* nearly = NW 345*).

11. "in a way befitting their ages" *vayaḥsthānām*: See 94.51 and note for the appropriate procedures. Varadacharya suggests, "to elders he would show the compassion of a son, to children that of a father, to his contemporaries that of a friend" (1964-1965, vol. 1, p. 184n). This is essentially the same as the old explanation of the commentators, Cv, Cm, Cg, Ct, Cr, though they take the compound as accusative

singular feminine, "[compassion] whose degree or measure was [according to] age." Cg's alternative gloss, "to the elders (of all four social orders)," Cm's, " 'to the youthful,' that is, ignorant," have little to recommend them.

12. After this verse S manuscripts and Ś1 insert: "On horse the best of men passed beyond three courtyards guarded by bowmen, and went through the other two of them on foot [perhaps as a sign of humility, see note to 5.4]" (350*). In 51.20 the royal palace is described as comprising eight courtyards.

Sarga 16

2. The NR inserts after this verse a passage showing Lakṣmaṇa to be present (351*; see note on verse 56 below).

7. "like that of the ocean under a full moon" *samudra iva parvaṇi*: Ck remarks, "Although it is from joy that the ocean is agitated when the moon rises on full-moon days, the simile here has reference merely to the fact of agitation."

10. "He seems desolate" *sa dīna iva*: Follows Ck, who against all other commentators takes *pādas* ab to refer still to Daśaratha (see verse 12 below; Ck however also interprets these as questions: "Why does he seem . . . ?").

12. "physical illness or mental distress" *śārīro mānaso . . . saṃtāpo vābhitāpo vā*: The commentators all join *saṃtāpo* with *śārīro*, and *abhitāpo* with *mānaso*, in a sort of *yathāsaṃkhyālaṃkāra*, and we follow them.

13. "misfortune . . . one of my mothers" *mātṝṇāṃ vā mamāśubham*: One might also take *mama* closely with *aśubham*, "misfortune through my doing" (so Cr, Cs).

15. "in whom . . . the very source" *yatomūlam*: *yato* forms part of an *aluk* compound (so Cm, Cg, Ck, Ct), and is not to be taken separately as a conjunction (Cr).

16. "Can it be" *kaccit*: Rāma's three previous questions (verses 11, 12, 13) were all framed with *kaccin na* ("It cannot be, can it?"); this last one pointedly omits the negative, and thereby implies the expectation of an affirmative reply.

17. After this verse S and NW manuscripts insert eighteen lines (363*), in which Kaikeyī alludes to the boon (singular) given her by the king and asserts she will tell Rāma about it if he will fulfil its conditions. Rāma replies that she ought not to speak that way to him (that is, mistrusting his obedience).

19. "Rāma need not say so twice" *rāmo dvir nābhibhāṣate*: That is, he need not repeat a promise. This seems to be supported by *MBh* 5.160.23, in reference to Kṛṣṇa: *na dvitīyāṃ pratijñāṃ hi pratijñāsyati keśavaḥ*. So Vedāntadeśika explains, "My word, once spoken, is enough to ensure that the needy will have what they need" (*ad Gadyatraya*, p. 65, where the *Rām* verse is quoted to corroborate God's promise to the devotee of their ultimate union). Cm, Ck, Ct, Cr understand: Rāma never tries to abrogate a promise; this seems to be indicated by 6.3314*.

21. "wounded" *saśalyena*: Cs appears to offer the interesting interpretation "(gave the boons [by swearing]) on his [arrow, that is,] weapon." For this type of oath-taking, see 18.13.

24. "guarantee" *saṃnideśe*: The reading [*sa*] *nideśe* ("order") is an editor's emendation (made on relatively weak grounds, see Vaidya 1962, p. xxvi). The manuscript consensus is definitely in support of *saṃnideśe*, which we accept (though it is otherwise unattested), and we interpret as "guarantee [to me]," "assurance," "solemn declaration." Daśaratha, of course, has not yet *ordered* Rāma to do anything.

30. "You need not worry" *manyur na ca tvayā kāryaḥ*: Ct comments: Kaikeyī ought not to be "angry" with him (so Cs) because of his questions, which seek to know the king's position; she should not be upset, Rāma will definitely go. Ck seems to understand: she should not be angry with the king for not greeting Rāma [and ordering him to go himself].

31. "who knows what is right to do" *kṛtajñena*: See note on 1.20 and 23.4 with note, and observe the NR's "gloss," *dharmajñasya*. The commentators seek too much specificity: Ck, Ct, "cognizant of Kaikeyī's deed, that is, how she had saved him"; Cm, Cg, "cognizant of his own deed, that is, his having granted the boons."

37. "without questioning my father's word" *avicārya pitur vākyam*: Cg too subtly, "without deliberating (or hesitating) because my father has not said, 'Go to the forest.' "

38. "she pressed Rāghava to set out at once" *prasthānam . . . tvarayāmāsa rāghavam*: *Tvaraya-* takes two accusatives here, as in 71.25 below (*contra* Ct, Cr).

41. "you needn't worry about that" *manyur eṣo 'panīyatām*: Literally, "let this anger [or depression] be removed." Thus, as referring to Rāma, is the best way to understand the *pāda* (so Cg, it appears, in his first interpretation; see also the N recension "gloss," *mā manyur kuru rāghava*, 382*). Cm, Ck, Ct are more artificial: [the king is upset only because you are not leaving straightaway;] let *his* dejection be removed by your going immediately.

42. "your father shall neither bathe nor eat" *pitā . . . na te . . . snāsyate bhokṣyate 'pi vā*: As if Rāma's presence, like that of a corpse, put Daśaratha into a state of *aśauca*, ritual impurity (note that in 60.8 Rāma is said to have gone away "dead in life").

45. "so dreadful in their consequences" *dāruṇodayam*: Cf. the use of *udaya-* at 18.39 (wrongly Cm, Ck, Ct, "[words which were] a cruel answer").

47. "I will do" *kṛtam*: On this aspect of immediate futurity of the past participle, see note on 3.5.

48. "and" *vā*: This should be taken *samuccayārthe*, for no alternative is being offered (see its use in 92.4; the commentators here are silent).

50. "Indeed, Kaikeyī" *nūnaṃ . . . kaikeyi*: Rāma's direct use of Kaikeyī's name (rather than "my lady" or something similar, as in verses 17, 19, 30, 46) may be significant, implying a growing irritation (similarly Varadacharya 1964-1965, vol. 1, p. 201 note).

51. "the vast forest of the Daṇḍakas" *daṇḍakānāṃ mahad vanam*: On the Daṇḍakas Cg reports: "There was a scion of the House of the Ikṣvākus called Daṇḍa. As a result of Śukra's curse [for Daṇḍa's having raped a brahman girl], his kingdom was destroyed by a dust storm and became a wasteland called Daṇḍaka after him" (the episode is related in the *Uttarakāṇḍa, sargas* 71-72; for a survey of the ancient literature on the Daṇḍakas, see Lüders 1940, pp. 626ff.). The plural he explains as designating a specific locale.

52. "that Bharata obeys father" *bharataḥ . . . śuśrūṣet . . . pitur yathā*: Rāma urges that Bharata "safeguard his father's promise" by ruling, just as he himself is doing by departing for the forest (so Varadacharya, 1964-1965, vol. 1, p. 202n). But as we shall see in the case of Bharata, fraternal devotion will prove a more powerful motivation than paternal obedience, though neither the poet nor the commentators ever explicitly addresses the problem implicit in Bharata's choice.

53. N manuscripts show Daśaratha fainting here (390*); see the following verse.

55. The NR adds that Rāma met his friends with a smile (394*), and that no one save Lakṣmaṇa knew the sorrow he felt (395*).

56. We must assume that Lakṣmaṇa was present during Rāma's interview with Kaikeyī (so Ck, Ct; see note to verse 2 above).

57. "not to gaze" *dṛṣṭiṃ . . . avicārayan*: So we read for *avicālayan* of the crit. ed., on the authority of Ś1, Ñ, G1, 3, M2, 3 (see 3.23.24 for an identical variation).

The commentators here are very concerned to demonstrate that Rāma is unaffected by his disastrous change of fortune. As an avatar of Viṣṇu, Rāma is never, in the eyes of most of the commentators, really emotionally involved with the happenings in which he participates; any emotional display is simply a pretense maintained in order to expedite his mission (see also note on 2.28). How far this theological preconception inhibits the commentators from appreciating the poem fully we shall have further occasion to observe in *Araṇyakāṇḍa*.

59. "In this verse Rāma is shown to suffer no mental change, as he was shown in the preceding verse to suffer no physical change," Cg.

"one who has passed beyond all things of this world" *sarvalokātigasya*: A *jīvanmukta*, "one liberated from transmigration while alive" (Ck, Ct) or a great yogin who is indifferent to pain and pleasure, respect and scorn (Cm, Cg). The first hint in the *Rām* of Rāma's unique characteristic, his renunciatory approach to political life, his revaluation of the kshatriya's *dharma* (see Introduction, Chapter 10).

60. "to tell . . . the sad news" *apriyaśaṃsivān*: Taken by Böhtlingk as a perfect participle (without reduplication), "with future signification and, most unusually, in compound with its object" (1887, p. 221).

Sarga 17

1. S manuscripts begin this chapter with a fourteen-line interpolation (403*) describing the lamentation of the women in the king's inner chamber. The commentators take this as the reason for Rāma's being "sorely troubled" (see note on 16.57).

"of his own accord" *vaśī*: See note on 10.1. He goes to visit his mother not because he is bidden, but out of a sense of propriety. Given the discrepancy between the description of Rāma's emotional state here and that in 16.58ff. (a problem noticed by the commentators), one might prefer, "but self-controlled nonetheless" (so Cg), but both the position of the word and the absence of any adversative particle make this difficult.

2. "the venerable elder" *puruṣaṃ . . . vṛddhaṃ paramapūjitam*: Presumably the watchman.

6. "worshiping" *akarot pūjām*: Literally, "performing *pūjā*"; one of the first appearances in Sanskrit literature of the term for Hindu worship.

N manuscripts omit the reference to Viṣṇu (see 407*).

7. "she was . . . pouring an oblation" *juhoti sma*: Cm, Cg, Ck, Ct, Cr, comparing the causative *hāvayantīm* in the next verse (see note there), all understand that Kausalyā is having the *agnihotra* or fire-sacrifice performed by a priest, rather than doing it herself. Cs, however, cites a *smṛti* text to the effect that "women of the highest *varṇas* have authority to perform vedic rites."

"pronouncing benedictions" *kṛtamaṅgalā*: The commentators are silent on the meaning of the compound. It is no doubt equivalent to *maṅgalavādinīm* (the glossing reading of the NR, 409*.1), as 22.1 verifies (*cakāra . . . maṅgalāni*, the prayers following in verses 2ff.).

8. "pouring the oblation" *hāvayantīm*: Taking the causative here as *svārthe* (with Cr and Cs [second gloss]); see 3.70.18 for a likely parallel.

12. "your father is as good as his word" *satyapratijñaṃ pitaram*: Note the deep irony on the poet's part.

14. "It will bring sadness to you, Vaidehī, and Lakṣmaṇa" *idaṃ tava ca duḥkhāya vaidehyā lakṣmaṇasya ca*: Rāma, according to Ck, implies by this that he himself feels no sadness at all.

15. "giving up meat like a sage" *hitvā munivad āmiṣam*: Since Rāma and Lakṣmaṇa will later break their fast by eating boar, antelope, gazelle, and deer (46.79; they will eat meat elsewhere, 49.14, etc.), Cm, Cg are forced to interpret: like a sage Rāma will have to give up finely prepared meats—but not plain meat. Ck, Ct suggest, " 'like a sage,' that is, give up meat except at *śrāddha* feasts" (see note on 69.22), but this appears to contradict Rāma's actual behavior later on, though see note on 48.15. Cr and Cs try, characteristically, to obliterate the signification "meat" altogether.

18. "He came to her side" *upāvṛtya*: The commentators read *upāvṛttya*, which they explain as "[the mare] having writhed [upon the ground]."

"like a mare forced to draw a heavy load" *vaḍavām iva vāhitām*: Observe how the simile here nicely takes up and advances the one in verse 9.

21. "only of the mind and only a single grief" *eka eva . . . śokaḥ . . . mānasaḥ*: Both qualifications are emphatic: a mother experiences untold physical agonies in the birth and rearing of her child, and risks multiple emotional sorrows as well (similarly Varadacharya 1964-1965, vol. 1, p. 212n). *Aprajāsmi* is possibly double *saṃdhi*, *aprajāḥ asmi* (on the form see note on 64.15).

22. "within my husband's power" *patipauruṣe*: It may be that we are to hear a stronger sexual overtone in the second element of the compound, despite its impropriety in a mother's conversation with her son (Cm, Ck, Ct gloss it, "a sort of gratification resulting from a husband's love"). The NR gives, "from (the time of my) marriage with my husband."

"in a son" *putre*: Cm, Cg, Ck, Ct understand the locative absolutely, "(I perhaps might find) 'were there a son,' if I bore him a son." But the point is not that Kausalyā hoped to win her husband's affection by producing a son for him, but rather that the joy she never had from Daśaratha and had hoped to find in her son is now being taken from her by Rāma's banishment.

23. "Having told of her past sorrows, Kausalyā is now going to tell of her future ones," Cg.

"being their senior" *varā satī*: Kausalyā's "seniority" derives in the first instance from her status as first or chief queen; it is not a status she acquired "by virtue of Rāma," as Ck, Ct appear to maintain (Cg, "if she were junior she would not suffer this sorrow [that is, being stigmatized]").

26. "The ten years and seven since you were born, Rāghava" *daśa sapta ca varṣāṇi tava jātasya rāghava*: Rāma's age is a matter of some uncertainty, for the manuscripts are divided on the issue and the crit. ed. has not been wholly consistent in its decisions over the seven volumes. A detailed consideration is in order here.

If there is unanimous testimony anywhere in the *Rām*, we must start from that and work back. There does appear to be one such datum. In 3.45.10 Sītā says that Rāma was twenty-five years old at the time of his exile; the context certifies that Sītā is speaking about the time of the exile, not Rāma's age at the moment of her conversation with Rāvaṇa, see verses 9 and 11; were we to take it otherwise, Rāma would have to have been eleven at the time of his exile (this conversation with Rāvaṇa taking place at the beginning of the fourteenth year of exile), which not only causes more problems than it solves, but is also patently ridiculous. The single variant reading here among the twenty-nine manuscripts is contained in Ś1, which gives Rāma's age as twenty-seven (see our present verse, 2.17.26 where D4, 5, 7 give twenty-seven also). (Ñ1 omits the verse, but omits also the necessary verse 9, which suggests a lacuna in its exemplar.)

The statement in our present verse, 2.17.26, appears to conflict with this. Kausalyā says, "seventeen years have passed since you were born, Rāghava" (NE and some NW manuscripts give eighteen). Although at first glance artificial, the explanation of the commentators (Cm in particular) seems probable. They understand "born" in the sense of "reborn," that is, at the initiation ceremony, which for kshatriya boys may take place in their eighth year. Kausalyā could hardly have expected solace for her troubles during Rāma's infancy and childhood. However, that she waited seventeen years during Rāma's manhood, when at any moment he might be consecrated as prince regent and so secure her a position of preeminence, is at least reasonable.

Other facts support this age of Rāma at the time of his banishment. In 3.36.6, all S and NW manuscripts (though not the crit. ed.) give the age of Rāma just prior to his marriage as twelve. This need not contradict 1.19.2, where Rāma is merely said to be "under sixteen." Moreover, in 3.45.4-5 and 5.31.13-14 Sītā says, again in the S and NW manuscripts (so too *PadmaP* 6.269.181-82), though not in the crit. ed. of *Araṇyakāṇḍa*, that she and Rāma lived together twelve years in Ayodhyā after their marriage (see also 1.76.14, reported by *all* manuscripts except Ñ1, which for this passage is not extant), and were sent into exile in the thirteenth year. This all construes with an age of twenty-five for Rāma. (There is no reason to consider this an "interpolation," with van Daalen 1980, pp. 213-14.) For a traditional statement on the age of Rāma, which is in harmony with these calculations, see note on 3.45.10.

Finally, when Rāma first goes off to the forest to perform his divine deeds, he would be just the age a god should be, twenty-five, "for gods are always this age" (3.4.13-14). Note too that in 2.38.15 Kausalyā says of Rāma at his departure that he is "in age like a deathless god." Since the forest is a place where most normal human social categories are suspended, we may assume this to be his age, in a sense, throughout the years of exile, and thus when he kills Rāvaṇa.

The one textual objection to all this is contained in the NE tradition. Putting Rāma's age at marriage at just under sixteen, it has Sītā and Rāma live only one year in Ayodhyā (variants on 3.45.4-5; 5.31.13-14), which would allow us to interpret our verse, 2.17.26, more "naturally," that Rāma is seventeen years old at the time of banishment. But this conflicts with Sītā's statement in 3.45.10, which the NE also reports. The NE is also self-contradictory elsewhere (see 2.17.26: Rāma is eighteen whereas according to 2.45.4-5, etc. and 3.36.6, he should be seventeen). It looks as if the NE tradition is mistakenly attempting to reconcile the other passages with our verse here—mistakenly, because it failed to grasp the true sense of "born."

Sītā's age is not mentioned anywhere except in one line in *Araṇyakāṇḍa* reported by all manuscripts except Ñ1 (and unjustifiably rejected by the crit. ed.), which states that Sītā was eighteen at the time of the exile (874*). This would make her six at the time of marriage (and at least thirty-three at the time of the birth of her children). There are no socio-historical arguments that can effectively impugn the credibility of this datum, for any such arguments for India of this period would have to derive from the *Rām* itself. (2.110.33, where Sītā says of herself that she was *patisaṃyoga-sulabhaṃ vayo . . . me*, "I had reached the right age for marriage," does not necessarily mean that she had reached puberty; note that according to Megasthenes, Indian women were considered marriageable at the age of seven [cited in Scharfe 1968, p. 298 n. 1]).

30. "under . . . crushing" *arpitam*: Literally, "afflicted by," a relatively rare usage (but see 3.53.2).

31. This verse disrupts the connection between verses 30 and 32, and N manuscripts suggest that it should in fact be read either before or after verse 29.

33. As the crit. ed. reads *pāda* d, we would have to translate the verse as follows: "When she looked at Rāghava, and saw how her son was bound . . . like a *kiṃnara* woman she broke out in lamentation." Ck and Ct remark, " 'bound,' that is, by the bonds of truth," but Kausalyā at present does not know the cause of Rāma's exile, and therefore would not think of him as being in any way "bound." Then again, while the simile of the *kiṃnara* woman is elsewhere attested (9.46), the placement of *iva* here is disturbing, and the simile itself meaningless. For these two reasons it seems virtually certain that the correct reading in *pāda* d is *saurabhī*, "cow" (for *kiṃnarī*), preserved in the three conservative D manuscripts, 4, 5, 7. The simile in the previous verse accords nicely with this reading, and the use of the particular word for "cow," *saurabhī*, finds support in the story related below, 68.15ff. (see also 85.52).

"being bound" *baddham*: "Even as a cowherd, desirous of breaking in a calf . . . will lead it away from its mother and tie it with a halter to a post planted somewhere out of her way" (*Sumaṅgalavilāsinī* on *Dīghanikāya*, cited in Warren 1896, p. 354). See also *MBh* 12.171.6.

Sarga 18

1. "in the heat of the moment" *tatkālasadṛśam*: Literally, "suitable to the occasion"; according to Cg, "befitting the moment of Kausalyā's grief." By this we gather that what Lakṣmaṇa is about to speak is not really heartfelt [e.g., verse 3], but is meant merely to assuage Kausalyā's sorrow."

2. "bowing to the demands of a woman" *striyā vākyavaśaṃ gataḥ*: Ct against all probability construes the phrase with verse 3, in order to avoid the implicit criticism of Rāma.

4. After this verse many S manuscripts insert: "Today I will kill the miserable old man, who is under the power of lust and utterly shameless, who consorts with a woman and not with righteousness, king though he is" (446*). (Similarly in 4.30.3ff. Lakṣmaṇa is prepared to kill Sugrīva.) This idea is repeated in interpolation 454* (after verse 11 below).

11. After this verse S manuscripts insert: "If our father, incited by Kaikeyī, has become corrupt [read *saṃduṣṭo*] and our enemy, then let him without compunction be imprisoned, even slain. Though our guru, he is arrogant, does not know right

from wrong, and has gone off the proper course, and so he must be punished [= *MBh* 12.138.48, a verse repeated elsewhere in that text]. What power does he rely on, or what argument, that he is ready to give to Kaikeyī the kingship meant for you, best of men?" (454*).

13. "I swear . . . by my truth and my bow" *satyena dhanuṣā caiva . . . śape*: According to *ManuSm* 8.113, brahmans are to take an oath by their truth, kshatriyas by their mounts and weapons, *vaiśyas* by their material possessions and *śūdras* "by all sins." Swearing "by one's truth" means to guarantee an oath by pledging one's *dharma* (so basically Cr here; on 45.4 he explains it as pledging the good *karma* that one has amassed). See *MBh* 13, App. I, No. 20, lines 181-82, "When one swears by one's truth in the presence of the gods, the sacred fire or one's gurus [and fails to fulfil the oath], King Vaivasvata [Death] destroys half his *dharma*" (see also Medhātithi on *ManuSm* 8.113, " 'I swear by my truth' means, 'May my *dharma*, which is dependent on truth and the like, prove fruitless for me [if I do not do or mean what I say]' "). As in the present passage, swearing by one's truth is elsewhere in the epics differentiated from swearing by one's good *karma* (here, "gifts of alms and sacrifices," see also 10.19 above), as in the *MBh*, *śape . . . sakhyena satyena sukṛtena ca*, "I swear by my friendship, by my truth and good deeds" (6.102.68), whereas the *dharmaśāstras* also distinguish them (see *NāraSm* 4.248). What precisely the difference comprises we do not know.

15. "the queen . . . Rāghava" *devī . . . rāghavaḥ*: It is unclear, perhaps intentionally so, whether we should understand "Kausalyā . . . Rāma" or "Kaikeyī . . . Daśaratha" (Cs offers both possibilities).

After this verse most S manuscripts insert: "I will kill our old father, who is so mindlessly attached to Kaikeyī—that miserable, feeble child, whose old age is a reproach to him" (458*).

17. "you have heard your brother . . . speak" *bhrātus te vadataḥ . . . śrutaṃ tvayā*: The genitives (*pace* Cr) form the object of *śrutam* (see 58.27 and note).

"Whatever is best" *tattvam*: "True, right, best thing," as in 3.11.8, 34.22; 6.11.40, 15.11, etc.

18. "heeding the unrighteous words spoken by my co-wife" *adharmyaṃ vacaḥ śrutvā sapatnyā mama bhāṣitam*: Kausalyā's main argument here is that it is not his father's order anyway, but his stepmother's, that Rāma is ready to obey (Rāma will speak to this point in verse 35).

20. "Kāśyapa obeyed his mother" *śuśrūṣur jananīṃ . . . kāśyapaḥ*: The story of Kāśyapa referred to here is unknown. "One may infer," say Cm, Ck, "that Kāśyapa reached the rank of Prajāpati only by virtue of the obedience he showed his mother in this world." We may suppose that the son wished to abandon home for a life of austerities in the forest, but bowed to his mother's wishes and still achieved his aim (Cs takes the patronymic to refer to Garuḍa, but this is difficult).

21. "In no way . . . less deserving than the king" *yathaiva rājā . . . tathā*: Ck and Ct quote *smṛti* here: "A mother exceeds a father one-hundredfold in dignity" (see *Nāradapāñcarātra* 2.6.7).

22. "a life of comfort" *jīvitena sukhena vā*: The second half of the verse plainly demands that we regard this as hendiadys, as in 45.9 (3.47.24 additionally demonstrates that the phrase is best taken thus).

23. "I will fast to death" *ahaṃ prāyam . . . āsiṣye*: An early reference to *prāyopaveśana*, fasting in order to force another to one's will (see 103.13-15 and notes).

24. "like the ocean . . . the guilt of brahman-murder" *brahmahatyām iva . . . samudraḥ*: Again we do not know the legend, nor do the commentators, who admit that the ocean is nowhere said to have slain a brahman. Cg reasons that, as Kāśyapa attained heaven through obedience to his mother, the ocean, "through unrighteousness," that is, causing his mother sorrow, incurred the worst sin of all—brahman-murder—and so went to hell. Cs, like other commentators, reports a "purāṇic story," but it does not quite fit: the ocean once offended his mother; in consequence of the unrighteousness engendered by this act, the sage Pippalāda exercised sorcery against the ocean who, attempting to counteract it, incurred brahman-"murder," that is, he was guilty of obstructing a brahman's ascetic practices.

27. Kaṇḍu: The son of the seer Kaṇva (see 6.12.13ff., where some verses of his are quoted regarding the obligation of protecting all who take refuge with one). We know from 4.47.18ff. that in consequence of the death of his ten-year-old son he turned a forest into a barren wilderness. But nowhere in epic or post-epic literature do we find a reference to the incident mentioned here.

"strict in his observances" *vratacāriṇā*: The reading "dwelling in the forest" (*vanacāriṇā*) appears both textually and contextually preferable: all three examples (verses 27, 28, 29) would thus have reference to the exceptional circumstances of forest existence, which obtain to some degree in Rāma's case, too.

"for he knew that it was right" *janatā dharmam*: That is, to obey his father above all else. Were we to take the phrase concessively ("though he knew what was right"), or with Ct to understand *janatā adharmam* ("though he knew that [to kill a cow] was unrighteous"), the verse would imply that Rāma believes what he is doing to be wrong, which is unlikely.

28. "and thereby met with wholesale slaughter" *avāptaḥ sumahān vadhaḥ*: The NR, attempting to make the example more apposite, offers: "a great slaughter of living things was brought about by them" (467*). Cm, Ck, Ct explain: thus a father's command is to be obeyed even at the cost of one's own life. The story of Sagara and his sons is related at *Rām* 1.37ff.

29. "an ax . . . in the forest" *paraśunāraṇye*: Ck reports a reading unrecorded in the crit. ed., *paraśudhāreṇa*, "with the blade of an ax," which is attractive (though see above, note to verse 27). For the legend see *MBh* 3.115-17.

31. "It is this that is my duty on earth, and I cannot shirk it" *tad etat tu mayā kāryaṃ kriyate bhuvi nānyathā*: This agrees with Cg; equally acceptable: "this is my duty on earth that I do, not anything else (or, not anything contrary to duty)" (Cm, Ck, Ct).

32. The constitution of the text is uncertain here. Translating what the crit. ed. offers, we must take *avijñāya* in *pāda* e as being governed by *tava* in c (either as a true continuative or as a finite verb [as frequently in the *MBh*, see 8.67.27, 9.36.18, and Dandekar's references there; see also note to *Rām* 3.45.4 and 5.25.10]). This is corroborated by a comparison of 474*.2 (NW) and App. I, No. 11.29-30, which also suggests that originally the passage contained a main verb and read something like: "You (and mother) fail to understand . . . and so are causing me much pain."

33. "on righteousness is truth founded" *dharme satyaṃ pratiṣṭhitam*: Several good D manuscripts (4, 5, 7) read *dharmaḥ satye pratiṣṭhitaḥ*, "and righteousness is founded on truth," which is more logical, and is supported by a previous SR passage, 234*.1 (*satye dharmaḥ pratiṣṭhitaḥ*).

34. "Having once heard" *saṃśrutya*: It is hard to see how this can mean "promise" here, though that is how Cm, Ct and Cr gloss it (and see the NR version, 478*, *kariṣyāmīti saṃśrutya*).

35. "and it is at father's bidding" *pitur hi vacanāt*: The NR offers, "for father gave his approval to what Kaikeyī told me." As noted, Rāma here responds to Kausalyā's argument in verse 18. But let us observe that neither previously nor later does Daśaratha himself ever explicitly order Rāma to go into exile.

36. Cg comments: "Having described the real meaning of truth, Rāma now goes on to describe the principle of self-restraint . . . 'the code of kshatriyas,' described in the *MBh* as 'a thing of savagery and villainy' " [12.22.5]. Rāma's explicit rejection here of the *dharma* of the kshatriya class is worth noting closely. We shall see, particularly in *Araṇyakāṇḍa*, that a certain contradiction underlies Rāma's behavior, as a kshatriya who is by nature inclined to deny his proper *dharma* and to accept the *dharma* of ascetics, or in other words, to "spiritualize" the conventional behavior of his class (see also 101.20, 30-31 and note, and the Introduction, Chapter 10).

Cg remarks further: "The main concern of this *śāstra* [the *Rāmāyaṇa*] is to validate *dharma*, and this it does by refuting the doctrines of the materialists, who maintain that expedient policy [*nīti*] plain and simple, to the complete exclusion of *dharma*, is the means of achieving political success. Thus Rāma validates *dharma* by refuting the materialist doctrine everywhere it is brought forward for consideration, as here by Lakṣmaṇa. Herein lies the secret of the work" (see *sarga* 100 and notes there).

38. "the promise" *-pratijñaḥ*: Daśaratha's to Kaikeyī (10.19), probably, rather than Rāma's own to her (16.19) (so too according to the SR interpolation, App. I, No. 11.43, *pituḥ pratijñām*).

40. "earnestly" *parākramāt*: Adverbial ablative. The word *parākrama-* frequently carries no sense of "bravery" or "valor" in the *Rām* (as Cr erroneously takes it here), especially in such compounds as *satyaparākrama-*, "striving for truth." See notes to 19.7 and 101.30 in particular.

"Then, in his heart, he reverently circled the woman who gave him birth" *cakāra tāṃ hṛdi jananīṃ pradakṣiṇām*: The expression is curious, and only Cr seems to understand it reasonably and grammatically. One normally circumambulates a person to the right before taking leave, but "he did it only in his heart, because a real circumambulation would have hinted at their [forthcoming] separation" ("he resolved to do it," Cg; "having performed the circumambulation, he 'put in his heart,' set his mind on, going," Cm, Ck, Ct).

Sarga 19

1. "like a mighty serpent" *nāgendram*: This can mean elephant as well as snake, but the more usual simile for an angry man is that he sighs or hisses like a snake (which is what the NR in fact reads, 489*.2 and see 20.2 below; but see 17.1 and Johnston on *Saund* 1.38).

4. "You must take care that our mother" *mātā naḥ sā yathā . . . tathā kuru*: This obviously, considering the position of this verse between verses 3 and 5, has reference to Kaikeyī (so Crā, Cm [second interpretation], Cg, Ct [second interpretation]), not to Kausalyā (Cm, Ck, Ct, Cr, Cs). See the version of the good D manuscripts 4, 5, 7: *mātā naḥ . . . yavīyasī*, "our younger mother" (485*.6). Kaikeyī's anxiety would be that Lakṣmaṇa might incite Rāma to a coup d'état (Cg).

7. "a truthful man, true to his word, ever striving for truth" *satyaḥ satyābhisaṃdhaś ca nityaṃ satyaparākramaḥ*: The three qualifications apply to the tripartite division of human action—thought, speech, and deeds—as in 88.18 below, see note there (so

Varadacharya rightly points out, 1964-1965, vol. 1, p. 240; contrast the note on 104.3 below). *-parākrama-*: A "strenuous undertaking" or "attempt to achieve," without any suggestion of "valor." Compare the use of the word in the Aśokan inscriptions, especially Rock Edict VI (Shahbazgarhi), lines 16-18 (Hultzsch 1925, p. 57). Similarly employed is *vikrama-*. See also below 58.50, 66.28, 101.30, 103.7, 104.3 and notes, 3.6.6 and note, and Pollock 1983, pp. 276-79.

"of what other people might say" *paraloka-*: Here lies one of those crucial details that must color our whole understanding of the psychological motivations underlying the action of the *Rām.* Is Daśaratha acting as he does because of his "fear of public opinion," or is it "in fear of the other world," of his fate after death (a second possible meaning of the Sanskrit)? Evidence favors the first explanation, but not conclusively, as follows:

First, both Cr here and Cs on 47.26 agree in giving the compound the sense of "public opinion." In 47.26, additionally, the NR reads *lokavāda-*, "public talk," for *paraloka-*, a glossing reading of the sort that we often see elsewhere, causing us to regard the NR as our oldest "commentary" on the *Rām* (see Pollock 1981).

Second, when the sense "other world" is intended in the *Rām*, the uncompounded form is preferred, as for example in 3.11.26 (and far more frequently replaced altogether by *param* alone [2.100.16], *svargam, tridivam*, etc.). There is only one instance in the critically constituted text of the *Rām* where the compound form indubitably bears the meaning "other world," 3.59.6 (note that it is picked up in 59.8 by the uncompounded form). But see also note to 54.6 below.

Third, in the context of our present verse, the charge made in the following verse, "to hear his truthfulness impugned," makes far better sense if Daśaratha's fear is what the people might say. In 20.6, Lakṣmaṇa is unquestionably answering Rāma's argument here when he speaks of being "fearful of losing people's respect on account of some infraction of righteousness" (see also the note there). Elsewhere the Northern tradition has Daśaratha explicitly state that he is afraid of what people might say (see note on 31.1).

Finally, in 11.6 Daśaratha makes it clear that the consequences of lying he most fears are unequaled infamy and inevitable disgrace in the eyes of the people (*loke*). If further evidence is required of how strong the power of public opinion was felt to be, we need only point to the events of the *Uttarakāṇḍa*, where Rāma drives Sītā from the kingdom because of what the people are saying (7.42ff.).

Against the translation offered stands the opinion of the majority of the commentators: Cm, Ct, "What causes fear in the world to come, that is, falsehood"; Cg, "What causes the loss of the world to come" (similarly Cg, Ck, Ct on 47.26). Although it is true that Rāma often shows himself to be very concerned with the eschatological implications of behavior (see 101.8, 11, 15, 30), it is easy, against all of these examples, to set passages that reflect an anxiety about one's duty and fame in *this* world (see 18.39, 101.7, 9, 10; see also 101.22 and note). A second objection to this translation lies in 54.6, but there either of the two meanings is possible (see the note there). In the end, the problem cannot be solved with absolute certainty. Although the translator is forced to choose, the reader should bear in mind the alternative possibility.

9. "the city" *puraḥ*: Reading *puraḥ* for *punaḥ* (see NR 489*.16, *itaḥ purāt*; so also Ck, Ct, Cr, and two good S manuscripts, G2, M1).

12. This analysis of the verse takes a hint from the NR version, 489*.21-22 and

understands *yena . . . tat* as "since . . . therefore," and *saṃkleṣṭum* as absolute (perhaps with "to cause [her, that is, Kaikeyī] more pain" understood; the verb might also be used in the sense of "delay, tarry" [see the NR gloss *vilambitum*, and possibly 6.64.49], but this meaning is nowhere attested). The commentators are quite confused. They read *tam* for *tat* in *pāda* c and understand: " 'I should not pain him,' that is, myself, by whom [*yena*]," Cg; " 'him,' that is, my father," Ck ("that is, god or fate," Ct; "Mantharā and the other people," Cm).

17. "speak to my harm" *brūyāt . . . matpīḍām*: The text is somewhat uncertain. Cm, Ck give "harm me" (*kuryāt* for *brūyāt*), whereas the NR has *brūyāt māṃ tathā*, "speak to me in that way" (489*.32).

18. "What cannot be explained" *yad acintyam*: We understand this as referring to Rāma's previous statements, especially verses 15-17, and take *api* almost in the sense of *ca*; Ck eliminates *api*, reading attractively, [*bhūteṣu*]*na vi*[*hanyate*] (not recorded in the crit. ed.). This is in general agreement with Cm.

"(which) clearly" *vyaktam*: On this sort of single-word enjambment, see note on 21.14.

19. "What man" *kaś ca . . . pumān*: Reading *kaś ca* with most NW and S manuscripts (see 489*.32 v.l.) and Cg, Ck, Ct, for the crit. ed.'s *kaś cit*.

20. "all things" *yac ca*: Reading *yac ca* with all but one S manuscript and the commentators. Neither Ct's *yasya* = *yat*, nor Cr's *yasya janasya*, is any explanation.

"birth and death" *bhavābhavau*: Glossed "transmigration and liberation" by Cm, Ck, Ct (we agree with Cg, Cr).

"things such as these" *kiṃcit tathābhūtam*: The cause of which is inexplicable (Cm, Cg, Ck, Ct).

21. "Comply with my wishes" *anuvidhāya mām*: Ck, "imitate me"; Ct, " 'follow me,' with a veiled hint that Lakṣmaṇa, too, will be going to the forest" (see note on 28.1).

22. "younger mother" *yavīyasī*: We translate the word strictly, as a comparative. The poet does not make it wholly clear who the youngest mother is. In 64.8 Sumitrā is called the "middle mother" (*madhyamā*, but note D4, 7, *sumadhyamā*, "fair-waisted"), while in 3.2.18 Kaikeyī is so termed (NE manuscripts read *yavīyasī* for *madhyamā*; in 3.15.35 all manuscripts name Kaikeyī the middle mother, and this is how Bhavabhūti alludes to her in *UttaRāC* 1.21.2). Cg sees the inconsistency, which he tries to rectify by arguing that, where "middle" is used with reference to Kaikeyī, it means "middle [in age] with regard to all the [350] wives of the king," not with regard to the three chief queens (among whom he says Kaikeyī is the youngest). Such incidents as 1.15.26, where Kaikeyī receives the divine food only after Kausalyā and Sumitrā have first received a share, and overall narrative propriety argue for Kaikeyī's being the youngest of the three principal queens (see *SkandP* 6.99.20).

Sarga 20

1. "midway between joy and sorrow" *madhyaṃ . . . duḥkhaharṣayoḥ*: Lakṣmaṇa's joy stems from seeing Rāma holding so firmly to righteousness, his sorrow from the loss, or abandonment, of the kingship (see 98.70; so Cm, Cg, Ct; Ck: when he called to mind the mental discipline regarding the power of fate, which Rāma had just taught him, Lakṣmaṇa was happy; when he forgot it by force of his inherent nature, he could not bear the loss of sovereignty and all the rest, and so grew angry. As an

avatar of Śeṣa, according to Ck [Cs finds this hinted at in the simile in verse 2], Lakṣmaṇa is characterized by a mixture of the qualities *rajaḥ* and *sattva*, Rāma by pure *sattva*).

2. "like a great snake seized with anger in its lair" *mahāsarpo bilastha iva roṣitaḥ*: The commentators wonder why a snake should become angry in its own lair, and try variously to explain it; presumably something harasses it in a moment of unpreparedness. The simile reappears in 4.6.1.

4. "from side to side, up and down" *tiryag ūrdhvam*: We connect the adverbs with *vidhunvan*; it is hard to see how they can be joined with *pādas* cd (as Cm, Cg, Ct construe).

5. "the source of this sheer folly" *yasya jāto vai sumahānayaḥ* (crit. ed., *-yam*): The dangling relative *yasya* is uncharacteristic of the poet and troublesome (though not to the commentators, who understand *yasya prasiddhasya te*. See also the NW gloss *yas te*). The text as constituted would require the following translation: "Now is not the time for this great (*sumahān ayam*) panic that has sprung up in you." The problem of the relative is solved if we conjecture, as here, *sumahānayaḥ* (see 8.14 above, *sumahān anayaḥ*; *anayaḥ* is a favorite word of Vālmīki, occurring also in 51.26, 72.4, 3.62.7 [see 12], 5.19.10, 20.29, etc.). Rāma's panic (*saṃbhramaḥ*) is causing him to make an egregious (*sumahān*) political misjudgment (*anayaḥ*).

6. "fearful of losing people's respect" *lokasyānatiśaṅkhayā*: Cm, Cg, Ck, Ct, Cs analyze *anatiśaṅkhayā*, in the sense "for the purpose of the nonexcessive doubts," that is, for the removal of excessive doubts—which is manifestly unsatisfactory. Cg's second interpretation is the correct one, by which we divide *lokasya ānati-* (this also agrees implicitly with the NR gloss, *lokavādabhayena*). In this way, too, a sensible connection is established with 19.7 above.

7. Cm, Cg, Ck, Ct join *pādas* ab with verse 6cd. We treat this *śloka* as a unit (so too Cr).

8. "suspicion" *śaṅkā*: "That they are evil and that therefore in not doing as they order Rāma will be guilty of no lapse from righteousness," Cm (so Cg).

After this verse most S manuscripts add: "They have acted very skillfully, eager to seize their own advantage through guile. For if they had not conspired before now, Rāghava, then long before now she would have raised the matter of the boon and he would have granted it" (503*).

9. "I despise that 'righteousness' " *sa . . . dharmo mama dveṣyaḥ*: Lakṣmaṇa will later deny the existence of *dharma* (6.70.14ff.).

"has so altered" *āgatā dvaidham*: That is, he had just been prepared to accept the kingship, and now he is prepared to go into exile (so the commentators). Note that Lakṣmaṇa addresses Rāma as king here, as in verse 17 below (the NR removes both references, but adds a new one in verse 34). In 3.1.19, 5.10ff., etc., Rāma is regarded as a king, though he does not so regard himself in Book Four (see for example 4.18.23).

10. "Even if you think it fate that framed this plot of theirs" *yady api pratipattis te daivī cāpi tayor matam*: The construction adopted is that of Cm, Cg, Ck, Ct (though Ct repeats *matam* as subject of *pāda* c, "your own notion"). Another possibility, which avoids the slight problem of the absence of concord in *pratipattiḥ . . . matam* ("corrected" to *matā* in many S manuscripts), would be: "Even if you have a presumption (*pratipattiḥ*) regarding fate (that is, if you presume that fate is involved), still, the plan (*matam*) of those two must be rejected."

"this course" *tad*: That is, Rāma's course of action in submitting to fate (Cm, Cg,

Ct gloss, "[I do not approve of that,] that is, fate"; Ck, "the fact that he does not reject what should be rejected," and he cites *smṛti*: "One should not perform an act, *dharma* though it may be, if it does not lead to heaven and if it is something hateful to people").

12. On the issue here, that of fate versus free will, see the Introduction, Chap. 5.

18. "their hopes" *tadāśām*: *Tatpuruṣa* compound, *pāda* b functioning epexegetically, *pitus tasyāś ca* (Cm, Cg take *tat* adverbially [= *tasmāt*], Ct adjectivally [= *tām*]), while *yā* is relative to *āśām* (Ct), not *tasyāḥ* (Cg).

19. "one fallen (within my mighty grasp)" (*madbalena*) *viruddhāya*: Some S manuscripts make the reference more explicit, reading *viruddhāyā*, "of her [Kaikeyī] fallen." *Pādas* cd literally, "(the power of fate would not be such [that is, for the benefit of the person so endangered (Cm, Cg); to be able to free the person (Ck, Ct)]) as my terrible strength is able to work grief [for the person]."

20. As the following verse indicates, Lakṣmaṇa's primary intention here is to advise Rāma on the proper time to go to the forest, that is, only after he has ruled (Ck, Ct), though additionally he may be suggesting that Bharata will never gain the kingship (Cm, Cg; also noted by Ct). The main idea of the verse is, somewhat awkwardly, contained in the locative absolute. For the irony of Rāma's fulfilling in his youth the "vow" that normally fell to aged Ikṣvāku kings, see *RaghuVa* 12.20, *UttaRāC* 1.22.

"many years from now" *varṣasahasrānte*: See the note on 2.6 above.

"my brother" *ārya-*: We read the compound *āryaputrāḥ* as *arya putrāḥ* following B2's gloss, against Ct, Cr, and Cg.

22. "without the king's wholehearted support" *rājany anekāgre*: Literally, "the king not being of one mind." We take this to mean that the king's allegiances are divided (and thus that Rāma's accession would not be wholly legal), and translate *vibhrama-* as "revolt," particularly in view of verse 24 (see also *ArthŚā* 3.11.13, *rājyavibhrama-*); Cm, Cg are close to this.

23. "may I never . . . if I do not" *mā bhūvaṃ . . . ca rakṣeyam aham*: Literally, "may I never . . . and I will guard," a rather unusual construction, clarified in D4, 5, 7, which read *yadi* for *aham*.

24. "kings" *mahīpālān*: "That is, the opposing (rebellious) kings," Ck (Ct).

25. "ornament" *ābandhana-*: So Cm, Cg, Ck; other commentators try to explain this as something related specifically to life in the forest, as Ct, "to be used for making holes in logs, in order to *bind* them together"; Cr, "to cut ropes for building huts, etc." Similarly with *stambhahetavaḥ* ("just for filling [a quiver]," so Cg, PW s.v. *stambha-*): " 'to be used as props,' for propping up logs to keep them from falling down," Ck, Ct; "to be banded together 'so as to construct a post,' " Cr.

26. "that anyone" *yaḥ*: Understood as reduced from *yat* (or *yadi*) *kaścit*, as often (see 3.41.45 and note, and Speijer 1886, p. 356).

"match" *śatruḥ*: Here and in verse 27 the word has the specific meaning of an equal or superior foe, a conqueror (as in *indraśatru*, *ŚatBr* 1.6.3.8; see the name Ajātaśatru, which means not "having no enemy born" but "no conqueror").

27. "I count" *kalpaye*: So essentially Ck; "I do not let him stand [*sthāpayāmi*], but rather cut him down," Cg (so Ct).

28. "trunks, flanks, and heads of elephants, horses, and men" *hastyaśvanaraha-storuśirobhiḥ*: For this figure, which is technically called *yathāsaṃkhya*, see also 3.38.12 and note there (and Brinkhaus 1981).

29. The two similes refer to two different aspects of the slaughter: "like clouds

with lightning," because Lakṣmaṇa's sword is "lustrous as flashing lightning," verse 27 (and the elephants are gray); "like mountains engulfed in flames," because of the red blood streaming from the massive animals (so, for the latter, Ck, Ct, Cr).

31. "now one man with many, now many men with one" *bahubhiś caikam . . . ekena ca bahūñ janān*: That is, shooting one formidable enemy with many arrows, many weak enemies with one (an epic commonplace, see *MBh* 1.219.26).

32. The verse contains a remarkable figure of speech: half of its words are derived from the root *bhū* + *pra* ("be powerful"). Much of the *sarga*, in fact, shows great verbal playfulness (verses 13, 14, 28, 31). This might seem inappropriate at such moments of high passion, but it was clearly felt that the tension of the situation was underscored by such figures of sound, for they are common (see 27.18, 3.60.26).

36. "father's command" *pitrye vacane*: Cf. 21.1; or "parents' command" (Cm, Ck; *pitroḥ* is in fact read by Ct, Cr).

Sarga 21

1. N manuscripts insert three extra *sarga*s before and within *sarga* 21, in which first, Rāma continues to placate Lakṣmaṇa, telling him to bear the burden of kingship with Bharata, while he (Rāma) bears his heavy burden of *dharma* (lines 23-24), at which Lakṣmaṇa protests that he too will dwell in the forest (27-46), and Rāma agrees (48; see note on 28.1 below); second, Kausalyā tries to dissuade Rāma; third, Rāma reasons further with his mother (App. I, No. 12).

4. "Who would believe it" *ka etac chraddadhet*: Cm understands, "who would [ever again] believe the king."

"who would not be seized with terror" *kasya . . . na bhaved bhayam*: The fear would come with the realization that, if the king can exile his own beloved son, he might all the more readily exile anyone else (Cg, "another might have fears for his own banishment"; Ct, "sons might fear banishment from their fathers"; Cr, "with Rāma away, the people of Ayodhyā would fear for their lives"; Ck, "the fear would result from suspicions aroused by the recollection of [instances of] laxity in the affections of one's own wife or sons" [that might presage a similar finale?]).

After this verse, both the NR and the SR show insertions (526*, 527*, respectively). By comparing these, it appears that the original must have contained a *śloka* or two here in which Kausalyā laments that she will be burned "by a fire whipped up by the wind of separation, stoked by grief, smoky for her tears of worry," and so on. The antiquity of the lines is further corroborated by their being imitated by Aśvaghoṣa in *BuddhaC* 9.29 (see Gurner 1927, p. 357).

5. "when winter is past" *himātyaye*: Cg, "late winter"; Ct, "summer" (this latter is preferable). An epic commonplace, see *MBh* 5.72.10.

8. "Deceived by Kaikeyī" *kaikeyyā vañcitaḥ*: This is the first intimation that Rāma is obeying his father even though he knows a fraud has been worked against him (see the Introduction, Chapter 4).

11. "recognized what was proper" *śubhadarśanā*: "Her thinking was [now] in accord with *dharma*," Cg; see the NR gloss *dharmadarśinī*. *Śubha-* has the sense of "just," "righteous" elsewhere, as in 3.49.28.

"without joy" *asuprītā*: The crit. ed.'s reading *suprītā* here is most improbable, in view of both the situation itself and the very next verse; in addition, the NR reads instead, "sick with grief" (the commentators are silent). The emendation to [*uvācā*]*suprītā* is easy, besides being necessary. The meter is no problem, for the heavy sequence is not uncommon, see 20.18a.

14. "Once I have passed" *vihṛtya*: According to Cm, Cg, Ck, Ct, Cr, Rāma is here making light of the hardship of exile ("after I have pleasantly whiled away"). We disagree, understanding *vihṛtya* in its old, neutral sense and construing "with the deepest joy" in the main clause. The one-word enjambment over hemistich boundary (*varṣāṇi*) is not uncommon (see 19.18, 41.2, 68.18, 79.21, 108.10, and for a dramatic example, 3.45.13).

16. "like a wild deer" *vanyāṃ mṛgīṃ yathā*: "The sense [of the simile] is: 'As a deer of the wilds lives contented in the wilderness, so too shall I live. I shall not cause you any trouble,' " Cg.

17. "Rāma wept, too" *rāmo rudan*: Again the problem of Rāma's showing human emotion (see note on 16.57). Ck, Ct, Cr alter the reading to *'rudan*, "not weeping," Ck explaining: "Were he to weep he would show himself to be irresolute, and thus his mother's hopes of accompanying him might be revived." Cg reads as in the text, noting, "Though Rāma was described earlier as follows: 'When misfortune strikes anyone Rāma feels the sorrow keenly' [2.28], nonetheless he had remained firm in the face of his mother's misfortune for fear he might be prevented from acting righteously, that is, from keeping his father's command. But now that he has received permission to go to the forest, he weeps so that, by demonstrating his own affection, he may guard against anything calamitous happening to his mother." (The NR eliminates "wept" altogether.)

18. "Bharata is righteous, too" *bharataś cāpi dharmātmā*: See verse 2 above. "Here Rāma addresses Kausalyā's complaint in verse 16," Cm, Cg, Ck, Ct.

20. "who earnestly undertakes vows and fasts" *vratopavāsaniratā*: "The performance, however complete, of optional observances cannot counteract the evil consequent upon the sin of not performing obligatory observances [such as obedience to one's husband]," Ck.

21. "revealed in the *veda* and handed down in the world" *loke vede śrutaḥ smṛtaḥ*: We take this as a chiasmus (so Ct, Cs).

23. "if the champion of righteousness should survive" *yadi dharmabhṛtāṃ śreṣṭho dhārayiṣyati jīvitam*: "Supreme (earthly) good comes not from a son alone, but also from having one's husband alive," Cg, Ck, Ct.

Sarga 22

1. "pure" *śuciḥ*: Various parallels (1.21.18, 2.46.14) and strong manuscript testimony in the SR (the NR reads the *pāda* altogether differently) cogently support Cg's reading *śuciḥ* for *śuci* of the crit. ed. He comments: "Since weeping is a cause of impurity, and supplication of the gods can be made only by one who is in a state of purity, she is said to 'sip water' and thus is described as 'pure.' " (*Śuci* can hardly bear the meaning "purifying.")

S manuscripts insert thirteen lines after this verse, which include a prayer that Rāma be protected by the weapons he acquired from Viśvāmitra (559*.7-8; see 1.26).

2. *sādhyas*: Like the other gods in the verse, an undifferentiated group of celestial beings (Cg glosses merely, "particular gods"; see Hopkins 1915, p. 175, and for the "All-Gods," Gonda 1975a, p. 102).

Dhātṛ and Vidhātṛ: Frequently mentioned in the epics (especially the *MBh*), if only formulaically and without elaboration. Presumably the "Arranger" and the "Disposer." Cm, Ck, Ct explain as Virāj Viṣṇu and (Viṣṇu in the form of) Prajāpati, respectively (both are, again, to Cg "particular gods").

Pūṣan, Bhaga, and Aryaman: Gods of the vedic pantheon, obsolescent from the very beginning of the epic period. We are not meant to associate particular attributes with any of these obscure gods; the whole verse appears to be intended only to lend an air of vedic solemnity to the invocation.

4. "learning, fortitude" *smṛtir dhṛtiḥ*: Cg, Ck understand as "contemplation" and "meditation" or "mental stability," respectively. The translation agrees with Cr.

Skanda: Son of Śiva and leader of the army of the gods (for his birth see 1.36).

Soma: Probably the moon is meant, as, by Bṛhaspati, the planet Jupiter.

5. "as you wander . . . through the great forest" *mahāvane vicarataḥ*: So we read with most manuscripts, for the crit. ed.'s *mahāvanāni carataḥ*.

6. "monkeys" *plavagāḥ*: So Cg, Ck, Ct (Cr, "frogs"). None of the commentators is troubled by the inclusion of monkeys in this list of annoying or poisonous creatures. The NR is perhaps correct in reading *patagāḥ*, "moths."

"in the jungle thickets" *gahane*: Ck reads instead *bhavane*, "in your dwelling" (not noted in the crit. ed.).

9. "way" *āgamāḥ*: So Cm, Cg, Ck, Ct; a rare usage, if not unique. To account for it, Ct suggests that the nuance is, "May the roads be fit for your speedy return."

10. "things . . . in heaven" *devebhyaḥ*: Not "from the gods" (*divyebhyaḥ* of N and G manuscripts appears to be a *lectio facilior*).

11. "sustainer of creatures" *bhūtabhartā*: We understand this epithet in apposition to Brahmā (some manuscripts, and Ct, read more explicitly *bhūtakartā*, "maker of creatures"). Cg, understanding the compound independently, glosses it Nārāyaṇa.

After this verse the NR includes a line mentioning Janārdana (Viṣṇu) (575*.1).

12. Hereafter the SR includes ten lines (577*) that supply a somewhat easier transition to Kausalyā's further benedictions in verses 13ff.

13. "when he slew the demon Vṛtra" *vṛtranāśe*: In the mythology of Indra, from early vedic times, his greatest feat is the killing of the serpent-demon Vṛtra.

14. Vinatā: The mother of Suparṇa (= Garuḍa), who fought the gods for the drink of immortality and brought it to earth (see 3.33.27-34). Before Suparṇa departs on his perilous journey, Vinatā pronounces blessings over him, similar to Kausalyā's (see *MBh* 1.24.8-9). This verse, like the former, seems clearly to intimate the action to come—Rāma's quest for Sītā and his killing of Rāvaṇa (noted also in part by Ct). The present scene between Kausalyā and Rāma had already achieved a paradigmatic stature by the time of the *gāthās* of the *Jayadissa Jātaka*: "As Rāma's mother made her prayers for him when he was about to leave for the wilderness of Daṇḍaka, so I make my prayers for you" (*The Jātakas* #513, p. 29.1).

After this verse the SR adds some lines in which reference is made to Viṣṇu's good fortune when he took his three strides (581*.3-4).

15. "that could ward off thorns" *viśalyakaraṇīm*: Or, "that could ward off arrows"; Cm, Cg, "that could extract thorns" (Ck, Ct, Cr take it as a proper name). The NR calls it a *rākṣasa*-slaying herb, and has Kausalyā tie it to Rāma's right hand (582*). In 6.40.30, the magical herb "*viśalyā*, made by the gods," along with the *saṃjīva* or revivification herb, is used by Bṛhaspati to heal the gods when the *dānavas* had mortally wounded them.

NW manuscripts include a line hereafter invoking Brahmā, Śiva, Viṣṇu, and Prajāpati (583*).

16. "had him bow" *ānamya*: With Cg we interpret the verb causatively.

17. "in the house of the king" *rājaveśmani*: A metonymical expression (the palace being the power center of the state; see Schlingloff 1969, p. 46). The reading has little manuscript support; with the majority of S manuscripts it might be preferable to read *rājavartmani*, "in the way (that is, position) of king," in the kingship, but the question must remain open, since the NR disagrees with both. It gives instead, "(When shall I see you again) endowed with royal splendor," which would establish an interesting contrast with verse 20, where we are shown that Rāma does not really require investiture with kingship to corroborate his true kingly power.

18. That there is not a single explicit reference to Viṣṇu in all the invocations Kausalyā pronounces in this *sarga* is remarkable, particularly in view of 4.33, 4.41, 17.6, where Kausalyā is shown to be a devotee of Viṣṇu. But if Viṣṇu is to be regarded exclusively as the superintending deity of kingship (see note to 6.1), his omission here (and Kausalyā's earlier worship of him) would make sense, since Rāma is not to be concerned with kingship for the fourteen years of his exile. A more likely explanation might be the belief that Rāma is an avatar of Viṣṇu himself, if we were prepared to ascribe any antiquity to that belief (see the General Introduction, and Introduction to the *Araṇyakāṇḍa*).

19. "she reverently circled Rāghava" *pradakṣiṇam . . . cakāra rāghavam*: As mothers do not normally circumambulate their sons, the act here is meant as a special apotropaic charm, according to the commentators.

Sarga 23

2. "Along the royal highway . . . the prince went illuminating it" *virājayan rājasuto rājamārgam*: Note the alliteration, the sort of which Vālmīki seems particularly fond.

3. "Poor" *tapasvinī*: See note on 28.18. Not, "characterized by the restraints of vows and fasts on behalf of Rāma's consecration," Cm, Cg.

4. "knew the rites" *kṛtajñā*: See 1.20 and note, 16.31 and note, and again the glossing lection *dharmajñā* (in D4, 7). Such is Cr's interpretation (similarly Cm, Cg, though they understand prospectively: knowing the rites that she was to do when Rāma returned). Less likely, " 'grateful': she worships the gods in gratitude for their beneficence in granting the kingship," Ct.

"kingly attributes" *rājadharmāṇām*: The compound here does not, as in 7.19 above, mean "the ways of kings" (that is, that they can be cruel and fickle; this erroneous interpretation probably called forth the hypermetric variant reading of some N manuscripts, *anabhijñā*, "ignorant of"), but rather the marks or accoutrements of kings, the white parasol, and so on. Cm, Cg: she knew the signs betokening the completion of the ceremony that she was to expect (see verses 9-16 below).

8. "ruled by Bṛhaspati" *bārhaspataḥ*: The constellations (*nakṣatras*) and lunar mansions are each under the superintendence of a particular god, Puṣya being under Bṛhaspati, family priest of the king of gods, Indra (see Kirfel 1920, p. 35; Kane 1962-1975, vol. 5.ii, p. 798).

13. "officials" *prakṛtayaḥ*: See note on 3.27 (so Cm, Cg here).

14. "Puṣya chariot" *puṣyarathaḥ*: According to Cm, Cg (citing *AmaK*), Ck, and Ct,

it was used on ceremonial occasions for spectacle (never as a war chariot): it would precede kings in processions and they would mount it or not as they wished.

19. "you are the daughter of a great house" *kule mahati saṃbhūte*: "Fearing that Sītā would be overwhelmed with sorrow at hearing such awful news, Rāma tries to fortify her by mentioning her different virtues, 'You are the daughter of a great house,' and so on," Cm, Cg, so Ct; Ck, "He speaks thus in order to ensure that she remain lucid during his discussion of the cause of his banishment." Perhaps additionally Rāma wishes to secure Sītā's approval of his (and his father's) observance of *dharma* by reminding her of her own natural commitment to righteousness (see 25.2).

20. "great boons" *mahāvarau*: "The boons are 'great' insofar as they are irrevocable," Cr.

21. "Since he had made an agreement," *sasamayaḥ*: As the crit. ed. prints *pāda* c, *sa samayaḥ* (and Cm, Ck, Ct understand it), we are required to supply a new subject (Daśaratha) for *pāda* d, and this is too hard a construction. Moreover, *pracodita-* seems invariably to take a personal subject (see above 12.3, 8, 15; 3.57.6, 22; 60.8, etc.). Cg (and Cr) interpret best, explaining *sasamayaḥ* as a *bahuvrīhi* compound.

23. Cg believes Rāma's advice to Sītā here and in the following verses to be a deliberate provocation by which he means to test her affection for him (see also notes on 27.26 and 47.10).

24. "You must not ever expect to receive any special treatment from him" *nāpi tvaṃ tena bhartavyā viśeṣeṇa kadācana*: There is a dispute among the commentators about the reading of the line. Ck gives *ahaṃ te nānukartavyo*, explaining "I am not to be thought back on" (Ct reports Ck's reading as *nānuvaktavyo*, "I am not to be mentioned, or, discussed," but this disagrees with Ck's manuscripts, and anyway it is redundant in view of verse 23). Ck notes further, "This is the ancient lection, which some other commentator [Cm?] has utterly spoiled." Ck's "ancient" reading, however, as is often the case, has virtually no manuscript authority. The NR version is similar to the SR but more pointed: "When I am gone to the forest you will have to be supported by him, and only by conciliating him will you get food and clothing" (605*).

28. "she has subordinated all to righteousness" *dharmam evāgrataḥ kṛtvā*: With Ck, we understand this as referring to Kausalyā rather than to Sītā (as per Cg, Ct); Rāma's mother can be said to have done this by acquiescing in her son's course of action.

30. "Bharata and Śatrughna" *bharataśatrughnau*: The reading of the crit. ed., *lakṣmaṇaśatrughna*, is an editor's emendation. The reasons for it are not compelling (see Vaidya 1962, pp. xxvi-xxvii), and would require us to reject the unanimity of our manuscripts. Why, moreover, would twins be shown different degrees of respect, which is based on age? Cg will later cite this passage as implying that Rāma has given [or rather, was intending to give] Lakṣmaṇa permission to accompany him; see note on 28.1.

32. "and sedulously attended to" *prayatnaiś copasevitāḥ*: The NR more powerfully, "attended to like gods—and if they are not, they destroy."

34. "offense" *vyalīkam*: Ck, Ct understand as "false": "do not give the lie to my command, or, word," but compare the use of the word in 58.7, 5.44.8, 49.18.

Sarga 24

2. "past deeds" *puṇyāni*: Literally, "merit," which is meant to include also demerit (*pāpa*) (Cg, Ck).

3. "But a wife, and she alone, . . . must share her husband's fate" *bhartur bhāgyam tu bhāryaikā prāpnoti*: A wife shares in her husband's *karma* because she participates with him in his ritual activity. (Cm cites, "One's wife is half of oneself," *TaiS* 6.1.8.5.)

6. The sense of the verse is this: Granted you may feel anger or resentment toward Kaikeyī and the others, still you should not "pass that on to me," should not feel that way about me, for I am not to blame.

"resentment" *īrṣyā-*: Not merely "impatience" with her for insisting on going to the forest (so Cm, Ck, Ct understand; Ck actually reads *roṣāmarṣau*, unrecorded in the crit. ed.). Cg feebly explains Rāma's resentment to be caused by a perception that by following her husband Sītā will be "wholly fulfilled" with respect to her duty (and so more highly regarded by people than Rāma?).

"like so much water left after drinking one's fill" *bhuktaśeṣaṃ ivodakam*: We follow Cg, Cr, Cs in attaching this simile to *pāda* a. It probably only refers to the custom of not passing on to another a cup of water from which one has already drunk (Cs cites a *dharmaśāstra* that prohibits the use of leftover water; see also Wezler 1978, pp. 23ff., p. 26n, who compares *Viṇayapīṭaka* 4.265.32, and discusses the impurity attached to foods partly consumed). The other commentators are unsatisfied with this plain interpretation; joining the simile to the following sentence, they try to explain more pointedly, while at the same time specifying what is meant by *pāda* d (literally, "there is no evil in me"): "A man who travels through a wilderness where water is hard to find can save the water from a meal in his water jug and it is not considered impure; in fact it will benefit him and so must necessarily be taken along." This appears to be more subtle an interpretation than the verse can bear.

7. "surpasses the finest mansions" *prāsādāgrair . . . viśiṣyate*: Syntactically the most reasonable analysis of the verse is to construe the first line with *viśiṣyate* (instrumental for ablative, see note on 42.26; so Cv, Cm [second interpretation], Cg, Cr, and see the NR gloss, *-vimānebhyaḥ . . . śreyān*, 618*). A possible but less convincing alternative: "The shadow . . . circumstances—whether *on* the finest mansions . . .—is [to be] preferred." The instrumental for locative is found elsewhere in the epic dialect, see *MBh* 8.7.15, 10.12.10, and De's notes there.

The NR's *-(ā)śrayaḥ*, "shelter of [a husband's] feet," for *-cchāyā*, "shadow," is an attractive variant reading, but apparently unsubstantiated by the SR. The phrase reappears in 42.14; see the note there.

"the finest mansions" *prāsādāgraiḥ*: Probably thus, in agreement with Cr (see also *vimānāgrāt* in 6.115.48, and Sukthankar on *MBh* 3.176.18), rather than "the tops of palaces."

"flying through the sky" *vaihāyasagatena*: By the power of yoga (specifically the attainment of "subtlety"), according to the commentators.

8. "in all these different questions" *vividhāśrayam*: So Cm (not, "with regard to a husband's different circumstances" [Ck, Ct]). The NR specifies, "They told me, 'You must never live without your husband' " (620*.2).

10. "practice . . . chastity" *brahmacāriṇī*: Although a woman's *brahmacarya* is normally just fidelity (see 110.9 below), the term is thus translated because it has specific reference to the sexual abstention that will prevail during their exile as ascetics (so here Cg [second interpretation], Ck); see note on 25.7.

"What pleasures I shall share with you" *saha raṃsye tvayā*: The phrase need not have any sexual connotations. The type of pleasure meant is described in *sargas* 88-89; see also 50.21 and note.

11. Before this verse, some N manuscripts include a line likening Rāma's bravery to Viṣṇu's (624*).

"any other person" *anyasyāpi janasya*: So Ct ("any person to whom you are the only refuge," Cm, Ck). Just possible: "(You were able [or, ready] to protect) another [that is, a stranger] in the forest" (for this sense of *janasya*, see 23.33). A reference to the Viśvāmitra episode of 1.29?

12. "can survive" *bhaviṣyāmi*: For the pregnant sense see 3.41.23, 60.49; 6.23.27.

16. The word order of the verse is noticeably dislocated; diagrammatically the construction of the main items is: A B A B A. This may be intended to convey a sense of high emotion in the climax of Sītā's speech (see 96.4 and note, and note on 3.29.24).

17. "teeming with deer, monkeys, and elephants" *mṛgāyutaṃ vānaravāraṇair yutam*: Cg sees here veiled references to Mārīca (the magic deer) and Sugrīva (the monkey king), who are to appear later in the epic, in Books Three and Four.

"in strict self-discipline" *saṃyatā*: The reading of the crit. ed., *saṃmatā* ("permitted," though Ct glosses, "following your commands"), seems to be based only on Dt (what Dd, Dm, and Ñ1 report is unclear). The best attested reading is *saṃyatā*, which we confidently adopt; see *niyatā* in verse 10 above.

19. "who so cherished righteousness" *dharmavatsalaḥ*: Cg glosses, "who could not bear that his wife suffer." But the NR reading *dharmavādinīm* ("speaking words of righteousness") suggests the emendation *-vatsalām* (Sītā "who so cherished").

Sarga 25

2. Sītā: According to Ct (on verse 4), Rāma's calling his wife by her given name (not normally done) is "not a lapse but is meant to represent the mental confusion consequent upon his sorrow." Note the threefold anaphora of "Sītā" (verses 2-4), which lends an importunate tone to his words.

4. "wild regions" *kānāram*: Cm, Ck, Ct treat this word adjectivally and make *bahudoṣam* the predicate ("the *dense* forest is declared to have many ills"), which is less meaningful. Oldenberg suggests a pun, and this is indeed the form such punning etymologies could take. But no commentator mentions it and we are not convinced by Oldenberg's odd solution ("the poet probably had in mind the *Dhātupāṭha* gloss *vana saṃbhaktau*, 'to grant a share' " [1919, p. 65 n5]). Presumably he means that the root *van* can signify "enjoy," as occasionally in Vedic and Pāli. But why the poet would want such a pun is hard to see.

5. For the style of this passage, particularly the refrain at the end, see the interesting remarks of Oldenberg 1918, pp. 452ff.; 1919, especially pp. 64ff.: in comparison with that of the epic, the *jātakas'* use of the figure is "far more archaic, the movement of the verses petrified." At the conclusion of his comparison of the *Vessantarajātaka* passage that parallels the present one, he remarks, "Does one not get the sense here, in respect of their artistic capabilities, of two entirely different ages?" p. 67. Compare also 61.8ff., 69.14ff., etc.

6. "redoubled" *-sambhūtāḥ*: So Cg, Ct, Cr; or, "(roars of lions and roars) coming from (torrents)" (Cm, Ck).

7. "broken off of themselves" *svayaṃ bhagnāsu*: The commentators remark that by this qualification we are to understand that the leaves are sere and brittle. The reference, however, is probably more specifically to the prohibition against injuring trees (see also 3.67.22, and Kane 1962-1975, vol. 2.ii, p. 895), which is especially enjoined upon forest hermits (see 646*: one must eat only fruit that has fallen of itself; also *ManuSm* 6.21). Recall that Rāma had promised Kaikeyī to live the life of an ascetic (16.28, 30). He will become subject to the rules of the *dharma* of forest hermits (*vānaprasthadharma*), and consequently many of the things he mentions here with regard to food and fasting, clothing, personal hygiene, and so on, are not simply natural consequences of forest life, but requirements or prescriptions. More of these prescriptions are listed in 648*, 649*, especially 655*.3 ("One must turn one's thoughts to ascetic practices"); for Sītā's promise in 24.10 to practice sexual continence, another such requirement, see *ManuSm* 6.26 and Kane 1962-1975, vol. 2.ii, p. 920. Note that in 46.55ff., Rāma intentionally mats his hair with juice of the banyan tree, and is said to take on the vow of a forest hermit (see also 28.9; Ctr also more or less supports this interpretation, vol. 1, p. 259).

8. See *ManuSm* 6.6: "[The ascetic] is to wear hides or barkcloth . . . bear matted locks of hair and (let) his beard and nails (grow)."

10. "of every size and shape" *bahurūpāḥ*: Cg glosses instead, "with large bodies," perhaps rightly.

13. "branches and blades" *-śākhāgrāḥ*: This applies by synecdoche to both the trees and the grass (Cg, Ct; Cm, Ck take *-agrāḥ* as construing specifically with the grasses).

15. "did not reply" *na . . . vacanaṃ cakāra*: Compare 11.14 (so Cr here? Note the well-attested variant reading *sā* for *tat* in *pāda* c); or, "would not accept what he said" (Cg, Ck, Ct; so Cm?).

Sarga 26

1. "trickling" *prasakta-*: Cg glosses, "(her face) partly (tear-covered)"; Cr, perhaps rightly, understands *prasaktā* separately ("attached [to her husband]," or better, "persistent").

2. Cg refers to the amplification of this idea in 27.11ff.

3. "By the order of" *-ājñayā*: Although the order might be that of Sītā's elders (see 24.8; Cm, Ct refer to 1.72.17, with 1327*.1), Cg is perhaps right to say that "as *śruti* declares, 'one's wife is half of oneself' [*TaiS* 6.1.8.5], and so a command to Rāma from his elders is a command to Sītā" (as Sītā has already asserted, 24.3; thus also Cr).

4. "Śakra . . . could" *śaknoti . . . śakraḥ*: There is a light pun here in the Sanskrit, the name *śakraḥ* being derived from the root *śak* (literally, "The Able One").

5. "regardless of" *kāmam*: Regardless of all Rāma's instructions on how to live in his absence (23.23ff.), Sītā will not be able to live at all. Alternatively, we may take *kāmam* with *pādas* ab: "Despite the fact that a woman . . . you [nonetheless] have given such instructions as these to me." The commentators do not shed any light on the problem.

7. "yearned" *-utsāhā*: See 3.26.4 and pw s.v.; note also the NR gloss *-spṛhā*.

8. "And it is with you that I would go there" *sā tvayā saha tatrāhaṃ yāsyāmi*: That is, I do not want to fulfil the prediction in any way other than in your company (see the NR version 668*, *na hīcchāmi tam [siddhādeśam] anyathā*). This seems more

persuasive than the explanations of the commentators: Ct, Cr: the prediction will not come true otherwise (that is, if I do not go with you); Cg (and apparently Ck): since it is thus prophesied for me, I will go with you, not otherwise; that is, not merely because I want to.

10. "unprepared" *akṛtātmabhiḥ*: So Cg; or, "without self-discipline" (Cm, Ck, Ct, Cr).

11. Cm, Cg, Ck, Ct suppose the verse to offer a corroboration of the brahmans' prediction (" 'I heard that living in the forest' would befall me"), rather than an explanation of Sītā's preparedness.

"in the presence of my mother" *mama mātur ihāgrataḥ*: This must refer to Sītā's adoptive mother, the king's chief queen. See below, 110.32.

13. "I have been waiting for the chance" *kṛtakṣaṇā*: Thus Cm; so also in 5.45.39, *kṛtakṣaṇaḥ kāla iva prajākṣaye*, "Like doom waiting for the chance to destroy all living things" (see also 5.62.20). Alternatively: "the opportunity has now been given me." (Ck, Ct: "[let me be] given permission"; Cg, Cr: "I celebrate (going)" [am eager to go].)

14. "I shall have no sin to answer for" *bhaviṣyāmi vikalmaṣā*: If she remains behind, people will impute some sin to her (Ct); nor can she stay and propitiate her household god for purity, because "Rāma is her highest divinity" (Cg).

15. "is sacred" *kalyāṇaḥ*: Cm, Cg, Ct explain predicatively, and we follow them. Ck supplies as predicate something like *siddhaḥ* ("[my holy union] is permanent"), which may well be right, for it is the perdurability of their union, not its sanctity, that Sītā is concerned with here, as the next verse shows (and see 674*.1-2).

16. "in accordance with their own customs" *svadharmeṇa*: So Cg, Ct (they gloss "each according to his own caste-*dharma*"). Cm and Cr connect it with *pāda* d: through her own *dharma*, that is, fidelity, a woman remains with her husband.

"fathers" *pitṛbhiḥ*: The plural is meant to include grandfathers, etc. (Cm, Cg, Ct). Near the conclusion of the marriage ceremony, the heads of the bride and groom are sprinkled with holy water, see *ĀśvaGS* 1.7.20 (see below 110.48; Kane 1962-1975, vol. 2.ii, p. 1,267, and vol. 2.i, pp. 529-30), and above, 1.1327*.2.

Ck indicates that, with the exception of the element *mahāmate* (it is added by the poet for the sake of the meter), the *śloka* is essentially a *yajurmantra* (untraced).

18. "I have always shared" *māṃ samām*: Not, "I am the same, unchanging, whether pain or pleasure befalls me" (Cg), for then she would hardly call herself "desolate."

Sarga 27

4. The future *vakṣyati* is not explained by commentators. Cg and Ck merely gloss it as present, Ct impossibly takes it as future of the root *vah*; indeed it does not seem to have a true future sense here (see *vakṣyante* in 4.21 above with note).

"Rāma's 'great power' is not at all" *tejo nāsti paraṃ rāme*: We understand the line not as a quotation of the people's statement ("Rāma's great power is not like [that is, excells] that of the burning sun," Cm, Cg [third explanation], Ck, Ct, so the NR, 686*), but as a contradiction of it (with Cg's second gloss, and Cs). Cr tries to temper the insult and his explanation is clever: " 'If' [reading *yadi* for *yad dhi*] you do not take me, 'the people in their ignorance,' of any reason why you should refuse to take me, 'will speak this lie, that Rāma's great power is not. . . .' "

6. Sāvitrī: The paragon of wifely devotion who, with half her own life, redeemed her husband from the god of death. Her story is told in *MBh* 3.277ff.

7. "I would not even think of looking" *na tv ahaṃ manasāpi . . . draṣṭāsmi*: "Thus, fear of that need not stop him from taking her," Ck. The location of the comparison in *pāda* d, in isolation from its referent, is awkward, but irremediable. Additionally *pāda* c ("were I to go with you") is taken as a conditional clause, not an independent sentence (so the commentators). Because of these syntactical problems, the Mylapore editors suggest understanding *yathānyākula-*: "I would go with you, as any other woman who is no disgrace to her family (would want to go with her husband)"—that is, were he not to allow her to go, he would be treating her as if he thought her a slut. Rāma wants not only to spare her the hardships of life in the forest, but also to preserve her from the eyes of other men (see also note on 30.8 below).

10. "no more . . . than" *na . . . iva*: The reading *iva* (crit. ed. *api*) seems clearly indicated by the testimony of the manuscripts (so too Cm, Cg, Ck, Ct, Cr); the sense is also superior.

"on our pleasure beds" *vihāraśayaneṣu*: We analyze the compound as a *tatpuruṣa*; Cm, Cg take it unconvincingly as a *dvandva*, in order to avoid the sexual reference (" 'as in strolling,' namely, through a garden, 'or in sleeping' ").

16. "you will not know any grief or displeasure on my account" *na . . . kiṃcid draṣṭum arhasi vipriyam / matkṛte na ca te śokaḥ*: Here, as elsewhere, Vālmīki charges Sītā's speech with a profound and tragic irony.

18. "But" *atha*: There is no need, with Cg and Ck, to take this as an interrogative particle.

The second half-verse contains an interesting alliteration: *viṣam . . . viśaṃ dviṣatāṃ vaśam* (see note on 20.32).

20. "ten years of sorrow, and three, and one" *daśa varṣāṇi trīṇi caikaṃ ca duḥkhitā*: There is a moving pathos in Sītā's computation of the years of separation. Cg points out that it is meant to show how, to a woman separated from her lover, the ten years at the beginning, the three in the middle, and the one at the end of the period all seem equally long.

22. "the tears she had held in so long" *cirasaṃniyataṃ bāṣpam*: There is a slight inconsistency in view of 26.21, where Sītā is already weeping. Cg tries to reconcile this by saying that "long" means all the while she was talking (see also note to 23). The NR (697*, 698*) makes Rāma the subject of both verses 22 and 23 ("He was bruised by her pitiful words . . . and began to weep"), which is far more powerful. It may be that the theological attitude discussed in the note to 16.57 motivated the SR alteration (if there was alteration), but our manuscripts no longer allow us to reconstruct confidently the original state of the verses.

23. "Water clear as crystal" *sphaṭikasaṃkāśaṃ vāri*: "The 'crystal-like' clarity of her tears gives us to understand that the kohl in her eyes must already have been washed away, and thus that her tears must have been streaming down for a long time" (Cg; he also takes "water" in the lotus simile as "sap" [Cs imagines the lotuses to have been torn from the pond], this being both warm and clear).

25. "Self-existent" *svayaṃbhoḥ*: "This must be Nārāyaṇa, not Four-faced [Brahmā], because the latter did feel fear of [the demons] Madhu, Kaiṭabha, etc.," Cg; " 'Self-existent' means Blessed Brahmā, who is not afraid of anything, because there is no other really existent thing distinct from him—and according to the scriptural passage, 'Fear comes from [the existence of] a second,' etc. [*BṛĀraU* 1.4.2]," Ck.

26. "without knowing your true feelings" *tava sarvam abhiprāyam avijñāya*: The NR offers, "to test your commitment . . . I said I would not take you" (702*), and this may be what is in fact implied in our verse. Cf. also Cg's comment noted on 23.23.

27. "determined" *sṛṣṭā*: Here and in 35.5 below the word is translated thus, though this sense is rare, if not unique (so Cm, Ck; see PW s.v.; Cg suggests, " 'sent,' that is, by fate" [see 26.6]).

"self-respecting" *ātmavān*: Compare the use of the word in 46.63, 3.43.37, and 6.106.18. Like many other epithets, *ātmavān* takes its color from the context, and interpretation is often uncertain.

28. "my smooth-limbed wife" *gajanāsoru*: Literally, "whose thighs are (smooth) as an elephant's trunk."

Here Rāma is informing Sītā that, for him, living in the forest will be an act of *dharma*, of the highest moral dimension, not a vacation, as she is repeatedly shown to view it (so too Daśaratha, 32.5). This interpretation is at odds with that of all the commentators. They understand *dharma* here as *vānaprasthadharma*, the customs and code of forest hermits, and believe Rāma to be saying that, in taking his wife to the forest, he is only doing what other good men of the past have done. But this is beside the point, and in any case conflicts with the definition of *dharma* given in the next verse.

"radiance" *suvarcalā*: Certainly not meant as the personification of the wife of the sun, which is late.

31. "bestow precious objects on the brahmans" *brāhmaṇebhyaś ca ratnāni . . . / dehi*: Gifts to brahmans (and the needy) are considered an essential preliminary for any important act, here Rāma's departure. Cg, Ck on 32.1 vulgate call it the *yātradāna*, giving of gifts before embarking on a voyage (we do not, however, find any mention of this in the *dharmaśāstras* or *nibandhas*); such is also the opinion of Ctr, vol. 1, p. 296, who cites a parallel from the *MBh* (5.149.56-57). They may be correct, but at the same time, insofar as Rāma is virtually renouncing the householder stage of life, he is divesting himself of his material possessions (see 28.18ff., 33.2; so Dhṛtarāṣṭra before going forth into the life stage of the forest hermit, *MBh* 15.21.5). Additionally, Rāma may wish to ensure that his dependents and friends have the wherewithal to maintain themselves in his absence.

33. The verse is a recapitulatory one, marking *sarga* closure.

Sarga 28

1. Before this verse both the NR and the SR include sections that on comparison indicate that the original contained a number of lines in which Lakṣmaṇa addresses Rāma, telling him that he wishes to accompany him to the wilderness, and that Rāma has already given him permission. Note 716*.7-12 (the NR), 717*.11-19 (D4, 5, 7), 718*.1-4, 13-15 (the SR), and especially lines 11, 16, and 13, respectively, of the three "insertions": *anujñāto 'smi* [*-taś ca*, SR] *bhavatā pūrvam eva vanaṃ prati* [*nararṣabha*, Ñ1; *yad asmy aham*, SR], "you have already granted me permission (to go) to the forest." The NR explicitly shows Rāma granting permission, see 21.1 and note; in the SR the commentators identify various passages where permission is implied: 19.21 (see note there; thus Ck, Ct; Ck notes that when Rāma told Lakṣmaṇa

to "imitate" him he meant not in going to the forest, as Lakṣmaṇa thought and here asserts, but in not resisting the cancellation of the the consecration); 23.30 ("here it is only Bharata and Śatrughna whom Sītā is told to obey," Cg; see note on 23.30—Cg adds here that Rāma gave Lakṣmaṇa permission at that time only to prevent him from doing anything violent on the spur of the moment).

3. "shower [them] with all they desired" *abhivarṣati [te] kāmaiḥ*: We must understand, as direct object, *te* (feminine dual); or perhaps we have in *kāmaiḥ* instrumental for accusative with verbs of raining, as in Greek.

4. After this verse the SR adds, "Once Bharata becomes the king he will be wholly in Kaikeyī's power and will take no thought for Kausalyā or Sumitrā in their sorrow" (725*).

6. Hereafter most of the SR inserts, "If, when he gains the kingship, Bharata grows corrupt and out of animosity and pride does not protect [our mothers], I will kill him without hesitation for his cruelty and ill will, and everyone else who takes his side" (728*).

7. "she has acquired a thousand villages as her living" *yasyāḥ sahasraṃ grāmāṇāṃ saṃprāptam upajīvanam*: A remarkable statement on Kausalyā's vast wealth, even if "thousand" is hyperbolic and means only "many." Leaving aside the general question of women's usual property rights in the epic (according to *MBh* 2.63.1, for example, dependent women can own no property, see *MBh* 5.33.64, *ManuSm* 8.416), the editor of the text volume is probably right in seeing this wealth as a payment by Daśaratha to Kausalyā when she was "superseded" (*adhivinnā*) by Kaikeyī (Vaidya 1962, p. 697; see *ArthaŚā* 3.2.38-42 for the compensation of supersession *adhivedanikā*), though nowhere in the *Rām* narrative are the grounds, or the fact itself, of supersession explicitly related (Cm, Ck, Ct, reading *upajīvinām* for *upajīvanam*, explain the line, "whose dependents [or, by whose grace her dependents] have acquired a thousand villages," that is, if she can bestow such wealth, all the more should she be able to support herself).

8-10. For Cg, this passage shows that at all times, in all places and circumstances, every sort of service is to be performed by the subordinate individual soul (*śeṣa*) on behalf of the Supreme Master (*śeṣin*) in conjunction with his goddess.

9. "proper fare" *svāhārāṇi*: "Fit to be easily [*su*] eaten," Cg; "proper [*sva*] food, and good [*su*] food," Ck.

10. This verse, along with a line inserted by the SR before verse 1 of the *sarga* (718*.3, "Lakṣmaṇa clasped his brother's feet"), holds a special place in South Indian Vaiṣṇavism. Vedāntadeśika explains the famous *mantra* called the Dvayam, recited daily by Vaiṣṇavas, as expressing the "two things" contained in these two verses, namely, the goal of the soul's striving (28.10), and the correct means of realizing that goal (718*.3) (see *Rahasyatrayasāra*, pp. 318ff.).

12-13. "that great Varuṇa himself bestowed" *ye . . . dadau . . . mahātmā varuṇaḥ svayam*: The episode of Varuṇa's presentation of weapons to Janaka, or Janaka's to Rāma, has not been previously referred to in the *Rām*. (In 110.38 mention will be made of the great bow Varuṇa bestowed on Janaka, but that is the one Rāma shatters at the marriage rite of Sītā; see note there.) Cm, Cg notice this inconsistency and they explain it as follows: It is Vālmīki's habit to neglect to mention an incident where chronologically it should be noticed, because of the pressure of treating the topic at hand. Later on, his brief recapitulation of the incident, as here, establishes it as a fact of the narrative. They cite two other instances: in 5.64.4, Rāma refers to a piece of jewelry given to Sītā by her father at the time of her marriage, mention of which was omitted in Book One; the story of the crow attacking Sītā on Mount Citrakūṭa is not related in Book Two, though Sītā speaks of it in 5.36.12ff. (but see note on 89.19); see also note on 52.12ff. Cm, Cg, Ck suppose that the weapons were given "at Janaka's sacrifice" by Varuṇa to Rāma himself; Ct, on the other hand, that they were given to Janaka and then to Rāma, as part of Sītā's dowry. Insofar as Rāma is shown in 3.11 to acquire magical weapons from the seer Agastya, these weapons (not to speak of those given by Viśvāmitra, 1.26 or Brahmā, 39.11 below), seem superfluous.

14. "preceptor's residence" *ācāryasadmani*: Vasiṣṭha's (so Cm, Cg, because of the phrase "guru of the Ikṣvākus" in verse 15); or Suyajña's (Ck, Ct).

"in perfect order" *satkṛtya*: Taken by the commentators as " 'honoring,' that is, the teacher," but this is weak, and inappropriate in verse 16.

16. "tiger of the Raghus" *raghuśārdūlaḥ*: The crit. ed. reading "tiger among kings" is marked as uncertain; "tiger of the Raghus" is preferable both on manuscript and contextual grounds (so too Ck; note Ñ1, D4, 5, 7 *naraśārdūlaḥ*).

17. "with full self-possession" *ātmavān*: A vague epithet, like so many others (contrast its sense in 27.27, see the note there). Perhaps Rāma's "self-possession" is stressed here in view of verses 18-19, where he is preparing to give away everything he owns.

18. "poor" *tapasvibhyaḥ*: = *kṛpaṇa-* in 29.21. See also 23.3 and note, 36.2, 58.25 and note, 3.46.16, 56.8, 60.8 for the larger sense of the word; "ascetics" would hardly have any use for Rāma's wealth.

Sarga 29

1. "most just and welcome order" *śāsanam . . . śubhataraṃ priyam*: His command is "just" insofar as it betokens benefits for the brahmans; "welcome" in that it signifies approval of Lakṣmaṇa's accompanying him to the forest (Cg).

3. "the twilight worship" *saṃdhyām*: The fire-sacrifice required at the time of the noonday "twilight," when the sun is at its zenith (Cm, Cg, Ct). The morning twilight is some time passed (see 13.1 above), and it will be close to evening twilight when Rāma departs (see note to 31.27). On the twilights and the accompanying ceremonies see Kane 1962-1975, vol. II.i, p. 312.

9. "worth a thousand others" *gajasahasreṇa*: Literally, "at, equal to, the price of a thousand elephants"; a rare locution, but see Renou 1968, p. 292 (several S manuscripts read, "with a thousand units of gold" [*niṣkā*], that is, for its maintenance). Cg distinguishes this Śatruṃjaya from Daśaratha's elephant of the same name (see 91.13).

11. "As Brahmā . . . Indra, lord of the thirty gods" *brahmeva tridaśeśvaram*: Ck, Ct, evidently considering the simile unusual—since Rāma is being coordinated not with the preeminent kshatriya god Indra, but with the preeminent priestly god Brahmā—assert that it is employed merely with reference to the relative power of the commander and the recipient of the command. But the comparison of Rāma to Brahmā reappears in other sorts of contexts (see 93.27, 96.27, and note on 46.64), and is evidently meant to signal a special feature of Rāma's character (see the Introduction, Chapter 10).

12. Āgastya: The son of Agastya; Kauśika, the son of Viśvāmitra. We follow Cg who, like Ck (and Ct), must have read *āgastyam* (so the Kumbhakonam ed., *contra* the report of the crit. ed.). That Agastya himself should be in Ayodhyā is absurd; Rāma is not to meet him until 3.11.

13. "the learned preceptor of the Taittirīyas" *ācāryas taittirīyāṇām abhirūpaḥ*: The commentators offer no identification of this teacher of the Taittirīya school of the vedic tradition, with whom Rāma's mother appears to have had a special intimacy. But note that Vālmīki (or rather, a Vālmīki) is named as an authority of this school (in the *TaiPrāti* 5.36, 9.4; the work is to be dated before 350 B.C., see Keith 1914, pp. xxxix-xli). The poet probably quotes the *TaiS* in 85.42 below, and may well be alluding to other *Taittirīya* scriptures in 39.8-9, 101.28, 102.3, 110.17 (see notes there).

15. Citraratha: No previous mention has been made of this charioteer, who is different from Sumantra (as Cg, Ck, Ct tell us); perhaps his son?

Rāma throughout the passage is taking pains to secure the maintenance of his and his mother's friends and dependents (the older men in Daśaratha's entourage would still be provided for by the king), lest they suffer from Kaikeyī's studied neglect.

16. The presents listed here are presumably given to other brahmans. For the obscure terms employed one is forced to take refuge with the commentators:

"oxen" *bhadrakān*: So Cm, Cg. Ck, Ct gloss "a type of grain."

"dairy needs" *vyañjana-*: The word appears to be unique in the sense Cg here attributes to it. Ck, Ct read *vyañjanārhān* [not recorded in the crit. ed.], but this is equally obscure ("[grains] suitable as condiments"?).

22. After the first half-verse, the SR, Ñ1, and the good D manuscripts (4, 5, 7) insert eight lines showing Trijaṭa's wife, oppressed by her poverty in the forest, urging her husband to seek refuge with the beneficent Rāma (763*).

"sallow" *piṅgalaḥ*: An effect of his life of poverty (Cg, Cs). Possibly also, or instead, a proper name?

24. The brahman is asked to throw his staff (possibly instrumental for accusative with verbs of throwing, as in Greek, see Smyth 1966, pp. 346-47) above the extensive herd of cows. He will receive as many cows as are covered by the flight of the staff (Cm, Cg, Ck, Ct; see 770*). The commentators do not address the issue of the insensitivity (indeed, cruelty, as it must strike us) of Rāma's "joke." Cm merely remarks, "it is meant to show how shamelessly avaricious brahmans can be about cows" (so Ck, Ct). One can well appreciate the aesthetic requirement for comic relief between the dramatic confrontations of *sargas* 7-28 and the hysteria to come in *sargas* 30ff., but the humiliation of poverty does not offer much.

Sarga 30

1. "they went to see their father" *jagmatuḥ pitaraṃ draṣṭum*: "Though already given leave by his father, Rāma goes to Daśaratha to ask that Lakṣmaṇa and Sītā be granted permission to depart," Cg (see 30.20-21).

2. "weapons, which Sītā had ornamented" *āyudhe . . . sītayā samalaṃkṛte*: The weapons would have been adorned by Sītā as an act of *pūjā*, worship (Ct), with sandalwood paste and such (Cm, Cg, Ct, Cr; see 6.23.17).

3. "wealthy" *śrīmān*: Though the word usually connotes royalty, here it must be taken to signify simply "rich" (the commentators point out that all the structures are grand ones; they are otherwise silent).

6. "a vast army of four divisions" *caturaṅgabalaṃ mahat*: The four parts of an Indian army are the horse, elephant, chariot, and foot-soldier units.

7. "has always met the needs of the needy" *kāmināṃ caiva kāmadaḥ*: The clause seems irrelevant to the context. The NR replaces it with *śaktimān api vīryavān*, "though he is powerful and mighty" (783*).

8. "whom even creatures of the sky" *yā . . . bhūtair ākāśagair api*: Sītā, like all women of noble birth, would have lived up till now a life of uninterrupted sequestration (see the phrase used of a king's wife, *asūryaṃpaśyā*, "who never sees the sun" [*MahāBh* on *Pā* 3.2.36]). This fact makes it all the more dramatic when the queens show themselves in public following Rāma's departure (35.24).

10. "some spirit that has possessed Daśaratha" *daśarathaṃ sattvam āviśya*: *Pāda* b as printed in the crit. ed., *daśarathaḥ sattvam āviśya*, is meaningless here, and the commentators cannot convincingly explain it. The NR's *sattvenāviṣṭa-*, "possessed by a spirit" (785*), makes almost certain the conjecture adopted here, *daśaratham* (accusative). The lection is found in one manuscript of Ck and is suggested also by the Mylapore editors.

13-14. The similes in these two verses seem to have been transposed, though no manuscript reports this.

14. After this verse most S manuscripts (and Ñ1) add by way of explanation: "For he is the root of human beings, the glorious one whose essence [or, sap] is righteousness; the fruit, flower, leaf, and branches are the rest of the people" (791*).

22. "even (when Rāma looked) at the people" (*pratīkṣamāṇo*) *'pi janaṃ . . .* (*rāmaḥ*): The reading *'bhijanam*, which is never found in the *Rām* in the sense required here (see note to 53.15), seems to be based exclusively on Ct, who glosses " 'the place,' that is, the people in it." Cm, Cg, Ck all read *'pi janam*, and are supported by most of the NR. We confidently accept this (the concessive particle is also necessary here).

"not the least anguish touched him" *anārtarūpaḥ*: *-rūpa*, as in verse 23 below, is an intensifier (see note on 14.24).

23. "only then" *tatpūrvam*: Literally, "that being the first time." He halted only when he had to; none of the earlier signs of grief having stayed him. There seems to be no other way to construe the adverb, which has the sense given here also in 6.115.16.

24. This verse is preserved only in the SR, and is accordingly marked as uncertain in the crit. ed.

Sarga 31

1. The NR inserts before this a *sarga* in which Daśaratha again renounces Kaikeyī, and Bharata too (line 5), and accuses her of being in league with others (9-12). He expresses the hope that Rāma might disobey him, but knows he will not (31-32). He reproaches himself, fearing what people will say (*kiṃ māṃ vakṣyati loko 'yam*, line 39), and only wishes that he could die before having to consign Rāma to such a miserable fate (App. I, No. 13).

3. "He has given away all his wealth" *dhanaṃ dattvā sarvam*: As Ck and Ct remark,

the implication here is that Rāma has absolutely no intention of remaining in Ayodhyā.

6. It would seem as if the poet protests Daśaratha's innocence too much. See the Introduction, Chapter 9.

7. "in the company of all my wives" *dāraiḥ parivṛtaḥ sarvaiḥ*: Why does Daśaratha want all his wives present? The commentators are silent. Perhaps he hoped that their anguish (verse 16) might check Kaikeyī, or that their very presence might shame her (32.13, 33.6) into relenting.

10. "Half seven hundred" *ardhasaptaśataḥ*: Not 750 as per PW s.v. (see 34.32).

Ck and Ct observe that the fact that the women surround Kausalyā substantiates Lakṣmaṇa's previous statement [28.7] regarding her power. Though high-born women (and men, see 4.2 and note) are usually said to have coppery or red eyes, the commentators all remark that here it is due to weeping.

16. "countless" *sahasra-*: Here as often (such as verse 25 below, where Cg glosses *aneka-*, and see note on 2.6 above) for any large number. (Had he realized this, Cs would have been spared the problem of how to transmute 350 into 1,000.)

"made all the louder by the noise of their jewelry" *bhūṣaṇadhvanimūrchitaḥ*: Their jewelry would be shaking and falling off as the women beat their breasts and heads (Cm, Ck, Ct).

17. "and with Sītā's help" *sītayā sārdham*: Cr seems to construe this phrase only with *rudantaḥ* ("in tears"), taking the plural verb as epicism for dual (this is possible, see 3.67.20 and note). The commentator may in fact be correct: not only would Sītā shrink from touching her father-in-law, but she later explicitly says that she would never willingly touch any other man than Rāma, not even with her foot (see 3.43.34, 5.35.62-63).

18. "overwhelmed by a sea of grief" *śokārṇavapariplutam*: Four conservative N and S manuscripts (D4, 5, 7, M3) apply this adjectival phrase to Rāma rather than to Daśaratha.

21. "as Prajāpati once gave his children leave" *prajāpatir iva prajāḥ*: Brahmā (Prajāpati) permitted his children, Sanaka and the others, to depart when they wanted to go off and perform religious austerities, according to Ct and Cr. The legend seems not to be attested elsewhere.

23. "I was deceived by Kaikeyī into granting a boon" *kaikeyyā varadānena mohitaḥ*: This follows the natural interpretation indicated by Cm and Cg (and made explicit in 821*.4 below, *channayā calitas tv asmi striyā*). Ck and Ct, presumably in order to eliminate the narrative inconsistency (see note on 9.13 and Introduction, Chapter 4), explain, " 'Because of my granting the boon to Kaikeyī I have become deluded,' that is, utterly lost in grief and so unworthy or incapable of executing kingly duties."

25. "on my account" *me*: A sort of "ethical" dative.

26. For direct discourse to commence without a speaker introduction, as the crit. ed. has it here, is most unusual. The NR and SR differ completely here (though see 815*.17-18). But since the crit. ed. elsewhere includes unanimous SR readings when essential for the narrative, the necessary introductory verses in 816*, which have precisely the same manuscript authority as, for example, 30.24, must be put in the text before verse 26, as we have done.

"Go in safety" *gacchasvāriṣṭam*: An adverbial usage; possible also as adjective to *panthānam* (Cg). Cm, Ck, and Ct understand it as a sort of interjection, "farewell," for which we find no evidence. (On the meaning of *ariṣṭa-*, see note on 37.19 below.)

"to good fortune, prosperity" *śreyase vṛddhaye*: Cm, Cg, Ck, Ct distinguish the two as heavenly and earthly good, respectively.

27. "in the company of" *saṃpaśyan*: Literally, "seeing"; also possible: "out of regard for."

"you may set out" *sādhayiṣyasi*: So Cm, Cg, Ck, Ct. Though common in the Sanskrit drama, the verb is rare in this sense in the *Rām* (see however 32.8). But it is quite unlikely that the poet intends a *double entendre*: "you may achieve your purpose" (that is, that there may still be a way to achieve the coronation).

With respect to the chronology of the narrative, Ck, Ct observe that it was early in the day that Kaikeyī had banishment decreed for Rāma; that Rāma spoke with his mother and made the donations through the afternoon; and that it was early evening when he came to take leave of the king. (The sun sets in 41.10ff., soon after Rāma reaches the Tamasā River.)

29. "Who will confer" *kaḥ . . . pradāsyati*: That is, sooner or later his royal pleasures (so Cm, Cg, and Ct; see NR v.l.: *yān adya bhogān prāpsyāmi*, "the delights I shall have tonight") will have to come to an end, and it might as well be sooner (note too that Rāma had promised to leave that very same day, 16.51, and see 16.22 and 40). Ck and Ct suggest an alternative, but less persuasive, interpretation: who will give me [ascribe to me] tomorrow [if I should go tomorrow] the virtues [that is, *dharma*] I shall gain [if I go] today?

30. "its kingdom" *sarāṣṭrā*: Though somewhat awkward, this sense appears to be authorized by verse 33 below. Perhaps otherwise: "along with its vassal kingdoms" (see note on 43.11, and 102.31).

34. "this kindly land" *mahīm imāṃ . . . śivām*: Cg suggests that we are to understand by the adjective "kindly" that Rāma is not abdicating because of the rigors of kingship.

"as you have said" *tvayā yad uktam*: To Kaikeyī, as Cm and Ck note. Daśaratha himself has never yet *ordered* Rāma to go into exile (see 16.24 and the end of the note on 12.16), though Rāma often speaks as if he had (see verses 33 and 35, 43.1, 97.21, 98.38, etc.; see the Introduction, Chapter 4).

Sarga 32

1. Before this the SR inserts a *sarga* (App. I, No. 14) in which Sumantra vehemently reproaches Kaikeyī, saying among other things that he himself shall go with Rāma, "for no brahman ought to live in your domain" (line 21), and explaining that her evil character derives from her mother's. On this point he tells the following curious story: Kaikeyī's father had been granted a boon, which enabled him to understand the speech of animals. Once when he overheard what a bird was saying he laughed out loud. His wife, lying in bed with him and thinking him to be laughing at her, demanded to know the reason for his laughter. The king replied that, were he to tell her, he would straightaway die [for breaking the condition of the boon]. His wife persisted in her demand, regardless of whether he might live or die. The king then related the incident to the sage who had granted him the boon. The latter cautioned the king against telling, whatever his wife might do. Thereupon the king divorced his wife, "and enjoyed himself like Kubera" (33-54). For folkloric parallels to this story in India and elsewhere, cf. Ruben 1950, p. 294 note 1.

"in an urgent voice" *punaḥ punaḥ*: The reading has little manuscript authority (better *punar vacaḥ*), though cf. 46.14.

3. "eminent courtesans" *rūpājīvāś ca śālinyaḥ*: On the status of courtesans in the epics and the auspicious character of their presence, see Meyer 1930, pp. 264ff.

"with choice wares to display" *suprasāritāḥ*: This translation accords with Cm and Cg, "(merchants) making a display of their wares in the area of the camp" (cf. 42.3).

4. "all whose acts of strength have pleased him" *ramate yaiś ca vīryataḥ*: According to Cm, Ct, Cr, this refers to wrestlers whose bravery or strength he delights in testing. The SR adds that all the munitions, as well as townsmen and hunters, are to go, too (839*).

7. By a half-verse inserted after this verse (or in place of *pādas* cd), the NR makes explicit what Daśaratha intends by all these appointments: "Let Rāma enjoy the virtues of kingship even while living in the forest" (843*; cf. 840*).

8. "Great-armed" *(ca) mahābāhuḥ*: The NR reads more pertinently, *('py) uddhṛtadhanām*, "[Ayodhyā] emptied of its wealth" (cf. note on verse 10).

"Let . . . be sent off" *saṃsādhyatām*: Translated according to Cm, Cg, Ck, Ct; perhaps also: "let all the objects of desire fall to the share of Rāma." By either translation, however, the intended contrast is clear.

10. On manuscript evidence (as well as for sense) the readings *vivarṇā* ("pale," for *viṣaṇṇā*, "disconsolate") and *gatadhanam* ("its wealth gone," for *gatajanam*, "its people gone") are far more likely (cf. T3, G1, 2, M1-3, *vivarṇā*, and Dg, Dt, M3 *gatadhanam*, supported by NR 846*, *vivarṇa-*, *hṛtasāram*), and are therefore adopted here.

Note that Kaikeyī's demands of Rāma in 16.26 did include Bharata's control of the treasury of Ayodhyā.

11. "large-eyed wife" *āyatalocanām*: Cg remarks, rather cryptically, that "the reference to her beauty [when she is acting so perversely] is a function of the reference to his sadness," that is, apparently: it is used to show that his misery is inextricably connected with her physical attraction for him.

12. "dispossessed" *upārudhat*: *Pace* Cg, who claims that the word denotes only "exile" (Ct glosses, "to be shut out from the luxuries of kingship"). The whole point of the story is dispossession, not just exile (for which the poet normally uses *pra* or *vi* + the root *vas* or *vraj*).

15. The strange story of the psychopathic prince Asamañja, the very oddity and ignominy of which lend it a certain semblance of historicity, is related elsewhere in the *Rām* (1.37.16-21) and in the *MBh* (3.106.10-15, 12.57.8-9).

Sarayū: A river running to the north and west of Ayodhyā.

20. The SR continues: The minister knows of no crime on Rāma's part, and if Kaikeyī does, she should speak out before the assembly. He also cautions Kaikeyī to guard herself from the ill fame she will incur as a result of these actions (859*).

Sarga 33

4. "must refuse" *anujānāmi*: cf. below 37.8, 44.19 and note.

5. "a small basket, too, and a spade" *khanitrapiṭake cobhe*: To be used for digging and collecting tubers, roots, and so on (Cm, Cg, Ct, Cr).

6. Ct notes: "Up to this point Kaikeyī has effected what Mantharā set in motion;

now she commences the act that will make her an object of universal scorn, as the brahman's curse ordained. The curse is explicit[ly narrated] in the *Adhyātma Rāmāyaṇa*" (we are unable to locate the episode there; cf. the interpolation of the NR noted above on 9.27).

7. "a pair of them" *cīre*: The two articles of clothing are the upper and lower garments.

12. After this verse the SR (and Ñ1 and D) insert fifty-four lines, in which the other wives cry out that Sītā has not been ordered to live in the forest, and beg Rāma not to take her. Vasiṣṭha then reviles Kaikeyī, saying that Sītā should not go but rather, being Rāma's "self" (cf. note on 24.3), should govern in his absence (lines 18-20); or she may go, if she would, and all the people will follow. He asks finally that Sītā be allowed to wear her jewels, if she insists on going (App. I, No. 15).

13. "as if defenseless, though her defender was at her side" *nāthavatyām anāthavat*: Or, "like a woman without a husband, though she had one" (according to Varadacharya, bark clothes were also the dress traditionally worn by widows [1964-1965, vol. 1, p. 375 note]). But cf. the use of *nātha* elsewhere, such as 36.2.

"A curse upon you . . ." *dhik tvām*: The execration against Daśaratha, for his remaining passive and failing to prevent this outrage against Sītā even though her exile was not included in the stipulations of the boon, is eliminated in the NR (compare however the denunciation spoken by the villagers, 43.3-4).

14. "*kuśa* grass" *kuśa-*: This would have been woven into a belt.

Within this verse the NR interpolates four lines in which Daśaratha exclaims that neither Lakṣmaṇa nor Sītā was meant, by the provisions of the boon granted Kaikeyī, to go into the forest (cf. the SR interpolations 873*.8 and 875*), and that therefore there is no reason for Kaikeyī to give them bark clothes (872*). After the verse the SR interpolates eighteen lines in which Daśaratha says that Sītā may go if she would [Cm, Ck, Ct on verse 16 below take this as Daśaratha's granting her leave], but let her do so wearing her jewels.

15. "it suffices" *paryāptam*: This agrees with Cm, Cg, and Ct on the meaning of the word (they add, "that is, it suffices to send her to hell for as long as her soul shall exist"). Possible also: "Have you not already secured (Rāma's exile)?"

18. "higher" *bhūyaḥ*: That is, higher regard than Kausalyā has been accustomed to receive from her husband (cf. 17.22, note on 10.40). Less likely, "(show her) continued (favor)."

"granter of boons" *varada*: Note how this common epic epithet applied to great and generous kings (cf. 2.34 and note) is invested here with a poignant and tragic appropriateness.

Sarga 34

4. "made many childless" *vivatsā bahavaḥ kṛtāḥ*: Cg, Ck, Ct supply *dhenavāḥ* ("cows") with *vivatsāḥ* ("childless," literally, "calf-less," cf. 38.16 below), though this is unnecessary, as the latter construes well enough with *prāṇinaḥ* by enjambment (such is Cr's second interpretation, and see NR 881*, *kṛtāḥ . . . viputrāḥ putravatsalāḥ*). Daśaratha's memory will become clearer later in the story (*sargas* 57-58).

For similar metaphysical explanations of otherwise inexplicable suffering, see 38.16 (Kausalyā), 47.19 (Rāma), and the Introduction, Chapter 5.

11. "Such . . . must be the reward" *evam . . . phalam*: Cm, Ck, and Ct heighten the sarcasm: since a good and heroic man is going into exile, *śāstra* must (somewhere) declare that such is the reward of virtue. One of the sources of *dharmaśāstra* is *sadācāra*, the doings of good people.

14. "He was a meticulous and altogether honest man, with an accurate knowledge" *deśakālajñaṃ niścitaṃ sarvataḥ śucim*: We read the second half of the verse differently from the crit. ed.: *-jñam . . . śucim* (thus also Cg), on equally strong, if not stronger, manuscript testimony and for contextual reasons (cf. note on 15). The crit. ed. reading would give something like, "(the king) knowing the proper time and place, announced his decision (which was) altogether honest"—not wholly nonsense, but almost.

15. "calculating against the number of years" *varṣāṇy etāni saṃkhyāya*: That is, estimate the number of garments and so on that Sītā will require for the fourteen years of exile. Thus the propriety of the epithet in verse 14, "had an accurate knowledge of times and places."

17. "Noble" *sujātā*: Literally, "well-born." Glossed "not born from the womb" by Cm, Cg, and Ct (cf. below 110.27ff., 1.65, and note on verse 28 below).

22. "what was right and good" *dharmārthasaṃhitam*: Cg and Cr interpret: "(words) endowed with a motive (*artha*) which was righteousness."

23. "I have learned well" *śrutaṃ ca me*: That is, from her own mother and father (Cm, Cg, Ck, Ct, and Cr); cf. 24.8.

26. A famous verse, found also in *MBh* (12.144.6), *PañcT* (3.148), *MatsyaP* (210.18), and elsewhere. There is no reason to believe that the *Rām* is the borrower (as Kane supposes, 1966, p. 29 note); the very image of lender-borrower for such gnomic verses is misleading, for many of them were, like proverbs, the common property of the culture (see also Introduction, Chapter 6).

27. "I . . . understand this" *evaṃgatā*: Here we follow Ck, Ct, Cr, and Cs (Cm and Cg: "who have acquired this *dharma* of marital fidelity").

"high-born woman" *śreṣṭhā*: This agrees with Cs; all other commentators, attempting to avoid the apparent self-praise (but cf. 46.24), construe in compound with *pāda* b (though compounding over *pāda*-boundary is extremely rare in the *Ayodhyākāṇḍa*): "I have learned . . . from the best women," that is, from women worthy of respect (Cm, Ck), or who are themselves faithful (Cg): her mother, mother-in-law, etc.

"right from wrong" *-dharmaparāvara*: Literally, "the higher and lower aspects of righteousness"? (so Cr); Cm, Cg, Ct specify "the general rule [of righteous conduct] and the exception" (cf. 6.22 and note).

28. Kausalyā addresses Sītā again in a NR insertion after this verse (908*), saying at one point, "These words of yours do not surprise me, my daughter Maithilī, who cleaving the earth arose like lovely truth itself" (cf. above note on verse 17 for references to Sītā's birth).

30. "Do not be (sorrowful)" *mā (duḥkhitā) bhūs tvam*: Were we to accept the widely attested S variant reading *bhūtvā* (for *bhūs tvam*) we would have, "Mother, do not look upon my father sorrowfully (that is, with a sorrowful face)."

31. "safe and sound" *samagram*: As in 3.55.18, *sītāyāḥ sāmagryam* (not "having

executed his father's order, or, with his wishes fulfilled," Cg; nor "with his beatitude complete," Cm; Ck, Ct, and Cs are on the right track: "with his brother and wife"; cf. *MBh* 7.50.15).

"my loved ones" *suhṛt-*: Lakṣmaṇa and Sītā, as Cm also takes it (Ct, " 'surrounded by friends,' that is, insofar as he will [then] be king").

32. It is best, with Cm, Cg, to take *mātaraḥ* as epicism (for the sake of meter) for *mātṝs*.

36. "where . . . tambourines and bass drums rumbled like stormclouds" *murajapaṇavameghaghoṣavat*: Cm, Cg, Ct, and Cr suggest that *megha-* ("stormclouds") may also signify a musical instrument, but this is unexampled in epic literature. Cg, Ck, and Ct are all explicit in taking the compound as a *rūpakasamāsa* (metaphor compound), "where stormclouds—tambourines and bass drums—used to rumble," though it is as easily *upamānottarapada* (a simile compound) as translated here.

Sarga 35

5. "to your loved ones" *suhṛjjane*: With Cg and Cr, taken as referring to Rāma [and Sītā] (cf. note on 34.31); if with Cm, Ck, and Ct, it is to be understood as "your loved ones here," the clause will be concessive: "(you are determined to live . . .) although devoted." (Cg in his second explanation proposes to understand *sṛṣṭaḥ* as "born": "Just as Kausalyā brought forth a son for the protection of the world, so . . . you were 'engendered' by me for following Rāma into the wilderness" [= Ctś], but cf. the use of the word above, 27.27 and note.)

After this verse the NR adds, in the desire to account for Lakṣmaṇa's wife (cf. 110.51, 1.72, and the General Introduction): "I and my kinsmen have been saved by having so good a son—you, who are ready to abandon your beloved wife and me in your devotion to Rāma" (917*).

8. "Look upon Rāma as Daśaratha" *rāmaṃ daśarathaṃ viddhi*: Cm, Cg, Ct observe that Sumitrā provides Lakṣmaṇa with these substitutes lest in living in the forest he weaken his resolve by thinking back longingly on his father and the others.

This simple admonition on the appropriate emotional stance Lakṣmaṇa is to adopt (and that he might have some other attitude toward Sītā she herself will come to suspect, see 3.43.6, 8, 22-24), caught the imagination of the more inventive or theologically inclined commentators, who offer a large number of interpretations. Two of these we offer from Cm and Cg by way of illustration: first, know that Rāma is "Daśaratha," he whose chariot *(ratha)* is the Biter *(daśa)* [Garuḍa], that is, that Rāma is Viṣṇu; know that the daughter of Janaka is "me" (Sanskrit *mām*), that is, *mā* (= Lakṣmī); that the wood is Ayodhyā, the "Impregnable City," that is, Viṣṇu's city (Vaikuṇṭha). (See note to 39.1 on the traditional ascription to Sumitrā of the knowledge of Rāma's divine nature.) Second, know that Daśaratha is [will as a result be] dead [*rāmaḥ* = *uparataḥ*]; that I will be [once again] the daughter of my father *(janakātmajā)* (that is, as a widow she will have to return to live in her father's house); that Ayodhyā will be a wood, because everyone will depart with Rāma.

9. Mātali: The charioteer of Indra.

11. "which the queen has forced upon you" *yāni devyāsi coditaḥ*: For *codita-* to take a secondary object in the accusative (a *gauṇa karma*) is somewhat unusual, but it seems more awkward to take the final clause as an independent sentence: "The

queen has compelled you," that is, to leave this very night. Sumantra gives this advice either in the belief that for Rāma to have behind him even one day of the exile is a blessing (Cg), or in the awareness that *dharma* requires Rāma to leave immediately (Cr).

13. "leather basket" *sacarma kaṭhinam*: Comparing *MBh* 3.281.1, it seems certain that *kaṭhinam* means "basket" (so too Cnā cited in CSS on *Rām* 2.39.20); Cm, Cg, and Ct understand it as "spade," and *sacarma* as " 'leather,' that is, basket."

15. "for his long (stay)" *cirarātrāya*: So Cm, Ct, and Cr; Ck: "(When) 'at last' " (cf. 6.22 and note); Cg: "(a wave . . .) 'for a long time' (passed)." The adverb is used, as noted by Varadacharya, to distinguish Rāma's departure now from any brief excursions out of Ayodhyā he might have made in the past (1964-1965, vol. 1, p. 393 note).

16. "clangored" *-śiñjita-*: The word refers to the rattling of the horses' trappings, according to *AmaK* (cited by Cg, Ck; similarly Cm, Ct).

20. "godlike child" *devagarbhapratimaḥ*: This agrees with Cm and Cg; Ck and Cs, with unnecessary specificity, gloss "Hiraṇyagarbha"; Ct, "Skanda"; Cr, "a god."

21. "no more . . . than sunlight . . . Mount Meru" *merum arkaprabhā yathā*: See note on 3.19. The sun revolves clockwise around the mountain and so always partially illuminates it.

Notice the attractive comparison of Sītā first to a shadow and then to the gleam of the sun.

24. "accompanied by his desolate wives" *vṛtaḥ strībhir dīnābhiḥ*: See note on 30.8 regarding the presence of the royal women outside the palace.

28. "Oh mother of Rāma" *rāmamāteti*: Note the irregular *sandhi* (expect *-mātar iti*).

"while . . . the women . . . lamented over the crying king" *antaḥpuram . . . krośantam paryadevayan*: The line as printed in the crit. ed. is unclear. With some hesitation we understand *antaḥpuram* as the subject, *krośantam* as object (with *nṛpam* understood, cf. the NR's version 941*, *krośamāṇā* [v.l., *krośanto*] *nṛpam*), and *paryadevayan* as plural for singular (either through *pariṇāma* or with the collective singular *antaḥpuram* treated as a plural). This agrees in general with Cg, though like most S and N manuscripts he too reads *krośantaḥ*. *Krośantam* could be a neuter singular epic participle (cf. Renou 1968, p. 337; Hopkins 1901, p. 69), but the king must be introduced somewhere, both for reasons of context and to explain the NR version 941*, *nṛpam . . . parivavruḥ*.

31. "sight . . . was like a goad . . ." *darśanam . . . totra- . . . iva*: Differently Ct: Rāma was like an elephant tormented by a goad, the goad being Kaikeyī's words.

32. "who seemed almost to be dancing" *nṛtyantīm iva*: A striking image, reported nearly unanimously by the manuscripts. The commentators suggest that the likeness consists in her oscillating movements. An NR insertion before this line shows Kausalyā raising her arms (950*), which might have been felt to enhance the simile (cf. note on 89.8).

33. "very soul" *ātmā*: The poet could have used any number of words had he meant merely "mind," as Cg glosses. The situation demands the heightened sense (cf. also 58.55 and note).

"between two wheels" *cakrayor iva cāntarā*: The one at the front, the other at the back of the cart (Cg), so that if the cart goes forward, the back wheel crushes one, if backward, the front wheel.

34. "rebuke" *upālabdhaḥ*: Or, reading with several S manuscripts, *upalabdhaḥ*,

"(even though you) did perceive it." Concerning the lie that "ever-truthful Rāma" (cf. his words to Sugrīva in 4.7.21 and 14.13) urges his charioteer to make, the commentators are uncharacteristically silent, except for Cr, who attempts to preserve Rāma's truthfulness by way of a rather complex argument turning on a fine point of linguistic philosophy: what Rāma tells him to deny is the necessary volition (*kṛti*, signified by the personal ending of the verb) motivating the effort (*vyāpāra*) that is required to secure the end result of the verbal root "hear"; this does not entail a denial of the contact of the sense-organ with the sense-object, which would indeed be untruthful.

35. "the people" *taṃ janam*: Apparently Kausalyā and other women of the inner chamber (Cg; cf. verse 32 above; called "the king's people" in the next verse), not the townspeople (Cm, Ck, Ct), some of whom are said to follow Rāma up to the Tamasā River (cf. *sarga* 40). The NR calls them the "wives of the townsmen," 952*.2.

36. "but their hearts did not, nor the rush of their tears" *manasāpy aśruvegaiś ca na*: The artificial construction of Cm and Ct for the second half of this verse ("the other people, the townspeople, did not return 'even with their hearts,' let alone with their bodies") attempts to account for the continued presence of the townsmen as noted above. *Janaḥ* and *mānuṣam* here refer to the same group of people (cf. the NR adaptation, 952*.3-4).

38. "his perfect son" *sarvaguṇopapannam . . . sutam*: Despite their being so far separated from one another, these two items are here construed together (the adjective having considerably less propriety with *vacaḥ*, "what they said"). The dislocation may have been felt to be particularly emphatic or emotive (cf. note on 24.16).

It is not necessary to describe in detail Jacobi's arguments (1893, pp. 47ff.) for considering *sargas* 36-39 an interpolation. They are based on a subjective appreciation of poetic verisimilitude (cf. note on 57.3), on verses which are themselves interpolated (1369*, 1370*; even if one were to grant some authenticity to these lines, they do not have to be interpreted with the strict literalism Jacobi adopts; Rāma need not "just" have left; cf. 45.14 note for a similar case); and on an analytical text criticism whose fortunes have waned since Jacobi's day.

Sarga 36

5. "of the entire world" *jagataḥ*: The item is less likely to be construed with *kva*, "where in the world." Ct interprets it as an interjection by a second speaker ("who knows the true nature of the Blessed One").

9. "and the sun vanished" *sūryaś cāntaradhīyata*: The clause instead might be concessive, "even though the sun vanished." Fire-offerings are required at the evening twilight as at sunrise.

The sun disappears at Rāma's misfortune, Ct cleverly suggests, because Rāma and the sun belong to the same clan (the Ikṣvāku clan traces its descent from the sun; cf. 102.5). Crā notes, "By saying, instead of 'the sun set,' that the sun 'vanished,' we are given to understand that, though a little of the day still remained, the sun was wasted by the tragedy of Rāma's going into the wilderness and so disappeared." Ct suggests further that the portents presage the death of Daśaratha (so Cm and Cg on verse 11), and of the demon-king, Rāvaṇa. Cm comments: "What the verse means is that, since Rāma is the Self of all creatures, when he suffers everyone suffers. And for that reason we must understand that every single thing that is set forth in this *Rām* is [not mere poetic convention, but] absolutely real" (similarly Ck).

The anthropomorphic response of all nature to Rāma that we see here (as in 40.28ff., 42.8ff., 53.4ff.), perhaps the first appearance of the motif in the literary tradition, is a theme that will be developed throughout the Vaiṣṇava poetic corpus (cf. *BhāgP* 10.21, especially verses 15ff., for one particularly lovely example).

10. Triśaṅku: A dynast of the Ikṣvāku clan. His story is related in *Bālakāṇḍa* 59. Though not a planet (apparently some constellation, but probably not the Southern Cross as per PW, which cannot be seen in India and in any case consists of four, not three visible stars), Triśaṅku is included in the general reference, by the *chatrinyāya* [whereby one can characterize a whole group by properties that may apply only to a few members of it] (so Cg).

Lohitāṅga: Mars.

Bṛhaspati: Jupiter.

Budha: Mercury.

Cg is troubled by certain contradictions, too abstruse to detail, in the astronomical data here. But in commonplace descriptions of omens and portents such as this one we are wrong to expect astronomical precision on the part of epic poets.

11. "the constellation Viśākhā" *viśākhāḥ*: Four stars of Libra, according to Kirfel (1920, p. 36). It was the family constellation of the Ikṣvāku House; see 6.4.45, *nakṣatraṃ param asmākam ikṣvākūṇām* (according to Cm: "because Ikṣvāku was born in the clan of the sun, which sprang from the constellation Viśākhā"). Cm (second interpretation), Ck, and Ct erroneously gloss *viśākhāḥ* as an adjective referring to the planets and constellations ("out of their orbits").

12. "suddenly" *akasmāt*: Though the word is not infrequently used in this sense, all the commentators take it in its more usual signification, "without apparent reason," and then attempt to explain it in various ways, all of them unsatisfactory because that meaning is impossible here.

15. "children became indifferent, and brothers, too" *anarthinaḥ sutāḥ . . . bhrātaras tathā*: The verse is elliptical; we must understand: children become indifferent to their parents, brothers to their brothers. Cm's remarks are worth recording in full: "On the grounds that Kausalyā did not stop Rāma when she saw him going to the forest, children forsook their mothers, thinking them to be of no avail; mothers forsook their children, thinking them to be of no use, since even Rāma left his mother and went to the forest; husbands, observing how treacherously Kaikeyī had acted towards her lord, forsook their wives, and wives in turn forsook their husbands after observing how the king, in disregard of Kausalyā, made her son go to the forest; brothers forsook their brothers, thinking that Bharata was the reason the kingship was taken from Rāma, and in the same way even younger brothers left their elder brothers. So everyone turned his back on everyone else and thought about Rāma—thought, that is, that he was their only true kinsman, and that there was no need for others."

16. "As for Rāma's friends" *ye tu rāmasya suhṛdaḥ*: According to Cg we are meant by this "to differentiate these friends from those previously mentioned [that is, the loved ones]: the emperor permitted Rāma to go, Kausalyā gave him her blessings and so neither was really a 'friend'; not one of them did anything [to stop him]. The friends here mentioned are those to whom Rāma would tell things he would

not tell even his parents. . . . So why did they not grasp his feet and stop him? 'They were bewildered.' "

17. "just as the earth would . . . if abandoned by Indra" *puraṃdareṇeva mahī*: Cm takes this to mean: because Indra is the lord of the three worlds, the earth if destitute of him would have no protector, and so would quake (so Ck and Ct). Less likely is Cg's second suggestion: "as the earth quakes at the hands of Indra [in his aspect of] the splitter of mountains."

Though the manuscript support is not overwhelming, *-rathā(ḥ)* ("chariots," for *-gaṇā(ḥ)*, "hosts") seems to be a superior reading: the city, even with a complete army of four divisions (elephant, [foot-]soldier, horse, chariot), shook with fear when Rāma left.

Sarga 37

2. "he seemed to stand firm on the ground just to have him in sight" *vyavardhatevāsya dharaṇyāṃ putradarśane*: The line is problematic. Daśaratha is taken here as subject of the verb (and *asya* construed with *putra-*, literally, "[in order to have a view] of his son"). Not dissimilarly Cg (second interpretation), Ck, Ct, Cr, though they supply *deham*, "so long could 'his body' stand upright on the earth." Quite differently Cm: " 'It,' that is, the dust 'on the ground, seemed to increase,' as if it thought, 'The king might remain yet a little while untroubled if with my help he can continue to watch his son.' "

4. "to his left side came Kaikeyī" *vāmaṃ cāsyānvagāt pārśvaṃ kaikeyī*: The detail is emphasized by the commentators as symbolically distinguishing Kaikeyī from Kausalyā both in her behavior toward the king and in his attitude to her.

"whose only love was for Bharata" *bharatapriyā*: = *priyabharatā*, *paranipāta* occasioned by the verse cadence (cf. note on 42.27).

5. "The king, a man of prudence" *nayena . . . saṃpannaḥ . . . rājā*: Considering what Daśaratha proceeds to say, the first half-verse should probably be understood concessively: "The king, though a man of prudence" (the commentators are silent).

8. "I renounce it all" *anujānāmi tat sarvam*: Daśaratha renounces the earthly prerogatives of matrimony, that is, his sexual relationship with Kaikeyī (Cm, Ct), and either the performance of religious ritual with his wife (Cm) or the results of such ritual, that is, heaven (Ct).

9. "sovereign kingship" *rājyam avyayam*: Not just the prince regency, because Daśaratha will be dead (cf. 47.7, 11-12; 69.6).

"any funeral offering he makes" *yat . . . sa dadyāt pitrartham*: That is, the *śrāddha* offering to the dead (cf. note on 71.1).

10. The crit. ed. misspells here (for *samuddhvastam*), as do virtually all the vulgate editions and commentators—a curiously persistent error.

"began to lead him home" *nyavartata*: In agreement with Cs, we explain the form as an unmarked causative.

12. "he collapsed in the ruts of the chariot" *sīdato rathavartmasu*: Ck and Ct understand less literally: "suffering at the sight of the path of the chariot."

13-14. Translated here following a hint from Cs: Daśaratha looks again at the ruts into which he has fallen (verse 12) and, momentarily discomposed, imagines them to be the tracks of the chariot *returning*. Ct and Cr straightforwardly interpret,

"Realizing that his son had reached the outskirts of the city, he said . . . ," but it is hard to see how this fits with verse 14.

"to the city" *nagarāntam*: *-anta-* here probably does not mean "the outskirts" (of the city; so Ct), but either functions as an "otiose, suffix-like element" (see Gonda 1938, pp. 453ff., especially pp. 464 and 476), or has the sense of "middle" (as in the common *vanānta-*, or *veśmānta-* in verse 20 below).

16. "like the bull" *ivarṣabhaḥ*: The simile is weak, unless some unattested sense of *prasravaṇa-* ("mountain stream") lurks here, though this appears to be the meaning of the word in the *Rām* (cf. 5.54.12, 33.45, 33.55, etc.), except, of course, where it means Mount Prasravaṇa (as in 3.60.14, 5.34.38, etc.).

19. "the way a mourner enters a cemetery" *apasnāta ivāriṣṭam*: Literally, "as one who has performed the funeral bath enters an inauspicious place" (a burning ground, or cemetery). The translation is a rather desperate solution, but the problems of the line are insoluble, there being some irremediable corruption. In light of *BuddhaC* 7.7, *puraṃ śanair apasnātam ivābhijagmatuḥ* ("those two came slowly to the city as if going to a funeral bathing rite," Johnston, see his note ad loc.), which is clearly adapted from our *Rām* verse, we would expect *apasnātam* (or *apasnānam*), which we would translate, "a place for funeral bathing" (rather than the rite itself; for *apasnānam* cf. *Pā* 3.3.117). The difficulty of *ariṣṭam*, however, remains intractable. In the *Rām* the word always has its ancient (vedic) and authentic sense, "free from evil or danger" (cf. 31.26, 5.1.179, etc.; here is another small point to consider in locating the *Rām* historically, for the use of the word in this sense is limited almost exclusively to vedic texts). The one exception is 6.55.120, where the variant reading *arighnam* seems compelling. The negative connotations of the word appear only later in the epic period (*MBh* 12.69.47 is perhaps the earliest example; cf. also Vaidya on *MBh* 8.2.5), and it is unreasonable to suppose that the poet would have used the same word in two diametrically opposed senses. Hence the suspicions of corruption, and the stopgap character of the translation. The commentators understand, "as a man who has performed the funeral bath might enter a polluted place, such as a lying-in chamber" (and so be polluted once again; or, extrapolating considerably, the lying-in chamber where the infant son he just cremated had been born—so Varadacharya 1964-1965, vol. 1, note on p. 409), but this signification of *ariṣṭa-* is post-epic. The NR points altogether elsewhere: "as if seized with an epileptic fit." For an interesting discussion of "le cas curieux du terme *áriṣṭa-*" cf. Renou 1939-1942, p. 7.

20. "the people haggard, feeble" *klāntadurbala-*: Cm and Cg remark that this implies that all who were able to walk had followed after Rāma (see *sarga* 40).

22. "like a . . . pool, from which Suparṇa has snatched the serpents" *-hradam iva . . . suparṇena hṛtoragam*: The simile is a bit odd, in making "serpents" the *upamāna* or standard of comparison of Rāma, Lakṣmaṇa, and Sītā (it is repeated in 1032*.3-4 below). Cm, Ck, Ct unsatisfactorily explain that the illustration has reference merely to the king's being able to enter his home without fear of enemies (that is, they do not relate *pādas* ab to cd). We take it somewhat more closely with Cg, whose comment however is highly elliptical: "[He entered the house which was previously] like a pool that was not to be penetrated [by hostile creatures] because it had serpents [and which then becomes penetrable after Garuḍa has taken the serpents away]." Cf. note on 75.14.

23. After the first half of this verse, the SR adds: "For nowhere else will my heart

find consolation" (974*). It is, again, only in such passing references that the subordinate drama of Kausalyā's relationship with Daśaratha—their marriage, her childlessness and supersession by Kaikeyī, her renewed position of trust and authority after Kaikeyī's repudiation—is adumbrated in the received text (cf. the Introduction, Chapter 8).

25. "Looking around" *tac ca dṛṣṭvā*: All but several NE manuscripts (which consequently alter the reading in *pāda* a) precede this verse with a line that supplies some antecedent to *tac*. In all cases it is "house," and that is doubtless what we must understand.

26. "at the hour" *taṃ kālam*: Accusative of time at which (cf. 63.2, 75.1, 5.65.26, Cm, Cg on 5.38.14, and Böhtlingk 1896, p. 250).

27. "touch me" *māṃ . . . spṛśa*: According to Ck, Daśaratha wants to find out whether Kausalyā is in fact present; to Ct, whether he is still really alive.

"My sight has followed after Rāma" *rāmaṃ me 'nugatā dṛṣṭiḥ*: Note the attractive rhetorical figure (technically an *utprekṣā* or "poetic fancy").

Sarga 38

2. "like a snake that has shed its skin" *nirmukteva hi pannagī*: Cg suggests, "with boundless cruelty." Herpetologists say that shedding the skin is a traumatic process for a snake, which may well result in increased aggressiveness. But the point of the simile is probably simply that Kaikeyī will now act with "naked cruelty."

3. "like a vicious serpent in the house" *duṣṭāhir iva veśmani*: The implication, as Cr points out, is that Kaikeyī should be driven from the palace.

4. "You had the freedom to grant such a boon" *kāmakāro varaṃ dātum*: A problematic line, for which the commentators are no help. The key to it is to be found by comparing the poet's use of *kāmakāraḥ* elsewhere (98.15, 3.57.6, 6.98.23, 104.8 [cf. also 2.2201*]). Invariably the sense is "an act of one's own free will." (Both here and in the next verse Kausalyā suppresses naming the agent, Daśaratha. Only by verse 7 can she no longer maintain her tactful reticence; similarly in 55.16ff.) Kausalyā recognizes that Rāma's succession could legally be set aside, but she cannot forgive her husband's truly senseless act in freely allowing Kaikeyī a boon by which to *exile* Rāma (here, as noticed elsewhere, the "boon" is obviously regarded as a single one, given during the interview in *sarga* 10; the "two boons" are unknown).

5. "But you let Kaikeyī . . . throw" *pātayitvā tu kaikeyyā*: Technically *kaikeyyā* is the *prayojyakartā* of the verbal, Daśaratha (unnamed) the *prayojaka*: "[you,] letting Kaikeyī throw Rāma . . . have assigned him" (so Cm, first interpretation).

"from his place" *sthānāt*: Ck, "from dwelling in his own house"; Cm, "or, from the kingship." Cm's explanation of the simile is a good one: "As the sacrificer at the half-month (that is, new- or full-moon festival) assigns the heap of husks from the rice[-cake offered during the rite] as portion for the demons, so Kaikeyī has delivered Rāma up as portion for the demons [Ct: and thus, "we can never hope to see him again, for he will be slain by them"]. This donation is prescribed in the *Darśapūrṇānukrāmaṇikā* ["The Index to the New- and Full-Moon Rite"], [with the liturgical expression:] 'Hail to the demons! This is for the demons, it is not mine' " (thus also Ctr, vol. 1, p. 313, with citations from *śrauta* literature). Cg understands differently: " 'the share' of the kingdom that should have been given by you [Daśaratha] to Rāma, 'was assigned to Kaikeyī [taken as genitive], as a sacrificer [might assign] a portion' of an oblation 'to the demons,' when it should have been given to the gods."

7. "yielded to Kaikeyī" *kaikeyyānumate*: Cg rightly takes this as double *saṃdhi* (that is, *kaikeyyāḥ* as genitive).

13. "my two . . . sons" *mamātmajau*: The NR removes the reference, reading "the two Rāghavas" (cf. Kausalyā's explicit statement in verse 18).

After (or somewhere near) this verse all manuscripts save B add: "When shall I see them entering Ayodhyā, with their lovely earrings, their weapons and swords upraised, like two high-peaked mountains" (980*).

14. "When will maidens" *kadā . . . kanyāḥ*: The ceremony is unknown to the commentators; "An auspicious ritual observance of the northerners," is all Cg can say. Reading differently, Cm, Ck, and Ct understand, "When will Rāma and the others give flowers to maidens and fruits to brahmans, and circle. . . ."

15. "young as a deathless god" *vayasā cāmaraprabhaḥ*: That is, "twenty-five years old, for the gods always remain twenty-five years old," Cm and Cg; cf. Rāma's own words in 3.4.13-14, and note that this is almost certainly the age of Rāma at the time of his exile (cf. note on 17.26).

Sarga 39

1. Sumitrā's presence during Daśaratha's interview with Kausalyā has not in any way been indicated prior to this; the NR transfers the whole *sarga* to a place later in the narrative (after *sarga* 56). The commentators are more disposed here than previously in the *Ayodhyākāṇḍa* to interpret anagogically; Ctś perhaps explains this when he mentions the traditional belief that, like Tārā and Mandodarī (who appear later in the *Rām*, in Books Four and Five respectively), Sumitrā possesses, by reason of her merit accumulated in a former birth, knowledge of Rāma's transcendent divinity, *paratvajñāna*, which she here expounds. Partially similar is Cm on verse 8 below; cf. also note on 35.8.

5. In the traditional manner of counting the *Rām*, its 24,000 verses are correlated with the twenty-four syllables of the *Gāyatrīmantra* [*ṚV* 3.62.10] (the first syllable of the *mantra* coming at the commencement of the poem). The first syllable of this verse (*va*, corresponding to the fifth of the *mantra*) indicates that 4,000 verses of the (vulgate) *Rām* have been completed (noted by Cm, Cg).

6. We agree with Ct (and Cm, Ck, more or less), who sees in verses 5 and 6 further reasons why Rāma should not be mourned, and is in fact a lucky man (Cm accordingly understands *rāmasya* in 5d), rather than with Cg (and Ctś), who believes Sumitrā to be saying: Kausalyā should rejoice that both Sītā and Lakṣmaṇa are so firmly devoted to their respective duties (and he accordingly understands *lakṣmaṇasya* in 5d; the NR does, however, support this interpretation, cf. 985*, 988*).

Ct observes, with reference to verses 5-6, that by Lakṣmaṇa's "compassion to all creatures" it is implied that he is an avatar of Śeṣa, the supporter of the all-supporting earth; that by Sītā's following Dharma [incarnate in Rāma] it is implied that she is Śrī, and by this that Rāma is the Blessed One (Viṣṇu).

7. "What gain has your . . . son failed to reap" *kiṃ na prāptas tavātmajaḥ*: We follow Ct and Cr; Cm, Cg, and Ck gloss, "for what blessing is he not fit."

8. "purity" *śaucyam*: We translate the reading of the crit. ed., though the variant *śauryam* ("valor") of several S manuscripts is authenticated by the NR's *sattvam* ("courage").

In support of their anagogical interpretation Cm and Ct (so too Ctś) appositely cite the scriptural passage, "From fear of him the sun rises" [*TaiU* 2.8], on which Cm remarks, "It is unreasonable to hold that the sun would burn the supreme soul when the sun fears the supreme soul, as we know for certain from this scriptural passage." Perhaps the poet truly intended the allusion (cf. note on 29.13).

9. Cm (so Cg) again quotes scripture, "From fear of Him the wind blows" [*TaiU* 2.8].

10. Ctś cites, "By command of the Imperishable One, the sun and moon are held in their places" [*BṛĀraU* 3.8.9].

11. "was given divine weapons by Brahmā" *dadau cāstrāṇi divyāni yasmai brahmā*: Contrast 28.12-13 and note. The event here referred to is not mentioned elsewhere in the *Rām* (though cf. 3.48.23 and note). There is consequently considerable uncertainty among the commentators. Cm and Cg: "Timidhvaja is Śambara, cf. 'the city called Vaijayanta, where Timidhvaja ruled, the same who is called Śambara' [9.10-11 above, cf. note there]. When Brahmā saw Śambara's son, the Dānava king, killed [by Rāma], he gave Rāma divine weapons. This is referred to above, 'Whenever he goes forth with Saumitri to battle in defense of a village or city, he always returns triumphant' [2.24 above]. Once Rāma went to the Daṇḍaka forest and laid siege to the city of Vaijayanta, where he slew the son of Śambara, who had shown hostility to Daśaratha. Pleased by this act, Brahmā gave him the weapons." Ct calls their explanation "desperate conjecture." Ck (so Cr, Cs) suggests: " 'Brahmā' is the Brahmā-like maker of creation [or just, "the brahman" (so Ct)], that is, Viśvāmitra [so too the NR, 992*]; the 'son of Timidhvaja' is Subāhu" (a demon slain by Rāma, see 1.29). Ct again criticizes this latter equation on the grounds that Viśvāmitra gave the divine weapons to Rāma after the death of Tāṭakā (1.25-26), and prior to that of Subāhu. He also maintains that Subāhu could not possibly be the son of Śambara, inasmuch as he had already been identified as the brother of Mārīca [this is not actually so, but according to 1.19.24-25 we would at least be justified in assuming that Subāhu is the son of Upasunda, and Mārīca the son of Sunda]. Cr, for his part, disputes Ct's reasoning, but not altogether cogently.

After this verse the SR includes a ten-line insertion (993*) which further extolls Rāma's virtues. Ct comments (on 44.15 vulgate) that these verses show Rāma to be the *antaryāmin* or inner-controller of all things (cf. for example lines 7ff.: "He is the Sun of the sun, the Fire of fire . . . he is the Divinity of the gods").

Sarga 40

1. "men loyal to him" *anuraktāḥ . . . mānavāḥ*: On these followers, see the note on 35.36.

5. "his people . . . as though they were his children" *tāḥ prajāḥ svāḥ prajā iva*: The words for "people" ("subject") and "child" here are, untranslatably and significantly, the same: *prajā-*. On the significance of this, see the Introduction, Chapter 3.

7. "welfare" *hitāni*, "happiness" *priyāṇi*: Agrees with Crā. Cm, Ck, and Ct want to distinguish between *priya-* and *hita-* as earthly and heavenly good (the latter specified as Bharata's preservation of the duties of caste and stages of life).

8. "though gentle he is endowed with all the virtues of a hero" *mṛdur vīryaguṇānvitaḥ*: We accept the view of Cm, Ck, and the indications of symmetry, in identifying *mṛduḥ* ("mild") as concessive, rather than *vīryaguṇānvitaḥ* ("endowed with all the virtues of a hero"). Ct reverses it ("He is gentle though endowed . . . ").

Rāma, we have seen (note on 17.26), is about twenty-five years old at the time of his exile. His calling his brother Bharata a "boy" gives further credence to the inference about his youth (see note on 8.9).

9. "I myself have shown you, you must obey" *mayā śiṣṭaiḥ kāryaṃ vaḥ*: We understand *vaḥ* as instrumental (so too, it seems, Ck; this is an epicism, cf. Sen 1956, p. 268, where, however, he neglects to note this case), and construe it with *śiṣṭaiḥ* (derived from the root *śās*). The commentators fail to make sense of the verse.

Rāma has "shown" the citizens by way of his own example that they, too, must accede to the king's decisions, however displeasing they may be—a very important point for the significance of the poem as a whole, and one which the poet is not content to make merely by way of implication.

12. "By their virtues . . . seemed to bind" *iva guṇair baddhvā*: The verse works on a common pun, *guṇa-* meaning both "virtue" and "string" or "rope."

13. "authority" *ojasā*: Or, according to the commentators, the "power" acquired by the brahmans' religious austerities (Cm, Cg, Ck, Ct).

"began to cry out from afar" *dūrād ūcuḥ*: Since they are physically incapable of running up to Rāma (Cm, Ck, Ct, Cr).

16. "Rāma then . . . proceeded on foot" *padbhyām eva jagāmātha . . . rāmaḥ*: Rāma was unwilling to proceed by chariot lest the brahmans hurt themselves (in trying to run after), nor could he turn back in deference to them lest his vow be broken. He thus continues forward, but slowly, so that the brahmans might catch up (Cm, Cg, Ct). Ctr (vol. 1, p. 317) finds a scriptural precept for Rāma's conduct: *tasmāj jyāyāṃsaṃ kanīyān pratyavarohati* ("Therefore a younger person must descend [from his vehicle] before an elder [who is on foot]").

19. "brahman order" *brāhmaṇyam*: Cm (first explanation) and Ck interpret this as the "activity," that is, accoutrements of the brahmans (by *karmaṇi ṣyañ* [*Pā* 5.1.124], rather than by *samūhe yat* [4.2.42], as we analyze it [so too Ct]).

"sacred fires . . . borne on the shoulders" *-skandhādhirūḍhāḥ . . . agnayaḥ*: It would be the receptacles and fire-sticks that the brahmans carried on their shoulders (Cm, Cg, Ck, Ct), not the live fires themselves, in fire pots (as presumably is the case in 69.9).

20. "umbrellas given to us at the *vājapeya* rite" *vājapeyasamutthāni chatrāṇy etāni . . . naḥ*: "One who performs the *vājapeya* rite [a *soma*-sacrifice, performed only by brahmans and kshatriyas] acquires a [white] umbrella, just like a king's, according to the statement of scripture, 'Therefore (for the rest of one's life [*addit* Cg]) the performer of the *vājapeya* does not rise up [as a mark of respect] before anyone. (One becomes a bearer of the white umbrella [*addit* Cg]),' " so Ck, Cg [on verse 21 below]. We find something very similar in *TaiBr* 1.3.9.2 and *PañcBr* 18.6.12 (see *ĀpaŚS* 18.7.18 and Kane 1962-1975, vol. 2.ii, p. 1,210 and note).

Geese—these would be the white royal geese, corresponding to the white umbrellas—migrate after the monsoons, in the autumn.

22. "our minds are made up . . . to turn to a life in the forest" *sā kṛtā . . . vanavāsānusāriṇī*: Cg remarks that with this [their intention to abandon vedic study, Cm, Ck, Ct], the brahmans are placing a heavy burden of responsibility on Rāma, and

by so doing hope to persuade him to return (as Cg explains more fully on verse 19 above).

24. "will any regard now be paid to what is right?" *kiṃ syād dharmam avekṣitum*: A difficult quarter-verse. We understand *kim* as an interrogative particle, and *syāt* with infinitive as "is there a chance that?" "will you?". The point seems to be this: since Rāma is so wise in *dharma*, can he not see the transgressions that he is forcing them to commit because of his departure? The brahmans in the following verses appear to be cataloguing the breaches of *dharma* that have occurred and will occur if they follow Rāma (as they must if he continues). This explanation is relatively close to Ck: "Since you have constant regard for *dharma*, do you have a mind [repeated from *pāda* b] to regard our *dharma*?" The other commentators are perplexed.

25. "We have bowed our heads . . . we have pleaded" *yācitaḥ . . . śirobhiḥ*: Several commentators, troubled that the verse shows (aged) brahmans bowing down before a (young) kshatriya, remark, "It is because they know he is the Supreme One" (Cg), "or, because there is no fault in bowing down to a king, insofar as kings are a portion of Viṣṇu" (Ct). Ck offers a more elaborate explanation: "Why for that matter do we [brahmans] at the present day bow down [apparently before icons of Rāma]? If we answer that by listening to the *Rām* we come to believe in Rāma as the supreme god [*kuladaivata*], whereby our belief in him as the son of a kshatriya mother terminates, we can conclude that precisely the same reason obtains here: these brahmans came to understand that Rāma is *brahma*, and all the more easily [than we], because they actually experienced, with their very senses, the different properties of his divine nature."

26. If Rāma does not return he will be guilty of obstructing the sacrifices, presumably because the brahmans will not return without him.

28. "because their roots prevent their movement" *mūlair uddhataveginaḥ*: The crit. ed.'s *-vegibhiḥ* is marked as dubious. The preferable lection is *-veginaḥ*, "(trees) whose movement (is prevented by their roots)," adopted here (though it is just possible to dissolve the instrumental compound in the same sense, the *-in* suffix being otiose).

"as the gusting wind uplifts them" *unnatā vāyuvegena*: To be construed as a unitary phrase (cf. the NR v.l. *ūrdhvaśākhāḥ*): through the force of the wind the trees are raising up and waving their armlike branches in their misery (exactly as in 3.50.32, when Sītā is abducted). This is also the typical posture of mourning (cf. 51.23, 59.14, 60.15).

29. "They sit in one place in the trees" *vṛkṣaikasthānaviṣṭhitāḥ*: That is, the birds do not alight on the earth even to find food (Cm, Ck), and implore Rāma to turn back even if they must die in the process. Cg remarks, "Thus animals and unmoving things were pained, and it is because Rāma is the embodied soul of all things. When the embodied soul is discomfited, the body is seen to be tormented."

Sarga 41

2. Translated in accordance with the commentators (Cm and Cg in particular) and the indications of the parallel verse, 47.2 (and cf. the NR's version, 1017*). Alternatively: "This is the first night, Saumitri, that [we] have gone to [spent in] the forest. [But] please, do not feel sad at our living in the forest [*karmaṇi ṣaṣṭhī*]."

According to Cm, Rāma wants to emphasize that the period of their exile is already beginning to diminish, and for that reason Lakṣmaṇa should not feel sad.

3. "all around they seem to weep" *rudantīva samantataḥ*: The forest appears to be sobbing, presumably, because of the animals' nighttime sounds (as Cg notes, though he seems to contradict this when he goes on to say, " 'empty' means gloomy . . . and this gloominess makes for the poetic fancy of the forest's weeping"; Cm, Ck, Ct gloss the verb *rudanti* as "seem downcast").

4. Cg comments, "His memories are awakened by the poetic fancy of the forest's weeping, and he thinks back on what is happening in the city."

7. It is not certain (despite the *hi*, for this particle has a protean character in the epics) whether the second line supplies the reason for the first, or its consequence. The implications are, in the one case, that otherwise Rāma would have had to seek protection for her, which Lakṣmaṇa all by himself can now provide (Cm and Cg, especially Ct and Cr); or, in the other, that since Lakṣmaṇa has fulfilled his duty by the very act of his following Rāma, it is as something over and above this that Rāma must seek his attendance on Sītā. This would be a polite circumlocution for asking Lakṣmaṇa to fetch her food and drink, which would tally nicely with the following verse; this is what Ck intends, and how we understand it.

8. Rāma will fast because it is the inaugural day of his exile (and fasting is ancillary to the commitment to undertake exile in the forest [*vanavāsasaṃkalpāṅgātvena*], Ck, Ct). On their first night of exile the Pāṇḍavas likewise drink only water, *MBh* 3.1.40 (Ctr adduces this, claiming that on entering the forest one is required to abstain from food on the first night). Another reason to fast is the holiness of the place, according to Cg, Cm, and Cr. Cs believes the implication to be that Rāma fasts at the pilgrimage site in view of the fact that his father may have only a short time to live [that is, as an apotropaic rite?], cf. 44.24 below and note. Rāma finally does eat, and ravenously, after he crosses the Ganges (46.79).

11. "When Rāma had worshiped . . . and saw" *upāsya . . . dṛṣṭvā . . . rāmasya*: The subject of the gerunds in *pādas* ab is *rāmasya*, to whom in the first instance the ritual is always ascribed elsewhere (43.2, 44.24, 47.1, etc.; for this kind of "dangling" gerund, see 48.18, 84.5, 106.7, and Gonda 1967, pp. 264-65). Cg and Cr unwisely construe the gerunds with *sūtaḥ*, "charioteer," being then forced to explain: " 'worship' here means greeting. Even the *sūta-* caste [offspring of a *pratiloma* marriage, cf. *ManuSm* 10.26; but cf. also above 32.1 note, where Sumantra appears to be a brahman] is allowed to make the greeting, but only that [and not use the *Gāyatrīmantra*]."

12. "Escorted by Saumitri" *saumitreṇa sārdham*: The translation here agrees with Cm (first explanation). Word order might more cogently suggest the following: "Rāma found . . . and then with Saumitri and his wife," but common sense and the procedure in 44.25 speak against this. A strong variant reading, attested in all recensions, for the second half of the *śloka* is: "Rāma bade goodnight to Saumitri and. . . ."

13. "he engaged . . . in conversation, talking about Rāma's many virtues" *kathayām āsa . . . rāmasya vividhān guṇān*: Lakṣmaṇa talks about Rāma's virtues simply to pass the time and stay awake (Ck, Ct; Cg on the following verse).

15. "at a little distance" *vidūrataḥ*: Ck, Ct maintain that the specification (glossed "near by" by Cg in the VSP, who thus appears to have understood *avidurataḥ*)

indicates that Rāma camped away from the crowd of twice-born so that he could depart more easily after deceiving them (see below). The herds of cattle on the bank may have been a more powerful reason (Cr feebly suggests that Rāma was afraid he might commit some infraction like spitting in the river, were he too close to it).

16. "good . . . Lakṣmaṇa" *lakṣmaṇaṃ puṇyalakṣaṇam*: Literally, "of good, auspicious marks, traits," that is, particularly his devoted service to his elder brother.

19. "(a path) free from danger" *akutobhayam*: cf. verse 28 below. The NR offers *tapovanam*, "(along the path) to the grove of asceticism," a reading substantiated by the SR in a recapitulative verse (1029*.4).

20. "now, or ever again" *ato bhūyo 'pi (n)edānīm*: We differ from all the commentators in our understanding of the *pāda*. Cm and Cg: "They should not sleep again as [but whence the *iva*?] now" [or, "will not?" that is, they will return home?]; Ct: "Since they are loyal, they will not sleep [much longer] beyond this"; Ck seems to read without the negative: "They will sleep beyond this because they did not have anything to eat or drink on the previous day, and spent the night wakeful because of grief."

24. "head northward" *udaṅmukhaḥ*: Toward Ayodhyā.

Rāma does not go himself lest by making even this partial return to the city he break his vow (Cm, Cg, Ct, Cr).

Cg comments on Rāma's deception as follows: "If Rāma is so compassionate, is it not wholly improper for him to deceive those who love him so dearly and cannot stand to be separated from him? The answer is that this is not in fact deception. It cannot be a *deception* insofar as it is something done in their own best interests. The people of the city ran the risk of dying from the excessive bliss [of being with Rāma]. By the proverb of "healing a wound" [whereby initially the medicine may be more painful than the wound itself], Rāma contrived to separate himself from them under the pretext of going to the forest, and this was intended almost as a therapeutic regimen for them. If Rāma had not *contrived* this, then how to explain the fact that every single person was put to sleep? For some one among them, like Sumantra and Lakṣmaṇa, must otherwise have remained awake."

26. "on returning" *pratyāgamya*: That is, by another route (Cm, Cg, Ck, Ct).

27. "eddying" *-ākulāvartām*: Note *paranipāta* of *āvartā* (expect *-āvartākulām*). The phenomenon is not uncommon in the epics (cf. 37.4, 43.12, 45.13 and notes there; 5.12.8, 39.14, 6.40.1; *HariVaṃ* 40.44, 41.12, 55.3, 78.1, etc.).

The SR, by transposing verses 24-26 and 27-28, has Rāma first cross the Tamasā and then send the charioteer back to confuse the townsmen.

29. With this verse the vulgate commences a new *sarga*. For the rest of this *sarga* the NR substitutes simply: "When the townsmen awoke at the close of night, they saw that the chariot had turned back, and in the belief that the prince had returned to the town they went back to the city themselves" (1031*).

30. After this verse, the SR inserts twenty lines (1030*), reporting the incredulous and mournful outcry of the townsmen, their shock that Rāma could have done something so unfair to them (5-8), their threat to commit suicide (9-12), their anxiety about returning to the city without Rāma (13-18).

31. "when it gave out" *mārganāśāt*: That is, the chariot track heading toward the city; it would of course have to continue in another direction, but presumably the

townsmen are by now sufficiently convinced that they have been deceived ("by fate," verse 32) and that it would be futile to search further.

33. "good people" *-sajjanām*: "The qualification is meant to exclude Kaikeyī and her partisans," Ck, Ct.

Sarga 42

3. "would have no meals prepared" *apacan*: Very possibly an unmarked causative. Cg (understanding as simplex) hastens to point out that "it is only because their wives are 'half their bodies' [cf. note on 26.3], that the householders themselves can be said to have any connection with cooking" (that is, the men do not actually do any cooking themselves).

6. Ct (and Cm, who is similar) comments on what he takes to be the theological implication of the verse: "Those who did not attentively keep blessed Rāma in sight, but returned out of attachment to their homes, sons, wives, pleasures, and so on, will transmigrate again and again, and will never attain liberation. For even the sight of his phenomenal form renders the mind clear, and by means of this one becomes qualified for the knowledge requisite for ultimate liberation."

8. "Fortunate" *kṛtapuṇyāḥ*: Literally, "will realize [reap the benefits of] their [previously won] merit"; equally possible: "[must have] built up merit." For the anthropomorphic response, cf. note on 36.9.

9. "will adorn" *śobhayiṣyanti*: None of the commentators clarifies the sense of the word (in 1044*.6 it is Rāma who is said to "adorn the forests," as in 3.12.8). The NR reads either "delight" or "attract" (could such be the sense, otherwise unattested, of *śobhaya-* here?).

14. "before he is too far away from us" *purā bhavati no dūrāt*: The translation of *pāda* a (*purā* as conjunction) is in accordance with Cg's intention (though he takes it as "he will soon be far, so . . . "), and many N manuscripts (cf. 1039*, *yāvad dūraṃ na gacchati*). Cm, Ck, and Ct, reading *'dūrād*, gloss, "he will be [*purā* adverbially as a simple future-tense marker, according to *Pā* 3.3.4] near us" [that is, to protect them, as per verse 13].

"the shadow of the feet" *pādacchāyā*: That is, attending on him (Cm, Cg, Ck, Ct).

18. "we would have no further use" *na . . . naḥ . . . arthaḥ*: The second half of the verse forms the apodosis (so according to the interpretation of Cm), not *pāda* b, as Cg takes it. He argues this on the grounds that "this is a statement made under the supposition of what will occur," that is, Daśaratha's death. But the very conditions in which Kaikeyī acquires the kingship would be "against all that is right" and it would necessarily be "with our one defender gone"—Rāma, not Daśaratha.

20. "so long as she lives, or we do" *jīvantyā . . . jīvantyaḥ*: Cg is correct to take the participles as indicating temporal extent rather than as simple attributives ("living as her servants," so Cm, Ck, Ct).

22. "total devastation" *vilopaḥ*: Usually by enemy troops (*ArthŚā* 7.4.22, 8.4.15, etc.), but in view of verses 19 and 24 it is probably despoliation by Kaikeyī and her son that is meant.

23. "impoverished, luckless men" *kṣīṇapuṇyāḥ sudurgatāḥ*: "Their greatest wealth—Rāma—has been lost, so they are 'impoverished' " (Cg), and since Rāma is gone,

the merit acquired in their previous existences must have been used up, and thus they are called "luckless" (see the note on 42.8).

"mix" *āloḍya*: As in *MBh* 4.20.33, *viṣam āloḍya pāsyāmi.*

"you shall never be heard from again" *aśrutim . . . gacchata*: That is, "die" (see the following verse; so the NR, *praṇāśam . . . anugacchata*; against Cm, Cg, Ck, and Ct, who suggest, "Go to some distant place whence not even your names ["where not even Kaikeyī's name," Ct] will be heard").

26. "than their own sons" *sutaiḥ*: Instrumental of comparison (cf. also 82.10, and Renou 1968, p. 292).

Note how the women's affection for Rāma is said to be only either maternal or sisterly (though one B manuscript reads, "as though . . . a husband had been banished"). It is as if the poet were attempting to differentiate their attitude from that of the cowherders' wives for Kṛṣṇa.

Sarga 43

2. "the frontier of the realm" *viṣayāntam*: The southern border of Kosala (but cf. note on verse 7 below).

3. "wide-spaced boundaries" *vikṛṣṭasīmāntān*: That is, the plots were large and not crowded together. Cm, Cg, Ct, Cr interpret as "exceptionally well-plowed boundaries," but this gives *vikṛṣṭa-* a sense it does not have elsewhere in the epics.

"he proceeded swiftly—though it seemed so slow" *atiyayau śīghraṃ śanair iva*: As Varadacharya remarks, Rāma's progress seemed slow because he was so zealous [to enter the Daṇḍakas and] to commence his exile (1964-1965, vol. 1, p. 453 note). Less acceptable Cm, Cg: the horses were so skilled in running and the sights of the countryside so attractive that Rāma believed himself to be going very slowly.

4. "who made their homes in the villages" *grāmasaṃvāsavāsinām*: Cg, Cm, Ct, Cr gloss, "living in villages and hamlets"; we agree with Ck, *-saṃvāsavāsin-* forming a cognate accusative construction (cf. note on 48.33).

6. "steadfast" *atandritam*: Many S manuscripts, including the recensions of Cm, Cg, Ck, Ct, Cr, read instead *jitendriyam*, "self-controlled."

7. "he passed beyond the land of Kosala" *atiyayau . . . kosalān*: This seems to indicate that the Vedaśrutī River (mentioned in the next verse) formed the southern border of Kosala (contrast 4.8.6, where the land under the jurisdiction of the Ikṣvākus seems to be much vaster). No other mention of the southern border will be made (but see note on verse 11 below).

8. "toward the region where Agastya lived" *abhimukhaḥ . . . agastyādhyuṣitāṃ diśam*: The south. Agastya was the legendary seer who brought Brahmanism to south India; Rāma encounters him in 3.10ff.

9. "its shores teeming with cows" *goyutānūpām*: The phrase furnishes something of an etymological figure (cf. note on 65.2-3) for the name Gomatī, which means literally, "rich in cows."

11. "the land . . . bestowed upon Ikṣvāku" *mahīṃ . . . dattām ikṣvākave*: The commentators are less concerned with what appears to be a contradiction between this verse (on which they remark that the Syandikā forms the southern border of Kosala), and verse 7 (see note there), as they are with the question of how Ikṣvāku could be universal emperor (*sārvabhauma*) as he indeed was, if he was given only *this* land.

They respond that Kosala was merely his home base, whereas he had rights of taxation over, and correspondingly defense obligations toward, all other kingdoms (Cg, Ck, Ct).

"vassal kingdoms" *rāṣṭra-*: The qualification "vassal" is shown to be necessary by 102.31, *anuśādhi medhinīṃ prabhūtarāṣṭrām*, "govern the earth with its . . . abundant vassal kingdoms."

12. "charioteer" *sūta iti*: Both Cg and Ct notice the absence of *saṃdhi* after *sūta*, the former claiming that phrase-*saṃdhi* is in any case not obligatory, the latter (quite plausibly) that *pluta* is present, by which *saṃdhi* would be impeded (*pluta* being *pragṛhya*); cf. note on 95.26.

"in a voice like the call of the wild goose" *haṃsamattasvaraḥ*: Ct understands as *paranipāta* for *mattahaṃsa-* (so the NR), probably rightly (cf. note on 41.27; for the simile, 76.9 and note, 104.15).

14. "(I) so (long)" *atyartham* (*abhikāṅkṣāmi*): The reading *nātyartham* ("not very much"), accepted by the crit. ed., seems to be an absurd alteration of an original *atyartham* (preserved either literally or in spirit in the NR, in D1-7, M1, G1, 2).

Since addiction to hunting later came to be considered a vice (there is no evidence the *Rām* considered it such; note that it is not included among the fourteen "errors" listed at 94.56ff.), the commentators clearly felt it necessary to alter the text in order to explain away Rāma's declaration: Rāma enjoyed hunting "not very much"; he was not so addicted to it that he neglected his other duties. But observe that Rāma's zeal for hunting is elsewhere emphasized (cf. 3.6.17ff. and notes; 4.18.36), and in a sense it is narratively essential. His one foolish act is partly a result of his enthusiasm for the chase—his going out to capture the magical deer, despite Lakṣmaṇa's sound arguments to the contrary (3.41, especially verses 29-32).

15. Cg remarks that Sumantra will later reveal these sentiments to Daśaratha, but we do not find what he is referring to.

Sarga 44

1. An SR insertion shows Rāma dismissing the villagers who had been following him (1058*).

Śṛṅgaverapura: Literally, "Ginger Town" (*śṛṅgavera*→Greek *zingiberi*→Latin *gingiber*).

2. "river that goes by three paths" *tripathagām*: The three paths of the Ganges are in heaven, on earth, and in the netherworld. See Viśvāmitra's account of the origin of the epithet in *Bālakāṇḍa* 34ff.

5. "almond tree" *iṅgudīvṛkṣaḥ*: Actually the Bengal almond or *bādām*. It is glossed "ascetic's tree" (*tāpasataru*) by the commentators, and indeed it is often mentioned in descriptions of hermitages (cf. *Śāk* 1.14, *RaghuVa* 14.81). It bears sweet-smelling nuts which are pressed for oil, and of which a cake is made to be used as an offering to the dead in 95.24 and 96.10 below.

9. "of the Niṣāda tribe" *niṣādajātyaḥ*: Or, "of the Niṣāda caste"?

"chief" *sthapatiḥ*: "Originally the political and cult chief of a semi-barbaric or nomadic tribe, who nominally at least was subordinate to a more powerful king. . . . Later the *sthapati* may have been a dependent vassal prince or governor" (Rau 1957, p. 114; cf. Hazra 1979).

The Niṣādas (see 1.2.10ff. above) were a tribe of forest-dwelling hunters and fishermen (cf. *sarga* 78 below). Other epic texts treat them in what can only be described as a racist fashion (see for example the story of Ekalavya, *MBh* 1.123.10ff.). Vālmīki's treatment, especially given his historical context, is eloquent testimony to his profound and rare humanism. Some of the commentators, by contrast, are concerned that Rāma is shown to have an intimate friendship with a man of such a "caste." Ck claims that, since the verse implies Guha's authority, and so military might, Rāma's friendship with him in the present circumstances, when an army of woodsmen would be eminently useful, is proper; and that the strictures of the lawbooks, which number associating with low castes like the Niṣādas among the minor sins [he cites *YājñaSm* 3.241] apply only to brahmans. Cg makes two observations: first, since a chief of the Niṣādas is authorized to perform vedic sacrifices [*MīmāSū* 6.8.20; the commentary of Śabara ad loc. is cited by Cg; cf. *MaiS* 2.2.4, upon which the *MīmāSū* passage is based], we infer that friendship with a Niṣāda cannot be wholly reprehensible. But he claims the true explanation is that Guha is a devotee of Rāma—his love for the Blessed One is demonstrated by 1.59* [where Cg comments that by mentioning Guha in the same verse as Lakṣmaṇa and Sītā, the poet shows that he had the same affection for Rāma as the other two]—and so is in fact a very great person, as the following verse serves to indicate: "They are not *śūdras* who are devoted to the Blessed One—they are Bhāgavata priests, as tradition shows. The real *śūdras* are people of any caste who are not devoted to Janārdana" (cf. *Dharmaśāstrasaṃgraha* p. 636, verse 22).

11. The action here involves a point of protocol: Rāma rises and goes out to Guha as a mark of respect.

12. "Guha . . . in anguish" *ārtaḥ . . . guhaḥ*: Guha's pain comes from seeing Rāma dressed in an ascetic's clothes (Cg, Cm, Ct).

14. "our kingdom is yours to rule" *rājyaṃ praśādhi naḥ*: Merely a grandiloquent invitation to accept a host's hospitality (rather than implying any real political subservience, though cf. 78.5); cf. *MBh* 2.17.10.

18. "(with . . .) your treasury" *dhaneṣu*: A number of S manuscripts and Ck, Ct instead read *vaneṣu*, "in the forests."

19. "I must . . . refuse" *anujānāmi*: For this sense of the root *jñā* + *anu* cf. 33.4 and 37.8 above.

20. Ś1 and some D manuscripts insert by way of explanation: "[I would have you know that I will be] living [as an ascetic] for fourteen years at the command of my father" (1070*). For the *kuśa* grass, cf. note on 33.14.

Ct sees here, as more obliquely in verse 9 above, the implication that Guha has knowledge of Rāma's true nature (and so is not really low-caste any more). He reasons rather circuitously: Rāma is represented as refusing the food for no other reason than because he is under a vow. If Guha did not have such knowledge [and so become casteless], then his being a Niṣāda would have been sufficient reason for Rāma not to accept the food, for it would be impure. Or again, Guha would not have brought cooked food in the first place. (Note that in 81.14-16 Guha explains that Rāma refused the food on the grounds that kshatriyas may not accept gifts.)

21. "My honored friend" *atrabhavatā*: Cg separates *atra-*, glossing it, "on this occasion."

24. Rāma drinks only water, since presence at a pilgrimage site requires one to

fast (Ct, Cr, Cs), or, he fasts because, being omniscient, he knows his father is soon to die (Cs); cf. note on 41.8.

25. "and his wife's" *sabhāryasya*: cf. 81.20. The more fastidious commentators (Cg and Cr) make a futile attempt to avoid this, the only natural interpretation.

Sarga 45

1. "wide awake" *adambhena*: Literally, "without pretence," that is, without pretending to wake while really dozing. Cs, adducing *ViśvaPra*, claims *dambha-* can have the sense of "bed," but this is unattested in the literature.

4. "by my truth I swear it" *satyenaiva . . . śape*: Cf. note on 18.13.

9. "happiness in life" *jīvitaṃ vā sukhāni vā*: A kind of hendiadys (so interpreted also by Ck, "a happy life"); cf. 18.22 and note.

10. "(Look . . .) Guha" (*paśya*) *guha*: For the inappropriate *sukha-* ("comfortably") of the crit. ed., we read the vocative *guha*, with the NR and T2. This reading is validated by manuscript testimony in 80.11 below, where the verse recurs.

11. "This" *eṣaḥ*: Cg and Ck, as several S manuscripts, read instead *iṣṭaḥ*, "[the single most] beloved [son]"; this removal of the correlative adjective makes construing verses 11 and 12 together even more likely than it at first appears (so Cr understands).

"austerities, vedic recitations, and all kinds of heavy labors" *mantratapasā . . . vividhaiś ca pariśramaiḥ*: They form the subject matter of *Bālakāṇḍa* 8-17.

13. "the din . . . has ceased" *nirghoṣoparatam*: So Cm, Cg, Ck, Ct understand, taking the compound as a *bahuvrīhi* with *paranipāta* of *uparatam* (see the note on 41.27 above; though it may be as easily an ablatival *tatpuruṣa* [Cr]). It is surely the noise of lamentation, not of blessings (Ck) that Lakṣmaṇa imagines finally to have ceased.

14. "this night" *śarvarīm imām*: It is, of course, the second night of the exile. This slight and only apparent inconsistency led Jacobi to reject *sargas* 40-43 as an interpolation (Jacobi 1893, p. 47, note 1; to prove his point he relies on what has now been shown to be an interpolation, 1058*). These temporal adverbs are often used elastically, without rigorous attention to chronology; see for example, the note on 46.34, where "today" is used of events that have happened two days earlier (and Jacobi did not consider *sargas* 44-45 an interpolation). Thus we must understand, not "this very night, the first of our exile," but "these nights."

15. "Kausalyā's sorrow is such that" *tadduḥkham yat*: The parallel passage 80.16, *duḥkhitā yā tu*, suggests strongly that *yat* is meant to introduce a result clause, and is thus translated (*pace* the commentators).

16. "with its pleasant aspect" *sukhāloka-*: Cr quite as plausibly divides *sukhā loka-*, "a happy city (that brought) its people (gladness)."

17. "that just eluded him" *atikrāntam atikrāntam*: Evidently we have here a type of repetition (*āmreḍita*) not covered by *Pā* 8.1.1ff. Three other interpretations are offered by the commentators: (having never got his wish, [crying,]) "it is gone, it is gone" (Ck, Ct, Cs); "everything will have gone," that is, will have lost its purpose, since the king will die without installing . . . (Cm, Cg); (having never got his wish) "that grew and grew" [as Rāma grew] (Cg).

18. The verse refers invidiously to Bharata and his supporters, as Ct notes. He

explains further that Lakṣmaṇa in his anger refuses to use their names. Cm, Cg interpret more charitably: fortunate the people who will be able to perform the funeral for the king—we will not have even that.

Pāda c construes with the verb in d (Cm, Ct), not as a locative absolute with *upasthiteṣu* understood (Cg).

19. Again, we should understand Bharata and his partisans as subject (Cm, Ct; not the citizens of Ayodhyā [Cr]), and the description of the city as a general, timeless one; Lakṣmaṇa envisions the city as it had always previously been, not (with Ck) as it will again become.

22. "to find him well and his promise fulfilled" *satyapratijñena sārdhaṃ kuśalinā*: This must refer to Daśaratha (so Cg), not to Rāma (Cm, Ct, Cr, Cs).

23. After this verse Ś1 and several D manuscripts insert eight attractive lines beginning "Saumitri fell to brooding [*cintām*, feminine], and sleep [*nidrā*, feminine] avoided him, as a jealous mistress, disappointed at a rendezvous, will avoid her lover," and which go on to show that Rāma did not sleep either, for "His disappointment over the loss of the kingship, his having to leave his home and repair to the forest, all three things at once had taken sleep from him" (1076*).

24. "good" *prajāhite*: Literally, "good to his subjects." The epithet is inapposite, but the commentators are silent and the manuscripts suggest no alternative. Conjecture: *prajāgrite* [or *prajāgṛte*], "kept awake," or *prajāgrati*, "waking."

"in deep compassion" *gurusauhṛdāt*: Possible too, but less probable: "friendship, affection for his guru(s)" (brother, father, etc.), construing with the locative absolute clause, "(spoken) in affection" (Cg; Cm, Ck, Ct allow both constructions).

Sarga 46

1. "good Lakṣmaṇa" *lakṣmaṇaṃ śubhalakṣaṇam*: See note on 41.16.

2. "the jet-black bird, the cuckoo" *sukṛṣṇo vihagaḥ kokilaḥ*: The commentators are curiously reluctant to allow the natural meaning, with "cuckoo" in apposition (some cuckoos being quite dark). Ct explains, "The 'jet-black bird' is the crow, and since it is the protector of the cuckoo [which lays its eggs in the crow's nest] it is referred to by the word 'cuckoo.' 'Crow' itself is not used because to speak that word in the early morning is considered unlucky" (= Cs, Cr); Cg supposes asyndeton, glossing, " 'the black bird,' that is, the skylark [*bhāradvāja*], *and* 'the cuckoo.' "

4. After this verse, the SR adds twelve lines in which Guha orders his men to bring a boat, and then informs Rāma that it is at hand (1079*; an interpolation to account for the otherwise unexplained presence of a boat in verse 61 below).

5. "strapping on their quivers and buckling on their swords" *kalāpān saṃnahya khaḍgau baddhvā ca*: Cm, Cg, Ct, Cr take *saṃnahya* absolutely, " 'strapped on,' that is, armor," and construe both the other substantives with *baddhvā* (an unusual, and unlikely, syntax).

"down to the Ganges" *yena gaṅgā*: Literally, "to where the Ganges (flowed)." The adverbial use of *yena* (frequent in Buddhist Sanskrit, cf. Edgerton 1953b s.v. ["rare in Skt. Epic"; he cites *MBh* 3.137.15]) requires the nominative, cf. 30.15 above for example. This is what Cv reports to be the correct reading, and it is adopted here in place of the crit. ed.'s *gaṅgām*. The commentators are forced to the labored explanation, "they went (there) where (people reach or cross) the Ganges" (Cg, Ck, Ct, Cr; Cm joins with the following verse, "*since* they went to the Ganges without the chariot, therefore the charioteer approached").

9. "expected" *atikrāntam*: The word is unattested in this sense, but this is how the NR appears to have interpreted (*atarkitaḥ*), and the meaning is sensible (contrast its use in 45.17). Some commentators gloss "accepted, approved" (Cg; Ck, "Sumantra means that Rāma's banishment was totally unreasonable [read '*nyāya-*] and that thus he should stay with Rāma"), but this meaning appears to be unique as well, and anyway is very weak. The other options are not acceptable: "No man . . . can *escape* [fate, by which] your living," Cm, Ct; "no man . . . could *surpass*," *Poona Dictionary* s.v. *atikrāntam*.)

10. "chastity" *brahmacarye*: Actually "studentship," but one of its principal features is strict sexual continence, as already noted (on 24.10).

For the sentiment of the verse, and its possibly significant parallelism with a later event in the book, cf. 57.32 and note.

11. "an end" *gatim*: "Fame" (Cg), "liberation" (Cm), "supreme bliss and the world of Brahmā" (Ck), "supremacy" (Ct, Cr).

12. "even you have misled us" *tvayāpy upavañcitāḥ*: Sumantra speaks both on behalf of the townsmen (cf. *sarga* 41; so Cg [the published editions of Cg's commentary misplace this statement]), as well as on his own account, for having been brought this far he was naturally led to believe he would continue on.

13. "precious to him as life" *ātmasamam*: This is better taken as an adjective referring to Rāma (cf. 44.9, 64.24) than as a substantive, "(speaking what was) fit, appropriate to him" as counselor (Cm [first explanation], Ct, Cr).

"And as he looked at Rāma, so far from home" *dṛṣṭvā dūragataṃ rāmam*: This may also mean, "seeing him [in his mind's eye] far away from him" (such is probably what Cm, Ck, Ct intend).

For this whole episode we may compare the parting scene, modeled after our passage, of the Buddha and his charioteer Chandaka in *BuddhaC* 6, which includes Chandaka's dismissal, his anguish, the message he is to deliver to the king (verse 16, " 'You [father] should not grieve for me' ") and his tearful entreaties (verse 36, "I cannot leave you as Sumantra left Rāghava").

14. "sipped water, and when he was thus purified" *spṛṣṭodakaṃ śucim*: Cf. note on 22.1 above.

16. "(That is why I tell you) this" (*tasmād*) *etad* (*bravīmi te*): We follow Cm, Ck in regarding *etat* as introducing the statement that follows; Daśaratha's "desire" is specified in the next verse.

19. "displeasure" *alīkam*: Translated in accordance with Cm, Cg, Ck, Ct (Cg cites *AmaK*).

The NR inserts some verses here in which Rāma tells the charioteer to greet Vasiṣṭha (1082*).

20. "self-controlled" *jitendriyam*: One might naturally be disposed to think it an ornamental epithet, but perhaps Rāma means to reassert, in the face of all evidence to the contrary, his father's kingly virtue (contrast however his private sentiments, 47.9 ff., but see note on 47.7).

21. "we must live" *vatsyāmaheti*: Double *saṃdhi* (expect *-maha iti*).

22. "(you shall look upon) each of us again" *punaḥ punaḥ* . . . (*drakṣyasi*): The

repetition of *punaḥ* is taken distributively (*vīpsā*, *Pā* 8.1.4; rather than iteratively, *nitya*, Cg; so too in the following verse); the construction *punar āgatān punar drakṣyasi* (Cm, Ct) will not do.

24. "ask . . . after their health" *ārogyaṃ brūhi*: "Tell, inquire after, another's health," is no doubt the true meaning of the phrase (so too, it seems, for Cm, Ck; cf. below 52.13 and note; so *kuśalaṃ brū* in 1.72.3), rather than "tell them I am well" (Ct, Cr).

"I, her noble son" *mama cāryasya*: There appears to be no way to eliminate Rāma's using this epithet in reference to himself (cf. 34.27), though Cm and Cg (who construe with *lakṣmaṇasya*), Ct ("= eldest") and a number of N and S manuscripts make the vain attempt.

25. "in office with the approval of the kings" *nṛpamate pade*: That is, installed in the office of prince regent with the (formal) approval of, presumably, the vassal kings (as Rāma was "approved" by them in *sarga* 2).

26. Cm (first explanation), Ct, Cr improbably if understandably want to take the verse as addressed directly to Sumantra (with *abhiṣicya* as simplex for causative), since to some extent it is still Sumantra's grief that is under discussion.

28. "Kaikeyī and Sumitrā" *kaikeyī sumitrā ca*: Recall Śatrughna's special position in the eyes of Bharata (cf. note on 1.17.10), which would ensure Bharata's goodwill toward Sumitrā.

After this verse (or one interpolated after it) the NR ends the *sarga* and inserts an extra one (App. I, No. 16), in which Lakṣmaṇa informs the charioteer what he for his part wishes him to tell the king: why was Rāma exiled, when he had done nothing wrong? Since Daśaratha gladly abandoned them he should not have any regrets about them, any more than an ascetic who drinks an alcoholic beverage (lines 23-24); anyway, rich and powerful people like Daśaratha never feel remorse when they consider what they have done (25-26). Rāma, predictably, tells Sumantra not to repeat to the king what Lakṣmaṇa has said (but see below the note on 52.12ff.).

32. "how (the people were)" *tathā* (*janaḥ*): *Tadā* (*janaḥ*), the reading of the crit. ed., is intolerably elliptical, for no predicate is supplied. The correct reading is no doubt preserved in T1, 3 and M3: *tathā* (for *tadā*). The idea is amplified in verses 34 and 35.

33. "only a charioteer survived" *sūtāvaśeṣam*: Cg joins the compound with *pādas* ab ("the chariot empty except for the charioteer") and understands the remainder, "like an army seeing its brave warrior slain" (*hatavīram* as *karmadhāraya* compound); Cm, (Ck?), Ct also take *svasainyam* [sic] as subject of the simile, but then need to supply *ratham* as object, "like an army seeing (the chariot) with only the charioteer . . . while all its. . . ." Both are possible interpretations; we agree with Cr, and cf. 5.17.12 *hataśūrāṃ camūm iva*, which tells against Cg's analysis.

34. A difficult verse, but as throughout this passage the idea seems to be: it was bad enough when the citizens knew you would be leaving—how much worse will it be when they realize that you are gone for good. The translation here accords to some extent with that of Cm. The alternatives (of Cg, Ct, Cr and the Mylapore editors) in one way or another turn the sense around ("though you are far away, they think of you as nearby"), but with impossible, or jejune, consequences.

"Just now" *adya*: Literally "today," but here used loosely (it happened two days ago; so at 47.26, etc.).

36-37. "And what am I to tell" *ahaṃ kiṃ cāpi vakṣyāmi*: Cm (first explanation) and Ck, because of the presence of *api* in 37a, want to understand, "Then again, I will tell your mother this . . . *even though* it is untrue; I could not say such a thing as this (namely, that I have taken you to the forest)." This agrees with Cm, Cg (second explanation), Ct, Cr. All commentators cite in support of their interpretations the famous dictum of Manu's: "One should say what is true, one should say what is pleasing; one should not give voice to an unpleasant truth [nor to a pleasant falsehood. That is the eternal way of righteousness]" (*ManuSm* 4.138).

38. "it is true" *tāvat*: Note the concessive force of the particle.

"you and your kinsmen" *tvadbandhujana-*: We follow Cm, Ck, Cr in analyzing the compound as a *dvandva*.

39. The good D manuscripts 4, 5, 7 remove this verse to the end of the speech, after verse 48 where, as Sumantra's final desperate threat, it may well have more propriety.

41. The problem here is not what the first half of the verse says, but what it really means. We are told in 34.10 that it is Daśaratha who bids Sumantra convey Rāma to the forest. Cm, Ck, Ct suggest that Sumantra was in the past a counselor, who "by or for the favor, or for the sake of" Rāma, gave up his position for that of a lowly charioteer. Cm and Ct go on to suggest that Sumantra was prompted in his decision by his knowledge of Rāma's divine nature. (Cg's first suggestion, which he seems to abandon, is to divide *-kṛte na* [Ck, who appears to do the same, is in fact misprinted], and to interpret: " 'because of you I did not have the joy of tending your chariot,' that is, after your consecration into the kingship.")

43. "the world of the gods" *devalokam*: "What the phrase suggests is that a devotee of Rāma's should abandon even the desire to attain the world of the gods, since it is an impediment to devotion," Ct.

44. "the capital of great Indra" *rājadhānī mahendrasya*: Amarāvatī, the principal city of heaven.

48. "cherished your servants" *bhṛtavatsala*: The majority of N and S manuscripts give *bhaktavatsala*, "cherished your devotees," but the crit. ed.'s decision seems correct: cf. the responsive epithet *bhartṛvatsala*, "cherish your master," in verse 50 below.

53. "This is my first consideration" *eṣa me prathamaḥ kalpaḥ*: Cg combines the three motives—Kaikeyī's conviction (verse 51), her trust in the king (52) and her obtaining the kingship—as constituting Rāma's "first consideration." But the language does not indicate this.

"that it may thrive under Bharata's protection" *bharatārakṣitaṃ sphītam*: The qualifications must be understood proleptically.

54. Most of the NR inserts a *sarga* ending here.

55. After this verse the SR for the most part adds: "I can no longer rightly live in this forest where there are people, Guha. I must live in an ashram and carry on its way of life. I must take on the vow that is the ornament of ascetics, in my desire for the welfare of my father, and again, of Sītā and Lakṣmaṇa" [commentators differ] (1091*).

"I will mat my hair" *jaṭāḥ kṛtvā*: Recall his promise to Kaikeyī (16.25 and 28), which perhaps explains why his words "were purposeful" (cf. also note on 25.7).

58. "forest hermits" *vaikhānasam*: Cg shows a keen interest in the question of whether or not Rāma actually enters wholly into the stage of life of the hermit: "If he does, then he could not reenter the householder stage, for returning to an earlier stage after one has entered a later is censured: 'He is called one who has fallen after rising' [*ārūḍhapatito hi saḥ* = *ParāSm* 2.1.373; cf. also Kane 1962-1975, vol. 4,

p. 114]. But if he does not really enter it, then as a householder who wears the matted hair and so on, which are exclusive to hermits, he becomes a renegade from his stage of life, much the same as a renegade from a vedic school. But really this dilemma does not present itself, for there is nothing contradictory in the adoption of a special vow with a definite purpose, deriving from the command of one's father—and in this way Rāma's renunciation-*dharma* approximates that of Yudhiṣṭhira and others—for Manu himself says, 'The very root of *dharma*, it is handed down, is a desire springing from a right intention' " (actually = *YājñaSm* 1.7). Ct notices that Rāma does not shave his head, either here at the Ganges or later at Prayāga, or even when he hears of his father's death; and he interprets this as a prohibition, by way of "paradigmatic narrative" [*parakṛtirūpārthavāda*], against any kshatriya's doing so.

61. "saw a boat" *dṛṣṭvā . . . nāvam*: Cf. note on verse 4 above.

62-63. The point of etiquette at issue here is not clear. Rāma tells Lakṣmaṇa to board first and *then* to help Sītā aboard (*anvakṣam*, "then," "next," is the reading of the SR only, but its very difficulty speaks in its favor; N manuscripts read *kṣipram*, "quickly," which of course solves the problem, but we still must explain how the problem could have arisen). Lakṣmaṇa does just the opposite, and the poet takes pains to justify his action. Does Rāma want Lakṣmaṇa to go first, as a token of higher respect, which Lakṣmaṇa then accords to Sītā in the belief (the correct belief, according, it would seem, to Cg) that this is what Rāma really wants him to do?

64. After this verse, the SR inserts some lines in which Rāma "prays like a brahman and a kshatriya too" [*brahmavat kṣatravac caiva jajāpa*; commentators differ] for his welfare, sips water, and bows to the Ganges (1096*).

66. "guided by the helmsman" *karṇadhārasamāhitā*: "Made ready by the helmsman," Cm, Ck, Ct; "with attentive sailors," Cg.

67. "Sītā addresses the Ganges both because it is a great divinity and a woman's divinity," Ck, Ct. One is reminded by the following scene of Hecuba's supplication of Athena, *Iliad* 6.297ff.

68. "let him carry out his instructions" *nideśaṃ pālayatv enam*: The manuscripts are almost equally divided between the readings *pālayatu* and *pārayatu* (/r/ and /l/ being nearly homophonic, as Ct points out). The latter would give, appropriately to the circumstances, "let him *cross over* [that is, fulfil] his instructions."

69. "may he return" *pratyāgamiṣyati*: The NR has the optative in place of the future, whereas Cg, Ct, Cr supply "when" or "if," making a protasis to verse 70. In the epics the future often has an optatival nuance (as translated here), though it may in the present verse intimate, not prayer or conditionality but a stubborn optimism.

70. "for making all my wishes come true" *sarvakāmasamṛddhaye*: The reading -*samṛddhaye* (marked uncertain) is that of the NR (its more natural meaning, "for the fulfilment [of all *your* desires]," is unlikely here). S manuscripts (and Cg, Ck, Ct) have -*samṛddhini*, "O you who grant all desires," or one of several other similar locutions.

72. This agrees with Cr (thus Cg, Ck, Ct also appear to construe) in joining verses 72 and 73; it is less likely that we should understand the present tenses here as future ("I shall pay").

73. "I will give the brahmans" *brāhmaṇebhyaḥ pradāsyāmi*: "Gods accept offerings by way of the brahmans," Cg.

74. "courteous" *dakṣiṇā*: Perhaps meant in part to suggest the tactfulness of Sītā's address to the Ganges, the epithet is nevertheless used principally for the figure of sound, *dakṣiṇā dakṣiṇaṃ tīram.*

76-77. "Go in front, Saumitri" *agrato gaccha saumitre*: Under more normal circumstances the elder brother would precede the younger and the woman (in 3.10.1 Rāma goes first, Lakṣmaṇa last).

"Vaidehī will come to know the pain" *duḥkham . . . vaidehī . . . vetsyati*: Recall *sarga* 25, where "the pain of living in the forest" is described.

After verse 77 (or at the end of the *sarga*) the NR inserts some twenty-three lines that mainly describe the forest and show Lakṣmaṇa collecting lotuses for Sītā (App. I, No. 17).

78. An SR insertion after this verse (1108*) shows Rāma reaching the land of the Vatsas (in the Ganges-Yamunā doab).

79. "meat" *medhyam*: This follows Ck, though the word is rarely used in this sense; alternatively, and perhaps preferably, we should read with T1, 2, G1, 3 *medhyāṃs*, "pure," that is, animals, those fit to consume; cf. 49.14, *medhyān mṛgān*, so in 50.16. In the NR substitution (1109*) the brothers kill only one beast (a dappled antelope), light a fire, cook, and along with Sītā eat the meat, and then retire for the night beneath a tree.

Finally, and with a vengeance, Rāma breaks his fast (cf. note on 41.8 above), and it is noteworthy that he does so by eating meat (cf. note on 17.15, and contrast his words to Guha in 44.19-20, and to Bharadvāja in 48.15 [but see note ad loc.]). Ct (similarly Ck) remarks, "Meat is included in 'forest fare,' so there is no fault here; nor is there any in his killing animals, since it is part of the *dharma* of hunting." Cr's gloss displays an amusing perversity: " 'He struck great animals,' that is, he knocked them about in fun and then took 'pure' food, fruits, etc."

Sarga 47

1. "Rāma, the most pleasing of men" *rāmo ramayatāṃ śreṣṭaḥ*: An etymological figure (cf. also note on 9.24).

"Prior to this, in the presence of other people, Rāma had steadfastly held in his sorrow; now, in solitude [cf. also verse 27 below], he lets it all out," Ck; contrast Cg on verse 7 below, and Ck himself on verse 10.

2. "we shall spend outside our country without Sumantra" *yātā janapadād bahiḥ / yā sumantreṇa rahitā*: *Pādas* bc form one complex idea (Cr), not two distinct ones (Cm, Ck, Ct): Rāma had already spent one night (the second night of exile, and third of the narrative) beyond Kosala—out of which he passed in *sarga* 43—in Guha's domain on the bank of the Ganges.

4. "as best we can" *kathaṃcit*: They have not yet had time to build a leaf hut and so have to sleep on the open forest ground (Ck; similarly Cm, Ct; Cg: night has come before they have had time to make a proper bed).

5. "heartfelt words" *kathāḥ śubhāḥ*: As in 15.9, 48.21 ("forthright"), 4.2.18, etc.; not "good": there is nothing "good" about the suspicions to which Rāma proceeds to give expression. The NR apparently found the adjective troublesome and so substituted, "He carried on a conversation with Sītā [cf. verse 30 below] and Lakṣmaṇa in the night."

7. Rāma anxiously wonders whether Kaikeyī, emboldened by Bharata's presence (considering how she acted even in his absence), might not assassinate the king in order to secure her son's coronation, not merely as prince regent, but as *mahārāja* (Cm, Ck, Ct; cf. 52.16 below), or in order to stabilize his position (Cg). In the next verse, however, Rāma says that the king will be able to do nothing about Kaikeyī's actions, and in verse 12 it is said that Bharata will be sole head of state because the king is "on in years." Daśaratha's passion surely cannot be so overpowering that he would not defend himself from a murder attempt (the NR felt the need to affirm this, however: "He would pay no heed to his own life, since he is under the power of Kaikeyī" [1114*]). Perhaps we have an ancient corruption of some sort that has substituted *prāṇān* for an original *sthānāt*: Kaikeyī will try to "drive him from his place," that is, to dethrone him (cf. 58.20, 1.31.17 for the idiom).

Cg comments that Rāma's invidious supposition might be thought to contradict his own admonition later to Lakṣmaṇa not to speak ill of Kaikeyī (3.15.34-35 and note there, and compare also 97.17-18 below); but in fact Rāma is only playing on Lakṣmaṇa's own fears, in hopes of convincing him to return (verse 16).

10. Ck (like Cg on verse 7) claims that Rāma does not really believe what he is saying here—he knows full well that Daśaratha loves him more than life itself and sent him into exile only under the compulsion of his promise—but only wants to inspire Lakṣmaṇa to return (or, according to Ct on the following verse, to find out what Lakṣmaṇa is really thinking; cf. note on 23.23, and 27.26 and note).

12. "with father well on in years" *tāte ca vayasātīte*: Since Rāma has already conjectured (according to the crit. ed.) that Kaikeyī might murder Daśaratha, it seems gratuitously inconsistent to translate "with father dead of old age" (as PW s.v. *ī* + *ati*); the translation offered is supported by Cr. A possible alternative: "with father passed over, ignored, because of his age."

13. A gnomic statement (so Cr), rather than, as Ct takes it, one meant to refer specifically to Bharata (cf. 4.37.20-21).

14. "came among us" *saṃprāptā*: The NR replaces the vague locution with "was born" or "was married."

18. "You must commit" *paridadyāḥ*: Ck, Ct, Cr read instead, "She might give poison to your mother or to mine."

19. "by my mother's doing . . . (and so this has happened) to her" *jananyā*: This construes with both halves of the verse, and probably as genitive rather than instrumental.

21. "one who parts her hair" *sīmantinī*: A general designation of "woman"; Indian women as a rule part their hair down the center. The verse, the first line at least, is a very old one, appearing also in the *Vidurāputra* episode of the *MBh* (5.131.28), on the antiquity of which see Jacobi 1903, pp. 53-55 (not later than the fourth century B.C.)

22. "even her myna bird is a greater source of joy than I" *prītiviśiṣṭā sā mattaḥ* . . . *sārikā*: The myna, like Rāma, was raised and taught to speak by Kausalyā, but unlike him the bird is there to cry out (or, does not hesitate to cry out) in the woman's defense. The "enemy" can be that of the birds (such as a cat [Cm, Cg, Ct; similarly Cnā on CSS 2.52.24]), or more probably Kausalyā's (that is, Kaikeyī [Cg, Ck, Cr]). Mynas were often kept with parrots; the two are associated in *ManuSm* 5.12, *BhāgP* 5.24.9, and cf. especially *KāmSū* 1.3.15, where forty-third among the sixty-four arts is teaching mynas and parrots to speak.

Cg has a long theological comment on this verse from the viewpoint of Teṅgalai

Vaiṣṇavism, and it is worth summarizing. What the verse (allegorically) states, he argues, is that resorting to a teacher is a more efficacious means of salvation than even worshiping the Blessed One. This is suggested as follows: The teacher is represented in the verse by the bird (the myna), the teacher having two possible philosophical "positions" (*pakṣa-*)—action or knowledge—corresponding to the bird's two wings (*pakṣa-*); the feminine gender (*sārikā*) is meant to indicate dependence on [and so difference from] the Blessed One, for "everything besides [the Supreme Primal Man, that is, Viṣṇu-Kṛṣṇa] is feminine" (*strīprāyam itarat sarvam*); and it serves to show that in comparison with the Blessed One a teacher is an even more effective means of producing the "bliss" of liberation. The teacher is the "one from whom can be heard the word," the secret *mantra* passed down through the succession of gurus; and this word is: "O parrot" (the parrot, being of the same blue color as Viṣṇu, is equated with Viṣṇu), "bite the enemy's foot," that is, destroy the basis of man's great enemy, transmigration. The teacher from whom this is heard (says Rāma) "is greater . . . than I" [is better than Viṣṇu]. Cg goes on to read the whole episode (*sargas* 40ff.) as an allegory of this idea, man's quest for liberation: One leaves (Ayodhyā =) Vaikuṇṭha, Viṣṇu's heaven; crosses (the Ganges =) the Virajā River in heavenly Gokula; enters the forest (of transmigration); betakes oneself with one's individual soul to (a tree =) the body; eats, that is, experiences the fruits of one's *karma*; longs for a wise teacher [= Bharadvāja?], and finally comes to the certainty that of the four spiritual paths [*karmayoga*, *jñānayoga*, *bhaktiyoga* and *ācāryaniṣṭhā* or absolute confidence in one's teacher] the last one is the superlative means of release [= reaching Citrakūṭa?].

25. "force is useless" *vīryam akāraṇam*: Ck, Ct, "that is, in effecting what is beneficial for the world to come; only *dharma* can do that"; Cg, "Force should not be resorted to in order to effect something that would cause the loss of *dharma*."

26. "what other people might say" *paralokasya*: We agree with Cs's analysis (= *parakīyajanam*), which is clearly substantiated by the NR (1122*, *lokavāda-*); cf. 19.7 and note. Cs specifies further that the "danger of unrighteousness" is that, if Rāma does not follow his father's command, no one else will obey his own father [or the king]; cf. Rāma's own words in 101.9 and note there.

27. Cm, Ct, Cs try to explain away Rāma's lamentation and/or weeping, either as (literally) the histrionic performance of god in a human incarnation, or (if real) as being sympathy felt for his loved ones and not sorrow on his own account (cf. the notes on 2.28 and 16.57).

28. After this verse most of the NR inserts four lines, wherein Lakṣmaṇa says that people like Rāma should not grieve, and in any case the calamity is not really to be counted a calamity, but rather a blessing, since through it Rāma has learned how much affection the people have for him (1123*; a few manuscripts go on to show how this is so: "No one feels sorry for an evil man in misfortune . . . but since you are lauded even in misfortune . . . " 1124*).

30. "to (no) avail" *aupāyikam*: This agrees with Ck; Cg, Cm, Ct, Cr on the authority of *AmaK* gloss "right" (*yuktam*): because he is a "bull among men" it is not "proper" for him to grieve.

32. "(I would not care) to see" (*na* . . .) *draṣṭum* (*iccheyam* . . . *aham*): "Much less to go and protect them," Cm, Ct. Lakṣmaṇa speaks here, as in the preceding verse, in response not to Rāma's remonstrance against feeling "sad" or homesick (verse 2; so Cg, Ck, Ct, Cr take it), but to his order to return (Cm).

33. "at last, recognizing it as the way of righteousness" *prapadya dharmaṃ sucirāya*:

Cm, Cg, Ck, Ct all interpret this as "having betaken himself to the *dharma* of a forest hermit for a long time to come," which is acceptable for the Sanskrit, but makes little sense in the present context. Cs is somewhat better, " 'having accepted *dharma*' that is, that of his [Lakṣmaṇa's] obedience to himself." For *pra* + *pad* in the sense of "give in, admit, recognize," cf. 82.27 below.

"considerately gave him permission to live in the forest" *vanavāsam ādarāt* . . . *vidadhe*: Cm, Ck, Ct by a most unlikely syntax make the adverb and the substantive dependent on *vacaḥ*, "words (spoken) considerately about living in the forest." Cg, on the other hand, "After considerately listening . . . he was prepared to undergo (?) life in the forest," *vidadhe* as conative perfect (the simple past being impossible, as he sees), apparently in the sense "to undergo." The other commentators including Cs gloss the main verb as translated here.

Sarga 48

2. "the place where . . . the river Ganges" *yatra* . . . *gaṅgā* . . . *taṃ deśam*: Prayāga. The majority of manuscripts and the vulgate have, "where the Yamunā meets the Ganges" (glossed, "where the Yamunā starts, at the Ganges," Cm, Ck, Ct ["a locution meant to suggest the extreme holiness of the Ganges," Ct]).

3. "glorious (party)" *yaśasvinaḥ*: This probably refers to Rāma and the others, rather than to the places ("so called because their inhabitants were honored [by Rāma's visit]" Cg), or to "sages famous for their austerities" (Cr).

5. Agni: The god of fire. The smoke Rāma sees is that of the evening fire-offering (cf. verse 11).

7. "around [Bharadvāja's] ashram" *bharadvājāśrame*: Ct and Cr read instead *chinnāś cāpy āśrame*, "(trees) at the ashram that have been hewn off" (not recorded in the crit. ed.). Forest hermits and their dependents are often represented as cultivating trees, and so the hermitage would stand out distinctly from the surrounding wild forest.

8. "bearing their bows" *dhanvinau*: It is indeed curious that Rāma and Lakṣmaṇa carry their weapons into the sacred precinct (Bharata will deposit his before entering, 84.2; cf. *Śāk* 1.14.6 for one good example among many of disarming before entering an ashram). Similarly 3.1.9. *Dhanvinau* could also, of course, be a static epithet—"the two bowmen"—but even so we should expect some mention of their laying down their weapons before entering; in the NR interpolation 1131* Rāma is explicitly said to be armed, and then again, it is precisely because of this, say Ck and Ct, that he is said to frighten the animals in the next verse. The oddity of Rāma's bearing weapons is heightened by his ascetic clothing and matted hair; other characters later in the story will specifically refer to this antinomy—Virādha, for example (3.2.11), and Śūrpaṇakhā (3.16.11); note also the emphatic statement of the *MBh*: "(Rāma) had all the marks of an ascetic (and yet) was bearing a bow" (3.261.37). In fact, these references seem to invite us to a repeated consideration of the self-contradictory nature of Rāma, one in whom the ethos of a kshatriya and of a renunciatory brahman are fused (see note on 16.59, the insertion noted above on 46.64, and the Introduction, Chapter 10).

10. "stood some distance off" *dūrād evāvatasthatuḥ*: They stand at a distance either

to wait until the fire-sacrifice is completed (Cg), or to receive permission before entering (Ck, Ct). The NR and the SR each inserts its own verse describing the entrance of the sage (1132*, 1133*).

15. "we are to enter" *pravekṣyāmaḥ*: A number of both N and S manuscripts read the singular ("I am to enter . . . ," etc.) in part or throughout.

"the way of righteousness" *dharmam*: Here surely the *dharma* of forest hermits (Ck, Ct, Cr), not that of guarding his father's command (Cg).

"living only on roots and fruit" *mūlaphalāśanāḥ*: Rāma again professes his vegetarianism, though he has eaten meat (46.79) and will do so again (49.14). (The suggestion of Varadacharya [1964-1965, vol. 1, p. 503n] that " 'roots and fruit' is a general designation for unrefined food" seems implausible.) It may well be that the dietary restrictions come into play only when Rāma is actually in the grove of asceticism, not while he is traveling through the forest, for at no time after he reaches Mount Citrakūṭa do we see him eating meat (though cf. the interpolated passages noticed in the notes to 89.19 and 90.1, and cf. notes to 3.42.21 and 45.19).

16. "presented him with a cow" *upānayata . . . gām*: The cow, according to Cg, Cm, Ct, Cr, is required to provide (according to Ck it means) the *madhuparka*, the offering of curds and honey or butter which is to be given to "one who studies the *vedas*, a teacher, a priest, a religious student completing his studies [*snātaka*] or a righteous king" (thus a *smṛti* text cited by Cg and Ck ad loc.); or is it in fact, by the ancient custom, the cow to be slain in honor of a guest, especially a king (according to *AitBr* 3.4)?

17. "with deer and birds" *mṛgapakṣibhiḥ*: Some commentators join the phrase with "showed . . . hospitality," Cm rather fancifully explaining, "By the sage's power they were no longer animals, and being thus no different from the sages they realized that Rāma was the lord, and served him, too" (similarly Cg).

19. "at last I see" *cirasya . . . paśyāmi*: One might naturally have understood the verse to mean, "Since long ago have I [fore-]seen [that is, by his *jñānacakṣu* or "eye of wisdom"] . . . (and I have [recently] heard)," but no commentator supports this. In 6.112.14 Bharadvāja knows by means of his ascetic power everything that has happened (as does Agastya, 3.12.15).

23. Cm offers a long theological interpretation here, claiming that the real meaning of verses 22-23 is that Rāma is requesting the sage not to reveal his divine nature (criticized vigorously by Ct as philologically and contextually unsound).

24. "in a way that carried conviction" *vākyam arthagrāhakam*: Literally, "words that convinced with their sense." This seems to be the meaning of *grāhaka-* in the only other instances of its use in the *Rām* tradition (Book 4. App. I, No. 19.24; 4.1325*; Ck, Ct, "that informed him of the requirement he had spoken of"; Cg, "full of meaning").

25. "twenty miles" *daśakrośa*: Literally, "ten *krośas*." A *krośa* (Hindi *kos*) is the farthest distance one can hear another shout—a little more than two miles. The compound is accusative of extent of space. (Ck, Ct take *daśakrośa* as locative, Cm, Cg as nominative, "[situated] ten *krośas* away.")

26. "Langurs . . . monkeys and apes" *golāṅgūla- . . . vānararkṣa-*: For the zoological problems see note on 1.16.10. "By his mentioning just these three types of animals we understand Bharadvāja to be hinting that Rāma's only companions [in the later books of the *Rām*] will be creatures of this sort," Cg.

"Mount Gandhamādana": A name of at least two different mountains; here, it probably refers to the one included among the seven chief mountains (*kulaparvata*) of Bhāratavarśa, which is also called Ṛkṣavat or Ṛkṣaparvata ("Monkey-mountain").

27. "meditates" *samādhatte*: Perhaps also, "acquires" (Cg, Cr), or, "undertakes" (Cg).

28. "hundred autumns" *śaradāṃ śatam*: The proverbial span of human life (cf. note on 8.9).

"skull-white heads" *kapālaśirasā*: According to PW the B recension [= Gorresio] reads *kalāpaśirasā* (not recorded in the crit. ed.). The word is unique, and its signification uncertain. We take it as an (inverted) simile compound, attributive in function, the singular being collective (*upameyasamāsa, upalakṣaṇe tṛtīya jātyekavacanam*), that is to say, close to Ck, Ct. It may be useful to list the suggestions of, or reported by, the commentators:

> 1. "with head(s) like skull(s)"—for example, of men dead by famine—that is to say, "white"; they ascended to heaven by austerities that were full, performed throughout their lives, even in old age (Ck, Ct). 2. "with head(s) reduced to skull(s)," skin and hair having been rubbed away by continuous yogic headstands performed in the course of austerities (Crā, Cm, Cg). 3. "skull-head" connotes, or we are to supply, "body"; they ascended to heaven with their bodies (Cv, Cg, Cm; Ck, Ct dispute this: "but the body is not worthy of heaven; even Rāma, Yudhiṣṭhira, and so on went only a little way with their bodies—and only to demonstrate the power of their *dharma*—and then abandoned them before entering heaven, where they took on heavenly bodies"; but cf. the bodily ascensions mentioned in 102.10 and especially 4.13.18). 4. attributive of *tapasā*, that is, austerities in or from which "their head(s) were left nothing but skull(s)" (Cg). 5. proper name of a seer (Cm, Cg; = D3-5, 7 in 1147*). 6. Śiva (to be construed with *pāda* b, "Śiva waits there continually in order to see Rāma . . . and this intimates that he is most enamored of Rāma," Cr).

33. "Last night" *śarvarīm . . . adya*: An idiom, cf. 56.14 and note, 66.8 and note.

"we made our dwelling here" *uṣitāḥ . . . vasatim*: *Vasatim* with the root *vas* forms a cognate accusative construction (cf. for example, 33.5 above, *vāsam . . . vasataḥ*); grammar and sense argue against construing *vasatim* with *anujānātu*, as Cm, Cg, Ck, Ct, Cr all would have it.

36. "lapwing" *koyaṣṭika-*: So Ingalls 1965, p. 573, though, as this is a water bird (cf. also 3.71.11), we might not expect to find it on a mountain.

Sarga 49

2. After this verse the SR inserts a *śloka* in which the party is directed to go to the confluence of the Ganges and Yamunā, and follow the Yamunā where it flows westward (deflected by the Ganges) (1160*).

3. Kālindī: The Yamunā.

"the daughter of the sun" *aṃśumatī*: We follow Cm, Cg (who divide *āṃśu-*), Ck (on verse 11 below), Ct, Cr in their explanation. The Yamunā's descent from the sun is narrated at *HariVaṃ* 8.6-7. However, as an epithet for a river the word is as old as the *ṚV* (8.85.13), and here may mean simply "radiant."

4. Śyāma: We agree with Cm, Cg (first explanation), and Ct in taking this as the proper name of the tree here and in verse 12 below. This is corroborated both by Kālidāsa, *RaghuVa* 13.53, *vaṭaḥ śyāma iti pratītaḥ*, "the banyan tree known as Śyāma," and by Bhavabhūti, *UttaRāC* (after 1.23), *kālindītaṭe vaṭaḥ śyāmo nāma*, "the banyan tree on the bank of the Kālindī named Śyāma."

Both the NR and the SR (no manuscript excepted) insert hereafter one verse (1164*, 1165*), in which the sage says that Sītā should make a wish before the tree (cf. verse 13 below; the tree is named *satyābhiyācana*, "Granter-of-Wishes" in the NR, 1163* and 1177*; cf. below 62.12).

7. "How fortunate we are" *kṛtapuṇyāḥ*: cf. above note on 42.8.

10. "she was half embarassed" *īṣatsaṃlajjamānāṃ tām*: Her embarassment comes from grasping the hand of her beloved, and from the necessity of having to do so (Cg).

An SR insertion after this verse shows Sītā praying to the Yamunā (1173*, especially 5-8), much as she did to the Ganges.

14. "ate" *ceratuḥ*: So Cm, Cg, Ck, Ct. Note that curiously Rāma and Lakṣmaṇa are once again said to hunt and eat alone (cf. 46.79 above).

Sarga 50

1. "but straightway" *anantaram*: Literally, "afterwards," that is, immediately after Lakṣmaṇa had fallen asleep. Differently the commentators: "afterwards," that is, after Rāma himself had awakened (Cm, Cg, Ct).

Ct remarks that the popular belief that Lakṣmaṇa spent the entire fourteen years of exile without eating or sleeping is laid to rest by this verse. (Lakṣmaṇa is said to remain awake throughout the fourteen-year period in the Telugu *Dvipada Rāmāyaṇa* of Raṅganātha, sung in Andhra Pradesh).

The day now beginning is the seventh of the narrative, and more importantly for the coming action, the sixth of Rāma's exile (for the latter, the chronological signposts are found in *sargas* 40, 45, 47-50).

2. "Let us be off . . . it is time" *saṃpratiṣṭhāmahe kālaḥ*: Ct reports the reading (not recorded in the crit. ed.) *saṃpratīkṣāmahe kālam* (he explains, "we know it is time").

4. "sipped . . . water" *spṛṣṭvā . . . jalam*: This connotes the performance of all the obligatory morning rituals, bathing, etc. (Cg, Cm, Ct).

7. "in bloom" *phullān*: All but four manuscripts read instead *bilvān*, "bael" or Bengal quince, a plausible lection, for this is a medicinally valuable tree, like the marking-nut, and "one of the most useful . . . of Indian trees. A gum is obtained from the stem. A mucous is obtained chiefly from the fruit which is used as a cement . . . it is also used as a soap substitute. The fresh ripe fruit is eaten" (McCann 1959, p. 122).

"I shall be able to live" *śakṣyāmi jīvitum*: Most S manuscripts and the earliest commentators read the plural, "we shall be able" (the NR has the impersonal passive, 1192*).

8. "buckets" *droṇa-*: The word signifies not only a container but also a measure (of weight or liquid), which is how the commentators take it here ("filled with honey to the measure of a *droṇa*" [a little more than 21 pounds; cf. Kane 1962-1975, vol.

3, p. 145n], Cm, Cg, Ck, Ct). The image of bucket-like honeycombs appears elsewhere in the *Rām* (cf. 6.4.59).

9. "moorhen" *natyūhaḥ*: *Dātyūhaḥ* is the more common spelling of the name (so read here in the NR); it appears in this form in 4.1.14.

10. The fourfold anaphora of *paśya* ("look") in verses 6, 7, 8, 10 lends a quality of almost childlike excitement to Rāma's description.

11. The NR twice (verse 9cd v.l.; 1197*) indicates the party's proximity to the Mandākinī River (probably not the Ganges; cf. note on 86.11); cf. note on verse 22 below.

12. "he said": The commencement of direct discourse here is in fact uncharacteristically and jarringly left unmarked. The NR eliminates the problem, which is contained also in the vulgate.

An SR insertion within this verse mentions the sages who live on the mountain (1198*.4), and a later one (1200*, a particularly inept interpolation) shows the party going to greet one of them, who turns out to be none other than Vālmīki himself. The commentators show no surprise at this, but are interested only in the fact that in the *Bālakāṇḍa* (2.3) Vālmīki is said to live on the banks of the Tamasā. They reconcile the two accounts by asserting that Vālmīki first lived on Citrakūṭa and moved to the Tamasā when he composed the *Rām*, after Rāma became king (Cm, Cg, Ck; Ct dissents: the truth, he says, is that this is some other Vālmīki than the son of Pracetas and author of the *Rām*).

13. "Fetch wood" *ānaya dārūṇi*: It is probably because ascetics are not supposed to cut down trees (cf. note on 25.7) that the NR specifies, "trees broken by elephants" (1201*). It also indicates that two houses were constructed (1201*, 1202*), possibly, as Vaidya suggests (1962, p. 698), one for Rāma and Sītā, and one for Lakṣmaṇa (cf. 93.4 and note; in 86.12, *parṇakuṭī*, we no doubt have a singular rather than dual).

14. In an insertion after this verse, the NR shows Sītā smearing the house with fragrant earth (1203*).

15. No manuscript presents this succession of half-verses, which actually leaves the subject of the verse unidentified.

"to our hut" *śālām*: That is, to the tutelary deities of the hut. The SR expands Rāma's words with remarks on the *vāstuśānti* (1206*), the rite performed upon entering a new house, by the power of which, according to the *BrahmāṇḍP*, "one no longer fears disease, one's kinsmen do not perish, one will live a hundred years as though in heaven" (cited by Cg). The interpolation goes on (line 3) to assert that the sacrificial injunction they will be following—namely, animal sacrifice—is envisaged by *śāstra* (and so no crime of violence will attach to them, Cm, Ck, Ct). No extant *gṛhyasūtra* authorizes animal sacrifice for *vāstuśānti*. Note that the ceremony performed at the construction of their hut at Pañcavaṭī (3.14.23) consists of an offering of flowers. The tutelary deities to be propitiated are, according to Cm, forty-six in number (Ct, fifty), including the rain god, the fire god, etc. (or, Kāma at the bedstead, Space at the threshold, etc. [Cg, Ck]).

18. "The black deer has been roasted black" *ayaṃ kṛṣṇaḥ . . . śṛtaḥ kṛṣṇamṛgo yathā*: Or, "It has been roasted black and looks just like the black deer itself" (this on the assumption that Lakṣmaṇa skinned the animal before cooking it).

"with all its limbs intact" *samāptāñgaḥ*: The sacrificial animal was apparently immolated whole, head and all, something not encountered elsewhere in Sanskrit literature.

19. Both the SR and the NR expand the ceremony, the former with the intonation of vedic hymns, offerings to the Viśvadevas, Rudra, and Viṣṇu, etc. (1210*), the latter with offerings of grains to the ancestors and an offering to the *bhūtas* or spirits (2111*).

No manuscript appears to have the sequence of half-verses offered by the crit. ed. for verse 19, and indeed the repetition of Rāma (deleted in the translation) is suspicious.

"for averting evil" *pāpasaṃśamanam*: The "evil" is specified as either savage creatures that stalk the day and night (Cg), or the five dangers of the householder mentioned in *ManuSm* [3.68-71] (that is, the five "slaughter-houses"—the hearth, the grinding stone, the broom, the mortar and pestle, and the water-pot; by using these a householder runs the risk of incurring sin, against which he can protect himself by sacrifice—Cg, Ck).

After this verse the NR has Rāma and Lakṣmaṇa eat the leavings of the sacrifices, and Sītā their leavings (1212*), whereas the SR shows Rāma constructing religious structures of a dimension appropriate to the ashram (altar sites, a *caitya* or shrine), and placating the *bhūtas* with fruit and the like (1213*).

21. "wild animals" *vyālamṛga-*: This appears to be the true sense of the compound in the *Rām*. Cg takes *vyāla-* as elephants (possible, cf. 5.46.16) or snakes (impossible).

"all the while holding their senses under control" *jitendriyāḥ*: Cg notes that the phrase is significant: their pleasure on the mountain was of a quite different order from the vulgar pleasures most people enjoy in the country— swimming, gathering flowers, and so on (the phrase is eliminated in the NR).

22. The NR again (cf. note on 11 above) names the river Mandākinī, substituting for the otherwise unknown Malyāvatī. It has evidently preserved the correct reading here, cf. 86.11.

The three successive lyric meters, verses 20-22, serve to bring to a close this movement, as it were, of the narrative symphony. We should observe with what sense of contentment Rāma settles down to his rustic life, and how it is able to make him forget the attractions of the city. As mentioned in the Introduction, here (and elsewhere) in the *Rām* the tension between town and country is intimated perhaps for the first time in Sanskrit literature, although it becomes something of a commonplace in the later literary texts.

Sarga 51

1. With this *sarga* we pick up the action three days prior to the close of the previous one (that is, the fourth day from the beginning of the narrative and the third since Rāma left Ayodhyā). An SR insertion after this verse (1218*) reads, "Their visit to Bharadvāja, their stay at Prayāga, their going up to Citrakūṭa was reported by those there." The commentators take this to mean that Sumantra was informed—whether by Guha's scouts or others is not clear—of the progress of Rāma's journey. The motivation behind this interpolation is unclear, for Sumantra will make no use later (*sargas* 52-53) of the intelligence he is here supposed to have received. Daśaratha

has no precise idea where Rāma is (53.20, 21), nor has Sumantra or Bharata later in their search for Rāma (78.12, 84.18). For the commentators' remarks here on the chronology of the narrative, see the note on verse 4 below.

2. "Given leave to depart" *anujñātaḥ*: Either by Guha (Cm, Cg, Ct, Cr) or by Rāma (Ck).

4. "on the third day at dusk" *sāyāhnasamaye tṛtīye 'hani*: Sumantra returns "on the third day," that is, two and one-half days after being dismissed by Rāma. There is no reason to believe that it took Sumantra any longer than Rāma to make the journey between Ayodhyā and Śṛṅgaverapura, that is to say, one and one-half to two days (note that he proceeds "directly" and "speeds along," 51.2-3). The commentators, especially Ck, clearly show their sense of the need for uniformity in the two travel periods, for three of them, and two of the manuscripts, change the text here to read that Sumantra arrived "on the second day." But this leaves us with one extra day. If we now read with the NR in 53.3b that Sumantra spent "one day" with Guha—and there is no reason not to, for unquestionably the SR reading that has Sumantra spend "many days" with him depends exclusively on the athetized verse 1218* noted above on verse 1—our chronology is perfect: Rāma leaves Śṛṅgaverapura on the third day since his departure from Ayodhyā; Sumantra, waiting one day and traveling for two, returns three days after leaving Rāma, late on the afternoon of what must then be the sixth day of Rāma's exile. And in fact in 56.14, a scene that takes place on the evening of Sumantra's arrival, we shall be told that five nights of Rāma's exile have already passed (that is, it is the evening of the sixth night); and in 57.3, also on the same evening, that it is the sixth night since his exile. (These data find confirmation in the *PadmaP* [cited by Ct. This verse is not found in the Nāgarī vulgate of the text; presumably it is contained in the Bengali recension, which is unavailable to us].) The commentators, given their corrupt text, are adrift here.

The whole scene of Sumantra's return and the lamentation in the palace (*sargas* 51ff.) has been closely adapted by Aśvaghoṣa in *BuddhaC* 8.

6. After this verse several D manuscripts add that the people lost their minds when they saw just one man in the chariot (cf. 46.32) (1224*).

9. "have crossed the river" *tīrṇāḥ*: So all the commentators. Possible, too: "(realizing that) they (themselves, the people) had been overpowered" (that is, by fate; for the use of the verb, cf. 47.25); or, "(realizing that) they (themselves, the people) had (in fact) been deceived" (*tīrṇāḥ* abbreviated for *pratīrṇāḥ*, as in 1.34 above, *amanyata* for *anvamanyata*).

10. "we shall not see Rāghava here again" *neha paśyāma iti rāghavam*: The *iti* probably closes off the statement of one group of people, as Cm, Ct, Cr appear to take it; it is difficult to make it a causal adverb: "we who . . . are *therefore* lost" (with Cg).

11. "We shall . . . show ourselves" *drakṣyāmaḥ*: We explain this verbal form as (future) passive, or rather reflexive, with active termination, cf. 57.16 (and Sen 1949, pp. 102-103, though he neglects to note this example).

"since . . . Rāma will not be there" *rāmam antarā*: The NR understands the phrase in its correct sense (*vinā tam*, 1227*); *antarā* cannot be taken absolutely ("[We shall never again see Rāma] in [our] midst, among [us],") nor in construction with the distant locatives (with Cm, Cg, Ck, Ct, Cr).

Cg suggests that Rāma's presence at all these events is in order to present gifts, make corrections of any lapses in the ceremonies, and so on.

12. "pondering what was advantageous" *kiṃ samartham*: False are Cm, Ck, Ct (similarly Cr), "The city, which had been watched over . . . became worried, thinking 'what will be advantageous (from now on).' " The NR sufficiently clarifies the construction intended (1228*: *iti cintayatā tena*).

13. "inner shops" *antarāpaṇam*: Apparently shops inside of houses rather than stalls open on the street (Schlingloff 1969, p. 8, n. 7); the word is in compound with *anu*. The NR tries variously to supply the women's statements (1229*, 1230*, where Sumantra is called "shameless" or "hopeless").

14. "Sumantra covered his face" *sumantraḥ pihitānanaḥ*: Covering one's face appears to be not so much a way to avoid being seen as a response to embarrassing or mortifying criticism, here presumably the women's abuse (cf. *HariVaṃ* 63.14, though in *MBh* 2.71.3 Yudhiṣṭhira is said to cover his face lest he accidently cast the evil eye; Cg guesses, "he does so because he could not bear the sight of the people").

15. "crowded with men of importance" *mahājanasamākulāḥ*: Perhaps, as Cg suggests, as a result of the fact that the king has not been coming out (to transact royal business).

16. "hushed" *mandam*: Because of the presence of the king? (Cm, Ck, Ct).

18. "no easier to die" *na sukaram*: Literally, "to put an end (to life)"; cf. the NR v.l. *sumaram*, which may well be original (cf. *durmaram . . . aprāpte kāle*, "it is impossible to die before one's appointed hour," *MBh* 11.20.22, also *MBh* 8.1.21, and cf. *MBh* 14.60.9, where *durmaram* is replaced in the SR with *duṣkaram*). The inability to die except at one's fated moment is continually asserted throughout the *Rām* (see 17.30, 34.5; 5.23.12, 26.3, etc.).

"despite" *ācchidya*: See PW s.v. The only other example in the *Rām* (aside from the interpolated 557*.5) is 6.23.15, which may be similar (*mayācchidya*, "in spite of me"). The whole verse is admittedly difficult, but the commentators do not persuade us to translate otherwise (Cg: "Just as I think my own life is difficult to live, so surely it is not easy [*na sukaram*] that Kausalyā continues stubbornly [*ācchidya* = *prasahya*; so Cm] to live"; similarly Cs, Ck, save that for the latter and Ct, Cr, *ācchidya* = "[when her son left] abandoning [the consecration]"; Cm tautologically, "that she lives . . . is surely difficult; such a life is not easy").

20. "pale white chamber" *pāṇḍare gṛhe*: Cg claims that the qualification is meant to indicate that the splendor of royalty has disappeared.

26. With Ck, Ct, the first half of the *śloka* is taken as a question.

"set things right" *sukṛtaṃ te 'stu*: This is the most reasonable way to understand the phrase, considering the other instances of *sukṛtam* in our text (cf. 53.18, 58.1, 103.29, etc.). Cm, Ck, Ct: "You have your good deed," that is, you have kept your word, what are you afraid of (so, too, Varadacharya 1964-1965, vol. 2, p. 8n). But this interpretation requires us to invest the words with a sarcasm uncharacteristic of the poet.

"Grief will render you no aid" *śoke na syāt sahāyatā*: A formula (cf. Lüders 1940, pp. 103-104; he cites parallels from Buddhist *gāthā* literature), but usually spoken in a tone of solace rather than of anger, as apparently here.

Sarga 52

1. "had revived and recovered from his faint" *pratyāśvastaḥ . . . mohāt pratyāgataḥ*: The tautology is irremediable. The glosses on *pratyāgataḥ* by Cg (" 'he went' toward the charioteer") and Cm ("[he summoned the charioteer] 'who had come' [from Rāma]") are fruitless attempts to cure it.

2. The SR (by reason of "interpolation") and the NR (through a different reading) refer this verse not to the charioteer but rather to the king. Nonetheless the crit. ed. may be correct: the simile of the captured beast nicely describes Sumantra in his predicament of having to speak a painful truth (cf. above 46.36-37 and note).

4. With Cs we take the futures here as present (cf. note on 4.21).

6. "Wild animals" *vyālamṛgaiḥ*: Cf. note on 50.21 (Cm, Cg, Ct, Cr gloss the compound "boas").

8. "as the two Aśvins . . . onto Mount Mandara" *aśvināv iva mandaram*: The point of comparison in the simile here, say Ck and Ct, is the blackness of the mountain (corresponding to that of the forest), but this is uncharacteristically vapid for Vālmīki. Varadacharya suggests isolating *mandaram* from the simile ("handsome as the two Aśvins") and understanding it adverbially (= *mandam*): being delicate and unused to the forest, they would enter it "slowly" (1964-1965, vol. 2, p. 11n). The NR reads instead, "like Nara and Nārāyaṇa" (1251*).

9. After this verse the SR rather movingly adds, "I shall live on this, as Yayāti [when he fell from heaven and attained some consolation by falling] among good men" (1253*) (cf. note on 11.1; when Yayāti fell from heaven, he came down among his grandsons, who ultimately saved him).

10. "in a sob-choked and breaking voice" *sajjamānayā . . . vācā . . . bāṣpaparirabdhayā*: Cs suggests taking this *apo koinou*, with both *coditaḥ* ("pressed") and *uvāca* ("answered").

11. "Rāghava . . . bowed his head" *rāghavaḥ . . . śirasābhipraṇamya*: Apparently because they feel there is some impropriety in having Rāma bow to the (presumably) lower-caste charioteer, Cm, Ck, Ct ignore word order and interpret, "Rāghava in his solicitude . . . said, 'Cupping your hands . . . and bowing your head' " [to be construed with verse 12]. It may be that, reading the verse naturally, we are to picture Rāma adopting with Sumantra the posture Sumantra, as Rāma's proxy, is to adopt with Daśaratha; or, more probably, Rāma may be bowing in the direction of his absent father (so the NR, 1255*; cf. also 76.14, 5.15.31 and 56.6, and *MBh* 12.217.30).

12ff. As we can ascertain by a comparison with *sarga* 46 above, Sumantra's report of Rāma's message is not very faithful, despite Rāma's express desire for precision (46.54). There are, of course, a number of close parallels: 52.12 / 46.20 (though Rāma's optimistic words in 21-22 are omitted by Sumantra; the NR here inserts something approximate, 1257*); 52.13 / 46.23bcd-24a; 52.14 / 46.24ab (Sumantra, however, adds an extra admonition to Kausalyā; and Rāma's advice to have Bharata brought and crowned is omitted); 52.15 / 46.27. 52.16, a strong line, is not in Rāma's original message. But the most startling divergence is Sumantra's report of Lakṣmaṇa's words (verses 18ff.). It is only the NR that offered this (cf. note on 46.28), one would assume *ex post facto*, though for a later fabrication the number of parallels is very small (52.18 / App. I, No. 16.7-8; 52.19 / 16.9-10; the rest differs), and Rāma's warning to Sumantra, to hush it all up ("for the king is old . . . and sorrowful over my banishment; if he hears such insults he will die straightway," App. I, No. 16.31-32) is ignored here. (Cg [GPP 58.33] defends the narrative propriety of reporting indirectly Lakṣmaṇa's speech when it was never directly related: "By virtue of its being recounted here—though never mentioned when Sumantra was being sent away—we are given to understand that it must have been spoken then" [this is his standard rationalization of narrative inconsistency, cf. note on 28.12-13 above].) It is impossible to determine whether the variations are intentional or simply consequences of the special exigencies (such as inconsultability) of oral poetry (though cf. the verbatim report of the later message, 62.7 = 64.3).

13. "ask . . . after their health" *vācyam . . . ārogyam*: The idiom *ārogyaṃ vac* (or *brū*) is here correctly interpreted by Ck and Ct (cf. the NR gloss, *praṣṭavyā kuśalam* [1258*]; contrast above 46.24 and note).

14. The crit. ed. constitutes a text exhibited by no single manuscript, and one that is highly elliptical. *Vācyā* is easily supplied from the previous verse, though this is not typical of Vālmīki's style.

17. "the tears rolled in a flood" *bhṛśam aśrūṇy avartayat*: Rāma cries (cf. 1264* and Cg; Cr wants to supply *mām* with the causative verb, "made me cry"), Cg suggests, "only because of the impropriety of his saying anything further [lest he reveal his true thoughts?] since 'one can find out the true feelings of a person by what he says when asleep, drunk, or angry'; this idea will come up again after the abduction of Sītā" (it is unclear what verses he is referring to).

20. "that must provoke protest" *janayiṣyati saṃkrośam*: For this sense of *saṃkrośa-* cf. *ArthŚā* 1.17.39 ("public outcry"). Two possible alternatives to the translation offered: "that will bring forth censure (upon the agent)" (Cm, Cr); or, "that will bring forth, that must have, its denunciation."

21. "Rāghava shall now be brother, father" *bhrātā . . . pitā . . . rāghavaḥ*: Cm, Cg, Ck, Ct, all quote, "One is authorized to abandon a person, guru though he may be, who is proud, who does not know the difference between right and wrong, or follows an evil course" (*MBh* 5.178.24 and elsewhere in that epic). Cg interprets allegorically: "Those who are directed solely to the Supreme One should abandon their natural fathers and other kin; the Blessed One alone is father, master, kinsman, and one without qualification."

22. "could . . . feel loyalty to you" *anurajyeta . . . tvā*: That is, to Daśaratha. The change of address from third to second person does not have overwhelming manuscript support, but no clear alternative presents itself.

"devoted to the welfare of all the world" *sarvalokahite ratam*: The compound, rather surprisingly, occurs only here in *Rām* 2-6; it appears also in the Aśokan inscriptions (cf. for example Rock Edict VI, lines 9, 11). (Cg's reading is not recorded in the crit. ed.: *sarvalokāhite ratam* [joined with *tvā*], "[you] so keen to harm all the world.")

The SR inserts after this verse its logical conclusion: "Why should you remain king after going against the wishes of all the world by exiling Rāma?" (1271*).

Sarga 53

1. Before this verse an NR insertion (contained also in T2, 3) has Sumantra report how Rāma matted his hair, crossed the Ganges, and headed for Prayāga (1272*; in verse 21 below Daśaratha has no idea where Rāma is).

"as I was about to return" *nivṛttasya*: Genitive absolute (*pace* Cm, Cg, Ct, Cr). The past participle has an inchoative aspect, as does *prasthitaḥ* in verse 2.

Horses weep in 6.94.26 below, and elsewhere in Sanskrit literature: in the *MBh* (4.37.6; 5.141.11; 6.2.33, 3.42), and the *BuddhaC* (6.53; modeled on the *Rām*); cf. *Iliad* 17.437ff. In Indian literature this generally represents an evil omen, rather than, as here, an emotional response.

2. "sorrow . . . for them" *tadduḥkham*: Not understood as a compound by Cm, Cg ("such a sorrow"). We agree with Ct, Cr.

3. "But I waited the whole day" *kṛtsnaṃ ca tatraiva divasaṃ sthitaḥ*: We read *pādas* ab with the NR, against the SR's version accepted by the crit. ed., "(I waited) many days" (see note on 51.4).

4. The transition between verses 3 and 4 is abrupt, but all manuscripts support it. Before verse 4, therefore, we must understand: on the next day I departed and soon entered your realm.

5. "no beasts stirring forth" *vyālā na prasaranti ca*: That is, even to get food (Cm, Cg, Ct; cf. 40.29, 46.54). Again some uncertainty about *vyāla-*; the translation follows Cm, Cg (Cg's second explanation is "elephants"; Cr, "snakes").

10. "dimly" *'vyaktam*: We accept the reading of Cm, Cg, Ct, Cs (so B manuscripts and the Mylapore editor), although *pūrvarūpasaṃdhi* at *pāda*-boundary appears to be rare in the *Rām* (if anything there is a tendency, very slight, toward hiatus [exaggerated by Böhtlingk 1887, pp. 213-214]). The crit. ed. reading *vyaktam* is very weak ("clearly [more anguished]").

"bright eyes" *vimalair netraiḥ*: Cg suggests instead that the women's eyes are "clean," because they have stopped using kohl (in Rāma's absence).

11. "enemies" *amitrāṇām*: The commentators try to explain away this reference to the "enemies" of Rāma. But obviously, as Varadacharya points out, if there were no enemies the verse would not make any sense: sorrow would then be perfectly uniform, and in addition no one could be said to be either friend or enemy, but only "neutral" (1964-1965, vol. 2, p. 21n).

13. "Ayodhyā, like Kausalyā" *kausalyā . . . iva ayodhyā*: The similitude is heightened by the feminine gender of the name of the city.

15ff. Daśaratha here is confessing his personal responsibility, apparently in response to the accusations implicit in Sumantra's statements in this chapter (so Cm, Cg, Ck, Ct): natural disasters, as described in verses 4-5 above, were often attributed to a king's unrighteousness, in India (cf. *MBh* 12.91.33ff.) as elsewhere in the ancient world.

15. "a woman of evil family and evil designs" *pāpābhijanabhāvayā*: The compound is problematic. Comparing verse 10.40 above, where Kaikeyī is called *pāpaniścayā* ("evil-scheming woman"), we follow Ct in the main (but *abhijana* in the *Rām* seems always to mean only "family" or "descent" [cf. 2.1.18, 98.48], never "birthplace," which eliminates Ct in part, and Cm, Ck). But what is evil about Kaikeyī's family? The account of her mother's perversity, to which Cg refers, is an interpolation (cf. note on 32.1). Cg's analysis of the compound ("with an evil intent coming through her family") is attractive if we understand it, not as Cg himself does, that she is hereditarily prone to do evil, but as referring to the *rājyaśulka*, the "brideprice consisting in the kingship," which was exacted at the time of Daśaratha's marriage to her (cf. 99.3), and in which the king of Kekaya must have had a hand (this

implication can also be gleaned from the translation offered). It may be to this that Daśaratha is referring in these verses.

16. "wise brahmans" *naigamaiḥ*: We follow Cm, Cs, Cr ("those who know the *vedas* and *śāstras*"), but the meanings "merchants, guildsmen" (cf. note on 1.14) or just "(leading) townsmen" (Cg) are also possible.

17. With a final pitiful attempt at self-exculpation, and perhaps with a hint of his recollecting the incident soon to be related (*sargas* 57-58), Daśaratha offers the alternative cause, fate (so essentially Cg; Ct wrongly has *vā* = *vai*).

18. Daśaratha asks first to have Rāma brought to him (verse 18), hoping that his direct command will compel him to return (verse 19), but then realizing that Rāma may have traveled far already, he offers to go himself, one supposes, to avoid the insufferable delay of a return journey.

19. "If only . . . might . . . make . . . turn back" *yadi . . . nivartayatu*: *Yadi* (+ imperative) used absolutely, without apodosis (cf. Speijer 1886, p. 371, recording, however, only optative constructions). The commentators take *pāda* a as protasis to b, "if the command is still mine (to give)," and variously explain the third person singular verb ("let some one," "let you," etc.).

21. "with pearly teeth" *vṛttadaṃṣṭraḥ*: Literally, "with rounded teeth" ("like jasmine buds," Cm, Cg, Ct, Cr). The epithet is eliminated in the NR, but note that Daśaratha elsewhere at moments of severe emotional stress dwells on Rāma's physical beauty, cf. for example 58.51ff.

"if I am to live" *yadi jīvāmi*: Again, there is some problem with the conditional clause. Ck, Ct, recognizing the syntactical impossibility of the construction "if I may see him I shall live" (Crā, Cm, Cg, Cr), suggest, "I would see him, if I [may] live [long enough]." The translation offered attempts to account better for verse 22, while also respecting syntax.

23. Ct discusses what he takes to be the real meaning of verses 21ff.: "The Blessed One separated himself from his father in order to ensure that he would be continuously thinking about Him at the hour of his death, which is drawing close. For one who thinks [about the Blessed One during that time] secures for himself a place in heaven."

24. "You did . . . know" *jānīta*: Understood as second plural indicative active (augmentless imperfect); Cr takes it as third singular optative middle.

"my lady" *devi*: The sudden switch to direct address of Kausalyā is the reading of the SR (the NR reads for the most part, "charioteer.") And the crit. ed.'s decision to accept it makes no contextual (or manuscript) sense without the SR insertion that precedes the line: "His heart crushed by sorrow, the king was plunged into a sea of grief, one whose further shore was far beyond his reach. He said, 'The sea . . . in which, without Rāghava, I am sinking, Kausalyā . . . ' " (1297*).

25. "What misfortune" *aśobhanam*: Against Ct ("[it is a result of] my sin that"). Half of the manuscripts that preserve this verse alter to *suśobhanam*, "handsome" (agreeing with *rāghavam*), and so locate the antecedent to the relative *yaḥ* in verse 24.

26. "terror seized her once again" *bhayam agamat punar eva*: Kausalyā first feared for her life when Rāma departed (cf. 17.24), and now fears again, lest Daśaratha die leaving her a widow and at the mercy of her enemies (so, too, in the opinion of Varadacharya, 1964-1965, vol. 2, p. 25n). Cg, Ck, who construe "doubly" with

"terror," suggest she feared first for Rāma's life and now for Daśaratha's, but this seems less convincing. Kausalyā's anxiety throughout has been principally on her own account (cf. especially 17.23ff.).

Sarga 54

4. "The charioteer . . . in a breaking voice" *sa vācā sajjamānayā...sūtaḥ*: Presumably because it seems self-defeating to have Sumantra try to console Kausalyā in a tearful voice, Cm suggests joining the instrumentals in *pādas* ab (as attributives, *upalakṣaṇe*) with *devīm*, but this is very hard.

6. "is winning the higher world" *ārādhayati . . . paralokam*: Or, "winning the regard of other men," see note on 19.7. The translation adopts the first alternative, in hesitant agreement with all the commentators, for two main reasons. The NR version of the clause runs *paraṃ lokaṃ arjayan*, "securing the higher world" (1301*). (The variant is interesting in showing that both the compounded form *paraloka-* [cf. note on 19.7] and the use of the verb *ārādhayati* were felt to be obscure or ambiguous; see below.) It is, however, possible that the variant here is to be viewed as a revision rather than a gloss. More compelling evidence is provided by a parallel found in the Aśokan inscriptions, Kalinga Rock Edict II [Jaugad], line 7: *hidalogaṃ ca paralogaṃ ca ālādhayeyū*, "that they might gain both this world and the other world." See also 35.23. Speaking against the translation are several factors. First, the compounded form *paraloka-*, on which see the note on 19.7. More serious is the use of *ā* + the root *rādh*. This verb generally construes with a personal object in the *Rām* (4.40, 23.32, 99.4, 3.10.86, etc.), and with one uncertain exception (cf. 3.10.89 and note there), there is no other example in the *Rām*, or indeed in Sanskrit literature in general, of its being employed with an impersonal object, as it is here (PW s.v. records only the present verse). The very important set of D manuscripts, 4, 5, 7, obviously found the usage impossible, offering instead, "(Lakṣmaṇa will be dwelling in the forest) winning the regard (*ārādhayiṣyan*) of Kākutstha by his righteousness" (1302*). Finally, there are the frequent references to the esteem Lakṣmaṇa has won in the eyes of the people for his selfless sacrifice (cf. 35.22, 42.7, 80.1). The Aśokan parallel may be enough to tip the balance here, but the arguments to the contrary are too strong to allow the interpretations of 19.7 and 47.26 to be affected. If the translation chosen here is indeed the correct one, we must posit for the *Rām* a bivalence in the term *paraloka-*, perhaps reflecting a process of ethical reorientation.

7. "as if she were at home" *gṛheṣv iva*: Compare Sītā's own words above, 24.9, 17.

8. "I did not perceive that Vaidehī felt any despair" *nāsyā dainyaṃ kṛtaṃ kiṃcit . . . lakṣaye*: How easy the courtier Sumantra finds it to alter his story—cf. 52.23ff.—perhaps to spare the innocent woman any further pain (as he did not feel to be necessary in the case of the more culpable Daśaratha?).

"the hardships of exile" *pravāsānām*: For this sort of plural cf. Renou 1968, p. 275 ("noms d'action envisagés au point de vue des actes ou des moments").

10. "with her full-moon face" *-bālacandranibhānanā*: There is a question whether to understand *bāla-* with the crit. ed. (and Crā), or *(sīt)ābāl-* with Cv, Cm, Cg, Ct, Cr (supported by the NR; cf. also verse 14 below). One trouble with the latter is that *saṃdhi* (*savarṇadīrgha* or otherwise) at the *pāda*-boundary is rare in the *Rām* (cf.

above, note on 53.10; though it does occur, for example, in 110.30). But this seems less a problem than the text reading, which must mean either "new moon," obviously awkward, or, "newly (risen)" (as Varadacharya suggests, 1964-1965, vol. 2, p. 27 note). But in Sanskrit literature the moon is usually said to be of a darkish hue (red or orange) when it rises (cf. Ingalls 1965, p. 272; thus Rāma, who is *śyāma*, "dark," is properly compared to a *bālacandra* "just risen moon," in 3.36.12). *Abāla-* also establishes a familiar sort of contrast with *bāla-* in *pāda* a. The translation thus agrees with the majority of the commentators.

"like a young girl" *bāleva*: "The simile refers either to her inveterate playfulness, or to her insensibility to sorrow," Cg (Ck and Ct accept the second alternative).

12. After this verse the NR includes a *śloka* comparing Sītā in the midst of Rāma and Lakṣmaṇa to Śrī between Viṣṇu and Indra (1307*), while the SR continues with two verses in which the charioteer, claiming he cannot recall anything Sītā might have said against Kaikeyī, is shown to repress his recollection, preferring to report only what will positively cheer Kausalyā (1309*; the commentators have some difficulty in locating these words attributed to Sītā—understandably so, since they are nowhere recorded).

13-14. Contrast Kausalyā's own impression of Sītā in 96.22-3.

14. "Sweet" *vadānyāyāḥ*: "Sweet-voiced," according to Cm, Cg, Ct, Cr, who cite *AmaK* in support of their gloss (contrast the use of the word in 55.2). The epithet in any case is principally for alliteration: *vadanaṃ . . . vadānyāyā vaidehyā . . . vikampate*.

After this verse some D manuscripts add several lines comparing Sītā to Śrī, Umā, and Rati (wife of the god of love) (1310*).

15. Red liquid lac was applied to women's feet; Sītā's feet are said to be naturally such a hue and to remain so despite her traveling on foot.

16. "when she has cast off her jewelry out of love for him" *tadrāgānyastabhūṣaṇā*: The *pāda* is a little unclear. One naturally expects the verse, insofar as it is both juxtaposed to verse 15 and similarly constructed, to contain a comparable conceit (that is, that she moves as gracefully as if she were wearing ornaments, though she has removed them out of her desire to live as an ascetic with Rāma); this is how Cg (second explanation) and Cm (first) interpret. We follow them, despite the fact that Sītā is shown to have put on ornaments when they departed (34.17, 35.12), and still to be wearing them when Bharata comes to search for Rāma (82.13). The ornaments will take on a great importance later in the story: Sugrīva will find them after Sītā's abduction and show them to Rāma, 4.6.13ff. (unless these are supposed to be Anasūyā's gift, 2.110.17ff.).

18. "For theirs are exploits the world will keep alive in memory forever" *idaṃ hi caritaṃ loke pratiṣṭhāsyati śāśvatam*: Ck believes that the "exploits" include both the famous deeds of Rāma and the infamous ones of Kaikeyī. Ct comments that, by asserting that Rāma's deeds will live forever, the poet intimates Rāma's divinity ("for no one else's deeds attain to an eternal existence"). Although this view is an interesting example of the medieval understanding of the *Rām*, it is alien to the spirit of the work, which stresses the nobility of human suffering in adherence to righteousness, and the ignominy of victory in violation of it. The verse is powerful in its simplicity. It calls to mind, by its wording, the first *śloka* chanted by Vālmīki (*mā . . . pratiṣṭhām . . . agamaḥ śāśvatīḥ samāḥ*, 1.2.14) and, by its substance, though the point of view is instead pessimistic, *Iliad* 6.357-58 ("Zeus doomed us that we might

be a grand theme for singers in times to come"). Cf. 6.88.53 where, before slaying Rāvaṇa, Rāma says, "Now I will do a deed that people . . . shall talk about as long as the earth lasts" (and of course 1.2.35).

19. "are making good" *śubhāṃ . . . paripālayanti*: Notice the proleptic character of *śubhām*.

Sarga 55

Several D manuscripts have Sumantra sent from the room before Kausalyā begins to speak (1319*), whereas the NR substitutes some verses showing Kausalyā (in a way quite out of keeping with her actual words) reviving and gently stroking the king while she addresses him (1320*).

2-3. The crit. ed. presents the reading of the SR (the NR substitutes for 2cd, "I think that fame of yours has perished because of the banishment of Rāma" [1321*]), and the expression is unclear. We understand an *iti* after *rāghavaḥ* (with all commentators), taking the whole of verse 2 as the concessive protasis to verse 3, and understand *duḥkhitau* predicatively. The commentators for the most part are forced to supply a supplement to the verses (for example, though Daśaratha's fame is widespread, how could he have done so infamous a thing [Cm, Cg], or, how could he have abandoned them [Ck, Ct, Cr]; Cg's second alternative is not much better: even though Daśaratha's fame, from keeping his word at the cost of abandoning a son so dearly obtained, will be widespread, and so will Rāma's from returning the kingship promised him; and even though the fame of both of them is a worthy thing, how will they bear . . .).

After verse 2 the NR includes a long interpolation (App. I, No. 18), in which Kausalyā argues that Daśaratha has indeed broken his word by not consecrating Rāma after promising to do so (lines 1-10; cf. 11.6 and note); she goes on to praise truth (it is worth more than a thousand horse-sacrifices, is the first cause of the universe, etc. [11-32]), asserting that Daśaratha's infamy will be eternal, and expressing gratitude that Kaikeyī did not demand Rāma's execution, for Daśaratha would probably have complied (43-44). Kausalyā ends by saying that her grief has made her disobey Rāma's entreaties not to reproach the king (53-58) and by asseverating the power of fate (63ff.).

In place of, and after, verse 3, many N manuscripts insert a lament for Lakṣmaṇa and lengthen the one for Sītā (1323*, 1324*).

4. "a woman in the bloom of youth" *taruṇī śyāmā*: A woman's life is divided by the Sanskrit tradition into four periods: childhood (up to 16), young womanhood (16-30), middle age (30-55), old age (55-). Cm and Cg remark that the two words (which they gloss, "beyond childhood, in the middle of young womanhood," respectively) being used together here mean that Sītā was somewhat less than halfway through young womanhood (cf. note on 17.26 and 3.874*).

7. "like the banner of great Indra" *mahendradhvajasaṃkāśaḥ*: "By reason of his giving everyone cause to rejoice" (as people rejoice at the festival of Indra, where the banner is raised, cf. note on 68.29), Ct, Cr. Cg, Ck take the word in the sense of "rainbow," a meaning it seems never to have in the *Rām*; cf. 71.9, 24, etc.

10. "since Bharata will have possessed them" *bharatenopabhokṣyate*: We should

understand *yad* before *bharatena*, or *iti* after *upabhokṣyate* (which itself is future perfect).

13. "the oblation, clarified butter, rice cakes, *kuśa* grass or posts of *khadira* wood" *havir ājyaṃ puroḍāśāḥ kuśā yūpāś ca khādirāḥ*: The list of sacrificial materials not to be used again varies somewhat in different sources. Cg, Ck, Ct, Cr cite one authority that exempts from the prohibition "*mantras*, the black-antelope skin, *darbha* [nearly = *kuśa*] grass," and try to explain away the last item; according to the *TaiS* (3.4.9.4) the *havis* ("oblation") remains reusable.

14. "drained to the lees" *hṛtasārām*: Literally, "with its essence taken away" (cf. the similar expression used by Kaikeyī, 32.10). In the *soma*-sacrifice the officiants consume the *soma* or sacred drink after libations have been poured to the gods.

16. "Such a man" *tādṛśaḥ*: The adjective (eliminated in the NR) has no natural referent when we eliminate the SR verses in 1345*. It must therefore be taken absolutely.

17. "If only" *yadi*: Absolutely employed, in an optative sense. The only reasonable alternative offered by the commentators is Cg's "*yadi* in the sense of an interrogative particle," that is, "Did you keep . . . ?"

18. Cg compares the famous verse, "A woman's father guards her in childhood, her husband in womanhood, her children guard her in old age. She should never have independence" [*ManuSm* 9.3].

19. "you are no recourse for me" *tvaṃ . . . me nāsti*: The third singular verb, well-attested in the manuscripts, is to be taken with *gatiḥ* understood, *tvaṃ gatir nāsti* (as Varadacharya [1964-1965, vol. 2, p. 38n] and the Mylapore editors have also seen).

Two problems requiring attention here are the absence of any further mention of Kausalyā's third recourse, her kinsmen, and her sudden disinclination to go to the forest (cf. 54.3). The solutions offered for the first problem are not convincing (Ct: "her kinsmen are not in the vicinity"; Varadacharya: there were no relations between Kausalyā's kin and Daśaratha [this he claims is shown by the omission of their name in the passage cited at the note on 1.35], or, Kausalyā being the eldest wife and thus aged herself, her father and other kinsmen would be presumed to be dead [1964-1965, vol. 2, p. 37n] but cf. 46.36 above). Nor is one persuaded by the solution offered for the second (she did not want to go to the forest because she still did have a husband, Cg, Ck, Ct). Both problems would be lessened if we were to read, for *vanam* in *pāda* c (is it an ancient dittography?) something like *gṛham*, "(and) I will not go home," where as a divorced woman her social degradation would be intolerable.

20. "Your son and your wife" *sutaś ca bhāryā ca tava*: The expression is a pregnant one: Daśaratha has now in effect only one son and one wife (Varadacharya 1964-1965, vol. 2, p. 38n).

Sarga 56

1. "he . . . fell to brooding" *cintayām āsa*: Cm, Cg, Ck, Ct (presumably because of 1349*.4, "he noticed Kausalyā at his side and fell to brooding once again") understand by the king's pondering here his reflection on the truth of Kausalyā's words in *sarga* 55, rather than on his evil deed (55.21), but of course it is the latter, as verse 2 shows, that we have to understand here.

2. "shooting arrows by the sound of the target alone" *śabdavedhinā*: Cf. below 57.16ff. (Cg, Ck, Cr also take the compound as instrumental of means referring to the arrow).

4. "strangers" *pareṣu*: Cm, Cg, "disagreeable people"; Ck, Ct, Cr, "enemies." The NR substitutes the more powerful lines, "You ought not to throw salt on my chest . . . my heart is split open in my grief for my son" (1353*, cf. 67.3 for the image).

5. The bathos of Daśaratha again; cf. 11.12 and note. Ruben seeks to explain it as the effect of a heavily burdened conscience (1950, p. 296).

6. "you can tell good people from bad" *dṛṣṭalokaparāvarā*: A phrase used with reference to Rāma, 6.22 above (see note there). The commentators differ again: "who have seen among people their rise and fall" [Cg, Cm, Ct]; "the higher and lower world" [?] [Ck]; We are close to Cr.

"one more sorrowful still" *suduḥkhitam*: This agrees with Varadacharya (1964-1965, vol. 2, p. 40n) in seeing a comparative aspect in the adjective: Daśaratha is not, like Kausalyā, merely a parent commiserating for his child's misfortune; he is the cause of it.

8. "before the king" *rājñaḥ*: Here the genitive is understood according to Renou ("un gén. de la personne interéssée" [1968, p. 307]); Cm, Cg, Ct, Cr make it a subjective genitive, that is, she grasped and brought to her head the king's folded hands (which seems unnatural).

"alarmed" *trastā*: Ck and Ct note that her fear is that she has become a second Kaikeyī, saying things that break her husband's heart.

9. "and you ought not to hurt me" *hantavyāhaṃ na hi tvayā*: Cg and Ck, who alone of the commentators read with the crit. ed., seem to interpret the *pāda* as a question: "[I have offended you and so] should I not be struck by you [like a common slave]?" We understand, "You should not strike me again," that is, by beseeching her. The other commentators and most of the SR give, "I do not deserve your forgiveness," reading *kṣantavyā*.

10. "She is counted no real wife in this world or the next" *naiṣā hi sā strī bhavati . . . ubhayor lokayoḥ*: This agrees with Cg in construing together *pādas* a and c; cf. the NR "gloss" 1359*.4, *hatā seha paratra ca*, "She is lost both in this world and the other." Cm, Ck, Ct, Cr want to join *pāda* c with *ślāghanīyena*, "(a lord deserving to be praised) in this world and the next." The verse is no doubt reminding us of Kaikeyī's behavior in 10.40-41, 11.11ff.

12. "all one has learned" *śrutam*: "The sure sense of *dharma* that results from learning the *śāstras*," Cr.

14. "Only five nights all told have now passed" *pañcarātro 'dya gaṇyate*: That is, the previous night was the fifth; the sixth is coming on now. *Adya* + *rātrī* idiomatically "last night" (cf. 48.33 and note, 66.8 and note); the NR makes it rather clearer: "Five days have passed" [1362*]. The poet will call the coming night the sixth since Rāma's exile (57.3; cf. note on 51.4. The commentators' chronological computations here are false, and in any case immaterial, occasioned as they are by the spurious reading noted at 51.4 and 53.3).

15. "just as the waters of the ocean grow great with rivers ever rushing in" *nadīnām iva vegena samudrasalilaṃ mahat*: Cg and Ck remark that the comparison is founded on a popular belief (Ck: "one extrapolated from seeing what happens to smaller bodies of water like ponds; the ocean does not really increase by waters running into it—in the rains it actually diminishes in volume—but rather by the waxing of

the moon"). The NR alters the simile, "like the current of the Ganges after summer [that is, in the monsoons]" (1363*).

16. "heartfelt" *śubham*: Cf. note on 47.5. The commentators understand "good": "The 'goodness' of her words lies in her trying to conciliate her husband even in her state of extreme grief," Cm, Cg, Ct. (Cm reads locative for genitive in *pādas* ab [not noted in the crit. ed.].)

17. "gladdened . . . and overburdened" *prahlāditaḥ . . . samākrāntaḥ*: Varadacharya (1964-1965, vol. 2, p. 43n) seems to think the two states—of contentment with his wife and grief for his son—cancel each other out and give way to sleep, as one or the other alone would not. The commentators are silent.

Note the reduplicated perfect participle *eyivān* used as a finite verb (against *Pā* 3.2.108ff.; cf. also 6.47.126, below in 66.43, *upapedivān*, and Böhtlingk 1887, p. 221).

Sarga 57

2. "the equal of Vāsava" *vāsavopamam*: For alliteration, *vivāsād vāsavo-*.

"the demon's darkness" *tamaḥ . . . āsuram*: An eclipse, thought to be caused by the demon Rāhu swallowing the sun.

3. "that sixth night" *rajanīṃ ṣaṣṭhīm*: Significantly, the action is contemporaneous with *sarga* 50 (cf. note on 50.1). Jacobi believed that it was Vālmīki's intention, according to the demands of "poetic authenticity" (*poetische Gerechtigkeit*), that Daśaratha die on the very day of Rāma's departure (he consequently considered *sargas* 36-43 to be an interpolation via "thematic variation," but cf. above, notes on 35.38, 45.14). That Daśaratha dies six days later Jacobi claims to be due to one or both of the following reasons: either it is a result of the "error" that narrative time must coincide with chronological time, that is, that after the description of Rāma's journey to Citrakūṭa, the narrative of the events in Ayodhyā would be placed ahead, erroneously, the same amount of time, six days; or "Rāma's exile and return were celebrated on the ninth day of the bright half of [the month] Caitra. The full moon appears six days after this. Probably this date was decided on for the death of Daśaratha," for "according to [6.4.45] Viśākhā is the *nakṣatra* [constellation] of the Ikṣvākus. With the full moon in Caitra a cycle, in a certain sense, ended, and a new one began with the first day of Viśākhā" (Jacobi 1893, pp. 47-50 and addendum p. 255). The possibility that Vālmīki's narrative as we have it in the crit. ed. is a coherent and, indeed, brilliant piece of literary art, with its own inner motivation, is explored in the Introduction, Chapter 6.

"fully" *sam-*: The preverb here is doubtlessly significant. Daśaratha has had momentary flashes of memory already in 55.21 and 56.2.

The NR adds, "He said, 'If you are awake, Kausalyā, listen attentively to my words' " (1371*.4).

4ff. It seems as if Daśaratha were here thinking about two things at once: the evil deed of his youth (verse 4) and his marriage promise to Kaikeyī (verses 5-7).

5. "who sets about a deed . . . what he stands to gain" *ārambhe karmaṇāṃ phalam*: Cm, Cg take *ārambhe karmaṇām* together, construing *phalam* (*doṣaṃ vā*) also with *arthānām*. It is more sensible to join *karmaṇām apo koinou* with both *ārambhe* and *phalam*. (Ck, Ct want to distinguish *arthānām* from *karmaṇām* as "secular" and "re-

ligious" acts, respectively, which is unnecessary. They add with regard to *pāda* d: "such a man is the real ["fool," literally,] child, not the infant at the breast.")

6. "A person who . . . instead waters flame trees" *kaścid . . . palāśāṃś ca niṣiñcati*: "The person thinks the flame trees will bear fruit commensurate with their flowers, which are enormous and colorful, and he cuts down the mango trees—whose flowers are small and pale—because they are obstructing the flame trees. . . . The fruit of the flame tree is inedible [whereas the mango's is delectable]" (Cg; the idea is a commonplace in Sanskrit literature; cf. Ingalls 1965, p. 577).

7. This verse can be interpreted in two different ways. Daśaratha can be said to have "cut down a mango grove" by withdrawing his affection from Kausalyā, and by transferring it to Kaikeyī he "watered a flame tree." By "watered" Daśaratha may be referring either to the boon he offered Kaikeyī or, more probably, to the bride-price promise he made in order to gain her hand (99.3). Kaikeyī never bore the sweet fruit her appearance promised, but the bitter fruit that meant the exile of Rāma (so Cm, Cr; the commentators otherwise fail to understand the verse satisfactorily). Whereas this interpretation seems appropriate to the terms of the simile, it does not construe well with what follows, for Daśaratha proceeds to discuss the "fruits" borne by his "shooting by sound" (verse 9), which actually turn out to be his repudiation of Rāma (and eventually his own death). To make the present simile more relevant to this, we would have to equate the flame tree with his flamboyant archery, and the mango grove with the more temperate and virtuous pleasures of a prince—which would be a weak solution. In fact, Daśaratha again may be thinking of two things consecutively but unrelatedly: his beguilement by Kaikeyī (verses 5-7) and his youthful intemperance (verses 8ff.).

8. "it has now come home to me" *tad me 'nusaṃprāptam*: "[Normally] the good or evil deed a person does bears its fruit in some other world or in some future life. Because his deed was so heinous it bore its fruit in this very world," Cg.

9. "just as a child might eat something poisonous out of ignorance" *saṃmohād iha bālena yathā syād bhakṣitaṃ viṣam*: The simile underscores the fact that, with respect to the karmic effect of the deed, his youth and the accidental character of the act are both immaterial (Ck).

All S manuscripts include a line before *pādas* cd supplying the simile of the man deluded by the flame tree (1377*), which causes the commentators then to interpret variously the second half (for example, Daśaratha was deluded by his fame in archery and did not realize the bitter fruit it would bear, Cm, Cg). As the text stands (and as the NR in part confirms) the simile in *pādas* ab refers merely to the ignorance (and youth) of Daśaratha.

10ff. The following episode is closely paralleled by the *Sāmajātaka* (*Jātakas* #540, cf. *Mahāvastu* pp. 209-19 [prose version], pp. 219-31 [metrical version]); points of significant agreement or divergence will be noted in their appropriate places. Oldenberg offers an interesting stylistic comparison with the *jātaka*, which he judges archaic in comparison with the *Rām* version (1918, pp. 456ff.). There is an unusually large percentage of first-person pronouns here and in *sarga* 58, which lends a dramatic dimension to the narrative (cf. Gonda 1942, pp. 271-72).

10. "not yet married" *anūḍhā*: Perhaps because Kālidāsa in his retelling of this story shows Daśaratha to have been married already to his three wives (*RaghuVa* 9.22), Cm glosses *anūḍhā* as "not old" (*apraudhā*). (Daśaratha does not in Kālidāsa's version take his wives with him on the hunt, as Vaidya says [1962, p. xxv.; he misunderstands *RaghuVa* 9.48].)

11. "awful region" *bhīmāṃ . . . diśam*: The south. After the autumnal equinox the sun's vertical rays begin to move south of the equator; the sun is thus said in Indian literature to "follow the southern course." Yama Vaivasvata, king of the dead, is supposed to have his realm in the south. It is interesting that Kālidāsa should eliminate the vague sense of foreboding by transferring the events to the springtime (*RaghuVa* 9.24-25).

12. "cuckoos" *sārañga-*: Glossed "dappled antelope" and/or *cātaka* (cuckoo) by the commentators here, and "elephant" in the next verse. We are evidently forced to give it the same sense in both places (see the note on verse 13).

13. "the mountain with its wild white cuckoos" *mattasārañgaḥ . . . acalaḥ*: There are two problems here: in which of its several senses are we to understand *sārañga*; and whether *acalaḥ* is substantive or adjective. We take *sārañga* as the *cātaka* (the black and white pied-crested cuckoo, which is said to drink only the water of the monsoon clouds), forming part of a *bahuvrīhi* compound modifying *acalaḥ*, "mountain" (= Ct?): the white-breasted birds would presumably look like flecks of foam. Alternatively, "the mountain with its rutting elephants looked like a (motionless) [*acalaḥ* repeated] ocean" (Cg); "the rutting elephant looked like a motionless ocean" (Cr).

14. "the Sarayū River" *sarayūm . . . nadīm*: Cf. note on 32.15 and Rāma's words in 43.13. Kālidāsa sets the scene at the Tamasā (*RaghuVa* 9.72).

16. "being filled" *pūryataḥ*: Passive participle with *parasmaipada* termination. The NR offers *bṛṃhitam* (the "trumpeting" of an elephant) in *pāda* d, as Kālidāsa (*RaghuVa* 9.73).

Kālidāsa adds (9.74) that Daśaratha should not in any case have been shooting at an elephant, for that is prohibited (except in battle, as noted by the commentator Mallinātha; it is a crime punishable by death in the *ArthŚā*, cf. 2.2.8). Perhaps the later poet felt the need to affirm that Daśaratha was in some way guilty, lest such grievous retribution for an accidental deed appear unjust (cf. also *BrahmP* 123.47-48, "Although the king [Daśaratha] knew that lords of earth must never slay forest elephants, he sought to kill it—what will a man not do whom fate has driven mad?").

17. "like a poisonous snake . . . like a poisonous snake" *āśīviṣopamam . . . āśīviṣopamam*: Note the highly effective repetition here (technically an *ekāntarapādayamaka*). The simile of the snake (admittedly not uncommon) will be employed again in 4.23.17 of the arrow Rāma uses to kill Vālin, and in 6.97.8 of the one he uses to kill Rāvaṇa.

20. "renounced violence" *nyastadaṇḍasya*: Literally, "put down the staff."

"who lives in the wilderness on things of the wild" *vane vanyena jīvataḥ*: Rāma used this phrase in reference to himself, 33.2 above, a parallel that may be more than formulaic (cf. notes on verses 27 and 32 below, and on 58.48-49).

21. "The one burden I carry is my matted hair" *jaṭābhāradharasyaiva*: That is, he has no possessions worth stealing and he has never given cause for vengeful anger (and, as Ck and Ct add, no man eats human flesh [so he could not have been killed for food], as the *jātaka* makes explicit, p. 77.11).

22. In order to right the apparent asymmetry of the verse (*ārabdham* must [*pace* Cr] be *karmaṇi kta*, whereas *gurutalpagam* must be [*kartari*] *ḍa* [cf. *KāśiVṛ* 3.2.48]), we understand *tena* in *pādas* ab, and *tam* in *pādas* cd (so in part Ct). (The NR substitutes, "the murder of a guru at the hands of his student.")

"like the man who violates his guru's bed" *yathaiva gurutalpagam*: Sexual intercourse with the wife of one's guru is numbered among the major sins. This would include incest as well as adultery with one's teacher's wife (cf. *ManuSm* 11.59 and the note on 76.27).

24. "dead" *pañcatvam āpanne*: Literally, "gone to the elemental state."

25. "(all) slain" *hataḥ*: As Cm, Cg, Ck, Ct correctly perceive, *hataḥ* is to be construed sylleptically with both *pādas* (rather than making *pāda* a an independent clause, with Cr); cf. verse 30 (and compare the elaboration in *Mahāvastu*, pp. 213.10, 214.1-2, 222.14, 19, 223.1ff.).

26. "who had always striven to do right" *dharmānukāṅkṣinaḥ*: So the commentators. Quite possibly, however, the root *kāṅkṣ* is used in the sense we find in Buddhist Sanskrit, "feel apprehensive about" (see Edgerton 1953b, s.v.); this is corroborated by the NR "gloss" *adharmabhayabhītasya*, "afraid of the danger of [that is, that he had committed an act of] unrighteousness" (1402*). This is to say, Daśaratha was frightened not that he had killed a human being but that he might have killed a brahman (cf. verse 37). Note that in the *RaghuVa* (9.76) the very first thing Daśaratha does on finding the boy is to ask him his caste ("this suggests that he is afraid of having committed a sin," Mallinātha ad loc.).

"(the bow) and arrow" *saśaraṃ* (*cāpam*): Being a dexterous archer, Daśaratha would have drawn from his quiver a second arrow the moment the first was shot (Cg).

27. After this verse some N manuscripts add that the ascetic was just out of childhood and not too far into adolescence (1407*.1), which would make him roughly the same age as Rāma at the time of his exile according to the northern tradition (cf. note on 17.26 above; in the Pāli version the boy Sāma is "almost sixteen," p. 74.9).

29. "Your Majesty" *rājan*: Cf. note on 34 below.

31. "on the strength of hope" *āśākṛtām*: Ck suggests, "made [that is, increased] by hunger." The translation agrees with Cm, Cg, Ct.

32. "there is no reward for austerity" *na . . . tapaso vāsti phalayogaḥ*: The boy is probably referring, not to his own ascetic practices and learning (Cg, Cr), but to his father's (Ck, Ct; cf. the words of Śyāma's mother, *Mahāvastu* p. 228.10-11). On the first alternative, however, we would have a sentiment very similar to the one expressed in reference to Rāma (cf. 46.10), and this would add yet another parallel (cf. 58.48-49 and notes) between the story of Rāma and Daśaratha and that of the ascetic boy and his father.

33. "unable even to move about" *aparikramaḥ*: It is not certain whether the father is supposed to be truly lame (Cg, Cr) or, as is more likely, simply "immobilized" by his blindness (Ck, Ct; so the Buddhist versions) or old age.

34. "Rāghava": Daśaratha has not yet identified himself to the ascetic, so the latter's addressing him by his proper name (cf. also verse 29, "Your Majesty") is a slight, though not exceptional, inconsistency (unnecessarily Cg, "We understand by this that the boy knew Daśaratha already from his frequently having hunted on the banks of the Sarayū").

"lest . . . he consume" *na . . . anudahet*: It is best, with Cg, Ct, to take the optative + *na* as a "negative purpose clause" (again at 61.7; cf. Speijer 1886, pp. 318-19 and Ck on verse 35), that is, "if you do not go and tell him he will find out and destroy you" (cf. 58.19), rather than as simple declaration, "you may go . . . he will not destroy you," which forces us to interpret the simile quite awkwardly as a contrary one (*vaiśamyadṛṣṭānta*; so Cm and indirectly Cr).

36. "is tearing . . . apart" *ruṇaddhi*: Literally, "presses, pains," as the commentators

gloss it. The root *rudh* is rare in the sense it must have here; *AV* 19.29.3 (*runddhi darbha sapatnān me,* etc.) is a possible parallel.

"rushing" *sotsedham*: Translated thus by reason of *MBh* 8.67.33-4, *sotsedham apatac chiraḥ*; *śiraḥ . . . sotsedham iṣuḥ . . . apāharat* (cf. the same simile in *Ayodhyākāṇḍa* 17.28 and especially 58.55). The commentators gloss it "high (bank)," which is pointless here (perhaps they erroneously equate it with *samutsedha,* cf. 6.17.4).

Kālidāsa has Daśaratha carry the boy to his parents with the arrow still in him and extract it in their presence, thereby killing him (9.77-8).

37. "I was born of a *vaiśya* father and a *śūdra* mother" *śūdrāyām asmi vaiśyena jātaḥ*: This is the mixed caste called *karaṇa* (Cm, Cg [adducing *AmaK*], Ct, Cr; cf. *YājñaSm* 1.92). The NR has, "the son of a brahman father," 1416*; cf. the notes on 58.46,47. Kālidāsa calls him "other than a twice-born" (9.76), whereas Bhoja follows the SR (*RāmāCam* 2.58). (In the Pāli version he is *nesādaputta,* a son of a forest hunter, p. 78.11, whereas according to the *Mahāvastu* both his parents are brahmans, p. 209.9-13, as quite emphatically in the *BrahmP,* 123.49,74, 152-53). The boy identifies his caste lest the king, believing him to be a brahman, hesitate to draw out the arrow. For were that to kill him, the homicide would then in a sense be intentional and Daśaratha would be guilty of the most impious of crimes, brahman-murder (made explicit in the SR insertion 1415*.8).

38-39. With insertions after verse 38 both the NR (1420*.4) and the SR (1421*) show that the boy dies. Cm and Cg accordingly take verse 39 as a "recapitulation of Daśaratha's first view" of the boy (Ck and Ct note, " 'lying,' that is, dead").

Sarga 58

1. "how might it be righted" *katham nu sukṛtaṃ bhavet*: Thus in agreement with Cr (and cf. note on 51.26). The other commentators explain unsatisfactorily: "how the boy's order might be done," Cg, Ck; "whether it were better to inform the sage of the murder or not," Cm, Cg.

4. "talking about him" *tannimittābhiḥ . . . kathābhiḥ*: The instrumentals are attributive (*upalakṣaṇe,* so Cm, Cg; Ck, Ct, Cr, reading *apariśramau,* take them as causal, *hetau*).

9. "the more frightened I became" *bhīto bhītaḥ*: Thus the probable sense of the repetition. Perhaps to be read, with most manuscripts, *bhītabhītaḥ* (cf. *bhīrubhīruḥ* 5.64.12), "sufficiently terrified (just to look at him)" (cf. *Pā* 8.1.12).

10. "With effort I managed to collect my thoughts and recover the power of speech" *manasaḥ karma ceṣṭābhir abhisaṃstabhya vāgbalam*: Cm alone explains the syntax reasonably, and we follow him. The asyndeton is somewhat troublesome (though we find it elsewhere, as in 62.1, 66.6). One alternative is to understand *karma* in compound, *karmaceṣṭābhiḥ,* "by efforts made upon the action (of my heart)."

14. The word order of the verse is carefully wrought, climactically postponing by four qualifications the main object, "ascetic."

17. "Whatever awaits me now may the sage forgive me" *śeṣam evaṃ gate yat syāt tat prasīdatu me muniḥ*: Ck, Ct (and it seems Cm) understand the line artificially: "Now that your son has departed, may the sage favor me by ordering me to provide whatever assistance I might offer you for the rest of your life" (though cf. *Sāmajātaka* p. 87.25-28, *Mahāvastu* pp. 217-18, 227-28). Ck and Ct want to see

this offer of service as another reason, besides the unintentionality of the crime, why the sage does not immediately destroy Daśaratha. This, however, is uncompelling.

19. "your head would have . . . burst" *phalen mūrdhā sma te*: Causing the head of one's adversary to explode is a common threat in Sanskrit literature from at least the time of the *Upaniṣads* (*BṛĀraU* 3.6) through the medieval period (cf. the *VetāPañ*). It sometimes is shown to come true (*BṛĀraU* 3.9.26).

20. "(it topples) him" [*taṃ*] (*cyāvayet*): We must supply *tam* in *pāda* d (so, too, the Mylapore editors), in order to restrict the punishment to the perpetrator. Not every intentional murder carries with it cosmic consequences (as Ck suggests: "that is, if intentional, this murder would topple Indra—not to speak of the likes of Daśaratha—by reason of the sage's anger").

22. "We want to see" *draṣṭum icchāvaḥ*: That the blind father should express the desire to "see" his son rings oddly (Ck tries to solve the problem by glossing "to have a (last) *experience* of him by touching him, etc."). Most of the NR reads *spraṣṭum icchāmi*, "I want to touch (my son)" (1453*), and it would be a simple matter to alter the crit. ed. here to *spraṣṭum . . . paścimasparśanam* (cf. *asparśayam* in verse 24 and *spṛṣṭvā* in 25). But why, in that case, has no S manuscript emended? Furthermore, the visible objects in verse 23 seem to require the crit. ed. reading here (and cf. *Sāmajātaka* p. 88.23-24: *tattha netvā sāmaṃ dassehi*). The Mylapore editors argue plausibly that there is really no contradiction, the desire for "one last sight" being a normal, unpremeditated expression of grief in parents. (A similar case would be presented by *MBh* 15.36.25, when the blind king Dhṛtarāṣṭra speaks of being "purified by seeing" the great seers.) There might also be a suggestion here, or so they claim, that the poet himself is so overcome with grief that he forgets the aged couple is blind.

23. "King of Righteousness" *dharmarāja-*: Yama Vaivasvata, god of death. *Dharma* probably has the specific meaning here of "essential characteristic" of human beings, that is, mortality (as in *martyadharma, MBh* 14.60.33).

25. "wretched couple" *tapasvinau*: So *tapasvinīm* in verse 30 and contrast verse 7 above. The choice between the two senses of the word ("wretched," "ascetic"), both frequent in the *Rām*, is often subjective (cf. note on 28.18 above).

After this verse the NR inserts a short lament by the boy's mother, where she addresses him as Yajñadatta, the name he will have in later Sanskrit versions of the story (1456*).

26. "My son, don't you love me" *na nv ahaṃ te priyaḥ putra*: There is some disagreement among the commentators about the correct reading of *pāda* a; Cm, Cg, Ct, Cr (in different ways) give, "If you do not love me (at least) have regard. . . ."

27. "so sweetly reciting" *adhīyānasya madhuram*: Cm, Cg, Cr want to construe *madhuram* as direct object with *śroṣyāmi* (" 'sweet' sounds or words"). We instead take *kasya* as *karmaṇi ṣaṣṭhī* with the main verb (for the genitive with verbs of hearing, cf. 2.18.17, 60.9; 3.60.3; 5.56.43; *MahāBh* 1.4.29, Edgerton 1953a, p. 47, para. 7.68, and the genitive with *kluein* in Greek), and *hṛdayaṃgamam* and *madhuram* adverbially with *adhīyānasya*.

"or other works" *vānyat*: The epics and *purāṇas*, according to Cm, Cg, Ck, Ct, Cr. "Because he is of the [mixed] *karaṇa* caste, no mention is made of the possibility of his reading the *vedas*" [which were reserved for twice-borns], Ck, Ct. That, however, is probably what "sacred texts" (*śāstram*) refers to here.

28. "after the twilight worship" *saṃdhyām upāsyaiva*: "He would have performed

the twilight worship [not with the *Gāyatrīmantra*, as a twice-born does, but] according to the Tantric way ["the sectarian way," *āgamamārgataḥ*, Ck], with a salutation only," Cm, Cg, Ck, Ct. Troubled by the performance of the fire-sacrifice on the part of a non-twice-born (though see 57.37 and references ad loc.), Cm, Cg, Ct remark that since the *dharmaśāstras* permit a *śūdra* to perform the five great daily sacrifices (to the gods, ancestors, spirits, men [brahmans], and *brahma*) with a *mantra* appropriate to his caste, that is, a simple salutation (they cite *YājñaSm* 1.121, "He may perform the five sacrifices with a salutation as the *mantra*"), so may the son of a *vaiśya* and *śūdrā* do so.

"allay" *ślāghayiṣyati*: So basically Cm, Cg. The word is apparently unique in this sense.

29. "without leader" *apragraham*: Despite the tautology, this appears to be the only acceptable meaning here (Ck; Cm, Cg understand, "without a store [of rice]" that is, impoverished, but there seems to be no parallel for this usage; elsewhere in the *Ayodhyākāṇḍa* [1.20, 76.1] the senses of the word appear to be different).

33. "May the King of Righteousness forgive me" *kṣamatāṃ dharmarājo me bibhṛyāt*: What Yama is being asked to forgive is the father's audacity in asking for his son back (not any delay in arriving [Cg], or the sin incurred by the victim from dying by the sword [Ck], or the father's bad *karma* that gave rise to the tragedy [Ct, Cr]; these interpretations are motivated by an SR insertion here following, that has the father ask Yama to take his boy to heaven [1465*]); cf. the NR paraphrase *vaivasvataṃ . . . bhikṣiṣye . . . putrabhikṣāṃ pradehīti*, "I shall beg Vaivasvata . . . 'Give me these alms—my son' " (1464*).

34. The father, perhaps realizing the impossibility of negotiating with the god of death, performs an "act of truth" in order to convey his son to the world of heroes. (The literature on the act of truth is large and growing; two informed analyses can be found in Lüders 1951, pp. 486ff., and in Thieme 1952, pp. 108ff.) The "truth" is the indubitable veracity of the declaration in the first half of the verse (the purity of the son), not the seer's own (or, the son's) truth, his *tapas* (Cm, Cg, Ck, Ct, Cr; and thus the murder should not be interpreted as a penance for some unspecified previous sin, which reestablishes the purity of the boy, that is, "You have become pure by being killed" [Cm, Cg, Ct; so too implicitly Ck]). Note that in the *Sāmajātaka* the stricken boy is actually revived by three successive acts of truth. A similar prayer, though not an act of truth, occurs in 3.64.29ff. (spoken by Rāma at the death of Jaṭāyus).

Cg (similarly Cr) observes here, "Ought the father not to have asked that his son gain the world of Brahmā, being an ascetic as he is? Then too, he speaks of the world of heroes as something to be gained merely by dying by the sword. How does this all fit? The problem is solved by the declaration that heroes [also] gain supremely high worlds: 'There are two kinds of men in the world who [at death] pierce the disc of the sun [and so reach the world of Brahmā; cf. *MaiU* 6.30], the wandering ascetic disciplined in yoga and the one who dies face-front in battle' " [cf. *MBh* 5.178* and reference ad loc., and also 11.26.16 and *Rām* 6.54.22].

36. Most of these men are Rāghava heroes, and probably all are intended to be considered members of the solar dynasty. Sagara: cf. 1.37ff.; Śaibya: cf. note on 12.4; Dilīpa: according to the *Rām* the father of Bhagīratha (cf. 102.21; 1.41.7 and 69.26); Janamejaya: normally the great-grandson of the *MBh* hero Arjuna; Nahuṣa: also a *MBh* hero, father of Yayāti, but in the *Rām* a member of the Rāghava lineage (102.27; 1.69.29; cf. also note on 5.9 above); Dhundhumāra: an Aikṣvāka king, son

of Triśaṅku (102.11; 1.69.21), who "slew the demon Dhundhu," hence his name (*MBh* 3.192ff.).

37. "faithful to his one wife" *ekapatnīvratasya*: "This vow is incumbent on a man only in the case of a wife who is agreeable and who has produced a son," Cg.

38. "who lay their bodies down" *dehanyāsakṛtām*: That is, who commit ritual suicide either by commencing the "Great Journey" to the Himālayas with the intention of dying en route (Cg, Ck, Ct), or by abandoning their bodies in fire or water at Prayāga or some other holy place with the explicit resolution of attaining the higher world (Cm, Cg, Cr).

After this verse the SR adds, "He shall go that [accursed] way by whom you were slain" (1469*).

39. "funeral libation" *udakam*: See the note on 70.23.

41. "because I took care of you" *bhavatoḥ paricāraṇāt*: "The implication here is that taking care of one's father and mother, even if all other acts of *dharma* should be neglected, is sufficient to bestow residence in Indra's heaven," Ct. This filial devotion is the whole point of the story in the Buddhist versions (*Sāmajātaka* p. 94, *Mahāvastu* p. 230).

"presence" *mūlam*: The word is rare in this sense; Cg adduces the *Nigh* as authority.

42. "of wonderful construction" *vapuṣmatā*: The *-mat* suffix here connotes commendation (*praśaṃsāyām* [*KāśiVṛ* 5.2.94], Cm, Cg, Ck, Ct, Cr).

46. "Just as I now sorrow" *duḥkhaṃ yad etan mama sāmpratam*: The NR, like the puranic accounts (cf. *BrahmP* 123.76, *AgniP* 6.38) and Kālidāsa (9.79), is more explicit: "Just as I must necessarily lose my life, grief-stricken over my son" (1480*).

In Kālidāsa's somewhat idealized retelling, the curse itself has a beneficent aspect: the childless king can at least be sure of fathering a son (9.80).

After this verse the SR adds ten lines, which show the sage mounting a funeral pyre (cf. *RaghuVa* 9.81), after saying that no sin of brahman-murder will attach to Daśaratha, because the murder was accidental (a verse difficult for the commentators to explain away in light of 57.37 [cf., however, note there]).

47. "The words of the noble sage have thus come home to me" *tasmān mām āgataṃ . . . tasyodārasya tadvacaḥ*: The NR reads, "The brahman's curse has come upon me" (1484*; cf. note on 57.37). "The epithet 'noble' is meant to refer specifically to his bestowing [indirectly, by means of the curse] a child on the childless king" (Cg), though in fact it is more often used to designate a twice-born (cf. note on 77.7).

48. "or speak" *ālapeta vā*: In *pāda* b, the crit. ed. constitutes the text on the reading of Cg alone, *ālabheta*, which he glosses "come within sight." This is weak. In view of the NR paraphrase, *saṃbhāṣeta* (1487*), one would have conjectured the true reading to be *ālapeta*, but in fact one need not conjecture, for two good manuscripts offer it, G2 and M1, and we accept it. (Two S manuscripts offer *anvālabheta*, which may, in fact, be the ancient reading: the word appears in *MBh* 5.35.10, glossed *vade* by the commentator Devabodha.) Compare also the sage's words in verse 26 above ("embrace . . . speak"), and the note on verse 49 for the no doubt intentional parallel.

"How unlike me it was" *na tan me sadṛśam*: Daśaratha is making his final attempt to exonerate himself: Rāma's exile was not a thing he willingly did, but rather resulted from an implacable fate. The NR eliminates the line, offering instead, "(If only Rāma . . .) I think I might live, like a sick man given nectar. But no, even were I to see my beloved son, I would still die—in death I would no more feel this burning grief for my son" (1487*).

49. "(see you) with my eye" *cakṣuṣā* (*tvām . . . paśyāmi*): The singular is unexplained; it seems to be idiomatic in the phrase, cf. 6.61.17.

Daśaratha, blind, weak, and virtually childless, has now been reduced to the state of the ascetic's father.

50. "truthful" *satyaparākramam*: Literally, "who strives for truth." See note on 19.7 (and cf. 104.3 and note).

51. "lovely" *cāru*: Read here uncompounded, as adjective to *mukham* (cf. 5.33.78, *cāru tac cānanam*; 5.34.4, *cāru vadanam*).

54. Śukra: Venus.

"moving forward on its course" *mārgagatam*: A good omen (cf. 6.4.42); moving in a retrograde motion (*vakragata*) is a bad omen (cf. *Yavanajātaka* 75.3, where the words used to describe the position of Venus [in regard to military astrology] are *anuloma* ["facing with," that is, at the back] and *urasi* [at the front]; see Pingree's note ad loc.). The commentators are totally off track (Cm, Cg, for example, seem to take Śukra as referring, not to the planet, but to the preceptor of the demons, who "gave up his madness [of helping the demons?] and returned to his own station"). The NR reads, "like Śakra come from heaven," while Ck (not reported in the crit. ed.) has, "like a parrot [*śuka*] which had flown away from one's hand or perch and finally returned home"; Cs suggests in desperation, "or, 'like seeing, as the result of one's great merit, the son of Vyāsa' [that is, Śuka]."

55. "The grief arising here in my very soul" *ayam ātmabhavaḥ śokaḥ*: Cf. note on 35.33 for this charged sense of *ātman*. Less likely, "(grief) arising from myself," that is, by my own doing (so Cr), for Daśaratha seems no longer to be concerned with his guilt (the point of this and the previous *sarga* is in large measure to demonstrate that the king is far less "guilty" than he may seem), but rather with the intensity of his sorrow, and how it touches the very core of his being.

56. The SR adds in the middle of the verse, "in the presence of Rāma's mother and Sumitrā" (1496*.4); cf. the note on 59.9 below.

57. "a man of noble vision" *udāradarśanaḥ*: The commentators are regrettably silent on this final epithet given Daśaratha. The compound occurs in *KumāSaṃ* (5.36), where Mallinātha glosses, *unnatajñāna*, "of high intelligence" (it could here also mean "of noble appearance [so pw s.v.; Vallabhadeva on *KumāSaṃ* 5.35 argues plausibly for "lovely-eyed"], but such banality on Vālmīki's part is improbable). Is it reading too closely to suppose the poet's last comment on Daśaratha to be that he was a man "whose intentions were noble" but who was continually frustrated in realizing them? (The adjective will be used only once again in reference to Bharata [84.20], who seems similarly to be conceived as a noble figure that, indirectly and against his will, causes suffering.) Or that Daśaratha was a man who only "saw nobility" in others (cf. Cg on 64.7) and never suspected them of base motives, as he should have in the case of Kaikeyī; who, unlike Rāma, was not *dṛṣṭalokaparāvara*, able to "tell good people from bad" (6.22)?

Sarga 59

1. Before this verse the NR adds: "When the king had lamented in this manner and fallen silent, Kausalyā thought he was asleep and did not wake him. Without saying anything to her husband—she was haggard with grief and fatigue—she fell asleep on the bed"(1498*). Cf. note on verse 9 below.

4. "auspicious articles" *maṅgalālambhanīyāni*: This agrees more or less with Cm, Cg (Ck, Ct: "things to be touched for good fortune, cows, etc.").

"refreshments" *prāśanīyān*: "Things like crushed sesame seed, coconut, or caraway to be taken as a mouth-freshener after cleaning the teeth," Cm, Cg, Ct (Ck, "Ganges water, basil[-scented water], etc.").

"accoutrements" *upaskarān*: These would include the king's clothes, a mirror, and so on. Cg takes *striyaḥ* as accusative, " '(they brought) women,' that is, courtesans."

After this verse the SR adds some lines showing the attendants beginning to worry when the king does not appear (1503*).

5. "who waited in attendance" *yāḥ . . . pratyanantarāḥ*: Presumably some of Daśaratha's 350 "wives" are meant.

9. "sound of their crying" *ākrandaśabdena*: Probably thus, rather than "cry for help" (so Scharfe 1968, p. 129); cf. 3.41.2.

"Kausalyā and Sumitrā awoke" *kausalyā ca sumitrā ca tyaktanidre babhūvatuḥ*: Several versions are at pains to show us that Kausalyā (and Sumitrā) had fallen asleep *after* the king had finished his tale (so the NR, 1498*, cf. note on verse 1; the central D manuscripts, 1508*A; not explicit in the SR), but none of this can be admitted into the crit. ed. Are we therefore to infer that the king, waking up in the middle of the night (57.1-3, see the note on verse 3), tells his entire pathetic tale and reveals the only facts that, in some measure at least, can exonerate him, to one who never hears it? A fine irony, but perhaps overly fine.

11. Kosala: Ct wants to distinguish Kosala (with dental sibilant) as Kausalyā's father's country, from Kośala (with palatal) as the country around Ayodhyā. In fact both forms are current as referring to the latter (cf. Sircar 1967, p. 72). There was, however, another Kos(ś)ala in the Deccan; is this the homeland of Kausalyā?

"like that of a star" *tāreva*: The simile of the fallen star (*tārā*) will be used again, with etymological aptness, in reference to Tārā lamenting over the slain Vālin (4.21.1).

An SR interpolation (1516*.3) after this verse shows Kaikeyī mourning with the other women (cf. note on 77.6).

12. "throngs of heartbroken people" *paryutsukajanākulam*: This seems the obvious sense of the compound, against the commentators (Cm, Cg, "formerly thronged with eager people"; Ck, Ct, Cr, "with people curious to learn what happened").

14. "stretching out their arms" *pragṛhya bāhū*: The normal posture of lamentation in the epics is stretching out and raising up one's arms, as in 37.25, 51.23, 60.15, etc. (*pace* Cm, Cg, Cr, "they took each other's arms"; Ct, "they offered their arms").

Sarga 60

1. "dead" *svargastham*: Literally, "in heaven."

"like a . . . fire" *agnim iva*: These same three similes will be used of Vālin in 4.18.2, except that there "cloud" replaces "ocean." On "emptied of water" Cs remarks, "at the time when Agastya drank it up" (cf. *MBh* 3.100ff.).

2. "double" *dvividham*: This would appear to be the true reading for the crit. ed.'s *vividham* "various," as the NR version proves, *dvividhenāpi duḥkhena*; cf. also verse 4.

3. "You should be satisfied . . . for now you can enjoy the kingship unchallenged"

sakāmā bhava . . . bhuṅkṣva rājyam akaṇṭakam: Tārā screams the same words at Sugrīva in 4.20.19 (cf. Sītā's cry in 3.47.28).

"forsook" *tyaktvā*: The NR reads "slew."

4. After this verse the NR inserts eighteen lines, in which Kausalyā complains that her longing for the sight of Rāma (line 6), her own unworthiness (11-12), and the fact that time, not man, chooses the moment of death (13-14), are all that prevent her from following the path of good wives (5) and repaying her husband's goodness to her by immolating herself on his funeral pyre (App. I, No. 20; similarly in D4, 5, 7, App. I, No. 21, lines 11ff.); cf. also note on verse 10 below.

6. "A greedy person" *lubdhaḥ*: The analogy is unclear. We understand it as follows: Kaikeyī, hungry for power as she was, did not reckon the dangers of the hunchback's poisonous counsel, like the hungry man who will precipitately eat "fruit that makes one sick" (*kiṃpākam*, cf. *MBh* 5.122.20; Rāmacandra on *ŚatTrayī* of Bhartṛhari 2.48; Ingalls 1965, p. 545; in later literature apparently a specific fruit, though earlier the word was evidently adjectival, "badly cooked" [or better, "indigestible"], applied to food, *kim* as pejorative prefix [Mayrhofer 1956-1980, s.v. *kim*]). Unlike such a man, however, Kaikeyī ruins not only herself but the entire Rāghava clan (the commentators are unhelpful here).

How Kausalyā knows about the role of Mantharā has not been made clear. The NR excises the reference to her here.

8. "dead in life" *jīvanāśam*: None of the commentators who have this reading cites *Pā* 3.4.43 (*ṇamul* suffix; our form itself is recorded in *KāśiVṛ* ad loc.; Renou 1968, p. 131 also ignores it), by which this vocable is to be analyzed (Cs does explain it thus on 86.24; Cm, Ct, reading *jīvan*, get much the same sense). They consequently misunderstand, "(not knowing [cf. 1528*]) the destruction of the life of the king"; whereas the NR paraphrases, "he has gone . . . for the destruction [that is, with the effect being the destruction] of his father's life" (1530*). But *tathā* in *pāda* d indicates that Kausalyā at present is contemplating the personal fates of Rāma and Sītā only, not of Daśaratha.

"poor" *tapasvinī*: Thus correctly glossed by Cg; cf. note on 58.25 above (Ck, "strenuously engaged in *tapas*, ascetic practices").

9. "will hear the . . . cries" *nadatāṃ . . . niśamya*: For the genitive with the verb of hearing cf. note on 58.27.

Hereafter the NR inserts fourteen lines in which Kausalyā asks Kaikeyī how she, who had been righteous, could have turned so cruel. She goes on to warn her that Bharata will not commend her scheme (1532*).

10. After this verse the NR shows Vasiṣṭha having Kausalyā led away by waiting women "almost by force" (1533*, 1535*), whereas in the SR Kausalyā exclaims, "I will die today, faithful to my husband; I will enter the fire with his body in my embrace" (1534*).

11. "her maidservants helped her up" *tāṃ . . . sampariṣvajya . . . vyāvahārikāḥ*: *Sampariṣvajya* is governed by *vyāvahārikāḥ* (as understood by Cm), rather than by *tām* [*kausalyām*] (with "the king" or "the king's bed" as object understood [Cr]; cf. 1535*).

Some D manuscripts show Vasiṣṭha purposely clearing the room (1537*); in the NR he proceeds to deliberate the question of how Bharata and Śatrughna might be recalled (1540*-41*).

12. "placed him in a vat of sesame oil" *tailadroṇyām . . . saṃveśya*: Embalming is

rare in Sanskrit literature, though references are to be found in the ritual literature (cf. Kane 1962-1975, vol. 4, p. 233-34, adducing *SatyāSS* 29.4.29 and *ViṣṇuP* 4.5.7; Ctr [vol. 2, pp. 419-20] cites from *ĀpaŚS*, but the passage seems not to be found in that work, and in fact it agrees with *SatyāŚS*). There, however, it is said to occur only in the case of death away from home of a man who has maintained the sacred fires. His body is to be placed "in a vat of sesame oil" (*SatyāŚS*), and transported home.

"empowered" *ādiṣṭāḥ*: "By Vasiṣṭha," Cm, Ct, Cr note, but this specification is not necessary: the ministers would customarily be authorized to assume the duties of kingship during an interregnum.

13. "prudent" *sarvajñāḥ*: See the commentators cited on 3.31.19.

The funeral rites for Daśaratha will not, in fact, be performed until *sarga* 70, upon the return of Bharata. Ctr (vol. 2, pp. 419-20) refers to "some *smṛti* or other" that declares, "When sons are alive no one else should perform the funeral rites. The man who does so thereby injures the sons." There are, however, substitutes who are authorized to perform a man's funeral rites in the absence of his son (cf. Kane 1962-1975, vol. 2.i, pp. 256ff.). Is the real issue here that a hasty funeral, unsupervised by any of the princes (that is, possible successors), might raise suspicions about the circumstances of the king's death or about the ministers' own political ambitions? The commentators are silent, except for Cg, who blurs the political dimension by taking *sarvajñāḥ* in the sense of "knowing all [aspects of] *dharma*."

14. There is a slight chiasmus in the verse, *paryadevayan* governing the direct speech, *jñātvā* the participial phrase in *pādas* ab.

15. The NR shows the women "beating their breasts and heads and knees" (1544*).

16. "Like a night without stars" *niśā nakṣatrahīneva*: Three good S manuscripts, the NR, and Cm, Cg, Ck read "moon" for "stars" (but see the recapitulatory verse 18).

There is a light play on words in the main clause, reinforcing the sense: *nārājata* ("cast into gloom") . . . (*hī*)*nā rājñā* ("without its . . . king").

18. "the city went dark" *purī babhāse . . . na*: The enjambment of *na*, which must construe with *pāda* c, is startling. The commentators who read thus (there is some dispute about the lection) are silent. The position appears to be emphatic.

The inconsistency between verses 17 and 18 regarding the absence, or presence, of people in the streets, is eliminated in the NR.

19. "and found no comfort" *na ca śarma lebhire*: The phrase will be used again at the death of Vālin (4.22.25). The parallels between the two scenes (cf. 59.11, 60.1, 3 and notes) may be more than formulaic: both kings erred, and paid for their error with their lives.

Sarga 61

1. "deputies of the king" *rājakartāraḥ*: Cf. 60.12, *rājñaḥ* (*sarvāṇi*) . . . *cakruḥ karmāṇi*, "they assumed all the royal duties," that is, vice-regents (so Ck, Ct, "who execute all the business of the king" and Cr, "who carry out the duties normally belonging to the king"). Otherwise Cm, Cg ("those who perform the consecration of the king," so Hillebrandt 1916, p. 42; Altekar 1958, pp. 81-82), Cs ("those who make [one] a king, that is, counselors" [on 73.11], Dharma 1947). The NR reads instead, "gurus of the king."

4. "dead" *pañcatvam āpanne*: See the note on 57.24.

6. Rājagṛha: Cf. note on 8.22.

7. "here and now" *ihādyaiva*: These emphatic adverbs, and verse 25 below, clearly rule out the interpretation of Cg and Ck, who understand *ikṣvākūṇām* as "(one) of the four (above-mentioned) Ikṣvāku princes." What is meant is that some other collateral member of the dynastic house, a nephew or brother of the king, for example, should accede to the throne (cf. also the NR paraphrase, "What member of the House of the Ikṣvākus is to become king?" 1554*).

8ff. For this catalogue of calamities occurring in the state of anarchy (on the refrain cf. note on 25.5), we may compare in particular *MBh* 12.67-68. For a number of the verses here close, occasionally verbatim, parallels are available: 8-68.23; 9-68.17; 9, 17-68.21; 10-67.12; 12-68.25; 13, 1561*.5-68.22; 1561*.7-8, 1562*- 68.32; 16-68.30; 20, 23-68.13; 21-67.17; 1573*-67.14 (cf. also *MBh* 12.15.32-33, which approximate our verses 23 and 22, respectively).

8. "heavenly" *divyena*: Cg believes the qualification implies that other sorts of showers—of hailstones, for example—do occur.

9. "handfuls of grain are not sown" *bījamuṣṭiḥ prakīryate*: For fear of plunderers, with no king on hand to suppress them (Ck, Ct).

10. "one cannot have a wife" *nāsti bhāryā*: Because in a kingless state kinship relations are disrupted (? *bandhunigrahāt*) (Cg), or because wives become unfaithful (Cr; cf. Cs, "they are corrupted by rogues"), or simply because they are stolen away (cf. *MBh* 12.67.15).

The *MBh* refers to this line (and quotes it with some variation): "This *śloka* about kings was sung long ago by the great Bhārgava [= Vālmīki?] in his famous *Rāmacarita*: 'One must first secure a king, then a wife, then money. For without a king in the world, how could there be wives or money?' " (*MBh* 12.57.40-41; cf. 1.148.12). This parallel, incidentally, makes Roussel's suggestion unnecessary, namely, that *bhārya-* here has the sense of "soldier" (Roussel 1912, p. 20).

"And there is yet further peril" *idam atyāhitaṃ cānyat*: Translated in agreement with Cg, because of the position of *ca* (Cm, " 'There is [no] great fear,' that is, in those who would do wrong"; Ck, Ct, Cr, "this—that is, what is described in *pādas* ab—is a great danger"); cf. also, for the idea, 101.10 below.

12. "sacred rites" *sattrāṇi*: Defined as "[a sacrifice] where all the people are patrons [or, "consecrated" (Ck)] and all likewise priests" (Cg, Ck, Ct; according to *MīmāSū* 10.6.61, a sacrifice extending over more than twelve days; cf. also Kane 1962-1975, vol. 2.ii, p. 1,133 and note).

14. "litigants receive no satisfaction" *na . . . siddhārthā vyavahāriṇaḥ*: "Because there is no one (fairly) to adjudicate their disputes, and because corruption is rampant" (Cg); the line may also, but with less probability, refer to "tradesmen" who "achieve no purpose" by their trades (Cm, Cg, Ct, Cr).

"storytellers" *kathāśīlāḥ*: So Cm, Cg; compare *yajñaśīlāḥ* in verse 12. (Ck, Ct understand, "Storylovers [audiences, *kathāśīlāḥ*] are not pleased by storytellers [*kathāpriyaiḥ*].") The verse may also, according to Cg, refer to "debaters" who are not "satisfied" because there is no king to reward them.

18. "there wander no solitary . . . sages" *caraty ekacaraḥ . . . muniḥ*: Because no one will give them alms (Cg, Cr). Jain monks were actually prohibited from visiting kingless states (cf. Jayaswal 1955, pp. 82-85).

22. This verse (like the previous one) is omitted in the three good D manuscripts 4, 5, 7 (and read wholly differently in the NR). Here we probably have a late

insertion, borrowed from *MBh* 12.15.33. The *MBh* version runs, "Atheists, who break all bounds and denounce the *vedas*, become available for [the king's] purposes [*bhogāya*, so read in our verse by Crā; cf. also Belvalkar's note ad loc.] when punishment suppresses them." To translate it reasonably in its present context requires some twisting, though not quite as much as Cg, Ck find necessary ("Atheists too, who break all bounds, whom royal punishment had once suppressed, tend to gain in power, for all their fears are put to rest [in a kingless state]"). We agree in the main with Cm.

The atheists ("those who deny there is a world to come," Cr) "break all bounds," say Cg, Ck, Ct, "since they transgress the limits of their own caste, subcaste and stage of life."

23. "Ah" *aho*: The NR (and the parallel verse in *MBh* 12.15.32) reads instead *andham*, "It would be like blinding darkness." (Ct wants to take *tama* as locative singular of an a-stem form of *tamas*, "[this world would be] in darkness," but this is unneeded.)

"it would be like darkness" *tama ivedam*: This may refer either to the world (Cm, Cg, Cr) or, as seems more probable, to the condition of anarchy (Cg, Ck).

25. "what awaits us" *vṛttam*: Past participle with immediate future sense (cf. note on 3.5 above).

"Name some prince" *kumāram . . . vadānyam*: Again it is quite evident that the counselors do not mean that Vasiṣṭha should "name" one of the sons of Daśaratha (Cg, Ck), but some other member of the dynasty who is present in Ayodhyā (cf. note on verse 7 above).

Sarga 62

1. "the brahmans and the hosts of ministers and allies" *mitrāmātyagaṇān . . . brāhmaṇān*: The line shows asyndeton (as Cg and Ck, Ct seem to agree), but whether *mitrāmātya-* is *karmadhāraya* (Cg) or *dvandva* (as translated) cannot be firmly determined (though on the first alternative it does seem superfluous to specify that the counselors are "friendly").

2. "in the city of Rājagṛha" *pure rājagṛhe*: Ck and Ct read differently, "he to whom the kingship has been given."

3. The NR offers instead, "Let them bring him here by the word of the king, which he spoke when he was dying [? *atyayavādinaḥ*]" (1577*).

5. The NR (1580*) mentions only three messengers, whereas Ck interprets the SR (= crit. ed.) as giving only four names (cf. 1581*). With the exception of Nanda, the names are those of some of the counselors mentioned in 1.7, and there is no reason (*pace* Cm, Cg, Ck) not to assume these are the same men.

6. "on my authority" *śāsanād . . . mama*: The NR reads, "on the order of his father," and, in verse 7, " 'Your father asks.' "

9. "for the king" *rājñaḥ*: For Aśvapati, king of the Kekayas.

In the descriptions of both the messengers' route here to Rājagṛha on the Vitastā (Jhelum) in the northwest, and Bharata's route to Ayodhyā in *sarga* 65, there is considerable uncertainty in the constitution of the text and in the identification of many place names. (Aid was provided by the most recent compendium, Schwartzberg 1978.) Both accounts give the impression of archaic tradition, with which the poet had no personal familiarity.

After this verse the SR inserts, "By the west of Mount Aparatāla to the north of Mount Pralamba, between these two they went along the Mālinī River" (1584*). According to the commentators, these two mountains to the west of Ayodhyā extend north and south parallel to each other; the messengers traveled north between them along the river, and then headed west after reaching the northern slope of Mount Pralamba.

10. "at Hastinapura after reaching" *hastinapure . . . āsādya*: We agree with Cm in the admittedly unusual construction, joining *pāda* c with a and *pāda* d with b. Hastinapura is [Kuru-]Pañcāla country, whereas the Kuru jungle is to the west of the city, beyond the Yamunā.

Hereafter the NR (1586*) shows them crossing the Sarasvatī River (west of Kurukṣetra), but then coming to Puṣkar[l]āvatī, which seems to be recorded only as the name of a city 150 miles *west* of Rājagṛha.

11. Śaradaṇḍā: The name is attested only here. A few D manuscripts replace it with Śatadrū (Sutlej), which does flow to the east of the Vipāśā (Beas) (cf. verse 13). *Śaradaṇḍām* has otherwise full manuscript support; is it perhaps the name of the Śatadrū northeast of its confluence with the Vipāśā?

12. "the venerable tree" *nikūlavṛkṣam*: For a similar wishing-tree see note on 49.4. The NR calls it a *caitya* or shrine.

There is no mention elsewhere of a *city* named Kuliṅgā. A region of that name (or "Kulinda") appears to be located by the *MBh* considerably further to the east, due north of Kurukṣetra. The NR for the most part reads Bhūliṅga, but this area is far to the southwest.

13. "Abhikāla . . . Tejobhibhavana": We agree in desperation with Cm, Ck, Ct, Cr in identifying these as names of two villages, and Śālmalī (besides the well-known Vipāśā) as the name of a river (unattested elsewhere, as is Mount Sudāman). Raghavan (1943) has argued that the correct reading here is (*te*) *bodhibhavana-*, "Abode of the Bodhi tree" (there is indeed strong manuscript support for this in the SR), but there is no evidence that *bodhi* is ever used of any peepul except for the celebrated one in Gayā.

"the Foot of Viṣṇu" *viṣṇoḥ padam*: A mountain located near Kashmir (cf. *MBh* 3.130.8; cf. Belvalkar's note on *MBh* 12.29.31 with references).

Within this verse the SR adds, "They crossed the hereditary river Ikṣumatī [that is, the villages on whose banks belonged by hereditary right to the Ikṣvākus (Cg)]" (1588*; cf. 1.69, especially 3, to which Ck refers the reader). But this only adds to the confusion if the *Ikṣumatī* is to be identified as a tributary of the Ganges flowing through Farrukhabad district (with Agrawala 1963, pp. 43-44).

14. The NR reads here, "(they arrived) on the seventh night." Bharata will similarly spend seven nights on the road (65.14), but even this is something of an exaggeration for a journey of more than seven hundred miles.

15. "master" *bhartuḥ*: This refers to Bharata. He will be called their "king" in 64.2 (see note there).

"to bring the news" *priyārtham*: Cf. 3.29 and note. The commentators explain otherwise, and unsatisfactorily, as for example Cm, Cg: "It is a '*kindness* to their master' [Daśaratha] insofar as his reaching the other world depends on Bharata's being quickly brought and performing the funeral rites."

Sarga 63

2. "just as night was ending" *vyuṣṭām eva tu tāṃ rātrim*: "[This specification of time] is made in order to hint that, being an early morning dream, it will come true immediately" (Cg, cf. below, note on verse 18; similarly Ct). According to our chronology, and theirs, it already has, of course. Syntactically the phrase is an accusative of time at which (cf. note on 37.26).

4. "and sang" *gānti*: The reading of the crit. ed., *śāntim*, has no syntactical relationship here. The commentators are forced to understand with it *uddiśya* ("in order to pacify him"); PW s.v. *vad* cites this verse as an absolute use of the verb, whereas s.v. *śānti* it takes *vad* with the noun in the sense of "wish one well," which simply does not fit here (the parallel cited by PW, 5.69.28 vulgate, is removed in the crit. ed., 66.29). The correct reading, *gānti*, is preserved in D4, 5, 7. This was apparently misunderstood by the editor to be a corruption, but we now know that the form is part of the epic dialect: in *MBh* 5.107.9c *gānti* is correctly restored by the crit. ed. (cf. also 2.10.9 and Edgerton's note ad loc. and 7.48.48). It is, moreover, confirmed by the gloss in the NR, *jaguś* (1594*). Note also the common collocation of singing, dancing, and playing music (together called *saṃgīta*), as for example in 1.31.11, 2.85.23.

8ff. Compare the dream of Trijaṭā in 5.25.18ff.: Rāvaṇa, wearing red garlands and smeared with red cream, drives a team of asses south; the women of Laṅkā drink oil; Kumbhakarṇa and the other *rākṣasas* enter a dung-filled pond. Karṇa (*MBh* 5.141.27ff.) sees in his dream the victors in battle dressed in white, the vanquished in red and driving toward the south on camel carts.

13. "were . . . mocking him" *prahasanti*: Several S manuscripts read *praharanti*, "were beating him."

"part yellow, part black" *kṛṣṇapiṅgalāḥ*: In such a form does time personified come to the Vṛṣṇi tribe, *MBh.* 16.3.2.

14. "a righteous man" *dharmātmā*: Bharata's statement in verse 15, substantiated in 16, makes sense only if the referent of this noun-phrase is indefinite, and so we take it (despite the explicit mention of "my father" in the NR; but cf. its version of verse 15, noted there). For the significance of the south, cf. note on 57.11.

15. "terrifying dream" *bhayāvaham*: Not "terrifying night," with the crit. ed. The best S manuscripts and the NR coordinate *bhayāvaha-* with the dream (*etat*); there is not the slightest reason not to accept *bhayāvaham* here.

In the second half of the verse the NR reads, "Clearly Rāma or the king has died and gone to heaven."

16. "For when in a dream" *svapne . . . hi*: Ck cites *śruti* to authenticate the premonitory power of such dreams: "When in a dream one sees a black man with black teeth, who kills him [cf. *Rām* 6.26.25] . . . when [in a dream] one drives a team of asses or boars" [*AitĀ* 3.2.4; cf. the remarks of Keith 1909, p. 254 n14]. Compare Śaṅkara on *BrahmSū* 2.1.14, "By an unreal phantom in a dream we can be informed of a real fact, such as death," also on 3.2.4; and cf. the moving apostrophe to Sleep in *AV* 6.46.2 ("O sleep . . . agent of Yama . . . protect us from evil-dreaming" [Whitney]).

18. "that never before had entered my mind" *avitarkitāṃ purā*: Cg remarks, "The implication of the phrase is that the dream will come true, for when one thinks consciously [about something before dreaming it, then the dream] does not come

true. . . . The scriptural passage [*AitĀ*, see note on verse 16] is corroborated in this *sarga*, the special significance here being as follows: A dream concerning something one has previously [consciously] thought about does not come true; [when the content of a dream is totally unpremeditated] and it occurs at dawn, the dream will come true the same day; the earlier the hour, the less immediately does this happen [cf. *MatsyaP* 242.15-20, which claims that a dream seen in the last watch of the night comes true within a month; cf. also Kane 1962-1975, vol. 5.ii, pp. 778-79]; and finally it is the dreamer himself or a relative of his who comes to experience what is dreamt."

Sarga 64

1. Before this verse some D manuscripts insert a passage in which Bharata's friends explain that dreams are but half-true delusions and result from the bodily humors; that the divine (or fate, *daiva*) is the one recourse for those afflicted by the divine; therefore he should pray to the gods and pay homage to brahmans and cows, and these acts will release him from this "mental evil" (1614*).

2. "of the king" *rājñaḥ*: That is, Bharata himself. We follow Cg, Ck, Ct, Cr here; Ct adds that "other" commentators take "king" as referring to Kaikeya. That the envoys and everyone else in Ayodhyā already consider Bharata to be their king is clear from 65.22 (see note there).

4. "two hundred million" *viṃśatikoṭyaḥ*: A fascination with large figures is often found in Sanskrit literature, and any attempt at realistic computation is misplaced.

5. "his loved ones" *suhṛjjane*: Cg, Ck, Ct, Cr understand this to refer to Bharata's uncle and so on (supplying, "made the presentations to them"). Considering the questions that follow it would be more reasonable to see here a reference to his family in Ayodhyā.

7. "looks to it [righteousness]" *dharmadarśinī*: Cg explains differently, "She sees only the righteousness in her people; she accentuates the positive, not the negative."

8. "middle mother" *jananī . . . madhyamā*: Cf. note on 19.22.

9. "And Kaikeyī, too" *cāpi kaikeyī . . . kim uvāca ha*: We take *cāpi* as a connective, and *kim* as the interrogative particle, after which we are to supply *iti*, *uvāca* as often closing the discourse (with or without *iti*, cf. 41.9).

"my ever-selfish, hot-tempered, and irascible mother" *ātmakāmā sadā caṇḍī krodhanā*: The poet is a little too eager here (as in verse 5) to dissociate Bharata from Kaikeyī's wicked designs, and the effect is to strain credibility. For not only has no prior indication been given of Bharata's feelings toward his mother, but everything in the early chapters testifies that Kaikeyī was by nature a good woman, and only corrupted by an evil servant. Cg comments, "The epithets 'selfish' and so on are meant to suggest that Bharata, by reason of the nightmare and the arrival of the messengers, suspects that Kaikeyī has done something wrong."

10. "All fare well" *kuśalās te*: The NR magnifies the messengers' deceit by continuing, "Your father says you are to come quickly" (1623*, though cf. notes on 62.3 and 62.6); the SR has them add, "Lotus[-bearing] Śrī chooses you," which according to the commentators is not supposed to have its normal meaning (namely, that the kingship has passed to him), but rather is intended as a declaration of good fortune to put Bharata at ease (improbable, but see 73.15).

15. "has a worthy son" *suprajāḥ*: Nominative singular feminine, as if from the stem *-prajaḥ* (Renou 1968, p. 102; not infrequent in the *Rām*, cf. 90.5, 3.3.17; for a possible example of compounding with the mother's name [which is how Ck impossibly wants to read here], see above 14.11 and note there).

18. "gold ornaments" *niṣka-*: The commentators are in agreement that some sort of breast ornament is meant. There is no evidence to suggest that these would be [minted] coins, as per Vyas (1967, pp. 217 and note, 247); cf. Rau 1973, pp. 52-53 (= a necklace or choker, also used as a unit of weight).

19. Aśvapati: Cv notes, "Aśvapati is here called the grandfather, but how could this be the case since we read earlier, 'his maternal uncle Aśvapati' [1.6 above, where asyndeton is probable]? This really presents no problem; Aśvapati ["lord of horses"] is a family name of the Kekayas, for they possessed many horses."

20. "Mount Irāvata and Mount Indraśira": The commentators are not unanimous in identifying Irāvata (perhaps a back-formation from Airāvata, Indra's elephant) and Indraśira as either mountains or regions. The names appear to be unattested elsewhere.

21. The SR adds after this verse that Bharata, hurrying to depart and full of foreboding because of the dream and the messengers' haste, did not find any pleasure in the gifts (1636*).

23. "circle-wheeled" *maṇḍalacakrān*: A literal translation, for the phrase is obscure, though Ck may well be right: "A wheel used for starting a chariot under way, situated in the middle of the wheels at the four corners; we still find it used in Kāñci and other places" (Cg, "round wheels" [!]; Cm, "wheels fitted on in a circular formation"). Cm (and Ck apparently) takes *pādas* ab and cd separately, *yojayitvā* then having to signify, "having assembled."

24. "whom his grandfather trusted like himself" *āryakasyātmasamaiḥ*: *Ātma-* here is by exception reflexive not to the main subject but to *āryakasya*. Some S manuscripts, Ck among them, read in place of this *sabhāryakaḥ*, "along with his wife."

"Gṛha" *gṛhāt*: Instead of being short for *rājagṛhāt*, this could of course just mean "from the house."

"untroubled by enemies" *apetaśatruḥ*: The epithet is principally for alliteration, *śatrughnam apetaśatruḥ*.

"as a perfected being . . . the world of Indra" *siddha ivendralokāt*: It is not usual for such mythopoeic similes to have any narrative value (cf. note on 2.29), but this one seems to, suggesting that Bharata was suddenly transported from the Kashmirian paradise to the real world of personal, familial, and political turmoil in Ayodhyā.

Sarga 65

1. Cg comments, "The messengers had taken the straight though difficult route in order to reach Girivraja as quickly as possible; Bharata follows the great way, circuitous though it is, because he has a four-part army with him. That is why the names of the rivers, mountains, and so on mentioned here are different [from those in *sarga* 62]" (similarly Ck, Ct). With a few obvious exceptions, there is virtually no information on any of the geographical features mentioned in this *sarga*.

"deep" *hrādinīm*: The name of a river, according to Cg, Ct, Cr (so Cm, Ck, who read *hlādinīm*; *hrā-* is authenticated by the NR). The position of *ca*, however, and the use of the word in verse 4 below, clearly suggest that the item is an adjective (cf. PW s.v. *hradin*).

The SR has Bharata first cross the (otherwise unattested) Sudāmā River (1638*).

2-3. Cg believes (the unknown) Eladhāna to be on the Śatadrū.

"the 'river trailing stones' " *śilām ākurvatīm*: With Cm, Cg, we take this to be an epexegetical epithet of the river Śilāvahā ("bearing stones"), which we have in 3b (cf. another etymological figure for the name of a river at 43.9). (No river of this name is mentioned elsewhere in Sanskrit literature. Perhaps it is the Dṛṣadvatī, the "Stony River," a tributary of the Sarasvatī, known from the *ṚV*.) Otherwise we follow Ck in the main for the remainder of the two *ślokas*.

"honest, majestic and ever true to his word" *satyasaṃdhaḥ śuciḥ śrīmān*: For the intrusive commendation of Bharata, cf. note on 64.9.

After this verse the SR has Bharata cross the Sarasvatī and Ganges (which some commentators take to mean the Indus), and enter the Bhāruṇḍa forest beyond the land of the Vīramatsyas (1642*, 1643*).

4. Kuliṅgā: To be distinguished from the Kuliṅgā in 62.12, which is the name of a city.

5. "he took a store of water" *ādāya codakam*: That is, for his journey through the wilderness mentioned in the next verse (as Cg observes [so Cs]; not out of regard for the river as a holy place, as per Ck, Ct).

6. "as the wind (passes through) the sky" *mārutaḥ kham iva*: Ck reads in place of this, *meruprakhyam atha*, "(passed through the wilderness) called Meru" (not recorded in the crit. ed.).

An NR insertion hereafter shows Bharata crossing the Hiraṇvatī (1645*), and an SR (1646*), the Ganges.

7. "the southern end of Toraṇa" *toraṇaṃ dakṣiṇārdhena*: The accusative is prescribed by *Pā* 2.3.31.

9. "Bharata took leave of the army" *anujñāpyātha bharato vāhinīm*: Cg, Ck, Ct observe that since the land east of Ujjihānā was his own country, Bharata could allow the retinue to proceed at its own pace without fear, while he himself hurried on ahead. They also agree (citing *AmaK* in support) that *sāla* has here the [rare] sense of "tree" in general (contrast verse 12); and that *āsthāya vājinaḥ* means not "mounting horses" but yoking them to the chariot, inasmuch as later (verse 14) Bharata is shown to be riding in a chariot.

11. "the Gomatī": In 43.9 the Gomatī appears to be due south of Ayodhyā; cf. *MBh* 13.31.18, with Dandekar's note there (placing the river in Oudh).

15. "white-clay" *pāṇḍumṛttikā*: Or, "white-chalk." Presumably plastering or whitewashing is meant. Cm, Ck, probably rightly, understand this as a general epithet of the city, rather than one specifically indicating absence of joy ("because the practice of smearing the walls with cowdung [as a sign of, and means of securing, good luck] has been suspended," Cg, Cr; "despite its being protected . . . it looked like a mass of white clay, that is, worthless," Ct).

18. "since dusk" *sāyāhne*: Bharata has arrived at Ayodhyā in the early morning, and what he describes here should accord with that fact. We thus follow Cg, Ck, Ct, Cr on the temporal aspect of the compound; cf. also note on verse 19.

19. "to be weeping" *anurudantīva*: Because of the dewdrops? Compare a similar image in 3.15.16.

21. "various portents" *vividhāni . . . nimittāni*: Such portents, according to the commentators, would be the cry of a jackal [see 3.55.2], the appearance of a crow, the twitching of the left eye [cf. 3.55.20] (birds and animals passing on the left, 3.55.11; tripping, 3.58.1; etc.).

22. "the Gate of Victory" *dvāreṇa vaijayantena*: We agree with Cg, Cr in taking *vaijayantena* as a proper name (Cm [first explanation], Ck, Ct [first explanation], "so called because it had a palace similar to Indra's palace [Vaijayanta]").

"with cries of 'Long live the king!' " *vijayaṃ pṛṣṭhaḥ*: This means to call out [*vi-*] *jayatu devaḥ*, "May the god be victorious." It is the greeting that causes Bharata's puzzlement in the next verse, for it is only given to kings (cf. 6.23.34, to Rāvaṇa; 6.109.1, to Rāma; note that Bharata is already regarded as king by the people, cf. 64.2, 75.1). A nice touch by the poet, which the commentators overlook.

By the syllable *re* (in *dvāreṇa*), which is the sixth syllable of the *Gāyatrīmantra*, Cm, Cg observe that at this point in the text 5,000 verses of the (traditional) *Rām* have been completed (cf. note on 39.5).

Sarga 66

3. "his house" *svagṛham*: That is, his mother's house (Cs).

"the royal splendor was absent" *śrīvivarjitam*: Probably simply grandiloquence for "the king was not there" (cf. verse 12). Bharata would normally have done obeisance to his father first (cf. verse 13).

4. "drew . . . to her breast" *aṅke . . . āropya*: It is a curiously persistent error to translate *aṅka-* as "lap." That, in fact, it usually does not mean this in the *Rām* is indicated by such verses as 3.49.15, *aṅkenādāya . . . papāta bhuvi*, "Clutching [her] in his embrace he lept to the ground."

6. Note the asyndeton in *pādas* ab (confirmed by verse 8 cd).

8. "Last night" *adya . . . rātriḥ*: Cm, Cg, Ct here correctly explain the idiom (cf. 56.14 above).

9. "but they were an encumbrance, and so I left them on the road" *pariśrāntaṃ pathy abhavat*: The NR's *pathi tac chrāntam utsṛjya* supports Cg's interpretation of the syntax here (Ck explains, "[the gifts, that is, the animals] grew tired on the way").

14. "an artful mother to an artless son" *ajānantaṃ prajānantī*: This *pāda*, a very common syntactical schema (cf. 10.3), is taken independently and the verbals absolutely; Cg, Ck, Ct want *prajānantī* to govern *priyavat*, which is perfectly possible, but the syntactical design and symmetry seem deliberate.

"Your father has followed" *te pitā gataḥ*: Cg thinks this is a gentle locution employed in order not to arouse sorrow in Bharata; but it seems impersonal and cold, intimating that Kaikeyī did not much grieve for her husband's death (first because, as a young woman married to an old man, she always knew that she could be widowed at any moment; then too, she had married Daśaratha only because she had been able to extract the promise of her son's succession [cf. 99.3 and note]; thus Varadacharya 1964-1965, vol. 2, p. 123n).

15. "of a righteous family" *dharmābhijana-*: We agree with Cm, Ct, Cr in understanding the compound as a *madhyamapadalopi*, that is, with the middle element (such as *yukta-*) suppressed.

19. "prince" *rājaputra*: Some S manuscripts (and Ck and Cs) read, perhaps authentically, "king."

24-25. "the great and illustrious king" *mahārājaḥ . . . kīrtimān*: Despite the indications of Ck (and Varadacharya 1964-1965, vol. 2, p. 125n), Ct, and the NR (which in fact reads "my aged father"), there is no doubt that these verses refer to Rāma and not to Daśaratha. Bharata's use of *mahārāja*, "great king," in reference to Rāma is a fine artistic touch: skillfully but unobtrusively the poet hereby underscores both the absolute lack of any kingly ambitions on Bharata's own part (recall his confusion at being addressed as king in 65.22, and cf. 75.1), and his unquestioned, innate conviction that Rāma should and would naturally succeed (cf. verse 21).

28. "truthful" *satyavikramaḥ*: See notes on 19.7 and 104.3.

"just" *sādhu*: Apparently, "before you summon Rāma." (Ck on verse 29 takes *sādhu* in compound with *saṃdeśam*, "good message.")

29. "Kaikeyī replies with the intention of destroying his affection for his father, by saying, 'his last thoughts were not about you at all, but only about Rāma,' " Cg.

34. "promptly" *yugapad*: Cm, Cg, Ct understand in its more usual sense, "simultaneously," that is, at the same moment as she told of the king's death. We prefer the interpretation of Varadacharya, who comments, "One might expect, in relating something so vicious, that she would have to pause time and again, being unable to get the words out; but in fact she tells everything without any reluctance or difficulty" (1964-1965, vol. 2, p. 127n).

36. "about his brother's conduct" *bhrātuś cāritra-*: The NR eliminates Bharata's doubt about Rāma, reading "mother" for "brother."

37. "of any brahman" *brāhmaṇa- . . . kasyacit*: The indefinite adjective is to be construed with the noun in compound, against classical usage (not to be taken independently, "for some reason," Cm, Cg, Ct; "[or] of some one [else]," Cr).

38. "unborn child" *bhrūṇa-*: Cm, Cg implausibly want to interpret this as "brahman" (cf. Kane 1962-1975, vol. 2.i, p. 131 n290; p. 148 n334; vol. 3, p. 612 n1,161). Committing an abortion is considered a great sin as early as the *Nir* (6.27).

39. "with the same" *tenaiva*: The commentators refer this to the disposition Kaikeyī has shown throughout her interview with Bharata. We agree with Varadacharya in seeing a reference to her original transgression (1964-1965, vol. 2, p. 128n).

44. "as you know to be right" *dharmajña*: Literally, "knower of *dharma*." The commentators attempt to be more specific: "knower of political wisdom," Cm, Cg; "knower of the *dharma* requiring one to obey one's father's command, as Rāma did," Ct.

The NR here has Kaikeyī admit the contemptible nature of her deed (1715*), which does not seem to be implied in our verse by *evaṃvidham*, "such a thing," that is, "all that I could do."

Some S manuscripts hereafter insert a vigorous passage (1717*) in which Bharata violently rebukes his mother (exclaiming at one point, "You who exiled Rāma, who killed your husband, did I pass ten months in your belly! Oh god, I am an object of contempt to all the world"); he exhorts her to kill herself, saying he hesitates to kill her himself only because he shrinks from having it said of Rāma that his younger brother is a matricide, etc. (cf. 72.21, 98.47).

Sarga 67

4. "the night of doom" *kālarātriḥ*: "The all-destroying energy arising at the time of universal dissolution," Cm, Cg; "the night of universal dissolution," Ck, Ct.

7. "far-sighted" *dīrghadarśinī*: "Seeing the misfortune that would come at a later date ["from Kaikeyī," Ct]," Cm, Cg, Ct (we follow their indication of the concessive nature of the epithet).

9. "What possible purpose" *kiṃ nu paśyasi kāraṇam*: Translated thus in view of verse 10 (so, too, Cg, Ct explain); in view of verse 9ab, possible also: "what charge could you have brought against him" (see the note on 32.20).

12. "like Mount Meru behind its forest" *merur meruvanaṃ yathā*: The simile is not particularly effective. The commentators explain: "The Meru forest, springing up from Mount Meru [as Rāma from Daśaratha], acts as its guardian by making the way impassable" (Cm, Cg; so Ct). It is attested nowhere else in epic literature. Various NE manuscripts and D4, 5, 7 give, "[I resorted to Rāma] as the sun to Mount Meru" (1731*.7; see the note on 35.21), a sensible alternative.

14. "stratagems" *yogaiḥ*: As in *ArthŚā* 9.1.15, (*sāmādibhir*) *yogo*(*paniṣadbhyām ca*), "(conciliation and the other political means) or stratagems [such as spies, etc.] (or alchemical manipulations)" (cf. also 5.1.54; Cm, Cg wrongly take as = *sāma*, etc.).

"force of intellect" *buddhibalena*: Again see *ArthŚā*: "Power (*śakti*) is of three sorts: 'force of intelligence' (*jñānabala*), or the power of counsel (*mantraśakti*)" (6.2.33). Falsely Cm, Cg: "that is, when the intellect is endowed with the eightfold capacity for learning, retaining, and so on" (cf. *ArthŚā* 1.5.5 for the enumeration); Ck, Ct, "force—that is, physical force—joined with intellect."

"a woman so blindly ambitious for her son" *putragardhinīm*: The NR has the attractive variant *mātṛgandhini*, "you who only faintly resemble a mother" (1733*.2; cf. 73.12). Here the SR adds a verse to some extent confirmed by the NR (though not by the NW): "For in this family, among all our ancestors, the eldest (son) is consecrated to the kingship, and the other brothers show him strict obedience. You never considered this law of kings [SR; you destroyed this commendable practice (NR)]" (1735*.5-7 nearly = 1732*.9-11).

15. "inside a mountain cave" *parvatagahvarasthaḥ*: The qualification refers not to the supposition that lions roar louder when comfortably ensconced in their caves (Cg), but to the fact that the roar would be painfully amplified in an enclosed space (thus too Varadacharya 1964-1965, vol. 2, p. 138n).

Sarga 68

2. "you . . . should be expelled from the kingdom" *rājyād bhraṃśasva*: "That is, as her mother was," Cg, Ck (cf. note on 32.1 above).

"may you weep your eyes out without me" *mām ṛte rudatī bhava*: The meaning of the *pāda* is uncertain. The crit. ed. prints *mā mṛtam*, where *mā* is taken by the commentators either as the negative or = *mām*. The first would be translated, "do not weep for the dead (your husband)," do not perform those actions, such as weeping, which a woman should; you are no longer fit to do so since you have lost the feelings appropriate to a wife (Ck, Ct, Cg [second interpretation]); the second would mean, "considering me dead may you weep": since you have done a deed that could kill me, consider me dead ["because you have abandoned *dharma* your son cannot be expected to live" (Ct)] (Cm, Cg). As for the first alternatives, no evidence has been provided that Kaikeyī has been weeping for Daśaratha; if anything, just the contrary. The second alternative, on the other hand, not only fits in poorly with *pāda* c ("abandoned by *dharma,* weep for me who am, whom you may consider, dead"), but would be a solecism unique in the *Rām,* for the *pāda* would then commence with an enclitic. What Bharata seems to be saying is this: According to justice you should be thrown out of the kingdom and, "in disgrace with fortune and men's eyes," have all alone to weep for your outcast state, without me, for whom you claim to have done all this. Reading *mām ṛte* (cf. the NR's *mām ṛte* in a related context [1741*.6]) seems the most reasonable solution. Significantly, the rather rare accusative + *ṛte* is attested elsewhere in the *Rām* (for example, 5.36.5, 6.23.31; cf. also the critical apparatus on *MBh* 1.69.27a for a similar case).

4. "You are guilty of murdering the unborn" *bhrūṇahatyām asi prāptā*: "Guilty of a sin equal to the murder . . ." Cg. Or perhaps Bharata's charge is to be taken literally: What Kaikeyī has in fact done is to annihilate the future generations of the House of Ikṣvāku.

5. "(such evil . . .) renouncing" (*īdṛśaṃ pāpam . . .*) *hitvā*: Here *pāda* c is construed appositionally in the relative clause. Bharata's fear would be that, if Kaikeyī could abandon Rāma, whom all the world loves, what might she do to him (cf. 42.19, 21 above). The alternatives of the commentators are not persuasive: Ck, "the fear that by reason of her transgression Rāma will abandon him"; Ct, "fear, that is, of the people's reproach, namely, that Kaikeyī's son is naturally as corrupt as she is; or that equal guilt may attach to him by associating with her" (that is, on the principle that "one who closely associates or dwells with any one of the four [five] great sinners himself incurs *mahāpātaka* [equal sin]" [Kane 1962-1975, vol. 4, p. 25]).

6. "infamy" *ayaśaḥ*: Probably "that Bharata would be thought to have colluded with his mother to have his father killed and brother exiled" (Cg), rather than "that Bharata is the son of an evil mother who killed her husband" (Ck). *Ca* in *pāda* c coordinates the three acts, and does not imply "also in the world to come" (Cm, Ct).

10. We understand this *śloka* closely with verse 11; less likely is Cg's construction, taking it as a substantiation of the statement in verse 9, for the acts mentioned in verse 10 would not necessarily endanger the House of Kekaya.

13. "(that Rāma) arose from Kausalyā's very self" (*rāmaṃ*) *kausalyāyātmasaṃbhavam*: Considering the context—verses 12 and 14ff.—we understand the *pāda* (note double *saṃdhi, kausalyāyātma-*) as containing the predicate of the object clause (so Ck); Cg (and Ct) prefer, "you were not aware that Rāma, Kausalyā's son, is temperate" ("that is, she thought he would, like some baser man, slay his [affinal] kin").

"very self" *ātma-*: Quite possibly the word means "body" here (compare verse 23 below).

14. "Limb from mother's limb is a son born" *aṅgapratyaṅgajaḥ putraḥ*: The line is a near quotation of a famous *mantra* (cited in the *ŚāṅkhāĀ* 4.11, *Nir* 3.4 and elsewhere; see Kane 1962-1975, vol. 3, p. 641 n1, 220; the verse continues, "you are the [parent's] self with the name of 'son.' May you live a hundred autumns").

"Being born 'limb from limb' means that a child arises from the vital sap [*tejas*] collected from all the limbs . . . [sperm in the man's case], blood in the woman's," Cg, Ck, Ct.

"because he is her very own, and not mere kin" *priyatvān na tu bāndhavaḥ*: The *pāda* is problematic. Cg, Ck, Ct read differently, *priyā eva tu bāndhavāḥ*, "while relatives are merely dear." Cm, reading with the crit. ed., presses it to mean, "because he is 'dear' he is not (like) (some other) relative, an adopted son, for example." Neither explanation is convincing. The translation of *priyatvāt* as "because he is her very own" relies on an admittedly archaic sense of *priya-* (compare Homeric *phílos*; cf. Mayrhofer 1956-1980, s.v., and, for the connotations of the word, Stanford on *Odyssey* 1.60), but this sense may well have remained in currency through to the late vedic period (perhaps the *KauṣīBrU's indrasya priyaṃ dhāma* [3.1, p. 73] presents an example), and it might have been thought to harmonize with the archaizing character of the citation in the first half of the verse; it appears to fit well with the content of those *pādas*.

15ff. The story of the divine wish-granting cow Surabhi (also the *homa*-cow of Vasiṣṭha; often, as here, conceived of as residing in heaven [cf. verse 17], though in the *MBh* [5.100.1, for example] she is said to dwell in Rasātala, the seventh level of the subterranean world), is told also, with some few variations, at *MBh* 3.10.7-18.

15. "held in esteem by the gods" *surasaṃmatā*: For alliteration (a *yamaka*): *surabhiḥ surasaṃmatā*. So, too, in verse 17, "fragrant" *-surabhi*.

23. After this verse the NR continues with a narratively irrelevant but interesting story: Indra tells Surabhi not to be sad, for their suffering is a consequence of a decision the cows made themselves. They had practiced austerities and begged Brahmā that they might gain the highest worlds by their own acts. He told them to betake themselves to the world of men: all their sufferings there will be austerities to burn away sin. Any man that hurts them will reap evil, and any that succors them good. In the *MBh* version, Indra in commiseration causes rain to fall, impeding the labors of the farmer and releasing the ox (for here only one is mentioned) from its toil.

26. "amends" *apacitam*: The commentators all understand the word in the sense of "honor": "must pay full honor," but this is less apposite.

29. "like the banner of Indra, Śacī's lord" *śacīpateḥ ketur iva*: "Raising the banner [a bamboo staff decorated with garlands, etc.] in honor of Indra was a [late summer] festival [called Indramaha] prescribed for kings" (Kane 1962-1975, vol. 2.i, p. 398; cf. also Gonda 1966, pp. 74-77).

Sarga 69

1. Before this verse the NR includes eighteen lines, in which Bharata, addressing Śatrughna, ponders the power of fate; wondering then what he will say to Kausalyā, he begins to weep (1771*). The SR has Bharata vilify his mother in the midst of the counselors, maintaining that he did not lust after the kingship nor conspire with his mother; that, living far away, he knew nothing of the planned consecration of Rāma or of all that followed (1772*).

2. "Far-sighted" *dīrghadarśinam*: That is, malevolently forethoughtful, scheming (so Varadacharya [1964-1965, vol. 2, p. 148n] who refers to verse 6 below [cf. also 3.2.18]). Contrast Bharata's application of the epithet to Kausalyā, 67.7.

6. "how quickly" *śīghram*: Even more speedily than he might have anticipated, by reason of the king's untimely death (Varadacharya 1964-1965, vol. 2, p. 149n).

7. "what advantage" *kaṃ guṇam*: "For it was possible for her to acquire the kingship even without exiling Rāma," Cg; "Had he been present, Rāma, in accordance with his father's order, would have behaved just like Bhīṣma [in the *MBh* epic], and have consecrated you and stood by your side," Ck, Ct.

8. "Why doesn't Kaikeyī . . . drive me out as well" *mām api kaikeyī prasthāpayitum arhati*: "I must be equally an unwitting source of sorrow to her," Ck.

Hiraṇyanābha: Literally, "Of the golden navel" (or, "of the golden chariot-wheel"). This unusual epithet appears to be some kind of cognomen of the offspring of Kosalan women. See *PraśnaU* 6.1, *hiraṇyanābhaḥ kausalyo rājaputraḥ* (cf. also *ŚāṅkhāŚS* 16.9.13).

9. "and the sacred fires carried at our head" *agnihotraṃ puraskṛtya*: Since Kausalyā suspects Bharata of having conspired with Kaikeyī, she allows him no authority to perform the funeral rites of Daśaratha, and asserts here that she will take with her the king's sacred fires [cf. 70.13 and note] and by implication the body of the king to Rāma for cremation (Cm, Cg, Ck, Ct).

10. "it is up to you" *arhasi*: Invidiously acknowledging Bharata's new kingly authority.

"send" *netum*: Taken as unmarked causative (cf. Cg on verse 11).

14ff. "Bharata gives voice to imprecations in order to repudiate the charge that Kausalyā levels at him," Cm, Cg; "Bharata's claim—that he loves Rāma even more deeply than in the past, since he now invests him with the status of father—is not now open to Kausalyā for confirmation by personal observation, and so he tries to certify it by his imprecations," Ck, Ct.

The curses, while expressed in a general way, refer particularly to Bharata (namely, "may my mind . . . if I sanctioned," etc.), by the exegetical rule that "there is no general statement without particular application" (*nirviśeṣaṃ na sāmānyam*) (Cm, Cg, Ct). This will be made explicit in verses 30-31.

"Here the poet, by the artifice of the curses, expounds various aspects of *dharma*," Cg. It is equally probable that, by demonstrating Bharata's deep knowledge of *dharma*, the poet wishes to invite the inference that Bharata could never have done something so unrighteous as to conspire against his elder brother. For another example of how Vālmīki invests conventional epic didacticism with narrative and aesthetic function, see note on 94.7ff.

There appears to be no particular *dharmaśāstra* that offers an identical catalogue of offenses. Parallels can be cited only eclectically. A rather similar list of imprecations occurs in the *MBh* (7.51.25ff.).

For the style of the refrain, see the note on 25.5.

14. "May that man never come to think in harmony with the sacred texts" *kṛtā śāstrānugā buddhir mā bhūt tasya kadācana*: That is, may he lose all awareness of the commandments and prohibitions propounded in the sacred and secular texts. "This is the greatest misfortune of all, so it is presented as the first curse; all the rest is simply amplification of this," Ck ("the implication is, may he die; cf. 'from loss of mind one dies' " [*BhagGī* 2.63], Cr).

15. "most wicked of men" *pāpīyasām*: Low-castes (Cg, Cr); for being the servant of a *śūdra* cf. *ManuSm* 11.69.

"pass urine" *mehatu*: Cf. *YājñaSm* 1.134 for the prohibition (1.16 for the positive prescription).

"kick a sleeping cow" *hantu pādena gāṃ suptām*: Cf. *Āpastamba* [cited by Ctr, vol. 2, p. 453], "One must avoid touching with one's foot [images of] the gods, a king, a brahman and a cow" (cf. *pādena spṛśate gāś ca* in a similar list of imprecations in *MBh* 13, App. I, No. 20, line 151, and *MBh* 7.51.30). The qualification "sleeping" means to exclude cases of self-defense (Cg). The verse does not mean "killing" a cow, as Cg seems to interpret, for although that of course is prohibited (see *ManuSm* 11.59), it is difficult to accomplish by kicking.

The NR adds: touching, when impure, a cow, fire, or a brahman; reviling a guru; lusting after the wife of a friend or guru (1788*).

16. "without remuneration" *anarthakam*: We follow here Ck, Ct, Cr (so Cm?); just possible is also, "(forces . . . to do a deed) of great improbity" (cf. *GautDS* 21.10, *pātakasaṃyojaka*, one who incites another to commit a crime that causes loss of caste).

17, 18. The reciprocal duties of king and subjects: loyalty in exchange for protection, and taxation only in consequence of protection (*BaudhDS* 1.10.1; Kane 1962-1975, vol. 3, pp. 36ff. and references).

21. The sin of *brahmojjhatā*, forgetting the *veda* (Ck, Ct; *ManuSm* 11.56; *YājñaSm* 3.228, *adhītasya nāśanam*).

After this verse D3 adds the sin of a brahman's teaching the *vedas* and *vedāṅgas* to a Niṣāda (1789*), the NR, the sin of those who bear (false) witness in a dispute (1790*).

22. "to no purpose" *vṛthā*: That is, without ritual motivation, without the pretext of a *śrāddha* feast (Ck, Ct). The foods mentioned are to be used only in a ceremonial context: cf. *ManuSm* 5.7 (a close parallel to our verse, cited by Ctr vol. 2, p. 456; cf. also *MBh* 7.51.28). For the use of meat (goat or sheep) in the *śrāddha* ceremony, cf. 1.48.9, 2.71.2, 3.10.55, and Ck, Ct noted on 17.15 above (also *SatyāŚS* 28.4.1; *YājñaSm* 1.258-61, 269, 272). According to Cm, Cg, the sin is that of cooking for oneself only, and not for gods, ancestors, guests (*ManuSm* 3.118; *YājñaSm* 3.238). The NR seems to have "interpreted" with Ck, Ct, for it reads verse 27 below as though that referred to the sin Cm, Cg mention here.

"may he show contempt for his gurus" *gurūṃś cāpy avajānātu*: Cf. *ManuSm* 11.55.

After this verse the SR inserts the sins of touching a cow with one's foot (as if it had "interpreted" verse 15 with Cg), criticizing one's teacher, being treacherous to a friend, divulging confidences, and so on (1793*).

23. "while he alone eats delicacies" *sa eko mṛṣṭam aśnātu*: Whereas the others have to eat spoiled food (Cg) or are starving (Ck, Ct). Compare *MBh* 5.33.40: "Who is crueler than the man who eats fine food all alone . . . without sharing with his dependents?" (cf. also verse 46). Ctr (vol. 2, p. 458) cites *VāmaP* [untraced]: "He who eats by himself, alone, when his dependents are starving, is reborn as a *caṇḍāla*" (cf. also *Suttanipāta* 1.6.102 and *MBh* 7.51.32).

Some S manuscripts add, "May he never get a seemly wife, and die childless, without performing the rites of *dharma*" (1794*).

24. "dependents" *bhṛtya-*: For this general sense of the word (usually "servants"), cf. 98.32 (also Cm, Cg, Ck, Ct, Cr on 1795*.2). The sin is covered by *ManuSm* 11.95 and 62, *YājñaSm* 3.237, 239.

After this verse the SR adds the sin of selling lak, salt, meat; of being killed while fleeing in battle; of wandering begging like an idiot, carrying a skull in one's hand; of addiction to liquor, dice, women; of never turning the mind to *dharma*, of giving alms to people who do not deserve it, and so on (1795*).

25. Cf. *VāsiDS* 1.18.

The NR adds, "May he be an incompetent who gains political power and governs with the help of incompetents; may he reside six months in a village and pimp for his own daughter" (1796*).

26. "violation of a guru's bed" *gurutalpage*: Cf. note on 57.22.

27. "obedience to the gods" *devatānām . . . śuśrūṣām*: "This consists of satisfying them with clarified butter, rice or barley oblations, sacrificial animals, cakes, and so on, collected for the fire-sacrifices; 'obedience to the ancestors' consists of propitiating them, on eclipse days, on the death days of the mother and father, and so on, with the previously mentioned things as well as rice, and so on," Cg. The NR substitutes, "May he eat on his own without offering to . . ." (see the note on verse 22 above).

28. Hereafter the SR inserts a long list of sins and misfortunes, including: having many children while being poor and sick; disappointing suppliants; engaging in deceit and fearing royal punishment; missing one's wife's proper period for intercourse; renouncing a lawful wedded wife and having adulterous affairs; the crimes of a brahman's allowing his family line to become extinct, of polluting water and giving poison, of impeaching the honor shown to a brahman, of milking a cow that has recently calved, of denying a thirsty man when water is available, of remaining silent during a legal dispute though able to supply corroborative evidence (1802*).

30. "called down upon his head" *śapamānam*: The *ātmanepada* here and in verse 31 is taken as reflexive.

31. "chokes the very breath of life" *prāṇān uparuṇatsi*: Cg suggests, "You 'hold back,' restore, my life-breath which was ready to depart because of my separation from Rāma; that is, by making these curses you have reassured me." But cf. the use of *upa* + *rudh* with *prāṇa*- in 3.64.11 (Jaṭāyus on the point of death), *uparuddhyanti me prāṇā* (*dṛṣṭir bhramati*), "My breath is coming harder (everything is swimming before my eyes)."

32. "If what you promise me is true" *satyapratijño me*: We agree with Cm and Ct in seeing a conditional aspect here. What precisely the phrase means is more difficult to ascertain: "(If) you are telling me the truth," Cm; "What is suggested is that he should fulfil what he promised to Kaikeyī [68.27], and bring back Rāma," Ct. Perhaps simply, "if your promises—the protestations implied by your oaths—are true, sincere."

After this the NR inserts a passage in which Kausalyā blesses Bharata, informs him that his father has been embalmed, and urges him to cast off his sorrow and protect the subjects (1806*).

33. "confusion" *mohāt*: Ck understands this as "faintness." May it not rather mean that Bharata was racked not only with sorrow over the loss of his father and brother but also by the "confusion" that he was being held responsible?

34. Hereafter the NR adds that when night was over the ministers and others entered the king's chamber and found Bharata nearly unconscious with grief (1810*).

Sarga 70

1. The crit. ed. incorrectly registers two chapters of the NR (App. 1, No. 23) after *sarga* 74. They rightfully belong here, being the NR version of crit. ed. *sarga* 70, to be followed by 1812*. The *sargas* consist of the following: Bharata's lament (lines 1-26), including his repudiation of the kingship and his expression of the desire

either to immolate himself or enter the forest; Vasiṣṭha's admonition and instruction to perform the funeral of Daśaratha (27-54); Bharata's sight of, and lament over, the dead king (55-90); further admonitions from Vasiṣṭha and Jābāli (90-110, including a reference to "good king Bhūridyumna," who after death was caused to fall from heaven by reason of his kinsmen's excessive lamentation, 99-102; cf. *Saund* 11.46); Bharata's recovery of firmness and his readiness to perform the funeral (111ff.).

2. "obsequies" *saṃyānam uttaram*: All the commentators appear to have read *uttamam*.

3. "regained his composure" *dhāraṇāṃ gataḥ*: Ck criticizes the reading as artificial, offering instead *dharaṇīṃ gataḥ*, "[gone to the earth, that is,] making a prostration before Vasiṣṭha; such a salutation to the guru being preparatory to the commencement of every sacred rite" (but cf. the NR, 1812*.23, *śokavegam . . . dhārayan*).

"commenced the performance" *kārayām āsa*: Understanding the tense as a simple past, Cm, Cg allude to a "synoptic" or "abbreviated" aspect (*saṃgraha-*, *saṃkṣepa-ukti*) of the verb (the poet going on then to supply details). It seems clearly inchoative (cf. 1.23.4, 73.2; 3.47.1 and notes).

4. "laid upon the earth" *bhūmau niveśitam*: "To cleanse off the oil," Cg.

"protector of the earth . . . laid upon the earth" *bhūmau niveśitam . . . bhūmipam*: Note the poignant iteration.

6. "Why did you take this decision" *kiṃ te vyavasitam*: That is, to go to heaven (in agreement with Cg). Reproaching the dead's "decision" to die and forsake those who love him is a common motif of the ritual lament in epic literature (see for example *HariVaṃ* 77).

7. "your people" *imaṃ janam*: Less likely, "this person" (that is, Bharata himself).

11. "Let it all be done" *tāni . . . kriyatām*: A rare case of lack of concord without clear metrical exigency (cf. Michelson 1904, p. 145 [the single example he notes is rejected in the crit. ed., 3.874*], who cites Hopkins 1901, p. 245; see also Edgerton 1953a, p. 129, especially paragraph 25.14). Cg, Ck read the plural.

13. "The sacred fires . . . had been placed outside" *agnayaḥ . . . bahiṣkṛtāḥ*: Because of the presence of a corpse within (Cg, Ck, Ct).

The three *śrauta* fires of the dead *agnihotrin* are taken to the place of cremation and used to kindle the fire (cf. *ŚatBr* 13.8.4.11).

15. "silver" *hiraṇyam*: So glossed by the commentators attempting to distinguish it from *suvarṇam* (perhaps this is not so far from the truth; cf. Rau 1973, p. 18). They suggest also that these were "flowers made out of gold and silver."

The corresponding verses in the NR clarify the significance of the verse: "Wagons full of jewels and gold went distributing riches to the people, miserable now without their leader. All the servants distributed various jewels as the funerary gifts [*aurdhvadehikadāna*] of the king" (1812*.41-4). Giving gifts in honor of the dead (particularly kings) appears elsewhere in the *Rām* (4.24.5; related are the gifts mentioned in 71.2-3 below; see Hopkins 1889, p. 17n, for *MBh* references) and is attested in historical times (Kane 1962-1975, vol. 4, p. 182 n426).

The NR inserts at this point a verse describing how bards, panegyrists, and genealogists went in front of the procession "sweetly praising the king with a recitation of his deeds" (1812*.45-6).

18. "made offering to the fire" *hutāśanaṃ hutvā*: A kind of etymological periphrasis for "made it blaze." Cg, Ck, Cr read, "gave the fire," that is, lit the pyre.

"intoned prayers" *jepuḥ*: "That is, the *paitṛmedhikamantras* [*ṚV* 10.15.1-13, or more generally 10.14-18]," Cg, Ck, Ct. The NR has them recite the *mantras* "in their minds." In addition, it describes how the priests cleanse his sacrificial utensils—the plates, ladles, firesticks, etc.—and place them upon the pyre, and then sacrifice an animal [the *anustaraṇikā* (*sic legendum*) or "covering animal"] and place it [its parts] around the king [cf. 3.64.32]; how Bharata has the area to the east of the pyre dragged with a plow [this should, in fact, have been the first ritual act], releases a cow with its calf, and finally sprinkles the pyre with butter, oil, and suet and ignites it (1812*.66-76).

19. The NR shows that Kaikeyī is in attendance (1812*.53).

20. "as the flames engulfed" *agnicitam*: Cm, Cg, Ck, Ct understand the compound as "one who has erected the fire altar [*agnicit*], that is, a performer of the great sacrifices." We agree with Cr.

"leftward" *prasavyam*: We follow Cm, Ct (is *apasavyaṃ cakāra* in 4.24.41 to be understood so too? but see *MBh* 7.162.48-50 with De's note there). On inauspicious occasions, left rather than right predominates in ritual activity; the sacred thread, for example, which is normally worn so as to come under the right arm, is at funerals (when not brought round one's body), worn over the right shoulder so as to come under the left arm (cf. *KātyŚS* 25.8.13 and Paranjpe's note on *MBh* 11.23.42; also Kane 1962-1975, vol. 4, p. 206). Cg claims that this circumambulation (which he interprets as both leftward and rightward) is normally done while the corpse is still on the litter; that it is mentioned at this point in the ceremony, he suggests, may be because the poet does not intend to suggest any specific sequence, or it may be due to variation in local custom.

22. We are to understand that the whole cortège proceeded afterward to the riverbank to perform the water-offering to the dead. Otherwise the verse seems quite out of order. The NR, indeed, has the funeral take place at the bank (1812*.57, very frequently the site of funerals in the epic, for example, *HariVaṃ* 78.44), and suggests the following, more probable, order of verses for the crit. ed.: 14, 19, 15-17, 22, 18, 20-21, 23.

23. "After making the funeral libation" *kṛtvodakam*: "When [the mourners] have come to a place where there is standing water, having once plunged into it and raised their heads out of it they pour one handful of water, pronounce the *gotra* name and the proper name (of the deceased)" (Kane 1962-1975, vol. 4, p. 209). The rite is both a purification for the living and an offering to the dead.

"the ten-day period of mourning" *daśāhaṃ . . . duḥkham*: The commentators are troubled by this reference to a ten-day period of ritual impurity, when the standard *śāstras* required twelve (or sixteen) days for kshatriyas; they adduce *YājñaSm* 3.22 (cf. *ManuSm* 5.83; in the *MBh*, the twelve-day period was standard, see for example 1.118.30 [in honor of Pāṇḍu]). They reconcile the contradiction by pointing to [the prescription attributed to Vṛddhaparāśara in] *ParāSm* [3.4], which justifies the procedure here. See the note on 1.17.11-12.

Sarga 71

1. "*śrāddha* rites" *śrāddhakarmāṇi*: A memorial service consisting of offerings of balls of cooked rice (*piṇḍa*) to the departed ancestors, gifts to and feeding of brahmans (cf. next verse), and similar largesse (see the note on 100.13).

2. "goat's flesh and much white rice" *bāstikaṃ bahu śuklaṃ ca*: We take *pāda* c in apposition to b. The commentators disagree about the meaning of *śuklam* ("adjective to 'goat's flesh,' or, 'silver,' Cg; "pure, fit to be given," Cm; "silver," Ck, Ct, Cr); thus, either "(plentiful) white (goat's flesh)" or more probably (comparing 85.63), "(goat's flesh and much) white (rice)." But in fact, considering *YājñaSm* 1.260 and *ManuSm* 3.272, where among the foods to be given at a *śrāddha* we find *mahāśalkam*, perhaps the original reading was *śalkam* (a crustacean, specifically prawns [here a collective singular, *jātyekavacana*]), a rare word that even the commentators on the *dharmaśāstras* are uncertain about, and thus easily corrupted. For goat's flesh cf. note on 69.22 above; *bāstika* appears to be a unique usage.

5. "the ceremony of purification" *śodhana-*: The collecting of the charred bones (cf. verse 8). The ritual texts are at odds about the correct time for this rite, though the procedure here appears to agree with *ĀśvaGS* 4.5.1. Cg adduces *Baudhāyana*[*pitṛmedhasūtras* 1.14.1 (p. 395)], which allows a wide variety of options. Ck believes that the collection of the bones must have been done earlier and that the activity meant here is the cleaning of the place, removal of ashes, and the like.

"His throat choked with sobs" *śabdāpihitakaṇṭhaḥ*: Although not impossible, *śabdāpihitakaṇṭhaḥ* is attested nowhere else in epic literature, and is suspect. It looks like an old metathesis of *bāṣpāpihita-*, which is offered here by three good D manuscripts, and reappears at 93.38 below.

7. After this verse the NR has Bharata strew garlands upon the pyre and walk counterclockwise around it (1818*).

8. "the place where . . . body had met extinction" *śarīranirvāṇam*: Follows Cm, Cg, Ct, in accordance with *Pā* 3.3.117; Ck, "(and) his father's extinguished body."

9. "the way a pole-banner in honor of Śakra" *śakrasya yantradhvaja iva*: This translation of the simile accords with Cm, Cg. Ck, Ct, "Since Śakra's banner stands in the sky [that is, the rainbow, but see note on 55.7 above] it cannot 'fall to earth'; thus the word 'mechanical' [*yantra-*], that is, a mechanical contrivance in the form of a banner used for decorating houses" (?). The NR lucidly reads, "like a banner of Śakra fallen from the pole" (1820*; cf. *MBh* 7.67.68, 68.65).

10. "at his final hour" *antakāle*: That is, when his merit had been exhausted (cf. note on 11.1 above). Since the seers in the story of Yayāti are his grandsons, Cg would like to take *amātyāḥ* ("ministers") as "kinsmen," which is doubtful.

12. "another of . . . virtues" *guṇāṅgāni tāni tāni*: Literally, "another side, feature of" Cg, Cr (so too Cm?) understand the compound as *dvandva*, Cs explicitly glossing "his virtues and his [gentle] limbs"; Ck, Ct, "the acts—giving pretty clothes, etc.—which were 'parts' of his 'virtue,' that is, of his favoring them."

16. "does not dissolve . . . it never will" *nāvadīryate*: We agree with Cm, Cg in taking the verb *apo koinou* with both half-verses.

21. "their" *eṣām*: The plural (dual expected) is used in order to include Rāma (Cg), but see note on 3.67.20.

"the wise" *vaidyaḥ*: "Omniscient one" (Cm, Cg, Ck, Ct), though perhaps "physician" (that is, of the soul; Cr) is correct (all commentators cite *AmaK* for the two senses), or simply "learned brahman" (cf. 94.51 and note).

"maintaining his usual composure" *prakṛtimān*: Literally, "having his normal nature"; *contra* Cm, Cg, Cr, who take the suffix as commendatory (*praśaṃsāyāṃ matup*, "of excellent nature"), and Ck, Ct, "having a nature consisting of pure *sattva*" (quite improbably Cs, "with the subjects").

After this verse the SR adds, "This is the thirteenth day since your father's death (that is, since his cremation [according to commentators]). Why are you delaying in collecting all the bones?" (1831*).

22. Read *arhasi* (*arhati* must be a misprint).

"There are three dualities" *trīṇi dvandvāni*: It is curious that the three pairs of opposites are not recorded in the text. The commentators try in various ways to make good the omission; Cm is probably closest: "birth and death, happiness and sorrow, gain and loss" (cf. 19.20).

After this verse D3 adds the following poignant verses: "Like a flock of birds that for a night gathers together in one place and at dawn scatters to the ten horizons—such is one's union with sons and friends. Like travelers who exchange a few words at a roadside well and then go their separate ways—such is one's union with kinsmen" (1834*; cf. *Saund* 15.33-4).

23. "born and so must die" *-bhavābhavau*: The *samāhāradvandva bhavābhavam* appears to have greater manuscript support (its sense would be, "the nature of the life cycle").

25. "the other rites" *aparāḥ kriyāḥ*: "Taking away the ashes, sweeping the ground, pouring out an offering of milk, and so on," Ck.

After this verse the NR inserts a passage (App. I, No. 22), in which Bharata makes a water-offering to his father, grieves further, and even threatens to fast to death in order to follow his father (line 26), until he is deterred by the consoling words of a minister named Dharmapāla [note the apparently Buddhist name], who convinces him to return to Ayodhyā.

Sarga 72

1. "making the journey back" *yātraṃ samīhantam*: In disagreement with the commentators, who understand " 'preparing for ('contemplating,' Cm, Ct) the journey,' that is, to Rāma," Cm, Cg, Ck, Ct, Cr.

The repeated use of the phrase "Lakṣmaṇa's younger brother" (verses 1, 5, 23) is more than mere epic mannerism: it is meant to suggest that Śatrughna shares Lakṣmaṇa's character traits, particularly his propensity to violent behavior, as we witness in this *sarga*.

3. The first line is contemptuous in tone, the particle *nāma* (like *yo 'pi*) expressing scorn (Cg, citing *Vaija*).

4. "both sides of the issue" *nayānayau*: Literally, "the [relative] policy and impolicy," that is, of the two options, Rāma's exile or the king's dethronement. Śatrughna speaks, as Ck notes, in accordance with the political theory that holds, "Guru though a man be, if he is haughty . . . he must be punished" (cf. note on 18.11).

"would have deposed the king" *nigrāhyaḥ . . . rājā*: As Daśaratha himself had urged Rāma to do (31.23).

7. "the gatekeeper (. . . seized)" *dvāsthaḥ* (. . . *gṛhitvā*): Unless Mantharā's political influence had already begun to wane, it seems presumptuous, not to say dangerous, for a simple gateman to treat her thus. *Dvāḥsthām* has manuscript support, but then Bharata becomes subject (as he would also be if we were to take *dvāsthaḥ* adjectivally), and against this the use in verse 8 of the second plural *vaḥ* (though there are variant readings, or *vaḥ* could be majestic plural), and Bharata's words in verse 20 seem to

testify. For these reasons and despite the fact that most of the NR explicitly attributes the deed to Bharata, it appears best to accept the crit. ed.'s decision.

9. The NR here shows Śatrughna seizing Mantharā straightway by the throat and, as she screams, filling her mouth with dirt (1841*).

17. "like the sky in autumn" *śāradaṃ gaganaṃ yathā*: "That is, [when the monsoon clouds are gone and] the stars can be seen clearly," Cg.

18. "holding . . . in his powerful grip" *balavat . . . gṛhitvā*: Cg understands *balavat* in compound with *krodhāt* ("towering rage").

"(heaping scorn on) Kaikeyī" *kaikeyīm* (*abhinirbhartsya*): "We infer by this that Kaikeyī had come to set Mantharā free," Cm, Cg, Ck, Ct.

The NR adds Śatrughna's address to Kaikeyī here: "How will you ever set yourself free. . . . When you die you shall reap the fruits of your evil," and so on. He then threatens to kill the hunchback (1847*).

19. "she sought refuge with her son" *putraṃ śaraṇam āgatā*: Either because Śatrughna attempts to strike her (Cg, Ck) or in order to secure the release of Mantharā (Cm, Ct, Cr).

21. Some N manuscripts add: "Restrain your anger, righteous prince—she is already slain by her own deed, and she is the slave of another, a hunchback, and a woman on top of it all" (1848*).

Sarga 73

1. With regard to the possibility that *sargas* 73-74 are later additions, see note on 75.1ff.

"deputies of the king" *rājakartāraḥ*: See note on 61.1; the NR substitutes "counselors."

2. "our most revered guru" *no gurutaro guruḥ*: Ck comments: "Statements like 'First one must acquire a king, then a wife, then wealth' [*MBh* 12.57.41, cf. note on 61.10] demonstrate that a king, because he is the most obviously effective in providing protection, is an even more highly revered guru than one's mother or father."

3. "by mere chance" *saṃgatyā*: Comparing *MBh* 1.145.8 and 175.18-19, where the word clearly has the sense "by chance" (cf. Nīlakaṇṭha ad 1.184.18 vulgate; this appears to be its meaning in *Rām* 6.113.16 also, as well as in *MBh* 12.171.10), and not finding any epic instance of the word in the sense of "agreement," we concur with Cm [second interpretation], and Cg against Ck (who comments, " 'because of the agreement,' [embedded] in his father's command, with regard both to Rāma's exile and Bharata's succession").

"come to harm" *nāparādhnoti*: In agreement with Cm (second option), though there appears to be no parallel for use of the verb in quite this sense (Ck understands, " 'You [supplying *bhavān*; but cf. the second person singular in *pāda* a] would not be transgressing' if you became king, that is, Bharata would not be in conflict with *dharma*, his elder brother or worldly custom"). The "harm" meant would principally be invasion by neighboring states (cf. 82.20-22).

8. "I will live" *ahaṃ . . . vatsyāmi*: "That is, as Rāma's substitute," Cg, Ck, Ct; cf. 103.26-29.

11. "like a sacred fire" *havyavāham iva*: Is the common characteristic (*sādhāraṇa-dharma*) of the simile (*upamā*) Rāma's brilliant power (his *tejaḥ*), as well as the respect he deserves? The commentators are silent.

12. "who but faintly resembles a mother" *mātṛgandhinīm*: Most of the NR reads, "who is so blindly ambitious for the kingship" (cf. note on 67.14).

13. "Let a road be made" *kriyatām . . . panthāḥ*: "Since Rāma will be king it is correct form to come to him in company with a royal escort; thus there must be preparation of the road," Ck. The Pāṇḍavas march out to see the retired king Dhṛtarāṣṭra in much the same fashion, with large numbers of troops, grand rest houses, and the like (*MBh.* 15.29.18ff.).

"men to scout out the trackless regions" *durgavicārakāḥ*: Perhaps instead, "to lead the people through . . . " (so Cm; Cg, "people to prepare the trackless regions, or, guards who know . . .").

14. "prayer for majesty" *śrīmadvākyam*: The translation agrees with Ck, Ct, to the extent that *pāda* d cannot construe with *pādas* ab (so Cm, Cg, Cr), but the presence of *śrī* in the next verse requires the translation given here.

15. "of the lotus" *padmā*: Who dwells in the lotus (Cg), who carries a lotus (Cm), who is called "lotus" and whose emblem is [or who is marked with] the lotus (Ck, Ct). Is the statement a simple benediction, or does it carry the suggestion that Bharata too may some day succeed to the kingship, of which Śrī is a superintending deity? Cf. note on 64.10.

16. "for all to hear" *saṃśravaṇe*: cf. 3.57.25, *sudūrasaṃśravam* (*svaram*), 5.29.1, 6.38.5; so Ck here. Cm, Cg, Cr: "(spoke out) 'with regard to the promise' of bringing Rāma back" (citing Halāyudha; there appears to be no corroboration in the literature for the word being used in this sense).

Ck, supported by little manuscript evidence and less grammar, but with the enthusiastic endorsement of Ct, reads, "The prince, hearing their words (their blessing) (became happy) and tears of joy over (the people) fell down from the noble man's noble face," and observes, "One commentator [we do not know which] thinks this verse irrelevant, and says he offers some comment only because [of the maxim] 'Find some way of accounting for whatever is in the text.' Well, if it is true that the verse is irrelevant, he could do without the whole *Rāmāyaṇa*; he could get the entire matter from a little epitome and all the rest would be unnecessary." He goes on to say that the purpose of the verse, in fact, is the reference to the change in Bharata's countenance, which must be mentioned because of the action that follows.

Sarga 74

1-3. There is some disagreement among the commentators about the precise meaning of many of the terms appearing here. Reasonable alternatives to, or amplifications of, the translation follow:

"surveyors" *bhūmipradeśajñāḥ*: "Familiar with high and low, or various, tracts of land," Cg, Ck; "knowing which areas do or do not contain water," Ct, Cr.

"men trained in measurement" *sūtrakarmaviśāradāḥ*: "Trained in working with lines ("by making machines," Ck) for hauling water out of deep tanks, wells, etc., in dry areas; or, weavers," Cg, Ck; "trained in employing lines for measuring out the rest-areas; or, weavers," Cm, Ct, Cr (in *HariVaṃ* 86.12 the *sūtrahastāḥ* perform measurements).

"who were zealous in their work" *svakarmābhiratāḥ*: "Guards," Cg, Ck; "adjective to diggers, that is, who would dig even under enemy attack," Ct.

"engineers" *yantrakāḥ*: "Builders of auxiliary constructions, by means of logs, etc., for crossing large streams; or, trappers," Cg, Ck, Cr ("that is, builders of machines for trapping birds and animals," Cm); "makers of fountains, etc.," Ct.

"craftsmen" *sthapatayaḥ*: "Chief carpenters," Cm; "girders, builders of chariots" ("that is, chief carpenters," Ct) Ck, Ct (cf. Hazra 1979, especially pp. 420-22; contrast the sense of the word in 44.9).

"men" *puruṣāḥ*: "Royal foremen," Cg.

"skilled in machinery" *yantrakovidāḥ*: "Skilled in constructing catapults, etc. ("or, fountains," Cm)," Cm, Cg, Ct, Cr.

"road-levelers" *mārginaḥ*: "Men appointed to guard this or that particular forest road," Ck, Ct, Cr.

"cane-weavers" *vaṃśakarmakṛtaḥ*: "Arrowsmiths; or, men who measure off the earth with cane-sticks" [read *-dalair* in the crit. app.], Crā.

4. "joyfully" *harṣāt*: "Though the work is basically painful, the people go 'joyfully' because of their eagerness to see Rāma," Cg.

5. "bright and early" *purastāt*: There seems no other way to translate the adverb than in this unattested sense (PW "*vorher, zuerst*" makes little sense). It looks like a corruption of some sort; the NR, reasonably, gives *purataḥ* or *puraś ca* ("from the city").

7. "transplanted trees" *vṛkṣān aropayan*: Apparently full-grown trees, to provide shade.

8. "cleared" *vidhamanti*: Cg understands the verb to mean "burn" (a rare sense, if at all possible, and one that makes the qualification "stronger men" uncalled for; elsewhere, 5.12.20, 6.4.60, etc., it is used in the simple sense of "destroy"). The verb is construed with the remainder of *pādas* cd (in general agreement with Ct); though such a zeugma is rather hard, we do find parallel instances (cf. 73.13, 90.10, 3.55.10).

9. "dry wells" *kūpān*: As the NR makes clear, *jīrṇakūpān*, "old, disused wells" (1871*); cf. Cr, "wells that are dry and [dangerously] overgrown with grass."

11. "various kinds of reservoirs" *udapānān bahuvidhān*: "Different ones for men, elephants, horses, and so on ["tanks, wells, and so on," Ck, Ct, Cr]; the benches would be for resting [during drinking]," Cg.

12. "whitewashed" *sasudhā-*: "In those particular areas where the rest houses were [to be situated]," Ck ("elsewhere only clay-surfaced," Ct); so, too, with regard to the sprinkling of sandalwood water in verse 13 (Cg). The compound in *pāda* c should be understood as *paranipāta* for *mattadvijagaṇodghuṣṭaḥ* (cf. note on 41.27).

14. "diligently following the orders they had received" *yathājñapti yuktāḥ*: That is, from Bharata (so Ct, Cr).

15. "rest areas" *niveśaḥ*: *Jātyekavacanam*, both here and in verse 16. For the rest areas of a king out on expedition cf. *ArthŚā* 10.1ff. (they were grand constructions).

17. "spread heaps of sand" *bahupāṃsucayāḥ*: We follow Cg here, who glosses *pāṃsu-* as "fine sand." Ct, understanding the word in its more usual sense, believes the compound to suggest the removal of dirt, but this seems less likely.

"erected poles and crossbeams and bars" *yantrendrakīlaparighāḥ*: In *pāda* c there is a serious corruption. The crit. ed.'s reading, *tatrendrakīlapratimāḥ*, is nearly nonsense ("They [the sites?] had the look of Mount Indrakīla there," so the commentators). *Indrakīla-* is a rare word, meaning "bolt, crossbar, crossbeam"; it is found in

MBh 6.55.119 (cf. Belvalkar's note there), in juxtaposition to *yantra*, which we find here in our NR. We thus read with the NR, *yantrendrakīlaparighāḥ*, though without absolute confidence. (See further Rhys Davids and Stede 1921-1925 s.v. *indakhīla*, and Edgerton 1953b s.v. *indrakīla* ["not recorded in this sense in Skt."].)

19. "spire-topped mansions" *viṭaṅkāgravimānakaiḥ*: Or, "mansions with friezes, cornices (or, dove-cotes?) on their roofs" (*vitaṅka*, glossed *kapotapālikā* by *AmaK*, cited by Cm, Cg, Ck, Cr; cf. Cg, Ct, Cr on 5.42.6 "a beam installed horizontally atop a pillar").

20. This verse is to be construed with 21, in agreement with Cm, Cg, Ck, Ct, Cr. Cg adds, "The epithets applied to the Ganges suggest that the rest houses [or rather, the road itself] could not be constructed any farther"; note that Mount Citrakūṭa, where Rāma is dwelling, would still be at least twenty miles beyond the end of the road, assuming it reached to the Ganges at Prayāga (cf. 48.25).

21. It may be that we are supposed to arrange the tenors and vehicles of the simile thus: road-Ganges-fish—sky-moon-stars (the water of the Ganges is always described as white).

Sarga 75

1ff. The bards come to awaken Bharata, treating him as if he were the king. Bharata protests that he is not (verse 4). Vasiṣṭha calls an assembly to offer the kingship to Bharata (verses 8ff., 76.1-7), but the prince refuses, declaring instead that he will bring Rāma back from the forest (76.8ff.). Finally he orders an expedition (76.21ff.). Now, in light of *sargas* 73-74, all this is either inconsistent or redundant. In addition, nothing is later said either of the road (only in an SR interpolation, cf. note on 76.18; Guha is unaware of it in 78.15 [see Cg's weak defense ad loc.]), or of the decorated campsites (cf. especially 77.20). The inference one is forced to draw is that *sargas* 73-74, though attested in all manuscripts (somewhat differently placed in the NR, but this is not decisive), are a later addition. Varadacharya rather desperately suggests that Vasiṣṭha was not among the "deputies of the king" mentioned in *sarga* 73, and consequently proceeds with Bharata's consecration until Bharata himself rejects it in his presence (1964-1965, vol. 2, p. 191n).

For remarks on the (misplaced) NR insertion (App. I, No. 23), cf. note on 70.1.

1. "in the night" *rātrim*: That is, in the second half of the night (so Cm, Cg, and in general Ck, Ct). Note the accusative of time at which (cf. note on 37.26).

Nāndīmukha: Obscure. PW s.v. wants to connect it, in some unspecified way, with the *pitṛ*s of this name. Indeed, the *pitṛ*s are thus designated in the *vṛddhiśrāddha*, a *śrāddha* offered to secure good fortune (cf. Kane 1962-1975, vol. 4, p. 359 n920, and cf. *ŚāṅkhāGS* 4.4.1ff.). We should thus probably understand it as a ceremony to be undertaken the coming day in anticipation of Bharata's presumed consecration. The commentators themselves are quite uncertain, though Ck, Ct in a general way support this interpretation.

2. "the drum of the nightwatch" *yāmadundubhiḥ*: "That is, signaling when a watch had ended," Cm, Cg, Ck, Ct; "signaling that only one watch of the night was left," Cr.

3. "it brought . . . lacerating (grief)" (*śokair*) *arandhrayat*: The verb is a denominative from *randhra*- (apparently a unique usage).

5. "what great wrong these people are doing because of Kaikeyī" *kaikeyyā lokasyā-*

pakṛtaṃ mahat: The line is translated in agreement with Cg, Ck (Ct specifies that the wrongdoing is with regard to Bharata [their treating him as a king]). Alternatively: "how terribly Kaikeyī has offended against the people" (Cg, second interpretation).

6. Hereafter the SR inserts, "And our great leader, too, Rāghava himself, has been banished by this mother of mine, who abandoned righteousness" (1883*).

7. "the women" *yoṣitaḥ*: Or, "his wives" (cf. note on 8.5).

8. The NR has Vasiṣṭha enter in company with Bharata (and accordingly alters verse 13 below).

9. "with his attendants" *saganaḥ*: " 'With his troops' that is, of students" (Cm, Cg, Ct, Cr; "or, of assemblymen," Varadacharya 1964-1965, vol. 2, p. 193n).

Sudharmā: The assembly hall of the gods.

11. "commanders" *-vallabhān*: The word appears to be unattested in this sense, but thus do Cm, Cg, Ct, Cr gloss it (cf. also 98.71 and note). There is additionally some redundance here, which Ck, Ct (and Cg, Cr?) eliminate by reading "*vaiśyas*" for "soldiers." Does the verse give us an archaic list of the *prakṛtis*—the "limbs" of the state, cf. verse 13—later developed into a standard group of seven (cf. 84.6-7 and note for a nearly complete listing on the classical model)? The NR names those to be brought (Sumantra, Jaimini, Sumitra, Vijaya, etc. [1888*]), similarly the SR hereafter (Bharata, Śatrughna, Yudhājit ["another name for Vijaya," Cg], Sumantra, and so on. [1889*]).

13. "subjects" *prakṛtayaḥ*: Perhaps in the sense of "estates," referring back to those mentioned in verse 11.

14. "like a pool" *hrada iva*: Ck may be right to take it in the sense of "great pool, that is, the ocean"; in any case, clearly an oceanside pool (Cg, Ct). Cg and Ck equate the placid water with Vasiṣṭha [cf. 71.21; does it suggest instead the intense but controlled excitement of the assembly?], the fish and serpent with Bharata and Śatrughna (cf. 37.22 and note), and the gems, etc. with the ministers, etc.; whereas Ck (and Ct) goes on to remark that, while *hrada*, "pool" (masculine), and *sabhā*, "hall" (feminine), are different in gender, the relationship between them of tenor and vehicle can still hold, on the analogy of *candraḥ* (masculine) *iva mukham* (neuter), "a face like the moon" (Ct, "because the sensitive reader is not troubled by it"). Ct rejects these equations, saying that the qualifications in *pādas* ab construe actually, by morphological change, with *sabhā* (the fish, shells, etc. would be represented in paintings, the jewels would be found on the pillars, and so on), because if we take it any other way the poet would be guilty of the fault of "deficiency" (*nyūnatā*) (in that the actual *upameyas* are not mentioned in the verse?).

Sarga 76

1. "favorably inclined toward Bharata" *bharatapragrahām*: *Pragraha-* appears never to be used as an independent adjective (in the *Rām* or anywhere else), as the crit. ed. prints and the commentators understand. We read with the NR, which gives it in compound with *bharata-*, and makes Vasiṣṭha the subject of the verse. On this reading the simile would make better sense, Bharata = the moon (the nobles = stars).

2. "when the clouds have vanished" *ghanāpāye*: "In autumn, when the stars—to which the ornaments worn in honor of Bharata's anticipated consecration would be compared—are visible," Cg.

4. "in the performance of righteousness" *dharmam ācaran*: "Keeping his word," Cm, Cg, Ck, Ct.

5. Cg, Ck, Ct cite: "A son is a son indeed if he obeys his parents when alive, feeds [brahmans] plentifully year by year [at *śrāddha* ceremonies], and makes the ancestral offering for them at Gayā" (attributed to Manu in *SūktiRa* 74.4).

6. "gladden the ministers" *muditāmātyaḥ*: We take the adjectival compound as a prolepsis. Varadacharya (1964-1965, vol. 2, p. 196n) suggests, "the ministers are happy with you," that is, executing the duties of kingship will be easy since the ministers have no animosity toward him (an interpretation made with 67.11 in mind).

7. "sovereigns" *kevalāḥ*: Or, "tyrants" (so Cg, "those who have no [legitimate?] throne"; Ck, "no 'consecration of the turban' " [both construe only with *pāda* c]).

"the westernmost ones" *aparāntāḥ*: Thus, despite the tautology, in light of Aśokan Rock Edict V [Mansehra], line 4 (see Mookerji 1962, p. 140 n 6, and *ArthŚā* 2.2.[15], which he cites). Cg is in agreement: "living in the (western) region, the Yavanas [Greeks]."

"who live by the sea" *sāmudrāḥ*: "Islanders," according to Cm, Cg; "merchant mariners," Ck, Ct.

9. "like the call of the gray goose" *kalahaṃsasvaraḥ*: Cf. 43.12. Cg claims that the phrase suggests Bharata's "intense determination," by which he presumably means that Bharata, grieved by remembering Rāma, yet steadies his voice to proclaim his intention clearly. The indistinctness of the bird's call and of Bharata's words may in fact be the common property (cf. *MBh* 11.18.14). But in any case we should probably not look for too much narrative significance here, alliteration being a prime motive for the phrase, *-kalayā . . . kalahaṃsa-*. Cg goes on to add that the appellation "young prince" is a pregnant one ("how wonderful that he is ready to give up the pleasures of kingship even at the stage in life when he is most capable of enjoying them"), and that, being under the sway of his sorrow, Bharata fails to remember the prohibition against criticizing one's gurus in public.

10. "a person like me" *madvidhaḥ*: "Who follows *śāstra*," Cm, Cg. Ck, Ct believe that Bharata hereby means that he too has practiced chastity, and so on. But there seems no reason to assume that Bharata arrogates to himself the same qualities as Rāma. The qualification seems to suggest just the opposite, that Bharata is emphasizing his own inferiority to Rāma, about which he is explicit elsewhere (98.59-60).

12. "best" *śreṣṭhaḥ*: Or even, "most regal," as superlative to (an unattested) positive adjective of *śrī*?

"Dilīpa and Nahuṣa": "Named as representing the best kings of the solar and lunar dynasties [respectively]," Cg, but cf. notes on 5.9, 58.36 regarding Nahuṣa. For Dilīpa see 58.36 and note, and 102.21.

13. "followed only by ignoble men, and leading to hell" *anāryajuṣṭam asvargyam*: A quarter-verse reappearing at *BhagGī* 2.2c (with reference to Arjuna's "cowardice"), briefly discussed by Jacobi 1918, p. 324.

"in the eyes of all the world" *loke*: Cg wrongly wants the word to be qualified by *ikṣvākūṇām* ("in the eyes of the people of the Ikṣvākus").

16. The awkward irruption of this verse is removed in the NR by transposition and insertion.

17. "noble brother (Lakṣmaṇa)" *āryo* (*lakṣmaṇaḥ*): "The application of the term 'noble' to the youngest brother is because of his zeal in *dharma*, namely, compliance with the eldest," Cg.

18. "to force him to return" *vinivartayituṃ balāt*: Literally, "to bring him back by

force." This translation of the crit. ed.'s *balāt* is made with some hesitation. Both Cm and Ck read *vanāt*, "from the forest," and the NR diverges (the word probably can not construe with *vartiṣye*; the commentators are silent), but note that Bharata will attempt to force him by means of the hunger strike (cf. 103.13ff.).

After this verse the SR finds it necessary that Bharata mention the workers he has already sent out to prepare the road for the contemplated expedition (1899*).

22. "subjects" *prakṛtayaḥ*: Cg, citing *AmaK*, takes the word here in the sense of "guildsmen of the town"; cf. note on 75.13 above.

25. "in the midst of his gurus" *gurusaṃnidhau*: "This is added to show that permission had been granted him," Cg.

27-30. These verses recapitulate the contents of the *sarga* (Cg).

27. "His . . . guru" *gurum*: In contrast to its narrow signification as an English loanword ("spiritual teacher"), *guru* is in addition applied both to one's mother and to one's father (cf. 103.2-3); and in Bharata's eyes, now that Daśaratha is dead, Rāma is his father (cf. 66.26-27).

"and beg his forgiveness. The words he spoke were fitting" *bruvan suyuktaṃ . . . prasādayiṣyan*: Cm and Cg construe, "ready to beg his forgiveness with fitting words." We agree with Cr.

29. "charioteer" *sūtaputraḥ*: Here *-putra-* signifies merely "hereditary affiliation" to the *sūta* (charioteer) "class" (cf. Alsdorf 1950, pp. 357-60).

Sarga 77

3. "according to precept" *yathāvidhi*: That is, in formation (cf. *ArthŚā* 10.5), as Ct intimates; Cm, Cg, "in accordance with Bharata's order"; Ck, "at pleasure" (this perhaps with verse 20 in mind; see the note there).

6. Trying to explain why Kaikeyī is mentioned first in the verse, the commentators believe the implication to be that she is rushing ahead because of her deep remorse (Cg, so also Ct). They see importance, too, in the singular "carriage": either we are to understand that each woman went in a separate conveyance (Cm, Cg), or that all three went in one conveyance, out of (renewed) affection (Ct). It is indicative of the poet's indifference to Kaikeyī (she is a mere narrative device) that he has not prepared us for her apparent repentence here and in 86.16-17 (see the Introduction, Chapter 8).

7. "nobles" *ārya-*: "Men of the first three *varṇas*," Cm, Cg, Ck, Ct; "Vasiṣṭha and so on," Cr.

9. "the mere sight of Rāghava" *dṛṣṭa eva . . . rāghavaḥ*: "They mean that Rāma does not have to be close to them and smile at them, or even glance at them and say something, nor would they themselves have to make any effort. By a mere glimpse of him their grief will disappear," Cg.

11. "subject" *prakṛtayaḥ*: "city-guildsmen" (Cg, Ck, Ct, cf. note on 76.22; we agree with Cr).

"merchants" *naigamāḥ*: So the commentators (cf. note on 1.14).

12-15. As in 74.1ff., there is some uncertainty about the identification of several of the occupations mentioned here. Possible alternatives and clarifications follow:

"weavers" *sūtrakarmakṛtaḥ*: Contrast note on 74.1-3.

"workers in peacock-feathers" *māyūrakāḥ*: "Trappers of peacocks" ("and parrots, etc.," Ct), Ck.

"bauble-makers" *rocakāḥ*: "Those who bring out a high sheen on ivory, walls, pedestals, etc.," Cm, Cg, Cr (apparently "polishers").

"workers in ivory" *dantakārāḥ*: Artisans who carve as well as paint on ivory (Ct).

"blanket-cleaners" *kambaladhāvakāḥ*: Presumably dry-cleaners, in contrast to the "washermen" (*rajakāḥ*) in verse 15.

"valets" *-ācchādakāḥ*: Literally, "coverers"; most S manuscripts and commentators read, more attractively, *-ucchādakāḥ*, "masseurs" (cf. note on 85.50).

"headmen of villages and hamlets" *grāmaghoṣamahattarāḥ*: "Village heralds," Cm.

The "women" of the actors were employed both as actresses and as prostitutes.

Entranced by the catalogue style, the NR (1904*, 1905*) extends the list by some thirty to forty occupations.

Note the present in verse 15c. Vālmīki appears to invest this tense with a particular vividness or vivacity in some contexts (cf. 13.7, 8; 70.13, to cite only a couple of notable examples).

18. An SR insertion here has the train reach the Ganges close to Śṛṅgaverapura (1909*).

19. "stop" *anutthitām*: The authority for the crit. ed. reading (*a*)*nugatām* ("following") is not in the least compelling. It appears that both the SR (which we adopt) and the NR support some form of *-sthitām* (*anutthitām, ca sthitām*, etc.), whose sense is also superior. We have a slight *hysteron proteron* in *pādas* ab (the river causes the army to halt).

20. "anywhere it chooses" *abhiprāyeṇa sarvaśaḥ*: We agree with Cm, Cg, Cr, particularly in light of verse 22 below; Ck (so apparently Ct), "encamp them 'with the intention' of crossing; that is to say, not with the intention of spending two or three days there because the river is so pleasant."

The reason why Bharata does not have the army pitch a regular camp, and insists on informality, is not wholly clear. In addition to Ck's argument, we might suppose Bharata does not wish to arouse any suspicion that his is an army embarked on a hostile expedition, as a well-protected, formally ordered camp could imply. He will be suspected of this nevertheless.

"straightway tomorrow" *śva idānīm*: Perhaps we have an idiom here; it is neither possible, with Cg, Ck, Cr, to construe *idānīm* with *viśrāntāḥ*, nor, with Cm, to combine it with *niveśayata*.

21. "as part of his obsequies" *aurdhvadehanimittārtham*: "By omitting to report similar rites at any of the other rivers that had been reached during the journey, the poet means to imply that only the offering made with water of the Ganges will enable his father's to reach the other world," Ct.

Sarga 78

2. "purpose" *antam*: Lexica do not record this meaning for the word, but cf. Gonda 1938, p. 485. Less probably "end" in a spatial sense (though this in fact is how the NR interprets it, cf. 1913*, *antam asyā . . . vistṛtāyāḥ*, "[I do not see] any end to this expansive [army]").

Note the double *saṃdhi* in *asyāntam*.

3. "standard . . . marked with a *kovidāra* tree" *kovidāradhvajaḥ*: That is, emblazoned with the device of the *kovidāra*. According to Cm, Cg, Ck, Ct, this constituted the family standard of the Ikṣvākus (but note that the same device is found on the standard of Dhṛṣṭadyumna in the *MBh*, 6.50.89). Benthall describes the *kovidāra* as follows: "a small or middle-sized tree with a short trunk and dark brown, slightly rough bark. . . . During the cold season the foliage falls and . . . the large purple, pink, or white flowers appear among the falling leaves, until eventually they almost cover the otherwise bare branches, making this one of the most beautiful of all Indian trees" (Benthall 1946, p. 204).

"fishermen" *dāśān*: This, as per *ManuSm* 10.34, = *kaivarta* (cf. verse 7).

6. "with your troops" *balayuktāḥ*: Several S manuscripts and Ck read instead, *jālayuktāḥ*, "provided with your nets."

8. "is not ill-disposed" *aduṣṭaḥ*: For the *tuṣṭaḥ* of the crit. ed. we read *(a)duṣṭaḥ*, on the basis of manuscript evidence, sense, and 79.1 below. This is an unusually common scribal error; cf. 3.43.22, *-duṣṭaḥ*, v.l. *-tuṣṭaḥ* (also note on 3.19.10); *MBh* 12.97.13, *[saṃ]duṣṭaḥ* corrupted into *-tuṣṭaḥ*.

9. "fish, meat, and wine" *matsyamāṃsamadhūni*: The victuals Guha brings are, by later standards at least (recall the five Tantric ritual materials), peculiar. The commentators are silent save for Cr, who characteristically tries to etymologize them off the page. Do they suggest that Guha stands quite outside aryan-brahmanical civilization?

15. "This region is your pleasure-garden" *niṣkuṭaś caiva deśo 'yam*: That is, you may use it as you wish; another cliché, as in 44.14 ("it is fit to be enjoyed by you," Cg, Cr; "there is no need to worry that it is a jungle," Ck).

"caught . . . quite unawares" *vañcitāḥ*: "They were 'caught unawares' by not being informed of his arrival; had they been, they would have come out to welcome him. . . . Even though the road had been built as far as the Ganges [74.20], Guha says that since no messenger had up to then been sent he had no idea of Bharata's arrival," Cg, so Cm, Ck, Ct; the latter two call it "an expression of courtesy," Cr, "of regret, at not going out to meet him" (lame explanations to solve the problem noted on 75.1). As Guha is not relieved of his suspicions about Bharata until 79.11ff., the sense cannot be that he is "deceived" about Bharata's hostile intentions.

"us here" *te vayam*: Like *te sarve* in the next *pāda*. Cm, Cg, Ck, Ct, Cr all understand, "we are yours," that is, your servants.

"we all bid you" *nivedayāmas te sarve*: Ck, Ct, Cr read *sarvaṃ*, explaining, "we shall tell you everything, that is, about Rāma" (Ck, Cr), or, "we make over to you our kingdom" (Ct).

Sarga 79

1. "reasoned and purposeful" *hetvarthasaṃhitam*: That is, presumably, containing the reason why he refuses (Guha's offer is in itself sufficient expression of hospitality), and implying the motive behind his refusal (his wish to hasten on to Rāma, cf. verse 4).

4. "to Bharadvāja's ashram" *bharadvājāśramam*: How Bharata knows that Rāma had visited Bharadvāja is unclear. One suspects the poet nods: cf. note on 51.1, where the crit. ed. shows that Sumantra's knowledge of Rāma's whereabouts is

unquestionably an interpolation—perhaps motivated by such inconsistencies as the present one? (Cf. also note on 83.21.)

7. "This great army of yours" *iyaṃ te mahatī senā*: Nowhere, in fact, does Bharata clearly explain why he goes in the company of such a vast force (but cf. note on 73.13).

8. "pure as the sky" *ākāśa iva nirmalaḥ*: "The faults suspected by Guha do not attach to Bharata. If one tries to smear mud on the sky it does not stick, and all that is dirtied is one's hand. . . . 'Even voice,' because Bharata is not angry even though faults are [unjustly] being imputed to him," Cg. As students of Vedānta will recall, the sky (also, "space") is considered immaculate and whatever impurities are observed there are in fact superimpositions caused by ignorance.

12. "blessed" *dhanyaḥ*: Or perhaps, "beneficent," for although elsewhere the adjective usually has a passive sense ("to be blessed"), it seems to have an active one here ("to bring blessings").

16. "such a man" *tādṛśaḥ*: Against the commentators (except for Cg's second interpretation), this is taken as genitive rather than nominative.

17. "like the flame" *agnir iva*: The simile here is somewhat askew. Cr suggests that what is intended to be compared with the "forest fire" is Bharata's grief for Daśaratha. Is the "flame hidden within a tree" supposed to be spontaneous combustion (following the heating) deep within the hollow of a tree?

18. "(sweat) poured down . . . (Himālaya) pours down" *prasrutaḥ . . . (svedaḥ) . . . (himavān) prasrutaḥ*: The juxtaposition of the intransitive and transitive aspects of the same verbal form is considered inelegant. Many manuscripts have tried to eliminate the former instance because, as Cg remarks, the intransitive locution "does not accord with the simile."

19-20. We must not expect too close a coordination of vehicle and tenor in this extended metaphor, though it is worth recording Cg's attempt to provide it: "because his 'brooding' was continuous it is likened to a stream of rocks (falling) when 'split off from crevices' [*nirdara-*, see below]; the variety of 'sighs' [Cg extracts this from the *vi-* in *viniḥśvasita-*] is similar to the variety of 'minerals' [Ct is obscure: "because the sighs bring forth a change in color of his ornaments" (just as the minerals would?)]; 'desolation'—the disinclination of one's operative organs [hands, feet, etc.] to execute their proper tasks—is similar to the trees of the 'thickets,' in point of their insensibility; the 'grief,' etc. [Ck, Ct, Cr understand instead *adhi*, that is, *adhirūpāṇi*, "high"] are like 'peaks' because of their solidity; 'delirium' is similar to [wild] 'creatures' in its endangering one's life; 'misery' is similar to 'plants,' etc., because it is so hard to make one's way through it."

"gorge" *nirdaraśailena*: Literally, "mountain gorge," with *paranipāta* for *śailanirdara-*. *Nirdara* is a rare word, but one Vālmīki is fond of. Comparing its use in 3.63.5, 4.42.17 (and 4.13.5, where it must be read in place of the crit. ed.'s *nirjhara-*), we find that Cm's explanation in 3.63.5 is correct: "paths through openings in rocks." Cg, Ck, Ct, Cr, like Ck, Ct here, gloss "shattered rocks"; Cm, Ct on our present verse are led astray by the context: "rocks 'that will not shatter.' "

21. "high-minded Bharata . . . utterly distraught" *mahānubhāvaḥ . . . sudurmanāḥ*: The adjectives in *pāda* b (cf. the NR construction, 1935*.2) and *sudurmanāḥ* (a not unusual epic enjambment, cf. note on 21.14) refer to Bharata. The syntax proposed by the commentators is improbable, except possibly for Cg's joining *sudurmanāḥ* with *guhaḥ*, explaining, "seeing Bharata's pain Guha became even more distraught than he."

We understand the verse to mean that, after attempting to sleep, Bharata comes out again to speak with Guha, and after their conversation and Bharata's further lamentation (*sargas* 80-82), Bharata retires again and Guha departs. Alternatively, the verse is a recapitulation ("So Bharata . . . had met [that day] with Guha"); the events of *sargas* 80-82, then, would occur *before* Bharata retires here (verse 15) (suggested by Varadacharya 1964-1965, vol. 2, p. 216n).

Sarga 80

1. Before this the NR, rather clumsily, inserts eighteen verses, in order to introduce by way of a question from Bharata the otherwise abrupt and unmotivated account of Lakṣmaṇa's vigil. Cg prefaces the *sarga* with the following comment: "There are no differences in the modern as against the ancient way of teaching about the Blessed One. The teacher speaks and the auditor listens respectfully. So [the poet] here shows us. The preverb *ā* [in *ācacakṣe*, "began to describe"] has the sense of 'partially'; he told only what was within grasp of his speech and senses, not everything. . . . One who would teach such a thing [the complete nature of the Blessed One] . . . is attempting to take the measure of the ocean with his hand."

3. Verses 3-23 are nearly verbatim repetitions of 45.2-23 (45.16 is omitted here except in several N manuscripts [1942*]).

6. "simple" *kevalām*: Cg takes the adjective here to mean "obtained according to reasonable procedures" (in 45.5, "even the mere"; Ctś, "free of hindrances").

9. "Lakṣmaṇa entreated us all, with righteousness alone in view" *lakṣmaṇena . . . anunītā vayaṃ sarve dharmam evānupaśyatā*: It is not possible to understand an ellipsis in *pāda* b (such as *uktam*), and to have *pādas* cd spoken by Lakṣmaṇa (as in 45.8; for *anunītāḥ* cf. also 81.16). Both the SR and the NR agree in presenting what appears to be a clear corruption in *pādas* ab (irremediable) and in *pāda* c (*anunītāḥ* for *nātra bhītā*): Lakṣmaṇa's response has nothing to do with "righteousness."

17. "that just eluded" *atikrāntam atikrāntam*: Cm and Cg (again) explain this as an independent sentence, " 'everything has gone beyond,' that is, everything has lost its purpose" (cf. note on 45.17).

22. "his promise fulfilled" *satyapratijñena*: Cm, Cg here take the compound as referring to Rāma (in 45.22 they rightly apply it to Daśaratha; cf. note there).

25. "glanced back often" *vyavekṣamānau*: Apparently a unique usage, but cf. 3.43.37, *avekṣamānaḥ* in the same sense ("attentive in every direction," Cg).

Sarga 81

2. "By the attributes mentioned in the verse the poet means to express how little Bharata deserved to suffer such grief," Cg. Ck, Ct interpret the verse as containing Bharata's meditation on Rāma.

3. "pierced near the heart by goads" *totrair hṛdi viddhaḥ*: An odd image (though thus understood by Ck, Ct, Cr), given the nature and general use of elephant goads in contemporary India. The NR substitutes for the *pāda*, "like a tree fallen from a river bank [or, mountain slope]" (1946*).

7. "As a loving cow . . . her calf" *vatsalā svaṃ yathā vatsam*: Agrees with Cr; alternatively, "Lovingly . . . as if he were her own son" (Ck, Ct).

8. "you have no illness . . . ?" *vyādhir na te kaccit*: Cg artificially: "It is not physical illness Kausalyā is asking about, but the pain of separation from Rāma. Nor does she actually mean that, with Rāma in the forest, Bharata is ruler and protector, but rather this: All of us live only in the hopes of Rāma's return; were he to hear that you [Bharata] are no more, not only would he not return, he would never again even look in this direction."

15. "refused" *pratyanujñāsīt*: Cf. note on 44.19. The commentators are unsure: "he 'ordered,' ('let it be taken) back,' " Cg; "returned it," Cm; " 'accepted it' merely to please me (and then gave it back to me [Ct, Cs])," Ck; " 'promised,' that 'I will not eat it,' " Cr.

In 44.20 Rāma refuses the food by reason of the ascetic's *dharma* he is following (cf. Cs, "the 'code of kshatriyas' is either the keeping of his promise to live in the wilderness on things of the wild, or the *dharma* of [not] accepting gifts. On the first alternative we should understand the following verse to mean that Rāma suppressed his real meaning and avoids accepting the food on other grounds"). Cg reports, "Some are of the opinion that Rāma refuses the presentation because it is made by a low-caste man, since he will indeed accept food from seers" [cf. 48.18, 3.6.22, 11.24].

16. "It is not for us to take. . . . Ours is always to give" *na hy asmābhiḥ pratigrāhyaṃ . . . deyaṃ tu sarvadā*: On the vow itself, which Sītā is eager to repeat to anyone who will listen, see 3.45.15: "Rāma has taken a solemn vow . . . never to be broken: always to give and not to take, to tell the truth and not to lie" (cf. also 5.31.21). One might have thought the plural here to be simply majestic, but for the parallel in *MBh* 12.60.13: "I shall explain to you the *dharma* of the kshatriya: a king is to give, not demand (*dadyād rājā na yāceta*).

As on 44.20, the commentators are particularly interested in the sociological implications of the verse. Cg, " 'entreated us': By this we gather that the fruit and so on presented by Guha—the foremost of those devoted to his [the Blessed One's] feet—was purified by his devotion and perfectly acceptable by reason of his being a supreme Bhāgavata, on the model of Śabarī [who though apparently a tribal woman shows ardent devotion to Rāma, cf. *Araṇyakāṇḍa sarga* 70] or Vidura [in the *MBh*, the low-caste half-brother of Pāṇḍu and Dhṛtarāṣṭra, who is devoted to Kṛṣṇa]. Rāma therefore refuses to accept it [not because Guha's caste renders it impure, but] only because of his desire to fast on the bank of the holy river. And he wishes to fast because of the profound dejection he feels at the grievous, sorrowful experiences of separation from so many people, foremost among them his beloved mother and father." Ck, "If this [reason given in the verse] is true, why does Rāma accept *pūjā* [food offered by way of homage] from Bharadvāja etc. [see previous note]? The answer is, because that is customary. A king is to be honored by a brahman with the milk and honey mixture; and the king must accept it, insofar as it works to his [spiritual] benefit. The sixth portion of tax from his own country is accepted by a king for the same reason, because it is customary to do so. Guha, however, as a Niṣāda, has no qualifications to make the *pūjā* according to precept, and therefore it cannot be accepted. Nor could it be accepted as if it were a tax, because Guha is not a subject in Rāma's country." Ct adds, "The real explanation is that, while Guha knows the truth [about Rāma's divine nature] and so does have the qualifications to offer *pūjā* to the Blessed One, Rāma cannot eat it because he has taken a vow."

18. "had" *akarot*: Note the use of the polysemic root *kṛ*, with the instrumental (Cg, Ck, Ct, " 'made' a drinking by means of").

In 44.24 Rāma is shown to perform the twilight worship first and then drink water. Cm tries unwisely to adjust the sequence of verses 17-18 here to accord with the earlier narrative, whereas Cg remarks that, since Rāma's repast was the topic of discussion, Guha describes that first, though the sequence was just as it had originally been.

"all three" *te trayaḥ*: "Sītā too," Cg; "including Sumantra," Ct. Women do not normally perform the twilight worship.

20. "washing their feet" *prakṣālya ca tayoḥ pādāu*: Cg again adds an oversensitive note: "We are to understand that he washed Rāma's feet with his own hands, and Sītā's only insofar as he provided her with water" (cf. note on 44.25).

22. "a pair of quivers" *iṣudhī*: Heroes wear two quivers because they shoot ambidextrously.

"the whole night through" *niśām . . . kevalām*: The two oldest commentators, Cv and Crā, read *kevalām*, and we follow them. The crit. ed.'s *kevalam* cannot be satisfactorily explained ("that is, without bed or sleep" [Cm, Cg, Ct]; "that is, without the desire for any allies" [Cr]).

23. Cg curiously suggests that Guha takes up guard in the belief that Lakṣmaṇa had been forced by Rāma to accompany him into exile, and in retribution for that he might be driven to try to harm Rāma while he slept; that Guha's retainers come lest Guha himself do some harm to Rāma, and finally that all these fears were empty, as the poet implies, because Rāma is "the equal of great Indra."

Sarga 82

4. "on a pile" *varāstaraṇasaṃcaye*: Cm, Cg, Ck, Ct, Cr analyze the compound as a *bahuvrīhi*, with "bed" understood.

5-6. Both the NR (v.l. ad 5b) and the SR (1964*) supply for these verses the verbal *uṣitvā* ("having passed the night . . . [he would always wake (verse 7)]"), which we accordingly repeat, though there appears to be a certain verisimilitude in the rambling anacoluthic structure established by the crit. ed.

"in the finest palaces, mansions" *prāsādāgravimāneṣu*: Certainly a *dvandva*, cf. 24.7 above and note there for the translation (against the commentators).

"dazzling with bouquets of flowers" *puṣpasaṃcayacitreṣu*: Cg is possibly right to see *paranipāta* here (for *citrapuṣpa-*); we agree with Cr.

7. "ornaments" *-ābharaṇa-*: Those belonging to Rāma's servants (Cm, Cg, Ct, Cr).

10. "Fate" *kālena*: Literally, "time." Ck, "There is nothing at all that is 'divine,' that is, able to realize its purposes independently. . . . Everything must submit to the compulsion of time, even divinity"; Ct, "There is no divinity more powerful than time, for when time had come, Rāma himself was forced to sleep upon the ground." On the instrumental of comparison, see note on 42.26.

12ff. One is reminded, by Bharata's "reading" of these signs, of the famous scene in the cycle of Kṛṣṇa legends, where the village women interpret Kṛṣṇa's footprints (*ViṣṇuP* 5.13.31ff., *BhāgP* 10.30.24ff.).

13. "dressed in all her jewelry" *sābharaṇā*: "She fell asleep without taking off her jewelry because she was exhausted from traveling," Cg. A slight inconsistency: in 54.16 Sumantra said Sītā had taken off (or was not wearing) her ornaments (but cf. note there).

14. Recall that Sītā is wearing her bark clothes over her silk garments (33.12; cf. 34.15).

15. "(such pleasure) that" (*sukhā*) . . . *yena*: The verse is not absolutely clear, but the best way to understand it is probably in opposition to verses 16-17, and to take *yena* as introducing a result clause. Such is the construction of Cr.

18. "thrown into jeopardy" *saṃśayitāḥ*: Perhaps with an intended play on *śayitaḥ* ("[how could he] sleep") in verse 17. We agree with Varadacharya, who compares 47.31 above (1964-1965, vol. 2, p. 231n), against the commentators: Cg, "We are 'thrown into doubt' about whether Rāma will receive our ministrations or not" (so in general Ck, Ct); Cm, "We have 'come to doubt' [whether we will attain] our own purposes in life [*puruṣārtha*]."

20. "And yet" *ca*: Note the adversative force; see 6.5.4 for a good parallel.

"no one" *na . . . kaścit*: "That is, no vassal king," Cg; wrongly Ck, Ct, Cr, "any one like me."

23. *vā = eva* (so Cr).

24. "for what time remains" *uttaraṃ kālam*: The remainder of the fourteen-year period.

25. "Śatrughna shall live with me" *śatrughno mānuvatsyati*: On Bharata's relationship with Śatrughna, Varadacharya (1964-1965, vol. 2, p. 233n) points to 1.17.19.

26. "If only . . . allow" *api . . . kuryuḥ*: For this absolute use of the optative with *api*, see 38.9 above, 3.35.4, 43.31, etc., and Speijer 1886, p. 263. Cg, Cr, wrongly: "*api* in the sense of a supposition," that is, "can it be the gods will . . . ?"

27. "if I stay" *vasan*: "That is, he will become his servant. But will Rāma accept his attendance? Yes, he 'will not be able to ignore' one who is simultaneously brother, pupil, and slave," Cg; "because he loves those who are devoted to him," Ck, Ct.

The NR hereafter adds that the night then came on, and Guha departed (1970*).

Sarga 83

1. "in that very place" *tatraiva*: Where Rāma had slept (Cg).

2. "the army" *vāhinīm*: Cg (and Cr) takes this to mean "river" (a sense not found for the word elsewhere in the *Rām*), and is thus forced to supply *asmān* as *prayojyakartṛ*. We translate with 65.9 in view, understanding the causative with ellipsis of *karma*.

3. The NR supplies Śatrughna's musings: "Will Rāma show his grace to us, when you and I and our counselors beg his grace?" (1975*).

6. "subordinating all other considerations to Rāma" *rāmasyānuvaśaḥ*: Literally, "subordinate to Rāma." Varadacharya explains the use of the qualification: "Bharata does not want to waste time recounting the emotional difficulties he had experienced during the night. He is totally absorbed in going to see Rāma. Realizing that he has to reply to Guha's question to avoid further [time-consuming] inquiries, and with an eye only to his coming business, he responds in the affirmative, but not because he actually passed a comfortable night." For this and the rest of the line the NR

substitutes, "to pay honor to the courteous reception [Guha had shown], though he was deeply sorrowful at heart" (1978*.2).

7. "your Majesty" *rājan*: "Bharata uses the honorific 'king' insofar as Guha is a devotee of Rāma," Cg. But see note on 44.9.

11. "distinguished" *-vijñeyāḥ*: "To be recognized by, distinguished by," cf. NR "gloss" *-cihnāṅkāḥ* (so too Cr, second interpretation); Cm, Cg, Ck, Ct explain, "known as, called 'swastika,' " Cg adding, "these swastika boats are two boats lashed together." The swastika in ancient India is a symbol of good luck.

"sailboats" *patākinyaḥ*: Ct takes *patāka-* in the sense of "oar" or "pole"; contrast Cg on verse 16, "fitted out with *patākas* for catching the wind" (that is, sails), whom we follow in both places.

"that easily caught the wind" *yuktavātāḥ*: Uncertain; the commentators differ: " 'where the wind was (made) pleasant' ('decreased,' Cm) by partitions and windows which blocked off the gusts," Cg, Cm; " 'of appropriate motions,' *-vāta-* as past passive participle in the sense of 'going,' " Ck.

12. "that gave out sounds of festive music" *sanandighoṣām*: Ck, Ct, "with the sounds of auspicious instruments played by people upon the deck"; Cm, Cg, "with the delightful sounds of bells."

13-14. "the other wives of the king. . . . Before the women . . . next the wives of the king" *yāś cānyā rājayoṣitaḥ . . . tatpūrvaṃ rājadārāḥ*: The boarding procedure here is unclear, and it looks as if the poet is correcting himself. Cm, Cg (reading 13cd with 14, and taking *rājadārāḥ* in 14c in apposition to Kausalyā, etc.) assume that the mothers cross in different boats, whereas Ck, Ct have them in the same boat with Bharata (understanding in 14c, "attendant royal women").

15. "fired the camp" *āvāsam ādīpayatām*: "It is well-known that a king's soldiers, at the time of their departure, burn their camp for good luck [*śrīsamāgamārtham*]," Cg; "this is part of a king's [army's, Ct] procedure (*dharma*)," Ck, Ct; Cr would have them "illuminate" the camp with large lamps in order to see the equipment better; but of course, as Varadacharya reminds us [1964-1965, vol. 2, p. 237n], they are leaving in the morning, so there would be no need for lights.

17. "the vehicles and teams" *yānayugmam*: This agrees with Cm, Cg, Ck, Ct, who analyze this compound as a *dvandva*.

"the great treasures" *mahādhanam*: May well be *bahuvrīhi* to *yānayugmam* ("the valuable vehicles"). But presumably the army would be carrying with them the valuables of Ayodhyā, which has been left unguarded (82.20-22).

18. "lovely formations" *kāṇḍacitrāṇi*: This appears to be a unique usage. We translate in basic agreement with Cm, Cg, Ck, Ct, Cr (though they all explain *kāṇḍa-* as "water," adducing *AmaK*). "This describes the fishermen's sport during their return journey, the boats becoming exceedingly light once the cargo had been unloaded," Cg.

19. "caparisoned" *savaijayantāḥ*: So Cm, Ck, Ct, Cr; Cg suggests also, "with howdahs."

"like flag-topped mountains" *sadhvajā iva parvatāḥ*: The simile does not seem very pointed. Ct, Cr read *sapakṣāḥ*, "like winged mountains," that is, before the time when Indra clipped off their wings (see the story of Maināka, 5.56.14). Cg artificially interprets *sadhvajāḥ* as "moving."

21. "auspicious" *puṇyā*: Unexpectedly referring to the army (one manuscript reported by Varadacharya [1964-1965, vol. 2, p. 239n] reads *puṇyām*, modifying the

Ganges). The commentators attempt to explain: "[that is,] 'purified', by bathing and the like in the Ganges," Cg; " 'purified' by the continuous presence of Vasiṣṭha and the others," Cr. Perhaps the adjective is meant to suggest the army's peaceful intentions.

"at the hour of Mitra" *maitre muhūrte*: About 8:00 a.m. Cg comments: "The day [from sunrise to sunset] consists of fifteen parts [called *muhūrtas*, each approximately forty-eight minutes long]. . . . The (fifteen) *muhūrtas* are [named,] numbered [and ordered, starting with the dawn hour] by Bṛhaspati: 'Raudra, Sārpa, Maitra, Paitra, Vāsava, Āpya, Vaiśva, Brāhma, Prājaiśa, Aindra, Aindrāgna, Nairṛta, Vāruṇa, Āryaman, Bhagi' " (Cm gives a similar list but omits Bhagi, thus apparently understanding "Prāja *and* Īśa"; this agrees with Ct, Cr, who, however, are corrupt in other respects). Considerably different is the list given by Cm on 3.68.12 vulgate, while the names Vinda (3.64.13) and Vijaya (6.4.3) do not seem to appear in any of the catalogues.

After verse 21 the NR inserts a passage (App. I, No. 25) in which, after crossing the Ganges, Bharata asks Guha where to go to find Rāma (but cf. 79.4 and note). Guha, though he "knows where Rāma is living" (line 6; cf. note on 51.1), merely tells Bharata to go first to the Prayāga forest, then to Bharadvāja's ashram. Bharata sets out, reaches the forest one and a half *yojanas* from the Ganges ford and, one *krośa* further, the ashram of Bharadvāja.

There is no indication in this *sarga* that Guha continues on with Bharata, despite his statement in 79.6. He will, however, later reappear (see 92.15, 93.40 and notes).

22. We understand (*contra* Ct) the verse to be recapitulatory, as is often the case with the final lyric (cf. 76.26ff. for a good example). Cg reports the reading *-pravarṣam*, "old," for *-pravaryam*, "preeminent" (not recorded in the crit. ed.).

The SR inserts hereafter a verse in which Bharata is shown to arrive at the ashram (1982*).

Sarga 84

2. "equipment" *-paricchadaḥ*: "His jewelry, and so on, plus the coronation pitcher and the rest. . . . He also took off his turban and armor [contrast Rāma's entry into the ashram, 48.8 and note], putting on a lower and upper garment [of linen]. . . . Bharata will don the bark garments he vowed to wear [82.23] later, after leaving the ashram," Cg.

The NR hereafter inserts six lines describing the ashram: "filled with tranquil animals . . . an open door to heaven, blazing with the glory of the wilderness," and so on (1984*).

5. "Since he had come in the company" *samāgamya*: The gerund is surely governed by *bharatena* (*pace* Cg). See 41.11 and note for other examples where the subjects of the main verb and a gerund are different.

"knew him to be a son" *abudhyata . . . sutam . . . tam*: The NR offers a variant in the dual, "he recognized that they were two sons" (cf. Ck on verse 6, who takes the dual to mean Bharata and Śatrughna).

7. "But knowing that Daśaratha had passed away" *jānan daśaratham vṛttam*: If we must explain how Bharadvāja knows of Daśaratha's death, we can refer his knowledge to the magic power he has acquired through his religious austerities (*tapas*), cf. note on 48.19.

We have in these two verses a closer approximation to the classical list of the seven "limbs" of the state ("house" taking the place of "kingdom"; the deficiency is made good by the NR, 1985*; contrast note on 75.11). In this list "king" would naturally appear, but Bharadvāja tactfully suppresses it.

8. "Since, for ascetics, the body, the sacred fires, and so on are the means by which asceticism is achieved; and because the birds and animals, insofar as they live in the ashram, are as beloved as the students ["and are a means for the ascetics to acquire *dharma*, by offering them security," Ck, Ct], it is proper that inquiries are made about their health," Cg, Ck, Ct.

9. "in his abiding affection for Rāghava" *rāghavasnehabandhanāt*: (Rāma, of course [Cm, Cr],) "and not because he found fault with Bharata," Cg. But no doubt, like Kausalyā (69) and Guha (78-79), Bharadvāja initially suspects treachery on Bharata's part (verse 13), as the natural response of a rival claimant to the throne, and apparently, despite his admission in verse 20, he still does even after Bharata's protest to the contrary (cf. note on 85.10).

16. "on my behalf" *madantare*: We agree with Ct, "the word *antara-* can have the meaning 'without' only as an indeclinable in the instrumental" (cf. also note on 14.13); "in my absence," Cg, Ck; "without me," Cm; "at a time when I was far away," Cr.

18. "the lord of earth" *mahīpatiḥ*: "Bharata calls Rāma this to underscore his own lack of desire for kingship," Varadacharya (1964-1965, vol. 2, p. 245n; cf. note on 66.24-25).

After this verse, the SR inserts 1996*, in which the priests (Vasiṣṭha, etc.) beseech Bharadvāja on Bharata's behalf.

20. "to hear it openly confirmed" *dṛḍhīkaraṇam astv iti*: In basic agreement with Ct: " 'to make it firm,' to remove the possibility of his changing. Something declared before a multitude cannot be altered." Cg suggests, " 'that it might be made resolute,' according to the proverb of 'driving in a post' " (*sthūṇānikhanananyāya*, that is, fixing a post securely in the ground by repeatedly driving it down).

21. "You are mindful of the desires and needs of others" *kāmārthakovidaḥ*: We translate the compound literally, with some uncertainty as to the true sense. Cm, Cg, Ck, Ct, Cr all agree in their gloss, "who are proficient in bestowing objects of desire." Cs appears to support the version adopted.

22. "a man of noble vision" *udāradarśanaḥ*: Note the recurrence of the epithet used previously only of Daśaratha (cf. 58.57 and note).

"overjoyed" *pratītarūpaḥ*: Cg is correct to take *-rūpa-* here as the emphatic suffix *rūpap* (cf. note on 14.24); Ck, Ct, "whose fame [*rūpa-*, so defined by *Nigh*, cited by Cg] is well known."

Sarga 85

1. "offered of hospitality" *ātithyena nyamantrayat*: Perhaps literally, "invited as guest," predicative instrumental of abstract substantive (a late epic construction, it would appear). Ck, Ct gloss, " 'with,' the purpose being, hospitality" (Cg understands as dative in function).

2. "the hospitality appropriate to the forest" *ātithyaṃ vane yad upapadyate*: *Ātithyam* is included in the relative clause, against all the commentators. Cg, " 'hospitality' has been shown '[by that which is available] in the forest' " (so Cm, Ck, Ct).

3. "With a chuckle" *prahasann iva*: "Because he knows that Bharata thinks him incapable of supplying anything more than what he already has ("since he is a poor forest anchorite," Ct)," Ck, Ct.

4. "It is for this army of yours" *senāyās tu tavaitasyāḥ*: Ctr mentions a *Taittirīya śruti* text: "One must offer hospitality to all the attendants with whom a king arrives" (vol. 2, pp. 490-91).

"you . . . deserve no less" *yathārūpā tvam arhaḥ*: Literally, "(My pleasure is) [only] such as you deserve" (so essentially Cr), though the syntax is admittedly difficult. PW s.v. *yathārūpā* translates, "extraordinarily great" (a unique usage), which is unlikely and requires a hard asyndeton. The other commentators understand, "my pleasure is such as you ought (that is, to be pleased with)" (Cg), "to accept" (Cm, Ct), "to permit," (Cg, Ck, Ct). The NR reads, "I too would find pleasure in this" (2005*).

6. The SR adds, "Kings and princes should always assiduously avoid ascetics in their own domains" (2006*).

9. The *saṃdhi* at the seam of *pādas* ab, *senety / ā-* (for Vālmīki uncharacteristically harsh), is removed in the NR.

10. "entered the fire-sanctuary" *agniśālāṃ praviśya*: "In order to purify himself, insofar as it is a place where divine powers are present. . . . He would sip water three times, wipe his mouth twice and touch [with water] once his head, eyes, nostrils, ears, and heart, in accordance with the *śruti* prescriptions of sipping, which is preparatory to all rites," Cg (cf. *ManuSm* 2.60).

Several N manuscripts add that Bharadvāja wants to provide an exceptional type of hospitality, since Vasiṣṭha and other sages had come (2008*). Indeed, some explanation is called for, as the motive behind the magical entertainment is not clear. In view of such verses as 5 and 54ff., Bharadvāja may still be suspicious of Bharata, and either like Guha (see 78.17) is hoping to learn more of Bharata's intentions by keeping him in his presence as long as possible; or is actually attempting to disaffect (or disrupt) his army (see verse 77 below). For a traditional interpretation, see Ct on verse 36 below. It would appear that 1.52 is a recollection of this episode.

11. "Viśvakarman and Tvaṣṭṛ": Tvaṣṭṛ ("The Builder") and Viśvakarman ("The All-worker") are demiurgic gods, the later Viśvakarman wholly usurping the position of the vedic Tvaṣṭṛ. The commentators find the juxtaposition of the two troubling. Cg says Viśvakarman is the architect, Tvaṣṭṛ the builder; Ck, Ct, Cr understand them as one individual: "Viśvakarman who is endowed with the skills of a builder" (so too alternatively Cg, who claims that the cognomen Tvaṣṭṛ is added to exclude the Viśvakarman of the demons, that is, Maya).

For this episode compare *HariVaṃ* 86.20ff., where Viśvakarman, summoned by Kṛṣṇa, magically builds him a mansion in Dvāravatī.

After this verse many manuscripts insert, "I invoke the three gods who guard the world, under the lead of Śakra" (2009*).

13. "date-palm liquor" *maireyam*: "A type of intoxicating drink made from the wild date-palm (*kharjūra*) belonging [particularly] to the region of Mira [?]," Cm, Cg (cf. *Arth Śā* 2.25.22).

14. "the *gandharvas* of the gods" *devagandharvān*: "That is, as opposed to human musicians," Cg; so Cr.

"Haha, Huhu" *-hahāhuhūn*: Thus are the two names to be divided. The compound is generally treated as a *dvandva* of the old vedic type (*devatādvandva*, cf. note on

3.45.37), with both members in the dual; the former member retains the dual sign even when the compound is plural (as in the vedic *indrāmarutaḥ*).

"the *apsaras* goddesses" *apsaraso devīḥ*: There appear to be two classes of *apsarases*, those of the gods and those of the *gandharvas* (so Cg, Cr).

15. Tumburu: "The singing instructor of the *apsarases*," Cg (cf. the story of Virādha, 3.3.18).

16. "Kubera's . . . forest" *vanaṃ . . . kauberam*: "This is the forest called Caitraratha, which is found in the land of the northern Kurus" [a fairy-tale land beyond the Himalayas], Cg.

"(whose foliage is) raiment" *vāsobhūṣaṇapatravat*: *Vāso* should be printed in compound with the following item.

17. "(the blessed) moon" *(bhagavān) somaḥ*: By way of a complex mytho-linguistic identification with the sacrosanct *soma* "plant" (already in *AV*; for example, 7.81.3, 4), the moon was given the name and ancient epithet of *soma*, "lord of plants" (cf., for example, *ṚV* 9.114.2), and so came to be considered the source of all food.

18. "dropping" *-pracyutāni*: The garlands grow naturally on the trees, and do not require stringing (so intimated by Cm, Ct; Cg glosses simply, "new, fresh").

19. "his words accented in full accord with the rules of pronunciation" *śikṣāsvarasamāyuktam*: The compound is to be taken adverbially (with Cg, Cr; Cm adds *mantram*). With regard to the verse, Ck, Ct cite the famous lines [from *MahāBh* on *Pā* 6.1.84], "One word, fully understood and correctly employed, becomes a wishing-cow in the heavenly world"; Cg quotes the same text (vol. 1, p. 30): "A word corrupt in point of accent or phoneme, incorrectly employed, does not express its meaning. It becomes a language-thunderbolt to injure the sacrificer, as the word Indraśatru [injured Tvaṣṭṛ] by reason of [Tvaṣṭṛ's] mistake in point of accentuation."

21. "with a faint touch of the spice hills of Malaya and Dardura" *malayaṃ darduraṃ caiva . . . upaspṛśya*: The hills mentioned are, in the epic, the principal sources of sandalwood and other fragrant aromas. Cg places them near the Malabar hills; cf. *MBh* 2.52.34 [Chitrashala ed.], where the two mountains are paired and identified as the source of sandalwood (cf. *RaghuVa* 4.51) and aloe.

22. "clouds" *ghanāḥ*: Cm, Cg, Ck, would understand, "thick (*ghana-*) showers of blossoms"; we agree with Ct, Cs on *ghana-*, and take *kusumavṛṣṭayaḥ* as *bahuvrīhi*.

23. "Gentle winds" *uttamā vātāḥ*: Most of the NR avoids the redundancy (cf. verse 21; remarked on by Cg, Cr) by reading "fragrances" for "winds."

24. "rhythm" *laya-*: Or, "tempo": "The simultaneous cessation [that is, periodic rests] in singing, dancing, and music," Cg; "the measure of the beat [*tāla*] in dancing and singing," Ck, Ct, Cr.

28. "the forest" *vanam*: Kubera's (verse 16).

"the heavenly river" *nadī divyā*: The NR reads, "the Sarasvatī"; the commentators take the crit. ed. reading as a collective noun, save Ck, who identifies it as the Jambūnadī.

29. "four-room houses" *catuḥśālāni*: Understand *gṛhāṇi* (cf. *MBh* 1.132.8). (Cg glosses *sañjavanam*, a building enclosed on four sides.) This was the standard urban house: four long rooms (originally separate) arranged in a rectangle with a courtyard in the middle (cf. Schlingloff 1969, p. 25 and the Barhut relief reproduced as Figure 24).

35. "as if the king were there" *rājavat*: The commentators are divided in their understanding. Cm, Ct, Cr, "fit for a king" (as modifier of *rājāsanam* [by *Pā* 5.1.117]);

Cg, "as if [it, the throne, etc., were like] the king, that is, as if it were Rāma" [cf. *Pā* 5.1.115]. Possible too: "He approached like a king," with a surprise reversal in the next verse. In view of verse 36, we follow Cg and interpret slightly, though the usage itself is inherently ambiguous, and perhaps intentionally so.

36. "He paid homage to the throne" *āsanaṃ pūjayām āsa*: "Bharata imagines Rāma to be upon the throne, and takes up the fan as appropriate to his subordinate station," Cg (so in general Ck). Here Ct reflects: "The great seer, even though it cost him much of his ascetic power, has provided this hospitality so that Bharata by his actions might convince all the world of his total lack of desire for kingship [shown here by his taking not the throne but the minister's seat], which hitherto had only been asseverated in speech, and which people might consequently mistrust. A second reason is to please Bharata, who is a portion of Viṣṇu, the show of hospitality being like the *pūjā* one offers [to Viṣṇu] with flowers and the like. . . . Moreover, the sage wants to demonstrate the greatness derived from [his] loving Blessed Rāma—since those who are wholly absorbed in the Blessed One experience the joy of heaven here on earth—and by demonstrating this, to awaken in them an even greater love of Rāma."

37. "palace supervisor" *praśāstā*: Thus Kangle on *ArthŚā* 1.12.6, supported by Cr; Cm, Cg, Ct, "officer who manages the camp"; Ck, "guard [chief police officer?] of the city."

38. "running with rice pudding" *pāyasakardamāḥ*: Literally, "with rice pudding forming their sediment."

41. "coral" *pravālena*: The NR eliminates the reference; cf. note on 13.25.

42. Nandana: The pleasure garden of Indra.

"who could madden with passion any man they took in their arms" *yābhir gṛhītaḥ puruṣaḥ sonmāda iva lakṣyate*: According to Cg, Ck, and certainly quite rightly [see also note on 29.13], this alludes to the scriptural statement [of the *TaiS*], "It is the *gandharvāpsarases*, to be sure, who madden the man who goes mad" [3.4.8.4]. The variant reading reported for our verse by Cg, "any man they take in their arms, it is said, becomes wild with passion," attempts to make this allusion more explicit.

43. Nārada: Cg wants to distinguish this Nārada from the [*brahmarṣi*] son of Brahmā, but the two are identical in the early literature (cf. Hopkins 1915, pp. 153ff.).

Sūryavarcasa: The unusual a-stem lengthening in *sūryavarcasaḥ* (expect *-varcāḥ*, thus in *MBh*) has occasioned a host of variants here.

44. "at Bharadvāja's command" *bharadvājasya śāsanāt*: "By this we are to understand that the seer is testing Bharata's feelings toward Rāma under the pretext of this show of hospitality," Cg. On verse 45 he remarks further, "Having described how Bharata remains fully subordinating himself to Rāma and has no lust for pleasure, the poet goes on to describe the army's pleasure."

46. "beating the time" *śamyāgrāhāḥ*: See the explanation of the term in Raghavan 1963, pp. 559-60.

47. "becoming hunchbacks or dwarfs" *kubjā bhūtvātha vāmanāḥ*: Presumably what is meant is that these trees become servants ("hunchbacks") and/or jesters ("dwarfs").

48. The trees mentioned in this verse are all feminine in grammatical gender (contrast the trees in verses 46-47, which are usually masculine), hence the roles assigned them (noticed also by Cm, Cg, Ct).

50. "rubbed . . . with oil" *ucchādya*: The reading of Cm, Cg, Ck is *ucchādya* (*contra*

the crit. ed.'s report), and most of the NR supports *-cch-* here; thus we read with the S commentators.

52. "by strong men who bade them eat" *codayanto mahābalāḥ*: The line is not entirely clear as the crit. ed. constitutes it. Perhaps, like the celestial women brought down from heaven to serve the men, the "strong men" are stable hands magically provided by Bharadvāja (so Cg), since the soldiers themselves have become incapable of looking after the animals (verses 53, 56; cf. also verse 60).

55. "we will . . . go" *gamiṣyāma*: Instead of *gamiṣyāmo*, for the sake of the meter (as in 87.7, *sma* for *smaḥ*).

"may . . . fare well" *kauśalam astu*: This is not an expression of gratitude to Bharata (so Ck, Ct), but indicates indifference to him, as the second expression indicates indifference to Rāma (so Cg).

58. "turn their thoughts once more to eating" *abhavad bhakṣaṇe matiḥ*: Several manuscripts try to correct the rather uncharacteristic playfulness here, reading, "and no more turned their minds to eating."

59. "accompanying the army" *balasthāḥ*: Cg wants this to modify all three previous substantives, but the connective *cāpi* tells against this.

"all . . . dressed in fresh garments" *sarve cāhatavāsasaḥ*: We may understand either *ahata-*, "new" (Cg, Ck, Ct, Cr), or *āhata-*, "freshly washed" (Cg, whom we follow).

61. "begrimed with dust" *rajasā dhvasta-*: The entertainment being a divine one, the men were treated like gods (cf. verse 75), upon whom dust never settles.

62. "soups prepared from fruit-stock" *phalaniryūhasaṃsiddhaiḥ sūpaiḥ*: Some commentators want to take the compound independently, "treacle with ripe fruits," or, "preparations of fruit-stock" (Cm, Cg, Ck); we agree with Ck's second interpretation, on which he remarks, "This type of soup is common in Kerala" (Ct, Cr would have the compound, as translated, modify the meats in *pāda* a).

64. "wishing-cows" *kāmadughāḥ*: That is, cows from which anything one desires might be milked.

65. The translation follows the commentators, who take *pādas* cd in apposition to *pāda* b.

"prepared in steaming cauldrons" *prataptapiṭharaiḥ*: By *Pā* 4.2.16, with *luk* (though cf. Ck, Ct, v.l. *-paiṭharaiḥ*) of *aṇ*; Cm understands inversion, for *piṭharaprataptaiḥ*, whereas Ck, Ct gloss, "prepared in cauldrons and heated."

"peacock" *-māyūra-*: Until the Mughals outlawed their slaughter, peacocks were prized as a food throughout northern India, even by such quasi vegetarians as Aśoka (cf. Rock Edict I [Shah-Bazgari], line 3).

66. "well-fired" *susaṃskṛtāḥ*: In agreement with Cr.

"(buttermilk) scented with . . . woodapple" *kapitthasya sugandhinaḥ* (. . . *rasālasya*, verse 67): This follows Ck's indication, making *kapitthasya* dependent on *sugandhinaḥ*, which itself is adjective to *rasālasya* in verse 67. (Cm, Cg, Ct, Cr construe *kapitthasya* directly with *pūrṇāḥ* in verse 67, "woodapple milk," differentiating it from *rasāla*, which is milk flavored with such spices as ginger, pepper, cardamom, and clove.) The woodapple leaves would lend an aroma of aniseed.

69. "bristled" *aṃśumataḥ*: If Cg, Ck, Ct, Cr, whom we follow, are right (Cm instead glosses, "glistening"), we have a unique reference to bristle toothbrushes (toothpicks were and still are generally used).

70. "Shoes [*pāduka-*] are made out of wood, sandals [*upānaha-*] out of leather," Cm, Cg, Ct, Cr.

72. "just right for bathing, with lovely landings" *avagāhyasutīrthān*: We read the *pāda* thus, as a single *dvandva* compound (for the absence of the usual contrast between the adjectives, see Renou 1968, p. 105), and analyze with Ck; this is supported by the NR, *avagāhyān* or *-āḥ*. Ct (alone explicitly) construes *pādas* cd with b, which we understand as constituting a separate clause along with *pāda* a.

"watering" *pratipāna-*: "Water drunk after eating in order to help digest the food," Cg, Cm ("according to the *śāstra* of Bāhaṭa" [that is, Vāhaṭa]), Ck, Ct, Cr.

77. "To show that this was all real and not false ["as in a dream," Ck] is the poet's purpose in this verse," Cm (so too Cg, Ck, Ct, Cr). Ck goes on to add, rather cryptically, "The enjoyments here were just as real as the food enjoyed by a person who eats his fill at the horse-sacrifice of an emperor, real to the point of being actually digested."

Sarga 86

1. "of his own accord" *kāmāt*: A common meaning of this adverbial form. Varadacharya correctly, "of his own free will, before Bharadvāja had called him" (1964-1965, vol. 2, p. 268n). Cm, Cg, Ct, Cr, " 'in his desire' to reach Rāma."

3. "content" *samagraḥ*: The word is rare in this sense (contrast verse 5 below and the note on 34.31), though thus by the commentators.

Ct comments: "In this verse Bharata is being informed that it is ascetic power which is the great source of all good things, not kingship."

4. Bharadvāja strides out "the moment Bharata arrives in order that all the people, Kausalyā and the rest, might behold him" (Cg, so also Ct).

7. "though" *kāmam*: The syntax indicates that *kāmam*, as so often in the *Rām*, is concessive (cf. 5.22.7, to cite but one example).

9. Cg assumes that Guha and his kinsmen knew where Rāma had gone (cf. note on 51.1) and had told Bharata, who here is only asking the sage out of politeness.

10. "two and a half" *ardhatṛtīyeṣu*: Numerical compounds with *ardha-* are ambiguous. Here, as often when an ordinal is used, half of the *uttarapada* is added to the next lower number ("the third being a half," cf. German *drittehalb*). In 48.25 Bharadvāja says Citrakūṭa is ten *krośas* away from Prayāga; at the usual computation of four *krośas* per *yojana*, two and a half would indeed be correct (cf. Varadacharya 1964-1965, vol. 2, p. 270n).

11. Mandākinī: Though this name is often used of the Ganges, Cm, Ck are quite explicit that some other river is meant (see also notes on 50.11 and 22).

12. "(Between the stream) and Mount Citrakūṭa" (*anantaraṃ tatsaritaś*) *citrakūṭaṃ ca parvataṃ*: The crit. ed. is apparently wrong to read the nominative in *pāda* b. Much of the SR and the entire NR preserve the correct reading, the accusative, which we are to take by anacoluthon for genitive (restored in 2050*).

"their leaf hut" *parṇakuṭī*: Probably singular rather than dual (though cf. note on 50.13). The "two of them" surely refers to Rāma and Lakṣmaṇa (so Ck, Ct), rather than to Rāma and Sītā (Cr).

Hereafter some N manuscripts insert a few lines (2050*) stating that Vālmīki is living where Rāma has established his ashram (cf. note on 50.12).

13. "the southern road" *dakṣiṇenaiva mārgeṇa*: "On the southern bank of the Yamunā," Ck, Ct (cf. 49.3 above).

20. "(This woman whom) you see" (*yām imāṃ . . .*) *paśyasi*: We follow Ck, Ct, Cr on the syntax of the verb.

"grief and fasting" *śokānaśana-*: Or, "fasting because of her grief" (Ck, Cr).

21. Dhātṛ: Viṣṇu (Cg), Upendra [= Viṣṇu] (Cm, Ck; Ct, "Dhātṛ is Prajāpati, but Upendra can be meant by the name because Prajāpati is another form of him [Upendra]"); cf. note on 22.2.

22. "a *karṇikāra* branch stripped of its blossoms" *karṇikārasya śākheva śīrṇapuṣpā*: Cg glosses instead, "whose blossoms have faded." The blossoms of the *karṇikāra*, though large and fragrant, are not distinguished, and furthermore they open at night. On the other hand, the leaves—which is what most of the NR reads—are remarkable: "The lower surface [of the leaf] is covered with gray down. . . . The foliage, when ruffled by the breeze, appears silvery white, and can be picked out from that of all other trees at a great distance" (Benthall 1946, p. 58).

24. "dead in life" *jīvanāśam*: On the form cf. note on 60.8 (so Cs analyzes here).

29. "received his benediction" *saṃsiddhaḥ*: So Cm, Cg, Ck, Ct.

31. "like clouds" *jīmūtā iva*: The elephants resemble clouds not only by reason of their rumbling sound, but in their color: the gray of their massive bodies, as well as the yellow of their girths (which resemble streaks of lightning).

34. "standing ready" *niyuktām*: So Cm ("ordered, by Vasiṣṭha, etc.," Cg; "held up, by bearers," Ck, Ct, Cr).

35. After this verse the NR (2061*) has the army cross the Yamunā; the SR (2062*), the Ganges and other streams (commentators differ).

Sarga 87

2. We must here supply the verb "(were) thrown into confusion" from the previous verse (thus also Ct).

"monkeys" *ṛkṣāḥ*: Cg, Cr gloss, "bears" (cf. note on 1.16.10).

6. "he addressed Vasiṣṭha" *uvāca . . . vasiṣṭham*: The NR, probably rightly (cf. verses 11, 16), has Bharata address Śatrughna instead (Cg supposes Bharata to begin addressing Śatrughna at verse 10).

8. "at a distance" *dūrāt*: Ck understands *'dūrāt* ("near by").

10. Ct (and Ck) joins this verse closely with verse 9: "Because the elephants are striking the trees, their branches shake and their flowers drop."

13. We are at a loss to understand this elliptical verse. The probable antecedent to *amī* is "trees" (so Cm, Ct, Cr alternatively; Ck reads thus; Cg, " 'those,' that is, soldiers"), and we agree with Ck, Ct in understanding *phalakaiḥ* as "branches." It is presumably both in point of their chaplets of flowers and their dark limbs that the trees resemble men of the south: "southerners bind up their hair and decorate it with flower-chaplets," Cg; "the trees wear flower-chaplets just as southern men wear on their heads flowers that they have woven onto *phalakas* [unglossed] bound with dark leather," Cm. However, T3's *muñcanti* points persuasively to the conjecture *kiranti* (for *kurvanti*): "The trees, with their cloud-dark branches, *are scattering* flower-chaplets on their heads, and now the men look like southerners." Verses 9ff. are not merely descriptive; they report disturbances in the region caused by the army's approach. Verse 13 should conform to this, as the conjecture would permit.

15. "as if to do me a kindness" *kurvann iva mama priyam*: "Because his primary interest is catching sight of Rāma's ashram," Cg.

18. "pathway to heaven" *svargapathaḥ*: Against the commentators ("like a spot in heaven," Cg, Ck, Ct; "equal to heaven," Cr); contrast the sense of the word in 74.13.

19. This verse disrupts the train of thought. The NR either transposes or eliminates it.

21. "warriors with weapons in hand" *puruṣāḥ śastrapāṇayaḥ*: It is odd that a search party in a region where ascetics dwell is said to be armed. Perhaps the specification is meant only to prepare us for the events in *sargas* 90-91 (Lakṣmaṇa's rash inference as a foil to Rāma's calmness).

22. "the column of smoke" *dhūmāgram*: "Because it is just a 'spire of smoke,' a forest fire is ruled out and so their inference is sound," Varadacharya (1964-1965, vol. 2, p. 281n; Ct, "they can see the forest clearly and observe there is no forest fire").

24. "just and reasonable" *sādhusaṃmatam*: Or, "which the just would credit" (Cg, Ck, Ct).

25. "I . . . Sumantra and our guru" *aham eva . . . sumantro gurur eva ca*: It is curious that Śatrughna is not mentioned here, though he will be present at Bharata's interview with Rāma later (*sarga* 93). See also 95.33, 96.29, and notes.

Sarga 88

1. "the long time" *dīrghakāla-*: Although calculations are unavoidably conjectural after *sarga* 70, this day appears to mark the thirty-fifth of Rāma's exile. Ct on 108.2 calculates thirty-six days, though here he says "one month" (so too Ck, who notes, " 'long' is a relative term; in relation to two days even one month can be called a 'long time' "); Cr, "three months."

2. "wonderful Citrakūṭa" *citraṃ citrakūṭam.*

3. Ctś interprets the verse allegorically with regard to Rāma's avatar: " 'expulsion,' that is, from the position of Supreme Lord; 'being apart from my loved ones,' Garuḍa and so on," etc.

7. "all of them tame" *aduṣṭaiḥ*: Because of the beneficent influence of the sages who dwell there (Cm, Cg, Ck, Ct).

8-10. "soapnut trees" *ariṣṭa-*: Cg, Ct gloss instead, "the *neem* tree."

dhanvana-: The tree of Indra, according to Cg (so Ct).

"pomegranate" *bījaka-*: Following Cm, Cg, Ck, Ct.

12. *vidhyādhara*: Mythical creatures, apparently a type of wizard (the name means literally, "endowed with magical knowledge") or sprite, often associated with mountains.

"swords" *khaḍgān*: Cg, Cr assume the swords to be those of the *vidhyādharas*; Ck, Ct, those of the previously mentioned *kiṃnaras*. The epics refer to these and most other mythological creatures in so oblique and superficial a manner that virtually no specific information about them can be gained.

14. "with such pleasing redolence" *ghrāṇatarpaṇam*: Cg correctly takes the compound adverbially (so too Cm, but wrongly as modifying *praharṣayet*, whereas Ck interprets as substantive with *abhyetya*, whose subject he takes to be *naram*; Ct supplies *kurvāṇaḥ*).

15. "If I might live here . . . with you" *yadīha . . . tvayā sārdham . . . vatsyāmi*: "By the use of the conditional, their coming separation is intimated," Cg.

18. "marvels . . . to experience, to contemplate and talk about" *bhāvān manovākkāyasaṃyatān*: Literally, "things relating to the body, mind, and speech." The reading is disputed: Cm, Ck give *-saṃyatā*, "you, by whom the body, mind, and speech are restrained" (cf. *manovāgdehasaṃyatā* in *ManuSm* 5.165). Cg reads with the crit. ed. but explains, "things by which the body . . . are restrained," which seems impossible in this context.

"Body, mind, speech" is the classical tripartition of the psychophysical personality. Though known as early as the *ṚV*, it appears to become standard only in post-Buddhist times (replacing an earlier binary division, "mind and body," concretized as "word and deed." For related problems in Greek thought, see Barck 1976, especially pp. 8ff.).

19. "for kings" *rājñām*: The restriction did not seem relevant to many S and N manuscripts, which replace it with a vocative, "Sītā" or "queen."

"leads to well-being" *bhavārthāya*: Cf. the sense of *bhava-* in 95.3 below. The commentators are mistaken: Cg, "for the termination of rebirth"; Cm similarly, though he joins as if it were in compound with *pretya* (but for the absolute use of *pretya* see above, 39.4); Ck, "for the purpose of ending the torments of transmigration"; Ct, "for gaining the world of Bhava, that is, Śiva, Hiraṇyagarbha."

20. The verse contains a heavy alliteration, six instances of *ś* in two *pādas*.

21. "plants . . . blazing . . . in the beauty of their own luster" *oṣadhyaḥ svaprabhālakṣmyā bhrājamānāḥ*: On these magical plants cf. Mallinātha on *KumāSaṃ* 1.10, where he cites the scriptural statement, "The sun when setting deposits its luster in fire and [various] plants."

22. "Some parts . . . look like dwelling places" *kecit kṣayanibhā deśāḥ*: "Because of all the caves; others look like 'gardens' because of the vines and trees," Cg.

"sheer rock" *ekaśilā*: Literally, "monolithic"; Ck is obscure: " 'with one rock,' having a level surface capable of allowing many people to stand there."

24. "lovers" *kāminām*: Here and in verse 25 we are presumably to see a reference to the semi-divine creatures mentioned in verse 12.

26. Vasvaukasārā: The city of Śakra in the eastern quarter (Cm, Cg [citing *ViṣṇuP*]), or, the city of Kubera (Cg [citing the lexicographer Yādava], Cm, Ck, Ct, Cr, Cs).

Nalinī: Lake Mānasa, or, Lake Saughandhikā (Cm, Cg; cf. 89.4), or, the city of Śakra (Ck [citing the lexicographer Hari], Ct, Cr, Cs). Similar discrepancies among the commentators at 5.3.12; in *MBh* 3.186.94 Vasvaukasārā and Nalinī are juxtaposed and identified as rivers.

"the land of the northern Kurus" *uttarān kurūn*: Here the poet may finally be making explicit what appears to be his intention throughout this *sarga* and the next, of contrasting the two scenes, Bharadvāja's heavenly entertainments and Rāma's simple forest pleasures, to the advantage of the latter (compare also verse 25 with 85.77).

27. "Passing this time . . . will be a pleasure to me" *vijahrivān . . . prapatsye*: Rāma seems here to be repeating the sentiment earlier expressed (verses 16-17): his exile is both a pleasure to him and a benefit to his House. The temporal aspect of *vijahrivān* is thus coterminous with *prapatsye* (cf. the "perfect" in verse 16). Cm, Ck, Ct, Cr make the first verbal conditional, "if I may pass . . . I shall then find," whereas Cg sees the two verbals as consecutive, "After I pass . . . I shall find [another] pleasure, the kingship." But either such expression, in light of the whole *sarga*, would be a *non sequitur*.

Sarga 89

3. In this and the next verse "a figure of speech is suggested [that is, the following simile], that the river is like Sītā, Sītā's wide hips, sounding anklets and beautiful hands, feet, and face [corresponding to the shoals, calling birds, and flowers, respectively]," Cg. The erotic simile appears elsewhere in the *Rām* (see 4.29.28).

4. Nalinī: See note on 88.26. All commentators here gloss it Lake Saugandhikā.

8. "seems almost ready to dance" *pranṛtta iva*: "When in real life a person begins to dance, he first scatters flowers about and shakes his arms," Cg. For the inchoative sense of the past participle, see note on 3.5 above.

9. "The suggestion here is, like a broad-hipped woman [= the beaches], dressed in white [= the clear water], surrounded by admirers [= the holy men]," Cg.

10. "That is, [the river looks] like a woman whose dress is half falling off, after her lover has tugged at it," Cg.

11. "sheldrake" *rathāṅgāhvayanāḥ*: *Cakravāka* (cf. Ingalls 1965, p. 501).

12. "in your eyes" *tava darśanāt*: Literally, "from, according to, your viewpoint," as in 6.52.34. Cg, Ck, Ct agree on a sense we find unacceptable, "and better than seeing you, too" (Cg, "because it [more] inflames [my passion]," thus Cg's gloss of "my lovely" as "one without jealousy"; Cr offers, "[better] by reason of the fact that you are continuously looking at them [with me] in solitude"). It is awkward that the genitives in *pādas* ab should be objective while that in *pāda* d is subjective, but nonetheless this seems to be the poet's intention, as well as the only reasonable interpretation.

14. "as if it were an old friend" *sakhīvat*: So Cr. Rāma here and in the previous and following verses is assuring Sītā that the river is not an unfriendly one, that its agitation is not the result of the presence of dangerous animals, and that she should feel at home here. *Sakhīvat* construes with the accusative (as in the next verse). Cg would join it with the instrumental, "(Plunge in with me) as if with a female friend of yours" [that is, rather than as a lover], which is not only silly but against Sanskrit usage of *vatiḥ*. Ck, Ct explain as nominative, " '(Plunge in) like a friend,' that is, of the river's."

"submerging" *avamajjantī*: Note the *antarbhāvitaṇyartha*. "She 'submerges' them by the waves produced by the splashing of her breasts and loins; or perhaps we have here a poetic fancy (*utprekṣā*): 'submerge' them, that is, [put them] to shame at being worsted by the beauty of her face," Cg.

17. "at the time of the three oblations" *triṣavaṇam*: Morning, noon, evening.

18. As the verse is constituted in the crit. ed. (as in the vulgate), there is no verb for the accusatives in *pādas* a-c. Cm, Cg supply "bathing in" [*upaspṛśan*] from the previous verse, Ck, Ct, Cr, "plunging in" from nowhere; neither will do. We read *paśyan* for *ramyām*, with the entire NR.

"lions, monkeys, and elephants" *gajasiṃhavānaraiḥ*: "Their innate hostility toward each other has been mitigated by the beneficent influence of the ashram," Cg.

19. "fondly" *saṃgatam*: (Perhaps) literally, "attached," cf. 3.31.22, *viṣayeṣu saṃgataḥ* (cf. PW s.v. *gam* citing Hemacandra = *hṛdayaṃgama*; Cg, "desultorily" [? *prasaktānuprasaktam*]; Cr, "appropriately").

"a very balm to the eye" *nayanāñjanaprabham*: The commentators take this compound literally, "that looked like collyrium for the eyes—that is, black."

The entire NR includes hereafter a long *sarga* (given in App. I, No. 26), which it is worth summarizing and briefly considering critically: Rāma and Sītā return to the northern foothills of the mountain where, seeing a lovely grotto, they sit down and observe the countryside about them (the trees "crying tears of sap where elephant tusks have struck them, and seeming to weep aloud with the long cries of the crickets," etc.). They embrace, Rāma painting on her forehead a beauty-mark with glistening red arsenic and covering her hair with *kesara* flowers. The two set off walking again, when Sītā sees a monkey, who terrifies her; Rāma, after rebuking the monkey, calms Sītā with an embrace, whereby the red mark is transferred to his chest. Next they spot a grove of *aśoka* trees, proceed to it and adorn each other with flowers (lines 1-64). Upon their return to the ashram, Lakṣmaṇa shows them the ten deer he has killed. Sītā then prepares dinner for Rāma and Lakṣmaṇa [contrast note on 48.15], and afterwards for herself. She sets out the remaining meat to dry and on Rāma's order guards it from the crows. One such crow begins to assault Sītā; Rāma grows angry and shoots a magic arrow at it. Harassed by the arrow the crow throws himself upon Rāma's mercy, supplicating him in a human voice. Rāma cannot, however, render his arrow useless since he has cast a *mantra* upon it, and so, while prepared to spare the crow's life, he demands one part of its body. The bird resolves to give up one eye, and after doing so he departs (65-115). Rāma then hears the sounds of the approaching army.

The passage is referred to in various ways later in the narrative. In Hanumān's interview with Sītā (5.36.10ff.), when he asks her for some token of recognition to prove to Rāma that he has met with her, Sītā tells him what once happened "in the northeast foothills of Citrakūṭa": after bathing she gives herself up to Rāma's embrace (verse 14, see *Ayodhyākāṇḍa*, App. I, No. 26.30); all NR manuscripts mention here the red beauty-mark (5.834*, 835*), to which Sītā refers again in 5.38.4. A crow "greedy for meat" attacks her in the breast (verse 16; some NR manuscripts shift the scene to the ashram, having the crow grasp after the deer meat, 5.837*, which seems like a prudish revision, as does the *Ayodhyākāṇḍa* passage itself). The crow is said to be "the son of Indra" (who had taken the form of a bird). The rest of the incident is similarly reported (Sītā ending with the remarks, "For my sake, and at a mere crow, you released the Brahmā-missile; how can you tolerate that man's having stolen me from you?" 5.36.33). When Hanumān returns to Rāma he reports the incident of the beauty-mark, quoting Sītā's elliptical words, "Remember the beauty-mark of red arsenic" (5.63.21), and again the incident of the crow (5.65.2ff.).

On manuscript evidence the *sarga* appears to be an interpolation, although stylistically little argues that it is not Vālmīki's (the post-epic word *viṭa* in line 25 has hardly any manuscript support). Contextually the passage is necessary only to flesh out Sītā's otherwise cryptic remark reported by Hanumān (5.63.21). Intertextually, the picture is rather more complicated. The incident is absent from the *Rāmopakhyāna* (mentioned only at 266.67, in what corresponds to the *Sundarakāṇḍa* passage) and from Bhoja's *RāmāCam*. But the *PadmaP* knows the story (6.269.194ff.), as do Kālidāsa (*RaghuVa* 12.22-23; note that for both Kālidāsa and the *PadmaP* the bird is a son of Indra), and the *AgniP* (9.14). Most of these adaptations place the story after Bharata's departure from the ashram (cf. Ct on 2.108.2, where he cites at length the *PadmaP* version in what appears to be the Bengali recension; cf. also *RaghuVa* 12.21), whereas all the N versions of the *Rām* (and Kṣemendra, *RāmāMañ* 5.369ff.) place it before Bharata's arrival. (In 5.36.32 the bird bows to Daśaratha, which in a way suggests that Bharata had not yet arrived bringing news of his death.)

See further Jhala 1966, p. xxxiii, and Vaidya 1962, p. xxiii. Vaidya's strictures against the "interpolation"—"the suggestion of *śṛṅgāra* [the erotic sentiment] at this juncture is hardly justifiable [why? cf. notes on 89.3, 9, 10 which show that there was a tradition of erotic interpretation precisely in this *sarga*]. . . . The use of a reed sanctified by mantras . . . against a small bird for such a trifling purpose surely looks strange" [cf. however 5.36.33]—such strictures are impressionistic and unpersuasive.

Clearly, then, the passage is old, in good *Rām* style, and in part necessary for the narrative (though see the remarks on 28.12-13 for similar narrative inconsistencies). It is only impugned, as Vaidya notes (p. 701), by its exclusion from the SR. The commentators also regard it as an interpolation, even though they continue to transmit it. See General Introduction, Volume 1, p. 38.

Finally, attention might be called to an aetiological feature of the story: it explains why crows possess, so it is believed, only one eye, which rolls back and forth as they quickly move their heads.

Sarga 90

1. In order to establish a reasonable transition between *sargas*, the SR inserts before this verse four lines (2091*), in which Rāma, having shown Sītā around the mountain, sits down on the slope and gives her cooked meat to eat (thus attempting also to account for the fire mentioned in 87.21ff. and verse 10 below, cf. note on 89.19; it seems more likely that the fire is the one on the sacred altar, cf. 93.11 and 23, though whether one may unceremoniously douse a ritual fire, as Lakṣmaṇa will suggest in verse 10 below, is questionable).

6. "royal officer" *rājamātraḥ*: A rare word in Vedic and classical Sanskrit (attested elsewhere, it seems, only in *Śāṅkhā*(= *Kauṣī*)*Br* and *ŚāṅkhāŚS*; cf. PW s.v. and *KauṣīBr* 27.11.14), though not infrequent in Buddhist Sanskrit texts. Many manuscripts dispute the reading, but it recurs in 94.19 and 6.51.10. (Cg glosses, "equal to a king"; cf. *mahāmātra-* in 33.1 above, which in view of *ArthŚā* 2.5.5, *KāmSū* 1.3.12, signifies "state official"; Keith 1920, p. 513, "vicegerent," the term is "possibly [a sign] of later date," p. 27.)

7. "a flowering *sāla* tree" *sālam . . . puṣpitam*: "Because the tree was 'flowering,' its leaves would be sparse, and so his vision unobstructed," Ct.

10. "Put out the fire" *agniṃ saṃśamayatu*: Ck adds a personal note: "Living in the village of Gaṇaka we have often experienced this, the quenching of the fires at times of imminent danger."

"and take up" *kuruṣva*: The verb is to be construed by zeugma with *pāda* d as well as *pāda* c (Cg's second interpretation; cf. note on 74.8).

12. "raging" *ruṣitaḥ*: In agreement with Cr, taking this item as an adjective with "fire"; Cg (Ck?), Ct join with *lakṣmaṇaḥ* ("in a rage").

13. "wholly in his power" *saṃpannam*: We follow Cg, Ct in understanding this pregnantly (they gloss it, "without rivals"; cf. the D manuscripts, which read *akaṇṭakam*).

14. The second half of the verse is appositional to the first (Cm, Cg, *contra* Ct).

"spreading" *udgataskandhaḥ*: Literally, "with upraised branches"; it construes in sense with the (emblazoned) tree, though syntactically with the standard. For the *kovidāra* standard see 78.3 and note.

16. Most N manuscripts add another suggestion by Lakṣmaṇa, that Rāma retreat with Sītā, seeing as they are surrounded, while Lakṣmaṇa alone fights (2103*, 2106*, 2107*).

19. "first to give offense" *pūrvāpakāriṇām*: After this many N and S manuscripts insert, "And Bharata was the first to give offense [that is, by causing Rāma's banishment, not by coming to kill them (as Varadacharya suggests, 1964-1965, vol. 2, p. 304n)], and has abandoned righteousness, Rāghava" (2110*; Cg comments that, since Bharata is said to have "abandoned righteousness," we are to understand that Lakṣmaṇa considers his "offense" to have been intentional).

22. "O giver of honor" *mānada*: In the opinion of Cg, Lakṣmaṇa is implying: "do not deny me [the chance to win back] my honor."

25. "in great battles" *mahāhave*: The crit. ed. reading, *mahāvane* ("in the great forest"), makes very little contextual sense. We read with the commentators and the majority of manuscripts *mahāhave* (or, *-mṛdhe*, apparently read also by Ck; one might in fact conjecture *-raṇe*, cf. 16.2). For the identical problem see note on 3.34.22.

Sarga 91

2. Hereafter the SR adds twenty lines, in which Rāma asks what use the kingship could be to him if to get it he must kill Bharata; refuses to seek anything that would involve the misery of kinsmen or friends; asserts that he desires only the well-being of his brothers, and contends that Bharata has come out of affection to see him and to offer him the kingship (2112*). The similarities with *Bhagavadgītā* 2 are striking. See the Introduction, Chapter 10.

6. "How, after all, could a son kill his father" *kathaṃ nu putrāḥ pitaraṃ hanyuḥ*: Cg recalls Lakṣmaṇa's previously urging the assassination of Daśaratha (an interpolation, 454* above, cf. note on 18.11).

8. "For" *hi*: Cg reads instead *'pi* (not recorded in the crit. ed.), commenting, " 'when I but tell him,' that is, without even putting my heart into it."

9. After this verse all (save a few D) manuscripts add, "Lakṣmaṇa, having heard his words, and being ashamed, replied, 'I think our father, Daśaratha, has come to see you' " (2115*). The commentators here remark that Lakṣmaṇa says this out of embarrassment, hoping to change the subject; and that Rāma diplomatically complies in the next verse (Cm, Cg, Ck, Ct).

10. "the great-armed (prince)" *mahābāhuḥ*: Ck, Ct, mainly because of the insertion noted on verse 9, take Rāma's words here to refer instead to Daśaratha; Cr has them apply to Bharata, so too the NR (as it would appear from 2117*); the SR insertion 2119* explicitly mentions the father (Cm, Cg are silent). Verses 12 and 13 might, but do not necessarily, support Ck, Ct; whereas 94.2 gives no suggestion that Rāma assumed Daśaratha had come.

12. "the team of splendid horses" *turagottamau*: On the assumption that Rāma is in fact inferring the approach of his father, these would probably be the horses that carried Rāma from Ayodhyā, and which Daśaratha cherished (cf. above, 44.21-22).

13. Śatruṃjaya: Apparently not the elephant of the same name given to Suyajña (29.9 above).

"our wise father's . . . elephant" *nāgaḥ . . . tātasya dhīmataḥ*: Cr here, as Ck and Ct (cf. also Ctr, vol. 2, pp. 506-507), takes this as another sign by which Rāma infers Daśaratha himself to be approaching.

"aged" *vṛddhaḥ*: So Cr; Cm, Cg understand "tall" or "large" (and so tone down the force of *kampate*, "lumbering"), Ck, " 'great,' in years, size, and power."

Hereafter the SR inserts: "But I do not see the white parasol honored by the world, the heavenly parasol of my father. I am worried, my illustrious brother" (2121*).

16. "along" *āvṛtya*: Cg reads *āvṛttya* (not recorded in the crit. ed.), understanding thereby that the army encamped in a "circular" formation.

17. "with all the diplomacy at his command" *nītimatā*: Perhaps overtranslating the word (which is employed in part for alliteration), though there appears to be a special importance attached to the qualification. Mentioned as it is together with Bharata's righteousness and humility, his "social and political tact" (*nīti*) acquires an added emphasis: Bharata is going to employ all his powers of *nīti* to mollify his brother, which becomes even more apparent in the following *sarga* (so Varadacharya in part, 1964-1965, vol. 2, p. 313n).

Sarga 92

1. This *sarga* is suspect both on text-critical grounds (it is absent in three important manuscripts, D4, 5, 7) and for other, narrative reasons: Bharata has already had the forest reconnoitered (87.20ff.) and made his decision to proceed (87.24-25); for him to spot the ashram in verse 14 below and return to the camp, once again encamping the army, seems absurd (it is only added to form some transition to *sarga* 93), and moreover conflicts with *sarga* 93. The narrative is consistent if we pick up the action with *sarga* 93, eliminating 92 altogether. Perhaps this section owes its wide currency in the different versions, despite these narrative embarassments, to Bharata's dramatic proclamations and the moving refrain in verses 4-7.

"who was a guru to him" *guruvartakam*: Cf. 76.27; 79.2; 93.2, 24; 107.3 and note on verse 11 below. The suffix here is [*kartari*] *ṇvul* (*Pā* 3.1.113). The translation offered here runs counter to all the commentators (they gloss, irrelevantly, "who obeyed his gurus").

3. "these hunters" *lubdhaiḥ . . . ebhiḥ*: Ck, Ct identify them as Guha's servants (cf. 79.6).

Hereafter, in a four-line "insertion" (although all manuscripts that have the *sarga* have at least one or two of the lines), Bharata orders Guha to search with his kinsmen, and declares that he himself will proceed with all his ministers (cf. 93.7), the townsmen, gurus, and brahmans (2123*).

6. "all the signs of sovereignty" *pārthivavyañjana-*: According to Cm, Cg, signs of the thunderbolt, standard, lotus, goad, vessel of nectar, and so on (the usual markings said to appear on the soles of Viṣṇu's feet; Ck, Ct, Cr, "the line, standard, thunderbolt, parasol, and so on"). Perhaps, the wheel, fish, and so on, which were thought to be marked on the soles of the feet of the *cakravartin* or universal emperor (cf. Gonda 1966, pp. 92-93).

7. After this verse (or, where it has less propriety, after verse 5) all manuscripts in question (save D6) "insert": "Fulfilled indeed is Saumitri, who can look upon the lustrous face of Rāma, pure as the moon, with eyes like lotuses" (2124*).

9. "like Kubera in Nandana" *kubera iva nandane*: The simple implication "happily" is insufficient for the commentators, as Cg: "Just as Kubera who, though he actually lives in the Caitraratha garden, [enjoys himself when living] in Nandana, the garden of Indra, so Rāma on the unfamiliar mountain. Or again: he enjoys himself like Kubera, leaving his house and yet dwelling in his own garden, for according to the later statement, 'This land belongs to the Ikṣvākus, with all its mountains, forests, and glens' [4.18.6], Citrakūṭa would be within Rāma's realm, and the simile of Nandana would then express his deep sense of delight in the mountain." Some manuscripts, apparently regarding the simile as flawed, alter it to read, "(as Kubera dwelling) on (Mount) Mandara," since Kubera's dwelling place is actually Mount Kailāsa.

10. Cm, Ct note, "(The forest) has 'fulfilled itself' by being covered with the dust of Rāma's feet, which can release it from its insentient state."

11. "on foot" *padbhyām*: Bharata's going on foot is so often reiterated not only because he more properly deserves to be conveyed (Cg), but because this is the manner in which one approaches an ascetic and, more particularly, one's guru.

12. "The eloquent prince" *vadatāṃ varaḥ*: "He is thinking over precisely what he should say in the presence of Rāma," Cg.

13. "reaching" *āsādya*: Ct, Cr read instead, "climbing."

"banner of the fire" *agner . . . dhvajam*: Smoke. Ck, claiming Bharata has already seen the smoke (87.26), reads differently: "He saw an upraised banner atop [a *sāla* tree] at Rāma's ashram" (Varadacharya notes that even today in some areas banners are raised atop tall trees to indicate the special sanctity of a place [1964-1965, vol. 2, p. 316n]). Ck calls this the "commonly accepted reading," but again, as is often the case with such claims of his, no other manuscript confirms it. Cg tries to explain away the repetition by saying Bharata had previously seen the spire of smoke, and now because of his proximity sees its source (but see the note on verse 1 above).

15. "the holy men there" *puṇyajanopapannam*: We must wait until *sarga* 108 to have their presence fully explained (see however 89.6-7). The sudden mention of Guha is surprising (cf. note on 83.21), though recall 79.6, where Guha says that he will accompany Bharata (and verse 3 and note above). Guha will be mentioned only one more time, in 93.40, a reading disputed by the NR (but see also note on 105.22).

Sarga 93

1. "showing the way" *anudarśayan*: " 'Showing,' that is, the signs betokening the proximity of Rāma's ashram," Cm, Cg, Ck, Ct, Cr.

2. "his guru" *guru-*: That is, Rāma (so Cr).

3. "he was" *tasya*: Ck and Cr rightly understand *sumantrasya*.

4. Verses 4-5 (and by extension, verse 6), as they appear in the crit. ed., are clearly out of place. They belong, if anywhere, among verses 17ff. Most of the NR rectifies matters by reading, [4] "Bharata, questioning the ascetics in their abodes [4c-5 omitted] [6] saw in that forest the dry dung. . . ." Ck also queries, and alters, the vulgate order, but without appreciable improvement.

"leaf hut and thatched cottage" *parṇakuṭīṃ . . . uṭajam*: Ck, Ct distinguish the "leaf hut," as a sort of guest house situated beyond the "cottage," from this latter, a wooden structure with walls and doors, where Sītā would sleep; whereas Cm, Cg explain that the former is the fire-sanctuary [therefore the logs piled up in front of it, mentioned in the following verse], the latter the guest house (Cg offers still another alternative: the leaf hut is where Rāma sleeps with Sītā, the cottage a day-house. We probably cannot justify verses 4-5 by considering these to be outlying structures far removed from Rāma's main dwelling place). Perhaps we have here the two separate huts mentioned in the note on 50.13.

"situated within" *-saṃsthitām*: Cf. 108.1-2: there are ascetics living nearby (not, "situated like," Cm, Cg).

5. Ck's commentary on verses 5-38, said to be unavailable to the editor of the crit. ed., is printed in full in the Mysore edition (1965).

6. "for use against the cold" *śītakāraṇāt*: "They had set out in the latter half of Caitra [early April] and at that time, till the end of Vaiśākha [mid-May] it still gets cold at night" (Ct), and consequently a fire would be necessary.

7. "the ministers" *amātyān*: Cf. note on 92.3.

10. "And that one must only be a path beaten" *idaṃ ca . . . parikrāntam*: Ck, who like Cg rightly treats *parikrāntam* as *adhikaraṇe kta* (*Pā* 3.4.76), notes, "Having recognized the path leading to the ashram, Bharata now sees a forest path, out of possible confusion with which it was necessary (for Lakṣmaṇa) to mark the one leading to the ashram" (so essentially Ct).

11. "maintain a fire" *yam evāvadhātum*: For the morning and evening offering (Cm, Cg, Ct). Cg goes to great lengths here to show that the fire meant is the *smārta* household fire, which Rāma, he claims, maintained with a signal show of faith throughout his exile, until Sītā's abduction; only upon returning would he have established the three vedic fires, which is what Ck supposes this verse to refer to (cf. Cg cited in note on 3.7.3).

12. "his guru" *guru-*: His father, whom he honors by obeying his order to live in the wilderness.

13. "abuts the Mandākinī" *mandākinīm anu*: This follows Ck, Ct on the syntax of *anu*; cf. Bharadvāja's description of the location, 86.12.

14. "the 'heroic' posture in yoga" *vīrāsane*: With the left foot upon the right knee (Cg, so Vācaspati on *YogSū* 2.46); Ck (citing *YogVā*, as does Mallinātha on *RaghuVa* 13.52), with feet placed on opposite thighs. This would appear to be the earliest occurrence of the term in Sanskrit literature.

16. "again and again" *punaḥ punaḥ*: Ck (Ct) instead reads, "and Lakṣmaṇa's," claiming that "another" (Cm?) fabricated the reading "again and again" out of excessive piety, since an elder person is not to prostrate himself before a younger. Ck adds that, though highly unusual, such behavior is elsewhere attested, as for example in Daśaratha bowing before Kaikeyī.

19. "heavy" *bhārasādhanaiḥ*: That is, "heavy-duty," executing the heavy deeds of battle (Ck, Ct). Cm, Cg suggest that *bhāra-* is a technical term for the weight [that is, the draw-weight, not the actual weight] of a bow, 100 *palas*, or about eight and a half pounds (Cg cites as authority the *Īśānasaṃhitā*), but it is unclear how this construes with *-sādanaiḥ*.

20. Bhogavatī: The submarine abode of mythological serpents (*nāgas*).

23. "sloping to the northeast" *prāgudakpravaṇām*: Sacrificial altars are constructed so that they incline in a northeast direction (cf. *KātyŚS* 2.6.2-10 and Kane 1962-

1975, vol. 2.1, p. 1,034 note). *-pravaṇām* (for *-sravaṇām* of the crit. ed.) appears to be the correct reading, authenticated by *LāṭyāŚS* 1.1.14 [pw] and also *MBh* 12.40.12, *prāgudakpravaṇāṃ vedīm*). Compare *Rām* 3.70.19 and note there.

24. The final syllable of the verse (*ṇa*), corresponding with the seventh syllable of the *Gāyatrīmantra*, signifies that at this point 6,000 verses of the (traditional) *Rām* have been completed (Cm, Cg; cf. note on 39.5).

25. According to Cg the hide would form his upper garment, the bark cloth the lower.

27. "He looked like the eternal Brahmā" *brahmāṇam iva śāśvatam*: On the significance of the comparison, cf. note on 29.11.

28. Ct explains the repetition of "Bharata" as a sign of the poet's excitement; Cm, Cg join the second occurrence with verse 29; the NR eliminates it.

33. The distinction here is between the *dharma* acquired by way of vedic rituals performed by the strenuous efforts of priests, and that acquired by physical mortifications (so Ck, Ct).

36. "he reached in vain for Rāma's feet" *pādāv aprāpya rāmasya*: One is reminded of the earlier scene, the encounter of Kaikeyī and Daśaratha (10.41).

40. "The two princes" *rājasutau*: Rāma and Lakṣmaṇa. The NR for the most part eliminates the reference to Guha (cf. note on 92.15).

Śukra: Venus.

Bṛhaspati: Jupiter.

41. "The inhabitants of the forest" *vanaukasaḥ*: Presumably the ascetics among whom Rāma is living (cf. verse 4).

Sarga 94

2. "What has become of your father" *kva nu te 'bhūt pitā*: "In view of the fact that Rāma asks still more questions, we gather that Bharata fails to respond to this one," Cg.

"While he yet lives you should not be going off to the forest" *na hi tvaṃ jīvatas tasya vanam āgantum arhasi*: Bharata would not have come, were Daśaratha alive, either because he would be wholly absorbed in obediently serving his father, particularly given Rāma's absence (Cg, Ck, Ct), or because his father could not bear his absence (Cg).

3. "from so far" *dūrāt*: Rāma can hardly mean from the land of the Kekayas (Cm, Cg, Ck, Ct, Cr), considering the questions he proceeds to put, which imply that he assumes Bharata to have been consecrated prince regent in Ayodhyā.

"looking so somber" *duṣpratīkam*: The word is *hapax*. Ck, Ct would have it construe likewise, or only, with *vanam* ("somber forest"), but this is impossible word order, and anyway Rāma had just been remarking on the beauty of the landscape.

After this verse the SR inserts some lines in which Rāma baldly asks whether Daśaratha is indeed dead (2134*).

4. "still true to his given word" *satyasaṃgaraḥ*: For Cg the deeper meaning is: has the king, by honoring his promise, fallen ill from regret or remorse?

"royal consecrations" *rājasūya-*: Not in its aspect as an inaugural ceremony, but as a periodically repeated rite for the reinvigoration of the king's power (cf. Heesterman 1957, especially p. 7). For the horse-sacrifice, cf. note on *Bālakāṇḍa* 8.2 and verses 13ff. and notes.

6. "and Sumitrā" *sumitrā ca*: We agree with Cg in understanding *sukhinī* with both Kausalyā and Sumitrā.

7ff. Here commences a series of more general questions that will continue to the end of the *sarga*. A very similar, though longer list is present in the *MBh* (2.5; some thirty or so of our verses appear there in comparable, sometimes verbatim, form; another close parallel is furnished by *MBh* 15.9). There seems to be no conclusive evidence to determine the antecedence of either of the versions, and neither Vaidya's argument (1962, p. 702) nor Kane's (1966, pp. 51ff.) against the *Rām*'s priority is cogent. Such *kaccitparvans* were simply a stock feature of ancient Indian epic, intended to inculcate kingly *dharma* (as it is here explicitly said, 95.1), and so the question of borrowing is in a sense misleading. Yet the *kaccitparvan* of the *Ayodhyākāṇḍa* can lay claim to a special narrative propriety that is lacking in the case of the principal *MBh* version (where the questions are put in the mouth of the divine sage Nārada). For it serves to testify to Rāma's profound, encyclopedic knowledge of government, thereby validating his qualifications for the kingship and making his stern refusal to assume it not only the more regrettable and poignant, but incontestible: what arguments could be summoned against such wisdom as he is shown here to possess? See also note on 69.14ff.

7. Rāma assumes throughout that Bharata has already made the key appointments of his court (verses 8, 10, 20, 21, 24, 29). It appears, then, that here he is asking both whether Bharata has appointed a good family priest and whether he honors him (Cg, Ck), not just whether he honors the family priest, one with whom Rāma is already familiar— Suyajña or some other son of Vasiṣṭha (Cm, Ct, Cr).

8. Cg, Cr suppose this verse to refer also to the family priest. According to *YājñaSm* 1.313-14, however, it is not the *purohita* but the *ṛtvig* who performs the household sacrifices for the king.

9. Sudhanvan: Appears not to be mentioned elsewhere (the name means "good with a bow," or, "having a good bow").

"arrows and missiles" *iṣvastra-*: Cm, Cg, Ck, Ct, in their attempt to distinguish them, explain that the former are employed without spells (*mantrāṇi*), whereas the latter require them.

11. We understand asyndeton between *pādas* cd. Cg appears to join *mantradharaiḥ* adjectivally with *amātyaiḥ*, though the word is generally substantival.

13. "neither all by yourself nor with a multitude" *naikaḥ . . . na bahubhiḥ saha*: "A king framing his plans alone will fail to grasp properly the pros and cons of a matter because he lacks objectivity; and if he takes counsel with a multitude, not only is unanimity impossible, but the counsel can the more easily be divulged," Ct (so Cm, Cg).

15. "when fully accomplished, or nearly so" *sukṛtāny eva kṛtarūpāṇi vā*: Cr's construction would be attractive ("they regard the deeds once commenced as wholly achieved") except that it ignores the *vā*. *Kṛtarūpāṇi*, "nearly so" = *kṛtaprāyāni* in *MBh* 2.5.22 (so read by some manuscripts here). For the sentiment cf. *MBh* 12.57.32 and *ArthŚā* 1.15.17.

The "kings," according to the commentators, would be neighboring (or vassal, feudatory [*sāmanta-*]) princes (Cm, Cg, Ct).

16. Rāma has already enquired whether Bharata's counsels are betrayed before they are put into operation (verses 13-15). Now he asks if they might be found out in some other way. We therefore agree with Ck, Ct, Cr so far as to understand *mantritāḥ* in *pāda* b, but then construe it (by anacoluthon) as antecedent to *mantritam* in *pāda* d (for the grammatical irregularity cf. note on 98.6). One manuscript, however, D5, does offer what may well be the original reading in *pāda* d: *budhyante* . . . *mantritāḥ* (for the gender cf. verse 13). Cm, Cg's analysis of *pāda* b will not do (" '[in other ways] not mentioned,' such as, facial expressions"). The *MBh* parallel, supported generally by the NR, gives, "by reasoning or messengers who have gone unsuspected," but this looks like emendation.

"reasoning or supposition" *tarkair yuktyā vā*: Cg glosses, "*ūha* [a type of analogical reasoning] or inference"; Cm, "or presumption [*arthāpatti*]"; Ck, Ct, "inference or presumption."

17. "great benefits" *niḥśreyasam*: Cm, Cg gloss instead, "(bringing about for one great) power."

19. "his officer" *rājamātram*: Cf. note on 90.6 above.

20. "foremost . . . middling . . . lowly" *mukhyāḥ* . . . *madhyamāḥ* . . . *jaghanyāḥ*: Cg considers the qualifications to indicate subcaste (*jāti*) rank, and he exemplifies the three grades of duties from highest to lowest as follows: "1. cooking and serving up the king's food [? read *pacanapariveṣana-* for *vacanapari-* ?]; 2. fetching couches, chairs, and so on; 3. washing or massaging his feet, fetching his shoes, and so on."

21. "have passed the test of loyalty" *upadhātītān*: The technical meaning of the term is emphasized (*contra* Nīlakaṇṭha on *MBh* 2.5.43 vulgate, "beyond all fraudulence," and Ct, "beyond all bribery"), in agreement with Cm, Cg (Cr) (cf. especially *ArthŚā* 1.10ff.). They cite *Vaija* for the meaning and go on to remark, "Kings test their subordinates to see if they are corruptible. They will have someone bring them a precious garment or piece of jewelry and say that it was sent by a woman in the king's harem, or a rival king [if they refuse it, they are loyal]" (cf. *MBh* 15.9.14, a verse almost identical to ours).

22. "People have no reason to despise" *nāvajānanti*: For this sort of generalizing plural verb without expressed subject, cf. 101.12.

"as sacrificial priests . . . or women" *yājakāḥ* . . . *yathā* . . . *iva striyaḥ*: We agree with Cm (and Ctr, vol. 2, p. 516) in seeing two different similes here (against Ck, "the priests do not despise you as an outcaste"). The first refers to general transgressions against the people (*pace* Cg), the second to "brutal appropriations," as of taxes.

23. "a shrewd man with cunning schemes" *upāyakuśalaṃ vaidyam*: Ck understands differently: "A 'physician' who, for the sake of acquiring fees from the king, is skillful 'in the means,' that is, of aggravating the disease." Cm, Cg, Cr (so Ctr, vol. 2, p. 517) wrongly take the three qualifications as referring to one person; on this issue we agree with Ck. Additionally *bhṛtyam* is read here (for *bhṛtya-*), which is well attested in all recensions.

24. "bold" *dṛṣṭaḥ*: Divide thus (so Cg's second explanation).

28. "especially the men of good family" *kūlaputrāḥ pradhānataḥ*: Cm, Cg, Ct, Cr gloss "kinsmen" (Ck, "family slaves"), and they understand *pradhānataḥ* nominatively ("the chief ones"); Nīlakaṇṭha on *MBh* 2.5.50 vulgate, "from the counselor on down."

29. "a man of the provinces" *jānapadaḥ*: That is, someone not involved in court intrigue (cf. verse 30 and note)? Envoys would always, it would seem, be "countrymen" of the king's, and not foreigners.

30. "the eighteen chief officials" *tīrthāni*: Cg lists them (cf. *ArthŚā* 1.12.20): chief counselor, family priest, crown prince, general, lord chamberlain, commandant of the palace guards, warden of the prison, chief treasurer, chief of staff, minister of justice, quartermaster, city watchman, civilian paymaster [so Cg explains *kārmāntika*, though it usually = superintendent of mines and factories], chief usher of the assembly hall, chief authority on *dharmaśāstra*, superintendent of the executioners [so Cg; *daṇḍapāla* usually = officer in charge of the different branches of the army], guard of the fort, and chief border guard. The first three would be omitted from investigations carried out in one's own domain because they would be continually in contact with the king, who could thus determine for himself their true feelings. Cm and Cg both cite a *nīti* text to this effect: "A king should send out men—people such as heretics and the like, [and] who are not known to others or to each other—to spy on his enemies and his own chief officers, excepting his own counselor, crown prince, and family priest."

31. "hostile men who, once deported, have made their way back" *vyapāstān ahitān pratiyātān*: "They could not make their way back without someone's assistance, thus [they cannot be weak, and] one must pay close attention to them," Cg.

33. "derive their ideas from logic" *buddhim ānvīkṣikīṃ prāpya*: Cg cites [from *ManuSm* 12.106; the *Rām* verse is quoted ad loc. by the commentator Bhāruci], "Only he who, in order to resolve problems in the ancient [*veda*] and the teachings of *dharma*, employs logic *not in contradiction* with the *vedas* and the [*dharma*-]*śāstras*, knows *dharma*, no one else" (that is, logic cannot replace or be used to refute the *vedas* or *dharmaśāstras*; cf. also *Rām* 3.48.21 and note there). Ck enlarges here, claiming that in no revealed or traditional text is it shown that liberation is secured through logical knowledge, "dialectical reasoning"; all logicians (including Pañcaśikha, one of the founders of the Sāṃkhya system of philosophy) are materialists, and even those who accept the word of the *vedas* do so selectively, and deny that the soul is pure consciousness, nondifferent from *brahma*, and so on.

34. "true to its name" *satyanāmām*: We agree with Cm, Cg in taking the qualification proleptically. "Ayodhyā" literally means "The Impregnable (City)" (cf. 1.6.23).

37. "shrines" *caitya-*: Cm, Cg, Ck, Ct, Cr all gloss, "places where sacrificial altars are constructed," but see note on verse 52 below.

38. "the boundary lines are well spaced" *sukṛṣṭasīmā*: Cf. note on 43.3.

"disasters" *hiṃsābhiḥ*: Or, "acts of violence," of one villager against another (Cg).

39. "still nourished beyond the whim of the rain god" *adevamātṛkaḥ*: That is, well irrigated. Clearly in the eyes of this epic poet, the king was interested in supporting, if not initiating, irrigation projects (contrast Ritschl and Schetelich 1970).

Because of the repetition of the interrogative particle *kaccid* here (cf. verse 37), Cg supposes each qualification to be the subject of a question, and we follow him (so too in the preceding verses). Curiously, he quotes a *śloka* to this effect, which states that if the particle is used at the beginning and at the end of this verse, it should construe with the middle as well, questions being equally appropriate there too; further, that this shows Rāma's deep respect and affection for Kosala.

40. "a well-founded economy . . . promotes the world's happiness" *vārtāyāṃ saṃśritas . . . loko . . . sukham edhate*: Literally, "(well-)founded upon its economy, the world gains happiness." The latter half of the verse supplies the reason for the question in the former (*pace* Ck, Ct, Cr, who see two questions; cf. *MBh* 2.5.69 crit. ed.), whereas *pāda* c appears to be a syntactical unit (against Cm, Cg, "If there is a

[good] economy [*vārtāyām*], the people who have resorted to you" [*saṃśritaḥ* . . . *lokaḥ*]).

42. "your women" *striyaḥ*: Cf. note on 8.5.

"place . . . trust in them" *śraddadhāsy āsām*: This agrees with Cr on the genitive of person (Cm, Cg, Ck, Ct, " 'trust,' believe what they say to be true").

43. "display yourself" *darśayase*: "Otherwise the people might believe the king to be ill," Cg. Giving *darśana* or a view of the kingly (or holy) person is what is meant. Read the vocative for *rājaputraḥ*, a misprint.

44. "craftsmen" *śilpi-*: Cf. *ManuSm* 7.75 (*brāhmaṇaiḥ*) *śilpibhir* (*yantraiḥ*) (cited by Ctr, vol. 2, p. 526). But for this parallel, one would be inclined to interpret the word adjectivally, "crafty archers" (so Cr, and cf. the parallel verse Cg cites from *NītiSā* [4.58], which offers the glossing reading *vīrayodhaiḥ*, though the commentary *Upādhyāyanirapekṣā* ad loc. reads *dhīrayodhaiḥ*, glossing *śauryaśilpasampannaiḥ*).

45. "unworthy hands" *apātreṣu*: "Dancers, procurers, singers, and so on," Cm, Cg, Ck, Ct. The reference, however, may be to the control of the treasury passing into the hands of an untrustworthy superintendent.

47. "out of greed" *lobhāt*: Presumably in order to seize his property, whereas in the following verse bribery would seem to be at issue.

49. "engaged in a suit" *vyasane*: The word does not appear to be recorded elsewhere in this sense. It is thus explained by Cg, Ct, and see the NR gloss, *vivadato 'rtheṣu* (2161*).

50. Obviously this verse has greater propriety after verse 47 (noticed also by Varadacharya 1964-1965, vol. 2, p. 347n), though no manuscript offers such a sequence.

51. "brahmans" *vaidya-*: The parallel verse in *ManuSm* (8.395) shows clearly that *vaidya-* here does not refer to "physicians" (Ck, Ct), but rather to *śrotriyas*, brahmans learned in the *vedas* (cf. also the NR variants *vaidyān* or *viprān sasomapān*), and that *bubhūṣase* means, not "win over" (all commentators), but "honor" (*sampūjayet*). Though Kullūka ad loc. does suggest that the king should honor them with "gifts, high regard, and kindly deeds," our *pāda* c may in fact contain an old emendation, *dānena* displacing an original *kāyena* (cf. 88.18 and 101.21 and notes). This would give, "Do you . . . show regard (to them) in all three ways, in words and deeds and thoughts." The reason for the emendation is self-explanatory.

52. "shrines" *caitya-*: "Large trees at crossroads where divinities dwell," Cm, Cg, Ct; Cr, "a place where fire altars are constructed," with which he construes the adjective *siddhārthān* (glossed, "through which one's goals are achieved"). See note on 6.2.

53. "You never deny the claims of righteousness" . . . *dharmam* . . . *na vibādhase*: "Either: by pursuing *artha* in the morning (the time appropriate for *dharma*), *dharma* in the afternoon (the time appropriate for *artha*), or either of these two by pursuing *kāma* other than at its appropriate time, in the evening [the "seasons" or times mentioned in the following verse]; or, by pursuing *artha* to the exclusion of *dharma*, or *dharma* to the exclusion of *artha* (for example, failing to provide for one's family), or *kāma* to the exclusion of both (for example, if one were attached to a prostitute one would thereby destroy both *dharma* and *artha*)," Cg.

56. "atheism" *nāstikyam*: Actually, "belief that the world to come does not exist," Cg, Cr.

58. "auspicious rites" *maṅgalasya*: Such as looking in a mirror early in the morning (Cg; cf. *MBh* 12.53.9).

"indiscriminate courtesy" *pratyutthānaṃ sarvaśaḥ*: Literally, "rising [from one's seat, as a mark of respect] before everyone" (so Cg, Ck, Cr). Specific rules are prescribed in the *dharmaśāstras* regarding salutations. They are strictly regulated according to the age, caste, and degree of learning of the two parties involved in the exchange of greetings (cf. Kane 1962-1975, vol. 2.i, pp. 336-39). Cm, Cg also suggest as an alternative gloss for *pratyutthānam*, "a retaliatory campaign undertaken simultaneously against enemies in all directions," that is, attacking on more than one front. But there appears to be no evidence for the use of the word in this sense (though cf. *abhyutthāna-* in 6.80.55).

Hereafter the NR inserts (omitting or reordering verse 59), "Thus Rāma questioned him, and with a shaken mind, broken by grief, Bharata informed him of the death of their father" (2164*), whereas the SR extends the list of questions by fourteen lines (2165*).

59. "you never eat savory foods all by yourself" *svādukṛtaṃ bhojyam eko nāśnāsi*: Cf. 69.23 and note; in view of *MBh* 2.5.88, the implication would be that he should be feeding brahmans fine foods as well (rather than denying his family and dependents wholesome food).

Sarga 95

1ff. Cm, Ck (who argues vigorously against, most probably, Crā), Ct and a host of N and S manuscripts incorrectly read this *sarga* and the next after *sarga* 97 (which itself seems to be a later, clumsily integrated interpolation). Although this sequence would require the impossible succession of *sarga* 97 after 94, it would of course, conversely, result in the juxtaposition of *sargas* 96 and 98, which would seem to be authentic; Ck argues this point at the beginning of 98. There are lengthy arguments in the commentators both for and against the order presented in the crit. ed., but all of them are subjective and without much text-critical value.

1. "when I am wholly lost to righteousness" *dharmād vihīnasya*: Bharata's loss of righteousness is specified in the next verse, thus also Cr ("the ways of our family"); wrongly Cm, Cg, Ctś, "the chief *dharma*, that is, of serving Rāma"; Cg, Ck, Ct, "that is, the kingship itself."

4. "The purpose of the verse is to explain that not everyone [meaning Bharata] is capable of executing the duties of the kingship," Cg. Cm, Ct assume the verse to answer Rāma's unspoken question, "Why should I give up the performance of asceticism, which will secure divinity for me? What need have I of the kingship," whereas Cm goes on to say, "Divinity may be achieved either by way of self-torment, through asceticism, or by way of pleasure, through guarding the kingship."

"I esteem him a god" *devatve saṃmato mama*: The NR reads (and Ck understands), "But I esteem you to be a god."

The two "they say" phrases are suspect. Cg is forced to add for the first, "the common people."

5. After this verse the SR and some D manuscripts insert a verse (2171*) clarifying that Daśaratha died of grief (and not of illness).

6. "make the funeral libation" *kriyatām udakam*: Cf. note on 70.23.

7. The verse answers the implicit question, if Bharata and Śatrughna have made the funeral libation, why should it be repeated (Cg, Ck, Ct). Hereafter the SR adds the poignant verse, "It was you he was grieving for, you he wanted to see, it was

on you his thoughts were immovably fixed. Bereft of you, and broken with grief for you, your father passed away, thinking only of you" (2173*; the parallel with *Odyssey* 11.202-203 is noteworthy).

8. "piteous words" *karuṇāṃ vācam*: Crā, Cm (not Ck, as per the crit. ed.) understand, "pitiless words."

9. "flowering" *puṣpitāgraḥ*: Ct tries to find some point to the qualification: " 'like a flowering tree,' because he was still happy to see Bharata."

10. "striking a riverbank" *kūlaghāta-*: "As elephants will do when they are in rut and their tusks itch," Cg.

11. "sprinkled water upon him" *siṣicuḥ salilena*: Their tears, possibly, as Ctr takes it (vol. 2, p. 550), though cf. 6.70.12.

15. "no longer has direction" *anekāgrām*: So in general Cm, Cg, Cr. Ck, Ct, "has [now] many chiefs."

17. "noticed good conduct" *prekṣya suvṛttam*: The NR more persuasively offers, "would send me out and I would return," for as verses 15-16 show, Rāma would be thinking about other occasions on which he came home after an absence.

19. "sorrowful news" *duḥkam*: *Pāda* d stands in a sort of apposition to this (so Ct; Cm, Cg, Ck, Cr understand it adverbially, "sadly reported").

Note the editor's corrigendum here (Vaidya 1962, p. 706), which admits 2178* and 2179* (with SR reading) into the crit. ed. Vaidya wants 2179* to come first, but there is insufficient manuscript evidence for this (if anything, the verse should be rejected altogether, being absent in D4, 5, 7), and it would grate contextually.

21. "a cake of almond meal" *iṅgudipiṇyākam*: "A cake made of the nuts of the 'ascetic tree,' which are eaten by ascetics [cf. note on 44.5 and verse 31 below]. This would be only figuratively a 'cake'; actually the nuts would be just crushed and pulverized, and without their oil being extracted," Cg (so Ck, Ct). It is a coarse food, one prescribed for penances (cf. *ManuSm* 11.92, *YājñaSm* 3.321), for which Rāma makes apology in verse 31 below, and which Kausalyā beweeps in 96.9ff.

22. "the procession of mourning" *gatir . . . sudāruṇā*: A type of hypallage, for *gatiḥ sudārūṇām*. A prescription for the cortège is cited by Cm, Cg, Ct, Cr from the [*Bhāradvāja*]*pitṛmedhasūtras* [1.4.6]: "The youngest go first, the others behind them, women at the very head."

26. Cg discovers significance in each of the adjectives in verses 25-26; to cite a couple of examples: " 'lovely' implies that the river assuaged their sorrow; 'where the woodlands were always in flower' implies that they were shaded over until they completed the water-offering."

"Father, let this be for you" *tata etad bhavatv iti*: The reading of Cm, Cg, Ck is (*pace* the crit. ed. and the printed editions) *tataitat te*, that is, *tata* (vocative, = *tāta*, as often in vedic). Vaidya is probably right to print *tata etat*, with absence of *saṃdhi* (*pragṛhya*) by reason of the (presumed) *pluta* vowel (cf. 43.12 and note).

Normally the *gotra* name of the deceased would be proclaimed (cf. note on 70.23), for which "father," or so Ct claims, does duty. Others, he reports, adduce this very passage to show that such a proclamation is not obligatory.

27. "facing the direction of Yama" *diśaṃ yāmyām abhimukhaḥ*: Toward the south. Ct mentions a "recent digest" compiled by one Sumantu, which reports that kshatriyas are to offer water facing north. He dismisses this as groundless, precisely because it conflicts with the procedure here described, or as referring to low-rank kshatriyas.

29. "made the offering of food" *cakāra . . . nivāpam*: The procedure here is apparently out of keeping with traditional practice. Ct addresses the issue: "One must not raise the objection that, since a *smṛti* declares that a son enters a state of impurity for ten days upon hearing of his father's death (whenever the death itself may have occurred), the offering of food therefore should not be made now, on the first day, to the father for whom funeral rites have just been performed. For the *smṛti* in question must either apply to *varṇas* other than the kshatriya, or to ceremonial procedures of the Kali Age" (whereas the *Rām* is traditionally held to occur in the Tretā). Cg claims they simply "prepare" the cake, but do not offer it, since it is not to be offered till the tenth day.

31. The verse contains a hypermetric *pāda* (c) rare in Vālmīki; there is only one other in all of Books Two through Six: 3.10.70. It may be that *bhavati* is to be pronounced dissyllabically (a Prākritism). The NR eliminates the irregularity, reading for the most part *rājan* for *bhavati*, perhaps in recollection of *MBh* 13.65.59 (*yadanno hi naro rājan*; cf. *BrahmP* 123.175).

33. "Bharata and Lakṣmaṇa": Cr desperately notes, " 'Śatrughna' is included in 'Bharata' and need not be separately mentioned." As previously (note on 87.25), Śatrughna will again be ignored in 96.29 below; see the note there (for a discussion of the role of the junior brothers in the epic, see Goldman 1980).

37. "the delicate ones" *sukumārāḥ*: Cg (and Cm) applies the qualification to the first two groups as well: "Were one not exceedingly frail one would necessarily proceed on foot to the sorrowful Rāma" (see note on 92.11).

40. "Vehicles with hooves are horses, and so on; those with wheels, chariots, and so on," Ck, Ct, Cr.

41. "perfuming the way with their scent" *āvāsayanto gandhena*: Apparently their fear causes the bulls to exude ichor (Cg fancifully, "this implies that even the elephants of the wild were eager to see Rāma").

42. "cow-eared antelopes" *gokarṇa-*: The word is obscure. The commentators are uncertain (they suggest a type of gazelle, or deer).

43. "plovers" *plavāḥ*: It is not known whether this identification is ornithologically correct; the commentators are guessing when they gloss, "a type of plump crane." *Plavas*, however, like plovers, are shore birds (cf. for example, 3.33.18), and the two words are cognate (deriving from I-E **pleu*).

44. The SR inserts here some lines in which the people see Rāma and approach, all the while reviling Kaikeyī and Mantharā (2186*).

45. "he embraced them" *tān . . . paryaṣvajata*: "He embraced only those worthy of being embraced; cf. the next verse," Ct.

46. "restored to all . . . each according to his station, their one true kinsman or one true friend" *cakāra sarvān savayasyabāndhavān yathārham*: The *bahuvrīhi* compounds function predicatively. Highly improbable is Cr's explanation: "he showed appropriate honor [*yathārham*; Cm, Cg impossibly supply as direct object "esteem"] to all, with their kinsmen and friends." On Rāma's punctilious observance of degrees of social rank, cf. also 15.4 and note.

47. "the mountain caves" *guhā girīṇām*: *Guhāḥ* (feminine accusative plural) *girīṇām* should be understood thus separately (so Ck), and not in compound.

Sarga 96

4. A difficult verse, which we understand as follows: This spot on the river used to be deserted, never visited by men, but our children, who are used to comfort and have been driven from their home into the deep wilderness, are now using it, for one can see it has been disturbed. We reject all the commentators (Cm, Cg, because *kevalam* is nowhere attested in the sense of "surely, certainly"; Ck, Ct, Cr, Cs because, despite Ck's protestation that *kalanam* is the old reading, *kevalam* is clearly supported by manuscript evidence). The word order in the Sanskrit shows a complex interlacement (schematically a B a b A b). Again, the dislocation is probably by design, meant to suggest Kausalyā's deep anguish (cf. note on 24.16).

5. After this verse the SR inserts four lines in which Kausalyā explains that, humble though Lakṣmaṇa's task might be, it is virtuous, and expresses the hope that he will soon be released from his labors (2189*).

9. "how unseemly a food" *na . . . aupayikam . . . bhojanam*: Cf. note on 95.21.

10. "the whole four-cornered earth" *caturantāṃ mahīm*: The earlier geodetic conception, later to be replaced by the round disc model (see Lüders 1951, p. 79).

11. "should have only such meal to offer his father" *pitur dadyād iṅgudīkṣodam*: Normally a ball of fine rice would be offered to the departed.

17. "clingingly" *āsaktam*: Cm, Cg (citing the late lexicographer Halāyudha), "without ceasing"; Ck, Ct, Cr, "affectionately."

26. "lastly" *jaghanyam*: Cm, Cg, " 'directly after' Rāma and Vasiṣṭha seated themselves"; Ct, "behind."

Some N manuscripts include Guha in the company (cf. note on 92.15).

27. Bharata's folding his hands before Rāma would appear to be a signal that he wishes to address him (Ck, Ct include this verse in the next, as part of the people's reflections).

"like great Indra before Prajāpati" *yathā mahendraḥ . . . prajāpatim*: On the simile cf. note on 29.11.

29. Despite the position of the first *ca*, we apportion the adjectives one to each brother, which seems to be the poet's intention. Observe also that several trustworthy manuscripts (D4, 7, G3) read *sa* for this *ca*.

Note the omission, once again, of Śatrughna (cf. note on 95.33). Cs here tries to explain this by saying that, since Lakṣmaṇa and Śatrughna are twins, there is no need to mention them separately.

Sarga 97

1. On the text-critical questions relating to this *sarga*, cf. note on 95.1ff.

"comforted" *samāśvāsya*: Several manuscripts and commentators, with greater narrative logic, read "acknowledged" (cf. note on 96.27; Cm, Cg take "who so cherished his guru" predicatively with this verb).

2. "in barkcloth" *cīra-*: Cf. 82.23.

4. "holding them out stiffly" *pragṛhya balavad*: In light of such passages as 60.14, 95.9, 95.27, we must either read *bāhū* (for *bhūyaḥ*) with the NR or, what amounts to the same thing, understand an ellipsis of *-añjalim* with *pragṛhya*, as translated.

5. "grave wrongdoing" *karma suduṣkaram*: *Suduṣkaram*: = *suduṣkṛtam*, an unexampled usage.

17. Hereafter follows an SR insertion, in which Rāma explains that gurus have absolute license to act as they would toward their sons and wives (2201*).

21. "in the presence of all the world" *lokasaṃnidhau*: Perhaps "before witnesses," for Daśaratha made—or rather, acquiesced in—the apportionment in private, with only Kaikeyī (and, in a sense, Rāma) present (*sargas* 10-12, 16). The more "public" scene of *sargas* 31-34 cannot be meant, for no "apportionment" was made then.

"And after giving his orders" *vyādiśya ca*: Throughout the following six *sargas* (as in verse 24 below), Rāma will repeatedly make reference to his father's express "order" to live fourteen years in the wilderness of Daṇḍaka. As noted above (on 12.16), however, the text so far has made every effort to deny that Daśaratha had any direct involvement with Rāma's banishment, and nowhere has he given such an order. For further discussion of this problem, see the Introduction, Chapter 4.

Sarga 98

4ff. Many of these verses will be repeated in 6.116.2ff.

4. Having bestowed the kingship on Bharata, Daśaratha met the conditions of Kaikeyī's request and fulfilled his obligations toward her (he "honored" them, *sāntvitā* here = *pūjitā* in 6.116.2), and now that Bharata possesses the kingship it is within his rights to transfer it to Rāma; their father's word will still have been respected. Thus in the main Cg, Ck, Ct. On the proposed transfer of power, however, Cg remarks that, being Rāma's slave, Bharata wishes to make over to him the kingship according to the well-known proverb that "there are three who are propertyless" [a wife, a slave, and a son; cf. *MBh* 1.77.22], that is, that a slave's property is his master's.

5. "the kingdom will utterly disintegrate" *rājyakhaṇḍam idaṃ mahat*: The commentators all misunderstand the meaning of *-khaṇḍa-*, taking it in the sense of one of the nine "political sectors" of the world. *Rājyakhaṇḍam* here = *rājyacchidram* in 6.116.4.

6. Tārkṣa: Garuḍa.

Note the anacoluthon: the nominative construction in *pādas* ab (*kharaḥ* and *patatriṇaḥ*, requiring for example, *śaktāḥ*) is changed to an oblique one in *pāda* c, *na śaktir me*.

7. "depend" *upajīvyate*: Literally, "live off": Bharata's point is not that, although incapable himself of ruling (verse 6), he is reluctant to become dependent on others in order to acquire that capability (so Cg, Varadacharya 1964-1965, vol. 2, p. 385n). He is rather referring to the life of a king in exile in the wilderness, who must look to others for support (so Cr and, in the main, Cs). This may be not merely an inducement to Rāma to return and become his own master, but also a suggestion that forest life is not only "hard" but prohibited to kshatriyas (cf. *MBh* 12.22.7). The king is often referred to in Sanskrit literature as the one whom subjects "depend on," as creatures depend on rain (cf., for example, *MBh* 12.76.13, 36-37).

8-10. Cg analyzes the simile ("Bharata refrains from doing so himself out of deference . . . knowing Rāma is clever enough to understand it on his own") as follows: The planter of the tree = Daśaratha; the tree = Rāma; the flowers = the stage antecedent to the consecration; the fruit = the assumption of the kingship. (Ck, "The effort of the king in begetting you would be vain if you did not supply the means of subsistence to us who depend on you; you would then be 'fruitless,' like the great tree.")

"its being grown" *prabhāvitaḥ*: = *sa ropyate*, 6.116.7; Cg, Ck take as *kartari kta* ("he grew it").

Note in verse 10d the exceptional use of the imperative (with *na*) in a conditional clause. Curiously, none of the commentators remarks on it (the unusual terminal *hi* might suggest some indicative in *-si*, as read by several manuscripts, though it is hard to suppose that the strange imperative dislodged a simpler form).

12. There is a slight word play here between *nardantu* ("trumpet") and *nandantu* ("rejoice").

15ff. "Rāma begins to assuage Bharata's sorrow by showing him the true view of things, namely, that it was neither the king compelled by Kaikeyī nor Bharata who caused his exile, but fate," Cm, Cg. This is an artificial and unsatisfactory explanation for the narrative function of the following verses. However moving at times they may be, verses 15-36 are evidently *non sequitur* with regard to Bharata's plea. Perhaps the verses are out of place—note that the NR removes them to a separate *sarga*. Or maybe the poet has inserted here, rather awkwardly, material from a parallel legend, that of the Wise Rāma (*rāmapaṇḍitaḥ*), partly preserved also in the *Dasaratha Jātaka* (cf. note on verse 17 below, also Lüders 1940, pp. 38-39, 105ff., who calls attention to echoes in other *jātakas* for our verses 15, 18, 20, 21, 26). The wisdom verses in the *jātaka*, in fact, make considerably more narrative sense, insofar as there Rāma is shown never to grieve at all for his father (contrast above, 95.8ff., and his far more violent grief in *Araṇyakāṇḍa* 56ff.).

15. "No one acts of his own free will" *nātmānaḥ kāmakāro 'sti*: *Ātmanaḥ* is essentially reflexive. It has none of the theological overtones suggested by Ct, Cr: "the individual soul," as opposed to "the lord" (*-īśvara*, rendered here as "[not] independent"). They also overinterpret the phrase "this way and that": "from this body and world and from the other body and world it drags [the soul] in accordance with its *karma*."

"fate" *kṛtāntaḥ*: Like *daiva* ("chance," literally, "what comes from the gods"), *kāla* ("time"), *adṛṣṭa* ("the unforeseeable"), and so on, this signifies more or less our "fate." Observe again Rāma's profound fatalism (cf. for example 20.12 ff. and note). The foil to it in this section will be not Lakṣmaṇa but Jābāli, who discourses in *sarga* 100.

16. A famous verse, appearing in many texts, such as *MBh* 11.2.3, 12.27.29, *ViṣṇuP* 5.29. It is also found in the "consolation" *sarga* of some *dharmaśāstras*, such as *GobhiSm* 3.40 (cf. Kane 1962-1975, vol. 4, p. 237).

17. This verse, and it is the only such one, appears almost verbatim in the consolation scene of the *Dasaratha Jātaka* (*Jātakas* #461.85, cf. *Suttanipāta* 3.8.175). The one important difference is *niccam* (for *nānyatra*): "Ripe fruit need always fear falling, and men that are born must always fear dying." The Sanskrit version, as it is normally understood (by Lüders, for example) is suspiciously opaque; in the repetition of the verse in 7.10.16 it was felt necessary to add *nityam*. Either the transmission has been faulty, or perhaps we must take *nānyatra* in the sense "not at some other time," that is, "all the time." But as this signification is unattested, and conjecture is not efficacious, we let the opacity stand. Although the NR reading in *pāda* c is vindicated

by the (southern) Pāli version, as Lüders observes, the SR reading is authenticated by the northern Buddhist *Udānavarga* (ed. Bernhard 1965, 1.11).

18. After this verse the SR adds: "The night that comes on will never return, and the full Yamunā goes to the ocean, the abode of waters" (2208*).

20. "You should be grieving for yourself" *ātmānam anuśoca tvaṃ*: The commentators are not satisfied with the natural implication: Cg, "give thought to the world to come"; Cm, " 'you should be grieving for yourself,' who are engaged in seeking to attain ephemeral things"; Ck, Ct, "that is, you should think: death is ineluctably coming. What is to be my course in this world and the world to come?"; Cr, "make an attempt to free your embodied soul from suffering."

21. "Death walks" *mṛtyur vrajati*: "Because the lines etched on one's forehead by god are death's form," Cm (Ct, "because one's Inner-Controller has the form of death, and so it cannot be evaded").

23. "when the sun rises, or . . . when it goes down" *udita āditye . . . astamite ravau*: The translation agrees with Cr in seeing an alternative in *pādas* ab. Cg, however, is possible, too: "They rejoice when the sun rises, realizing that the hour to make money has come; *and* when it sets, realizing that the time for pleasure has come."

24. "the face of each new season come" *ṛtumukham . . . navaṃ navam ihāgatam*: Many manuscripts read instead, "(the face, or beginning, of a season) that seems to come each time brand new."

25-26. Famous verses appearing also in the *MBh* (12.28.36, 168.15).

27. "this course of things" *yathābhāvam*: The compound is virtually substantival (so Ck, Ct; Cm, Cg, falsely, " 'one cannot stay,' that is, with one's kinsmen '*as much as one wishes*' ").

30. "Since life trickles away" *vayasaḥ patamānasya*: *Pādas* ab form a genitive absolute construction (though not *anādare*). Note also *vā* in the sense of *iva* (compare *MBh* 12.138.3, with Belvalkar's note).

"happiness" *sukham*: Though used elsewhere in the *Ayodhyākāṇḍa* simply in the sense of "comfort" or "worldly happiness," the word must have a more transcendent meaning here, "ultimate happiness," as in 3.6.27, "One cannot derive happiness [*sukham*] from mere pleasure [*sukham*]" (see note there). Cg, Ct, Cr, " 'happiness,' that is, the cause of happiness, that is, *dharma*" (so read by the NR; note also *BuddhaC* 7.18, *sukhaṃ hi dharmasya vadanti mūlam*, "bliss is the ultimate end of *dharma*," Johnston).

"have found happiness" *sukhabhājaḥ*: Rather differently the commentators, such as Ck: " 'happiness is the proper lot . . .': creatures receive life that they may acquire the means to happiness."

34. "heavenly treasure" *daivīm ṛddhim*: Cg, "a heavenly body, etc."; Ck, "the attainments of lordliness, wisdom, high station, and bountiful bliss"; Ct, "ascetic power."

36. "different griefs" *bahuvidhāḥ śokāḥ*: At his father's death, his brother's exile, and so on (Cm, Cg, Ct). " 'Grief,' a mental affect; 'lamentation,' a verbal one; 'weeping,' a physical one" [the three aspects of the person, cf. note on 88.18], Ck.

37. "of his own accord" *vaśinā*: So Cr (cf. 10.1).

38. "where" *yatra*: Agrees with Cg (Ck, Ct, Cr, "with regard to what duty").

40. "wonderful" *citram*: "Since Rāma spoke in such a way that no response seemed possible, Bharata has to reply [as it were] with another mouth [with exceptional

eloquence], thus the adjective," Cg ("invested with remarkable argument and expressions, capable of amazing the audience," Ck, Ct [Cr]).

42. "in their existing and not existing both" *yathāsati tathā sati*: The meaning of the second half of this verse, particularly the change from nominative to locative, is not entirely clear (the NR reads locative in both *pādas*). Rāma's speech centered on the transience of life—on death in the midst of life—and this may explain one part of the verse (the nonexistence of the living); whereas verse 34 above may help us grasp the second part (the continued existence of the dead). The commentators explain more or less improbably, for example, Cm, Cg: " 'just as a dead person' is not an object of hate, 'so' neither should 'a living person' be; 'just as' there is no passion 'for a nonexistent object,' 'so' there should be none 'for an existent one.' " Ck remarks at the end of his rather confused (or at least confusing) analysis, "This verse [42cd-43ab] illustrates the meaning of the scriptural passage, 'If a person comes to know that *ātma*, that he is it, what would he want, in the desire for what would he cling to the body?' [*BṛĀraU* 4.4.12], as well as the meaning of the entire *Bhagavadgītā*. To our thinking, the verse offers opportunity for vast exegesis, treating as it does of the spiritual discipline of our innate ideas (intellect)."

44. "courage" *-sattva-*: So Cr; or, "power," Cs. Cf. 5.66.18.

45. N manuscripts hereafter insert (or substitute) a few lines in which Bharata explains that he himself is not so endowed, is all alone, suffers unspeakably, and cannot bear to live (2219*).

48. "a deed so abominable" *karma jugupsitam*: That is, usurping the kingship (Cm), not slaying his mother (Cs).

49. "he was a god to us" *daivatam*: So Cr (cf. 16.15 above, and *MBh* 12.41.4); equally possible, and perhaps preferable, "(now departed and become) a deity," which is how Ck understands (cf. also 95.31, verse 34 above, and especially 3.62.4 and 4.61.10).

50. "But still" *hi*: Note the adversative force of the particle.

"contrary to all that is right and good" *dharmārthayor hīnam*: That is, "based totally on the urgings of desire [*kāma*]" (Cm, Cg, Ct; cf. 47.13).

51. "There is an ancient saying" *purāśrutiḥ*: Cm, Ct call it a *gāthā*. We find no *śloka* exactly like this, though there are many verses of a similar import. In the *Rām* cf. 3.54.16: "When a man is to be ruined by implacable doom, he loses all sense of right and wrong—and it is this that dooms him." In the *MBh* cf. 2.72.8 and in particular 2.583*, which concerns the Rāma legend itself: "The nearer a man's downfall, generally the more wrong-headed his thoughts become."

52. "out of anger" *krodhāt*: Cm, Cg, Ct try to explain, "that is, [from fear of] Kaikeyī's anger," quite unsatisfactorily. D4, 5, 7 persuasively read, "from greed" (though see Rāvaṇa's words in 3.34.10). No doubt Rāma's declaration in 101.17 is to be juxtaposed to this.

53. "corrects" *sādhu manyate*: In view of the context here and verse 54, there seems to be no other way to interpret the phrase than in this unusual fashion, with the commentators (Cm, Cg, Ck, Ct; contrast its sense in 57.22). Most N manuscripts have the easier [*sādhu*] *kurute*.

Cm, Cg, Ck, Ct etymologize, "He is called a son—*apatyam*—because he prevents his father from falling—*patana*—[into hell]"; cf. 99.12.

54. "(do not) endorse" (*mā* . . .) *abhipattā*: What the crit. ed. means by *abhi*pattat* is unclear (is it an emendation? It is not so noted on pp. xxvi-xxvii of the Introduction

to the text volume). We read with Crā, Cm, Cg *abhipattā* (periphrastic future of the root *pad*; for the use of *mā* with the future in prohibitions cf. Renou 1968, p. 462).

56. Hereafter the SR inserts 2228*, in which Bharata says the first obligation of a kshatriya is the consecration, in order to govern, and that this clear and unequivocal duty should not be abandoned in favor of some other one that is ill-defined and uncertain.

58. "the foremost is that of the householder" *gārhasthyaṃ śreṣṭham āśramam*: Ck cites *GautDS* [3.3], "Of these [three other stages of life] the householder stage is the womb, because the others do not bring forth offspring," and he remarks, "One should envisage [entering] the other stages only when the householder's is no longer possible, and not when it is."

59. "rank of birth" *sthānena janmanā*: Literally, "in rank by birth." We agree with Ck, Ct in taking the two words thus closely together (see the next verse; Cr, "position [or station, stature] and birth"; Cg, "position, that is, the order of succession," but that, of course, is determined by birth).

60. "in both virtue and intelligence" *-buddhiguṇaḥ*: Note the "gloss" of B1 and G3 (*hīnabuddhir hīnaguṇaḥ, guṇair hīnaḥ*). Cm, Cg suggest instead taking the compound as a *tatpuruṣa* rather than *dvandva*, "virtues of intellect," "mental powers."

64. "Discharge the three debts" *ṛṇāni trīṇy apākurvan*: Cf. note on 4.14 above. Ck, Ct, adducing the *TaiS* [6.3.11] (which states that a brahman is born with three debts), claim that a kshatriya likewise incurs them, either because "brahman" is meant to include kshatriyas (Ct), or because the activities—studentship and so on—by which the brahmans pay off the debts are enjoined upon the kshatriya as well, and this implies his obligation to meet the debts.

65. "the ten directions" *diśo daśa*: The four primary and four intermediary points of the compass, plus the zenith and the nadir.

67. "Great lord" *maheśvaraḥ*: Usually the name of Śiva (occasionally, in the epics, of Indra, cf. Hopkins 1915, pp. 122-23). The identification with Śiva is made more certain by the fact that he is often called Bhūteśa (lord of creatures), or Paśupati (lord of beasts). Cg offers various reasons why the word must signify Viṣṇu, the least ridiculous of which is that Śiva, given the task of destroying creatures at the time of universal dissolution, could not possibly be said to "take pity" on them. Note that Rāma is compared to Śiva elsewhere, 2.15.39, 23.27, 24.10, 26.

71. "merchants" *naigamāḥ*: Cm, Cg, Ck, Ct, Cr gloss, "townsmen" (citing *Vaija*, which also gives "merchants"); cf. note on 1.14 above.

"commanders of the troops" *yūthavallabhāḥ*: Cm, Cg, Ct, "chief men of the troops" ("that is, of counselors, and so on," Cr); cf. note on 75.11.

Sarga 99

1. The crit. ed. notes here that Ck is absent for the rest of the second book of the *Rām*. The Mysore edition of the commentary (1965) is, in fact, complete.

3. "our father . . . made a brideprice pledge" *pitā naḥ . . . samāśrauṣīt . . . -śulkam*: On the significance of this startling piece of intelligence, see the Introduction, Chapter 4. The commentators try desperately, here and elsewhere in the *sarga*, to explain away a fundamental inconsistency in the narrative (see also on 4.25). Ck is naturally led to wonder why, if the kingship were given to Kaikeyī as her brideprice,

she used a boon to ask for it. He cites a passage from a *smṛti* text which states, "A lie is not considered reprehensible if told to a woman, at the time of a love-match, to protect one's livelihood, when one's life is in danger, on behalf of cows or brahmans when violence is offered them" [*BṛDharmaP* 1.47.69, *BhāgP* 8.19.43, and cf. Johnston on *BuddhaC* 4.67], and suggests that Kaikeyī was afraid the king would not actually give her son the kingship [since Kausalyā was already chief queen and Kaikeyī's marriage was a love-match], and so she uses the boon. Cg (on verse 6 below) adds that she only asks for the [two] boons because the brideprice agreement had happened long ago, when she was only a child. It is reasonable, he adds, that she might have forgotten what happened long ago since she had to be reminded even of the two boons [cf. 9.5 and note], though that incident occurred in her adulthood. (It is, of course, totally unreasonable.)

4. "a boon" *varam*: Some N manuscripts read, "two boons." Cm, Cg, Ct, Cr gloss "boon" as "pair of boons," that is, as *jātyekavacanam*; but this is to extend the grammatical principle beyond the range of usefulness.

5. Cm comments, "If Daśaratha at the time of his marriage had promised the kingship to Kaikeyī's son, how could he have been ready to give it to Rāma? According to the proverb, 'They say five lies entail no sin: one told at the time of marriage, at the time of love-making, when one's life is in danger, or one's whole property is on the point of being seized, or on behalf of a brahman' [*VāsiDS* 16.37; cf. *MBh* 1.77.16], Daśaratha realized there would be no fault and so acted as he did." As noted in the Introduction, if the agreement were not binding on Daśaratha, Rāma would not cite it as an argument here.

6. Cg remarks, "[Not only did Daśaratha think his deception about the marriage pledge no crime; cf. note on verse 5] but the king of Kekaya, too, being deeply impressed by Rāma's virtues, did not demand the kingship for his grandson [obviously he suspected nothing of Rāma's coronation; cf. also note on 1.35]. Rāma had heard about this secret (pledge) from Sumantra and others, and so we must assume that they approved [of Daśaratha's behavior in awarding the kingship to Rāma?] when they learned of it." We never learn from Vālmīki when Rāma is supposed to have come to know of the brideprice agreement (see also the Introduction, Chapter 4).

8. "brook no opposition" *apratidvandvaḥ*: So Cm, Cg, Cs; possible is Ck's, "without any animosity."

10. "Free the . . . king from his debt" *ṛṇān mocaya rājānam*: The king would remain in debt as long as Bharata is not consecrated king (so Cm, Cg, Ct, Cr).

11. "glorious Gaya" *yaśasvinā / gayena*: A Gaya is recorded as author of two vedic hymns (*ṚV* 10.63, 64), and is mentioned in both of them (line 17 of each), though the verses attributed to him here are not found in the *vedas*. Buddhist and Jain tradition considers Gaya a king of the environs of Gayā (it is located in Bihar state), one of the holiest regions in India, where sacrifices attain their greatest efficacy (and where the Buddha attained enlightenment). If a son performs a *śrāddha* at Gayā he most assuredly rescues his father from the torments after death (cf. note on 76.5).

12. "rescues" *trāyate*: The most ancient, and the standard, "etymology" of the word *putra*: "he saves [*trāyate*] his father from [the hell named] Put" (already in *Nir* [2.11]).

"or because he protects his ancestors" *pitṝn yat pāti vā*: As the text of *pāda* d is printed, one must agree with Ck, Ct in seeing a second possible "etymology" being proposed, *pāti* ("he protects") *pitṝn* ("his ancestors"). A variant reading found in Ctr, *vai* for *vā*, gives the more reasonable, "For a son indeed protects his ancestors" (the NR reads with *ManuSm* 9.138, *svayam eva svayaṃbhuvā*, "[was called . . .] by the Self-existent Brahmā himself").

A son "saves" his ancestors by conveying them to heaven by means of sacrifices, public works, and so on, which are performed in their name (Cm, Cg), and, as here, by preserving their truthfulness.

13. "journey to Gayā" *gayāṃ vrajet*: That is, to perform a *śrāddha* there for the father ("the field of Gayā is the place providing the most efficacious means of securing the release of one's father," Ck). The verse is famous, appearing in various forms in *MBh* (3.85.7), *VāyuP* (105.10), *KūrmaP* (2.34.13), and elsewhere.

17. "I shall become sovereign king of the beasts of the wild" *vanyānām aham api rājarāṇ mṛgāṇām*: "Perhaps this line plants the seed of events to come, of Rāma's pleasing [so they gloss *rājarāṭ*, "sovereign king"] Sugrīva [the monkey king], his slaying Vālin, and so on," Cm, Cg (Ct, "his coming overlordship over the monkeys is here intimated").

19. "his principal sons" *tanayavarāḥ*: Is the adjective significant, suggesting that the king had other sons by his lesser concubines? Otherwise, "us, his good sons."

"Do not despair" *mā viṣādam*: We understand ellipsis of a singular verb, that is, *kuru* (cf. the NR's *viṣīda*, so read also by Ct), cf. 3.59.13, 6.38.22 (Ck would supply *carāma* with *viṣādam* ("let us not despair").

Sarga 100

1ff. The minister Jābāli (mentioned also in 2.61.2, 105.2 where he is called "strictly observant," and elsewhere in the *Rām*) will present the *cārvāka* (Cg) or *lokāyatika* (Ck, Ct), "materialist" or "realist," position. On Jābāli, his disquisition, and related matters, see the instructive discussion of Ruben 1956.

1. "at variance with righteousness" *dharmāpetam*: The NR reads either "in accord with righteousness," or, "correct" (cf. also Ruben 1956, p. 40).

Several N manuscripts insert hereafter 2237*, containing some of Jābāli's preliminary arguments: Daśaratha had already given Rāma the kingship, Bharata is ready to return it, as is Kaikeyī; Rāma should relieve Lakṣmaṇa and Sītā of the burden that has been placed on them; gurus often act recklessly, renouncing their sons, as for example Ṛcīka, who renounced Śunaḥsepha [*sic*] (cf. *AitBr* 7.13ff.; *Rām* 1.60).

2. "in distress" *tapasvinaḥ*: Cf. note on 58.25 above. Ck's construction, "like some miserable commoner," is impossible. Cm, Cg and a number of good S manuscripts read, "and you a wise [*manasvinaḥ*, T1, 2, or, "powerful," *tarasvinaḥ*, M3], noble-minded man."

Jābāli here and in most of the following discourse is probably addressing the opinion Rāma expressed in 99.12 (so Ruben).

3. The idea here is indeed close to Rāma's own (98.25ff.), but in this instance directed not to consolation but to political action.

4. A very similar sentiment in *Saund* 15.31.

6. There is a light word-play here, "the wise," *sajjanāḥ*, "feel . . . attachment," *sajjante*. On the meaning of *sat-* cf. note on verse 17 below.

7. "kingship of your fathers" *pitryaṃ rājyam*: That Jābāli makes use of the idea of ancestry, though he had already denied that any kin relationships really exist (verses 3ff.) is merely a concession to Rāma, as Cm, Cg, Ct note: "If you want to convince someone you must use categories he understands."

8. "wearing her single braid of hair" *ekaveṇīdharā*: Faithful wives separated from their husbands would braid their hair into a single tress (note again that the word "city" in Sanskrit is feminine in gender).

10. "Expressed here on a deeper level is the notion of [perpetual] change, according to the [Buddhist] doctrine of momentary destruction. . . . The father [in the Buddhist doctrine] has no more relationship with the son than with the egg of a louse," Ct. Most manuscripts add: "The father is [supplies] but the seed of an offspring; the sperm and blood combine in a woman during her fertile period to bring about the birth of a person" (2239*).

11. "where he had to go" *gantavyaṃ yatra tena*: "That is, he has been reduced back into the five elements," Cm, Cg, Ct.

"deluding yourself" *mithyā vihanyase*: The verb in this sense appears to be Buddhist, cf. *Saund* 9.9 with Johnston's note (Ruben falsely, "*dulden*").

12. "who place 'righteousness' above what brings them profit" *arthadharmaparāḥ*: Since Jābāli goes on to consider actions by which *artha* is frustrated (and because we would naturally expect him to promote *artha*), the compound cannot mean, "devoted to *dharma* and *artha*." Ck (unrecorded in the crit. ed.) reads, *arthe dharmaparāḥ*, "who, when *artha* [exists ready to hand, abandon it and] devote themselves to *dharma*" (so Ct also understands). We suggest, thus, analyzing, *arthād dharmaḥ paro yeṣām*, rare though such a *vigraha* might be.

Jābāli mourns such people ("who abandon perceptible pleasure [for imperceptible goals]," Cg) because when they die no soul continues in existence, as they had falsely believed, to reap the rewards of *dharma* (Ct).

13. "the Eighth Day, the rite for the ancestors" *aṣṭakā pitṛdaivatyam*: *Śrāddha* offerings for the departed ancestors (cf. note on 71.1) were prescribed for the eighth day of three different months. Brahmans would be invited to partake as representatives of the ancestors (cf. *ĀśvaGS* 4.7.2), the food they eat being thought to feed the spirits of the departed.

14. This sentiment appears, attributed to the Cārvāka school, in the *SarvaDaSaṃ* (p. 14 verse 5); in the *ViṣṇuP* (3.18.28) it is voiced by Viṣṇu in his delusive avatar as the Buddha.

15. Cf. *SarvaDaSaṃ* p. 13 verse 2.

16. "world to come" *param*: Cg, "anything to be experienced in another world"; Ck, Ct, "anything beyond this world, whose purpose is for the world to come—that is, *dharma*."

The insertion after this verse, 2241*, is discussed in the note on 101.29.

17. "of the wise" *satām*: Cf. verse 6. "Wise" is not often the sense of this adjective (normally = "good," sometimes "wealthy"), but this is clearly what it means in both our places. Compare 5.26.3, where *santaḥ* corresponds to *paṇḍitaiḥ* in the first occurrence of the proverb at 5.23.12 (cf. for other remarks Ruben 1956, p. 41). Rāma pointedly employs the word again in 101.3, 19, and 30. (Ck, Ct, Cr understand, "realists," "those who maintain the doctrine that only those objects are real [*sat*] which we can perceptually validate" ["and not those which depend only on scriptural authority," Ct]; Cm, Cg deviously separate as *sa tām*, "to these [ideas].")

"concurs" *-nidarśinīm*: So Cm, Cg, Ct. Ck, "in harmony (with the whole world)"; Cr, "which enlighten (the whole world)."

After this verse some N manuscripts insert a passage (App. I, No. 27): a catalogue of kings is given, all of whom died, leaving their wives and children, "and no one knows where they have gone." Rāma is urged to devote himself to pleasure: those who are righteous are often unhappy, those who are unrighteous often happy (lines 21-22). Rāma is angered, replies that he will not disobey his father's command, and asks why Jābāli does not accept as valid [corroboration of a metaphysical reality] Indra's attaining heaven by means of sacrifices (lines 38-39, cf. 101.29), the successes of Viśvāmitra, and so on.

Sarga 101

3ff. In the following verses Rāma seems not to be directly addressing Jābāli's argument, but to be contemplating the contradictions between his own professions and actions were he to follow that advice. The *truly* wise (cf. note on 100.17) value virtuous conduct, not virtuous declarations. Principles are only authenticated by deeds, and if they are not thus authenticated, they are mere pretense.

5. This verse appears to be the apodosis of the conditional clause in verse 6 (Cm, Cg take the apodosis to be verse 7; Ck, Ct supply their own). Ck cites: "Whoever abandons the precepts of *śāstra* and acts according to his own will [*kāmakārataḥ*] does not find success or happiness, or the highest goal" [*BhagGī* 16.23]. In *pāda* b the conjecture *yathā* (for *tathā*) easily suggests itself, but has no manuscript corroboration.

7. "a corrupter of the world" *lokadūṣaṇam*: Cf. verses 9-10. (Ck, Ct, "resorting to a type of behavior that corrupts, destroys, the *world to come*.")

8. Only by conforming to the practices of one's ancestors can one hope to reach them in heaven. Ct gives the hint for the somewhat difficult *pāda* a by making oblique reference to a tenet we find in *ManuSm* 4.178: "Let him walk in that path of holy men which his fathers and his grandfathers followed; while he walks in that he will not suffer harm" (Bühler).

9. "the entire world would follow suit" *ayaṃ lokaḥ kṛtsnaḥ samupavartate*: The doctrine that the king sets the standard of behavior for his subjects in all matters of conduct is set out more explicitly in 3.48.8-9.

13. "Truth is the lord of this world" *satyam eveśvaro loke*: Ck, perhaps rightly, understands *samāśritaḥ* here, "In this world the lord resides in truth."

"goddess of the lotus" *padmā*: Śrī, goddess of wealth and royalty.

15. How is it that some men are able to achieve success in this world? Why is it that after death one man goes to heaven and another goes to hell? There must be some reason—and that reason is their adherence (or lack of adherence) to truth. Such seems to be the main point of the verse; see also *MBh* 12.183.3 (Cr, "The verse supplies proof that deeds are rewarded"; Cm, Cg, "The poet is showing the worldly and heavenly rewards of the man devoted to truth, and the damnation of the man who is not").

16. This follows Cm in construction of the verse; he refers to 16.19 above as the instance of Rāma's pledge (to Kaikeyī; Ck [on verse 17] refers to 16.49).

17. "Not out of greed or delusion" *naiva lobhān na mohād vā*: See the note on 98.52.

"the dam of truth" *setuṃ satyasya*: Cm, Cg (so Ck, Cr) construe *guror* with *satyasya*, "the dam of my guru's truth" (that is, 10.19 above). This seems improbable in light of verse 24 below (and 103.11), though of course there have been several promises: Daśaratha's to Kaikeyī (10.19), Rāma's to Kaikeyī (16.17, 16.49) and to his father (31.25), and all of these form a single complex.

19. "personal code of righteousness" *pratyagātmam . . . dharmam*: Not entirely certain. *Pratyagātmam* is evidently adjectival, construing with *dharmam*, and contrasting with *kṣātraṃ dharmam* in verse 20. It appears to have no theological overtones, though the word is attested with such as early as *KāṭhU* (2.1.1). We agree with Ck in taking *satyam*, "the true one," as the predicate.

20. "I reject the kshatriya's code" *kṣātraṃ dharmam ahaṃ tyakṣye*: Ck, Ct comment: "He means, I give up (only) the debased kshatriya code, where one takes the kingship against one's father's command, and I follow the true one." Not dissimilarly Ctr, who in his long comment here argues that Rāma is distinguishing between two levels in the code: one holding that protection of his subjects is a kshatriya's primary duty (cf. *ManuSm* 7.144), the other, that for a kshatriya to keep his promise is most important. It is the former aspect of the code, he claims, that Rāma is rejecting here (similarly Yudhiṣṭhira in the *MBh*; Ctr appositely cites 2.35.14, 21). We cannot know for certain whether the relative clause in *pāda* b ("where unrighteousness . . .") is nonrestrictive (so we punctuate) or restrictive, defining. But note that Rāma has often been shown to revise if not reject out of hand the conventional behavior of his social class (see, for example, 18.36 and the Introduction, Chapter 10).

21. "And sinful action is of three sorts" *trividhaṃ karma pātakam*: Here Rāma apparently wishes to show how all three types of sin are of equal weight, lest he be reproached with recoiling from the seemingly trivial lapse of breaking his word (for the tripartition see note on 88.18). Cr suggests that all three types of sin would be committed were he to break his word and take over the kingship. Ct quotes an interesting verse from the *BhāgP* [1.18.7] to show that in the present age, the Kali Yuga, whereas good *karma* can be produced from good thoughts, evil thoughts do not produce bad *karma* (not the case in the Tretā Yuga, that in which the *Rām* is traditionally thought to take place).

22. "the man who holds to truth" *puruṣaṃ . . . satyastham*: The crit. ed. offers *svargastham*, "when a man is in heaven." It is not clear how we can simply say, " 'a man,' that is, the truthful man" with Cm, Cg, Ck, Ct, Cr; but the verse would make little sense if we do not. But even then, that "land" should attend a man in heaven is as absurd in Sanskrit as it is in English. Considering the reading of Dt, Dd, Dm: *satyaṃ samanuvartante*; and 99.19: *narendraṃ satyastham*, we feel confident in conjecturing *satyastham* for *svargastham* in *pāda* c here.

23. "What you consider the best course" *śreṣṭham . . . avadhārya*: Translated in agreement with Cg, Cr with respect to the syntax of *śreṣṭham*. Might it not, however, be a superlative marker for *anāryam*, "(what you are suggesting is) a most ignoble thing"?

"mere sophistry" *yuktikaraiḥ*: Literally, "have the force of mere logic." Cf. the later idiom *yuktiṃ kṛ*, "to employ a stratagem"; cf. also 94.33.

25. "it brought delight to the heart of Queen Kaikeyī" *prahṛṣṭamanasā devī kaikeyī cābhavat tadā*: Ct comments, "[Rāma is saying], 'It would be totally inappropriate for me to take away the delight I once gave Kaikeyī [by my promise].' " Here Rāma appears either to be rejecting the argument that adherence merely to the letter of

Daśaratha's boon is sufficient, as Bharata claimed (98.4), or to be denying that Kaikeyī has had any change of heart (cf. the insertion reported at the note on 100.1).

26. "restricting my food to holy things, roots, fruit, and flowers" *niyatabhojanaḥ mūlaiḥ puṣpaiḥ phalaiḥ puṇyaiḥ*: Construing the verse in agreement with Cr. Ascetics, particularly those who "adhere to the Vaikhānasa doctrine" (as apparently is the case with Rāma, cf. 46.58 above and note there), are "to subsist solely on flowers, roots, and fruit," according to *ManuSm* (6.21, cf. 6.13) as well as the *MBh* ("Those who have adopted the Vaikhānasa doctrine . . . subsist, some on roots, some on fruit, some on flowers" [12.236.13-14]). Accordingly, in *Rām* 3.1.21 Rāma will be offered "fruit, roots, wild flowers, and other sorts of food." Alternatively, of course, we may adopt the easier syntax and join *pādas* c and d ("satisfying the gods and ancestors with holy things, roots . . ."), though offerings of roots are not commonly met with. (Note also that *pāda* d of our verse is one that frequently appears without expressed instrumental, cf. for example *MBh* 3.83.52, 125.11; 13.152.7.)

27. "the world on its course" *lokayātrām*: "The course of the world is obedience, the keeping of one's father's word," Cm, Cg, Ct (Ck, "the maintenance of one's body"). Rāma would "corrupt the world" (cf. verses 7, 9 above) were he to disobey, because kings are exemplary figures (cf. 101.9 and note, also *BhagGī* 3.21).

28. Cg rightly considers this verse to be a response to the denial of efficacy in vedic rites voiced above, 100.13.

"On entering this realm of action" *karmabhūmim imāṃ prāpya*: That is, having been born into this world. The *MBh* distinguishes between this world as the "realm of action," and the afterworld as the place where the fruits of those actions are reaped (3.247.35; cf. also Rāmacandra on *ŚatTrayī* 2.98; the distinction, and the terminology itself, are common in the Jaina tradition).

"Fire . . . have reaped them" *agniḥ . . . phalabhāginaḥ*: "In another birth fire and the others performed good works and thereby became Fire, etc.; therefore everyone should perform such works," Cm; Ck cites *śruti*, "Fire desired, 'Let me be the food-eater for the gods' [and having performed the appropriate rite, he became such" *TaiBr* 3.1.4.1]. Cf. note on 29.13 on Vālmīki's familiarity with the Taittirīya scriptures.

29. "king of the gods" *devarāṭ*: The designation is proleptic.

Contrast the *MBh* verse (12.22.11-12) cited in the Introduction, Chapter 10 (Indra becomes king of gods by slaying his ninety-nine "brothers").

S and most D manuscripts insert hereafter a number of lines in which Rāma continues to criticize Jābāli's position, two of which deserve notice: "A Buddhist [or, the Buddha, *buddhaḥ*] is like a thief; and know that a Cārvāka is (like) a Buddhist" [*tathāgata*, so Cm] (2241*.14-15; this is apparently the only occurrence of the word *buddha* in the *Rām* tradition). Jābāli thereafter responds (2249* = 2241*.21-26) with the denial that he is a Cārvāka, and declares that he only spoke as he did to win Rāma over.

30. "strenuous effort" *parākramam*: That is, the vigilant effort to be truthful and righteous. On this sense of the word see note on 19.7 and compare *satyadharma-parākrama* in 103.7. The commentators understand the word in its more frequent epic sense, "bravery," and are then forced to restrict the prescription here to the kshatriya class (so Ck). Or, in order to preserve the wider application of the ethics, they gloss it fancifully (for example, "ascetic acts," Ct). Attempting to maintain the sense "bravery," Ctr adduces an interesting parallel from the *MBh* (12.60.13ff.): "(I

shall explain to you the *dharma* of the kshatriya. . . .) He must be always ready to slaughter Dasyus, he must show bravery in battle (*raṇe* . . . *parākramam*). . . . Those are the ones who most effectively conquer the worlds" (that is, of heaven, as Ctr would understand). It would appear that this is precisely the kshatriya code as it was conventionally understood that we see Rāma revising here and in the next verse, as elsewhere in the poem. See the further remarks in the Introduction, Chapter 10.

Sarga 102

1. "the true course" *gatāgatim*: Literally, "comings and goings." Apparently a unique usage; perhaps similar is *āgatiś ca gatiś caiva lokasya* (*MBh* 12.16.6). Cg, Ct, Cr take it differently: "departing and returning, that is, death and rebirth," but Rāma was not addressing himself to such metaphysical questions.

2. Vasiṣṭha commences a genealogy of Rāma's lineage, in order to corroborate historically the right (and obligation?) of primogeniture (cf. 95.2 above), as a means of dissuading Rāma from his purpose (Cg; so Cm, Ck, Ct). Though Vasiṣṭha does not explicitly enunciate this purpose, it is implicit in the making of genealogies (cf. also note on verse 13 below).

"master of the world" *lokanātha*: "You were there to perceive all this," Cg; Ck, Ct likewise explain the vocative by reference to Rāma's being an avatar of Viṣṇu.

3. "He then became a boar" *sa varāhas tato bhūtvā*: In the later epic and purāṇic period the myth of the cosmic boar rescuing the sunken earth comes to be associated, like so many others, with Viṣṇu; it is only in vedic and *Brāhmaṇa* texts that Prajāpati (= Brahmā) has the main role, cf. *TaiS* 7.1.5: "This was in the beginning the waters, the ocean. In it Prajāpati . . . becoming a boar seized her. . . . She extended, she became the earth" (cf. also *ŚatBr* 14.1.2.11). The preservation here of this archaic feature (cf. also note on 12.8) is of some significance for the relative dating of the *Rām* (cf. the General Introduction; several N manuscripts alter the text to read, "Viṣṇu became"; Cm refers the pronoun to Nārāyaṇa, so essentially Ck, Ct; Cr alone resists the revisionist temptation, Cg remaining silent).

"sons" *putraiḥ*: That is, the ten (or eleven) sons of Brahmā, among whom are counted the seven seers.

4. Recall the line of descent reported in the *Bālakāṇḍa* (1.69.17ff.). We must not make too much of the discrepancies among the various genealogies of the sun dynasty. Beyond two or three generations from the principal heroes, most epic (not to speak of purāṇic) genealogy is confused and cannot bear close scrutiny (and is historically worthless).

"eternal" *nityaḥ*: "This must mean, 'long-lived in comparison with others,' otherwise it would conflict with his 'arising from space,' " Cg.

5. "he was the first lord of creatures" *sa* . . . *prajāpatiḥ pūrvam*: Literally, "he was a Prajāpati for the first time." Ct explains: Before Manu all progeneration had been "mental"; with Manu begins physical progeneration (thus Ck: Manu "was authorized to create mortal creatures by way of his sperm"; see also Hopkins 1915, pp. 201-202).

Cg cites 1.5.6 on Manu's founding of Ayodhyā.

9. Anaraṇya: The name means "[under whose rule there is] no wilderness." Cf. Johnston on *BuddhaC* 2.15 for other epic references.

10. The story of Triśaṅku's elevation to heaven by Viśvāmitra is told in 1.56ff. (especially *sarga* 59); cf. also note on 36.10 above.

13. By referring only to the son of the eldest, Druvasandhi, the law of royal primogeniture is implied (so Cg, Ck, Ct; cf. verse 29).

15. "became a contented sage" *babhūvābhirato muniḥ*: Ck, Ct suggest that Asita practiced asceticism in order to acquire the power to defeat his enemies (Cg, that he remained "contented" lest they drive him from the mountain as well). It is unclear who "exiled" him; Cr says his father, Ct implies it was voluntary. One would suppose rather that the enemies did it, after defeating him. The story of Asita and the birth of Sagara appears in a (sometimes verbatim) interpolation in *Bālakāṇḍa* (1274*). See note on 1.69.24.

16. The childless wives of Sagara himself will similarly approach Śiva, according to the *MBh* (3.104.9ff.).

On the Bhṛgu clan and its relationship with the *Rām* (and *MBh*), see Goldman 1976 and 1977.

17. "the sage greeted her" *sa tām abhyavadad vipraḥ*: Perhaps a modest allusion to *niyojana* (a sort of levirate). Compare the remarks on Ṛśyaśṛṅga in the Introduction to *Bālakāṇḍa*.

18. "along with that very poison" *gareṇa saha tenaiva*: The "etymology" of the king's name: "[born] with (*sa*) poison (*gara*)."

19. "when it swells under the full moon" *parvaṇi vegena*: This agrees with Cm, Cg on the syntax of *parvaṇi* (cf. 38.11, 74.4 above). Ck, Cr, however, may be right to join with *iṣṭvā*, "while sacrificing on a full-moon day," considering the use of the word in 1.38.7 (cf. 3.36.4). For the story of Sagara cf. 1.37ff.

20. Asamañja: Cf. 32.15ff. and note above.

21. On these three figures, and the descent of the Ganges finally achieved by Bhagīratha, see *Bālakāṇḍa sarga* 41.

23. The story of Kalmāṣapāda, his association with Viśvāmitra, his demonic possession (by reason of a curse called down by Vasiṣṭha's son), his devouring of the one hundred sons of Vasiṣṭha, and so on, is narrated in *MBh* 1.166ff. It is odd that he should be reckoned the son of Raghu, since Saudāsa is clearly patronymic ("son of Sudāsa"; in *Rām* 7.57.10ff. the story is told of Mitrasaha son of Sudāsa [called Kalmāṣapāda in verse 34], who slays a demon and is cursed by its companion to "suffer a deformation," and so on). For a discussion of the different versions of the legend, see most recently Ensink 1968. See too Goldman 1978.

24. "and whoever came up against his might perished utterly" *yas tu tadvīryam āsādya . . . vyanīnaśat*: We take this line as a general statement of Śaṅkhaṇa's prowess (cf. the NW variant 2271*). There appears to be no version of the Kalmāṣapāda legend in which he devours his own son, as Cm, Cg suggest in their interpretation of the *pādas* (*yaḥ* = Śaṅkhaṇa, *tad* = Kalmāṣapāda), or in which Śaṅkhaṇa perishes possessed by a demon (Cr). Even less likely appears the interpretation of Ck, Ct, that "Śaṅkhaṇa met by chance with the well-known [*tad*] force [death? doom?] and so perished" (though cf. the NE variant, *daivena vidhinā . . . vyanaśat*, 2270*, "he perished . . . by fate's decree").

27. Nahuṣa: Normally reckoned a member of the lunar dynasty, and father of

Yayāti (cf. notes on 5.9 and 58.36), which is how NW manuscripts read here, dropping Nābhāga.

29. "show regard for the world" *avekṣasva jagat*: Several manuscripts as well as Cg, Ck offer what may well be the correct reading here, *avekṣya svajanam*, "showing regard for your own people," that is, for your family tradition.

Sarga 103

3. "The father begets the man" *pitā hy enaṃ janayati puruṣam*: " 'Father,' is meant to include 'mother' also," Cg.

Cg, Ck, Ct cite *ĀpaSm* [1.1.1.15ff.]: "[One should never offend one's teacher; (he is the best of gurus [not in *ĀpaSm*])] for he brings about a second birth for the pupil by imparting sacred learning to him. This second birth is the better one; the father and mother produce only the body."

5. "The 'men of the assembly' are the brahmans; the 'guildsmen,' the townsmen, that is, kshatriyas and *vaiśyas*," Cg.

"in practicing righteousness on their behalf" *eṣu . . . caran dharmam*: That is, by protecting them (Cm, Cg, Ct).

6. "Your mother" *mātuḥ*: Cg, Ct cite, "A mother is to be revered a hundred times more than a father" [cf. *MBh* 14, App. I, No. 4.2530].

"disobey" *avartitum*: Note the rare use of the negative *añ* with the infinitive (cf. *ajīvitum* in 6.38.33).

7. "when supplicating you . . . you will not go astray" *yācamānasya . . . ātmānaṃ nātivarteḥ*: We agree with Ck, Ct, Cr in construing *ātmānam* (as second person reflexive pronoun) with *yācamānasya*, and taking *ativarteḥ* absolutely. Varadacharya, despite Ck's strictures, suggests, " 'you will not stray from yourself,' that is, from your own limits of propriety," which is quite possible (1964-1965, vol. 2, p. 441n; so also Ctr, vol. 2, p. 684).

8. "gentle fashion" *evaṃ madhuram*: Varadacharya points out the possible significance of this: Vasiṣṭha does not actually order Rāma to abandon his purpose, so there is no fault in rejecting his advice (1964-1965, vol. 2, p. 441n).

9. Compare the very similar verse in *ManuSm* (2.227): "The pains a mother and father must suffer in raising a child to manhood can never be repaid, not in a hundred years." Cg comments: "The parents provide one with life, which is the foundation for the execution of all acts of righteousness [*dharma*], according to the maxim, 'Only when there is a subject [*dharmin*, a person to possess *dharma*] can righteous acts be contemplated.' . . . So a father's command takes precedence over a teacher's" (similarly Cm; both these commentators wrongly take *tanaye* as " '[what parents do] for the purpose of [bringing forth] a child,' that is, vows, fasts, and so on").

11. "he begot me" *janayitā . . . mama*: The clause is meant to exclude any possibility of Daśaratha's being an adoptive father (Cm, Cg, Ct).

"promise" *ājñātam*: Rightly glossed *pratijñātam* by Cg (cf. the NR variants *saṃśrutam, pratijñātam*).

"He promised his father first [that is, by promising Kaikeyī], and so cannot fulfil the (later) requests of his mother or brother," Cg.

12. "(So Rāma) spoke" *uktaḥ*: The locative is widely attested in place of the nominative, which, despite its occurrence in several N and S manuscripts, need not be original (it is the type of scribal error that could arise independently). As the crit. ed. stands, however, we must take *pāda* a as an independent sentence (with *vasiṣṭhaḥ* understood).

13. "I will fast against" *pratyupavekṣyāmi*: See the note on 18.23. Ck, Ct describe the procedure of the hunger strike: "Before the front door of the person one aims to coerce, one lies down upon some *kuśa*-grass and fasts, covering one's face and lying on one side without turning over on the other, until the goal is reached."

14. "a penniless brahman" *dhanahīnaḥ . . . dvijaḥ*: "The phrase refers to the creditor who has lent out [all his] money for interest and, to recoup it, obstructs the house of the debtor" (Cm, Ct; this is the most common reason for such a public hunger strike).

17. "a brahman" *brāhmaṇaḥ*: "That is, a creditor (who acts thus) to recoup his principal plus interest from the debtor," Cm.

"those whose heads are anointed" *mūrdhāvasiktānām*: Kshatriyas. The verse suggests to Ct that if a kshatriya does attempt this, expiation is required (cf. verse 23 below).

20. "what Rāghava is telling Kākutstha is correct" *kākutstham . . . samyag vadati rāghavaḥ*: The reply of the people is ambiguous (perhaps intentionally so), for both patronymics can apply equally well to Rāma and Bharata. But we agree with Ck, Ct, Cr, Cs in identifying Rāghava as Bharata, Kākutstha as Rāma; and so give an adversative sense to the particles in verse 21a.

21. "truly" *añjasā*: Or "(incapable of dissuading him) at all quickly" (such is its sense in 62.14 above, and 3.11.6).

23. "sip water" *spṛśa . . . udakam*: Rāma asks Bharata to do this in order to atone for the fasting, which is prohibited to kshatriyas (Cm, Cg), and thus of course to reestablish his purity (cf. 22.1 and note; 46.14). Cg, additionally, interprets "touch me" as "swear to me you will never do this again" (Ck, "in order to redeem yourself from the sin of fasting against me").

25. "But I do recognize" *abhijānāmi*: The second half of the verse may be conjunctive rather than adversative: "And I know that my brother is supremely righteous," that is, most worthy of becoming king (so Ctr, vol. 2, p. 689), but this seems less plausible.

29. "substitute" *upadhiḥ*: Apparently unique in this sense. Contrast the use of the word in 3.41.5, "guise," which suggests that the word here connotes dishonesty or deceit.

It is "repugnant" insofar as a substitute is required only for something one cannot do oneself, and Rāma is perfectly capable of living in the wilderness. If he were not to do so, his abilities would be impeached (so Cr, Ck, Ct).

31. "shall rejoin my . . . brother and become supreme lord" *bhrātrā saha bhaviṣyāmi . . . patir uttamaḥ*: Or, "with my brother I shall be." On this second interpretation, Rāma would be saying that he will share the kingship with Bharata. So the construction of Cr implies (the other commentators are silent). But Rāma will make no such offer later in the story, except insofar as he appoints him heir apparent when Lakṣmaṇa refuses the office (6.116.79).

32. "her bidding" *tadvacanam*: In accordance with the entire NR, which explicitly

refers *vacanam* to Kaikeyī (2292*, 2293*); thus Cm, Ct also explain. One might have otherwise assumed "his bidding," given Rāma's frequent references to Daśaratha's order in the previous *sargas*.

"saved" *mocayānena*: Present participle *ātmanepada* (so too Ck, Ct understand); Cm, Cg, Cr divide [*mocaya*] *anena*, " '(save father) by this,' that is, by your guarding the kingship" (Cg), "by your doing my bidding" (Cm).

Sarga 104

2. "hosts of seers . . . supreme seers" *ṛṣigaṇāḥ . . . paramarṣayaḥ*: " 'Hosts of seers' = royal seers . . . 'supreme seers' = divine seers, cf. verse 7," Cm, Cg.

3. "who know and follow the way of righteousness" *dharmajñau dharmavikramau*: We consider the two compounds to be complimentary (so too Cr, Cs, who gloss the latter, *dharmapravartakau*, "promoting [acts of] *dharma*"). Cf. *satyaparākramaḥ*, 19.7 and note, and 58.50, *dharmajñam . . . satyaparākramam* (note the bipartition here, "knowing and acting," as opposed to the tripartition in 19.7, and cf. also note on 1.20).

"How envious we are" *spṛhayāmahe*: That is, we envy him, the father (against the commentators, "We are eager [to hear it again]," Cm, Cg, Ct, Cr; "We are pleased [with them]," Ck, Ct).

4. This would appear to be the first reference to Rāvaṇa in the (original) *Rām*, and to have it made in so offhand a way, without any preparation, seems narratively and artistically improbable. However, there are no variants for the *pāda* (at least the crit. ed. reports none). The line, in fact much of the *sarga*, may be late. As pointed out in the General Introduction, it often happens that passages which contain a sectarian element and which therefore on the grounds of "higher criticism" must be late, are unexpectedly well attested in the manuscripts and unusually free of variants. The very unanimity of the witnesses seems at times to suggest interpolation. However, whether the present passage is to be included in that category remains unclear.

"tiger among kings" *rājaśārdūla*: Two good S manuscripts (G2, M1) read, "tiger of the Raghus," but unlike the identical case in the note on 28.16, no N support is recorded. Here, of course, the reading accepted by the crit. ed. can claim greater narrative propriety.

6. "forever keep his father free from debt" *sadānṛṇam . . . pituḥ*: We agree with Cr (so also Ck, Ct, though they implausibly understand, not *sadā*, but *sad*, "by means of his good actions"). Possible but less likely in view of verses 5 and 6cd, "to be free from debt to his father forever."

"If Rāma were not to keep his father free from debt, if he were to go back on his word or employ a substitute, Daśaratha would fall from heaven," Ck, Ct.

13. "restore its stability" *sthāpaya*: Ck, Ct understand, "accept the kingship and afterwards '*entrust it*' to my guardianship [Ct, "to someone's care"; Cr, "to the ministers, and so on"]. By your simply accepting it you are able to guard the people; all that is required to protect them is the general belief that the kingship is Rāma's." This interpretation conditions their understanding of the significance of verse 22 (see note there).

15. "dark" *śyāmam*: In traditional pictorial representation, Bharata, like Rāma himself (and unlike the twins, who are always fair), is generally shown to be of a swarthy complexion (so Rao, 1914-1916, vol. 1.i, p. 191 and plate 57, and Goldman 1980, p. 154 and n21). In some schools of painting, however, such as that of Malwa, this seems not invariably to be the case.

16. After this verse several N manuscripts add an irrelevant but interesting passage in which Rāma explains how the ways of a king should approximate Indra, the sun, the wind, Yama, Varuṇa, the moon, the earth: as the earth, for example, bears all creatures equally, so should a king support all his subjects; when a king gladdens his subjects, he is following the moon's vow, which when full gladdens the mind; just as a person is bound by Varuṇa's bonds, so a king, by following the vows of Varuṇa, restrains brigands, and so on (App. I, No. 29; cf. 3.38.12).

18. "my promise to my father" *pratijñām . . . pituḥ*: Less likely, "my father's promise," but cf. 101.17 and note.

Note the rhetorical figure here (see also 10.39). Though very common in Sanskrit literature, it does not appear to have a technical name in the *alaṃkāraśāstra* (= Greek *adynaton*).

19. "on your behalf" *tubhyam*: This agrees with Cr; Ck, Ct understand as dative or genitive, "your mother (did this)."

"treat her as what she is, your mother" *vartitavyam . . . mātṛvat*: "According to the shastric precept, 'One must ever obey one's mother, even were she to be an outcaste,' " Ck.

21. Much of the NR gives this statement to Vasiṣṭha (Cm, Cg, Ct say Bharata is speaking under orders of Vasiṣṭha; cf. 105.9-11), and has Rāma simply take off his own slippers and give them to Bharata (cf. note on 105.12). By contrast, and likewise in an NR insertion (App. I, No. 30, lines 35ff.), the slippers are brought by the pupils of the sage Śarabhaṅga (cf. *Araṇyakāṇḍa sarga* 4), and are made of *kuśa* grass. Bhavabhūti knew this tradition (cf. *MahāvīC* 4.53ff. [pp. 172-73], and Raghavan 1968, p. 597).

22. Ct (on verse 21), Ck, "By his stepping into the slippers, which will be placed on the throne and which are a substitute for himself, Rāma has been made to accept the kingship . . . and consigning the slippers to Bharata he charges him with guarding the kingship as his proxy. Thus Bharata's request in verse 13 [see note there] has been answered." Ct continues: "By his stepping into the slippers they have become invested with a special power, so that by the mere sight of them one acquires wisdom. Thus in the *Padmapurāṇa* [Bengali recension?] 'By coming to know their command, and by means of them, Bharata ruled the land.' That is to say, merely by beholding the slippers Bharata learned what Rāma's command would be on each and every matter, and so administered the kingdom" (see 107.22 below).

Cs notes, "Bharata must have brought these slippers with him, for it would have been inconsistent for Kaikeyī to have given Rāma golden slippers when she took his clothes away and gave him only hides" (cf. note on 105.12).

Hereafter the SR inserts 2304*, in which Bharata declares that he will wear matted hair and hides for fourteen years, subsist on roots and fruit, and live outside the city, during which time the powers of the kingship will be invested in the slippers. If after fourteen years to the very day Bharata does not see Rāma, he will commit suicide by self-immolation.

23. "he placed them atop a splendid elephant" *cakāra . . . uttamanāgamūrdhani*: "That is, one fit to bear a king. He wishes it to seem as if the newly consecrated king were being mounted thereon; his purpose here is to make a public proclamation of this," Ck, Ct.

Sarga 105

1. "upon his head" *śirasi*: For Bharata to put the slippers upon his own head (after taking them from the elephant's, so Cm, Cg; alternatively Ct, " 'having placed them upon the head,' of the elephant," but cf. 107.12), is an act of profound self-abasement. Compare the scornful idiomatic expression "to put one's foot on another's head" (*MBh* 2.36.3, 41.31; to strike a person with one's shoe is considered a great outrage in contemporary India). Ctś comments, "Bharata is now delighted to be wearing a head-crest consonant with his express wish—see 92.6. Previously he was terrified by [the prospect of his political] independence; now, having the slippers, he is 'delighted.' "

2. Vāmadeva: In his note on *BuddhaC* 9.9, and in his introduction (p. L), Johnston offers the curious argument that our *Rām* knows of no visit to Rāma paid by Vasiṣṭha and Vāmadeva, and that Aśvaghoṣa's reference to them in *BuddhaC* 9.9 implies that "the entire passage recounting Bharata's visit to Rāma was not in the text the poet [Aśvaghoṣa] knew, that it had in its place an account of a mission headed by Vasiṣṭha and Vāmadeva," while "in the process of gradual sentimentalising, to which the epic was subject for many generations, this passage was deliberately replaced by one which it was thought would do more honour to Bharata's character, leaving as its sole trace the *MBh's* mention [3.261.36] of the *purohita* and minister." Johnston seems to have missed *Rām* 2.102-103, and the present reference, and additionally to have forgotten the old *gāthā* in the *Dasaratha Jātaka* (verse 81), which presupposes Bharata's presence.

"and strictly observant Jābāli" *jābāliś ca dṛḍhavrataḥ*: By the epithet the poet perhaps means to corroborate Vasiṣṭha's remark in 102.1 (note that he is "the glorious Jābāli" in 61.2).

4. "observing the thousands" *paśyan . . . -sahasrāṇi*: This detail suggests that Bharata is not as hurried to return as he was to arrive (so in general Cg and Varadacharya [1964-1965, vol. 2, p. 455n]).

9. "deeply displeased" *param aprītaḥ*: As in 8.6, cf. note there. His displeasure (cf. 102.1) comes from the suggestion that he should break his promise.

10. Again, the promise is probably Rāma's to Daśaratha (via Kaikeyī), rather than Daśaratha's own promise to Kaikeyī (so Cm, Cg, Ct). The genitives in *pādas* a and d are therefore to be taken as objective (note the variant readings, especially of the D manuscripts). Cf. 101.17, 104.18, and notes.

11. "Vasiṣṭha replied" *vasiṣṭhaḥ pratyuvāca*: Cf. note on 104.21.

12. "By the fact that the slippers are called 'gold-trimmed' we gather that Bharata brought them from the city, having had them newly made to present to Rāma," Cg (cf. Cs on 104.22). The verse implies, however, that Rāma had them on, and was asked simply to take them off (cf. note on 104.21). Ñ2 reads, "touch these shoes and give them."

17. The same words are addressed by Rāma to Lakṣmaṇa on a much less significant occasion, the construction of the house at Pañcavaṭī (3.14.27).

22. After this verse some N manuscripts add, "He dismissed Guha saying, 'I am pleased with you' " (2310*). Cf. 92.15 note, 93.40 and note.

Sarga 106

2. Here commences a series of seventeen similes (technically, a *mālopamā*, or "garland of similes," according to the rhetorical textbooks), which takes up most of the *sarga*. Note that all the vehicles of the similes are feminine singular, identical to the tenor (Ayodhyā).

"elephants" *vāraṇa-*: Ck, Ct understand this word to mean "doors," which is difficult to construe intelligibly in the compound ("the doors of the men"?).

"dark as night" *kālīm . . . niśām iva*: So Ck, Ct; or, "like a night of the dark [fortnight] (when the moon is waning)," Cm, Cg.

3. Rohiṇī: Five stars in Taurus (according to Kirfel 1920, p. 36). The constellation is considered to be the wife of the moon as early as the *AV* (13.1.22).

4. "scant, hot" *alpoṣṇa-*: Taking the compound as a *dvandva* (so Cr); or, as a *karmadhāraya*, "tepid" (Ck, Ct).

5. Ck, Ct, Cr understand that the flame is put out when the oblation is poured onto it, but this seems unlikely in view of other passages where fire is said to flare up smokelessly after an oblation is poured on (cf. 6.67.8, *MBh* 1.219.32).

7. "raised" *bhūtvā*: Böhtlingk finds the form to be a problem, since a continuative must construe, in his view, either with the grammatical or the logical subject of the sentence (1887, p. 224). But cf. note on 41.11 above. (His conjecture *bhūtām* finds no manuscript support.)

9. "herd of cows" *gavāṃ paṅktim*: The crit. ed. reading, *gavāṃ patnīm* ("wife of cows"), makes no sense, unless *gavām* is to be explained as a highly irregular (in fact, unattested) accusative singular. Ct, whose reading this is, does nothing to explain it. We read *paṅktim* with the best S manuscripts and Ck (one might hypothesize that Ct emended in order to eliminate the apparent incongruity of the collective noun, all the other *upamānas* being true singulars). Cm's lection *pattim* (misread by Ct) is unrecorded as a synonym of *paṅkti-*, despite his explicit claim.

11. "like a star . . . when its merit is exhausted" *puṇyakṣayād . . . tārām iva*: Stars were thought to have reached their eminent place in heaven by virtue of their good *karma*, and this is exhausted in the course of time. Apparently this is the popular explanation of shooting stars. Cf. 3.50.30 and note, and 6.23.19.

13. "All the merchants were in a daze" *saṃmūḍhanigamām*: Thus Ck. Alternatively with Cm, Cg, " 'The merchants' quarters were stupefied,' that is, devoid of people."

"bazaars and shops" *vipaṇāpaṇa-*: See Schlingloff 1969, p. 8 n7 (contrast the sense of the compound in *MBh* 12.139.19 [cf. Belvalkar's note there]).

16. "fitted out with loops" *yuktapāśām*: *Paranipāta* for *pāśayuktām*. The loops are for taking the nocks of the stave (so explained by Cm, Ct, Cs).

17. "one that should still be running free" *utsṛṣṭām*: We understand the adjective quite pregnantly (cf. Cg, "that is, one that should not [yet] have to bear a load"), and hear a critical tone in the first half of the verse.

20ff. Bharata's questions are, narratively speaking, illogical. One wonders whether the passage may not be a later thematic variation on 65.16ff.

Sarga 107

2. Nandigrāma: A village located some two and a half miles east of Ayodhyā (cf. 6.113.26).

9. "in great joy" *paramaprītau*: Presumably joy at leaving Ayodhyā and its painful memories, and commencing his period of penance. Or (as in 8.6 and 105.9) *param aprītau*, "in deep misery" (cf. verse 19)?

"together with their counselors and family priest" *vṛtau mantripurohitaiḥ*: We are to understand that, like the army and the people at large (verse 11), the ministers unexpectedly decide to accompany Bharata and share in what looks like an expiation for the injury done to Rāma.

14. "it is these gold-trimmed slippers that will guarantee its welfare and security" *yogakṣemavahe ceme pāduke hemabhūṣite*: "Bharata wishes to show that, though given the kingship in trust, he will arrogate to himself no autonomy in ruling," Cm, Cg; "that even the guarding of the entrusted kingship is not dependent on himself but on the inconceivable power invested in the Blessed One's slippers," Ck, Ct.

Many N and S manuscripts insert here after *pāda* d: "Hold up the parasol at once [over the slippers]; these are to be considered the two feet of my noble brother. In these two slippers of my guru has the power of the kingship been invested. This is a trust committed to me by my brother, out of love" (2326*). The antecedent to *tam imam* in *pāda* e of verse 14 is *saṃnyāsa-* in b, contrary to classical usage.

15. "tying them on . . . with my own hands" *saṃyojayitvā . . . svayam*: As in fact he will later do, cf. 6.115.42.

22. The NR ends the *Ayodhyākāṇḍa* with this *sarga*; Vaidya adequately vindicates the book division of the SR followed by the crit. ed. (1962, p. xx). It is not until 1.1 of the *Araṇyakāṇḍa* that Rāma is actually said to enter "the wilderness" (*araṇya*) of Daṇḍaka.

Sarga 108

1. "after Bharata's departure" *pratiprayāte bharate*: Ck, "These events do indeed take place after Bharata's departure, but considerably later" (cf. Ct on verse 2).

"uneasiness" *autsukyam*: Cm, Cg, Ck, Ct understand, "the 'yearning' to go to another ashram"; Cr, "an 'eagerness' to tell him something."

2. We agree with Ck, Ct in seeing double *saṃdhi* in *tāpasāśrame*.

Ct remarks here, "It was on Puṣya day—on the tenth day of the bright fortnight of Caitra [early April]—that Rāma was sent to the forest; it was [six days later, cf. note on 51.4] on the full-moon night, at midnight, that Daśaratha died; a fortnight later that Bharata came to Ayodhyā, while a fortnight elapsed with the funeral service. Vaiśākha [mid-April to mid-May] had thus passed, and in Jyeṣṭha [mid-May to mid-June] Bharata proceeded to Citrakūṭa. Between the time of the monsoons and the end of Kārtika [mid-October to mid-November], Rāma continued to live on Citrakūṭa, and thereafter he noticed the ascetics' uneasiness, that is, not directly after Bharata's departure. So in the *Padmapurāṇa* . . ." (he then goes on to quote at length the section in the *Padmapurāṇa* recounting the incident of the crow [cf. note on 89.19], apparently to demonstrate that some time at least does elapse between Bharata's departure and that of the ascetics).

6. We take *iva* as = *eva* (cf. verse 8, so Ct ad loc.; Cm reads *iha*, not recorded in the crit. ed.).

8. The NR adds two verses hereafter, in which the seer denies any wrongdoing on the part of Rāma or Lakṣmaṇa (2339*).

10. "because of the *rākṣasas*" *rakṣobhyaḥ*: We follow Cm, Cg, Ck, Ct, Cr, who all construe *rakṣobhyaḥ* with *pādas* ab (on the one-word enjambment cf. note on 21.14).

14. "show themselves" *darśayanti*: Ck, Ct, Cr correctly interpret the verb as reflexive (with active for middle termination, cf. 51.11 and note; Cm, Cg, " 'show,' that is, danger").

21. "does some harm" *ayuktaṃ* . . . *pravartate*: "That is, in revenge for Rāma's 'crime' of serving as their protector for so long," Ck.

25. This verse is in the very rare meter *asaṃbādhā* (cf. *ChandaḥSū* 7.5), which runs M,T,N,S,G,G, with *yati* after the fifth syllable (- - - - - / ˘ ˘ ˘ ˘ ˘ ˘ ˘ ˘ - - ⏓). There is a nearly irremedial corruption in the first *pāda* (*anugamanād*); uncertain conjecture: *anugacchan sa* (cf. 2362*, *anugamya*). A similar problem is in the second (what Vaidya's *tasmāc cid* is supposed to mean, or what manuscript it is based on, is unclear; all commentators drop the *cit* and, to avoid the submetric, read *abhivādya ṛṣim*, but this results in *yatibhaṅgadoṣa*, and wrecks the cadence); conjecture: *kasmāc cit*.

26. The meter of this verse appears to be corrupt (Cg alone notices this, remarking that the meters of both this and the previous verse are "questionable"), and not surprisingly requires some twisting to render it at all intelligible; the causal relationship between the two half-verses, however, if it is causal, remains obscure.

Sarga 109

1ff. In the *MBh* (3.261.39) Rāma is said to leave Citrakūṭa because he feared the townsmen might return (in *RaghuVa* 12.24 he is worried that Bharata might return, since Citrakūṭa is relatively near Ayodhyā-Nandigrāma). Recall that Kaikeyī had expressly demanded that Rāma live in Daṇḍaka forest (cf. 16.25), which he is said to enter only in *Araṇyakāṇḍa sarga* 1. In any case, the poet here wants to make it clear that Rāma is leaving for reasons other than fear.

2. "in their . . . grief" *anuśocataḥ*: Taking the participle as accusative plural (so Ct). It might equally well be genitive singular, "(the memory of me) grieving (for them)" (Cr), though the assertion that the source of Rāma's painful memory is their grief for him seems more to the point.

5. Atri: One of the legendary seven seers, son of Brahmā, father of Durvāsas.

9-10. "ten" *daśa*: Evidently the figure has some numerological significance in the Anasūyā legend.

"caused the Jāhnavī to flow" *jāhnavī* . . . *pravartitā*: Kālidāsa alludes to the story in *RaghuVa* 13.51.

11. "obstacles" *pratyūhāḥ*: "To the ascetics' austerities," Ck, Ct. Similarly the roots and fruit were created to feed the seers, and the Jāhnavī (Ganges) provided to allow them to bathe (so Ck, Ct, Cr).

12. "reduced ten nights to one" *daśarātram kṛtā rātriḥ*: Literally, "a period of ten nights was turned into one" (the verbal is attracted into the gender of the predicate). NE manuscripts seek somewhat greater intelligibility by reading *daśarātrī*.

The incident related here seems not to be recorded elsewhere in epic literature. Cg claims one may find it in the *purāṇas*, but we have not (*MārkP* 16.14ff. is similar, but differs in certain essentials). Ck reports: "[The sage] Māṇḍavya cursed a woman named Nālinī, that on the following day she would be widowed [the VSP of Cm, Cg (p. 1,310 note) gives, "at dawn on one of the next ten days"]. She countered with the curse that there would be no tomorrow, and as a result of the curse, night was indeed not followed by dawn. The gods [distressed by the interruption of the morning offerings to them] besought Nālinī's friend Anasūyā, who reduced the period of ten nights to one, and so obviated her friend's being widowed."

13. "ever amiable" *akrodhanām*: Literally, "never irascible." The word *anasūyā* itself means "never complaining or grumbling" (cf. also note on verse 16; there Cg suggests an alternative analysis of the name, " 'One against whom no complaints can be made,' because of her inimitable grandeur").

16. "Her name is Anasūyā, and her deeds have won her renown" *anasūyeti yā . . . karmabhiḥ khyātim āgatā*: More literally, "Through her deeds she has won renown . . . as [an] Anasūyā," Ck, Ct (similarly Cg) here remarking on the propriety of the name.

21. "when she saw how . . . Sītā was following the way of righteousness" *sītāṃ . . . dṛṣṭvā tāṃ dharmacāriṇīm*: This does not refer to Sītā's humble salutation (that would be expected), but to her clothing and general mien, which would indicate that she is adopting her husband's vow to live as an ascetic.

23. "good or evil" *pāpo vā yadi vā śubhaḥ*: That is, not *vā aśubhaḥ*. Given the contrast in the first *pādas*, it seems that a comparable opposition is wanted in the second (as Ct, Cr, accepting *śubhaḥ . . . vāśubhaḥ*). The reading of the crit. ed. is virtually tautologous, and the three negative traits in the next verse do not mitigate this. (The NR offers *śuciḥ* [again, not *aśuciḥ*, as per the crit. ed.], "[whether evil or] honest," which is also the lection in the *Hitopa* [cf. Sternbach 1966, p. 246].)

24. "indigent" *dhanair . . . parivarjitaḥ*: Note the parallel verse in *ManuSm* (5.154) where *guṇaiḥ* is read for *dhanaiḥ* (but cf. 34.21 above, which serves to authenticate the crit. ed. reading here).

25. "ascetic power . . . once acquired" *tapaḥ kṛtam*: Ck, Ct take these two items as a compound, "the performance of asceticism"; so Cr, "the effect, the reward of asceticism."

Sarga 110

1. "ungrudgingly" *anasūyā*.

7. For Kausalyā's instructions, cf. 34.19ff.

10. Sāvitrī: Cf. note on 27.6.

"Arundhatī, too, went up" *tathaivārundhatī yātā*: We reject the reading of the SR adopted by the crit. ed. in *pāda* c, *tathāvṛttiś ca yātā tvam*, "So you have behaved, and you too shall go to heaven." First, *yātā* would be very hard here. The sense of immediate futurity of the past participle is not of course impossible (cf. note on 3.5

above; so here Cm, Cg, Cs, and Varadacharya 1964-1965, vol. 2, p. 489n), but it is highly unlikely; even more unlikely is Ck's, " 'you have gone to heaven,' that is, in another form, and are present on earth now only for the sake of asceticism." In the second place, verse 12 requires another example of wifely devotion from out of the past. The NE and NW reading seems correct, *tathaivārundhatī yātā*. Arundhatī, the wife of Vasiṣṭha, is praised again in 3.12.7 (cf. 6.99.15). Like Rohiṇī in the next verse, Arundhatī is also considered to be a star (in the constellation Ursus major), and the phrase *yātā . . . divam*, "went up to the heavens" (as in verse 11), would be apposite in reference to her. The SR might have revised under the impression that some compliment to Anasūyā was in order here.

11. Rohiṇī: Cf. 106.3 and note.

17. "a cream . . . a precious salve" *aṅgarāgaṃ . . . mahārham anulepanam*: We follow Cm (first interpretation), Ck, Ct, in taking *anulepanam* in apposition to *aṅgarāgam*. Cg, Cr wish to distinguish the two, the first as saffron, sandalwood and other creams, the second as ointments perfumed with camphor, aloe, musk, and so on.

In reference to this episode, Jacobi (1893, p. 137) mentions the *stāgara alaṃkāra* (read *sthāgara*, a cosmetic powder made of the fragrant *sthagara* [plant?], so Sāyaṇa ad loc.) on the *TaiBr* (2.3.10), whereby one Sītā is able to win the love of King Soma ("the moon"; this, he claims, is perhaps partly responsible for the identification of Rāma with the moon); an interesting story but probably irrelevant to the *Rām* (but cf. also note on 29.13 on Vālmīki's familiarity with the Taittirīya corpus of vedic scripture).

Whether or not it is these flowers and ornaments that will later play a role in the search for Sītā (cf. 3.60.15ff., 4.6.13ff.) is unclear. Anasūyā's gift will not be explicitly mentioned again (except as noted on 3.50.15).

19. Note the reference to Viṣṇu, one of the few in Book Two.

20. "gift of love" *prītidānam*: "This implies that Sītā could accept it, though kshatriyas are normally prohibited from receiving any gifts," Ct, Cr (cf., for example, 81.15-16 above), but this seems hypercritical.

23. "self-choice rite" *svayaṃvare*: This is the literal translation of the term, though as the reader of *Bālakāṇḍa* will recall, the husband in this instance was not selected by the girl, but won her by a feat of strength (the *vīryaśulka*); see 1.65.15ff.

26ff. Although it would not be easy to demonstrate precisely how, Vālmīki does seem to invest Sītā's narrative with a wonderful simplicity and artlessness. Anasūyā in the next chapter will specifically remark on the "sweetness" of Sītā's storytelling.

26. After this verse the NR inserts twelve lines, which relate how Janaka once saw the *apsaras* Menakā flying through the sky, and expressed the wish to have a child born of her. A nonhuman voice from the sky tells him he shall one day acquire a daughter equal in beauty to the nymph (2385*).

27. "he was tilling the circle of fields" *karṣataḥ kṣetramaṇḍalam*: Cg understands the king's plowing as a purification of the sacrificial field (cf. 1.65.14) where a fire-altar is to be constructed (he cites *śruti*, the chapter on plowing the sacrificial ground [*TaiS* 5.2.5.2]; so Cm, Ck, Ct, Cr). Perhaps the ceremony is instead the ritual first plowing and sowing that a king is required to perform, as is familiar to us from the Buddhist tradition, where it is called *vappamaṅgalam* (cf. *Nidānakathā*, in *Jātakas* vol. 1, p. 57).

28. "sowing grain by the fistful" *muṣṭivikṣepa-*: Cm, Cg, implausibly cite *śruti* to

substantiate their view that the king is "strewing plants about" [?], whereas Ck believes he is casting about clay to level the land.

30. For the second line of the verse the NR offers, "This human child is yours, born of Menakā" (cf. note on verse 26), and adds, "Since she broke the earth and arose like a furrow [Sanskrit, *sītā*], she shall be called Sītā" (2389*). It is interesting to note that the word *sītā* occurs in the earliest work on statecraft in the sense of "crown lands" (*ArthŚā* 2.6.3; cf. Scharfe 1968, pp. 277ff., especially p. 281), and that Rāma's recovery of her will often be likened to the reacquisition of land (3.59.22, 5.14.23). See also 2.39.12.

31. "had obtained vast wealth" *avāpto vipulām ṛddhim*: Ct appears to take this literally, "after he obtained me he became very wealthy."

32. "favorite queen" *iṣṭavaddevī*: This agrees with Ck, Cr; alternatively, "the queen who wanted [me?]" (Cg), or, " 'who wanted' continuation of the line" (Ct).

33. "right age for" *-sulabham*: So Cm, Ck, Ct; Cr, "[an age at which] marriage would easily be arranged" (Cg, "[an age] able to be borne (?) only if one is married"). This of course does not prove that Sītā had reached puberty (on her age see note on 17.26).

"like a man impoverished by the loss of his wealth" *vittanāśād ivādhanaḥ*: The simile is probably not meant to refer us back to verse 31 in particular, but in general ahead to verses 34 and 36.

34. Compare *ManuSm* 9.4: "It is considered reprehensible when a girl is marriageable but not married, and the father of the girl is held responsible."

38. Several N manuscripts substitute: "When my father held a sacrifice long ago he was given a bow and inexhaustible quivers by great Śaṅkara [= Śiva] as a pledge" (2392*). In the *Bālakāṇḍa* version adopted by the crit. ed. (1.65.8ff.), the bow belongs to Rudra (Śiva), left as a pledge with Janaka's ancestors (Cm, Ck thus, "given by Varuṇa, that is, who was sent by the gods," Ck citing 1.30.8; such too is Cg's intention; cf. also 1.74.12, 20, and note on 2.28.12-13).

40. "put . . . on display" *sthāpya*: Reading with the NR for the crit. ed.'s vapid *prāpya* ("had gotten [the bow]").

43. "a sacrifice" *yajñam*: The reference may be to Janaka's sacrifice, mentioned in the *Bālakāṇḍa* (cf., for example, 1.30.6), or the *dhanurmaha*, the festival of the displaying of the bow; or finally, the "self-choice" rite itself, which is still in effect (cf. verse 52).

44. "and . . . Viśvāmitra" *viśvāmitras tu*: *Tu* has conjunctive force (the participle agreeing in number, as often, with the closest referent).

48. "raised up a splendid water vessel" *udyamya jalabhājanam uttamam*: To sprinkle the heads of the bride and groom, as part of the wedding ceremony (cf. above 26.16 and note).

51. Note that, with one unimportant exception, there is full manuscript support for this verse narrating the marriage of Lakṣmaṇa (cf. notes on 3.17.3 and 35.5 above), but none for the marriages of Bharata and Śatrughna (cf. 1.72.19-20). However, that Bharata was considered to be married by the poet of the *Ayodhyākāṇḍa* is clear from various references (cf. 8.5, 47.11, etc.).

52. "as is right" *dharmeṇa*: Most of the NR reads less frigidly, "with all my heart" (*bhāvena*).

Sarga 111

5. "carrying their waterpots" *kalaśodyatāḥ*: The crit. ed. prints the improbable *phalaśodhanāḥ*, "who have cleaned their fruits" (a suggestion of *karmaphala* is quite out of place here). All the commentators (whom we follow here) and the NR support *kalaśa-* ["waterpot"], with either "upraised" or "in hand" as second element—and this is also sensible (cf. also 3.15.3).

7. Even those trees with little foliage seem to have grown thick, because the space between their leaves has been obscured by the darkness. The reason for this is implied by the final clause (so Cm, Cg); Cr takes the final clause as the effect, "and so the horizons cannot be seen." Nevertheless, the verse is unclear and disappointing, particularly *pāda* c. Reading *nikṛṣṭe* [*hy api*], "even in the nearby areas," would improve matters somewhat, but there is no manuscript support for this.

9. Ct would like the verse to imply that it is now the occasion of the first day of the lunar fortnight after Kārtika (that is, early November); cf. his remarks noted on 108.2.

19. The sages point out the *one* safe path by which Rāma can travel through the forest (so Cr, and *pace* Vaidya 1962, p. 704); the copulative force of *tu* is not infrequent (cf. 110.44).

Glossary of Important Proper Nouns and Epithets

Aikṣvāka: "descendant of Ikṣvāku," patronymic used mainly of Daśaratha and Rāma
Anasūyā: wife of the sage Atri, famous for her devotion and chastity
apsarases: celestial maidens or nymphs, known for their beauty
asuras: class of demons, the brothers of the gods
Aśvapati: father of Kaikeyī and maternal grandfather of Bharata
Aśvins: twin deities of the vedic pantheon renowned for their beauty
Ayodhyā: capital city of the Ikṣvākus
Bhāgīrathī: epithet of the Ganges
Bharadvāja: sage who renders hospitality to Rāma and to Bharata
Bharata: Daśaratha's second son, by Kaikeyī
Brahmā: creator divinity of the Hindu "trinity," regarded as the "Grandfather" of all living creatures
Bṛhaspati: family-priest of Indra
Citrakūṭa: mountain where Rāma, Sītā, and Lakṣmaṇa live during their exile
dānavas: class of demons descended from Danu
Daṇḍaka: forest where Rāma, Sītā, and Lakṣmaṇa spent the greater part of their exile
Daśaratha: Rāma's father and king of Ayodhyā
Dāśarathi: "descendant of Daśaratha," patronymic used of Daśaratha's four sons, especially Rāma
gandharvas: class of semi-divine beings known for their musical abilities; *gandharva* women are noted for their beauty
Ganges: a famous and holy river
Guha: king of the Niṣādas and lord of Śṛṅgaverapura; he was an ally of Rāma, and assisted him during his exile
Ikṣvāku: family name of the royal house of Ayodhyā
Indra: king of the gods
Jābāli: a minister of King Daśaratha
Jāhnavī: epithet of the Ganges
Janaka: king of Mithilā and father of Sītā
Jānakī: "daughter of Janaka," patronymic used of Sītā
Kaikeyī: younger wife of Daśaratha and mother of Bharata
Kailāsa: mountain peak in the Himalayas
Kākutstha: "descendant of Kakutstha," patronymic used of princes of the Ikṣvāku dynasty, especially Rāma and his brothers
Kālindī: epithet of the Yamunā
Kaśyapa: son of Marīci and father of gods and demons
Kausalyā: senior wife of Daśaratha and mother of Rāma

Kekaya: name of the father of Kaikeyī, and of the country of her birth in northwest India
Khara: a brother of Rāvaṇa
kiṃnaras: mythical creatures with the head of a horse and a human body; *kiṃnara* women are famed for their beauty
Kosala: kingdom of the Ikṣvākus
Kubera: god of wealth, son of Viśravas and half-brother of Rāvaṇa
Lakṣmaṇa: son of Daśaratha and Sumitrā, and Rāma's constant companion
Maithilī: woman of Mithilā, epithet of Sītā
Mandākinī: river flowing near Mount Citrakūṭa in Rāma's place of exile
Mantharā: hunchbacked slave-woman of Kaikeyī
Manu: traditionally considered the father of the human race; the legendary founder of the Ikṣvāku dynasty
Maruts: companions of Indra
Mithilā: Janaka's capital city
Nandigrāma: village where Bharata lived during Rāma's exile
Nārāyaṇa: epithet of Viṣṇu
Niṣādas: forest-dwelling hunters and fishermen, ruled by Guha
Prajāpati: "lord of creatures," epithet of Brahmā
Rāghava: "descendant of Raghu," patronymic used especially of Rāma and his brothers
Raghu: son of Kakutstha and ancestor of Rāma; also used like "Rāghava"
Rājagṛha: capital city of the Kekayas
rākṣasa: class of violent and bloodthirsty demons, ruled by Rāvaṇa
Rāma: eldest son of Daśaratha and Kausalyā, and hero of the *Rāmāyaṇa*
Rāvaṇa: main antagonist of the *Rāmāyaṇa*, the ten-headed overlord of the *rākṣasas*
Śaci's lord: epithet of Indra, Śaci being Indra's wife
Sagara: an Ikṣvāku king, ancestor of Rāma
Śakra: epithet of Indra
Sarayū: river flowing on the outskirts of Ayodhyā
Śatrughna: son of Daśaratha and Sumitrā, and Bharata's constant companion
Saumitri: "son of Sumitrā," metronymic used of Lakṣmaṇa
Sītā: daughter of Janaka, wife of Rāma, and heroine of the *Rāmāyaṇa*
Śrī: goddess of royalty and consort of Viṣṇu
Śṛṅgaverapura: town on the Ganges, ruled by the Niṣāda king, Guha
Sumantra: charioteer and adviser to King Daśaratha
Sumitrā: youngest wife of Daśaratha and mother of Lakṣmaṇa and Śatrughna
Suparṇa: epithet of Garuḍa, Viṣṇu's mount
Tamasā: river near the Ganges
Vaidehī: "woman of Videha," epithet of Sītā
Vaiśravaṇa: "son of Viśravas," patronymic used of Kubera
Vaivasvata: "son of Vivasvān," patronymic used of Yama
Vāmadeva: a minister of King Daśaratha
Varuṇa: lord of the ocean
Vāsava: epithet of Indra
Vasiṣṭha: Daśaratha's family preceptor
Videha: country of Sītā's birth

Viṣṇu: one of the three main gods of the Hindu "trinity," along with Brahmā and Śiva

Yama: god of death

Yamunā: a famous and holy river

Yudhājit: son of the king of the Kekayas, brother of Kaikeyī and maternal uncle of Bharata

Emendations and Corrections of the Critical Edition

Below are listed the emendations and corrections of the critical text that have been adopted by the translator. For specific discussions the reader may consult the notes to the translation. Question marks identify conjectures.

	READING OF THE CRITICAL EDITION	*TRANSLATOR'S READING*
1.20	pragrahānugrahayoḥ	pragrahanigrahayoḥ (?)
6.10	cakre śobhāṃ purāṃ punaḥ	cakre śobhayituṃ purīm
6.15	rāmābhiṣeka-	rāmābhiṣṭava-
6.16	rāmābhiṣeka-	rāmābhiṣṭava-
8.1	abhyasūyya	abhyasūya
9.31	śāntam	śātam
11.3	katthase	katthyase
11.12	sādhuvṛttasya	sādhu vṛddhasya
12.6	samaye	samayam
12.22	rāmo 'bhiṣekārtham ihāyāsyati	rāmabhiṣekārtham ihāyasyati
13.16	saṃpratibuddhasya	saṃprati buddhasya
14.14	madirekṣaṇā	madirekṣaṇe
16.24	*sa nideśe	saṃnideśe
16.57	avicālayan	avicārayan
17.33	kiṃnarī	saurabhī
19.9	punaḥ	purāt
19.19	kaścit	kaś ca
19.20	yasya	yac ca
20.5	mahān ayam	mahānayaḥ (?)
21.11	uvāca suprītā	uvācāsuprītā (?)
22.1	śuci	śuciḥ
22.5	mahāvanāni carataḥ	mahāvane vicarataḥ
23.21	sa samayo	sasamayo
23.30	*lakṣmaṇaśatrughnau	bharataśatrughnau
24.17	saṃmatā	saṃyatā
27.10	api	iva
28.16	rājaśārdūlaḥ	raghuśārdūlaḥ
29.12	agastyam	āgastyam
30.10	daśarathaḥ	daśaratham (?)
30.22	abhijanam	api janam
31.25		add: 816*
32.10	viṣaṇṇā, gatajanam	vivarṇā, gatadhanam
34.14	deśakālajño, śuci	deśakālajñam, śucim
37.10	samudhvastam	samuddhvastam
40.28	uddhatavegibhiḥ	uddhataveginaḥ

43.14	nātyartham	atyartham
45.10	sukha-	guha
46.5	gaṅgām	gaṅgā
46.32	tadā	tathā
53.3	guhena sārdhaṃ tatraiva sthito 'smi divasān bahūn	guhena saha kṛtsnaṃ ca tatraiva divasaṃ sthitaḥ
53.10	vyaktam	'vyaktam
58.48	ālabheta	ālapeta
58.51	cāru-	cāru
60.2	vividham	dvividham (?)
63.4	śāntim	gānti
63.15	bhayāvahām	bhayāvaham
68.2	mā mṛtam	mām ṛte (?)
71.5	śabda-	bāṣpa-
71.22	arhati	arhasi
74.17	tatrendrakīlapratimāḥ	yantrendrakīlaparighāḥ
76.1	bharataḥ	bharata-
77.19	anugatām	anutthitām
78.8	yadā tuṣṭas	yadāduṣṭas
81.22	kevalam	kevalām
85.16	vāso bhūṣaṇa-	vāsobhūṣaṇa-
85.50	utsādya	ucchādya
85.72	avagāhya sutīrthāṃś ca	avagāhyasutīrthāṃś ca
86.12	citrakūṭaś ca parvataḥ	citrakūṭaṃ ca parvatam
89.18	ramyām	paśyan
90.25	mahāvane	mahāhave
93.23	-sravaṇām	-pravaṇām
94.23	bhṛtya-	bhṛtyam
94.43	rājaputraḥ	rājaputra
95.47	guhāgirīṇām	guhā girīṇām
98.54	abhi*pattat	abhipattā
101.22	svargastham	satyastham (?)
106.9	patnīm	paṅktīm
108.25	anugamanāt . . . tasmāc cid	anugacchan sa . . . kasmāc cid (?)
109.23	vāśubhaḥ	vā śubhaḥ
110.10	tathāvṛttiś ca yātā tvam	tathaivārundhatī yātā
110.40	prāpya	sthāpya
111.5	phalaśodhanāḥ	kalaśodyatāḥ

Bibliography of Works Consulted

TEXTS OF THE *VĀLMĪKI RĀMĀYAṆA*

Ramayana. (1928-1947). 7 vols. Lahore: D.A.V. College. Northwestern recension critically edited for the first time from original manuscripts by Vishva Bandhu. D.A.V. College Sanskrit Series, nos. 7, 12, 14, 17-20.

Ramayana id es carmen epicum de Ramae rebus gestis poetae antiquissimi Valmicis opus. (1829-1838). 3 vols. Bonn: Typis regiis. Edited and translated by August Wilhelm von Schlegel. Volumes numbered 1.1, 1.2 (text); 2.1 (translation).

Rāmāyan of Vālmīki. (1914-1920). 7 vols. Bombay: Gujarati Printing Press. With three commentaries called Tilaka, Shiromani, and Bhooshana.

The Rāmāyaṇa of Vālmīki. (1909). 3rd ed. Bombay: Nirṇayasāgar Press. With the commentary (Tilaka) of Rāma. Edited by Vāsudev Lakshman Shāstrī Paṇśīkar.

Śrīmadvālmīkirāmāyaṇam. (1911-1913). 7 vols. Bombay: Nirṇayasāgar Press. Also called the Kumbakonam Edition. Edited by T. R. Krishnacharya and T. R. Vyasacharya.

Śrīmadvālmīkirāmāyaṇam. (1935). 3 vols. Bombay: Lakṣmīveṅkateśvara Mudraṇālaya. Edited by Gaṅgāviṣṇu Śrīkṛṣṇadāsa. With the commentaries of Govindarāja, Rāmānuja, and Maheśvavatīrtha and the commentary known as Taṇiślokī.

Śrīmadvālmīkirāmāyaṇam. (1958). Mylapore, Madras: n.p. Second edition revised by K. Chinnaswami Sastrigal and V. H. Subrahmanya Sastri.

Śrīmadvālmīkirāmāyaṇam. (1960-). Mysore: University of Mysore, Oriental Research Institute. With Amṛtakataka of Mādhavayogi. Edited by K. S. Varadacharya et al.

Vālmīki-Rāmāyaṇa. (1933) Calcutta: Metropolitan Printing and Publishing House. Volume 2, *Ayodhyākāṇḍa.* Edited by Amareshwar Thakur. Calcutta Sanskrit Series, no. 2.

The Vālmīki Rāmāyaṇa: Critical Edition. (1960-1975). 7 vols. Baroda: Oriental Institute. General editors: G. H. Bhatt and U. P. Shah.

SANSKRIT TEXTS

Commentators are specified only when cited in the notes.

The Abhijñāna-Śākuntala of Kālidāsa. (1891). 3rd rev. ed. Bombay: Nirṇayasāgar Press. Edited by Nārāyaṇa Bālakṛishṇa Godabole and Kāshīnāth Pāṇḍurang Parab.

Adhyātmarāmāyaṇa. (1935). 2 vols. Calcutta: Metropolitan Printing and Publishing House. Edited by Nagendranāth Siddhāntaratna. Calcutta Sanskrit Series, no. 11.

Agnipurāṇam. (1966). Varanasi: Chowkhamba Sanskrit Series Office. Edited by Āchārya Baladeva Upādhyāya.

Aitareya Āraṇyaka. (1909). Oxford: Clarendon Press. Edited by Arthur Berriedale Keith. Anecdota Oxoniensia, Aryan Series, vol. 1, part 9. Reprint 1969.

Aitareya Brāhmaṇa. (1911). Bombay: Nirṇayasāgar Press. Edited by Vāsudevaśarma Paṇśikar and Kṛṣṇaṃbhatta Gore.

The Amarakośa. (1940). 11th ed. Bombay: Nirṇayasāgar Press. Edited by W. L. Śāstrī Paṇśikar.

Āpastambasmṛti. (1905). Poona: Ānandāśrama Press. Ānandāśrama Sanskrit Series, no. 48.

Āpastambaśrautasūtram. (1945). 2 vols. Mysore: University of Mysore. Edited by S. Narasiṃhācār. Mysore University Oriental Library Publications, Sanskrit Series, nos. 87, 93.

Āśvalāyanagṛhyasūtram. (1938). Poona: Ānandāśrama Press. Ānandāśrama Sanskrit Series, no. 105. Reprint 1978.

Atharvaveda (Śaunaka), with the Commentary of Sāyaṇācārya. (1960-1964). 4 vols. Hoshiarpur: Vishveshvaranand Vedic Research Institute. Edited by Vishva Bandhu et al. Vishveshvaranand Indological Series, no. 13.

Baudhāyanagṛhyasūtra. (1920). Mysore: University of Mysore. Edited by R. Shama Shastri.

Baudhāyanapitṛmedhasūtra. In *Baudhāyanagṛhyasūtra, q.v.*

The Bhagavad-Gītā. (1935). Bombay: Gujarati Printing Press. With eleven commentaries. Edited by Shastri Gajānana Shambhu Sadhale.

Bhāgavatapurāṇam. (saṃvat 1965 [=A.D. 1908]). Bombay: Veṅkateśvara Press.

Bhāradvājapitṛmedhasūtra. In *Bhāradvājaśrautasūtra, q.v.*

Bhāradvājaśrautasūtra. (1964). Poona: Vaidika Saṃśodhana Maṇḍala. Edited by C. G. Kashikar.

Bhāruci's Commentary on the Manusmṛti (The Manu-śāstra-vivaraṇa, Books 6-12). (1975). 2 vols. Volume 1, the text. Wiesbaden: Franz Steiner Verlag. Edited by J. Duncan M. Derrett.

Brahmapurāṇam. (1895). Poona: Ānandāśrama Press. Ānandāśrama Sanskrit Series, no. 28.

The Brahma Sūtra-Shānkarabhāshyam. (1934). Bombay: Nirṇayasāgar Press. Edited by Mahādeva Śāstrī Bakre. 3rd ed., revised by Wāsudev Laxmaṇ Śāstrī Paṇśīkar.

Bṛhadāraṇyakopaniṣat. (1891). Poona: Ānandāśrama Press. Edited by Kāśīnāth Śāstrī Āgāśe. Ānandāśrama Sanskrit Series, no. 15. Reprint 1939.

Bṛhad-dharma-purāṇam. (1888-1897). Calcutta: Asiatic Society of Bengal. Edited by Haraprasād Śāstrī. Bibliotheca Indica, no. 120. Reprint Varanasi: Chaukhamba Amarabharati Prakashan, 1974.

The Buddhacarita or Acts of the Buddha. (1936). Lahore: Motilal Banarsidass. Edited by E. H. Johnston. Reprint Delhi, 1972.

Das Çāñkhāyanagṛihyam. (1878). Leipzig: F. A. Brockhaus. Edited by Hermann Oldenberg. Indische Studien, no. 15. Reprint Hildesheim: Olms, 1973.

The Çatapatha-Brāhmaṇa in the Mādhyandina-Çākhā. (1855). Berlin: Ferd. Dümmler's Verlagsbuchhandlung. Edited by Albrecht Weber. Reprint Varanasi: Chowkhamba Sanskrit Series Office, 1964.

The Champū-Rāmāyaṇa of King Bhoja (1-5 Kāṇḍas) and Lakshmaṇa Sūri (6th Kāṇḍa), with the Commentary of Rāmachandra Budhendra. (1917). 5th ed. Bombay: Nirṇayasāgar Press. Edited by Wāsudev Laxmaṇ Śāstrī Paṇśīkar.

The Chandaḥśāstram of Piṅgalanāga. (1938). Bombay: Nirṇayasāgar Press. Edited by Paṇḍit Kedāranāth. 3rd ed., revised by Anant Yajneśvar Śāstrī Dhupkar. Kāvyamālā, no. 91.

The Çrautasūtra of Kātyāyana. (1859). Berlin: Ferd. Dümmler's Verlagsbuchhandlung. Edited by Albrecht Weber.

Dharmākūtam, vol. II: *Ayodhyākāṇḍa*, by Tryambakarāya Makhi. (1924-1926). 2 parts. Srirangam: Sri Vani Vilas Press.

Dharmaśāstrasaṃgraha. (1876). Calcutta: Sarasvatī Press. Edited by Jivānanda Vidyāsāgara.

Dhātupāṭha. In *Pāṇini's Grammatik, q.v.*

The Dīghanikāya. (1958). 3 vols. N.p. Pali Publication Board (Bihar Government). Nālandā-Devanāgarī-Pāli Series. General editor Bhikkhu J. Kashyap.

Gadyatraya, with the Commentary of Vedānta Deśika. (1910). Srirangam: Sri Vani Vilas Press. Edited by R. Krishnamācāriar.

Gautamapraṇītadharmasūtrāṇi. (1910). Poona: Ānandāśrama Press. Edited by Naraharaśāstrī Talekar. Ānandāśrama Sanskrit Series, no. 61. Reprint 1966.

Gobhilasmṛti. (1905). Poona: Ānandāśrama Press. Ānandāśrama Sanskrit Series, no. 48.

Inscriptions of Aśoka. (1925). Oxford: Clarendon Press. Edited by E. Hultzsch. Corpus Inscriptionum Indicarum I, new edition. Reprint Delhi, Varanasi: Indological Book House, 1969.

The Institutes of Nārada. (1885). Calcutta: Asiatic Society of Bengal. Edited by Julius Jolly. Bibliotheca Indica, no. 102.

Jāska's Nirukta. (1848-1849). Göttingen: Verlag der Dieterichschen Buchhandlung. Edited by Rudolph Roth.

The Jātakas. (1877-1897). 7 vols. London: Trübner and Co. Edited by V. Fausbøll. Reprint 1962-1965.

Kalidasa's Śakuntala. (1922). 2nd ed. Cambridge: Harvard University Press. Edited by Richard Pischel.

Kāmandakīyanītisāra, with the Jayamaṅgalā and Upādhyāyanirapekṣā Commentaries. (1964, 1977). 2 vols. Poona: Ānandāśrama Press. Ānandāśrama Sanskrit Series, no. 136.

The Kāmasūtram of Vātsyāyana Muni. (1964). Varanasi: Chowkhamba Sanskrit Series Office. Edited by Devduṭṭa Śāstrī. Kashi Sanskrit Series, no. 29.

Kāśikā of Vāmana and Jayāditya. (1969). 4th ed. Varanasi: Chowkhamba Sanskrit Series Office. Edited by Nārāyaṇa Miśra. Kashi Sanskrit Series, no. 37.

Kāṭhakopaniṣat. (1914). Poona: Ānandāśrama Press. Edited by Vaijanātha Rājavāde. Ānandāśrama Sanskrit Series, no. 7.

Kathāsaritsāgara of Somadevabhaṭṭa. (1970). Delhi: Motilal Banarsidass. Edited by Jagadīśalāla Śāstrī.

Kauṣītaki-Brāhmaṇa. (1968). Wiesbaden: Franz Steiner Verlag. Edited by E. R. Sreekrishna Sarma. Verzeichnis der orientalischen Handschriften in Deutschland, Supplementband 9, 1.

The Kaushītaki-brāhmaṇa-upanishad. (1861). Calcutta: Asiatic Society of Bengal. Edited by E. B. Cowell. Bibliotheca Indica, no. 39. Reprint Varanasi: Chowkhamba Sanskrit Series Office, 1968.

The Kauṭilīya Arthaśāstra, Part I. (1969). 2nd ed. Bombay: University of Bombay. Edited by R. P. Kangle. University of Bombay Studies Sanskrit, Prakrit and Pali, no. 1.

Kāvyālaṅkāra of Bhāmaha. (1970). 2nd ed. Delhi: Motilal Banarsidass. Edited by P. V. Naganatha Sastry.

Kāvyaprakāśa of Mammaṭa. (1965). Revised from the 6th ed. Poona: Bhandarkar Oriental Research Institute. Edited by Raghunath Damodar Karmarkar.

The Kumārasaṃbhava of Kālidāsa, with the commentary (the Sañjīvanī) of Mallinātha (1-8 sargas) and of Sītārāma (8-17 sargas). (1886). Bombay: Nirṇayasāgar Press. Edited by Nārāyaṇa Bhaṭṭa Parvaṇīkara and Kashīnātha Pāṇḍuraṅga Paraba. 9th ed., 1923. Edited by Vāsudev Laxmaṇ Shāstrī Paṇsīkar.

The Kūrmapurāṇam. (1971). Varanasi: All-India Kashiraj Trust. Edited by Anand Swarup Gupta.

Mahābhārata: Critical Edition. (1933-1971). 19 vols. Poona: Bhandarkar Oriental Research Institute. With *Harivaṃśa* (1969-1971). Critically edited by V. S. Sukthankar et al.

Mahābhārata, with the commentary of Nīlakaṇṭha. (1929-1933). 6 vols. Poona: Chitrashala Press. Edited by Ramachandrashastri Kinjawadekar.

Mahābhāratam Part VII, *Harivanshaparvan, with the Bhārata Bhāwadeepa by Neelakantha.* (1936). Poona: Chitrashala Press. Edited by Ramachandrashastri Kinjawadekar.

Mahābhāṣya: Vyākaraṇamahābhāṣye navāhnikam. (1951). Bombay: Nirṇayasāgar Press. Edited by Bhārgava Śāstrī Joshi.

Mahāvastu. (1882-1897). 3 vols. Paris: L'Imprimerie Nationale. Edited by É. Senart. Reprint Tokyo: Meicho-Fukyū-kai, 1977.

Mahāvīracarita of Bhavabhūti. (1910). 3rd ed. Bombay: Nirṇayasāgar Press. Edited by T. R. Ratnam Aiyar and S. Rangachariar.

Maitrāyaṇī Saṃhitā. (1881-1886). 4 vols. Leipzig: F. A. Brockhaus. Edited by Leopold von Schroeder. Reprint in 1 vol. Amsterdam: Philo Press, 1971.

The Maitri or Maitrāyaṇīya Upanishad. (1870). Calcutta: Asiatic Society of Bengal. Edited by E. B. Cowell. Bibliotheca Indica, no. 42.

Mānava-dharma Śāstra, with the Commentaries of Medhātithi [etc.]. (1886). Bombay: Ganpat Krishnaji's Press. Edited by Vishvanāth Nārāyan Mandlik.

Manusmṛti, with the commentary of Kullūka. (1929). Bombay: Nirṇayasāgar Press. Edited by Vāsudevaśarma Paṇaśīkar.

Mārcaṇḍeya Purāṇa. (1862). Calcutta: Asiatic Society of Bengal. Edited by K. M. Banerjea. Bibliotheca Indica, no. 29.

Matsyapurāṇam. (1907). Poona: Ānandāśrama Press. Ānandāśrama Sanskrit Series, no. 54.

Mīmāṃsādarśanam. (1970-1976). 7 vols. Poona: Ānandāśrama Press. Edited by Kāśīnāth Vāsudevaśāstrī Abhyaṃkar et al. Ānandāśrama Sanskrit Series, no. 97.

Mṛcchakaṭika of Śūdraka. (1896). Bombay: Government Central Book Depot. Edited by Nārāyaṇa Bālakṛṣṇa Goḍabole. Bombay Sanskrit Series, no. 52.

The Nārada Pancha Rātra. (1865). Calcutta: Asiatic Society of Bengal. Edited by K. M. Banerjea. Bibliotheca Indica, no. 38.

Pāda-Index of Vālmīki-Rāmāyaṇa. (1961-1966). 2 vols. Baroda: Oriental Institute. Edited by G. H. Bhatt. Gaekwad's Oriental Series, nos. 129, 153.

Padmapurāṇam. (1893-1894). 4 vols. Poona: Ānandāśrama Press. Edited by Viśvanātha Nārāyaṇa Maṇḍalik. Ānandāśrama Sanskrit Series, no. 131.

The Panchatantraka of Vishṇuśarman. (1896). Bombay: Nirṇayasāgar Press. Edited by Kāśīnāth Pāṇḍurang Parab.

Pāṇini's Grammatik. (1887). Leipzig: H. Haessel. Edited by Otto Böhtlingk. Reprint Hildesheim: Olms, 1964.

Parāśarasmṛti. (1893-1919). 6 parts. Poona: Director of Public Instruction. Edited by Vāman Śāstrī Islāṃpurkar. Bombay Sanskrit Series, nos. 47, 48, 59, 64, 67, 74.

Pātañjalayogadarśanam, with the Commentary of Vyāsa and the Subcommentaries of Vācaspatimiśra and Vijñānabhikṣu. (1971). Varanasi: Bhāratīya Vidyā Prakāśan. Edited by Nārāyaṇa Miśra.

Praśnopaniṣat. (1889). Poona: Ānandāśrama Press. Ānandāśrama Sanskrit Series, no. 8. Reprint 1932.

Pratīka-Index of the Mahābhārata and Harivaṃśa. (1967-1972). 6 vols. Poona: Bhandarkar Oriental Research Institute. Edited by Parashuram Lakshman Vaidya.

Raghuvaṃśa of Kālidāsa, with the commentary of Mallinātha. (śāka 1808 [= A.D. 1886]). 3rd ed. Bombay: Nirṇayasāgar Press. Edited by Kāśīnātha Pāṇḍuraṅg Parab.

Rahasyatrayasāra of Vedāntadeśika. (1968). Madrapuri: n. p. Edited by Uttamūr Ti. Vīrarāghavācārya. Translated from the Maṇipravāla into Sanskrit by Ku. V. Nīlameghācārya.

Rāmāyaṇamañjarī of Kṣemendra. (1903). Bombay: Nirṇayasāgar Press. Edited by Bhavadatta Śāstrī and Kāśīnāth Pāṇḍurang Parab. Kāvyamālā, no. 83.

Ṛgveda-Saṃhitā, with the commentary of Sāyaṇāchārya. (1933). 5 vols. Poona: Vaidic Samshodhan Mandal.

Sāhityadarpaṇa of Viśvanātha Kavirāja. (1967). Varanasi: Chowkhamba Sanskrit Series Office. Edited by Āchārya Kṛṣṇamohan Śāstrī. Kashi Sanskrit Series, no. 145.

Śāṅkhāyana Āraṇyaka. (1922). Poona: Ānandāśrama Press. Edited by Shridhara Shastri Pathak. Ānandāśrama Sanskrit Series, no. 90.

Śāṅkhāyanagṛhyasūtra, see *Das Çāṅkhāyanagṛihyam.*

The Śāṅkhāyana Śrauta Sūtra. (1888-1889). 4 vols. Calcutta: Asiatic Society of Bengal. Edited by Alfred Hillebrandt. Bibliotheca Indica, no. 99.

Sarvadarśanasaṃgraha of Sāyaṇa Mādhavācārya. (1978). 3rd ed. Poona: Bhandarkar Oriental Research Institute. Edited by Vasudeva Shastri Abhyankar. Government Oriental Series Class A, no. 1.

Śatapathabrāhmaṇa, see *The Çatapatha-Brāhmaṇa.*

Satyāṣāḍhaśrautasūtra. (1907-1932). 10 vols. Poona: Ānandāśrama Press. Edited by Kāśīnātha Śāstrī Āgāśe et al. Ānandāśrama Sanskrit Series, no. 53.

The Saundarananda of Aśvaghoṣa. (1928-1932). 2 vols. Lahore: Oxford University Press (for the University of the Panjab). Edited by E. H. Johnston. Panjab University Oriental Publications, no. 14. Reprint in 1 vol. Delhi: Motilal Banarsidass 1975.

Siddhāntakaumudī of Bhaṭṭojidīkṣita. (1967-1971). 4 vols. Delhi: Motilal Banarsidass. Edited by Giridharaśarma Caturvedi.

Skandapurāṇam. (1910). Bombay: Veṅkaṭeśvara Press.

The Śrauta Sūtra of Āpastamba. (1882-1902). 3 vols. Calcutta: Asiatic Society of Bengal. Edited by R. Garbe. Bibliotheca Indica, no. 92.

Śrauta Sūtra of Kātyāyana, see *The Çrautasūtra of Kātyāyana.*

Subhāṣitatriśatī (the Śatakatrayam of Bhartṛhari), with the commentary of Rāmacandra Budhendra. (1957). Bombay: Nirṇayasāgar Press. Edited by D. D. Kosambi.

Sūktiratnahāra of Sūrya. (1938). Trivandrum: Government Press. Edited by K. Sāmbaśiva Śāstrī. Trivandrum Sanskrit Series, no. 141.

Suttanipāta. Khuddakanikāye . . . suttanipāta. (1959). N.p.: Pāli Publication Board (Bihar Government). Nālandā-Devanāgarī-Pāli Series. General editor Bhikkhu J. Kashyap.

Taittirīya-brāhmaṇam, with the commentary of Sāyaṇācārya. (1898). 3 vols. Poona:

Ānandāśrama Press. Edited by Nārāyaṇaśāstrī Godbole. Ānandāśrama Sanskrit Series, no. 37. Reprint 1979.

The Taittirīya-Prātiśākhya. (1871). New Haven: American Oriental Society. Edited by William Dwight Whitney. Reprint Delhi: Motilal Banarsidass, 1973.

Taittirīya Saṃhitā. (1900-1908). 9 vols. Poona: Ānandāśrama Press. Edited by Kāśīnātha Śāstrī Āgāśe. Ānandāśrama Sanskrit Series, no. 42. Reprint 1961.

Taittirīyopaniṣat. (1889). Poona: Ānandāśrama Press. Edited by Vāmana Śāstrī Islāmpurkar. Ānandāśrama Sanskrit Series, no. 12. Reprint 1929.

Tāṇḍya Mahābrāhmaṇa (=Pañcaviṃśabrāhmaṇa). (1870-1874). 2 vols. Calcutta: Asiatic Society of Bengal. Edited by Ānandachandra Vedāntavāgīśa. Bibliotheca Indica, no. 62.

Udānavarga. (1965-1968). 2 vols. Göttingen: Vandenhoeck & Ruprecht. Edited by Franz Bernhard. Abhandlungen der Akademie der Wissenschaften in Göttingen, Philologisch-historische Klasse, Dritte Folge, Nr. 54. Sanskrittexte aus den Turfanfunden X.

Uttararāmacarita of Bhavabhūti. (1948). Bombay: Nirṇayasāgar Press. Edited by Nārāyaṇa Rām Ācārya.

Vallabhadeva's Kommentar (Śārada-Version) zum Kumārasaṃbhava des Kālidāsa. (1980). Wiesbaden: Franz Steiner Verlag. Edited by M. S. Narayana Murti in collaboration with Klaus L. Janert. Verzeichnis der orientalischen Handschriften in Deutschland, Supplementband 20, 1.

The Vāmanapurāṇam. (1968). Varanasi: All-India Kashiraj Trust. Edited by Anand Swarup Gupta.

Varahamihira's Brihat Jataka. (1929). Mysore: Government Branch Press. Edited by V. Subrahmanya Sastri.

Vasiṣṭhadharmaśāstra. (1883). Bombay: Government Central Book Depot. Edited by A. A. Führer. Bombay Sanskrit Series, no. 23.

Vāyupurāṇam. (1905). Poona: Ānandāśrama Press. Ānandāśrama Sanskrit Series, no. 49.

Vetālapañcaviṃśati. In *Kathāsaritsāgara, q.v.*.

Viṣṇupurāṇam. (saṃvat 1967 [= A.D. 1910]). Bombay: Veṅkateśvara Press.

Vyākaraṇamahābhāṣya. (1967). 3 vols. Delhi: Motilal Banarsidass. (Reprint [?] of the 6-vol. ed., Bombay: Nirṇayasāgar Press, 1935- .)

Yājñavalkyasmṛti of Yogīśvara Yājñavalkya, with the commentary Mitākṣarā of Vijñāneśvara. (1949). 5th ed. Bombay: Nirṇayasāgar Press. Edited by Narayan Ram Acharya.

The Yavanajātaka of Sphujidhvaja. (1978). 2 vols. Cambridge: Harvard University Press. Edited by David Pingree. Harvard Oriental Series, no. 48.

SECONDARY SOURCES

Agrawala, V. S. (1963). *India as Known to Pāṇini.* 2nd ed., rev. and enlarged. Varanasi: Prithvi Prakashan.

Aiyar, R. Narayana. (1950). "Svadoṣa-Paradoṣa-Vit." *JORM* 17, no. 3, pp. 105-28.

Alsdorf, Ludwig. (1950). "Pañcatantra-Miszellen." *ZDMG* 100, pp. 356-61.

Altekar, A. S. (1958). *State and Government in Ancient India.* 3rd ed. Delhi: Motilal Banarsidass.

Barck, Christophorus. (1976). *Wort und Tat bei Homer.* New York-Hildesheim: Olms. Spudasmata, no. 34.

Belvalkar, Shripad Krishna, ed. (1947). *The Bhīṣmaparvan.* Poona: Bhandarkar Oriental Research Institute. Vol. 7 of the critical edition of the *Mahābhārata.*

———, ed. (1949-1950). *The Śāntiparvan, Parts 1, 2 and 3.* Poona: Bhandarkar Oriental Research Institute. Vols. 13 and 14 of the critical edition of the *Mahābhārata.*

Benthall, A. P. (1946). *The Trees of Calcutta and Its Neighbourhood.* Calcutta: Thacker Spink and Co.

Binchy, D. A. (1970). *Celtic and Anglo-Saxon Kingship.* Oxford: Clarendon Press.

Bloch, Jules, trans. (1950). *Les Inscriptions d'Asoka.* Paris: Société d'édition "Les Belles Lettres."

Böhtlingk, Otto. (1879-1889). *Sanskrit-Wörterbuch in kürzerer Fassung.* 3 vols. St. Petersburg: Kaiserlichen Akademie der Wissenschaften. Reprint Graz: Akademische Druck u. Verlagsanstalt, 1959.

———. (1887). "Bemerkenswerthes aus Rāmāyaṇa, ed. Bombay Adhj. [*sic*] I-IV." *Berichte über die Verhandlungen der königlich sächsischen Gesellschaft der Wissenschaften zu Leipzig, philol.-hist. Classe,* vol. 39, pp. 213-27.

———. (1896). "Bemerkungen zu Manu's Gesetzbuch." *Berichte über die Verhandlungen der königlich sächsischen Gesellschaft der Wissenschaften zu Leipzig, philol.-hist. Classe,* vol. 48, pp. 245-50.

Böhtlingk, Otto, and Rudolph Roth. (1855-1875). *Sanskrit-Wörterbuch.* 7 vols. St. Petersburg: Kaiserlichen Akademie der Wissenschaften. Reprint Osnabrück-Wiesbaden: Otto Zeller Verlagsbuchhandlung-Antiquariat Otto Harrassowitz, 1966.

Bongert, Yvonne. (1963). "Réflexions sur le problème de l'esclavage dans l'Inde ancienne, à propos de quelques ouvrages récents." *BEFEO* 51, pp. 143-94.

Brinkhaus, Horst. (1981). "Yathāsaṃkhya und versus rapportati." *Studien zur Indologie und Iranistik* 7, pp. 21-70.

Bühler, Georg, trans. (1886). *The Laws of Manu.* Oxford: Clarendon Press. Sacred Books of the East, vol. 25.

Burling, Robbins. (1974). *The Passage of Power.* New York: Academic Press.

Buss, Andreas. (1978). *Société, politique, individu: Les formes élémentaires de la vie sociale en Inde ancienne.* Montreal: Les Presses de l'Université de Montréal.

Carey, William, and Joshua Marshman, eds. and trans. (1806-1810). *The Ramayuna of Valmeeki.* 3 vols. Serampore: Baptist Mission Press (?). Reprint 1823.

Chézy, A. L. (1814). *La Mort de Yajnadatta, épisode extrait et tr. du Ramayana, poème épique sanskrit.* Paris: Imprimerie de P. Didot l'ainé.

Cone, Margaret, and Richard F. Gombrich. (1977). *The Perfect Generosity of Prince Vessantara: A Buddhist Epic.* Oxford: Clarendon Press.

Dandekar, Ramchandra Narayan, ed. (1961). *The Śalyaparvan.* Poona: Bhandarkar Oriental Research Institute. Vol. 11 of the critical edition of the *Mahābhārata.*

———, ed. (1966). *The Anuśāsanaparvan, Part 2.* Poona: Bhandarkar Oriental Research Institute. Vol. 17 of the critical edition of the *Mahābhārata.*

De, Sushil Kumar, ed. (1958). *The Droṇaparvan.* Poona: Bhandarkar Oriental Research Institute. Vol. 8 of the critical edition of the *Mahābhārata.*

Derrett, J.D.M. (1976). "Rājadharma." *JAS* 35, pp. 597-609.

Dharma, P. C. (1947). "King Makers or Rājakartāraḥ in Ancient India." *ABORI* 28, pp. 219-25.

Dietrich, B. C. (1965). *Death, Fate and the Gods*. London: University of London, Athlone Press.

Dumont, Louis. (1962). "The Conception of Kingship in Ancient India." *Contributions to Indian Sociology* 6, pp. 48-77.

———. (1964). *La civilisation indienne et nous*. Paris: A. Colin.

———. (1980). *Homo Hierarchicus: The Caste System and Its Implications*. Revised ed. Translated by Mark Sainsbury et al. Chicago: University of Chicago Press.

Eagleton, Terence. (1976). *Criticism and Ideology*. London: Verso.

Edgerton, Franklin, ed. (1944). *The Sabhāparvan*. Poona: Bhandarkar Oriental Research Institute. Vol. 2 of the critical edition of the *Mahābhārata*.

———. (1953a). *Buddhist Hybrid Sanskrit Grammar*. New Haven: Yale University Press.

———. (1953b). *Buddhist Hybrid Sanskrit Dictionary*. New Haven: Yale University Press.

Ensink, J. (1968). "Mitrasaha, Sudāsa's Son, with the Spotted Feet." In *Pratidānam . . . Studies presented to F.B.J. Kuiper*. Edited by J. C. Heesterman et al. The Hague: Mouton, pp. 573-84.

Fairservis, Walter A. (1975). *The Roots of Ancient India*. 2nd ed., rev. Chicago: University of Chicago Press.

Fränkel, Hermann. (1962). *Dichtung und Philosophie des frühen Griechentums*. Munich: C. H. Beck.

Garde, D. L., and P. P. Apte. (1967-1971). "Bibliography of Political Thought and Institutions in Ancient and Medieval India." *Journal of the University of Poona* 25, pp. 99-133; 31, pp. 87-122; 35, pp. 131-66.

Geldner, Karl Friedrich, trans. (1951). *Der Rig-Veda*. 3 vols. Cambridge: Harvard University Press. Harvard Oriental Series, vols. 33, 34, 35.

Ghatage, A. M., ed. (1976-). *An Encyclopaedic Dictionary of Sanskrit on Historical Principles*. Vol. 1, parts 1, 2, 3; vol. 2, parts 1, 2 (all published to date). Poona: Deccan College Postgraduate and Research Institute.

Goldman, Robert P. (1976). "Vālmīki and the Bhṛgu Connection." *JAOS* 96, pp. 97-101.

———. (1977). *Gods, Priests, and Warriors: The Bhṛgus of the Mahābhārata*. New York: Columbia University Press.

———. (1978). "Fathers, Sons, and Gurus: Oedipal Conflict in the Sanskrit Epics." *JIP* 6, pp. 325-92.

———. (1980). "Rāmaḥ Sahalakṣmaṇaḥ: Psychological and Literary Aspects of the Composite Hero of Vālmīki's Rāmāyaṇa." *JIP* 8, pp. 149-89.

Gonda, Jan. (1938). "Altind. -anta-, -antara-, usw." *Bijdragen tot de Taal-, Land- en Volkenkunde* 97, pp. 453-500. Reprint in Gonda (1975b), vol. 2, pp. 101-48.

———. (1942). "Bemerkungen zum Gebrauch der Pronomina der 1. und 2. Person als Subject im Altindischen." *Acta Orientalia* 19, pp. 211-79. Reprint in Gonda (1975b), vol. 3, pp. 111-79.

———. (1947). "Skt. Utsava- 'festival.' " In *India Antiqua, a volume of Oriental studies presented . . . to J. Ph. Vogel*. Leiden: E. J. Brill, pp. 146-55. Reprint in Gonda (1975b), vol. 2, pp. 276-84.

———. (1966). *Ancient Indian Kingship from the Religious Point of View*. Leiden: E. J. Brill. Reprinted from NUMEN III and IV with addenda and index.

———. (1967). "On the Use of the Absolutive in Sanskrit." In *Kavirāj Abhinandana Grantha*. Edited by Baburam Saksena. Lucknow: Akhila Bhāratīya Saṃskṛta Pariṣad, pp. 262-65. Reprint in Gonda (1975b), vol. 3, pp. 91-94.

———. (1969). *Aspects of Early Viṣṇuism*. 2nd ed. Delhi: Motilal Banarsidass.

———. (1975a). *Vedic Literature (Saṃhitās and Brāhmaṇas)*. Wiesbaden: Otto Harrassowitz. *A History of Indian Literature*, vol. I, *Veda and Upanishads*, fasc. 1.

———. (1975b). *Selected Studies*. 5 vols. Leiden: E. J. Brill. Vol. 2, *Sanskrit Word Studies*; vol. 3, *Sanskrit Grammatical and Philological Studies*.

Goodwin, William Watson. (1893). *Syntax of the Moods and Tenses of the Greek Verb*. 3rd ed. Boston: Ginn.

Goody, Jack, ed. (1966). *Succession to High Office*. Cambridge: Cambridge University Press.

Gore, N. A. (1943). *A Bibliography of the Rāmāyaṇa*. Poona: the author.

Griffin, Jasper. (1980). *Homer on Life and Death*. Oxford: Clarendon Press.

Gurner, C. W. (1927). "Aśvaghoṣa and the Rāmāyaṇa." *JASB* N.S. 23, pp. 347-67.

Hazra, R. C. (1979). "The Word 'sthapati'—Its Derivation and Meaning." *Our Heritage* 150th Anniversary Volume, pp. 397-423. Calcutta Sanskrit College Research Series, no. 119.

Heesterman, J. C. (1957). *The Ancient Indian Royal Consecration: The Rājasūya Described According to the Yajus Texts and Annoted* [*sic*]. The Hague: Mouton. Disputationes Rheno-Trajectinae, vol. 2.

———. (1978). "The Conundrum of the King's Authority." In *Kingship and Authority in South Asia*. Edited by J. F. Richards. Madison: South Asian Studies, University of Wisconsin, pp. 1-27. Madison Publication Series, no. 3.

Hegel, G.W.F. (1975). *Aesthetics: Lectures on Fine Art*. 2 vols. Translated by T. M. Knox. Oxford: Clarendon Press.

Hill, Christopher. (1977). *Milton and the English Revolution*. New York: Viking Press.

Hillebrandt, Alfred. (1916). "Zum altindischen Königsrecht." *ZDMG* 70, pp. 41-48.

Hopkins, Edward Washburn. (1889). "The Social and Military Position of the Ruling Caste in Ancient India, as Represented in the Sanskrit Epic; with an Appendix on the Status of Women." *JAOS* 13, pp. 56-372.

———. (1901). *The Great Epic of India: Its Character and Origin*. New York: Charles Scribner's Sons.

———. (1906). "Modifications of the Karma Doctrine." *JRAS*, pp. 581-93.

———. (1915). *Epic Mythology*. Strassburg: Trübner.

Hultzsch, E., ed. and trans. (1925). *The Inscriptions of Aśoka*. Oxford: Clarendon Press. Corpus Inscriptionum Indicarum 1, new edition. Reprint Delhi: Indological Book House, 1969.

Ingalls, D.H.H. (1962). "Words for Beauty in Classical Sanskrit Poetry." In *Indological Studies in Honor of W. Norman Brown*. New Haven: American Oriental Society, pp. 87-107.

———. (1965). *An Anthology of Sanskrit Court Poetry: Vidyākara's "Subhāṣitaratnakoṣa."* Cambridge: Harvard University Press. Harvard Oriental Series, vol. 44.

———, trans. (1968). *Sanskrit Poetry from Vidyākara's "Treasury."* Cambridge: Belknap Press, Harvard University Press.

———. (1976). "Kālidāsa and the Attitudes of the Golden Age." *JAOS* 96, pp. 15-26.

Jacobi, Hermann. (1893). *Das Rāmāyaṇa: Geschichte und Inhalt nebst Concordanz der gedruckten Recensionen*. Bonn: Friedrich Cohen. Reprint Darmstadt: Wissenschaftliche Buchgesellschaft, 1976.

———. (1903). "Über ein verlorenes Heldengedicht der Sindhu-Sauvīra." In *Album-Kern*. Leiden: E. J. Brill, pp. 53-55. Reprint in Jacobi (1970), vol. 1, pp. 304-306.

———. (1918). "Über die Einfügung der Bhagavadgītā im Mahābhārata." *ZDMG* 72, pp. 323-27. Reprint in Jacobi (1970), vol. 1, pp. 307-11.

———. (1970). *Kleine Schriften*. 2 vols. Edited by Bernhard Kölver. Wiesbaden: Franz Steiner Verlag.

Jameson, Fredric. (1976). "Criticism in History." In *Weapons of Criticism*. Edited by Norman Rudich. Palo Alto: Ramparts, pp. 31-50.

———. (1981). *The Political Unconscious: Narrative as a Socially Symbolic Act*. Ithaca: Cornell University Press.

Jayaswal, K. P. (1955). *Hindu Polity*. 3rd, enlarged, ed. Bangalore City: Bangalore Print. and Pub. Co.

Jhala, G. C., ed. (1966). *The Sundarakāṇḍa: The Fifth Book of the Vālmīki Rāmāyaṇa: The National Epic of India*. Baroda: Oriental Institute.

Kale, M. R., ed. and trans. (1967). *Kālidāsa's Kumārasaṃbhava*. 6th ed. Delhi: Motilal Banarsidass.

Kane, P. V. (1962-1975). *History of Dharmaśāstra*. 8 vols. Poona: Bhandarkar Oriental Research Institute. vol. I, i (1968); vol. I, ii, 2nd ed. (1975); vol. II, i, 2nd ed. (1974); vol. II, ii, 2nd ed. (1974); vol. III, 2nd ed. (1973); vol. IV, 2nd ed. (1973); vol. V, i, 2nd ed. (1974); vol. V, ii (1962).

———. (1966). "The Two Epics." *ABORI* 47, pp. 11-58.

Keith, Arthur Berriedale, trans. (1908). *The Śāṅkhāyana Āraṇyaka*. London: Royal Asiatic Society. Reprint New Delhi: Oriental Book Reprint Corporation, 1975.

———, ed. and trans. (1909). *The Aitareya Āraṇyaka*. Oxford: Clarendon Press. Anecdota Oxoniensia, Aryan Series, vol. 1, part 9. Reprint 1969.

———, trans. (1914). *The Veda of the Black Yajus School Entitled Taittiriya Sanhita*. Cambridge: Harvard University Press. Harvard Oriental Series, vols. 18, 19.

———, trans. (1920). *The Aitareya and Kauṣītaki Brāhmaṇas of the Rigveda*. Cambridge: Harvard University Press. Harvard Oriental Series, vol. 25. Reprint Delhi: Motilal Banarsidass, 1971.

Kirfel, Willibald. (1920). *Die Kosmographie der Inder nach Quellen dargestellt*. Bonn-Leipzig: K. Schroeder. Reprint Hildesheim: Olms, 1967.

Kosambi, D. D. (1952). "Ancient Kosala and Magadha." *JBBRAS* N.S. 27, part 2, pp. 180-213.

La Vallée Poussin, L. de. "Notes bouddhiques." *Académie Royale de Belgique, Bulletin de la Classe des Lettres* 7, pp. 515-26.

Lévi, Sylvain. (1936). "Alexander and Alexandria in Indian Literature." *IHQ* 12, pp. 121-33.

Lewis, C. S. (1942). *A Preface to Paradise Lost*. London and New York: Oxford University Press.

Lüders, Heinrich. (1940). *Philologica Indica: Ausgewählte kleine Schriften*. Göttingen: Vandenhoeck & Ruprecht.

———. (1951). *Varuṇa*. 2 vols. Edited by Ludwig Alsdorf. Göttingen: Vandenhoeck & Ruprecht.

Mabbett, Ian W. (1972). *Truth, Myth and Politics in Ancient India*. New Delhi: Thomson Press.

McCann, Charles. (1959). *100 Beautiful Trees of India*. Bombay: D. B. Taraporevala Sons and Co.

Macdonell, Arthur Anthony, and Arthur Berriedale Keith. (1912). *Vedic Index of Names and Subjects*. 2 vols. London: J. Murray. 3rd reprint Delhi: Motilal Banarsidass, 1967.

Mayrhofer, Manfred. (1956-1980). *Kurzgefasstes etymologisches Wörterbuch des Altindischen: A Concise Etymological Sanskrit Dictionary*. 4 vols. Heidelberg: Carl Winter Universitätsverlag.

Merchant, Paul. (1971). *The Epic*. London: Methuen.

Meyer, Johann Jakob. (1930). *Sexual Life in Ancient India*. 2 vols. London: George Routledge and Sons.

Michelson, Truman. (1904). "Linguistic Archaisms of the Rāmāyaṇa." *JAOS* 25, pp. 89-145.

Mookerji, Radha Kumud. (1962). *Asoka*. 3rd ed. rev. and enlarged. Delhi: Motilal Banarsidass.

Mylius, Klaus. (1970). "Zur absoluten Datierung der mittelvedischen Literatur." In *Neue Indienkunde—New Indology: Festschrift Walter Ruben*. Edited by Horst Krüger. Berlin: Akademie-Verlag, pp. 421-31. Deutsche Akademie der Wissenschaften zu Berlin, Institut für Orientforschung, Veröffentlichung Nr. 72.

Narahari, H. G. (1960-1961). "Ideas about Karma in the Rāmāyaṇa." *Munshi Indological Felicitation Volume, Bhāratīya Vidyā* 20-21, pp. 111-15.

Oldenberg, Hermann. (1918). "Jātakastudien." *Nachrichten von der Kgl. Gesellschaft der Wissenschaften zu Göttingen. Philologisch-historische Klasse*, pp. 429-68. Reprint in Oldenberg (1967), vol. 2, pp. 1069-1108.

———. (1919). "Zur Geschichte des altindischen Erzählungsstiles. 1. Noch einmal Jātaka und Epen." *Nachrichten von der Kgl. Gesellschaft der Wissenschaften zu Göttingen. Philologisch-historische Klasse*, pp. 61-79. Reprint in Oldenberg (1967), vol. 2, pp. 1477-95.

———. (1922). *Das Mahābhārata. Seine Entstehung, sein Inhalt, seine Form*. Edited by Friedrich Carl Andreas. Göttingen: Vandenhoeck & Ruprecht.

———. (1967). *Kleine Schriften*. 2 vols. Edited by Klaus L. Janert. Wiesbaden: Franz Steiner Verlag.

Oppenberg, Ursula. (1965). *Quellenstudien zu Friedrich Schlegels Übersetzungen aus dem Sanskrit*. Marburg: N. G. Elwert. Marburger Beiträge zur Germanistik, 7.

Paranjpe, Vasudev Gopal, ed. (1956). *The Strīparvan*. Poona: Bhandarkar Oriental Research Institute. Vol. 12 of the critical edition of the *Mahābhārata*.

Pollock, Sheldon. (1981). "Text-Critical Observations on Vālmīki Rāmāyaṇa." In *Sternbach Felicitation Volume*. Edited by J. P. Sinha. Lucknow: Akhila Bhāratīya Samskṛta Pariṣad, pp. 317-25.

———. (1983). "Some Lexical Problems in Vālmīki Rāmāyaṇa." *Ṛtam, B. R. Saxsena Special Volume*, pp. 275-88.

Przyluski, Jean. (1926). *Le Concile de Rājagṛha: Introduction à l'Histoire des Canons et des Sectes bouddhiques*. Paris: Librairie Orientaliste Paul Geuthner.

Raghavan, V. (1943). "Bodhi and Viṣṇupada in N.W. India and Toponymic Duplication." *The Indian Geographical Journal* 18.3, pp. 98-104.

———. (1956). "Methods of Popular Religious Instruction in South India." In *The Cultural Heritage of India*. 2nd ed. Edited by Haridas Bhattacharyya, vol. 4, pp. 503-14. Calcutta: Ramakrishna Mission Institute of Culture.

———. (1963). *Bhoja's Śṛṅgāra Prakāśa*. Madras: Punarvasu.

Raghaven, V. (1968). "Rāmāyaṇa Quotations and Textual Criticism." In *Mélanges d'Indianisme à la mémoire de Louis Renou*. Paris: Publications de l'Institute de Civilisation indienne, vol. 28, pp. 595-604.

———. (1973). *The Greater Ramayana*. Varanasi: All-India Kashiraj Trust.

Raghu Vira, ed. (1936). *The Virāṭaparvan*. Poona: Bhandarkar Oriental Research Institute. Vol. 5 of the critical edition of the *Mahābhārata*.

Ramaswami-Sastri, K. S. (1944). *Studies in the Ramayana*. Baroda: Baroda State Department of Education. Kirti Mandir Lecture Series, no. 9.

Ranade, H. G., trans. (1978). *Kātyāyana Śrauta Sūtra*. Pune: the author.

Rao, T. A. Gopinatha. (1914-1916). *Elements of Hindu Iconography*. 2 vols. in 4 parts. Madras: Law Printing House.

Rau, Wilhelm. (1954). "Lotusblumen." In *Asiatica: Festschrift Friedrich Weller*. Edited by Johannes Schubert and Ulrich Schneider. Leipzig: Otto Harrassowitz, pp. 505-13.

———. (1957). *Staat und Gesellschaft im alten Indien nach den Brāhmaṇa-texten dargestellt*. Wiesbaden: Otto Harrassowitz.

———. (1973). *Metalle und Metallgeräte im vedischen Indien*. Mainz: Akademie der Wissenschaften und der Literatur. Abhandlungen der Geistes- und Sozialwissenschaftliche Klasse, Jahrgang 1973, Nr. 8.

———. (1976). *The Meaning of Pur in Vedic literature*. Munich: W. Fink. Abhandlungen der Marburger Gelehrten Gesellschaft, Jahrgang 1973, Nr. 1.

Renou, Louis. (1939-1942). "Sur certains emplois d'a(n)- priv. en sanskrit, et notamment dans le Ṛgveda." *BSOAS* 10, pp. 1-18.

———, ed. and trans. (1966). *La Grammaire de Pāṇini*. 2nd ed. 2 vols. Paris: École Française d'Extrême-Orient.

———. (1968). *Grammaire Sanscrite*. Paris: Adrien-Maisonneuve.

Rhys Davids, T. W., and William Stede. (1921-1925). *The Pali Text Society's Pali-English Dictionary*. London: Pali Text Society. Reprint 1972.

Ritschl, Eva, and Maria Schetelich. (1970). "Zu einigen Problemen der frühen Klassengesellschaft in Indien." In *Neue Indienkunde—New Indology: Festschrift Walter Ruben*. Edited by Horst Krüger. Berlin: Akademie-Verlag. Deutsche Akademie der Wissenschaften zu Berlin, Institut für Orientforschung, Veröffentlichung Nr. 72, pp. 29-37.

Roşu, Arion. (1969). "Note sur Rāmāyaṇa II, 4, 2." *JA* 257, pp. 37-40.

Roussel, Alfred, trans. (1903-1909). *Le Rāmāyaṇa de Vālmīki*. 3 vols. Paris: Librairie orientale et américaine.

———. (1910). "Les anomalies du Rāmāyaṇa." *JA* 10, no. 15, pp. 5-69.

———. (1910-1912). *Rāmāyaṇa; études philologiques (Extrait du Muséon)*. Louvain: J.-B. Istas.

Ruben, Walter. (1936). *Studien zur Textgeschichte des Rāmāyaṇa*. Stuttgart: Verlag W. Kohlhammer.

———. (1950). "Vier Liebestragödien des Rāmāyaṇa." *ZDMG* 100, pp. 287-355.

———. (1956). "Der Minister Jābāli in Vālmīkis Rāmāyaṇa." *Acta Antiqua Academiae Scientiarum Hungaricae* 4, pp. 35-53.

———. (1975). *Die homerischen und die altindischen Epen*. Berlin: Akademie-Verlag.

———. (1978). "The Development of the Town in Ancient India." In *History and Society: Essays in Honour of Professor Niharranjan Ray*. Edited by Debiprasad Chattopadhyaya. Calcutta: K. P. Bagchi, pp. 229-37.

Sastri, N. Aiyaswami. (1931). "References to Ancient Stories in the Rāmāyaṇa." *JORM* 4, pp. 101-107.

Satya Vrat. (1964). *The Rāmāyaṇa: A Linguistic Study.* Delhi: Munshi Ram Manohar Lal.

Scharfe, Hartmut. (1968). *Untersuchungen zur Staatsrechtslehre des Kauṭalya.* Wiesbaden: Otto Harrassowitz.

Schlegel, August Wilhelm von, trans. (1838). *Ramayana.* Bonn: Typis regiis. Vol. 2.1 of his edition of the *Rāmāyaṇa.*

Schlingloff, Dieter. (1969). *Die altindische Stadt: Eine vergleichende Untersuchung.* Mainz: Akademie der Wissenschaften und der Literatur. Abhandlungen der Geistes- und Sozialwissenschaftlichen Klasse, Jahrgang 1969, Nr. 5.

Schwartzberg, Joseph E., ed. (1978). *A Historical Atlas of South Asia.* Chicago: University of Chicago Press.

Sen, Nilmadhav. (1949). "The Secondary Conjugations in the Rāmāyaṇa." *PO* 14, pp. 89-106.

———. (1956). "Un-Pāṇinian Pronouns and Numerals in the Rāmāyaṇa." *JOIB* 5, no. 3, pp. 266-71.

Shah, U. P. (1980). "Rāmāyaṇa Manuscripts of Different Versions." In *The Rāmāyaṇa Tradition in Asia.* Edited by V. Raghavan. Delhi: Sahitya Akademi, pp. 93-102.

Sharma, J. B. (1968). *Republics in Ancient India, c. 1500 B.C.-500 B.C.* Leiden: E. J. Brill.

Sharma, Narendra Nath, ed. and trans. (1976). *Āśvalāyana Gṛhyasūtram.* Delhi: Eastern Book Linkers.

Sharma, Ramashraya. (1971). *A Socio-Political Study of the Vālmīki Rāmāyaṇa.* Delhi: Motilal Banarsidass.

Siauve, Suzanne, ed. and trans. (1978). *Aṣṭādaśabhedanirṇaya: Explication des dix-huit différences . . . de Śrī Vātsya Rañganātha.* Pondichery: Institut français d'Indologie. Publications de l'Institut français d'Indologie, No. 58.

Sircar, D. C. (1967). *Cosmography and Geography in Early Indian Literature.* Calcutta: Indian Studies: Past and Present.

Smyth, Herbert Weir. (1966). *Greek Grammar.* Revised by Gordon M. Messing. Cambridge: Harvard University Press.

Speijer, J. S. (1886). *Sanskrit Syntax.* Leiden: E. J. Brill.

Spellman, John W. (1964). *Political Theory of Ancient India.* Oxford: Clarendon Press.

Stanford, W. B., ed. (1967). *The Odyssey of Homer.* 2nd ed. 2 vols. New York: St. Martin's Press.

Sternbach, Ludwik. (1966). "Quotations from the Rāmāyaṇa in the Kathā Literature." *JOIB* 15, pp. 236-51.

Stoll, Elmer Edgar. (1961). "Source and Motive in Macbeth and Othello." In *Shakespeare: Modern Essays in Criticism.* Edited by Leonard F. Dean. New York: Oxford University Press.

Sukthankar, Vishnu S., ed. (1942). *The Āraṇyakaparvan, Part 2.* Poona: Bhandarkar Oriental Research Institute. Vol. 4 of the critical edition of the *Mahābhārata.*

Tambiah, S. J. (1976). *World Conqueror and World Renouncer.* Cambridge: Cambridge University Press.

Thapar, Romila. (1961). *Aśoka and the Decline of the Mauryas.* Oxford: Oxford University Press.

Thieme, Paul. (1952). "Bráhman." *ZDMG* 102, pp. 91-129.

Tiwari, Arya R. G. (1960). "The Kaccita [*sic*] Parva of Bk. II ch. 100, Vālmīki Rāmāyaṇa—A Study." *PO* 25, pp. 20-35.

Tod, James. (1920). *Annals and Antiquities of Rajasthan*. 3 vols. Edited with an introduction and notes by William Crooke. London, New York: H. Milford, Oxford University Press.

Trautmann, Thomas R. (1971). *Kauṭilya and the Arthaśāstra*. Leiden: E. J. Brill.

Tripathi, Gaya Charan. (1968). *Der Ursprung und die Entwicklung der Vāmana-Legende in der indischen Literatur*. Wiesbaden: Otto Harrassowitz. Freiburger Beiträge zur Indologie, 1.

Vaidya, Parashuram Lakshman, ed. (1954). *The Karṇaparvan*. Poona: Bhandarkar Oriental Research Institute. Vol. 10 of the critical edition of the *Mahābhārata*.

———, ed. (1962). *The Ayodhyākāṇḍa: The Second Book of the Vālmīki-Rāmāyaṇa: The National Epic of India*. Baroda: Oriental Institute.

van Buitenen, J.A.B., ed. and trans. (1973-1978). *The Mahābhārata*. 3 vols. Chicago: University of Chicago Press. Vol. I, 1973; vol. II, 1975; vol. III, 1978.

van Daalen, L. A. (1980). *Vālmīki's Sanskrit*. Leiden: E. J. Brill.

Varadacharya, K. S., ed. (1964-1965). *Śrīmadvālmīkirāmāyaṇam with Amṛtakataka of Mādhavayogi: Ayodhyākāṇḍa*. 2 vols. Mysore: University of Mysore, Oriental Research Institute.

Vyas, S. N. (1967). *India in the Rāmāyaṇa Age*. Delhi: Atma Ram and Sons.

Warren, Henry Clarke, ed. and trans. (1896). *Buddhism in Translations*. Cambridge: Harvard University Press. Harvard Oriental Series, no. 3.

Wezler, Albrecht. (1978). *Die wahren "Speiseresteesser" (Skt. vighasāśin): Beiträge zur Kenntnis der indischen Kultur- und Religionsgeschichte* I. Mainz: Akademie der Wissenschaften und der Literatur. Abhandlungen der Geistes- und Sozialwissenschaftlichen Klasse, Jahrgang 1978, Nr. 5.

Whitney, William Dwight, trans. (1905). *Atharva-Veda Saṃhitā*. Revised and edited by Charles Rockwell Lanman. 2 vols. Cambridge: Harvard University Press. Harvard Oriental Series, nos. 7, 8.

Zimmer, Heinrich. (1879). *Altindisches Leben: Die Cultur der vedischen Arier nach den Saṃhitā dargestellt*. Berlin: Weidmannsche Buchhandlung. Reprint Hildesheim: Olms, 1973.

Index

Library of Congress Cataloging-in-Publication Data
(Revised for volume 2)

Vālmīki.

The Rāmāyaṇa of Vālmīki.

(Princeton Library of Asian translations)
Includes bibliographies and indexes.
Contents: v. 1. Bālakānda — v. 2. Ayodhyākāṇḍa / introduction, translation, and annotation by Sheldon I. Pollock.

I. Goldman, Robert P., 1942- . II. Sutherland, Sally J. III. Title. IV. Series.

BL1139.22.E54 1984 294.5'922 82-61364
ISBN 0-691-06561-6 (v. 1 : alk. paper) ISBN 0-691-06654-X (v. 2)